Steven Spielberg

by the same author

for Faber and Faber Ltd

FRANK CAPRA
The Catastrophe of Success

HAWKS ON HAWKS

Other titles

Filmmakers on Filmmaking, Vols. I and II (editor)

HIGH AND INSIDE
The Complete Guide to Baseball Slang

ORSON WELLES
Actor and Director

KIRK DOUGLAS

JOHN FORD (WITH MICHAEL WILMINGTON)

FOCUS ON HOWARD HAWKS (EDITOR)

ORSON WELLES

PERSISTENCE OF VISION
A Collection of Film Criticism (editor)

Steven Spielberg
A Biography

Joseph McBride

faber and faber

First published in the United States in 1997
by Simon & Schuster
Rockefeller Center
1230 Avenue of the Americas
New York, New York 10020

First published in Great Britain in 1997
by Faber and Faber Limited
3 Queen Square London WC1N 3AU

Printed in England by Clays Ltd, St Ives plc

© Joseph McBride, 1997

Joseph McBride is hereby identified as author of this
work in accordance with Section 77 of the Copyright,
Designs and Patents Act 1988

A CIP record for this book
is available from the British Library

ISBN 0–571–19177–0

2 4 6 8 10 9 7 5 3 1

To Jean Oppenheimer

CONTENTS

He is arguably the most influential popular artist of the twentieth century. And arguably the least understood.

— MICHAEL CRICHTON, 1995

"CECIL B. DeSPIELBERG"

FIRELIGHTS CAPTURE EARTHLINGS IN FILM PREMIERING TUESDAY
— HEADLINE IN *THE ARIZONA REPUBLIC*

SEARCHLIGHT swept the night sky of downtown Phoenix as a limousine pulled up under the theater marquee. The director and his stars stepped out, bedazzled by the glare of strobes and exploding flashbulbs. Inside, a packed house awaited the world premiere of a science-fiction epic from American Artist Productions. For the next two hours and fifteen minutes, the audience watched enrapt at the spectacle of mysterious colored lights emerging from the heavens to abduct humans for an extraterrestrial zoo. At the night's end, the box-office take from that screening at the Phoenix Little Theatre, at seventy-five cents a head, was enough to put the movie into profit.

The date was March 24, 1964. The movie was *Firelight*. Its production cost was under $600, and it was the first feature-length film written and directed by a high school junior named Steven Spielberg.

The precocious seventeen-year-old billed himself as "Steve" in the credits, not Steven, but some of his classmates mockingly called him "Spielbug." He may have looked like a "nerd" and a "wimp" in those years, as he himself recalled, but he was already making a name for himself in Phoenix with his moviemaking. His mother proudly called him "Cecil B. DeSpielberg." A Jewish kid who "felt like an alien" while growing up in a succession of increasingly WASPish suburbs and turned to making movies as a way of finding the social acceptance he craved, Steve Spielberg had been shooting film obsessively for more than seven years, with a monomaniacal dedication that made him virtually oblivious to schoolwork, dating, sports, and other normal adolescent pursuits.

"I was more or less a boy with a passion for a hobby that grew out of control and somewhat consumed me," he said years later. ". . . I discovered something I could do, and people would be interested in it and me. I knew after my third or fourth little 8mm epic that this was going to be a career, not just a hobby."

One of Steve's grade-school classmates, Steve Suggs, has never forgotten the day in seventh grade when he received a phone call from a mutual friend who told him, "Spielberg's making a movie. Do you want to be in it?" It was a World War II movie called *Fighter Squad*.

Steve Suggs was one of the school jocks, and he was not close to Spielberg: "I had no insights into his level of talent. He wasn't athletic at all, nor was he necessarily a brainchild. On the surface, in the six or eight hours a day we spent in school together, he didn't have any redeeming qualities. I didn't know if he was going to have his Brownie out there pointing at us and have us dressing up as girls.

"I went to Spielberg's house and got into a car; Steve's father was driving. We went out to the airport. Somehow Steve had arranged access to a fighter and a bomber! He took a shot of me in the fighter with ketchup coming out of my mouth when I was shot. He had a script; he knew what he was doing. It wasn't just the boys going out and screwing around—he knew how to deal with people.

"I remember telling my mom about it afterward. Here was this kid who was sort of a nerd and wasn't one of the cool guys; he got out there and suddenly he was *in charge*. He became a totally different person, so much so that I as a seventh grader was impressed. He had all the football players out there, all the neat guys, and he was telling *them* what to do. An hour ago at home or on the campus he was the guy you kicked dirt in his eyes.

"It was miraculous. It just blew me away. It's as if you hear this nerd play piano and suddenly he's Van Cliburn."

P E O P L E all over Phoenix soon began to pay attention to the youthful filmmaking prodigy. A local TV news crew covered the filming of Spielberg's forty-minute World War II movie, *Escape to Nowhere* (completed in 1962), which won first prize in a statewide contest for amateur filmmakers. The filming of *Firelight* was the subject of two articles and photo spreads in *The Arizona Republic,* which hailed him in December 1963 as a "Teenage Cecil B." with "an amateur but honored standing and a professional outlook."

"We're all for Steve's hobby," his mother, Leah, told the newspaper. "This way we know and the parents of his teenage friends know where they are; they're not cruising up and down Central Avenue."

The Army surplus jeep Leah drove around town was prominently featured in *Firelight,* and she sometimes slapped a helmet over her short blond hair to play a German soldier in her son's war movies. "Our house was run like a studio," she recalled. "We really worked hard for him. Your life was not worth a dime if you didn't, because he nagged you like crazy. Steven had this way of directing everything. Not just his movies, his life. He directed our household. . . . He was a terrible student in school. But I never thought, What's going to become of him? Maybe if it had crossed my mind, I'd have gotten worried."

Leah was so tolerant of her son's lack of interest in school that she often let him stay home, feigning illness, so he could edit his movies. All he had to do to convince her was "hold the thermometer to a light bulb and put the heating pad over my face"—a trick he had Henry Thomas's Elliott play on his mother in *E.T.* Steve's father, Arnold Spielberg, a pioneer in the field of computer engineering, was frustrated by his attitude toward schoolwork. "The only thing I ever did wrong," Arnold says, "was try to coax him into being an engineer. I said, 'Steve, you've gotta study math.' He said, 'I don't like it.' He'd ask me to do his chemistry for him. And he would never even *do* the damn chemistry lab, he would just come home and say, 'Dad, I've gotta prepare this experiment.' I'd say, 'You don't have any data there. How am I supposed to tell you what you've done?' So I'd try to reconstruct the experiment for him, I'd come down with some answers. He'd come back and say, 'Jesus, Dad, you flunked!'

"Leah recognized that he really wasn't cut out for [science]. She would say, 'Steve, *I* flunked chemistry two times. Don't even try.' After about a year, I gave up. He said, 'I want to be a director.' And I said, 'Well, if you want to be a director, you've gotta start at the bottom, you gotta be a gofer and work your way up.' He said, 'No, Dad. The first picture I do, I'm going to be a director.' And he *was.* That blew my mind. That takes guts."

Arnold humored his rebellious son by bankrolling the production of *Firelight.* He also helped Steve design miniature sets, rigged the lights for scenes filmed in Steve's studio (the carport of their house), and built a dolly for the elaborate tracking shots that were already a hallmark of the Spielberg visual style. Steve enlisted his three younger sisters, Anne, Sue, and Nancy, in the production as well. Anne served as a script supervisor, Nancy played the key role of a little girl abducted by aliens, and all three of them bounced up and down on the hood of the jeep inside the carport to make the jeep look like it was speeding through the desert night around Camelback Mountain.

Steve Spielberg's ambitions were grandiose, if as yet intellectually circumscribed: he told his young collaborators during the making of *Firelight,* "I want to be the Cecil B. DeMille of science fiction."

Many of his schoolmates, teachers, and neighbors thought him an "oddball" and a "nut" for being so consumed by moviemaking, but "one thing I never heard anybody associate with Spielberg was that he was blowing smoke," recalled a high school friend, Rick Cook. "A lot of people were skeptical about his chances, but I don't think you can find anybody who didn't think he would give it his all."

B Y the time of the *Firelight* premiere, the teenaged Spielberg had already started the process of turning his dreams into reality. He had met a man at Universal Studios who recognized his extraordinary potential as a filmmaker, gave him advice about the making of *Firelight,* and eagerly awaited a chance to see the finished movie. Spielberg saw *Firelight* as his *entrée* to a career as a Hollywood director. He hoped to persuade Universal to back him in making a big-screen version of his sci-fi tale. But though Universal would sign him to a directing contract five years later, it was only after Spielberg had served an apprenticeship in television and directed what was then the biggest hit in film history, *Jaws,* that he was able to raise the $19 million he needed from another studio for his transmutation of *Firelight—Close Encounters of the Third Kind.*

After becoming a professional filmmaker, Spielberg publicly disparaged *Firelight* as "one of the five worst films ever made anywhere." But his extraordinary promise was obvious to everyone who attended the Phoenix premiere in 1964. *"Firelight* is just as good, although this may be construed as criticism, as some of the science-fiction movies seen by the late-late television viewers," wrote *Arizona Journal* reviewer Larry Jarrett. "The plot, the action, the basic material of the movie, is sound and not as far out as some of Hollywood's fantasies-de-science."

Allen Daviau, the cinematographer who has shot such Spielberg films as *E.T. The Extra-Terrestrial, The Color Purple,* and *Empire of the Sun,* was shown *Firelight* by Spielberg in the late 1960s. "It's what you expect with a kid's film, the acting and so on, but oh, God! Some of it was so audacious," Daviau says. "The effects were what was really amazing—that's what his heart was in. What he did with crumpled aluminum foil and bits of Jell-O on a kitchen table was pretty amazing."

S PIELBERG'S canny flair for self-promotion, which has served him so well in his professional career, was already much in evidence in his teenage years, although then, as now, it was carefully concealed within a personality that seemed outwardly shy and modest, even deferential. People in Phoenix still speak in awestruck tones of how Spielberg talked his way into shooting scenes for *Firelight* at a hospital and at an airport, using an actual jet plane.

"When he was making *Firelight,* and he had to get into a hospital," his father says, "he went down to the Baptist Hospital in Phoenix and talked them into letting him have a room. They lent him some oxygen tanks and stuff like that, and he put one of his actresses in a bed and put an oxygen mask on her. He did it all on his own. I didn't help him at all. He said, 'What do I do?' I said, 'Call the office and ask 'em.' 'Well,' he said, 'how do I get on an airplane?' I said, 'Just get down to the [Sky Harbor] airport and ask American Airlines if you can have the use of a plane for about ten minutes when it lands and before it takes off again.' And they let him!

"I would just give him the lead and then he'd go do it. Because I figured, if I ask for him, then he's not really doing it. He had more guts than *I* did, asking for things that I would say, 'Oh, they'll turn you down, Steve.' Besides, he was a novelty in Phoenix, a bright young kid there, and made the newspapers. So people cottoned onto that and they were very cooperative. He had something special. Mostly he had drive. He had a will to do it."

Betty Weber, whose daughters Beth and Jean worked on *Firelight,* let Steve shoot part of the film at her house. A volunteer stage manager at the nonprofit Phoenix Little Theatre, Betty cajoled the theater's board members into donating their facilities for the premiere. She barraged the local newspapers and radio stations with announcements about the young filmmaker, arranged for photo spreads in *The Arizona Republic,* and made sure the title of *Firelight* was displayed on billboards at businesses all over town. Beth Weber, the film's leading lady, typed and mimeographed the programs distributed to the opening-night audience. The limousine that brought Steve and his actors to the theater was supplied and driven by a cast member's father who owned a local brewery. The searchlight was borrowed from a nearby shopping center.

Arnold Spielberg helped Steve play the complicated soundtrack for the movie, and Leah Spielberg climbed a ladder to put the title of her son's first feature on the marquee. As she did so, she was thinking, "This is a nice hobby."

That triumphant evening in March 1964 marked a coming of age for Steve Spielberg. His debut as a feature filmmaker was also his farewell to his boyhood years in Arizona. The day after the premiere, he and his family moved to California. He told the local press that he hoped to be working for Universal that summer before finishing high school and going to film school at UCLA.

Making movies "grows on you," Steve declared. "You can't shake it. . . . I want to write movie scripts, but I like directing above all. All I know for sure is I've gone too far to back out now."

ONE

"HOW WONDROUS ARE THY WORKS"

MY FATHER WAS SO EXCITING. I HAVE MEMORIES—COLOR MEMORIES—OF WALKING THROUGH A SNOWSTORM IN CINCINNATI. IT WAS GLISTENING, AND HE LOOKED UP AND SAID, "HOW WONDROUS ARE THY WORKS." HOW WONDROUS ARE THY WORKS. THIS IS WHO I AM. THIS IS WHO STEVEN IS.

— LEAH ADLER, STEVEN SPIELBERG'S MOTHER

THE child's eyes were wide with awe as he was borne from the surrounding darkness toward the red light burning before the Ark of the Torah. Framed in a colonnaded marble arch inlaid with gold and blue, the Ark's wooden doors were hidden by a curtain that glistened in the candlelight with an alluring, unfathomable aura of mystery. Under the domed skylight with a bronze chandelier hanging from a Star of David, the child in his stroller was pushed down the blue-carpeted aisle. From all around he could hear the chanting of elders in beards and black hats, swaying rhythmically to the Hebrew prayers. "The old men were handing me little crackers," Steven Spielberg recalled. "My parents said later I must have been about six months old at the time."

This was the earliest memory of the child who would grow up to make *Schindler's List*. The year was 1947, and the place was the Adath Israel synagogue in Cincinnati, Ohio, across the street from the first home where Steven Spielberg lived during his peripatetic boyhood.

No other filmmaker has mined his childhood more obsessively or profitably than Spielberg, who has said that he "can always trace a movie idea back to my childhood." Indeed, the roots of his distinctive visual style can be seen, embryonically, in those images of the synagogue: the hypnotic tracking shots mingling a sense of wonderment with fear of the unknown, the dazzling light flooding his characters' field of vision ("God light," he calls it), the intensely emotional employment of subjective viewpoints, and the omnipresent delight in surprising apparitions and visual magic. He always has been fascinated by "what I think is there but cannot see." From *Jaws, Close Encounters of the Third Kind*, and *E.T. The Extra-Terrestrial* to *The Color Purple, Empire of the Sun*, and *Schindler's List*, Spielberg has shown a rare gift for making audiences throughout the world share his own primal fears and fantasies.

He describes his favored protagonist as "Mr. Everyday Regular Fella." That common touch is one of the keys to Spielberg's unprecedented level of success with the mass audience. It also helps explain the disdain of elitists who fail to recognize that the ordinariness of his protagonists encompasses a wide range of archetypal human conflicts. Spielberg's protagonist typically is either a child whose troubled life has caused him to evolve into a precocious maturity, or a childlike adult whose attempts to escape a grown-up's responsibilities are viewed by the director with deep ambivalence. Despite the relatively limited thematic range and intellectual scope of much of his body of work so far, Spielberg, like any major popular artist, has an instinctive awareness of shared contemporary psychological concerns and an uncanny ability to express those concerns with directness and simplicity. Perhaps his greatest artistic strength is his seemingly innate ability to conjure up visual images that evoke archetypal emotions and are nonetheless complex for being nonverbal.

When asked in 1991 to select a single "master image" that sums up his work, Spielberg chose one with powerful echoes of his first childhood memory: the shot of the little boy in *Close Encounters of the Third Kind* opening his living-room door to see the blazing orange light from the UFO, "that beautiful but awful light, just like fire coming through the doorway. And he's very small, and it's a very large door, and there's a lot of promise or danger outside that door."

P R O M I S E *or danger.* Spielberg gives the words equal weight, but for many years most American critics condescendingly regarded Spielberg as a child-man fixated on the toys of moviemaking and incapable of dealing maturely with the darker side of life. Pauline Kael, who praised *Close Encounters* in *The New Yorker* as "a kids' movie in the best sense," later complained, "It's not so much what Spielberg has done, but what he has encouraged. Everyone else has imitated his fantasies, and the result is an infantilization of the culture." Spielberg's public statements did little to discourage such belittling assessments of his life and work. He said in 1982 that he was "still a kid. . . . Why? I guess because I'm probably socially irresponsible and way down deep I don't want to look the world in the eye. Actually,

I don't mind looking the world in the eye, as long as there's a movie camera between us."

There was truth in that *mea culpa,* enough to make even his admirers uneasy about Spielberg's potential for growth and development. Would he continue to resist the responsibilities of full maturity as a man and as a filmmaker, indulging his boyish fondness for pulp adventure (the Indiana Jones movies), infantile humor and overblown production values *(1941, Hook),* and special-effects fantasy extravaganzas *(Poltergeist, Jurassic Park)* while becoming self-consciously skittish when he ventured into mature sexual territory *(The Color Purple, Always)*? Would he overcome his anxieties about confronting his audience—and himself—with the kind of socially conscious, controversial subject matter he has touched upon only intermittently throughout his career?

In his *annus mirabilis* (1993) that saw *Jurassic Park* break *E.T.*'s worldwide box-office record by grossing nearly a billion dollars, Spielberg finally silenced many of his detractors with *Schindler's List,* his masterful film version of Thomas Keneally's book about a gentile businessman who saved eleven hundred Jews from the Holocaust. The film was hailed as "a giant bar mitzvah, a rite of passage . . . his cinematic initiation into emotional manhood." Such praise was double-edged, for it implied that in his first twenty-five years as a professional filmmaker, Spielberg had never before made a serious, mature, adult film, an assumption that unfairly denigrated the best of his earlier work, from his landmark TV movie *Duel* to the timeless fantasies *Close Encounters* and *E.T.* and the flawed but deeply moving dramas *The Color Purple* and *Empire of the Sun.* After Spielberg started winning awards for *Schindler's List,* his grade-school teacher Patricia Scott Rodney, one of the first people to encourage his filmmaking talents, commented, "I've heard him say, 'Finally I've made a serious film.' I recognize that as Spielberg humor."

"The critics in awe of how much I've stretched just don't know me," Spielberg said. "This is no stretch at all. *Schindler's List* is the most natural experience for me. I *had* to tell the story. I've lived on its outer edges."

But few people, least of all Spielberg himself, questioned that *Schindler's List* marked both a profound enrichment of his art and a triumphant midlife point of personal maturation. "I feel a very strong pull to go back to traditions," he said at the time. The film was the culmination of a long personal struggle with his Jewish identity, a struggle that had helped determine his choice of a career and his orientation as a popular, mass-market filmmaker. He spoke of that struggle in interviews at the time of *Schindler's List:*

"I never felt comfortable with myself," he admitted, "because I was never part of the majority. . . . I felt like an alien. . . . I wanted to be like everybody else. . . . I wanted to be a gentile with the same intensity that I wanted to be a filmmaker.

"I was so ashamed of being a Jew, and now I'm filled with pride. . . . This film has kind of come along with me on this journey from shame to honor.

My mother said to me one day, 'I really want people to see a movie that you make someday that's about us and about who we are, not as *a* people but as people.' So this is it. This is for her."

Spielberg's early rejection of his Jewish roots, and his gradual return to them, was an experience he shared with many Jews in his post–World War II, post-Holocaust generation of baby boomers. He was a child of second-generation American Jews who broke away from their roots and for whom assimilation was part of the price of social acceptance and professional advancement. As a result, Spielberg, like many others in his generation, grew up questioning the relevance of his old-world heritage and the faith of his parents and grandparents.* In the white-bread culture of the Eisenhower era, Jewish baby boomers such as Spielberg became increasingly Americanized as they drifted from their cultural identity and became, in large part, a generation of outwardly assimilated but inwardly alienated suburb-dwellers. Spielberg and his movies came to typify the suburban experience, as he himself became, in Vincent Canby's phrase, "the poet of suburbia," a designation hardly suited to win honor with cultural elitists who scorned the middle-American ethos that suburbia had come to represent in the 1950s.

Spielberg once defined his approach to filmmaking by declaring, "I am the audience"; it was as if his own personality, through a self-abnegating act of will, had become indistinguishable from that of the majority. His prodigious popularity was a sign of how thoroughly assimilated he had become. Though his films sometimes engaged in social criticism, his refusal before *Schindler's List* to assume all the responsibilities of a socially conscious filmmaker—he once called himself an "atheist" on serious subjects—was bound up with his refusal to define himself as a Jew. He was in danger of losing touch with an essential part of himself, the part that stemmed from being part of a minority.

While associating himself with Jewish charities and liberal political causes, Spielberg tended to aim for the broadest mass appeal as a filmmaker, largely avoiding Jewish subject matter and not asserting his ethnic identity as overtly as such directors as Woody Allen and Paul Mazursky. Still, Spielberg chose Richard Dreyfuss ("my alter ego") as his protagonist in *Jaws, Close Encounters,* and *Always,* when other directors might have cast a WASP leading man in those roles, although Spielberg did not direct attention to the characters' ethnic backgrounds. The unleashing of the magical powers of the Ark of the Covenant to destroy its Nazi captors in *Raiders of the Lost Ark* reflected Spielberg's affinities with Jewish mysticism, but in the context of a frivolously escapist storyline; after making *Schindler's List,* Spielberg said he could no longer stomach the use of Nazis as figures of mere entertainment.

A more revealing exception to the rule of Spielberg's general avoidance of specifically Jewish themes was the 1986 animated film *An American Tail,*

* While Spielberg's maternal grandparents were Orthodox, his mother kept kosher only intermittently and his family attended Conservative synagogues.

on which he was an executive producer. It tells the story of a Jewish immigrant mouse named Fievel Mousekewitz, who comes to America to flee persecution (by Cossack-like cats) at home in Russia. Fievel, whose adventures continued in *An American Tail: Fievel Goes West* (1991), was named by Spielberg after his beloved maternal grandfather, Philip Posner, an impoverished Russian immigrant whose Yiddish name was Fievel.

T H E Spielberg family history reflects the archetypal Jewish-American journey of the last hundred years, from persecution in Russian cities and *shtetlach* (small towns) to religious freedom in the New World, and in succeeding generations from the comforts and limitations of a traditional midwestern Jewish-American community to the hazardous opportunities offered by the largely WASPish suburbs.

Spielberg's not atypical rejection of the values of his devoutly Orthodox maternal grandparents was in large part a defense mechanism against his feeling of growing up an "alien" in a predominantly Christian society. That feeling grew increasingly stronger in him as his college-educated parents moved the family up the socioeconomic ladder from Cincinnati to Camden and Haddon Township, New Jersey, and then westward to Phoenix, Arizona, and Saratoga, California.

Like many other successful Jewish creative artists in the twentieth century, Spielberg built his career not by declaring his "otherness" but by seeking acceptance and common cultural ground with the American majority, by trying to become one of them. "I've always worked to be accepted by the majority," he said in 1987. "I care about how I'm perceived—by my family, first; by my friends, second; by the public, third."

In choosing to concentrate his youthful energies on making movies rather than paying attention to his schooling, Spielberg rebelled against the traditional Jewish reverence for education and literacy. By declaring his independence from that part of his cultural tradition—and from the middle-class values typified by his father, who despaired because of Steven's refusal to finish college and follow in his footsteps—Spielberg was casting his lot with another kind of Jewish cultural tradition, the more disreputable but equally vital mass culture established in Hollywood by immigrant Jews of his grandparents' generation, popular fabulists who drew much of their inspiration, and their audiences, directly from the humbler elements of the *shtetl*. Those early Hollywood moguls created the homogenized popular image of the American Dream. As Neal Gabler wrote in *An Empire of Their Own: How the Jews Invented Hollywood,* "The movie Jews were acting out what Isaiah Berlin, in a similar context, had described as 'an over-intense admiration or indeed worship' for the majority, a reverence that, Berlin also noted, sometimes oscillated with a latent resentment too, creating what he sympathetically called a 'neurotic distortion of the facts.' Hollywood became both the vehicle for and the product of their distortions."

It was not until he became middle-aged that Steven Spielberg took the profound and irrevocable risk of redefining himself before the world by fully embracing his ethnic and religious heritage. Making *Schindler's List* was an act of psychic health and integration that took him back full circle to those first memory images of the synagogue in his Cincinnati childhood. "This is truly my roots," he declared. What finally enabled him to make *Schindler's List* was his long-deferred decision eight years earlier, at the age of thirty-eight, to leave his childhood behind by accepting the responsibilities of fatherhood:

"I had to have a family first. I had to figure out what my place was in the world. . . . When my [first] son [Max] was born, it greatly affected me. . . . A spirit began to ignite in me, and I became a Jewish dad at the moment of birth and circumcision. That's when I began to look at myself and think about my mom, my dad, what it was like growing up, what my childhood was like. I began crying at every movie. I began crying at bad television. At one point I thought I was having a bit of a breakdown. I tried to go back, seeing what I had missed, and I realized I had missed everything. . . .

"Suddenly I'm flashing back to my childhood and remembering vividly the stories my parents and grandparents told me. . . . My father was a great storyteller, and my grandfather [Fievel] was amazing. I remember hearing stories from him when I was four or five and I'd be breathless, sitting on the edge of his knee. My grandfather was from Russia, and most of the stories were very indigenous of the old country."

O N E of the stories Fievel told was of how he learned his lessons. As a Jew growing up in Odessa, Russia, in the late nineteenth century, Fievel was prohibited from attending secondary school by the czarist government's *numerus clausus* (closed number), a quota system severely limiting the number of Jews allowed to receive a higher education. But he found a way around the edict. Steven remembered what Fievel told him: "They did allow Jews to listen through open windows to the classes, so he pretty much went to school—fall, winter, and spring—by sitting outside in driving snow, outside of open windows."

A version of this memory made its way into *An American Tail*. Separated from his family after coming to New York, Fievel Mousekewitz forlornly presses his nose against a pane of glass to watch a group of little American mice attending school. Always the outsider, even in America, the strange new land of freedom, where there were supposed to be "no cats." Though Steven Spielberg failed to acquire his grandfather's yearning for education, he too became a storyteller, and he never forgot the image of the boy sitting outside the schoolhouse, or what it showed him about being a Jew in a hostile land.

Always convenient scapegoats during economic and political upheavals in a land of deep-seated anti-Semitism, Russian Jews in the late 1800s were subjected to increasingly frequent and brutal pogroms (the Russian word for "devastation"). In his childhood, Steven listened with fascination to his grandparents' tales of pogroms. The social and economic liberties of Russian Jews were restricted further by laws compelling them to live only in *shtetlach* and barring them from most occupations except for certain forms of trade. Nearly 2 million Jews fled Russia and Eastern Europe for the United States between 1881 and 1914, "a migration comparable in modern Jewish history only to the flight from the Spanish Inquisition," Irving Howe wrote in *World of Our Fathers*. America was seen "not merely as a land of milk and honey," observed novelist Abraham Cahan, "but also, perhaps chiefly, as one of mystery, of fantastic experiences, or marvelous transformations."

Steven Spielberg's ancestors were part of that vast migration, settling in the hospitable midwestern city of Cincinnati, which, in the words of historian Jonathan D. Sarna, was then "the oldest and most cultured Jewish community west of the Alleghenies." Some of his relatives remained in Russia for generations to come, and some eventually went to Israel, but many of those who did not emigrate were murdered along with the rest of their communities in the Nazi Holocaust. His father estimates they lost sixteen to twenty relatives in the Holocaust, in both Ukraine and Poland.

The original roots of the Spielberg family, Arnold Spielberg says, may have been in Austria-Hungary, where some of his ancestors, before emigrating to Russia, may have lived in an area controlled by the Duke of Spielberg. The Spielberg family name, which is German-Austrian, means "play mountain." *Spiel* connotes either recreation or a stage play (cf. the English word "spiel," meaning a recitation), and *berg* means mountain or hill. It is a fittingly theatrical name for a playful adult who works in show business and ever since his childhood has loved to build and film miniature mountains. A "play mountain" appears as a central plot device in *Close Encounters of the Third Kind:* Richard Dreyfuss obsessively constructs in his living room the image of the Wyoming mountain where, in the film's magical finale, the alien mother ship makes its landing. A film production company Arnold and Steven Spielberg formed early on, when Steven was a college student in Long Beach, California, was called Playmount Productions.

Steven's grandfather Shmuel Spielberg, who in America would change his name to Samuel, was born in 1873 in Kamenets-Podolsk, Russia. Once ruled by Lithuanian-Polish nobles and known in Polish as Kamieniec Podolski, it is now part of the independent state of Ukraine. In 1897, a few years before Shmuel's departure for America, Kamenets had a population of about forty thousand, including about sixteen thousand Jews.

Most of the Jews spoke Yiddish as their principal or only language, and they lived as all Russian Jews did, in a tightly knit, insular community whose religious and cultural tradition brought comfort and mutual support in the midst of hostility. Although anti-Semitism permeated many of the city's institutions during the reigns of Czars Alexander III and Nicholas II, the memorial book of Jewish life in Kamenets reports, "In general, relations between Jews and non-Jews in town were correct." Even during the Ukrainian pogroms of 1881 and the widespread pogroms of 1905, there were no massacres in Kamenets, although there was some vandalism of Jewish property.

Steven's grandfather Shmuel was the second son of a farmer, rancher, and huntsman named Meyer Spielberg and his wife, Bertha (Bessie) Sandleman, who also had three younger daughters. When Shmuel was about five years old, both his parents died in an epidemic, and he was raised by his brother, Avrom (Arnold Spielberg was given the Hebrew name Avrom in his honor). Shmuel worked on his brother's ranch as a cowboy, rounding up cattle and horses. Jews were conscripted into the czarist army for a six-year period, and Shmuel found his way into the army band, playing the baritone, a brass wind instrument. "By staying in the band," his son Arnold relates, "he managed to keep from getting killed or shot. And then he became a cattle buyer for the Russian army. He used to go up to Siberia and buy cattle, and he dealt with Manchuria. When the Russo-Japanese war started [in 1904], he just said, 'I will not get back into the army again.' He escaped to America in 1906, and then he brought my mother in 1908 [the year they married]."

Samuel (Shmuel) Spielberg's wife, Rebecca Chechik, "Grandma Becky" to Steven's generation, was the daughter of Nachman (Nathan) Morduhov Chechik and Reitzl (Rachel) Nigonova Hendler, who had eight other children. The Chechik family name, which is also spelled Tsetsik and means "linnet" in Russian, later was Americanized to Chase.

The Chechiks had a brewery in Sudilkov, a *shtetl* that no longer exists. Sudilkov was in the Kamenets area, near the larger town of Shepetovka, where some other family members lived. Arnold Spielberg relates that his grandfather Nachman Chechik "prayed and studied the Torah. His wife ran the brewery business. She was a shrewd woman. She and the children ran the business. My uncle Herschel, the oldest son, was the brewmaster. In those days, the old Jewish men, if they could get out of business and study the Torah, that's what they did." The brewery trade was forbidden to Jews by the Russian government in 1897, and some of Rebecca Chechik's siblings eventually emigrated to China. They lived in the Manchurian city of Harbin and then in Shanghai's British enclave, the setting for the opening scenes of Steven Spielberg's World War II film *Empire of the Sun*.

Samuel Spielberg, Arnold's father, worked for a few years as a grocer and a peddler in Cincinnati before he found a steady but modest living as a jobber, operating a store on West Third Street. "He'd go down to the small stores in Indiana, Kentucky, and Ohio," Arnold explains. "He'd buy up their merchandise that they had not been able to sell. He'd buy what they called job lots, or incomplete lots. He'd bring them to his store and he'd sell them to other merchants, or to retail; he had some retail trade. And, of course, in the wholesale trade he sold to even *smaller* stores."*

Arnold's mother, Rebecca, was "a very enterprising woman. She took care of the kids and ran the house. She was interested in politics—we were Democrats from way back—and she'd read a lot, go to plays, go to concerts. She'd join all the Jewish organizations." Mildred (Millie) Friedman Tieger, a longtime friend of Steven's mother, remembers Rebecca as "a strong, powerful woman, very smart, and more domineering" than her husband.

In addition to their son Arnold Meyer Spielberg, who was born on February 6, 1917, Rebecca and Sam had a younger son, Irvin (called Buddy or Bud), who became an aeronautical engineer and worked on NASA's space program, and a daughter, Natalie, who married Jacob (Jack) Guttman and with him ran a family business that manufactures cake decorations (Natalie died in 1992).

S T E V E N ' S mother's side of the family, the Posners, originated in Poland. "Posner" means "a person from Poznań," the name of a city and province in western Poland (also spelled Posnań or Poseń). Poznań was taken over by Prussia in the late eighteenth century, and as the late Dr. Jacob Rader Marcus, dean of American Jewish historiography, noted in a 1994 interview, "Germans despised Posners. If a German says, 'He's a Posner,' it means he's held in contempt." But the Posner ancestors of Steven Spielberg had a more worldly background in Russia than the Spielbergs, for the Posners' cosmopolitan hometown of Odessa, a bustling port on the Black Sea, was known as "The Paris of Russia."

In the end, however, Jews were scarcely more welcome in Odessa than they were anywhere else in Russia. Odessa was the site of regular anti-Jewish riots, and an unusually severe pogrom occurred there in 1905, the year of the attempted revolution and the mutiny by sailors on the battleship *Potemkin* (later the subject of Sergei Eisenstein's silent film classic *Potemkin,* which includes the famous Odessa Steps sequence). When Odessa's Jews celebrated the czar's promise of reforms, four hundred Jews were killed in retaliation during four days of mayhem. Such attacks—which also occurred in several other parts of Russia during 1905—were provoked by the authorities and executed by local ruffians with the help of policemen and Cossacks.

That year of turmoil was the year Philip Posner, born in Odessa in 1884, came to Cincinnati to make a new life for himself and his family, one he

---

* Steven Allan Spielberg's Hebrew name, Shmuel, is a tribute to his grandfather, who died before he was born. Asked why Steven was not given the first name of Samuel, Arnold says, "We gave him an Anglicized 'Steven.' We just artificially made it that. Leah and I wanted to give him a non-Biblical name. 'Allan' came from the Hebrew Aharon. And we just liked the name Allan, out of nowhere."

hoped would be safer from persecution and tyranny. He would remain devoutly Orthodox, resisting the modernizing influences of the Haskalah, the Jewish Enlightenment movement that flourished in Odessa, and the Reform movement in America. But Odessa's cultural ferment would leave an imprint on his consciousness, despite the deficiencies of his formal education. An artist *manqué,* Philip Posner would pass along his artistic inclinations to his daughter and his famous grandson.

Philip's parents, Simon Posner (son of Ezekiel Posner and Anna Fildman) and Miriam (Mary) Rasinsky (daughter of Benjamin Rasinsky), emigrated soon after him to Cincinnati, where Simon Posner, like Samuel Spielberg, became a jobber. The oldest of six children, Philip followed the same profession, selling *schmatte* (clothing) and other merchandise to support his wife, the former Jennie Fridman, and their two children, Leah and Bernard (Bernie).

Philip Posner was "a very emotional man," his son-in-law Arnold Spielberg recalls. "A religious, very observant man. He used to go to the synagogue in the morning, in the evening, *any* time. He was at one time quite well-to-do, and then the Depression took him under, along with many other people."

One time, Leah recalled, her family did not have enough to eat for several days until her father made ten dollars buying and selling old jewelry. He used the money to take them on a holiday. "We were poor, but there was no depression in our house."

Philip worked mostly out of his home, and Steven loved to play in his grandfather's attic, which was crowded with his merchandise—shoes and socks and shoelaces, belt buckles and tie clips. Norman Cummins, a fellow Jewish merchant who ran a discount clothing store, would buy Philip's discontinued stock "as a *mitzvah*—a blessing," Cummins's wife, Edith, remembered. "Mr. Posner was a little, slight, sweet sort of man. He had a very nice, pleasant little house. I would go there with my husband, and I'd talk to Steven. He was a real skinny tyke, very lively. Who knew he was going to be this big man? He'd sit there and eat a cookie and dip it in a glass of milk. When he had finished his glass of milk, his grandmother would strain the cookie out of the milk and put the milk back. I was very impressed by that. I don't know if it was poverty or just frugality."

Like the violin-playing Papa Mousekewitz in *An American Tail,* Steven's Grandpa Fievel poured his heart not into his business but into his music, playing the guitar and dancing ballet. Leah, who inherited her father's love for music, felt his creativity was sidetracked by his struggle to make a living. Fievel's brother Boris was the first known relative of Steven Spielberg to enter show business. He was a Shakespearean actor in the thriving Yiddish theater of the period; Leah remembers Boris declaiming Hamlet's "To be or not to be" soliloquy in their living room, in Yiddish. Boris was also a vaudevillian, singing and dancing with a straw hat and a cane, and he later became a lion tamer in the circus. (In Spielberg's 1995 animated film *Balto,* set in Alaska during the 1920s, there is a Russian Jewish refugee goose named Uncle Boris.)

Leah's mother, Jennie, born in 1882, was a native Cincinnatian. She was the second oldest of ten children born to Russian émigrés Louis Fridman, who had come to the United States by way of London in 1870, and Sarah Leah Nathan. Louis Fridman's father, a cigarmaker named Israel Fridman, was born in Poland in 1830—the earliest date of birth that can be traced for any of Steven's ancestors—and died of emphysema in Cincinnati in 1883. Louis practiced his father's profession for a while, but he also worked as a horse cart driver and a traveling salesman.

Steven's Grandma Jennie was a lively, hardworking, and self-reliant "American lady," as family friend Millie Tieger described her. "Both of [Steven's] grandmas were more assertive than the grandpas." Immigrant men often found that to be the case, for their traditionally dominant role in the old country tended to wither away in the face of the harsh economic realities and more liberal mores they encountered in America.

Before her marriage to Philip Posner in 1915, Jennie briefly ran a millinery shop with her sister Bertha. Jennie also majored in English at the University of Cincinnati, and Arnold Spielberg remembers her as "a very bright woman and a cultured, gentle woman." She called everyone she liked "Dolly," including her daughter Leah, who was born on January 12, 1920, and inherited her effervescent, outspoken personality from her mother.

Jennie "was never too domestic," Leah admiringly recalled. Jennie worked as a milliner and clerk for a while after her marriage. Later she taught English in her home to German Jewish immigrants, many of whom were refugees from Nazism and had their tuition paid by local Jewish charities to help them acclimate to life in America and to prepare for citizenship applications. And yet the husband of this thoroughly modern American lady never lost his old-world ways.

Fievel Posner had a long white beard and wore the traditional Orthodox garb of black coat and hat. While growing up, Steven became so embarrassed by his grandfather's appearance and frequent *davening* (praying) that he tried to keep his gentile friends away from the house when Grandpa Fievel came to visit. One day when Steven was eight years old and living in Haddon Township, New Jersey, he was playing football with some friends in the street, "and suddenly my grandfather, with the yarmulke, comes out of our house, two houses down, and yells: *'Shmuel! Shmuel!'* [Steven's Hebrew name]. I'm not answering him. I'm pretending I don't know him. I'm denying that name. My friend is saying, 'He's looking your way. Does he mean you?' They point at me, and I'm saying 'No, it's not me,' and I'm denying the existence of my own grandfather."

• • •

I F not quite the "paradise for the Hebrews" extolled by a nineteenth-century Ohio historian, what the Spielbergs and Posners found in the Queen City of the West was a stolid, largely German-American burg where Jews and gentiles lived in relative harmony and prosperity.

Arnold Spielberg had only "a little" trouble with anti-Semitism when he was growing up, such as an incident when a man wearing a Ku Klux Klan insignia on his belt called him a "Jewboy." "But my street was the best street in the world," he nostalgically recalls. "During the wintertime, the city would block it off and we had sled riding. The street went right down into a park. We had a ballfield there. We had a woods to go play in. It was a wonderful place for a kid to grow up. You couldn't have asked for a better place."

Even though its Jewish population has always been modest compared to those of cities on the East Coast—Jews made up only about 5 percent, or 22,000, of Cincinnati's 475,000 citizens when Steven Spielberg was born—Cincinnati was long regarded as "a Jewish version of the American dream," Jonathan D. Sarna wrote in his and Nancy H. Klein's 1989 history, *The Jews of Cincinnati.*

The roots of the city's Jewish community date back as early as 1814. As the birthplace of the Reform movement, founded in the mid-nineteenth century by Rabbi Isaac Mayer Wise to liberalize and Americanize traditional Judaism, Cincinnati is home to such renowned Reform institutions as Hebrew Union College, *The American Israelite* newspaper, and the American Jewish Archives. Spielberg's birthplace, the nonsectarian Jewish Hospital in Avondale, is the oldest Jewish hospital in the United States. Partly because of its strong German influence, Cincinnati has never been immune to anti-Semitism, and Sarna concludes that "in many ways, the Jewish vision of Cincinnati was simply too good to be true." But Jews arrived early enough in Cincinnati to have won the status of pioneers, and they have long been seen as an integral part of the city's social, political, and cultural establishment, even if they were not always as readily accepted in all parts of the business community.

Among the many hurdles Russian Jews, such as Spielberg's grandparents, faced when they began pouring into America in the late nineteenth century was the hostility of many German Jews who had preceded them. German Jews who had settled in America viewed themselves as far more educated, more solvent, and more cultured than the hordes of newcomers seeking their help and kinship. For much of Spielberg's grandparents' and parents' lives in Cincinnati, their German Jewish neighbors "held Eastern Europeans in utter contempt," Jacob Marcus said. "The German Jews were predominant socially, culturally, and financially, but for every German Jew there were at least five or six Eastern Europeans, which included Russians, Poles, Rumanians, and Eastern Hungarians. It was only around the 1930s or the 1940s that a few individuals of Germanic origin began to marry into the families of Eastern Europeans." In housing, too, the German

Jews were "always a street ahead [of the Eastern Europeans] and ne'er the twain shall meet," he observed. "The lines were drawn very sharply until about 1950."

With the coming of the automobile around the turn of the century, Cincinnati, like the midwestern city of *The Magnificent Ambersons,* found itself "heaving up in the middle incredibly." And as Cincinnati heaved and spread by annexing the outlying suburbs of the horse-and-buggy days, the old inner city was left a slum, occupied by Negroes and the poorest whites. Avondale, the genteel suburb of first remove for Jews leaving the West End, by the 1920s became the city's largely Jewish enclave. It was there Spielberg's grandparents and parents lived, where Steven was born and where he spent his first two and a half years.*

The more fashionable streets north of Rockdale Avenue in Avondale initially were the domain of German Jews. As the WPA's guide to the city put it, "The Orthodox Jews infiltrated the southern part of the suburb and gradually moved north, establishing a lively shopping district along Reading Road near Rockdale Avenue." Beginning less than a block from Arnold and Leah Spielberg's apartment at 817 Lexington Avenue, across the street from the Conservative Adath Israel synagogue on Reading Road, that district included the neighborhood movie house, the Forest Theatre. When Arnold was a boy, "Every Saturday we used to get a nickel and go to the Forest Theatre. I used to like to watch most adventure movies, all the Douglas Fairbanks movies, all the serials."

South Avondale was a *haimish*—warm and unpretentious—Jewish neighborhood of extended families and *landsleit*—people from the old country—who all pulled together to survive. Athough his grandfather Samuel Spielberg died a year before he was born, Steven grew up with an advantage few of today's children share, that of having three grandparents living in the same neighborhood.

Leah's parents, Philip and Jennie Posner, had rented a white frame house at 819 Glenwood Avenue since 1939, the fifth home they had lived in since their marriage. Arnold Spielberg remembers it as "a very nice home. When I was going to school at the University of Cincinnati, they lived just one block over. Leah would go over to their house, I'd come back after school, and we'd sit down and have a Sabbath lunch. Then we'd pray after lunch and sing songs. I learned all their songs."

Sam and Rebecca Spielberg had lived in ten homes before the family settled in 1935 into half of a red-brick duplex they rented at 3560 Van Antwerp Place. "Our street was ninety-five percent Jewish," Arnold recalls. "And all of them were successful people, doctors, dentists, or lawyers. It was very education-oriented. My brother and I were the only engineers that came out

---

* Spielberg announced in 1989 that he planned to make a movie dealing with his childhood years in Cincinnati, from a script by his sister Anne, *I'll Be Home.* The movie would have to be shot on location, he said, because "there's nothing in L.A. that looks like Cincinnati—nothing."

of that street. We used to brag to each other as to how religious the families were. My friends were almost all Orthodox. We were one of the few Conservative families on the street." After Sam's death, Rebecca continued to live there, supported by her children. Although Sam's grandson would amass a fortune estimated by *Forbes* magazine in 1996 at $1 billion, Sam's estate amounted to only $1,728.57, of which Rebecca received $1,182.15 after the costs of his final illness, burial, and probate.

By the time of Steven's birth, many of Avondale's old homes had been cut into duplexes or subdivided into three or four apartments, with the former maid's quarters on the top floor often serving as the tiny apartment of an elderly or unmarried family member. After Arnold's discharge from the U.S. Army Air Forces in September 1945, he and Leah rented their modest first-floor apartment on Lexington Avenue from Mrs. Bella Pritz, who lived upstairs with her daughter (the apartment occupied by the Spielbergs was one of two on the first floor). Though Avondale was already being vacated by German Jews, who kept moving northward into fresher and more rustic suburban acreage, it still was only "lower middle-class at worst" in those years, historian Jacob Marcus recalled. With housing growing scarcer as veterans began coming back from the war, the newlywed Spielbergs were lucky to find a decent apartment.

"It was a lovely neighborhood," recalls their neighbor Peggie Hibbert Singerman. The houses had "big backyards, huge porches on the front, swings. They were elegant houses, with wonderful woodwork in some of them." Many of those beautiful old homes remain well preserved today, long after the white flight of the 1950s that saw the Jewish population abandon Avondale to blacks climbing the economic ladder behind them. The house where Steven lived as a young child is still standing; it is a rental property owned by the Southern Baptist church, which in 1967 bought the Adath Israel building across the street, now a national historic landmark.

I N their growing restlessness with the comfortable but limiting environment of Cincinnati's Jewish enclave, Arnold and Leah Spielberg were typical of many second-generation American Jews whose postwar ambitions for themselves and their children would lead them to turn their backs on their aging hometowns and depart for the brave new world of suburbia.

Arnold Spielberg, his sister Natalie Guttman recalled, "was always a questioning, exploring, and highly intelligent youngster whose quest for learning was and has never really been quenched." But when Arnold was attending Avondale Grade School, he was regarded as "a nerd," according to a schoolmate, Dr. Bernard Goldman. "He didn't fit into the group. Other kids played ball, but he never seemed to join in that. He wasn't a spectator. He probably had his own interests."

From early boyhood, Arnold's primary interests were scientific: "The earliest influence was the son of the man who lived upstairs [in my building]. His son used to tinker around with radios. I was a little kid then, about six or seven years old, and I used to go down to the basement, watching him build stuff. Then another guy moved into the house next door—he was a radio repairman, and he gave me parts. And I was going to Avondale School one day—I'll never forget this—I was walking up the street on Windham Avenue, and I looked in the wastebasket. There was a bunch of radio stuff. I picked up that radio stuff, ran home, and opened the door—'Mom, don't throw this out!' I went to school, barely made it to class, came home—it was a crystal set that somebody had tried to fix. I just put the wires to the nearest connection and I got it to work. This was in 1927 or '28; I was ten years old at that time.

"I'll never forget putting the earphones on my uncle's ears when he came over from Manchuria to America. It was the first time he ever heard a radio. The family thought I was nuts, you know, a 'crazy-head scientist.' I was always into magnetics and electrical stuff. Making magnets, burning up batteries, making shocking machines out of batteries from the old battery-radio sets. I used to go around to people's houses and say, 'Have you got any used-up batteries?' They'd give 'em to me, I'd get some power out of 'em, connect 'em all in series, make sparks. Typical kid stuff."

Arnie and his brother Buddy, who was only a year younger, shared the same hobby. "They were into electrocuting rats in the attic," their nephew, Samuel Guttman, relates. "Arnold was a ham operator [from the age of fifteen], and somehow he had an antenna system that ruined the radio reception in the neighborhood. The two terrorized the neighborhood. My mother once got so crazy she threw a punch at 'em through a glass door." Arnold "was remarkably intelligent in school, and he would fool around at home— he did all kinds of smart scientific things," recalls family friend Millie Tieger. "He built a television set in the 1930s, before anybody else did, before anybody knew what a television *was*. Everybody said, 'Arnold, what *are* you doing?' "

Some of Arnold's visionary qualities can be attributed to his avid interest in reading science fiction, a habit he later passed on to his son. "I've been reading science fiction since I was seven years old, all the way back to the earliest *Amazing Stories,"* Arnold says. *"Amazing, Astounding, Analog*—I still subscribe. I still read 'em. My kids used to complain, 'Dad's in the bathroom with a science-fiction magazine. We can't get in.' "

Sam and Becky Spielberg, who spoke mostly Russian around the house, were struggling to make ends meet during the Depression, and they could not afford to send Arnold and Buddy to college. After his graduation in 1934 from Hughes High School, Arnold barely missed out on a college scholarship and had to take a job far beneath his potential, working as a clerk in a chain of small-town department stores across the river in Kentucky, run by his mother's relatives, the Lerman brothers.

Before becoming a store manager for the Lermans, Arnold worked as an assistant manager in Cynthiana, Kentucky, for his older cousin Max Chase, a nephew of Rebecca Spielberg. Starting the process that eventually would make Arnold's son Steven into a filmmaker, Max gave Arnold his first movie camera during the early 1930s. "I started taking home movies when I lived in Kentucky," Arnold recalls. "My cousin bought one of the earliest 8mm movie cameras. He didn't know how to use it, so he said, 'Here, you use it.' I was about seventeen years old when I started doing that. I used to take a lot of junk movies, you know what I mean? Family and stuff like that. But no class. Just pictures."*

Arnold continued to work for the Lermans until the coming of World War II. He enlisted in the U. S. Army Signal Corps in January 1942, but was soon transferred into the Army Air Forces. After serving as an airplane-parts shipping clerk in Karachi, Pakistan, he parlayed his ham-radio experience into a post as a radio operator. Stationed first in Karachi and then outside Calcutta, in the China-Burma-India theater of operations, he was part of a B-25 bomber squadron that destroyed Japanese railroad lines, shipping, and communications in Burma, earning them the nickname of "The Burma Bridge Busters." Arnold recalls that although he "flew a couple of missions," he spent most of the war running the squadron's communications room: "At first I signed on to be a radio gunner, but they said, 'No, if you know how to fix radios, you're better off on the ground.' They wouldn't let me fly anymore." He was rotated back to the United States in December 1944, serving out the rest of the war at Wright Field in Dayton, Ohio.

The country's shared sacrifices and its victory over fascism, coupled with the eventual discovery of the full dimensions of the Holocaust, contributed to the postwar advancement of social acceptance and economic opportunities for American Jews. The Cold War climate of fierce American competitiveness with the Soviet Union also helped open doors in higher education, science, and business during the postwar years, while helping make Christians somewhat more tolerant in their social interactions with Jews, or at least less overt about their anti-Semitism.

The most immediate and far-reaching benefit of wartime service for Arnold Spielberg was the GI Bill of Rights, which finally enabled him, like 2.2 million other American veterans, to attend college. The GI Bill gave veterans what one of them called "a ticket of admission to a better life."

It was that for Arnold Spielberg, making it possible for the former department store manager to earn a degree in electronic engineering from the University of Cincinnati in June 1949 and launching him on what would turn out to be a highly successful career in computer engineering. Arnold

---

* Arnold is still shooting home movies today, mostly of his travels, using a Sony High-8 video camera and a professional-quality Avid editing system his son gave him. In his current occupation as an electronics industry consultant, Arnold also has been making industrial films: "Ever since I retired, they say to me, 'With the name Spielberg, you've got to be able to make movies.' So they got me making movies."

remembers that just before his father died, he was "so proud" to see his son enter college.

"Arnold blossomed in an academic setting," family friend Millie Tieger observed. "Arnold was such a turn-around person. He married Leah and she encouraged him to go to college. She *pushed* him. She was already a graduate of the University of Cincinnati; she was a smart girl, talented, very outgoing. I think she wanted Arnold also to have a good education. He turned out to be a brain, absolutely brilliant, a pioneer in computers. When Arnold was working in New Jersey, doing early computer research, he used to come to Cincinnati, and he would sit down at our kitchen table and calculate numbers to the thirteenth power. I had no idea what he was talking about. I would say, 'Shut up, Arnold.' "

W H E N Steven Spielberg's mother attended Walnut Hills High School, the college preparatory school for Cincinnati public school students, she was "kinda mousy. So was I," recalls fellow student Edith Cummins. "We weren't the prom queen types. She was very plain." "I was different-looking," Leah told Fred A. Bernstein, author of *The Jewish Mothers' Hall of Fame.* "But I never wanted to change. If I had had a tiny pug nose, maybe I wouldn't have had to develop a personality. But instead, I learned to play piano. I was somebody. I loved my life, and I believed in me."

"She was so different from the Spielbergs," notes Millie Tieger. "She had a sparkle. They were all bigger, dark, and here is this under-five-foot young lady, blond, her eyes flash, she talks like this [moves her head and eyes rapidly as she talks]. Arnold was super-smart and accomplished, but I think Leah had a more all-encompassing 'people' personality. She's a very insightful creature."

Leah started dating Arnold Spielberg in 1939. Arnold attended high school with Leah's brother, Bernie. "We all played tennis together," Arnold's sister Natalie recounted. "Leah was going with somebody else at the time, but when she broke up with her boyfriend I introduced her to Arnold because I thought that would be a good match."

During the early 1940s, Leah pursued her musical ambitions as a student at the renowned Cincinnati Conservatory of Music, affiliated with the University of Cincinnati. She planned a career as a concert pianist and did some public performing, much to the pride and delight of her family. Leah was "a very talented concert pianist," Arnold says. "She contributed a lot of artistic talent to Steven."

Leah, a home economics major in college, was graduated and took a job as a social worker for the Travelers Aid Society at the city's Union Terminal. She married Arnold in South Avondale's Adath Israel synagogue on February 25, 1945, while he was still in active service at Wright Field. Joining him in Dayton, Leah worked for the local social services department. After his discharge later that year and their return to Cincinnati, Leah helped administer electrocardiograms for a few months at the Jewish Hospital, but quit that job shortly before Steven was born at the same hospital. With her own artistic career sidetracked by the demands of raising a family, she passed on her artistic ambitions to her son, but never stopped playing the piano.

"The first piece of furniture we got when we were married was a piano," Arnold says. "We borrowed a bed, and we bought a Baldwin spinet." Arnold, who took piano lessons as a boy, was always an avid music listener. "We had a big collection of classical records," he recalls. "We had classical music playing in the house all the time, way back, early on." While pregnant with Steven, Leah spent much of her time playing classical pieces on her piano, and when he was an infant in diapers, he would sit on her lap on the piano bench, listening and learning to tap out the music. Sometimes Arnold also got into the act: "I knew enough to know the notes, so when she'd play, I'd turn the pages."

Sometimes the music would affect Steven in unexpected ways. "Steven always had a highly developed imagination," said Leah. "He was afraid of everything. When he was little he would insist that I lift the top of the [piano] so he could see the strings while I played. Then he would fall on the floor, screaming in fear." But Millie Tieger, who remembers watching him as a small child sitting at the piano with his mother, suggests that the early influence of Leah's music is "the key to the understanding" of his creative development: "What went into Steve when he heard his mother play music so beautifully?"

Like fellow *wunderkind* director Orson Welles, whose father was an inventor and whose mother was a concert pianist, Spielberg acquired his dazzling blend of artistic talents from a synthesis of his parents' disparate abilities. He once said he is the product of "genetic overload." His father describes Steven's personality as "a lucky piece of synergy," explaining that Steven's mother is "a very musically creative person, she's a good dancer. And she's a zany type. I'm a little more grounded. But I also like creative things. I was a great storyteller. I love science fiction."

Arnold's pioneering creativity within his own field of computers has brought him several patents. When Steven was an infant, his father would put him to sleep by the imaginative means of using an oscilloscope to reflect wavy lines on the wall. Though Steven showed no interest in following his father into engineering, he picked up his interest in filmmaking from his father. Steven's fascination with all kinds of cutting-edge technology and his mastery of the tools of filmmaking have been evident from the earliest days of his professional career.

The influence of music is also strongly evident in Spielberg's career. He played the clarinet (though not very well) in his grade school and high school bands, and sat in as first clarinet for composer John Williams in the beach scene of *Jaws*. He still noodles on the instrument for pleasure and relaxation. He has been a passionate collector of movie scores since childhood, and has said, "If I weren't a filmmaker I'd probably be in music. I'd play piano or I'd compose. I'd probably be a starving composer somewhere in Hollywood right now, hopefully not starving, but I probably would not have been successful."

In the view of Williams, who has written the scores for most of Spielberg's films, he is being overly modest about his musical sense: "Steven could have been a composer himself. He has that rhythmic sense in his whole being, and I think that is one of the great things about his directing—this rhythmic, kinetic sense he has."

Through his parents, Spielberg inherited his love of music from Grandpa Shmuel, who performed in the Russian army band, and from Grandpa Fievel, the Russian immigrant Jew who was not allowed to go to school but used his music to proclaim "How wondrous are Thy works."

Perhaps the most joyous scene in all of Spielberg's movies is the ending of *Close Encounters of the Third Kind,* in which the scientists finally devise a way of communicating with the alien mother ship by using their computers to play synthesized music together. The musical interchange between the humans and their extraterrestrial visitors starts as a few tentative notes and quickly becomes a rapturous duet of spiritual celebration.

"When I saw *Close Encounters,*" Millie Tieger recalls, "I thought, There's Leah with the music and Arnold with computers. That's Steve, the little boy. Steve wrote a movie about Mommy and Daddy."

T W O

" M A Z I K "

WE HAVE A WORD FOR HIM IN YIDDISH. WE'D CALL HIM A *MAZIK* — IT'S SAID LOVINGLY, YOU
KNOW, BUT IT MEANS A MISCHIEVOUS LITTLE DEVIL. AND HE WAS THAT!

— STEVEN SPIELBERG'S AUNT NATALIE GUTTMAN

S T E V E N Allan Spiel-
berg's birth certificate shows that he was born at Cincinnati's Jewish Hospital
at 6:16 P.M. on December 18, 1946—not December 18, 1947, as has often
been reported.

Just why Spielberg has felt it expedient to appear a year younger than
his true age throughout most of his Hollywood career became a matter of
controversy in 1995, when the issue provoked an exchange of lawsuits between Spielberg and one of his former producers, Denis C. Hoffman. But the
truth about his age was not entirely unknown over the years. In 1981, when
Patricia Goldstone, a freelance feature writer for the *Los Angeles Times,* discovered college records indicating that Spielberg actually was born in 1946,
the director "would not comment," she reported. Spielberg's incorrect age
and birthdate have been given in innumerable articles and several books,
although all that was necessary to resolve the question was a request to the
Cincinnati Board of Health for his Ohio Department of Health birth certificate. Prior to 1995, the only book on Spielberg or his work that reported his
age correctly was *Outrageous Conduct: Art, Ego, and the "Twilight Zone"
Case* (1988) by Stephen Farber and Marc Green, which cited Goldstone's
article, commenting, "Almost everyone in Hollywood lies about his age; but

Spielberg, with a premature vision of the legend he wanted to build, may have started fudging earlier than anyone else."

Spielberg's birth notice appeared in the December 26, 1946, issue of *The American Israelite,* a national Jewish newspaper published in his home town of Cincinnati: "Mr. and Mrs. Arnold Spielberg (Leah Posner), 817 Lexington Avenue, son, Wednesday, Dec. 18th." Before he moved to California, Spielberg's age was reported accurately when his filmmaking activities were written up in the Phoenix papers. *The Phoenix Jewish News* reported on December 25, 1959, that his bar mitzvah (the ceremony that takes place when a Jewish boy turns thirteen) would be held the following January 9 at Beth Hebrew Congregation. Spielberg's true birthdate also appears in the records of the high schools he attended in Phoenix and in Saratoga, California, as well as in the records of California State College (now California State University) at Long Beach. But after Spielberg began making his first inroads into Hollywood, his attitude toward his past history became more creative, and as a result the chronology of his early career has become a self-generated tangle of confusion.

On October 26, 1995, in response to questions prompted by Hoffman's lawsuit, Spielberg's attorney Marshall Grossman and his spokesman, Marvin Levy, acknowledged to the *Los Angeles Times* that "the director was born in 1946, and that any references to 1947 are incorrect," the paper reported. "But they both refused to explain why Spielberg never corrected it, or why he lists it incorrectly in documents such as his driver's license." Grossman told the paper, "I'm sure there's an answer. Maybe he didn't care what people said about his age. He cares about one thing: making films."

C O U L D Spielberg, as Farber and Green suggested, simply have been lying about his age all those years in order to make himself seem even more of a *wunderkind* than he really was? Or was there another reason for his obfuscation, one that, as Hoffman alleged, involved "a deliberate and outrageous lie perpetrated by defendant Spielberg in a calculated and malicious scheme to avoid his legal obligations"?

Spielberg was a genuine novelty when he arrived in Hollywood. The movie industry at that time "was still a middle-aged man's profession," he has recalled. "The only young people on the [Universal] lot were actors. It was just the beginning of the youth renaissance." Spielberg already had learned some valuable lessons about publicity during his teenage years, when he was hailed as a youthful filmmaking prodigy in Phoenix. So he was acutely conscious of the novelty of his age in Hollywood and the potential advantages of exploiting his precocity in the press.

One of the first contacts he made in Hollywood was Charles A. (Chuck) Silvers, Universal Pictures' film librarian, who became his earliest mentor in the film industry. Silvers remembers Spielberg telling him, "The only thing

I want to do is direct before I'm twenty-one." Spielberg did manage to direct an independent short film called *Amblin'* in the summer of 1968, several months after his twenty-first birthday. *Amblin'* was what brought Spielberg to the attention of Sid Sheinberg, then vice president of production for Universal TV, who offered Spielberg a directing contract in the fall of 1968. As Sheinberg has recalled their first conversation, Spielberg told him, "I just have one request and I'd like you to give me not so much a commitment, Mr. Sheinberg, but a promise. I want to direct something before I'm twenty-one. That would be very important to me."

Sheinberg, who may not have been entirely clear about Spielberg's actual birthdate, promised that would happen. Spielberg's age was given as twenty-one when Universal announced his signing in the Hollywood trade papers on December 12, 1968. That was indeed recognized as newsworthy, for as *The Hollywood Reporter* put it, "Spielberg, 21, is believed the youngest filmmaker ever pacted by a major studio." But the trades didn't realize that Spielberg would turn twenty-two only six days later. Spielberg's first television assignment, a segment of the three-part TV movie *Night Gallery,* went before the cameras in February 1969. So in spite of his discussion with Sheinberg at the time he was hired, Spielberg did not direct anything for Universal until he was *twenty-two,* a fact that in later years has not stopped him from making frequent claims to the contrary, such as his 1991 comment to *Premiere* magazine that "I got my contract at age twenty to be at Universal for seven years."

When Spielberg was interviewed by *The Hollywood Reporter* during the first day of shooting on *Night Gallery,* his age was accurately emblazoned in the headline 22-YEAR-OLD TYRO DIRECTS JOAN CRAWFORD. Spielberg also told the truth about his age to a rabbi who interviewed him for a Jewish newspaper in November 1970, when he was twenty-three, but shortly after that the history of his life began to undergo rewrites.

By December 28, 1970, ten days after his twenty-fourth birthday, a year had been subtracted from Spielberg's age in Hollywood press coverage: he was still twenty-three when Universal announced it was extending his contract. And when the *Reporter* talked with Spielberg again the following April, the "23-year-old" filmmaker was quoted as saying he had first set foot on the Universal lot "one day in 1969, when I was 21." The story changed again the following year, when a profile in *TV Guide* stated that Spielberg arrived at Universal "[i]n 1968, just before his 20th birthday." In subsequent interviews, Spielberg gradually began moving the date of his arrival farther and farther back, giving it as 1967, 1966, 1965, and the summer of 1964. At least he was getting closer to the truth in that respect, for it actually was in late 1963 or early 1964 when Spielberg made his first visit to Universal and met Chuck Silvers. Spielberg was then only sixteen or seventeen years old and still a high school student.*

---

* The full story of that meeting is told in Chapter Five.

It's understandable that people could have been confused about how old Spielberg was when he started in Hollywood, for apart from his precocious knowledge of filmmaking, Spielberg appeared "very young for his age in all other respects" when Silvers first met him. "Physically he was very young—thin, slight—he looked a couple or three years younger than he was."

D E N I S Hoffman, who owned a Hollywood optical and title company, produced and financed the making of *Amblin'* in the summer and fall of 1968. Spielberg's first completed 35mm film was a slickly made short whose professionalism made it an impressive calling card for the young director. Hoffman paid Spielberg no salary for making the film, and in exchange for his investment, the producer acquired an option on Spielberg's services.

On September 28, 1968, Spielberg signed an agreement with Hoffman reading in its entirety:

> To recompense for financing my story to be made into a short film I agree to direct one feature film for DENIS C. HOFFMAN sometime during the next ten years.
>
> I will be paid $25,000 plus 5% of the profit after all expenses.
>
> I will direct any script of DENIS HOFFMAN's selection and I will perform my services for him anytime during the next ten years at his choosing unless I am involved in a project. In which case I will make myself available to him immediately following said project.

Although *Amblin'* won Spielberg his seven-year contract with Universal that December, Hoffman's plans to produce another film went nowhere. Hoffman claimed in his 1995 lawsuit that he tried unsuccessfully for the next few years to get Spielberg to commit to a project. When *Jaws* became a blockbuster hit in June 1975, making Spielberg the hottest director in Hollywood, Hoffman pressed Spielberg to comply with their agreement. According to the suit, Spielberg surprised him that July by asserting that the agreement was unenforceable. Spielberg and his attorney, Bruce Ramer, allegedly claimed that at the time he signed the agreement, he was only twenty years old and, as a minor, unable to enter into a contract under California law. Believing Spielberg's assertion that he was born on December 18, 1947, Hoffman, on January 3, 1977, accepted a $30,000 buyout offer from Spielberg for all rights to *Amblin'*, including the right to use the title of the film for the name of his production company. As early as July 1975, Spielberg formed a company called Amblin', but for unexplained reasons, his Amblin Entertainment, founded in 1984, never included the apostrophe in its name.

After obtaining a copy of Spielberg's birth certificate in 1994, Hoffman renewed his claim to an option on Spielberg's services.* Discussions with Spielberg's attorneys failed to produce a settlement, and Spielberg filed a preemptive lawsuit against Hoffman in Los Angeles County Superior Court on October 24, 1995. Spielberg's suit made no specific reference to the age issue but said Hoffman had demanded $33 million "based on specious claims that the 1977 Buy-Out Agreement had been procured by Spielberg through fraud. Spielberg refused to yield to these baseless claims and prefers that they be litigated in a court of law." Hoffman filed his suit the following day, charging Spielberg with "fraud and deceit" and seeking damages for the "many millions of dollars" a producing credit on a Spielberg feature might have been worth to his career. Although Hoffman claimed he had offered Spielberg several scripts to direct, Spielberg not only denied that but also alleged that when approached by Hoffman with the buy-out offer, he "offered to try to obtain a producer's position for Hoffman on one of Spielberg's next films. Hoffman declined that offer and responded that he did not want and was not equipped to be a producer and that he wanted the $30,000 instead."

The controversy provoked head-shaking surprise in the media, which had been fooled for so many years by Spielberg's false story about his age. Even the *Los Angeles Times,* which seemed to have no institutional memory that Patricia Goldstone had revealed the truth in its pages in 1981, called the age issue the "strangest twist in the case."

"I T O L D Steve, if I'd known how famous he was going to be, I'd have had my uterus bronzed," his mother quipped in 1994.

Steven Allan Spielberg arrived at the end of the first year of the greatest baby boom in the nation's history. Millions of returning GIs and their young brides were making up for lost time, starting families during 1946. As the first-born child and only son of Arnold and Leah Spielberg, and as the first grandchild born on either side of the family, Steven "was very loved," Millie Tieger remembered. "Everybody was so thrilled with him, this first grandchild. He was a smart little kid, very talkative, a lot of fun, and cute-looking, with bangs, a camel-hair coat with leggings, and a little hat."

---

* Hoffman's lawsuit stated that in August 1994, the author of this book (whom the suit did not identify by name) "contacted Hoffman for an interview about Hoffman's early associations with defendant Spielberg. The writer visited Hoffman at Hoffman's personal residence, and spoke with Hoffman for approximately three hours. At the end of the interview, the writer commented he recently had discovered defendant Spielberg actually is one year older than his stated age. Hoffman was so astonished that he asked the writer to repeat his remark several times, to be sure he had heard the writer's statement correctly."

In fact, the author first contacted Hoffman on September 12, 1994, and in their interview two days later, the author told Hoffman that Spielberg's fudging about his age had been reported in Goldstone's 1981 *Los Angeles Times* article. When Hoffman subsequently asked how he had verified Spielberg's age, the author replied that in February 1994 he had obtained a copy of the director's birth certificate, a public record.

"From the time he was able to open his mouth his first word, I think, was 'Why?,' " his aunt Natalie Guttman said. "He'd see a shadow on the wall and want to know why it was there. . . . I used to baby-sit for him, and I can tell you, he was something. You just had to answer every question, and then there would be more. Most of what I remember is Steve's curiosity and inquirious [*sic*] nature. He was just curiouser and curiouser . . . like his father, like Leah, really like the whole family. Steven comes by his genius honestly, I have to tell you. It's in the genes."

Photographs from the period, and Arnold Spielberg's home movies, show Steven as an elfin creature with a huge cranium, protuberant ears, pale white skin, a nimbus of soft blondish-brown hair, and wide, quizzical eyes. The child's expression is penetrating, amused, and serenely confident. It's hard to escape the feeling that there is something otherworldly about Steven's appearance in his early childhood pictures. With his oversized head and eyes and his spindly body, he looks more than a bit like E.T., whom Spielberg once described as "a creature only a mother could love."

"When he was growing up, I didn't know he was a genius," Steven's own mother later admitted. "Frankly, I didn't know what the hell he was. You see, Steven wasn't exactly cuddly. What he was was scary. When Steven woke up from a nap, I shook. My mother always used to say, 'The world is going to hear of this boy.' I used to think she said it so I wouldn't kill him. . . . His badness was so original that there weren't even books to tell you what to do. . . .

"He was my first, so I didn't know that everybody didn't have kids like him. . . . If I had known better, I would have taken him to a psychiatrist, and there never would have been an *E.T.*"

W H E N asked what Steven was like as a child growing up on Lexington Avenue in the Cincinnati neighborhood of Avondale, a next-door neighbor, Roslyn Mitman, replied in one word: *"Different."*

Mrs. Mitman, who had two daughters several years older than Steven, explained, "There were times when I really wasn't all that happy my children played with him. I remember one incident. We all had pressure cookers, and they would very often explode. When his mother's pressure cooker exploded and food hit the ceiling and messed up their entire kitchen, he thought it was wonderful."

Steven's anarchic sense of humor wasn't all that bothered Mrs. Mitman about the incident. She also found it troubling that Leah didn't scold him. An exploding pressure cooker "wouldn't have upset Leah," she commented disdainfully. "It would have upset *me*—I would have killed *my* kids."

From that conventional perspective, Steven did indeed seem hopelessly spoiled by his equally eccentric mother. "I'm certifiable, dolly," Leah joked to an interviewer in 1994. "If I weren't so famous, they'd put me away." Leah seemed to have an unusually strong sense of identification with her son, finding him endlessly amusing and encouraging his rebellious, creative nature. It seems clear in retrospect that she was transferring to him her own abandoned hopes for an artistic career. People who knew both families commented that little Steven even looked more like a Posner than a Spielberg, more like his short, slender, blond mother than like his tall, stocky, dark-haired father. And if Steven increasingly showed the signs of being a special child, Leah also was generally recognized as a special mother, though the virtues of her tolerance seem clearer in retrospect than they may have to most people at the time.

Asked to describe Steven as a small child, his father says, "Precocious. Energetic. Curious. Wanting to get into everything. Wanting to ask questions about things. When he was still in a little go-car, he'd go to the store and he'd want to stop and look in the window. He was a very precocious kid in terms of wanting to fill his brain. He learned quickly. He spoke easily and early. He was into asking questions relating to fire engines, relating to things that get destroyed."

Rabbi Fishel Goldfeder of Adath Israel offered Leah some advice on how to deal with her unusual son. One day, Millie Tieger remembered, the rabbi "saw Steve throwing a fit because he wanted some toy, maybe it was a fire truck. He raised a big fuss. The rabbi said to Leah, 'Buy it for him, you're going to buy it for him anyway.' "

Leah took the rabbi's advice to heart. "Nobody ever said no to Steven," she admitted many years later. "He always gets what he wants, anyway, so the name of the game is to save your strength and say yes early." Asked how she influenced her son's development, she replied, "I gave him freedom. Steven and I happen to be very much alike. Our nervous systems, everything. . . . And everything Steven wanted to do, he did. We lived very spur of the moment; there was no structure. He has an amazing talent—this cannot be denied—but he also had the freedom to express it."

W H E N Steven was a toddler, his father was earning his degree at the University of Cincinnati and "studying all the time," Millie Tieger recalled. Arnold's absorption in his studies and, later, in his electronics career reflected his determination to make something of himself after his unpromising prewar beginnings. But it also made Steven view him as emotionally distant.

"I always felt my father put his work before me," Steven has said. "I always thought he loved me less than his work and I suffered as a result. . . . My dad was of that World War II ethic. He brought home the bacon, and my mom cooked it, and we ate it. I went to my dad with things, but he was always analytical. I was more passionate in my approach to any question, and so we always clashed. I was yearning for drama."

Still, Steven acquired what he called his father's "workaholic" personality, along with such traits as his love of storytelling and his fascination with high technology (somewhat ambivalent in Steven's case). Steven's tendency to withdraw into his own world—so different from his mother's extroverted exuberance—also is a legacy from his father. "Steven's father was an intellectual," recalls Rabbi Albert Lewis, who headed the temple to which the Spielbergs later belonged in New Jersey. "Like Steven, he was sort of an introverted person." When asked about the period just before his marriage broke up in the 1960s, Arnold Spielberg said, "Whenever things hit me with stress like that, I plunge deeper into work, to compensate."

If his father often seemed an aloof, even forbidding figure to Steven as a child, his mother at times may have seemed too much the opposite, too flighty and childlike. "We're all for immaturity in my family," Leah once said. "The rule at home was, 'Just don't be an adult.' Who needs to be anything but ten?" "We never grew up at home, because *she* never grew up," Steven commented.

T H E combination of indulgence and emotional isolation Steven experienced in his childhood may have helped delay his own maturation process by allowing him to grow up as the privileged ruler of a narcissistic fantasy world. His mother often read him J. M. Barrie's *Peter Pan* as a bedtime story, "one of the happiest memories I have from my childhood. When I was eleven years old I actually directed the story during a school production." Doubtless he was mightily impressed by Peter's defiant declaration to Mrs. Darling, "I don't want to go to school and learn solemn things. No one is going to catch me, lady, and make me a man. I want always to be a little boy and to have fun." As Spielberg admitted in 1985, "I have always felt like Peter Pan. I still feel like Peter Pan. It has been very hard for me to grow up. . . . I'm a victim of the Peter Pan Syndrome." The issue of whether Spielberg would ever "grow up"—both as a man and as a filmmaker—was much worried over by critics and other members of the press as he reached middle age.

Dr. Dan Kiley's popular 1983 book, *The Peter Pan Syndrome: Men Who Have Never Grown Up,* was strongly influenced by feminist analyses of the problem of delayed maturation in baby boomer males. Men who suffer from the syndrome, writes Kiley, perpetuate adolescent modes of behavior because of a "poor adjustment to reality" in their interpersonal relationships, such as an avoidance of commitment and a compulsion to find self-acceptance by seeking the approval of others. Such men are typically the product of a permissive upbringing by parents who "nurture the development of irresponsibility . . . in which the child believes that rules don't apply to him." From childhood onward, sufferers from the syndrome "are filled with anxiety. Early in life, tension begins to pervade the atmosphere of the home. It grows every year. . . . The cause of this free-floating anxiety is parental unhappiness."

Spielberg, who still bites his nails to the quick, "combines an incredible security with an incredible insecurity. . . . I wouldn't have known it, but he says he comes to work every day wanting to vomit," reported Dustin Hoffman, who played the title role in *Hook,* Spielberg's 1991 contemporary gloss on *Peter Pan.* Spielberg dealt directly with the damaging effects of the Peter Pan Syndrome in that uneven but autobiographically very revealing film, with Robin Williams playing Peter as an anxious middle-aged yuppie workaholic who emotionally neglects his own son, making him hostile and rebellious while driving him into the clutches of Captain Hook, the child-hating surrogate father.

In a penetrating 1991 essay on Spielberg's work, Henry Sheehan wrote, "[I]n fragments, that story is the story of nearly every Spielberg film. . . . Although Spielberg's films are usually described as warm or even exhilarating and euphoric, their most prevalent temper is anxiety. Every Spielberg hero from *Duel* onward is, to one extent or another, worried that he is failing at some essentially male role, either lover or father. In *Hook* these twin fears are merged in Peter, who is plainly a poor father and who, less conspicuously, wants to retreat from the issue of sex in general."

Those prone to the Peter Pan Syndrome and all its attendant anxieties also tend to share some positive attributes, Kiley reminds us, and they are attributes Spielberg has had in abundance since childhood: "a rich imagination and a yearning to stay young at heart. Cannot these traits be portals to brilliance and serenity?" However stunting Spielberg's upbringing may have proved to his emotional growth, it allowed him the psychological license to explore his creativity with a rare degree of boldness and self-confidence. A "poor adjustment to reality" is not necessarily a handicap for a filmmaker, particularly one who often works in fantasy genres as Spielberg does, although it would help account for his frequent difficulties working himself up to dealing with adult subjects.

S P I E L B E R G grew up hearing his parents talking about "the murdering Nazis" and hearing stories from his "verbal grandparents who constantly spoke about" the extermination of the Jews. Since the Nazis' rise to power, European Jews had found refuge in the close-knit community of Cincinnati's Avondale, and there were many Holocaust survivors living in the neighborhood. In the English classes taught four times a day by Steven's grandmother, Jennie Posner, for eight or ten students gathered around the dining room table at her home on Glenwood Avenue, survivors told stories of what they referred to as "The Great Murder."

Steven would visit with his mother when the lessons were in progress, and he learned his numbers from one of Jennie's pupils. The man showed Steven the tattoo that had been burned into his arm at Auschwitz for identification. As Steven remembered, "He would roll up his sleeves and say, 'This is a four, this is a seven, this is a two.' It was my first concept of numbers. He would always say, 'I have a magic trick.' He pointed to a six. And then he crooked his elbow and said, 'Now it's a nine.' "

"Every person there had a history, either their own or about their family or someone they knew," recalled Leah, who often repeated stories she heard to Steven. "Some of the stories were so horrible that there was almost a movie-like quality to them. It was hard to imagine terrible things like that actually happening. It brought the Holocaust close to home, because you were talking to people who had lived through these unimaginable things. . . .

"I remember one woman's story. The Nazis wanted her ring. She couldn't get it off. They were about to cut her finger off, but the ring suddenly fell off on its own. I guess it was her panic. It just freaked me. I'm sure it affected Steven. . . . Who knows how much our children absorb when they're very young? Perhaps more than we imagine."

"In a strange way my life has always come back to images surrounding the Holocaust," Steven agreed in 1993. "The Holocaust had been part of my life, just based on what my parents would say at the dinner table. We lost cousins, aunts, uncles. When I was very young, I remember my mother telling me about a friend of hers in Germany, a pianist who played a symphony that wasn't permitted, and the Germans came up on stage and broke every finger on her hands. I grew up with stories of Nazis breaking the fingers of Jews."

M O V I N G from the traditional Jewish neighborhood of Avondale and choosing to raise her children largely among gentiles was "my one really big mistake," Leah once said, recalling the incidents of overt anti-Semitism that Steven began to encounter while growing up in mostly WASP suburbia. Although it was Arnold's career path that primarily motivated the family's movements around the country, Leah took responsibility for the fact that from 1950 onward, the family lived in neighborhoods that were progressively less and less Jewish. "I didn't want to be part of any community or deal with any labels," she explained. "I've never been very comfortable traveling in a pack."*

But the Spielbergs' living situation was never as simple or clear-cut as either Steven or his mother remembers. They had gentile neighbors in Avondale, some of whom looked upon them with barely repressed hostility, and they were not entirely lacking for the company of Jewish neighbors and friends in New Jersey, Arizona, and California. The distinctions among their living places were subtle, and helped shape Steven's evolving personality.

L I V I N G in a Jewish neighborhood such as Avondale could be fraught with nightmarish images for a small child in the immediate postwar years, but Steven did have the advantage of starting life in an insular, cocoonlike

---

* Leah also began to call herself "Lee," a name that sounded less Jewish; her husband and even her children called her Lee.

setting that shielded him from many of the harsher realities outside his middle-class ghetto. Relations between Jews and their minority of gentile neighbors were outwardly polite, but not without submerged tension.

"Being we weren't Jewish, we didn't know the people," admits Anastasia Del Favero, an Italian-American Catholic with three children who lived next door to the Spielbergs. "They were nice people, mostly all Jewish, but we didn't really know them. There was a family there with a baby, but I was so busy—I had three children, my husband was working—I didn't have time to socialize."

"It's a shame that I do not remember [Steven] at all, but as a teenager, I don't think I bothered much for two-year-olds," says Anastasia's sister-in-law, Dolores Del Favero Huff, who also lived in the house next door to the Spielbergs. "I did not baby-sit for him—they were Jewish. When I grew up in Avondale, as a gentile, I had no Jewish friends. The Jewish children stayed with their own kind. They didn't bother with the gentiles. I just think it's the breed—I believe that—I guess they feel they're different from us. They'd say hello, but as far as playing or going to a movie—I did not make the attempt."

Meyer Singerman, a veteran of the U.S. Army Air Forces who lived two doors down from the Spielbergs, had worked for the B'nai B'rith Anti-Defamation League. Although he recalls Avondale residents sharing Cincinnati's exclusionary attitude toward African Americans—"I don't think blacks could have moved between us and the Spielbergs"—he also says, "I don't remember any anti-Semitic incidents there involving me and my family. When you lived in a Jewish community and you're very young, you don't see the real world." Steven's cousin Samuel Guttman, who was born in 1949 and has a younger brother and sister, says that whatever anti-Semitism Steven might have encountered in Cincinnati, it would have been "no more than us —having fights as kids."

There were not many children of Steven's age in the immediate neighborhood; most of the people there were middle-aged. Steven, as a result, spent most of his time around adults, his parents and grandparents and their family and friends, Jennie's pupils from overseas, and the people at the shops and synagogues. Living his first two and a half years in a neighborhood that Peggie Singerman characterizes as "culturally advanced" and Millie Tieger describes as "a hotbed of brains," Steven no doubt acquired some of his sense of otherness, his precocious reserve and gravity, from learning to deal at an early age with people much older than he was, many of whom regarded him (benignly or not) as "different." A child who seldom spends time with other children learns to speak when he is spoken to, and he learns to live with solitude and his imagination, finding his sense of play not so much from others but from within himself.

What Steven experienced of Cincinnati, aside from his vividly remembered encounters with Holocaust survivors and his mother's music, may lie mostly beneath his consciousness. His family's devotion, especially that of his mother, no doubt fostered his early belief that he was a special creature, that his differences from other people were something to be cherished. Such a belief may have helped shield him from any conscious awareness that his more conventional and bigoted neighbors saw him as "different" in a negative sense. But he could not have helped internalizing the effects of their isolating gazes.

L o o k i n g back from the perspective of 1994 and her born-again Orthodoxy, Leah felt that, aside from the family's observance of the Sabbath and Jewish holidays during the years when Steven was growing up, Judaism was "a very nothing part of our lives."

"Leah's parents, while they were Orthodox, attended a Conservative synagogue," Arnold relates. "But they obeyed the Sabbath. They did not do anything on the Sabbath, except during the worst times in the Depression, when Mr. Posner just had to work. When Leah and I got married, first we were observant, then she said, 'I've got to get off the kosher standard. I want lobster and things like that.' So we'd go off the kosher standard, then her conscience would prick her, and we'd go back on the kosher standard. We'd go in and out of it. But when she married [her second husband] Bernie Adler, he was very religious, so she stayed totally Orthodox."

After leaving Cincinnati, the Spielbergs tended to observe the laws of *kashrut* (kosher food preparation) only when their rabbi or Leah's parents came for visits. As Steven put it, they were "storefront kosher." Leah once was preparing to boil three live lobsters for dinner when they heard the rabbi's car pulling up in their driveway. Steven hid the lobsters under his bed until the rabbi departed.

If Leah and Arnold felt limited, and perhaps even somewhat stifled, by the traditionalism of their decaying hometown environment, and were willing to brave alienation and loss of identity by leaving it, they were typical of their generation of Americans who were starting families and careers in the late 1940s and early 1950s.

"In the years following the traumatic experiences of the Depression and World War II, the American Dream was to exercise personal freedom not in social and political terms, but rather in economic ones," David Halberstam wrote in *The Fifties*. "Eager to be part of the burgeoning middle class, young men and women opted for material well-being, particularly if it came with some form of guaranteed employment. For the young, eager veteran just out of college (which he had attended courtesy of the GI Bill), security meant finding a good white-collar job with a large, benevolent company, getting married, having children, and buying a house in the suburbs. In that era of general good will and expanding affluence, few Americans doubted the essential goodness of their society."

Arnold Spielberg, thirty-two years old and newly graduated from the University of Cincinnati, was hired by RCA in June 1949 to work at its manufacturing plant in Camden, New Jersey, across the Delaware River from

Philadelphia. "I thought RCA hired me to work on television," he recalls. "When I showed up there, no, they didn't have a job in television: 'You're in military electronics.' I was doing circuit development, then I got involved in advanced circuit development leading toward computer technology. We were trying to prove, 'Do we use tubes? Do we use magnetics?' Transistors were just beginning to come in. 'Do we use transistors?' We had contests to see which design would win for the technology to be used in designing computers. It was that early. I hardly even knew about computers at college, other than about analog computers. I only became interested in computers while I was at RCA."

Arnold's chosen field of electronics at that time was still a profession dominated by WASPs, although the fact that RCA chairman David Sarnoff was Jewish helped make that company more hospitable to Jews than others. As the Cold War and scientific competition with the Soviet Union intensified in the 1950s, many of the long-standing barriers against Jews in American science and higher education began to fall. Arnold was one of the beneficiaries of that change, and he became a stellar example of achievement in his newly developing field. But his family paid a price in rootlessness and instability as he moved them around the country, responding to career opportunities and the eventual westward migration of the computer industry.

"Just as I'd become accustomed to a school and a teacher and a best friend," Steven has recalled, "the FOR SALE sign would dig into the front lawn. . . . And it would always be that inevitable good-bye scene, in the train station or at the carport packing up the car to drive somewhere, or at the airport. Where all my friends would be there and we'd say good-bye to each other and I would leave. This happened to me four major times in my life. And the older I got the harder it got. *E.T.* reflects a lot of that. When Elliott finds E.T., he hangs onto E.T., he announces in no uncertain terms, 'I'm keeping him,' and he means it."

The anxiety caused by the first of those moves may help account for the fact that, as Spielberg has said, "I've been biting my fingernails since I was four"; the move from his hometown of Cincinnati to New Jersey took place the year he turned three.

Explaining why he nevertheless has always felt a basic optimism, Spielberg said, "I think growing up I had no other choice. I guess because I was surrounded by so much negativity when I was a kid that I had no recourse but to be positive. I think it kind of runs in my family, too—my mother is a very positive thinker. One of the first words I learned, when I was very, very young, one of the first sentences I ever put together—my mother reminds me of this, I don't consciously remember it—was 'looking forward to.' And it always used to be about my grandparents. I loved it when they'd come to visit from Ohio to New Jersey, and my mother would say, 'It's something to look forward to, they're coming in two weeks,' and a week later she would say, 'It's something to look forward to, they'll be here in a week.' "

During their first three years in New Jersey, the Spielbergs lived in a huge complex of identical red-brick buildings at 219 South Twenty-ninth Street in Camden, the Washington Park Apartments. Although the complex looked like a barracks, it had the consolation of being considered the place where, as family friend Miriam Fuhrman put it, "All the young Jewish couples lived" (it is now populated largely by African Americans and Hispanics). While the Spielbergs were living in Camden, Steven's oldest sister, Anne, was born in Philadelphia on Christmas Day 1949.*

In August 1952, the Spielbergs moved a few miles to suburban Haddon Township, adjacent to Haddonfield, an affluent, quaintly picturesque village of seventeen thousand settled by English and Irish Quakers in the early 1700s. Many other RCA employees and people who worked in companies doing business with RCA also lived in the Haddonfield area. Although the Spielbergs were part of a migration of young Jewish families from Camden to Haddon Township, their move to the suburbs was a momentous step, culturally speaking, because it meant entering a more heterogeneous community in which Jews were expected to assimilate in order to be accepted.

"After 1945, the social and economic profile of American Jews was transformed into one that closely approximated the American ideal," Edward S. Shapiro wrote in *A Time for Healing*. ". . . The most important aspect of the postwar mobility of America's Jews was their relocation to the suburbs and their movement into the middle class. While mirroring national currents, these demographic trends were more intense among Jews. Historian Arthur Hertzberg estimated that, in the two decades between 1945 and 1965, one out of every three Jews left the big cities for the suburbs, a rate higher than that of other Americans. Jews tended to cluster together in suburbia, but some brave pioneers moved into suburbs that contained few if any Jews."

Throughout the United States, the decade of the 1950s saw the old urban patterns of vertical, tightly packed dwellings exploding kaleidoscopically into sprawling rows of look-alike suburban houses, with lawns and backyards and sprinklers and play sets for the rapidly arriving children. There was a numbing conformity in this rush to replicate Levittown, an intellectually arid, unimaginative, and ultimately illusory sense of safeness that would be increasingly decried and mocked and challenged by the end of the decade. The rise of the civil rights and feminist movements would shed an even harsher light on the exclusionism and patriarchy of middle-class American life in the Eisenhower era, which the suburbs came to typify. Many who grew up in 1950s suburbia, as a result, look back on that milieu with an unresolved mixture of nostalgic yearning and embarrassed distaste, and Steven Spielberg, "the poet of suburbia," has captured that ambivalence in his films.

---

* Steven's two other sisters also were born while the family lived in New Jersey, Susan on December 4, 1953, and Nancy on June 7, 1956. Anne Spielberg lives in Sherman Oaks, California, with her husband, Danny Opatoshu (son of actor David Opatoshu and grandson of Yiddish novelist Joseph Opatoshu). Sue (Mrs. Jerry Pasternak) lives in Silver Spring, Maryland, and Nancy (Mrs. Shimon Katz) in Riverdale, New York.

It is impossible to imagine John Ford never having seen Monument Valley, or Martin Scorsese never having walked New York's mean streets, and it is equally impossible to imagine Steven Spielberg never having grown up in suburbia. "I never mock suburbia," Spielberg has said. "My life comes from there." And yet, despite his expressions of affection for suburbia, Spielberg does not entirely believe in it, share its values, or depict it in quite such glowing terms on screen. In such Spielberg films as *Duel* and *Close Encounters* and *E.T.*, the suburbia to which his upwardly mobile parents escaped in the early 1950s becomes a place of entrapment from which his dissatisfied middle-class characters yearn to escape.

" M E S H U G G E N E H "

HE WAS DISAPPOINTED IN THE WORLD, SO HE BUILT ONE OF HIS OWN.

— JEDEDIAH LELAND ON
CHARLES FOSTER KANE IN *CITIZEN KANE*

T was early 1952 in Camden, New Jersey, when Steven Spielberg, who had just turned five, first went to a movie theater.

"My father told me he was taking me to see a circus movie," he remembered. "Well, I didn't hear the word *movie,* I only heard the word *circus.* So we stood in line for an hour and a half and I thought I was going to see a circus. I'd already been once before to a circus and I knew what to expect: the elephants, the lion tamer, the fire, the clowns. And to go into this big cavernous hall and there's nothing but chairs and they're all facing up, they're not bleachers, they're chairs—I was thinking, Something is up, something is fishy.

"So the curtain is open and I expect to see the elephants and there's nothing but a flat piece of white cardboard, a canvas. And I look at the canvas and suddenly a movie comes on and it's *The Greatest Show on Earth* [the Cecil B. DeMille spectacle that won the 1952 Oscar for Best Picture]. At first I was so disappointed, I was angry at my father, he told me he was taking me to a circus and it's just this flat piece of color. I retained three things from the experience: the train wreck, the lions, and Jimmy Stewart as the clown. Everything else went over my head.

"For a while I kept thinking, Gee, that's not fair, I wanted to see three-dimensional characters and all this was was flat shadows, flat surfaces. . . . I was *disappointed* by everything after that. I didn't trust anybody. . . . I never felt life was good enough, so I had to embellish it."

T o the exasperated Arnold Fuhrman, the Spielbergs' next-door neighbor in Camden's Washington Park Apartments, little "Stevie" was a *"vilde chai"* —Hebrew for "wild creature."

"That Stevie is *meshuggeneh,"* Fuhrman also would complain, using the Yiddish for "crazy." Once, he recalled, Leah baked a cherry pie and Stevie tossed it up onto the ceiling, watching fascinated as it dripped down to the floor. Fuhrman became incensed over Stevie's constant teasing of his little daughter, Jane. Stevie liked to terrify Janie in her playpen, and when he would see her outside wearing a dress, he would push her to the ground and grind her into the dirt with his foot. Every day when Arnold Fuhrman came home from work, he would say to his wife, Mitzi, "What did the little son of a bitch do today?"

"Our father would threaten to kill Steven for years because he was torturing Janie," her brother Glenn reports. "Later he took credit for Spielberg's success because he didn't kill him."

As upsetting as it was to the Fuhrmans, Stevie's fondness for scaring Janie was an early manifestation of his creative impulses. Even Arnold Fuhrman had to admit that Stevie was "bizarrely creative." He gradually would learn to express his aggression and hostility in more constructive ways, although his penchant for teasing younger children, especially girls, would long retain an edge of cruelty. He would delight in scaring his friends and his three younger sisters, whether it was with spooky stories, weird makeup, ghoulish games, or, eventually, with movies that made people scream.

From his early childhood, Spielberg has been intimately acquainted with fear. "He had a lot of phobias that were slowly worked out," his father says. "He had a lot of imagination, and it was not difficult for him to visualize anything scary or frightening or threatening out of simple things."

After his family moved in 1952 to the Camden suburb of Haddon Township, Steven was haunted by a single spindly maple tree in front of their house, illuminated by a streetlight. The moving shadows it cast at night on the wall of his second-floor bedroom seemed to Steven the shapes of monsters with gnarled heads and waving tentacles. Other monsters, he was convinced, were living under his bed and in his closet. And he would study the crack in the plaster above the closet door, persuading himself that more amiable creatures dwelled inside the crack. He remembered having the eerie experience of seeing the crack burst open and pieces of plaster tumble out of it.*

Steven began to find that the fears generated by his imagination could be strangely enjoyable, especially if he could discover ways of manipulating them and conjuring up new kinds of visual effects. "I used to be afraid of my hand shadow," he said. "I would sit in bed at night, see how white the ceiling was—there was a big stucco ceiling and I would put a small lamp on the floor and turn the light on with a naked bulb and I would do these hand shadows. I would scare myself with hand shadows."

The solitary burden of all these phobias increasingly demanded some kind of outward release. He was fortunate to have a captive and pliable audience to help satisfy his need for self-expression: "I had no way to sublimate or channel those fears until I began telling stories to my younger sisters. This removed the fear from my soul and transferred it right into theirs."

His sister Anne, who became a Hollywood screenwriter, once said, "At the preview of *Jaws,* I remember thinking, For years he just scared us. Now he gets to scare the masses."

N O T much has been written about Spielberg's years in New Jersey, the period in which he grew from two and a half to ten years old, a crucial time in anyone's psychological and social development. Perhaps this neglect stems largely from Spielberg's own fuzzy memories of that time and place. His boyhood reminiscences tend to focus on his subsequent years in Arizona, but it was while living in New Jersey that he first showed real signs of creativity.

His memory has created a distorted picture of his neighborhood in Haddon Township. In a 1994 interview with Julie Salamon for *Harper's Bazaar,* he spoke at length about his feelings of growing up Jewish, remembering how distressed he was that "everybody else" on his street put up lights on their houses during the Christmas season. His house, by contrast, seemed like "the black hole of Crystal Terrace." Spielberg's subjective childhood feelings of exclusion, of being "different," became so intense that his memory exaggerated the degree to which his family was seen that way by their New Jersey neighbors—many of whom, in fact, were also Jewish.

Crystal Terrace, which has changed very little since the Spielbergs lived there, is a lovely, tree-lined street curving in a gentle arc off one of the main thoroughfares in Haddon Township, Crystal Lake Avenue. The residents use the adjacent town of Haddonfield as their mailing address, and Spielberg never tells interviewers that he actually lived in Haddon Township. But

---

* As unlikely as that may seem, he probably was not imagining it. Loretta Knoblach, who bought the house from the Spielbergs with her husband, August, says stresses in the wall cause the plaster above the closet door to expand slowly, with the result that "the crack in his bedroom comes back every couple of years, then we paint it."

especially for Jews in that era, the more welcoming Haddon Township, with its plethora of newly arrived and upwardly mobile middle-class families, was quite different from staid, old-monied, WASPish Haddonfield.

The Spielbergs' two-story Colonial-style house at 267 Crystal Terrace, which they bought from Peter and Helen Rutan for $14,000, had been built in 1949, when the street was developed from rustic land, the site of an old potato farm. During Steven's childhood, vestiges of the farm could still be seen behind his house, a block away. He and his playmates ventured with some trepidation into the Gothic wooded area and field surrounding the weathered farmhouse and a rusting hulk of abandoned farm machinery. Steven evidently combined his memory of the old farm with the single tree on his front lawn to conjure up the synthetic memory image of a spooky "forest outside my window." He used that memory as the basis for the scene in his 1982 movie *Poltergeist* of a menacing tree bursting through a boy's bedroom window (*Poltergeist* also contains a scary clown doll, another object of Steven's childhood fears).

Many of the fathers in Steven's neighborhood were, like Arnold Spielberg, young veterans buying their first homes under the GI Bill. Crystal Terrace swarmed with dozens of children, and one of Steven's neighbors, Marjorie Robbins, remembers, "He looked like all the other boys—thin, with a crew cut and a baseball cap that covers the whole face, with the ears sticking out." "There were a lot of Protestants, a lot of Jews, Italians, Irish, Germans—we all got along," says Robert Moran Sr., an Irish Catholic who lived across the street from the Spielbergs. "It was a great place for kids to be raised. What made it nice is that it was a new neighborhood and people came in from different areas. Most of them were young people and they got along."

There were at least three other Jewish families among the twenty-six households on Crystal Terrace in that period, and the adjacent Crystal Lake Avenue was predominantly Jewish. "That was the Jewish neighborhood, the Jewish ghetto" for the Haddonfield area, according to Rabbi Albert Lewis of Temple Beth Shalom, who taught Steven in Hebrew school from 1953 to 1957.* Before World War II, Haddonfield was restricted against Jews, and despite the postwar migration of Jews from Camden and nearby Philadelphia, it "liberalized but very slowly," the rabbi says. "There were some country clubs in which Jews weren't allowed. That's why the Jewish community created our own country club."

"My sense of anti-Semitism as a kid wasn't so great [as Steven's]," says Marjorie Robbins, who grew up around the corner from Steven on Crystal Lake Avenue and, like him, is Jewish. "I think because the Jewish community was very warm, very loving, so that gave a security. We lived in a community where the doors were always unlocked. We had freedom to express our-

---

* Steven also attended kindergarten through fourth grade at Thomas A. Edison School in Haddonfield from December 1952 until February 1957. Earlier he had attended kindergarten in Camden.

selves, freedom to imagine, freedom to create. But the street where he lived was very Christian, and it was very obvious at Christmastime that we live in a Christian world. I remember seeing Santa Claus outside the A&P on Kings Highway, and we used to get in the car—we all did this—and drive through Haddonfield looking at the Christmas lights. It was spectacular."

Crystal Terrace had its own lavish Christmas displays. Each year the Morans prominently displayed a large Nativity scene, with spotlights and brightly colored Christmas lights, that the Spielbergs could not avoid seeing from their living-room window. Steven's next-door playmate Scott MacDonald, who was a Presbyterian, remembers Christmas being "a stressful time for him. We would bring our presents outside, and I remember him kind of being in a huff. It was not one of his more positive times. Nobody knew the difference about a Jewish kid, except they didn't have Christmas. He might have gotten some kind of ribbing about, 'What do you do? You don't get presents.' "

When Scott's sister, Jane MacDonald Morley, asked Anne Spielberg why they didn't celebrate Christmas, Anne "said their father was Santa Claus; he was so busy, and that's why they didn't have time to celebrate it. I knew he didn't look anything like Santa Claus, and he smoked a cigar. I couldn't imagine that Santa Claus smoked a cigar. So I asked my mother and she told me, No, Mr. Spielberg was not Santa Claus."

Steven was "quite inquisitive—he asked everybody else about their religion," recalls next-door neighbor Mary Devlin, a Catholic. Steven often quizzed her son, Charles F. (Cholly) Devlin, about his duties as an altar boy. "He would usually ask about the services—he would ask about the observances rather than about the faith," Devlin says. "He was interested in rituals—'What is that you are carrying?' I would be carrying a cassock and a surplice. 'Where are you going at six A.M.?' "

Another neighbor boy, Gerald McMullen, admits, "I was one of the kids who tried to convince him that Jesus Christ was really who he was. I was going to Catholic school and thought Christianity was *it*. Most of the kids were Christians; Steven was the only one who didn't recognize Christ. He told me something to the effect that 'My mother says no, Jesus was not the Messiah.' I remember telling him to go home and tell his mother that she was wrong. He wasn't upset to the point that he reacted with any kind of emotion or anger, but you could tell from the way he reacted to it that he felt bad. I don't recall him as being different, he was actually quite well liked, but he probably felt it more keenly. His parents were really nice people, even to me, in spite of what I told him to tell his mother. She always welcomed me when I came over. I felt pretty bad about it when I got older and realized what I had done. The older I was, the more embarrassed I was I didn't know the difference between Catholicism and Judaism."

The lesson Steven took from such encounters was: "Being a Jew meant that I was not normal. I was not like everybody else. I just wanted to be accepted. Not for who I was. I wanted to be accepted for who everybody else was."

At Christmastime, Julie Salamon related in her profile of Spielberg, he wanted his parents to put up lights for the holiday season. They told him, "We're Jews and Jews don't put up lights like the gentiles." Steven tried to compromise by suggesting that he could put up blue and white Hanukkah lights, but his father said, "We have a nice menorah. If you'd like, we can put the menorah in the window."

"_No! No! No!_" screamed Steven. "People will think we're Jewish."

One night before Christmas, according to Salamon's account, Steven created his own holiday tableau on the family's front porch. Using extension cords, he hooked up a color wheel—a revolving device that projected light patterns through colored gels—and had his four-year-old sister Anne wait at the switch. Then he draped himself in a white sheet and struck a Crucifixion pose, giving Anne the signal to start the color wheel turning. As people drove along Crystal Terrace to look at their neighbors' Christmas decorations, Steven could be seen on his porch playing the role of Jesus, dramatically bathed in a nimbus of shimmering colored lights, a precursor of the lighting effects that would herald the arrival of extraterrestrial creatures in such Spielberg movies as _Close Encounters_ and _E.T._

"His parents were furious," Salamon wrote. "They dragged their son, kicking and screaming and crying, away from the door, muttering that he was making a _shande_ (a shame) in front of the neighbors."

When that story was recounted to Arnold Spielberg by the author of this book, Arnold responded, "I don't remember him dressing up like Jesus. I think I would have said, 'No way.' " But Steven's father added, "I can _visualize_ him doing that. Because I know he wanted in the worst way to have Christmas lights. I said, 'No, we're Jewish. We can have Hanukkah lights, and we'll put up the Hanukkah lights in the window.' So I went and found a candelabra of some kind and I got blue little bulbs and put 'em in that, and I said, 'Keep that in the window for the eight days of Hanukkah.' "

Even if it may have been somewhat transformed in Steven's memory, the incident over the Christmas lights is a revealing illustration of the creative process by which he took his painful feelings of being different and learned to transform them into his own individualized form of art—an art that also would appeal to the widest audience he could think of commanding.

A YEAR and a half after joining RCA, Arnold Spielberg became the engineer in charge of advanced development on the company's first venture into computers, the Bizmac. Covering an entire floor at the Camden plant, the Bizmac contained 100,000 vacuum tubes and was built as a cost-inventory control unit for the U.S. Army Ordnance Corps. While it was being completed, transistors were introduced, revolutionizing the field of computers. RCA delivered the Bizmac to the Army, but it became a costly white elephant. Before leaving in 1957 to join General Electric in Phoenix, Arnold also worked on RCA's first transistor computer, a communications computer project, and a computerized sales recording system.

Arnold "had the reputation of being one of the way-out engineers," recalls his Camden neighbor Miriam Fuhrman, who also worked for RCA. "He was an absolutely brilliant guy." "He was the absent-minded professor," adds her niece, Jane Fuhrman Satanoff. "He once stopped to get gas. Leah got out to go to the bathroom. He was an hour on the road before he realized it." Arnold's superior on the Bizmac project, J. Wesley Leas, remembers him as "somebody you would give a job to and you knew he would do what it took to get it done. He would work his ass off. He would give his life for you. You would see him Sundays and late at night, if that was needed. He would stick with a problem no matter how difficult it was. But don't ever put 'creative' with him. His technical talents were very good, as were his managerial talents. He just wasn't imaginative. He was more methodical, more of a plodder. His wife was the one with vision, flair, creativeness."

In some ways, though, the dichotomy Steven and others have drawn between his mother (creativity) and his father (logic) is not quite so clear-cut. Whether or not Arnold Spielberg can be described as a "creative" or "imaginative" person in the way those words are used in the arts, his pioneering work in computers demonstrated an ability to break new technological ground while devising complex and innovative systems of communication. Steven Spielberg has mastered an equally complex modern art form that depends to a large degree on the creative synthesis of technology, including computer technology, which his films have helped pioneer. And when Steven started making his first amateur films, he was imitating his father, who had been shooting home movies since the age of seventeen. After the family moved to Arizona on Valentine's Day 1957, Arnold became an enthusiastic tutor and partner in Steven's amateur filmmaking ventures.

Unlike Leah, however, Arnold was not as encouraging as Steven would have wanted about his choice of filmmaking as a career. From an early age, Steven could not help disappointing his father with his overwhelming lack of aptitude for engineering. "I hated math in school," Steven admitted. "I didn't like when they'd stack the numbers on top of one another. My father used to say things like three into four won't go, and I'd say, 'Of course it won't. You can't put that three into the little hole on top of the four. It won't fit.' "

Nevertheless, Arnold is convinced that his technological background did have an influence on his son's career as a filmmaker: "At first he absolutely was against learning anything mathematical or scientific. He still doesn't care for it that much, but he has to now. It's his game. And he's caught up in it. His use of a computer is different from mine. I'll use it to do business on it, I hardly ever play games. He *only* plays games on the computer. His house has a whole row of video games. He's got a flight control simulator. I was over at his house the other day [in December 1995] and he was shooting down planes with a skill that a pilot would have."

Leah's attitude toward Steven's education eventually would become more *laissez-faire,* but after he entered Edison School in Haddonfield, she too was frustrated over his lack of interest in conventional intellectual pursuits. "His mother was quite upset because his marks weren't what she was expecting," Mary Devlin recalls. "He only got C's" during his four years at Edison, adds Jane Fuhrman Satanoff, "and she was always disappointed because he was so bright but he was just a mediocre student." Leah would compare Steven's marks with those of a certain neighbor boy, and "she couldn't understand how [Steven] wasn't doing better," Mary Devlin says. "He didn't have time for it—he was always playing. He was a nice boy, very small and thin, but just involved in what he wanted to do. We didn't sense he was very bright."

"He was a very quiet youngster and remained so for many years," says Rabbi Lewis of Temple Beth Shalom. Attending Hebrew school three afternoons a week, Steven and his fellow students would arrive on the bus "very exhausted" following a full day at public school, the rabbi says. "Steven sat there. He did what he had to do." Remembering his religious education as a "punitive" ordeal, Steven has tried to make his children's training in Jewish tradition more "fun" than his own. "I don't think I was really trained properly. I think it would have stuck with me a lot longer had the training been less like going to the dentist and having my teeth pulled."* Although Steven was also a member of the temple's Cub Scout troop, Rabbi Lewis could see he needed something more than school and Scouting to develop his social skills: "He needed a way to express himself. He needed that because he was pretty much a loner."

"I remember him just walking along in a daydream, with that kind of towhead," says Leah's friend Grace Robbins. "I never remember him with other children. To me he looked like he was in a dream world. Not that he was lost in oblivion, but lost in thought. I didn't see it because I didn't spend much time with him, but I know Leah thought he had something. She said, 'He is different. Without a doubt, he is different.' His mother got a big kick out of him, in spite of the things he did. I think she was the right mother for him. She had a lot of wit, she wasn't dull."

As a result of his father's long hours at work, Steven saw much less of Arnold than he would have liked. The elder Spielberg is remembered as a shadowy figure by most of his neighbors on Crystal Terrace. "I very rarely saw him," says Steven's next-door playmate Scott MacDonald. "I remember him being tall, on the portly side, with dark hair. He always wore a white shirt, and I remember he had a pocket protector with pens. I don't remember seeing him playing in the yard. A lot of fathers would play catch with their

---

* When his second wife, Kate Capshaw, converted to Judaism before their marriage in 1991, Spielberg studied along with her and said he had "learned more in one year than I had learned all through formal Jewish training."

kids or coach baseball, but Steve's father never did. He would never do anything with him."

Arnold's workaholic tendencies already were beginning to cause noticeable tensions in the household. When Arnold would come home from work, the neighbors would often hear him bellow, "Leah, I am home. Are you dead or alive?" According to the neighbors, Leah seemed to spend most of her time practicing on her piano or sunning herself in the yard, when she wasn't playing Scrabble or cards with her friends Grace Robbins and Cissy Cutler. Perhaps because of his growing distance from his father, Steven clung even closer to his mother emotionally. "Every time she had to go someplace he took sick," Mary Devlin says. "He didn't want her to go. She was a good person, very loving. Leah had a wonderful disposition—everything was a big joke. If you'd have a bad day, you'd talk to Leah and feel better."

"She seemed much more relaxed than our mothers, much more liberal, bordering on the artsy," says Cholly Devlin. "She was unique in our neighborhood. In a sense, my mother and the rest of the mothers were right out of the Betty Crocker mold. At the time housewives would clean house and serve food. They would be the model mother of the fifties. But she wasn't. She was much more 'with it.' "

A N incident that may have occurred near the end of the Spielbergs' stay in New Jersey symbolized for Steven his growing tensions with his father.

Arnold brought home one of the first transistors from RCA. Displaying it to his family, he proclaimed, "This is the future." Steven promptly took the transistor and swallowed it. His father, he recalled, laughed involuntarily, but quickly became upset. No wonder, for that primitive transistor was not only his Dad's prized possession, but a piece of hardware half an inch in diameter and a quarter-inch thick, with "a few wires sticking out of it," reports Arnold's boss at RCA, Wes Leas. Steven's impulsive gesture could be interpreted as a bizarre tribute to his father, his own literal way of internalizing Arnold's love of technology. But in Steven's telling of the tale, making the transistor disappear carried another, more defiant message to his father: "That's your future, but it doesn't have to be mine."

Arnold says he doesn't recall such an incident. But it amuses him to hear Steven's story. He allows it "could have" happened. Steven, he says, "has a good memory [of what happened to him] as a kid. Plus a little exaggeration. He's a good storyteller."

"I S E E pieces of me in Steven," Arnold told *Time* magazine in 1985. "I see the storyteller."

"When my kids were young," he explains, "I used to love to tell them stories. I used to have running serials of adventures that I told the kids when they'd go to bed. For Steve, I had one set of stories, and for the girls, another.

I always involved them in the adventures. They were climbing caves, and going here and there. I invented time machines that they would get into and go back and look at things in time and rescue somebody. I invented all kinds of animals. I invented characters, a girl and a boy, Joanie Frothy Flakes and Lenny Ludhead, my kids' age, so they related to 'em. We did serials all the time. 'Now I quit. Now you guys gotta go to sleep. I'll continue tomorrow.' "

Steven's own budding talents as a storyteller first manifested themselves when he lived on Crystal Terrace.

His neighbor Jane MacDonald Morley, who was six years old when Steven moved away, remembers, "On lazy summer afternoons when we were bored, we'd sit in the shade at the side of our house, five or six kids, and Stevie would be the one telling the stories. He always seemed to get the attention of the kids. The younger kids believed what Stevie said, because he was a good storyteller. They'd go, 'Uh-huh,' 'Really?,' 'Wow!'

"It was out of those sessions that the bogeyman story came. He told me, 'The bogeyman will get you.' I can remember telling him I wasn't afraid of the bogeyman because I slept on the second floor, and he couldn't get in my room. He said, 'Oh, but the bogeyman is twenty feet tall and he can look into your window.' He told me it didn't matter how safe you were, he was *there*. I remember that night being awake, worried about the bogeyman."

The stories didn't always convince kids closer to Stevie's own age, however, and sometimes the other boys would tell him to knock it off or would turn the tables on him.

"My sister would say, 'Stevie scares me,' " Jane's brother Scott recalls. "Stevie was very sincere, and my sister was very gullible. He was pretty slick about throwing a few zingers at my sister and his sister. He would be bragging about this or saying that. We would all roll our eyes and we would never believe him. I said I had an alligator in my basement, and day after day he would beg me to let him see the alligator. He would ask me, 'How do you feed him?' I said, 'I put hamburger meat on the end of a pencil. He's only four or five inches long.' He would ask me, 'Can I see it?' I would say, 'He's not well.' Finally he accused me of lying to him. I had him going for a while."

From telling scary stories to little girls, Stevie's imagination soon turned to ever more elaborate pranks.

"Even if he hadn't become famous, he's the kind of kid I would have remembered," says Stanley (Sandy) MacDonald, the older brother of Jane and Scott. "You could see he had a theatrical bent. We both used to love storms. Most of the kids in the neighborhood didn't, but he was one of the few who liked storms. He had a real nice screened-in porch in back of his house, and when the sky would get dark and stormy we'd wear yellow slickers and sit on his porch in lawn chairs, reading comic books and looking for lightning.

"One summer somebody got a set of golf clubs, and he and I built a golf course in his back yard. We dug holes and planted tin cans and flags. That summer we had the only tornado we ever had in the area. We could see the dark cloud and we had to go in our basements. But I liked to watch storms, so I looked out and saw Stevie out in his backyard running around knocking over the golf course flags, spinning around with his arms outstretched. I remember asking him later why he did it and he said, 'I didn't break the golf course. The tornado did.' I said, 'Stevie, I *saw* you.' He wouldn't admit it, but he *became* a tornado."*

W H E N it came to neighborhood sports, Stevie was hopelessly uncoordinated. "He would participate, but we would kind of tease him about not being able to throw a football or catch very well," Scott MacDonald admits. "We wouldn't really tease him in a cruel way, because he never reacted in a way for us to get a kick out of it. He would play for a while and then say, 'I'm going to go in.' Stevie wasn't ostracized or anything, but he had a different *style* of play. You might call him a slightly nerdy kid, but he really wasn't. We thought he was pretty cool in the areas he was interested in."

"One time someone got boxing gloves," Sandy MacDonald relates, "and we made a ring between our two houses. When it was Stevie's turn, he got hit and ran away. He got a bottle of ketchup from his house and every time he was hit he'd pour ketchup on himself. He had it all over his clothes and hair."

"Another time," recalls Scott, "Stevie put a tomato in a pot on his stove. Three or four of us were gathered around watching. He said, 'Watch what happens when I get this to explode.' Before it happened, we heard his mom or dad pulling in the driveway and we all took off. He thought it was a new way to make blood; he liked anything that would look like blood, that would explode all red. He used to love mulberries. He would squeeze them on his head and arms and run into his house screaming to his mother that he was bleeding."

Then there was the time Stevie managed to cause a commotion simply by locking himself into his bathroom on the second floor of his house. As Scott says, "Seeing the fire department coming through the window with ladders and everything, I thought that was really neat."

T H E future director of *Jurassic Park* had an early fascination with dinosaurs. That was not unusual for a boy growing up in the Haddonfield area, because the town, built on land once covered by a prehistoric ocean, was the discovery site of the *Hadrosaurus foulkii,* the first virtually complete dinosaur skeleton found in modern history. When Spielberg was a boy, schoolchildren often were taken on field trips to the site where the hadrosaur

---

* Spielberg's Amblin Entertainment made *Twister,* director Jan De Bont's 1996 action blockbuster about tornado researchers.

fossil was found. Some of the remains were on display at Philadelphia's Academy of Natural Sciences, which sold brass models of dinosaurs.

"I've been interested in dinosaurs since I was a child," Spielberg said while making *Jurassic Park*. "As most of my films originate, the interest of the subject matter originates from kidhood. And I remember always collecting dinosaur models, and being interested in the fantastic *size* of these creatures."

Like almost every American boy growing up in the 1950s, Spielberg also imbibed a sense of fantasy and adventure from comic books, which had a strong influence in shaping the bold, sometimes exaggerated clarity of his visual style as a filmmaker. Among his favorites were the superhero and fantasy genres—Superman, Batman, and the Bizarro characters—and the Disney comics featuring Mickey Mouse, Donald Duck, and Uncle Scrooge. Stevie and friends also devoured *Mad* magazine, which became a cult favorite among aspiring hipsters throughout the United States during the 1950s with its refreshing irreverence, "sick" humor, and clever movie parodies.

Mad paved the way for Spielberg and his fellow Hollywood "movie brats" to indulge their boyhood fondness for old movie clichés, reinventing and parodying genres and images with twists for the postmodernist era. A famous example can be seen in Spielberg's *Raiders of the Lost Ark*. The script called for an elaborate sword-and-bullwhip duel between Harrison Ford's Indiana Jones and an Arab foe. But Harrison Ford felt ill and Spielberg was trying to speed up the schedule, so they decided to have Indiana Jones abruptly terminate the duel by pulling out his pistol and casually blowing away his opponent. Spielberg said the scene reminded him of the *Mad* feature "Scenes We'd Like to See."

Perhaps it was largely through the influence of comic books that as a child in New Jersey, "Stevie had a surprising kind of morbid streak," Scott MacDonald says. "We thought it was really cool. I remember his elaborate torture chamber. We used to go down in his basement, and he would show us how he would put his toy men in a guillotine he had made out of a black shoebox. He chopped off heads, he sawed a few heads off—it was a great effect. When my brother and I saw *E.T.*, we said to each other, 'Gee, *that* doesn't seem like Stevie.' He seemed kind of warped when he was little. When he moved to Arizona, I got a fascinating letter from him telling us about scorpions and about the Gila monster, how it had really cool poison spikes on its head. We couldn't imagine what kind of lifestyle he had out there."

In Stevie's basement there was also a big cardboard box he used for puppet shows. "I began wanting to make people happy from the beginning of my life," he remembered. "As a kid, I had puppet shows—I wanted people to like my puppet shows when I was eight years old."

• • •

U N D O U B T E D L Y the single most pervasive cultural influence on Spielberg in his early childhood years was television. "I was, and still am, a TV junkie," he has said. "I've just grown up with TV, as all of us have, and there is a lot of television inside my brain that I wish I could get out of there. You can't help it—once it's in there, it's like a tattoo."

The Spielbergs bought their first television set, a round-tubed DuMont, in 1949. At that time, national TV networks had been in full operation for barely two years and only one in twelve American families owned a set. Although television was still in its infancy in the early 1950s when Steven lived on Crystal Terrace, that era was so rich with creative invention that it now is regarded as the medium's "Golden Age." Few kids were watching highbrow anthology programs like *Omnibus* or *Playhouse 90,* but Steven and his friends grew up huddled around their small-screen black-and-white TV sets (many of them made at his father's RCA plant in Camden), absorbing shows that are now considered classics. While the influence of TV on the baby boomer generation of filmmakers often has been lamentable—Spielberg's own big-screen productions of *The Flintstones* and *The Little Rascals* are among the more witless examples of recycled TV nostalgia—much of what he and his friends watched as children was considerably more sophisticated than most of today's TV offerings in terms of the quality of writing and performing.

Among their favorites were the brilliantly inventive comedy skits on *Your Show of Shows,* starring Sid Caesar and Imogene Coca; uproariously funny variety programs such as *The Milton Berle Show* and *The Colgate Comedy Hour,* with Dean Martin and Jerry Lewis; sitcoms such as *The Honeymooners* and *The Phil Silvers Show,* with Silvers as Sergeant Bilko; and Jack Webb's police drama *Dragnet* (which Stevie found frightening). They watched such kiddie programs as *Howdy Doody;* Don Herbert's *Mr. Wizard; Andy's Gang,* with Andy Devine showing jungle serials; and the adventure sagas *Captain Video and His Video Rangers, Superman, Hopalong Cassidy, The Roy Rogers Show, The Cisco Kid,* and *The Lone Ranger.*

Most popular of all with the kids in Stevie's neighborhood were Walt Disney's Sunday night *Disneyland* series, which began in 1954, and *The Mickey Mouse Club,* the daily variety program starring the Mouseketeers which first aired in 1955. Stevie had crushes on three of the girl Mouseketeers in succession: perky Darlene Gillespie, winsome little Karen Pendleton, and the sultry-yet-wholesome Annette Funicello, whose spectacular emergence into puberty awakened many American boys' libidos. For Steven, that was the time when puppy love turned into "sexual awe—I hate to use the word *sexual;* it's a little heavy, but there it was."

Playing Davy Crockett was a neighborhood obsession on Crystal Terrace for more than a year following the December 1954–February 1955 broadcasts of the *Disneyland* TV serial "Davy Crockett" (later released as a feature film titled *Davy Crockett, King of the Wild Frontier).* Unfortunately for Stevie, everyone else got a coonskin cap before he did, so he wound up being chosen to play the "bad guy," Mexican general Santa Anna. He and his playmates battled to the death with cap pistols and long toy rifles at their makeshift "Alamo," a stockade fence in the backyard of a neighbor family.

Steven was not only fascinated by what appeared on television, but by the tube itself. "I believe there's something in there trying to get out," he once said. "I used to stick my eye right up to the snow. I was _this_ far away from the TV set and there would always be some out-of-the-way channel, some far-off channel that was getting its signal through the station that wasn't broadcasting, and there would be ghosts and images of some broadcasting station five hundred miles away." In _Poltergeist,_ which Spielberg has described as "my revenge on TV," a little girl is sucked into the family TV set by ghosts she greets in the opening scene by staring into the snow on the tube and announcing, "They're _here._"

Steven often has claimed that, aside from such bland fare as _The Mickey Mouse Club_ and some comedy programs, he was "forbidden to watch TV." His parents, he said, not only rationed TV viewing on principle, but after he became distraught watching a documentary on snakes, they also tried to shield him from such potentially disturbing shows as _Dragnet_ and _M Squad._ Steven even remembered his parents trying tricks to discourage his surreptitious TV viewing: "Sometimes my father would attach hairs in exact positions so he could tell if I had lifted up the dust ruffle over the RCA nineteen-inch screen and snuck a peek. . . . I always found the hair, memorized exactly where it was and rearranged it before they came home."

Arnold Spielberg responds, "He used to complain I never let him watch television, that his parents were real strict. Well, he saw _plenty_ of TV. It just wasn't enough. The TV was on all the time. But, you know, we said, 'Homework time.' And I guess I was kinda hard-nosed about that. I would not let them watch too much television, so he resented that."

Steven's conflict with his father over that issue may help explain why he later declared that "my stepparent was the TV set." He also pointed out that before the advent of television, "[P]arents would read to the kids from a rocking chair, and families were very, very close. They used to gather around the reader, or the _seer,_ of the household, and in the twenties and thirties, usually it was the father. And then television replaced the father, and now it seems to be replacing both the father and the mother." Since his father's nightly storytelling ritual once had been so important to Steven, and since he had to turn elsewhere for entertainment when Arnold became consumed with his job in the 1950s, it was literally true, in that sense at least, that in Steven's house, "television replaced the father."

Spielberg's parents also tried to control his movie-watching habits in his preadolescent years. "I could only see films in their presence and usually pictures that appealed more to them." The Spielbergs attended family-audience movies such as _The Court Jester_ with Danny Kaye, the Fred Astaire–Audrey Hepburn musical _Funny Face,_ and of course, Disney movies. "And yet when I came screaming home from _Snow White_ when I was eight years old, and tried to hide under the covers, my parents did not understand it," Steven recalled, "because Walt Disney movies are not supposed to scare but to delight and enthrall. Between *Snow White, Fantasia,* and *Bambi,* I was a basket case of neurosis."*

Because his parents "didn't know what backfired" at the movie theater, Steven recalled, they "tried very, very hard to screen violence from my life." He and his friends occasionally went to Saturday matinees at the Westmont and Century theaters in neighboring Westmont and Audubon, paying a quarter to watch a program consisting of cartoons and a monster movie, a sci-fi movie, or a Western with Hopalong Cassidy or the Cisco Kid. But Steven's parents' concern over his moviegoing fare and the freer availability of TV discouraged him from becoming a movie addict until later in his boyhood, after he moved to Arizona. The most enduring feeling about movies he took away from that period in New Jersey was his frustration at being kept away from them. As he said later, "I feel that perhaps one of the reasons I'm making movies all the time is because I was told not to [watch movies]."

L I K E many other sons of veterans, Stevie was fascinated from an early age with World War II: "I love that period. My father filled my head with war stories—he was a radioman on a B-25 fighting the Japanese in Burma. I have identified with that period of innocence and tremendous jeopardy all my life. It was the end of an era, the end of innocence, and I have been clinging to it for most of my adult life."† As a boy he especially enjoyed building model planes and was, he said, "attached to flying," like his youthful protagonist in *Empire of the Sun.*

Stevie and his friends on Crystal Terrace would stage battle scenes with plastic and rubber soldiers (World War II or Civil War) and with cowboys and Indians. Stevie became known as the grand master of those war games. He found willing partners in Sandy MacDonald, who also enjoyed long, intricate games that stretched on for days, and his brother Scott, who remembers the unusual way Stevie used to start playing:

"Stevie had this big table and he would set up a village with Indians or the Civil War. He would show us how they would move around. We wouldn't really play—we would watch him set up the scenario of *his* play. He would say things like, 'This guy gets caught here. Ooh, this guy gets an arrow. This

---

* Steven was even traumatized by Disneyland: "My father took me to the Magic Kingdom in 1959. I was afraid of everything: the crazy eyeball of the sea serpent in the submarine ride; the witch from *Snow White* offering me a poison apple; Mr. Toad's Wild Ride. Yet it was the kind of scary that tickles. It took me several trips back and a little more growing up before I recognized the twinkle in Mr. Disney's eyes."

† As an amateur filmmaker in Arizona, Spielberg often made World War II movies. And as a professional filmmaker he has made *Schindler's List, Empire of the Sun, 1941,* and for his TV series *Amazing Stories,* "The Mission." He also remade the World War II flying picture *A Guy Named Joe* in a contemporary setting, as *Always.*

guy gets guillotined.' We had about five or ten minutes of him administering the play and then *we* could all play."

"I'd go across to Stevie's basement and we'd set up those huge battle scenes," adds Sandy. "He always played with a box of nails and a hammer. When the soldiers were hit by arrows, he'd put nails into them, and use ketchup for blood. At the end of the game he had fewer and fewer usable soldiers. I never used to bring my men over because he'd ruin them. I wouldn't do that to my men. For him, it was worth it to get an effect; it had to be real, to have an arrow stick out. It was just that little bit of extra that I wouldn't have thought of doing."

"We [girls] were never allowed to play, but we would stand around and watch," Sandy's sister Jane remembers. "Most kids would be content to say, 'Oh, this guy's killed.' Steven would make it seem that the guy *was* getting killed. To me that's why he seemed different."

FOUR

" A WIMP IN A WORLD OF JOCKS "

BY SOME IRONIC JUSTICE, THOSE WHO HAVE HAD A DIFFICULT CHILDHOOD ARE OFTEN BETTER
EQUIPPED TO ENTER ADULT LIFE THAN THOSE WHO HAVE BEEN VERY SHELTERED, VERY LOVED;
IT IS A KIND OF LAW OF COMPENSATION.

— THE SCHOOLTEACHER IN FRANÇOIS TRUFFAUT'S *SMALL CHANGE*

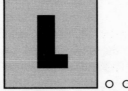 OOKING back on his
childhood, Spielberg always has thought of Arizona as "my real home. For a
kid, home is where you have your best friends and your first car, and your
first kiss; it's where you do your worst stuff and get your best grades."

Arizona was also the place where Steven's family ties grew increasingly
strained, almost to the breaking point, turning him more and more inward
for emotional sustenance. And, most important, Arizona was the place where
he set his sights on becoming a filmmaker. One of his boyhood friends in
Phoenix, Jim Sollenberger, recalls Spielberg saying "he could envision himself going to the Academy Awards and accepting an Oscar and thanking the
Academy. He was twelve or thirteen at the time."

"I've been really serious about [filmmaking] as a career since I was twelve
years old," Spielberg said in a 1989 interview. "I don't excuse those early
years as a hobby, do you know what I'm saying? I really did start then."

STEVEN'S mother later admitted that the very idea of moving to
Phoenix made her "hysterical" with culture shock: "I mean, in [1957] what
nice Jewish girl moved to Arizona? I looked in an encyclopedia—it was

published in 1920, but I didn't notice at the time—and it said: 'Arizona is a barren wasteland.' I went there kicking and screaming. I had to promise Steve a horse, because he didn't want to go either. I never made good on that promise, and he still reminds me of it today."

When they arrived in February 1957, the Spielbergs spent four months in a cramped two-bedroom apartment on the west side of Phoenix before moving into their newly built ranch house at 3443 North Forty-ninth Street, in the city's Arcadia neighborhood.* As a newcomer living in a suburban development carved out of citrus groves near the winter resorts at the foot of Camelback Mountain, Steven felt more like an "alien" than ever before. In that conservative western community on the fringe of the Arizona desert, Gila monsters still roamed, men wore string ties, some streets were unpaved, new commercial buildings on some streets had to have hitching rails out front, and his neighbors included Senator Barry Goldwater and a golf-playing youngster named J. Danforth (Dan) Quayle. The ten-year-old Jewish kid from back east could not help sticking out, like the ears protruding from under his baseball cap.

"He was the first person I knew who came with an accent," recalls Spielberg's grade school classmate Susan Smith LeSueur, a Mormon who is an Arizona native. "He talked a lot and gestured a lot. He was very funny-looking, and I guess very Jewish. I didn't know many Jews. I didn't know anybody who talked that way or looked that way. He was so different."

"I guess we were a pretty intolerant bunch of people back in the fifties and sixties," says Steven's Boy Scout counselor Richard (Dick) Hoffman Jr. "It was like being back in the thirties, practically. Phoenix didn't have a lot of Jews. With the kids I didn't see much anti-Semitic stuff, but I did see it among the parents. We have a lot of jackasses out here. People out here are small-minded. Being a liberal is almost like being a Communist."

Entering Ingleside Elementary School during the second semester of fourth grade, Steven reacted to his culture shock by withdrawing into himself. "He was very quiet," says his sixth-grade teacher, Eleanor Wolf. "I felt sorry for him because he didn't have any friends. You see, he was different from everybody else. Nerdy. He looked kind of prim and proper, he wore a little button-down collar; he looked kind of sissy. He was living in a dream world. He was rather nondescript, just a good little kid. He was so reserved —a lot of kids wanted to direct everything, but he didn't. I don't know what his problem was—maybe it was self-consciousness, low self-esteem. Oh, heavens, never in my wildest dreams did I imagine Steven Spielberg would have grown up to be anything like he is."

• • •

_____

* Their house was in Phoenix, not in neighboring Scottsdale, as has often been reported by Spielberg and others.

S O O N after he came to Arizona, however, there was a harbinger of things to come.

"One night my dad woke me up in the middle of the night and rushed me into our car in my night clothes," Spielberg remembered. "I didn't know what was happening. It was frightening. My mom wasn't with me. So I thought, What's happening here? He had a thermos of coffee and had brought blankets, and we drove for about half an hour. We finally pulled over to the side of the road, and there were a couple hundred people, lying on their backs in the middle of the night, looking up at the sky. My dad found a place, spread the blanket out, and we both lay down.

"He pointed to the sky, and there was a magnificent meteor shower. All these incredible points of light were crisscrossing the sky. It was a phenomenal display, apparently announced in advance by the weather bureau. My dad had really surprised me—actually, he'd frightened the hell out of me! At the same time, though, I was tremendously attracted to the *source,* to what was causing this."

Although Steven remembered being in a crowd of hundreds of people, "We were by ourselves," reports Arnold Spielberg. "There was a comet that was supposed to be visible in the sky. Some journal said there should be a comet, maybe tenth magnitude or something like that. I wanted to see the comet, and I wanted Steve to see the comet. So we drove up over the mountains and into the desert, away from the city lights. We just got out of the car and lay down in the sand and we started looking for that comet.

"For some reason, a bunch of meteors showed up. In those days, there wasn't that much smog in the air or dust in the air in Phoenix, and the stars were just tremendous. They were so intense it was *frightening.* When you got out of the car, there was this bright canopy of dust, bright lights over your head. And it was momentarily frightening—you know, you got disoriented a little bit. Then we settled down. And I could not find that damn comet."

His father, Steven recalled, "gave me a technical explanation of what was happening. . . . But I didn't want to hear that. I wanted to think of them as falling stars." That memory would inspire his first feature-length film, the Arizona-made *Firelight,* and its later "remake," *Close Encounters of the Third Kind,* in which Richard Dreyfuss bundles up his family in their station wagon, drives out into the country, and watches by the side of the road as strange and wonderful lights appear in the night sky.

W H I L E growing up in Phoenix, Steven "had more friends than he remembers having," his sister Anne has pointed out. But there were many people who looked down on the gawky kid with glasses and acne and considered him "weird" or "wacky," a "nerd" and a "wimp." Steven remembered being "a wimp in a world of jocks. . . . I was skinny and unpopular. I hate to use the word wimp, but I wasn't in the inner loop. . . . I had friends who were all like me. Skinny wrists and glasses. We were all just trying to make it through the year without getting our faces pushed into the drinking fountain."

Some kids bullied Spielberg and ostracized him from social events. Some called the gangly boy with the big ears and nose and the bulging Adam's apple "Spielbug." And a few taunted him for being Jewish. His frequent recollection that he was the only Jewish kid in his neighborhood, and in his Phoenix elementary and high schools, is factually incorrect, but he often must have *felt* that way. His awareness of being "different" in his new surroundings was so acutely painful that he secretly tried to alter his physical appearance in the privacy of his bedroom: "I used to take a big piece of duct tape and put one end on the top of my nose and the other end as high up on my forehead line as I could. I had this big nose. My face grew into it, but when I was a child, I was very self-conscious about my *schnozz*. I thought if you kept your nose taped up that way it would stay . . . like Silly Putty!"

Apart from a lackluster stint with Ingleside Elementary School's Little League baseball team, the C&L Service Mounties, Steven did not participate in sports, the main preoccupation of most boys in his neighborhood. But his mother's friend Marie Tice recognized other qualities in Steven: "I wouldn't have called him a wimp, because he had strength. Steven was always very involved in movies. I don't remember him ever being interested in anything else. I don't think Steven ever had any doubt about what he was going to do. He was very determined without being obnoxious about it."

Many who knew him could not help scoffing when he declared that he was heading to Hollywood. His friend Barry Sollenberger, who also made amateur movies, "didn't hesitate to give him some advice. I remember once when I went into high school and changed my interests to more important things like football games and chasing cheerleaders, I said, 'Come on, Steve, grow up—what are you going to do, film movies all your life?' He was really a perfect example of somebody that got the last laugh on the neighborhood."

One of those who did not mock Steven's dreams was his seventh- and eighth-grade social-studies and homeroom teacher, Patricia Scott Rodney, whom Steven knew as "Miss Scott." "I've heard him talk on television about not being a popular kid," she says. "He talks about people not liking him, how he was an outsider. That always makes me very sad. I've spent my life with kids, and *I* didn't see him as an outsider. I go, 'Wow, was I *that* stupid? Or was it much bigger to him being an adult?' I thought he was a force in this group. We always knew what he was thinking; he spoke up. He was very bright and he was a neat, funny little kid. He didn't care much about how he looked, he didn't have any real interest in haircuts or whatever the other kids were wearing. He would just come in as he was, and he presented himself as a really big personality."

"He had friends around him," says classmate Clynn Christensen, "but if he didn't, he wasn't upset about it. He could take it or leave it. Maybe he was just so far ahead of the rest of us that he knew where he was going in life and wanted to get an early start."

• • •

S H O R T L Y after he moved to Arizona, Steven started fooling around with his father's new movie camera. Arnold recalls, "Around that time, Leah, for a birthday or Father's Day present, got me this little twenty-dollar Brownie 8mm movie camera, a real cheap, no-frills camera. It worked fine. Steve glommed onto it pretty quick."

"I became interested in moviemaking," Steven explained, "simply because my father had an 8mm movie camera, which he used to log the family history. . . . I had an outdoorsy family and we would spend three-day week-ends on outings in sleeping bags in the middle of the wilderness in the White Mountains of Arizona. My dad would take the camera along and film the trips and we'd sit down and watch the footage a week later. It would put me right to sleep. . . . I would sit and watch the home movies and criticize the shaky camera movements and bad exposures until my father finally got fed up and told me to take over."

"If you know so much, why don't you try?" Arnold Spielberg said as he gave his son the camera.

"I became the family photographer and logged all our trips," Steven continued. ". . . I was fascinated. I had the power of choice. This is what I choose to show. This is my view of the trip. When the film was processed and screened, Dad was very critical and fussy about my choices: 'Why did you show this and not that?' But it was my view, my choice. . . .

"Then I began to think that staging real life was much more exciting than just recording it. So I'd do things like forcing my parents to let me out of the car a hundred yards before we reached the campgrounds when we went on trips. I'd run ahead and film them arriving and unpacking and pitching camp. . . . I began to actually stage the camping trips and later cut the bad footage out. Sometimes I would just have fun and shoot two frames of this and three frames of that and ten frames of something else, and it got to the point where the documentaries were more surrealistic than factual."

Steven's friends remember Arnold helping shoot some of Steven's early movies, but Arnold says modestly that there was little he could teach his son about using a movie camera: "All you could do with the camera was push the button and load it. That's all there was. You couldn't even focus it—it was a fixed-focus camera. He took over so fast that all I did was give him a little bit of coaching. When we'd go on vacation together, he'd take the camera and do the shooting, and it was always better."

"My earliest recollection of Steven with a camera," his mother said, "was when my husband and I were leaving on a vacation and we told him to take a shot of the camper leaving the driveway. He got down on his belly and was aiming at the hubcap. We were exasperated, yelling at him, 'Come on! We have to leave! Hurry up!' But he just kept on doing his thing, and when we saw the finished results, he was able to pull back so that this hubcap spinning around became the whole camper—my first glimpse at the Spiel-bergian touch and a hint of things to come."*

Steven soon made what he considered his first actual movie. The storyline was an impulse of sheer juvenile delight—"my electric trains crashing into each other." It came about because he had become so fond of staging train wrecks that his father threatened to take the trains away if he didn't stop. So Steven came up with the creative solution of putting together one final, spectacular crash for his own viewing enjoyment, composed of various angles of trains roaring down the tracks on collision courses, with cutaways to shots of plastic men reacting in mute horror. His cinematic inspiration was the scene "when that train came off the screen and into my lap" in the first movie he ever saw, Cecil B. DeMille's *The Greatest Show on Earth*. When he set up his own version, "Intuitively, I guess, I put the film together the right way. I figured if you shot one going right to left and one going left to right, it would be clear they were going to crash." He called his movie *The Last Train Wreck*. When it came back from being developed, he was "amazed at how my little trains looked like multiton locomotives."

When he made his first primitive little movies, Steven was "editing in the camera." Since Steven had no film splicer then, his father explains, "When he had two guys shooting it out, he'd say to one guy, 'Now, you pull.' And he'd photograph him pulling. Then he'd say, 'Stop right there.' The guy'd stop. He'd change the film, turn to the other guy, and say, 'Now *you* pull.' So you could see, in the continuity state, one guy pull before the other, and then *Bam!*

"I was over to his house a week and a half ago [in December 1995]. For Christmas and Hanukkah, he had put up a train set for Max [his ten-year-old son]. He takes it out once a year and sets it up. It's a real elaborate, German-made set, everything detailed. Max had invented a movie. Steve was the cameraman, Max was the director: 'Now, let's see, we gotta put this man on the rail, the train's gonna run him over.' Kids' gory stuff. Steve had this new video camera and he was videoing the thing up real close, because it had a lens that will allow you to get up within three or four inches. He was filming the trains and editing it in the camera, just like he did as a kid. He said, 'Yeah, Dad, I'm editing it in the camera!' Back to the beginning."

S T E V E N ' S filmmaking hobby was a natural outgrowth of what he admitted was his boyhood need for attention. That need grew following the

---

* One of Steven's playmates in New Jersey, Cholly Devlin, claims that Steven started experi-menting there with stop-motion filmmaking: "He had hundreds of toy soldiers, and he had a small movie camera. Steven would line up all his toy World War II soldiers on the living room floor, underneath his mother's grand piano. He would move them and film them, and move them and film them, and *move* them and film them." However, Arnold Spielberg does not recall Steven making movies in New Jersey. The family did not own a movie camera while living there, but Arnold says it is possible that Steven borrowed a movie camera.

births of his three sisters in six and a half years during the 1950s. With his father often absent, both physically and emotionally, Steven felt he lived in "a house of women. Even the dog was female. I was the only guy in the entire house. I was eight, nine, or ten at the time, and I was supposed to be the oldest in the family, but [my sisters] had the run of the house. I just remember my sisters were terrors. They'd run through the house, they'd come into my room and they'd knock my models off the shelf; they'd do anything. I had no choice, I had to do something to make my presence felt."

Steven spent much of his childhood thinking up increasingly sophisticated ways of bullying his three sisters. "I used to do anything in my imagination to terrify them," he admitted. "I was terrible. From seven to thirty-three I was really awful to them." It did not take him long to recognize that being a movie director was a socially permissible form of bullying: by casting his sisters in his films, he could subject them to any kind of violence and mayhem he desired, just as long as it was fictional.

Moviemaking enabled him to turn his feelings of sibling rivalry and powerlessness into something more positive: "I saw it as a way to compete with my sisters for my parents' attention. It was my way of saying, 'Hey, I'm here, too. Look what I can do!' I wanted approval and applause. Well, the camera gave it to me. . . . I discovered something I could do, and people would be interested in it and me."

"Steven didn't get involved too heavily in the neighborhood activities until he came around with his little movie camera, and that kinda caught our attention," says Phoenix schoolmate Steve Lombard. "He got interaction that way with all the kids in the neighborhood, as he directed them. Everybody was excited to be in his movies and they couldn't wait to see themselves onscreen."

W H E N a visitor enters Steven's old neighborhood in Phoenix today, with its 1950s-era ranch houses still lining a broad, tranquil street crisscrossed by friendly kids riding bicycles, the feeling is inescapable: You're not only going back in time, you're entering into a Spielberg movie. If Steven's anxiety-ridden life as a small boy in Haddon Township lends that neighborhood the aura of *Poltergeist,* this suburban neighborhood, with its deceptively idyllic surface hiding powerful undercurrents of tension, is redolent of *E.T.*

E.T. is "a very personal story," Spielberg has said. ". . . I'm not into psychoanalysis, but *E.T.* is a film that was inside me for many years and could only come out after a lot of suburban psychodrama. . . . *E.T.* was about the divorce of my parents, how I felt when my parents broke up. I responded by escaping into my imagination to shut down all my nerve endings crying, 'Mom, Dad, why did you break up and leave us alone?' . . . My wish list included having a friend who could be both the brother I never had and a father that I didn't feel I had anymore. And that's how *E.T.* was born."

Although Arnold and Leah Spielberg were not divorced until 1966, after the family had moved to California, the problems in the marriage became obvious to Steven and his sisters while they were living in Phoenix. The children's daily lives were clouded by their parents' unspoken antagonisms, and at night those differences would find expression in arguments the children could not help overhearing in their bedrooms. Steven and his sisters came to dread their parents' nocturnal talk of divorce, a melodrama that dragged on for years and left the children emotionally ragged, clinging to each other for support. The mounting tension at home during Steven's boyhood years "was hard on him," teacher Pat Rodney observes, "but I think it made him a caring person."

Living under such strain heightened Steven's sense of social alienation and took away some of the solace that a happy home life could have provided for a boy who felt uncomfortable being Jewish in a mostly gentile environment and often was bullied at school and on his way home.

Although people who lived near the Spielbergs at the time agree that the neighborhood was generally harmonious and that blatant expressions of anti-Semitism were not everyday occurrences, ugly incidents occasionally did take place. Janice Zusman, who grew up in the house directly behind the Spielbergs, remembers a neighbor boy drawing swastikas on the sidewalk so that she and another Jewish girl would see them on the way to school. Steven's mother recalled that the children in one neighbor family "used to stand outside yelling, 'The Spielbergs are dirty Jews. The Spielbergs are dirty Jews.' So one night, Steven snuck out of the house and peanut-buttered all their windows."

"All of us are part of some minority," Spielberg reflected after making *The Color Purple,* his film version of Alice Walker's novel about a southern black woman. "I was Jewish and wimpy when I grew up. That was a major minority. In Arizona, too, where few are Jewish and not many are wimpy."

ARNOLD Spielberg was chief engineer for the process control department of General Electric, working long hours at its plant in Phoenix and on field trips throughout the United States and abroad. Process computers, then in their early developmental stages, run the controls for complex industrial processes, such as utilities, steel mills, and chemical plants. Arnold later shifted to GE's business-computer department, which he had started as a spinoff from the process-control department.

"Arnold is tremendously intelligent, and sort of like a kid, like his son," says Walter Tice, a GE application and sales engineer who was responsible for the industrial marketing of Arnold's process computers. "Arnold was not the typical engineer—he really wanted to learn about the processes, he wanted to go to steel mills and see the steel being made. He's like Steve, he's always interested in the whole story. Some of the best engineers are deadheads, no personality, zero. Arnie's not dull, he has a lot of charm and wit about him. As far as being an engineer goes, he was very creative."

Arnold insists he did not spend a great deal of time traveling while working for GE: "Leah had the impression I traveled a lot, because she hated to be left alone. So anytime that I was gone, it was like a big deal. When I went to Russia, I was gone for a month. I was offered an opportunity to go to Russia as a representative of GE at the first international control conference, held in Moscow and Leningrad. And I wanted Leah to come, but she couldn't bring herself to go: 'Oh, I can't fly, I'm afraid of flying.' Now she flies, reluctantly, but then she could not fly. I felt so bad that when I came home, I said, 'I've got to get you something.' We found an ad for a lovely Steinway grand piano. So we bought this piano, and she loved it."

Steven also felt Arnold's absences keenly. His sixth-grade teacher Eleanor Wolf has a poignant memory of a rare appearance Arnold made at the school. When he came back from the Soviet Union, Arnold "brought slides in to show us. That was the only time I saw the kid excited, maybe because his father would take the time to come in. I gathered his father didn't have too much time for him."

"I made some movies over in Russia, and Steve edited and titled them," Arnold adds. "I got him a titler. He spelled a couple of things wrong, but he'd do special effects. He'd put one letter at a time down and take a picture, then another letter, *dot-dot-dot-dot-dot,* like each letter in the title spelled itself out."

"His father traveled a lot, and I think that's why Steve was close to his mother," says his teacher Pat Rodney. "She was a really strong person in Steve's life. She gave a lot of time and energy raising her kids, and she didn't think her raising ended at 8:00 A.M. when they went to school. A lot of kids envied how she showed up at school. She wasn't a pain in the neck like some moms. She just would drop in and bring Steve his lunch, and she used to come in and clean tables in the cafeteria. She said, 'I'm the only person with a master's degree that you have cleaning tables. You may wonder why I spend so much time here. I have a neighbor who comes over and sits in my kitchen. She's the kind of person who has an orgasm over Beads of Bleach.' "

Although Leah "thought Steve was perfect," she was "concerned about his personal habits," his teacher adds. "She came in to my room one time and said they were going to condemn their house if he didn't bathe. She said, 'He likes you and his dog, not necessarily in that order. Would you talk to him about his personal cleanliness?' So I asked him, 'Listen, do you want those people to remember you as Smelly Spielberg?' " Steven shared his cluttered bedroom with an uncaged lizard and loose parakeets. Leah went in there only to pick up his dirty clothes.

The Spielbergs' living room was dominated by Leah's white grand piano, with its lovingly displayed photo of Brahms. "One time Steve ruined the whole top of the piano," neighbor Bill Gaines reports. "It was never quite the same after that." There was not much other furniture on their blue shag carpet, partly because Steven often took over the room for filming and partly because Leah didn't seem interested in that kind of domesticity. "They didn't have great stuff, except for an Eero Saarinen kitchen table and chairs," recalls family baby-sitter Susan Roper Arndt. "The TV was [often] broken. I remember when Steven blew up the TV set, the way he hooked it up."

Leah played classical piano with the Scottsdale Chamber Orchestra, which she helped organize. She also took ballet lessons and "said it was better than going to a psychiatrist," recalls her neighbor Katherine Galwey. "She used to practice by walking on curbs." The unconventional Leah also raised eyebrows in the neighborhood with her Army surplus jeep. When Leah drove around in her jeep, "she'd *haul,*" Sue Arndt says. "You knew she was coming. She was so creative and wonderful. She had short bobbed hair, she always wore short jean dresses, way above her knees, and she always had a great tan, a *major* great tan."

Bernard (Bernie) Adler, an engineer who followed Arnold out from New Jersey and worked as his assistant at GE, was a good friend of both Arnold and Leah Spielberg. Bernie, who was unmarried at the time, "was almost like a member of the Spielberg family," says Walter Tice. "He and Arnold got along great. The three of them would go on vacations together to California. The kids called him Uncle Bernie. He was always there. He did everything with them."

Later, after divorcing Arnold Spielberg, Leah would enter into an enduring marriage with Bernie Adler, returning to the Orthodox religious practices of her youth, from which she had drifted since marrying the more liberal and assimilated Arnold Spielberg (Bernie died in 1995). Leah found Bernie "so funny, so bright, so moral. I was madly in love."

Some of their Phoenix neighbors found Leah's romantic history a bit *outré.* "I was always confused as to who [Steven's] father was," says Steven's friend Chris Pischke. Katherine Galwey recalls that Leah "told me she loved both men. She said she couldn't marry 'em both, so she married Mr. Spielberg."

"We were bohemians growing up in suburbia," Steven's sister Sue recalled. Steven once yelled at his mother during his adolescence, "Everyone else's mother is normal. They go bowling. They go to PTA meetings, and they play bridge."

"The conventional always appealed to Steven," Leah once remarked. "Maybe because we weren't."

M U C H like Elliott in *E.T.,* who has to cope with an absent father and a mother who is so distracted she doesn't notice for quite some time that he has an alien living in his bedroom, Steven compensated for the instability, isolation, and myriad anxieties of his childhood by taking refuge in a soothing world of magic—in his case, the magic of filmmaking.

"To me, Elliott was always the Nowhere Man from the Beatles song," Spielberg said. "I was drawing from my own feelings when I was a little kid and I didn't have that many friends and had to resort to making movies to become quasi-popular and to find a reason for living after school hours. . . . I was always drowning in little home movies. That's all I did when I was growing up. That was my escape."

P E O P L E who live in the "Valley of the Sun," as the Phoenix area is known, are accustomed to seeing movies and television shows being filmed on location. For young movie buffs such as Spielberg and his friends, living in Phoenix was almost like living in a suburb of Hollywood. If Hollywood seemed an almost impossibly remote dream for a kid growing up in a small town in New Jersey, a career in moviemaking or other forms of show business seemed more tangible for a kid living only an hour's plane trip from Los Angeles. Three students from Spielberg's high school would become actors in Hollywood: Lynda Carter (TV's *Wonder Woman,* who grew up around the corner from him), Dianne Kay (the ingenue in his movie *1941*), and Frank Webb (who was directed by Spielberg in a 1970 episode of TV's *Marcus Welby, M.D.*). Many parents in the Spielbergs' comfortable middle-class neighborhood had 8mm or even 16mm movie cameras to document family activities, and there were at least a dozen other young filmmakers besides Steven who were busy making their own amateur movies in town on a regular basis.

One of their inspirations was the daily local TV kiddie show *Wallace & Ladmo,* a zany potpourri of studio skits, cartoons, and silent slapstick comedy footage (including frequent Western spoofs) shot off-the-cuff in the parks and desert around Phoenix. *Wallace & Ladmo* had a weekly showcase for young filmmakers, "Home Movie Winners." Spielberg appeared on the KPHO program in the early 1960s to show a brief piece of film he had shot that "looked like space guys glowing in the dark," according to series costar and writer Bill Thompson ("Wallace"). "He was very inventive, a bright guy. He was very highly thought of, even as a kid." When Steven was interviewed about his filmmaking on another local TV show, his father was "amazed— he just was so cool and collected. He was sixteen or seventeen, but he handled it just like he'd been doing it for years."

Steven was not the only kid in his neighborhood making movies. His budding interest in film was stimulated by his friendship and collaboration with three other amateur filmmakers—Barry Sollenberger, Barry's younger brother Jim, and Chris Pischke. "Most of us were considered kooks or goofs," Pischke admits. "When other kids were doing whatever—sports, chasing girls, playing with cars—we were playing with guns and making films. All of us were pretty much self-taught." "We got our ideas from watching movies and TV—Westerns, sci-fi, war movies, those were the popular types of movies in those days," Barry Sollenberger recalls. "We all appeared in each other's movies, and when we were all in a scene and had no one to film it, we'd say, 'Steve, come and film this scene,' and vice versa. The person who made the most movies was Steve."

"It was helpful to Steve, indirectly, that there were other people in the neighborhood equally interested in what normally would be considered an offbeat or off-the-wall type of thing—making movies," observes Jim Sollenberger. "If Steve had been a Lone Ranger, the only kid on the block making movies, he might not have been able to pursue it. But since there were two or three other kids, that gives you some support, instead of people looking at you as a complete geek. It was a pretty good place to incubate."

S T E V E N ' S budding interest in filmmaking remained unfocused, however, until he became a Boy Scout, a member of the Flaming Arrow Patrol of Ingleside's Troop 294. He made his first real attempt at a story film in order to earn his photography merit badge in 1958. "Scouting gave me my start," Steven has said. ". . . Boy Scouts put me in the center of the loop. It sort of brought out things I did well and forgave me for things I didn't." He found that the Boy Scouts helped him fill a growing emotional void. With his father becoming "as much a workaholic as I am today," he later explained, "as a child I didn't understand, and Scouting became like a surrogate dad."

Troop 294 went out into the desert in convoys of station wagons to pitch tents for weekend campouts and also made week-long visits to Camp Geronimo, the Phoenix area's organized Scouting camp. Arnold Spielberg was treasurer of Steven's troop. He went along on a few outings, and Steven wistfully remembered that on those weekends, "We became our closest." Dick Hoffman, who supervised the boys on many outings, says that Steven's father "wasn't a big participator in our activities. He was a hardworking engineer. Few parents will go out in the wilds for the weekend—they don't like that. Those of us who do get interested are zealots. I think we all felt we were filling a need for these kids."

"I always had the feeling [Steven] was somewhat embittered about his father," says fellow Scout Charles Carter. "He was really close to his mother and disowned his father."

Hoffman remembers "Stevie" Spielberg as "a skinny, little, inconspicuous fellow. I worried about him, because I liked him very much. He seemed to go in fits and starts—he would dash from one thing to another. I thought it was a disability, not being able to concentrate the way the rest of us would. I knew he was wildly enthusiastic about things, but I didn't think he had enough ability to analyze things. I tried to stabilize him, and that didn't work out very well.

"What stands out in my mind was a time they were all going off to cook wieners and marshmallows. The kids were going to scrape around, picking up combustible pieces of wood to build a fire. Stevie would rush around and pick up about three or four little twigs and start his fire. I told him, 'Stevie, that's no good. You've got to go out and get a big pile to start a fire.' He just couldn't do it. He was too impatient to get the fire started. I thought, When he grows up and gets into the real world he's going to have a tough time keeping up. I didn't dream anything would come of him. Of course, that was a complete misjudgment of the kid's personality."

Steven admitted he "was always doing doofy things" as a Scout. When he demonstrated ax-sharpening at a gathering of five hundred area Scouts, "On the second stroke, I put the blade through my knuckle." Another time, on an "absolutely freezing night," he was supposed to build a fire for cooking, but "I dropped my mess kit into the mud. Couldn't get the fire started. I was hungry and also very tired, and instead of putting the canned food into a pot, I forgot and put the cans unopened on the fire. They exploded, sending shrapnel in all directions. No one was hurt, but everyone within about twenty yards of my cookout needed new uniforms."

Nevertheless, Steven earned the respect of his fellow Scouts, becoming assistant patrol leader, then patrol leader, and working gamely to overcome his limitations to become an Eagle Scout. Completing his one-mile swim requirement was a major challenge. He was afraid of the water and "really couldn't swim a mile, but it was a case of mind over muscle, once I determined I was going to do it. I remember pulling myself out of the water after that in a complete sort of wet haze. . . . I got more respect for myself in being able to overcome those phobias momentarily."

"I was one of the leaders who had to initial their cards when they completed their requirements," fellow Scout Tim Dietz recalls. "Steve couldn't do the obstacle course. That was the only thing he couldn't do to get Eagle Scout. We worked on him and worked on him: 'Come on, Steve, you've got to complete the course!' We held onto Steve's legs to make sure that he could do all the pullups required. He was a good sport about everything—a *good guy*. He wasn't the kid we beat up or anything else."

Dietz admits, however, that they sometimes pulled pranks on Spielberg. He and a few others once persuaded Steven to take part in a "snipe hunt," a prank which involved sending a gullible boy out in the darkened desert hunting for birds with a pillowcase. Dietz laughingly remembers Spielberg "sitting on the side of a mountain about a hundred yards from us, yipping and yapping and callin' in the snipes."

But sometimes the hazing went too far for Steven. "A guy named Rechwald had his pants down taking a crap," Charles Carter remembers. "Rechwald was an underling in the pecking order; I think he was a little obese. Spielberg intervened because we were torturing Rechwald with a flashlight —everybody was shining lights on Rechwald, exposing him and chuckling at him. Spielberg got mad because they were embarrassing him. I think we tortured Steve a little bit [for protesting]—not seriously, we were just kids. But they laid off on Rechwald. I didn't think much about it at the time, but looking back, I was impressed. Most kids didn't stand up against peer pressure. He did. He took a stand."

• • •

S T E V E N became "much beloved of the boys because of his imagination," Dick Hoffman says. Steven "was always reading, always bringing books along" to camp, and when the boys pitched their pup tents and bunked down for the night, he would provide the entertainment with his own storytelling. Hoffman's son Bill remembers that Spielberg's stories "tended to be science-fiction—lots of monster-from-outer-space stories."

"I was a great storyteller in Boy Scouts," Spielberg recalled in 1982. "I used to sit around the campfire and scare forty Scouts to death with ghost stories." The image is archetypal: Spielberg's TV series *Amazing Stories* started each week with a montage showing the development of storytelling through the ages, beginning with a caveman spinning stories around a campfire. When Steven told stories to his fellow Scouts, "The whole semicircle would fall silent, all of them listening to what came out of the tent," Dick Hoffman says. "He's got the damnedest imagination of anyone I ever knew. The other kids were rapt in their attention to what he was saying. I don't think he was terribly popular except when he was telling those stories."

"It's what made him special," says fellow Scout Bob Proehl.

Steven's storytelling ability also manifested itself in teacher Ferneta Sulek's seventh-grade class, classmate Del Merrill remembers: "He would always write some short story or some kind of fantastic story that was fun to hear. We'd all read our stories aloud and you didn't *want* to hear some people's stories. But *everybody* always wanted to listen to his story. He brought mystery into it, too. He often would have a twist ending, and he could scare you. A lot of his stories were a blend of humor and science fiction. I remember him reading a lot of science-fiction books in seventh and eighth grade. He said it was his favorite kind of reading."

Spielberg, who has been described by Ray Bradbury as "probably the son of H. G. Wells, certainly the grandson of Jules Verne," acquired his passion for science fiction from the pulp magazines and paperbacks his father left around the house. Steven's tastes included not only the visionary fantasies of such masters as Bradbury, Arthur C. Clarke, and Robert A. Heinlein, but virtually any kind of sci-fi yarn between covers.

Spielberg's obsession with science fiction was "one of the fascinating things about him," says Gene Ward Smith, a fellow sci-fi buff who later attended high school with him in California. "Here I'd gone through my life, and if I met a guy who'd read one science-fiction book, I'd read fifty—and he'd read *all* this stuff. He'd read stuff *I* hadn't read. He'd also seen all these science-fiction movies I hadn't seen, like *The Day the Earth Stood Still.* He took me through the whole plots of *Forbidden Planet* and the sleazeball monster movies. We spent a lot of time talking about science-fiction shows on TV—he wasn't a big fan of *Science Fiction Theater,* but he thought *The Twilight Zone* was wonderful."

Outer space was brought close to home for Steven by the work of his uncle Bud, the rocket scientist, and Scout leader Dick Hoffman, who was program manager for Motorola on space communications equipment linking ground stations to astronauts on Apollo moon flights and sending photo transmissions from interplanetary satellites. Many of the Flaming Arrow Patrol meetings were held in Hoffman's backyard "hobby house," a guest house full of elaborate ham radio equipment he had built himself, along with a planetarium and a globe of the world that lit up to indicate places he was calling. Many years later Spielberg told Dick Hoffman how much he envied his son for having a father who was "the Mr. Wizard of Phoenix, Arizona." A huge antenna loomed above the hobby house, with a platform the boys could climb to peer into a four-foot-long telescope to study the stars over Camelback Mountain on cloudless nights. Steven, who later shot part of *Firelight* in the hobby house and the orange grove surrounding it, was fascinated by the telescope. He set up a smaller telescope to watch the skies from his own backyard. Once, when he found Saturn, he excitedly invited the neighborhood kids to come around and share the sight with him.

When Steven wasn't reading science fiction or making movies, he usually was watching television. His memories of TV-watching in Phoenix are somewhat distorted. He once complained that "Phoenix, Arizona, is not exactly the culture center of the United States. We had *nothing!* Except, probably, the worst television you've ever seen. They showed one movie on three different channels, *The Atomic Kid* [a 1954 comedy starring Mickey Rooney as a radioactive survivor of an atomic bomb blast]. They kept repeating that for years!"

But even if Phoenix TV was a wasteland for movies, there was a lot more to watch than *The Atomic Kid.* In addition to *The Twilight Zone,* Steven enjoyed *Alfred Hitchcock Presents* and Steve Allen's comedy-variety shows. When he attended high school in California, Spielberg (whose middle name is Allan) would introduce himself by saying, "I'm Steve Allan . . . Spielberg." He also liked the comedy of Ernie Kovacs and *You Bet Your Life* with Groucho Marx. But the comedy show that influenced him most when he was growing up in Phoenix was the locally produced favorite *Wallace & Ladmo.*

"These guys [Bill Thompson and Ladimir Kwiatkowski] were inventive and original, and they turned me on," Spielberg recalled. "They were my idols. I watched them every day. I grew up and I was supposed to be too old to watch them, and I still watched them, because they were very hip. They always kept abreast of the times. They were the *Saturday Night Live* before *Saturday Night Live.* Essentially they were contemporary humorists. They never talked down to kids, that's what I remember most about them. They never treated kids as children; they always treated them as peers. I will never forget the day they took Stan Freberg's album *United States of America* [i.e., *Stan Freberg Presents The United States of America,* a satirical revue of early American history], and they did the whole thing on their show, they lip-synched to the record. It was just great. I remember buying the album after that and memorizing it."

• • •

S T E V E N ' S movie fanaticism was nurtured at the Kiva Theater on Main Street in Scottsdale, which showed sexy "adult" movies in the evenings but had kiddie matinees every Saturday. Parents would drop off their kids and leave them all day with fifty cents' admission to a program including two features—grade-B Westerns and Tarzan movies, sci-fi and monster movies, and occasionally more prestigious films, such as John Huston's *Moby Dick* and John Ford's *The Searchers*—along with ten cartoons, *Our Gang* shorts, and two installments of the kinds of serials Spielberg would pastiche so affectionately in his Indiana Jones movies. "It was a great Saturday," Spielberg recalled. "I was in the movies all day long, every Saturday. I saw *Tailspin Tommy* and *Masked Marvel* and *Commando Cody* and *Spy Smasher* —serials like that."

"I've seen absolute duplicates in Spielberg movies of scenes we used to see back in the 1950s at the Kiva, in serials filmed in the 1930s and 1940s," reports Barry Sollenberger. "When Harrison Ford in *Raiders of the Lost Ark* rides his horse down the hill and jumps onto the truck carrying the ark, Spielberg got it from the 1937 serial *Zorro Rides Again,* with John Carroll, even the camera angle—Zorro is riding a horse chasing after a train, and he jumps into a semi truck going down a freeway."

Arnold Spielberg took Steven and Jim Sollenberger to see Alfred Hitchcock's *Psycho* at the Round-Up Drive-In in 1960, on a double bill with Roger Corman's *House of Usher.* "*Psycho* absolutely scared the living shit out of me," Jim remembers. "All three of us were in the front seat. Steve was in the middle, I was on the side, and I remember breaking his dad's little wind-wing window." Steven later told neighbor Tom Simmons how impressed he had been with Hitchcock's employment of the power of suggestion: "Steve talked about the shower scene in *Psycho,* how Hitchcock never showed any real violence—he showed you the knife and this and that, but most of it was in the viewer's mind."

Steven and his friends could get a bit rowdy when they attended movies at the Kiva Theater—once they were kicked out for making too much noise —and when they took the bus to see first-run movies at theaters in downtown Phoenix. The uproarious scene of the ghastly little title characters in Spielberg's 1984 production *Gremlins* tearing the theater apart while watching *Snow White and the Seven Dwarfs* is a homage to fondly remembered boyhood mischief.

When Irwin Allen's dinosaur movie *The Lost World* played one of Phoenix's biggest theaters in 1960, Steven recalled, "My friends and I took a lot of white bread and mixed it with milk, Parmesan cheese, creamed corn, and peas. We put this foul-smelling mixture into bags, went to the movie, and sat in the highest balcony. At the most exciting part, we made vomiting sounds and squeezed the solution over the balcony on the people below. We did it for laughs. Little did we realize that it would begin a chain reaction of throwing up. The movie was stopped, the houselights came on, and ushers appeared with their flashlights—ready to kill. We were so frightened that we raced out the fire-escape exit. Even though we had brought two cars, the seven of us ran about a mile and took a bus home."*

Spielberg and his pals especially liked the historical epics and other big-screen spectacles in vogue during that period. *"Ben-Hur* [1959] was in town for a year," Jim Sollenberger recalls, "but Steve, being Jewish, was reluctant to go see that movie because they advertised it as 'A Tale of the Christ.' I went to see it and thought it was fantastic. I finally persuaded him to go see it, and he said he was surprised a movie could be that good. Steve and I also saw *On the Double* [1961], a comedy with Danny Kaye, and we both thought it was hilarious. It's tough to imagine comedy coming out of Nazis, but Danny Kaye did it. He would disguise himself as Hitler, and I can remember Steve for years after that jumping up and giving Danny Kaye's Hitler salute."

The movies that impressed Steven the most in his Arizona boyhood were two epics directed by British master David Lean—*The Bridge on the River Kwai* (1957) and *Lawrence of Arabia* (1962). Spielberg later called Lean "the greatest influence I ever had." He has emulated Lean's magisterial sense of visual storytelling throughout his career, especially in the underrated 1987 World War II drama *Empire of the Sun,* a project he inherited from Lean himself.

Haven Peters, a classmate who acted in two of Spielberg's amateur movies, remembers that in theater-arts class at Arcadia High School, "Steve was promoting *The Bridge on the River Kwai* as the greatest movie because of its stupendous action scenes, especially 'the greatest scene ever' (or words to that effect), 'the way Alec Guinness falls, dying, onto the dynamite plunger.' And, animated by the thought, he acted out Sir Alec's famous fall."

Speaking at Lean's Life Achievement Award tribute from the American Film Institute in 1990, Spielberg declared that *River Kwai* and *Lawrence* "made me want to be a filmmaker. The scope and audacity of those films filled my dreams with unlimited possibilities."

I N the summer of 1958, shortly after finishing fifth grade, Steven "was working on Eagle Scout and doing merit badges, and he kinda ran out of ideas of what to do for a merit badge," his father recalls. "I said, 'Well, they have a photography merit badge. Why don't you take this little movie camera and go out in the desert and make a Western? See if the scoutmaster will accept it.' So I gave him three rolls of film and he went out in the desert and made this little Western."

The movie had no title cards. Steven subsequently referred to his first

---

* In Spielberg's 1985 production *The Goonies,* one of the kids, Chunk (Jeff Cohen), tells that story about himself, calling it "the worst thing I ever done." Spielberg later directed his own dinosaur movie called *The Lost World,* his 1997 sequel to *Jurassic Park.*

attempt at cinematic storytelling as *The Last Gunfight, The Last Gun,* and *The Last Shootout.** The primitive little Western, which was edited in the camera, had a cast made up of fellow Scouts and other pals, including Jim and Barry Sollenberger.

"A bunch of neighborhood kids went out in a station wagon with Steven's dad to a restaurant named Pinnacle Peak Patio [a Western steakhouse in Scottsdale], which had a red stagecoach parked in front of it," recalls Jim Sollenberger, who played the lead. "Steven's dad did most of the filming, or all of the filming. We were not old enough to handle a camera. The movie was Steven's idea. He had more of the director role; it was his toy.

"I played a bandit with a bandanna and a cap pistol. I robbed a stage with two people on top. The camera was positioned so that you couldn't see that there weren't any horses. The people threw the money down from the stage. Then we got in the car and drove out in the desert. I remember my cowboy hat blew off during one scene and, like in the old Westerns, we naturally left it in and in the next scene I was wearing my hat. It ended with me being shot and rolling down the rocks. [When Jim was tossed over a cliff, he was doubled by a dummy made up of pillows, clothes, and shoes.] Steve and his dad had broken a ketchup bottle for blood and poured it on the rocks. I was grinning ear-to-ear trying to be serious. I remember getting no end of crap from them over the years because I was lying there dead and grinning."

Making that early Western gave Steven "a sense of power bossing around a few kids who otherwise would be slapping me around. But that wasn't so important. I was making something happen that I could relive over and over again, something that would only be a memory without a camera in my hand."

When the film was shown at the next Monday night's troop meeting, Steven recalled, "the Boy Scouts cheered and applauded and laughed at what I did, and I really wanted to do that, to please again."

Steven began taking his camera along on every Scout trip, filming everything that happened, from the boys getting on and off cars and buses to their physical exertions and shenanigans at camp. When he showed the movies at troop and patrol meetings, some of which were held in his house, he enjoyed seeing "everyone come out of their seats, partly because they were in the picture."

Starting his moviemaking career shooting film without sound was excellent discipline in the art of visual storytelling, comparable to the training received by the great directors who started in silent movies and perfected their craft in the sound era, such as Hitchcock and John Ford. Steven's friend Terry Mechling also had a family 8mm movie camera, and over two Saturdays during seventh grade he and Steven put together a silent homage to Ford in

---

* He also has called it *Gunsmog,* although his memory may have been playing a trick on him, for that was the parodistic title of an apparently unfilmed Western comedy project he described to *The Arizona Republic* in 1962.

Mechling's backyard, a two-reel Western starring classmate Steve Swift. "It was pretty much action-packed, just a straight robbery-chase kind of thing, with the general store robbed and the sheriff chasing the robbers, more scenes than a thought-through movie," Mechling recalls. "We both liked the same movie—John Ford's *The Searchers*—and that was one of the movies we felt we could emulate."

Spielberg remembers having made about fifteen or twenty 8mm movies as an amateur filmmaker, but that rough estimate covers only his completed story films, not all the varied footage he shot while growing up. His movies sometimes had no stories, but were simply experiments in filming techniques. "He would look at *anything* and see how it would look through the lens," Mechling says. Steven even hooked up a camera cart behind his cocker spaniel, Thunder, and had the dog tow it around the neighborhood to make a movie called *A Day in the Life of Thunder.*

Steven "had an attitude about the use of film that I didn't," Arnold Spielberg says. "I'm a Depression baby. When I grew up, everything was expensive. When I used to put film in the camera, I tried to use every bit for taking pictures. He'd take several rolls and he'd experiment. He'd try out close-ups, he'd try out stop frames, he'd try out slow motion. I used to say, 'Steve! Use the film efficiently!' He said, 'Dad, I gotta experiment.' " Cinematographer Allen Daviau has described Arnold as Steven's "first producer." "That's right —'Watch the money!' " Arnold laughs. "That's what they say about George Lucas [who has produced Spielberg's three Indiana Jones movies]: Lucas would try to control the number of retakes that he wanted to do. Now Steve's good at it. He knows how to manage things."

Steven soon became impatient with the limitations of his 8mm home movie camera. "I remember I was over at his house," says next-door neighbor Bill Simmons Jr., "and I went in the bathroom and he was working on some kind of sound effects in the sink, making different sounds in the water." Jim Sollenberger recalls an even more remarkable experiment Steven made with him when they were thirteen years old: "He filmed me as a hideous intruder in the night, coming down the hallway in his house directly into his bedroom. He filmed it in 8mm—in CinemaScope. He bought an anamorphic lens that he had found in a catalogue, that would squeeze the image down. He put one adapter on the camera and one on the projector. For most of the filming, he was lying on the floor looking up at me. He'd bought a spotlight, and it was hotter than hell. I was holding a big butcher knife, and he filmed me quite effectively—I turned the knife in such a way that we saw a glint of it coming across his camera a couple of times."

When Steven was in eighth grade, teacher Pat Rodney had a "career exploration" project, encouraging students to show what they planned to do for a living. Steven went out in the desert with some classmates and made another 8mm Western, this time with a primitive soundtrack. His teacher recalls that Steven ran an accompanying tape of "dialogue, screaming, and galloping. They were rolling around in the desert shooting and stuff. One of the things I remember was the money he spent on props to make it look realistic. He spent his allowance on bags of blood. We had a great time—we ran the movie forward and backward, and we all hollered. We all knew he had some special talent."

"I'm going to make movies," Steven told the class. "I'm going to direct and produce movies."

"I WAS an exhibitor when I was twelve, thirteen, fourteen years old," Spielberg has recalled. "I exhibited 16mm movies for a charity in my dad's family room in Phoenix, Arizona. And I never made those movies. I never made *Davy Crockett* or *Toby Tyler* or any of the [other] Disney films that were available to me to exhibit for this charity. But in watching the reaction of the kids getting off on the movies, I felt as if I had made those films. . . . I wanted to run my amateur theater like the big time. It gave me the feeling I was part of a large industry."

In fact, as people who attended those screenings vividly recall, Steven *did* show his own movies, usually as curtain-raisers for the programs of Hollywood features, cartoons, and serials. Some of the profits were given to the building fund of a local school for the retarded, the Perry Institute. In July 1962, *The Arizona Republic* ran a feature on four benefit screenings of *Davy Crockett, King of the Wild Frontier* Steven held on a single day. "Producer-director-scriptwriter-cameraman Steven Spielberg, age 15, has now turned entrepreneur," wrote columnist Maggie Savoy. He told her he would have shown one of his own films to help the Perry Institute, but that most of the neighborhood kids had already seen all of his movies, and "anyway, they're nothing great. They don't have any stars in them—just all my friends."

Steven made his own posters and ran off advertising fliers on his father's office mimeograph machine. His father would bring home a GE 16mm projector. Anne and Sue took tickets and peddled popcorn, candy bars, Kool-Aid, and Popsicles at a refreshment stand during intermissions. "Leah would leave—she would abandon it," Steven's friend Doug Tice remembers. "They had an agreement he had to clean up when he was done." On summer nights, Steven devised his own equivalent of a drive-in movie theater by hanging a sheet on his mother's clothesline in the backyard and showing movies to kids gathered on his patio.

Between screenings, Steven quizzed his audiences about their reactions, using the neighborhood kids as his own early version of what Hollywood today calls a "focus group." It was invaluable feedback for a budding director who wanted to understand how to appeal to the mass audience. And by immersing himself in the nuts and bolts of exhibiting movies, he acquired knowledge that has enabled him to supervise the marketing and distribution of his Hollywood productions with a rare degree of expertise. Barry Sollenberger was impressed by Steven's precocious commercial savvy: "He would rent *Francis (The Talking Mule).* I thought it was a goofy movie, but the neighborhood kids loved it. He would rent what the kids would see, what would sell."

The primary purpose of Steven's screenings, Arnold Spielberg says, was "to make money for his movies." When he began making movies, Steven recalled, "My dad financed them—about twenty bucks per film." But after Steven's filmmaking became a steady habit, he found he needed an additional source of revenue. The money raised by selling concessions at the screenings "was used to finance his ongoing purchase of film," Arnold explains. "He'd give the girls a little, but the rest was his money to buy whatever film he wanted. I wouldn't let him keep the money for admission. I said, 'You can't do that. We're using somebody else's film. It's not licensed to us.' So he would donate that money to the Perry Institute for retarded children, and he would get a lot of publicity out of that. I said, 'You got more credit for donating that money to the Perry Institute than you would out of saving it and buying film.' "

From time to time Steven augmented his income from the screenings by whitewashing fruit trees to protect them from bugs and the blistering Arizona heat. Like other boys, he would pick up fifteen or twenty dollars spending a few hours whitewashing the trees in neighbors' yards. Another time, he went to the Scottsdale shop of his family hairdresser, Paul Campanella, and said, "You need something done here. I know I can earn fifty dollars. Let me look around." As Campanella remembered, "He looked around and went to the ladies' room, checked it out, and said, 'Your ladies' room is terrible. Let me do it all.' So I said, 'OK, go ahead, paint it all.' I went to look at it the next morning. I couldn't *believe* what he painted. He painted the faucets, he painted the handle on the toilet, he painted the trap underneath the sink, he painted the little [aperture] around the drain, he painted the chrome around the mirror."

For all of Spielberg's business enterprises, "He didn't really care about making money," Doug Tice points out. "That was not one of his goals. Even when he was showing movies at his house, he wasn't doing it to make money. He was doing it to support his addiction to making movies."

"People who don't know me think I'm just motivated by money or success," Spielberg told *The New York Times* in 1992. "But I've never been motivated by that. I've never based a decision on money."

STEVEN'S fascination with collecting soundtracks began when he bought the album for George Pal's 1950 sci-fi movie *Destination Moon,* and it became an enduring passion. He has hundreds of movie soundtrack albums, including some of the rarest titles. His intimate familiarity with classic movie scores and composers has helped him greatly in conceiving scenes with music as an integral component, and in talking the musical language of longtime collaborator John Williams. Spielberg would "make my 8mm home movies when I was a kid by taking the soundtrack from some score like

[Elmer Bernstein's] *The Great Escape* or [Miklos Rozsa's] *Spellbound* and inventing a movie *to the music.*"

"I can remember spending summer afternoons, when it was miserable outside, in Steven's room listening to soundtrack albums," says Bill Hoffman, who played the piano for high school musicals while Steven played the clarinet. Tom Simmons "never will forget" the day Steven came to his house, discovered his xylophone, and "hit notes playing songs from every single Western known to man on television—*Gunsmoke, Maverick, Cheyenne,* whatever was on TV in those days."

Influenced by his mother's love of music, Steven joined the Ingleside Thunderbird Band, spending several years playing the clarinet at school ceremonies, recitals, and football games, and marching in a black-and-white uniform with a gold-plumed high hat in local parades, including the annual Parado del Sol before 100,000 people in Scottsdale. The band's repertoire included the standard John Philip Sousa marches and the "Colonel Bogey March" from *The Bridge on the River Kwai.*

"He was a very energetic young lad, well liked by all of those around him," says band director Rodney Gehre. "He was obedient, he was a good listener, and he had discipline. I always gave him the top grade. But it's a good thing he did what he did [i.e., made movies], because he probably wouldn't have made it as a musician. Well, *maybe* he would have. He was very creative—he would take a little lick on his instrument and make a little jazz figure on it. It seemed that playing the clarinet was a good release for him."

W H E N Steven was in his second semester of fifth grade, teacher Helen Patton went to Ingleside principal Richard T. Ford and complained about his obsession with moviemaking. "He was driving her nuts," Ford recalls. "He did some filming at the school, and he was always talking about it. I remember having a talk with him in my office. He came in—I think he took his camera into the office—and talked about what he was doing. I said to her, 'Oh, for cryin' out loud, get off the kid's back and leave him alone.' I wasn't encouraging him because he was making movies, even though I'd *like* to say that—it was because he was active, because he was a busy little guy, and he never bothered anybody; and because I always liked to have kids be in a position where they could dream. If a kid wanted to sit by himself beside a wall and watch the clouds go by, that was fine with me. There has to be a time for dreams."

When called upon to read aloud in class, Steven, much to his embarrassment, was "a very slow reader." Even today he considers it "sort of a shame" that he does not have the same passion for reading that he has for motion pictures. It is an intriguing question how much his prodigious visual sense may be compensation for his difficulties with reading, and, conversely, how much his difficulties with reading stem from his intense inclination toward the visual. His mind would often wander while he was reading in school, and he would amuse himself by drawing stick figures on the edges and flipping the pages, making his own animated movie.

Although he never made the honor roll, during his last two years in grade school Spielberg impressed social studies teacher Pat Rodney as "a *good* student," demonstrating an especially keen interest in history. It was in her class that the future director of *Schindler's List* first saw film footage of the Nazi concentration camps. She ran a documentary about Nazism called *The Twisted Cross,* which "showed the real thing—dead bodies, people hanging from barbed wire—it was shocking. In order to show the movie I had to get permission from the parents. I did it for several years, and I always involved somebody who was a true Holocaust person, who'd been in the camps."

While on location in Poland making *Schindler's List,* Spielberg told a journalist that although he had relatives who died in the Holocaust, and although he knew Holocaust survivors as a child in Cincinnati, those stories did not become real to him until he saw *The Twisted Cross.*

T H E R E was a dark side to Steven in his childhood, a pent-up aggression stemming from the harassment he received from bigger boys and from the tensions between his parents. "He could be a little brat at times," remembers Sylvia Gaines, who lived across the street. "He was always out there pelting younger kids with oranges. At his bar mitzvah [open house at his home on January 10, 1960], they had to call the kids off—he was up on the roof throwing oranges. I'm sure he was venting some of his latent talent."

In the same 1978 interview in which he confessed to the vomiting prank in a movie theater, Spielberg described his most serious instance of youthful misconduct: "By today's standards, we were pretty straight. But I did have a six-month fling as a juvenile delinquent. One day I went with four of my friends to a modern shopping mall that was being built and threw rocks at plate-glass windows for three hours. We later discovered we had caused about thirty thousand dollars' worth of damage."*

He usually took out his frustrations by bullying his "three screaming younger sisters" and some of their little girlfriends.

"Every Saturday morning my parents would escape from the four of us kids," Anne Spielberg has recalled. "The minute they were out of the house I would run to my room and blockade the door. Steven would push it all away and then punch me out. My arms would be all black and blue. Sue and Nancy would get it next, if they had done some misdeed. Then when he was through doling out punishment, we would all get down to making his movies."

Nancy never has forgotten the time when she and her sisters "were sitting

---

* Spielberg did not mention in that interview what happened to him, if anything, as a result of his juvenile vandalism.

with our dolls, and Steven was singing as if he was on the radio. Then he interrupted himself 'to bring us an important message.' He announced that a tornado was coming, then flipped us over his head to safety. If we looked at him, he said, we'd turn to stone."

"When I would put Annie to bed," their mother recalled, "Steven would hide outside her window and say in this eerie voice, 'I am the *Mooooon!*' Annie would scream in terror. . . . Once I bought Nancy a doll for Hanukkah, and one night while I was out, he cut off the doll's head and served it to her on a big platter with a bed of lettuce and garnished with parsley and tomatoes. At this point Nancy didn't even freak out. Baby-sitters would not come into the house. They'd say, 'We'll take care of the girls if you take him with you.' "

"I remember being totally scared of him," says Janice Zusman, who lived in the house behind the Spielbergs. "One time Susie and I were playing Barbie dolls by the canal near our house, on Indian School Road. I would have been grounded for life if my parents knew I'd even gone near the canal. We were pretending it was the Grand Canyon. Steve was bugging us and teasing us: 'If you don't do whatever'—unfortunately, I don't remember what it was he wanted us to do—'then I'm going to throw your Barbie into the canal.' He grabbed my Barbie doll and yanked the head off and threw it into the canal. The most important thing in my life was this Barbie doll! It was so traumatic I've been talking about it ever since. The worst thing was that I couldn't tell my folks, so I had to go down and fish the head out of the canal."

"Steven loves to do that stuff—he was always doing something to scare somebody," says neighbor Bill Gaines. "He'd get younger kids in some kind of situation he wanted—when Sue and Anne were over at our house climbing trees or whatever—and he'd get it on film real quick. He always had a camera ready so whatever the moment was he'd catch it for future use later on. He was almost fanatical about having his camera with him."

Reminiscing about his behavior toward his sisters, Steven admitted, "I loved terrifying them to the point of cardiac arrest. I remember a movie on television with a Martian who kept a severed head in a fishbowl. It scared them so much they couldn't watch it. So I locked them in a closet with a fishbowl. I can still hear the terror breaking in their voices." He also used the closet as the setting for another exercise in creative sadism. The props included a plastic skull, a light bulb, a pair of goggles, and his father's Army Air Forces aviator cap. Out of them Steven fashioned the desiccated head of a dead World War II pilot. Luring the girls into the darkened closet, Steven switched on the light inside the skull and relished the sound of his sisters screaming at the grisly apparition.

His later penchant for scaring the wits out of movie audiences is a creative outgrowth of those childhood pranks. He has described *Poltergeist* as "all about the terrible things I did to my younger sisters." From Spielberg's boyhood fondness for mutilating dolls and smearing ketchup on the walls to make his sisters believe they were seeing blood, it was a short step to showing a little girl abducted by ghosts inside her suburban home and homicidal skeletons bursting out of the backyard swimming pool. And in the Indiana Jones movies, those extended homages to his boyhood moviegoing experiences at the Kiva Theater, Spielberg's relish in putting his heroines through the most grueling ordeals with such creatures as snakes, bugs, and rats has the unmistakable aura of an incorrigible overgrown adolescent's tormenting of the opposite sex.

N o t every girl in Steven's neighborhood was afraid of him.

"Of all those older boys, Steven was the nicest, because he just wanted to take pictures of us," says actress Lynda Carter, who is four years younger than Steven. "He at least interacted with us instead of torturing us and tying us to trees. He had an 8mm camera and he was always filming. My sister Pamela and I always put on shows in our backyard—singing and dancing—and he filmed some of them. I recall our begging him to film us. He would go, 'Oh, *OK.*' He *did* ask us to do crazy things, like hanging in trees, but he didn't ever really traumatize us."

Classmate Nina Nauman Rivera says that although Steven was "really shy" around girls, he had a crush on one of the prettiest girls in his neighborhood, who was in the class behind him, and he "used to try out some film ideas on her." His friend Del Merrill describes a certain "buck-toothed blond-haired little girl" as having been Steven's "girlfriend" in seventh grade. But Steven remembers his first romantic experience as somewhat traumatic: "I'll never forget the time I discovered girls. I was in the fifth grade. My father took me to a drive-in movie with a little girlfriend of mine. This girl had her head on my arm, and the next day my parents lectured me about being promiscuous at an early age."

That may have accounted for some of the reserve he showed around girls in his high school years in Arizona, a time when no one can remember him having a single formal date, even though he had female friends and worked with girls on school plays and on his movies. His friend and fellow moviemaker Chris Pischke thinks Steven didn't date because he was "a fanatic about doing film. Plus, it would have cost him money that he would have spent on his movies. What made Steven who he is is that he was single-minded—he didn't care about anything except making movies."

"I don't think he realized the crushes that some girls had on him," Anne Spielberg said. "Some of my friends had major crushes on him. If you looked at a picture of him then, you'd say, Yes, there's a nerd. There's the crewcut, the flattop, there are the ears. There's the skinny body. But he really had an incredible personality. He could make people do things. He made everything he was going to do sound like you wished you were a part of it."

• • •

W H E N he was in eighth grade at Ingleside, Spielberg's creative energies burst forth into a wide variety of cinematic genres, including his Western for Patricia Scott Rodney's "career exploration" project; a filmed record of a school play, the mystery *Scary Hollow,* made with his friend Roger Sheer, a member of the cast; and a slapstick comedy. The comedy featured trick photography of students' heads popping out from both sides of trees, speeded-up chases, and other sight gags reminiscent of Mack Sennett silent two-reelers. Spielberg screened it at Halloween 1960 as part of the school's annual outdoor fund-raising carnival, in a booth on the playground decorated with a sign reading "Steve Spielberg's Home Movies." The filmmaker would show his little movie to anyone for a quarter.

The Spielberg movie that people remember best from that remarkable school year—the one that pointed most clearly toward his future—was a World War II flying movie, *Fighter Squad.* He had begun filming it in seventh grade, and it was his most ambitious project to date. The subject itself was not unusual for a kid in Steven's neighborhood. "We all made films about World War II," Spielberg noted. "It was because our fathers had fought in the war and their closets were full of props: souvenirs, uniforms, flags, revolvers that had been fixed so they wouldn't shoot." But the *way* Steven (and his father) managed to bring World War II alive on screen despite an infinitesimal budget still has people who saw *Fighter Squad* shaking their heads in admiration.

The black-and-white movie, which ran about fifteen minutes, integrated 8mm Castle Films documentary footage of World War II dogfights with scenes Steven shot at the local airport using vintage fighter planes. "If *we* were making a flying movie," admits Barry Sollenberger, "it never would have dawned on us to say, 'Let's go to the [airport] and really shoot the scene in an actual airplane.' But Steve got permission to go in the cockpit to film. He would stand on the wings filming as if the plane was actually flying."

It was Arnold Spielberg who arranged for the use of the plane. "These planes were used for firefighting, aerial drops and things like that," he says. "We got permission to crawl over 'em and even sit in 'em, but no keys to turn anything on. Steve would climb up on a ladder and climb up on the nose and photograph into the cockpit, with one of the kids sitting there with a helmet on. When he wanted to show him turning, he took the camera and [tilted it], and, so help me, it looked like you're making a bank! He did his own planning. I would try to open doors to help him get things." Arnold helped Steven augment the scenes shot at the airfield with close-ups filmed in a backyard mockup of a cockpit, using a painted backdrop and a household fan for a wind machine.

Doug Tice, who is four years younger than Steven, remembers being shown part of *Fighter Squad* in the filmmaker's bedroom, which was jammed with movie photos and posters, camera equipment, props and masks, and model airplanes. "When you see a guy about your age in a fighter plane and it looks like a *real* fighter plane, you say, 'Wait a minute, how did you do this?' To this day I wouldn't know how he did it. I asked him, and he said, 'I can't tell you.' Steve was nice, but he would never tell you the secrets of how he did things."

"I'd buy seven or eight of those [Castle] films and pull out all the exciting shots and write a movie around them," Steven explained in a 1978 interview with *American Cinematographer* magazine. ". . . If I needed a shot of a young flier pulling back on the stick of a P-51, we'd go out to the Sky Harbor Airport in Phoenix, climb into a P-51 (after our parents got us permission), and I'd shoot a close-up of the stick being pulled back. Then I'd cut to a piece of stock footage of the airplane going into a climb. Then I'd cut back to a close-up of this fourteen-year-old friend of mine grinning sadistically. Then another close-up of his thumb hitting the button. Then another stock shot of the gun mounts firing. I'd put the whole thing together that way."

Jim Sollenberger, who played the squadron leader, remembers Spielberg also appearing as a flier in the movie: "Spielberg played a German—there were *always* Germans in Spielberg pictures, never Japanese. Spielberg's interest was in the Nazis, and I frankly was a little surprised it took him as long as it did to make a movie *[Schindler's List]* with them as real villains, not like *Raiders of the Lost Ark.* In *Fighter Squad,* Spielberg got shot, in a scene of a plane falling for a long time, spliced in with him in the cockpit trying to get out. He slumped forward and had black or blue food coloring coming out of his mouth. I filmed it; I was on the wing filming sideways into the cockpit to get the effect of the plane going down. I gradually tilted the camera to make it look like the front end was going down. I can remember him being all pissed off after he got back the film because I had shaken the camera too much. He wanted me to shake it a *little,* but I shook the camera more than he wanted. It was the only time in the years I was around him when he was angry."

"You know how kids are in eighth grade—all they wanted to do was screw around," recalls cast member Mike McNamara. "He would say, 'Everybody calm down—we're shooting a movie. We do this, we do that, and if you don't want to do it, leave.' Everybody else was doing it more or less as a game, and he was very serious about what the end result was supposed to be. It was his life. I was amazed how focused he was. It was unbelievable. It was scary."

W H E N graduation ceremonies were held on May 26, 1961, for Steven's class at Ingleside Elementary School, Pat Rodney wrote a Class Prophecy, imagining a reunion fifty years in the future:

"Some of us have aged a bit and may be difficult to recognize. We would like to take a little time out right now to introduce you to your classmates once more. . . . You there, with the tam and glasses, STEVE SPIELBERG, would you please stand so that we may see the producer of those great Smell-o-Rama Productions."

Pat Rodney insists she was only making a joke about the then-current exhibition gimmicks of Smell-O-Vision and AromaRama (processes that wafted odors around the movie theater) and that she was not poking fun at the bathing habits of "Smelly Spielberg." But otherwise the prophecy was remarkably on target.

Asked how she felt when Steven became successful in Hollywood, his favorite grade-school teacher replied, "I wasn't a bit surprised by his film-making. *He was a filmmaker.* Always, from the early days."

" B I G   S P I E L "

ONCE I COULD MAKE FILMS, I FOUND I COULD "CREATE" A GREAT DAY OR A GREAT WEEK JUST BY CREATING A STORY; I COULD SYNTHESIZE MY LIFE. IT'S JUST THE SAME REASON WRITERS GET STARTED, SO THAT THEY CAN IMPROVE THE WORLD OR FIX IT. I FOUND I COULD DO ANYTHING OR LIVE ANYWHERE VIA MY IMAGINATION, THROUGH FILM.

— STEVEN SPIELBERG

BECAUSE of its space-age design, students in Spielberg's day called Arcadia High School "Disneyland." Campus life centered around "The Flying Saucer," a circular library building raised up on stilts—today the building is often referred to as "E.T.'s spaceship." Affluent and bustling, the two-year-old Phoenix high school already had a strong reputation in both academics and athletics when Steve entered as a freshman in September 1961. He was one of 1,539 students, and by the time he moved to California in his junior year, the enrollment had increased to 2,200. In those days, Arcadia was "a typical suburban middle-to-upper-class white school [aside from its two families of Asian descent], where the kids had too much money, too many cars," says fellow student Craig Tenney. "But it was large enough that you could find a circle in which you were comfortable."

Steve's boyhood friend and classmate Del Merrill remembers him being "a lot more popular in grade school than he was in high school. In grade school he was outgoing, smart, always working, ready to tell his story—'I got an idea.' Everybody was listening to him. He was relatively popular. I think he had a lot of confidence until he got to high school. Then he got quiet. When he hit Arcadia High School, something happened. The first couple years of high school I think was a gloomy, quiet time for him. He did a withdrawal from us. We had a lot of bullies at that age, among the jock crowd. Steve was one of the skinnier little runts. He got pushed around a bit in freshman and sophomore years, [when] everybody [else] had a growth spurt. *I* never turned on him, even though I was part of the jock crowd, but I've *seen* it—he was taking some knocks, being bumped into and laughed at or put down."

One of Steve's closest friends at Arcadia, Clark (Lucky) Lohr, suggests that he developed "a skill blending in and not being high-profile, maybe because he was afraid of attracting unwanted attention." "Big Spiel," as he came to call himself, formed his own tight little social circle in response to his exclusion from the jockocracy of Arcadia High School. "He had a social life going," recalls Karen Hayden, who played in the school band with him. "He had friends and was going places and doing things. He was weird but *good* weird, independent-minded."

A notoriously indifferent student throughout his years at Arcadia, Steve was "very much preoccupied with filming—he carried around a camera all the time and he was always taking pictures," says his driver's education teacher, Howard Amerson. "I was impressed with his determination to do what he wanted to do. So many kids don't know what they're interested in."

Not everyone was so impressed with Steve's monomania. "The neighborhood was all upper-middle-class and up, and the kids came in with the assumption that they were going to college," says English teacher George Cowie. "That was fine, unless you happened to be a Steve Spielberg and were not interested in going to college." Because of his frequent absences from school when he was faking illness to stay home and edit his movies, Steve "spent a lot of time being disciplined," says his Drama Club adviser Phil Deppe. "He definitely did his own thing and went his own way, and that was fine for those of us who were going our own way as well. But the administration, oh, they didn't like that."

Arnold Spielberg had frequent clashes with his son while trying to steer him into becoming an electrical engineer or a doctor. Steve remembered his father being "very strict with me regarding all the high school courses that would lead me in those directions, such as math or chemistry, which I was intuitively horrible at. Of course I took the opposite trail and followed in my mother's footsteps."*

Steve's friends were mostly creative oddballs like him, and the things they were doing were not mainstream interests at Arcadia. When he became part of the drama group, it was the first time he "realized there were options

---

* Steve's unsuitability for a medical career was apparent when he took biology and was required to dissect a frog. He became nauseated and had to run outside to vomit along with other students, "and the others were all girls," he noted. Before leaving he set several frogs loose; he endearingly recreated that scene in *E.T.*, when Henry Thomas's Elliott liberates all the frogs in his school's biology lab, thereby earning a kiss from a pretty little blonde (Erika Eleniak).

besides being a jock or a wimp." But he still could not help regarding that group as "my leper colony."

"Arcadia was the most status-conscious, rigid school in terms of class lines, a very stressful peer situation," explains Steve's classmate Nina Nauman Rivera. "If you didn't fit into those parameters of having new clothes, having a boyfriend who was on the football team, you were worthless. Kids who were academically oriented, who were intellectual, or had big dreams just didn't fit in. Steven was really shy, and he was introverted in terms of girls. Nerds didn't get talked to. It tended to make people introverted."

One night in 1963, Arcadia student Sue Roper was baby-sitting for the three Spielberg girls. Steve was lying on a couch watching television, and Roper asked him to hold still so she could sketch him. He agreed, and she drew him staring placidly but intently toward the TV through dark, heavy-lidded eyes, his face soulful and handsome but entirely oblivious to her presence. While she was sketching, she could not resist leaning over to plant a kiss on his lips. "After being around him a while, I was attracted to him," Roper says. "It must have been hormones. I remember kissing him on the couch, and it didn't make a dent in him. I kissed him and he didn't kiss me. It was probably my fantasy. He never went to proms—I know because I was there—I don't think he had time. He wasn't depressed or moody, he was just too involved in being creative. It certainly wasn't *school* he was involved in, and there wasn't much interaction with real close relationships."

"A lot of us would have liked to spend more time with him, but he was very goal-oriented and very busy," admits Jean Weber Brill, who worked with him on plays and movies. Lucky Lohr remembers, however, Steve "had girlfriends, at least one or two, who would talk to him about their boyfriends or whatever. I heard one woman telling Steve how it was 'really rough waiting for that phone to ring.' I thought, 'My gosh, Steve is this person's confidant. They *trust* that guy.' Certainly he wasn't known as a big man on campus, but he seemed to inspire confidence in females. It impressed me he was mature enough to be able to talk to them. Whatever misery he might have been going through in high school, there was something very coherent and balanced about him."

S PIELBERG has given accounts of his high school years that have tended to conflate some of his experiences in Phoenix with experiences during his senior year at Saratoga High School in California. Some anti-Semitic incidents that actually happened to him in Saratoga, according to friends and other eyewitnesses, have been incorrectly described by Spielberg as happening in Phoenix. This may be a result of his tendency to confuse the locales and dates of events that happened in one of the five cities where he lived when he was growing up; a natural consequence, perhaps, of such a peripatetic upbringing. While Spielberg *was* bullied frequently in Phoenix, and at least some of that abuse did stem from anti-Semitism (overt or otherwise), the instances of anti-Semitism against him appear to have been more frequent and considerably more virulent later, in Saratoga.

However, Spielberg has recalled that he was tormented in high school by a bully who "made anti-Semitic slurs" and enjoyed pushing him around. The bully would shove his face into the drinking fountain between classes and bloody his nose during football games in physical education. The most frightening incident came when the boy tossed a cherry bomb at Steven while he was sitting on the toilet in the school lavatory; Steven barely escaped injury. These incidents can be placed with certainty in Phoenix because the boy appeared in a film Spielberg made while he was a student at Arcadia.

Steve gravitated toward Arcadia's drama group not only because his interests lay in show business, but also because it offered a refuge with congenial, like-minded students who accepted him for what he was. The proportion of Jewish students involved in drama was much higher than in the school at large, so that was a factor in easing his acceptance. Teasingly known to some of his classmates as "Spielbug," he was "a nerdy little Jewish kid, a nice guy, talented and dweeby," recalls Sherry Missner Williams, who was involved with him in the drama group and is also Jewish.

"One of the interesting things about that milieu," his friend Rick Cook comments of the Arcadia neighborhood in the early 1960s, "is that it was so new, everybody was from somewhere else, and a lot of the old ethnic associations didn't exist. Looking back, there were a fair number of Jews at the school—who knew? Who cared? The intense social status revolved around athletics—in the 1963 school year we were state champions in football—and the drama people were very much second-class citizens, neck-and-neck with academics.

"By the time I knew 'Spielbug,' he knew what he was going to do. But he was not narcissistic about it. The thing with him was not ego, not the shallow sense of 'I'm going to be a big movie director.' What interested him was *making the movie,* the whole process. He is still childlike in the sense that he is still fascinated with magic and a sense of wonder, but he was one of the least childish fourteen-year-olds I had ever seen. He was very focused, and that's not a fourteen-year-old's characteristic. If anyone I knew was going to make it, I thought he was going to, because he was so driven and committed."

Arcadia's stage facilities were of professional caliber. The school was locally renowned for its annual spring musical, an elaborate production on which as many as three hundred students would work under stage director Dana Lynch, musical director Reginald Brooks, and vocal director Harold Millsop. Spielberg was a member of both the Drama Club (joined by his sister Anne in her freshman year, 1963) and the National Thespian Society, an honorary group for drama students. Art teacher Margaret Burrell, who designed sets and costumes for the school plays, says that in addition to helping her paint sets, Steve would "organize everything—he would organize the crews and work with the actors. He was a nice young man, very cooperative and interested."

The headline on the page containing his class picture in the 1964 Arcadia High School yearbook reads, "Spelberg [sic] Seen As Talented Actor." No one who knew him in high school remembers Spielberg as a particularly talented actor, but he did have several inconsequential bit parts in school plays that he performed adequately. "He schlepped one of the bodies out of the basement in *Arsenic and Old Lace,*" remembers fellow actor Michael Neer. Spielberg played a soda jerk in *I Remember Mama* and, while serving as a prompter for the school's 1963 production of the musical *Guys and Dolls,* he was the offstage voice of garage owner Joey Biltmore in a telephone scene with Neer's Nathan Detroit. As a member of the school band, Spielberg also played clarinet in the pit orchestra for *Guys and Dolls,* as he had for the previous year's production of *Brigadoon.* But he was more prominent in the drama group for his work with director Dana Lynch as her sometime stage manager and general all-around assistant.

"Steve would try out for acting parts, but he usually wouldn't get anything because he wasn't too good in that area," recalls fellow drama group member Haven Peters. "He didn't have a lot of personality; he was kind of awkward. Even in class, where we were all friends, he had trouble. We had to give dramatic readings, and he wanted to do well, he worked hard at it, but he had trouble memorizing lines. He would kind of stumble through it. I bet he has a lot of sympathy for people in that position, because he was always very nervous and shy. And in terms of class work, he was *worse* than average —he would never read the textbook.

"He always volunteered for other things. He would stay after school for hours and hours. Mrs. Lynch was kind of disorganized, and he was always willing to help her out in any way possible, running errands, ringing telephones [offstage], doing makeup, helping with lights. Some kids would kid him about being Mrs. Lynch's pet, for hanging around her for hours asking to help with every little thing. I recall some of the girls, and [Steve's friend] Roger Sheer, kidding him with names like 'Nanny Spielberg,' because he was always fussing about production details. But other people wanted to be in the spotlight. He didn't. He had a good attitude about the theater: pitching in and doing anything."

But it was largely through his filmmaking, recalls *Firelight* cast member Warner Marshall, that Spielberg "created a circle of friends, a whole bunch of people who admired him and enjoyed him. It was a way of giving people a chance to know him and get to like him. He enjoyed the social interaction of doing the film; he wasn't just trying to use people. I had the sense of it being a communal effort, and he was the gentle leader."

"P H O E N I X has a young Cecil B. DeMille—young Steve Spielberg," a local TV newscaster announced in 1961.

Spielberg's first public notice came when a TV crew was sent to cover the making of his World War II movie *Escape to Nowhere* in the desert around Camelback Mountain. The forty-minute *Escape to Nowhere,* which began filming in 1959 and was finally completed in 1962, was a considerable advance in production values from *Fighter Squad.* With a cast of mostly adolescent actors shooting it out and emoting in a motley collection of makeshift uniforms, no one would mistake the movie for *The Bridge on the River Kwai.* Still, the 8mm color movie won first prize in a statewide amateur film contest, the 1962–63 Canyon Films Junior Film Festival (Canyon was a company that made industrial films). The prize was awarded in part because the director's battlefield props and special-effects explosions appeared so startlingly realistic.

"When we showed up in the morning at his house to come out to film," Barry Sollenberger remembered, "he had a pickup truck with a 50-caliber machine gun mounted in the back. I remember how awed we were: 'Man, where does this guy come up with this 50-caliber machine gun?' But I had enough foresight to say, 'The machine gun—heck, where does a [fourteen]-year-old come up with a *pickup truck?*' "

Chris Pischke, who helped Spielberg stage the battle scenes, recalls what happened next: "We got to the location first, and waited and waited, and he hadn't shown up. All of a sudden he finally pulled in—it turned out the police had pulled him over. They thought it was a real machine gun and he was going to spray the traffic or something. It was pretty funny."

During a later part of the prolonged filming schedule, Spielberg had another brush with the law.

"The Highway Patrol came after us," reports Haven Peters, who played one of the leading roles. "We were out in the desert, and some people drove by and reported to the state police that all these guys were trooping around in Nazi helmets and guns. Two or three cars of troopers came out to investigate. We thought, Are we all going to be arrested for trespassing? Somebody told them we were making a movie, and I remember Steve's dad talking to them and cooling them off. After that they were really interested, and they hung around to watch." Arnold Spielberg seemed to be the dominant personality in the making of *Escape to Nowhere,* says Peters: "I think he ran everything, that was my memory of it. Steve was running the camera, but his father was the adult—he was the one people really looked to for direction."

Escape to Nowhere was shot around Camelback Mountain and at Cudia City, a local Western studio where Steve and his fellow amateur filmmakers occasionally made movies without permission. The ambitious silent featurette tells the story of a group of American soldiers surrounded by Germans as they try to capture a strategic hill in North Africa. In the process of trying to break out, all of the GIs are killed except for one soldier, played by Haven Peters: "I was all alone at the end, lost and done for. It ends as I'm just sitting there all by myself. It was sad. But in that movie there wasn't any interpersonal stuff—except with bayonets. It was all action. I always felt that was what he was interested in. It was mass directing. What do you call it? Second unit. The whole movie was second unit. He reshot [some scenes] later because he wanted to have more close-ups. Even then, he would just kind of have the camera zoom in and show my face. It wasn't like I had to *act* or anything. I had no input. That was always the way I felt with him and his father. I was just a body that got filmed."

Although Peters was surprised to find that Spielberg had managed to round up as many as twenty or thirty boys for the battle scenes, they all had to double up as Americans and Germans to make the cast seem larger. Spielberg attempted to dye white T-shirts black to make German uniforms, but they didn't come out right, so his Germans wore blue with silver eagles. At other times, Spielberg resorted to old B-movie trickery to stretch his limited resources. He had a limited supply of German helmets, so he would have his soldiers run past the camera and pass their helmets to other kids, who then would dash around behind the camera and make their appearances. And as Esther Clark reported in her 1963 feature article on Spielberg in *The Arizona Republic,* to "give the impression in [one] scene of a long line of GIs sneaking past the enemy . . . Steve and a classmate simply went around and around a grinding automatic camera on the ground."

"Since we had a jeep in Arizona, and I was the only one old enough to drive it in that gang," Arnold Spielberg recalls, "I put on my Army fatigues, and I'd crunch down and drive the jeep, leading a column of American soldiers through the desert." Steve's mother also drove the jeep for some scenes in the movie, wearing a helmet over her short blond hair while playing a German soldier. Even Anne Spielberg found herself pressed into service. "We were shy a soldier the day we filmed the scene," Steve told the reporter, "so we had her put on a uniform and helmet and got rid of her in a hurry, wearing a German uniform and crawling on her stomach."

And he later recalled, "It was fun to get them dressing up. Difficult to keep them interested, though. I could only shoot on weekends. Monday through Friday, I was in school. Saturday and Sunday, when they really wanted to go out, have a good time, I needed them to come over to the house and be in a movie. For the first few weeks they loved it. They were great! After that, other interests developed. They got into cars. They got into girls. They wouldn't turn up and I'd replace actors, rewrite characters out of the movie. That was the major problem."

Jim Sollenberger, who had played the lead role in *Fighter Squad,* fought a hand-to-hand battle to the death as a German soldier in *Escape to Nowhere.* "This was the first time I can remember thinking that Steve had some talent," he says. "*Fighter Squad* was just kids goofing around. It got pretty serious after that."

"One time on *Escape to Nowhere* he had *six cameras* on a big battle scene —it was awesome," Pischke remembers. "That scene was spectacular and sweeping—the way he set it up against Camelback Mountain in Echo Canyon, all the guys he mustered together, the explosives—can you imagine a kid filming a huge battle with explosions and firebombs? And it was on 8mm!"

"My special effects were great," Spielberg boasted in a 1980 interview. "For shell explosions, I dug two holes in the ground and put a balancing board loaded with flour between them, then covered it with a bush. When a 'soldier' ran over it, the flour made a perfect geyser in the air. Matter of fact, it works better than the gunpowder used in movies today."

Even more ingenious than the special effects was the way that Spielberg used *Escape to Nowhere* to deal with a vexing problem in his personal life, the bully who "made anti-Semitic slurs" against him at Arcadia High School: "He was my nemesis; I dreamed about him." Struck by the boy's resemblance to John Wayne, Spielberg had the brainstorm of asking him to play the squadron leader in *Escape to Nowhere*. Initially scoffing at the request, the bully soon found himself co-opted into acting under the command of the "wimp" he loved to torment.

"Even when he was in one of my movies, I was afraid of him," Spielberg said. "But I was able to bring him over to a place where I felt safer: in front of my camera. I didn't use words. I used a camera, and I discovered what a tool and a weapon, what an instrument of self-inspection and self-expression it is. . . .

"I had learned that film was power."

"THREE people in the neighborhood, within ten houses, were filming movies all through late grade school," Barry Sollenberger recalls. "And when we got to high school, Chris Pischke and the Sollenbergers lost interest. Spielberg kept the interest and kept doing it, and the rest is history. Relatives of ours discouraged us—'What are you going to do, film movies all your life?'—and Spielberg was encouraged by relatives of his. That made the difference."

Friends who knew Spielberg in Phoenix have observed that, painful as he found his parents' impending breakup, it also may have had some beneficial side-effects. "They didn't hover, they let him have the space to go about and do it," says Warner Marshall. "It seemed they had a lot of wisdom—they were either distracted or they realized he knew what he wanted to do." The Spielbergs' departure from Phoenix for California in 1964, putting Steve one step closer to the movie business, was in part a response to the marital tensions between Arnold and Leah, a last-ditch attempt to start anew in fresh surroundings. When the attempt failed, Leah and the girls returned to Arizona, but Steve went to Hollywood.

"The best thing that ever happened to Steven Spielberg was his parents getting divorced," Barry Sollenberger believes. "If Steve had never left Arizona, he wouldn't have had the opportunities to succeed that he had in California."

• • •

I N 1962, the same year he completed *Escape to Nowhere,* Spielberg first set foot on a Hollywood soundstage.

While visiting relatives in the Los Angeles area, he managed to insinuate himself onto Stage 16 at Warner Bros. in Burbank, where a battle sequence for *PT 109* was being filmed (Spielberg himself would film part of *Jurassic Park* on that same stage thirty years later). A rah-rah adventure movie about the World War II exploits of U.S. Navy Lieutenant (j.g.) John F. Kennedy, *PT 109* starred Cliff Robertson as the future president and was directed by Leslie H. Martinson (whose Mickey Rooney comedy *The Atomic Kid* had driven Spielberg to distraction with its frequent appearances on Phoenix late-night TV).

Spielberg recalled that he "stayed on the set up until the moment when the Japanese destroyer sliced the PT boat in half." Then, to his disappointment, "They made us visitors leave."

T H E stimulus for Spielberg's first feature film, *Firelight,* was an unidentified flying object he did *not* see when he was growing up in Phoenix.

Fascinated by heavenly lights ever since that night in 1957 when he and his father saw a meteor shower, Steve, like virtually every American boy growing up in the 1950s, was intrigued by reports of flying saucers and other UFOs. He longed for the real thing—the chance to see a UFO with his own eyes. So he was devastated when he missed a Boy Scout outing, "the only overnight I missed the entire year. Wouldn't you know," and his fellow Scouts came back and told him how, at midnight in the desert, they all saw "something they couldn't explain . . . a blood-red orb rising up behind some sagebrush, shooting off into space. I felt so left out not being there." Patrol leader Bill Hoffman says, "One overnight Spielberg was absent out in the desert. I don't recall who did it, but the story was told to Spielberg that someone had seen a flying saucer. Spielberg was very interested. It wasn't true at all. As far as I can tell, it was a complete fabrication."

The making of *Firelight* was made possible by the prizes Steve had won for *Escape to Nowhere* in the state amateur film contest. "He won a whole bunch of stuff," his father recalls. "He won a 16mm Kodak movie camera. I said, 'Steve, I can't afford to spend money for film for 16mm. Let's swap it for an 8mm, and we'll get a good one.' So we bought a real good Bolex-H8 Deluxe, the big camera that was built on a 16mm frame, but cut for 8mm, and so you could get 400-foot reels on it. It had telephoto lenses, single-frame motion, and slow-motion, so he could make all kinds of stuff with that. And he won a whole library of books relative to filmmaking. He loved those books, but he said, 'I'm going to donate them to the school library. I don't need them. I have the feel for it.' As a gift for being that generous, I said, 'OK, we're going to up the ante.' We bought a Bolex projector, and we also bought a sound system. It was the first sound system out for consumer use, a Bolex Sonerizer."

The Bolex Sonerizer enabled Steve for the first time to record sound directly on film. After editing his footage, he would have a laboratory put a magnetic strip on the side of the film. He then would lay the sound onto the strip, post-synching the dialogue, music, and sound effects in his living room. With the Bolex camera, he could do multiple exposures, making it possible for him to produce professional-looking visual effects. "A lot of the technique was dictated by what the camera could do," he recalled. The equipment he used for *Firelight* is "antique now, just as Lionel trains are now antiques, but I was able to use the state-of-the-art such as it existed in [1963] and still make films that were pretty sophisticated."

Steve's sixty-seven-page, fully dialogued screenplay for *Firelight* was completed in early 1963, near the end of his sophomore year in high school. He spent about six months filming it, from June through December of that year, with a cast recruited from *Guys and Dolls* and other school plays. Asked how the film was financed, Arnold said, "We paid for it." The cost was "somewhere between $400 and $600, and I think Steve took in about $700 or $800. He made a little money."

The characters in Spielberg's script are cardboard figures reminiscent of dozens of grade-B 1950s sci-fi movies, especially *Quatermass II* (1957), British writer Nigel Kneale's tale of alien invaders controlling the minds of humans (Spielberg admitted that Kneale's Hammer Films featuring Brian Donlevy's Professor Quatermass were a major influence). Much of the dialogue in *Firelight* is unintentionally comical, with overblown rhetoric and frequent malaprops (the script also contains many ludicrous spelling and grammatical errors). Everyone who saw *Firelight* agrees that Spielberg, who was making his first film with trained actors and a carefully detailed screenplay, had not yet developed into much of an actor's director. But Spielberg's innate narrative sense, his precocious flair for visual storytelling, and his already evident ability to orchestrate complex movement and character interaction (as outlined in the script) make *Firelight* a gripping, well-constructed (if overlong) yarn about a small group of scientists investigating mysterious red, white, and blue balls of moving light coming from the sky to abduct people, animals, and objects.

Set in the fictional town of Freeport, Arizona, *Firelight* focuses on scientist Tony Karcher (Robert Robyn) and his wife, Debbie (Beth Weber), whose marital problems threaten to disrupt Tony's career, and the obsessed UFO expert Howard Richards (Lucky Lohr), whose quest to prove the existence of extraterrestrial life has won only grudging support from his skeptical patrons in the Central Intelligence Agency. Among the abductees are a dog named Buster, a squad of National Guardsmen, and a small girl named Lisa (played by Nancy Spielberg), whose disappearance causes her mother (Carolyn Owen) to die from a heart attack. Lisa's abduction by an overpowering red light descending in her backyard is strikingly similar to the scene

Spielberg calls his "master image," the abduction of little Barry Guiler by the unseen UFO—also represented by a flaming red light—in *Close Encounters of the Third Kind.*

Various locations around Phoenix were used for *Firelight,* including the desert around Camelback Mountain, Sky Harbor Airport, the Baptist Hospital, the National Guard Armory, the Middleton Institute of Electronics, Dick Hoffman's radio shack and orange grove, and the home of cast and crew members Beth and Jean Weber. But much of the "American Artist Productions" film was shot in and around the Spielberg house, with the family carport used as a studio for both interior and "exterior" shots. Steve and Arnold gave the shoestring production the illusion of a Hollywood spectacle with ingeniously designed visual effects. These included various optical tricks to conjure up supernatural firelights and the filming of some elaborate miniatures, including a map of the area with flashing lights to show where the firelights were attacking, an Arizona town under glass, and a papier-mâché mountain for a stop-motion sequence of firelight disintegrating National Guardsmen, tanks, and jeeps.

Much of the summer shooting took place at night, because of the heat. After school resumed, Steve had to film mostly on weekends, working around school and work schedules and Arcadia High's staging of *See How They Run* and *I Remember Mama.* Postproduction, including postsynchronization of dialogue and recording of a musical score, continued until the March 1964 premiere. "I used the high school band to score [the] movie," Spielberg recalled. "I played clarinet and wrote a score on my clarinet and then had my mother (who played piano) transpose it to her key. We made sheet music, the band recorded it, and I had my first original soundtrack."

"It was a huge undertaking," marvels Rick Cook, who now writes science-fiction novels. "He wrote a professional-looking script, he had to be the production manager, he had to scare up props, he had to convince actors to be in it—although that wasn't too hard—he had to juggle everything. He was the damnedest promoter. He knew how to get things out of people, and he did it without being pushy or obnoxious. He was not a braggart, he was not one who would talk about what he was going to do. He just did it. He knew what he wanted, he was young and kind of attractive, and it was a matter of enthusiasm and dedication being contagious."

S PIELBERG has suggested that the emotional core of *E.T.* is a response to his parents' divorce and his longing for a friend/brother/father, even one from another world. So it is logical that *Firelight,* made during the time when he was actually living through the trauma of the impending divorce, sprang from the same emotional needs as *E.T.* and *Close Encounters.* The metaphors of childhood and rebirth pervade those films, as indeed they do the entire science-fiction genre.

"Close Encounters was actually a remake of *Firelight,"* says jean Weber

Brill, who did the makeup for *Firelight*. "There were scenes in *Close Encounters* that were almost direct copies from *Firelight,* such as the lights appearing on the highway and the scene when the little boy looks out the door at the bright light. The storyline of *Close Encounters* was very similar, but obviously rewritten and more sophisticated."

Firelight introduces the themes of supernatural intruders, suburban alienation and escape, broken families and abducted children, scientific adventure, and spiritual renewal that would become familiar in Spielberg's mature work. The young couple on the run in *Firelight* also point toward the Richard Dreyfuss and Melinda Dillon characters in *Close Encounters,* and the earlier film's UFO expert, Howard Karcher, is an older, more fallible, less blissful version of François Truffaut's Lacombe. But unlike *Close Encounters,* which radically departed from sci-fi movie tradition to depict its extraterrestrials as benign rather than menacing, *Firelight* derives in large part from the mood of anxiety and paranoia that characterized the genre in the 1950s, when Spielberg became hooked on sci-fi. "It was a Cold War movie," says cast member Lucky Lohr. "They talk about it being his [first] version of *Close Encounters,* and it *was,* in a sense—a sky movie, about sky gods—but the 'cinematic vision' of *Firelight* owed more to horror movies about aliens dusting humans."

Firelight expresses the lack of confidence some of the more liberal sci-fi movies of that era displayed toward the U.S. government's ability to cope with alien invasion. The movie has a typical postnuclear age skepticism about scientists. Spielberg's portrayal of ufologist Howard Karcher's callousness and obsessiveness, and his depiction of Tony Karcher as a husband with an eye for another man's wife (Helen Richards, played by Margaret Peyou), may reflect the young filmmaker's problems in dealing with his father's career and his parents' unsettled marriage.

Spielberg's vision of alien life is also somewhat ambiguous. His sense of the healing possibilities of higher intelligence links the movie with the more optimistic strain of science fiction exemplified by Arthur C. Clarke's classic novel *Childhood's End* and Robert Wise's film *The Day the Earth Stood Still.* In a twist ending showing the influence of Rod Serling's *Twilight Zone* series on Spielberg's early artistic development, it turns out that the aliens in *Firelight* are transporting Freeport and its residents piece by piece to their planet, Altaris, to serve as a miniaturized zoo. As *Arizona Journal* reviewer Larry Jarrett wrote, "The meaning of all this is brought to light when three shrouded spacefolk explain via their conversation that they are higher forms of life who have taken the life of earthpeople and given them a sort of brainwashed heaven. The reason for this is to save the entire universe from the destructive nature of we earthpeople."

Spielberg's Altarians, who feel threatened by humankind's stockpile of nuclear weapons, are divided on the wisdom of brainwashing humans to eradicate their past tendencies toward violence, hatred, and prejudice. The dilemma Spielberg proposes (like Anthony Burgess and Stanley Kubrick in *A*

Clockwork Orange) is that those tendencies are inevitable consequences of free will. *Firelight* ends with the aliens flipping a coin to decide whether to begin by reprogramming the capitalist countries or the Communist countries (a somewhat irrelevant question in the overall scheme of things, but one that reflects the film's Cold War origins). The audience never finds out which way the coin will land, and is left wondering whether the interplanetary zoo will become a prison or a place of spiritual rebirth for the human race, a new Garden of Eden in outer space.

"S TEVE' S parents were totally behind the film," Jean Weber Brill remembers. Leah not only kept the cast and crew supplied with snacks, but cheerfully put up with "constant commotion at her home" weekend after weekend, *The Arizona Republic* reported. She even allowed Steve to set up a flashing red light by the carport door to signal the neighbors to keep quiet while filming was in progress. "The things we did in this poor woman's house!" Jean marvels.

Since the time in Cincinnati when he so enjoyed seeing the mess made by his mother's exploding pressure cooker, Steve had been fascinated by the pop-art potential of kitchen mayhem. He dreamed up a comical scene for *Firelight* in which Beth Weber's inept maid (Tina Lanser) forgets to watch the pressure cooker while making dessert. "His mom actually loaded [thirty cans of] cherry pie filling in her pressure cooker and let him blow it up," Jean recalls. "We spread cherries all over the cabinets, the floor, the face of the actress. It was a real mess—it was fun."

For some night exterior scenes around Camelback Mountain, Steve used a light meter to guide him in the filming method known to professionals as "day for night"—putting a blue filter over the lens to turn daylight into night. For the visual effects involving the firelight, Steve ingeniously employed a variety of simple but effective techniques. Charles G. (Chuck) Case II, now a federal bankruptcy judge in Phoenix, played a love scene with Dede Pisani in the orange grove behind Dick Hoffman's house. The scene ends with the young couple being chased by a firelight and Case calling the police. "The firelight was just a red gel on a light," Case recalls. "It descended from the trees, and the illusion was effective. In the film it really looked like something strange was happening."

Arnold Spielberg explains how Steve showed "the firelight picking up Nancy [his little sister]. She was crawling along the ground. He had her crawl from here to a tree, and he timed it in his head, backed up the film, then reexposed the same thing, but with a firelight coming right down to where Nancy was. In order to get this effect of a whirling piece of flame, of energy, he took two glass plates and a red gel and put Vaseline between the plates. Sue or Anne would take the plates and pull them back and forth, and that would make the jelly wiggle and move, and then he'd film through it. If you imagine a bunch of clouds in fast motion whirling around, that was his effect of firelight. And it came out! It looked like it took her and she disappeared."

"I was intrigued by the contraptions he dreamed up," says crew member Warner Marshall. "The one I remember most vividly was a scene in his parents' carport with Carol Stromme. Somebody was sitting on the hood bouncing the jeep, and he had pulleys with a couple of white Christmas lights—a clothesline of lights would move past the jeep so it would look like the jeep was driving in the country passing a house. He had floodlights shining down on the jeep to make it look like moonlight. He had a big piece of cardboard with triangular holes in it that would pass in front of the light to make shadows. He conceived all that! It made a heck of an impression on me when I was fifteen years old—this guy really knew what he was doing. But he didn't exude an *air* of a guy who knew exactly where he was going and what he was doing. He was humble and kind of quiet."

Perhaps the most remarkable visual effect was Steve's use of a series of quick lap-dissolves in showing the attack of the firelight on the UFO expert (played by Lucky Lohr). "He collapsed on the floor and we filmed him disintegrating," recalls makeup artist Jean Weber Brill. "We filmed the scene in the Spielbergs' front room. Steve had the camera on a tripod and we filmed about eight frames at a time, then we would change the setup and the makeup and film another eight frames. We did that all day long."

"They had red and brown makeup and wet Kleenex on my face," Lohr remembers. "I had a cold at the time, so I was shivering. I thought I was being a real trouper. At the end of the scene, Steve pulled out a plastic skull, moved me out, set the skull down, and shot a couple of frames of the skull." Spielberg redid that scene at the end of *Raiders of the Lost Ark,* when the blazing light from the Ark hits the Nazi villain Toht (Ronald Lacey) and disintegrates him right down to his skull.

During the months-long filming process on *Firelight,* the sixteen-year-old director "could be firm, he could coax people, but he did everything from an emotional place of such calm that I never had trouble doing what he wanted," Lohr says. "He'd say in a low-key voice, 'Luck, I want you to do this or that,' and it would move swimmingly. I might have screwed up, but I never got a sharp word from him. I never saw *anybody* get a sharp word from him."

Even when the two actors originally cast in the lead roles (Carol Stromme and Andy Owen) quit after the first two weeks of shooting, Spielberg did not become discouraged. He recast the parts with Beth Weber and Bob Robyn and reshot the opening scenes in December. "I remember the energy level starting to flag, people starting to wonder, 'Gee, do I want to spend my *entire* Saturday doing this?,' " says Warner Marshall, who also played a National Guardsman in the film. *"He* was having a great time. He'd say, 'I want to get this one last thing. Would you mind staying?' He was extremely gracious. He created an atmosphere where everybody had an affectionate respect for him.

He wasn't anywhere in the forefront of *Guys and Dolls,* but when he made *Firelight,* everybody grew to really love him."

"We had so much fun filming *Firelight,*" says leading lady Beth Weber Zelenski. "Steve was methodical, thorough, and pleasant to work with. It turned out very professionally considering what he had to work with. There were a couple of times when I didn't exactly know what to do. He's much better now with actors than he was then, and it was a brand-new thing for me, being in a film. But Robert Shaw [who acted in *Jaws*] said that Steven Spielberg is a man with a heart, which is what struck me too."

S T E V E had experimented with sound effects and music accompaniment on other films,* but the synchronized soundtrack of *Firelight* was a remarkably ambitious undertaking. "I got some guys from GE" to help him, Arnold says, "and I put all the sound together for him." After editing many hours of 8mm film down to his final cut running two hours and fifteen minutes, Steve set up a microphone in his living room with the assistance of sound technicians Bruce Palmer and Dennis LaFevre. He brought in the actors to postsync their dialogue on the Bolex Sonerizer as the film was projected on a wall.

"The soundtrack of the voice was lip-synched on the film," Arnold explains. "But all the special effects and the music and the background noises were on tape. The sound on the tape machine would slip out of sync with the motion, and when we showed *Firelight* at the Phoenix Little Theatre, I was working with him like mad in the projection booth to try to make it in sync."

Steve had made the actors follow his script fairly closely during shooting, but at some points in the dubbing process he had to resort to lipreading to understand what they were supposed to be saying. "It took a lot of sessions, trying to get the hang of it and not have it look stupid," Warner Marshall remembers. "But when *Firelight* was shown at the Phoenix Little Theatre, on a big screen, with bright colors, sound, it didn't look at all what you would expect from a group of goofy high school kids. To me, and to most of the people in the audience, it seemed incredible."

When he first saw the final print of *Firelight* with the cast in his living room, Spielberg later recalled, "I knew what I wanted, and it wasn't what my dad wanted for me: I wanted Hollywood."

The day after the premiere of *Firelight,* he and his family left Phoenix and moved to California.

---

* While working on *Firelight,* he helped another amateur filmmaker, Ernest G. Sauer, make a feature film called *Journey to the Unknown,* which also had a premiere at a local theater. Sauer, who owned some fairly sophisticated sound equipment, filmed most of his sci-fi fantasy in a soundproofed studio at his parents' house. Spielberg was credited with the special effects on the film and also had third billing as spaceship mechanic Ray Gammar. Haven Peters, who played the lead, says Spielberg's "main interest was in learning about sound technology."

• • •

"**P**OKE a Hollywood legend with the needle of fact and it usually blows up in your face," *TV Guide* noted in a 1972 profile of Spielberg. Although the magazine insisted that Spielberg's story of his first visit to Universal Studios "checks out as truth," that oft-told tale can't survive a poke from the needle of fact.

In one of his earliest tellings of the tale, to *The Hollywood Reporter* in 1971, Spielberg claimed: "One day in 1969, when I was twenty-one [*sic*], I put on a suit and tie and sneaked past the guard at Universal, found an empty bungalow, and set up an office. I then went to the main switchboard and introduced myself and gave them my extension so I could get calls. It took Universal two years to discover I was on the lot."

In a previous (1969) interview with the *Reporter,* Spielberg had said, "Every day, for three months in a row, I walked through the gates dressed in a sincere black suit and carrying a briefcase. I visited every set I could, got to know people, observed techniques, and just generally absorbed the atmosphere."

And in his 1970 interview with Rabbi William M. Kramer for *Heritage-Southwest Jewish Press,* Spielberg confessed, "To get by the guard at the gate I lied a lot."

Spielberg also claimed (to *Time* magazine in 1985) that the visit occurred when he wandered off a tram ride on the Universal Studios Tour during the summer of 1965. He said he was looking around the soundstages when he was stopped by Chuck Silvers of the Universal editorial department: "Instead of calling the guards to throw me off the lot, he talked with me for about an hour." Silvers became interested in seeing his movies, Spielberg recalled, "so he gave me a pass to get on the lot the next day."*

"I've heard a lot of stories about how I met Steven," Chuck Silvers says with a wry smile, before telling what he calls "the most accurate one."

The soft-spoken, avuncular Silvers, born in 1927, started in the film business as an assistant editor at Republic Pictures, working on John Ford's *The Quiet Man* and other films, before moving to Universal in 1957. At the time he met Spielberg, Silvers was assistant to David O'Connell, editorial supervisor for Universal TV, and had been given a special assignment to reorganize the studio's film library. The temporary quarters of the library were on the second floor of a functional building adjacent to the headquarters of the editorial department.

Silvers says he doesn't remember the exact date when he met Spielberg, but says that "Steven was probably fifteen to sixteen years old. He was still in high school," and visiting Universal on a break from his school in Arizona. Spielberg was in postproduction on *Firelight* at the time of his meeting with

---

* A 1996 interview with Spielberg in *Reader's Digest* dates that meeting in "the summer before his senior year" (1964).

Silvers, which would mean that the meeting occurred sometime between the fall of 1963 and March 1964, when he was sixteen or seventeen (and, as Silvers put it, "looked a couple or three years younger than he was"). In his *Arizona Journal* review of *Firelight* that March, Larry Jarrett wrote, "Steve plans to go to the coast this summer with the hopes of working for Universal International. It seems he knows the head librarian Chuck Silvers."

Silvers says that one rainy day when he was in his office at Universal, he received a telephone call from Arnold (Arnie) Shupack, manager of information services (i.e., computers) for Universal's parent, MCA Inc. As Silvers recalls, "I had met [Shupack] and gone through a course in computer administration under his aegis. Arnie called me and said, 'The son of an old friend of mine from GE is here. He's in high school and he's a real film bug. Would you mind showing him around postproduction?' I said, 'Fine.' Steven was on some kind of long weekend from school. So he sent Steven."*

Arnold Spielberg, however, recalls that the person who set up his son's meeting with Silvers was Stu Tower, who lived in the San Fernando Valley and was a cousin of Bernie Adler, the friend of the Spielbergs whom Leah later married. A salesman for Honeywell, Tower had become acquainted with Silvers after selling Universal a computer that was used in the studio film library.

Whether it was Shupack or Tower who arranged the meeting, Silvers gave generously of his time when Steve arrived at his office: "Because it was raining, I didn't try to show him a hell of a lot of stuff. I showed him postproduction, editorial, Moviolas; I do remember him saying he had seen Moviolas. We spent the rest of the day talking and walking. He said, 'I make movies.' He told me about the movies he had made. I asked basic questions of him, how he became involved in film. That first conversation was a mind-blower for me."

Spielberg told Silvers how his early interest in film was nurtured in the Boy Scouts and how it had progressed through his increasingly elaborate 8mm movies about World War II to the making of *Firelight*. He explained how he wrote, photographed, and directed his own pictures, casting them with neighborhood and school friends, devising the special effects, and even making the costumes.

"Steven was such a delight," Silvers felt. "That energy! Not only that impressed me, but with Steven, nothing was impossible. That attitude came through—it was so clear. He was so excited by everything. When we walked onto a dubbing stage, how impressed he was! At some point in time, it dawned on me that I was talking to somebody who had a burning ambition, and not only that, he was going to accomplish his mission.

"He was very young for his age in all other respects. In the sophisticated parts of life, he wasn't involved. But when it came to motion pictures, God

---

* Shupack, who is now president of studio operations and administration for Sony Pictures Studios, declined to be interviewed for this book.

damn! I knew he was gonna do *something*. I didn't know *what* the hell he was gonna do, but he was gonna do something. You can't walk away from a kid like that. Just out of curiosity, you want to sit and watch."

After Spielberg went back to Arizona, he occasionally corresponded with Silvers, asking advice about production matters on *Firelight,* such as how to go about requesting permission to use an existing piece of music in his score. Eventually he returned to show Silvers the final print of *Firelight.* He had been telling people who worked on the movie that he was planning to show it to Universal, and that he hoped to convince the studio to let him make a big-screen version of *Firelight.* Silvers does not recall Spielberg discussing that idea with him, but he vividly recalls the astonishment he felt while watching *Firelight:*

"I thought, How the hell did Steven ever manage that? *Firelight* was fascinating. What a project! Something that really impressed me was that he had done a stop-motion animation sequence that involved movement of armored vehicles, cannon and so forth, through terrain. I recall him saying he went to the National Guard and asked to borrow tanks and equipment and they wouldn't allow it, so he did stop-frame animation. I asked him, 'How the hell did you do that?' He said, 'I had a lot of trouble. The lights would keep burning out.' The lighting was uneven, I'll grant you, but it was a *totally* credible sequence. Steven Spielberg is as close to a natural-born cameraman as anybody I've ever known.

"The other thing that impressed me was that he had recorded dialogue, various effects, and music, and he had mixed this. There was no doubt that he was special. There was this tremendous confidence everything was going to work out the way he wanted it."

At the beginning of Spielberg's senior year at Saratoga High School in northern California in September 1964, the school paper reported, "Steve Spielberg worked with Hollywood directors this summer at Universal Pictures." Silvers confirms that Spielberg "spent that whole vacation" working as an unpaid clerical assistant in the Universal editorial department. The job enabled Spielberg to roam the lot watching films and television shows being shot and to hang out with film editors and other postproduction people, kibitzing and learning the craft of professional filmmaking. He would continue hanging out on the lot all through his college years, until, with Silvers's help, he was hired as a director.

"The first time he came back there [in 1964] I got him a pass to come on the lot," Silvers adds. "I couldn't get him a permanent pass on the lot. Steven found his own way of getting on the lot. Steven was able to walk onto the lot just about any time he damn well pleased."

At the time of his signing to a directing contract by Universal in December 1968, Spielberg first told the press the story of how he broke into Hollywood. To Ray Loynd of *The Hollywood Reporter,* he stated simply, "Through private auspices, I got a gate pass and studied filmmaking."

S I X

" H E L L   O N   E A R T H "

HE MADE AN ENORMOUS IMPRESSION ON ME. . . . I THOUGHT HE WAS SO DEVELOPED — SO
MUCH OF HIS PERSONALITY WAS IN PLACE BY THE TIME HE WAS SEVENTEEN.

— GENE WARD SMITH, SPIELBERG'S CLASSMATE
AT SARATOGA HIGH SCHOOL

PIELBERG began
his unofficial Hollywood apprenticeship at Universal in the summer of 1964,
following his junior year in high school in northern California. His mentor,
Chuck Silvers, recalls that the ambitious teenager gradually "worked out his
own curriculum" on the lot, visiting sets and kibitzing with editors and sound
mixers. Silvers offered Steven a place to hang out in the television editorial
building, provided he could justify his presence by helping in the office for
a few hours every day: "I said to him, 'There's a certain amount of scut work
you can do that's not involved with the union.' There we had to be very
careful. He couldn't even be a junior apprentice—he was a kind of guest, a
self-appointed observer who made all his own arrangements with the people
who responded to him."

Silvers shared an office with a middle-aged woman named Julie Raymond,
the Universal Television editorial department's purchasing agent, in charge
of filling orders with laboratories and other subcontractors. "Spielberg was
sixteen when I first met him," she remembers. "He was working on the lot
when he was still in high school. Chuck told him he could use our office to
take phone calls. Chuck brought him into the office and told me the kid was
floating around the lot. Spielberg used to come in to take calls and work on

scripts. I was working my butt off and going up to see my husband [who had cancer] in the Veterans Hospital in Sylmar. I had so much work to do, I gave Spielberg things to do."

Spielberg helped her during the summers of 1964 and 1965 by "tearing down" purchase orders—separating colored sheets and carbons—and routing copies to various departments. He also ran errands to the Technicolor laboratory adjacent to the studio lot, and to other suppliers housed in that building.

In his accounts of his early days at Universal, Spielberg has never mentioned his office work with Julie Raymond. Instead he has gone to considerable lengths to turn mundane reality into romantic myth, saying that after bluffing his way past the guard and finding an empty office, he commandeered it, listing his name in plastic letters next to Room 23C in the building's directory.

"I've never been in that office, let's say," Chuck Silvers comments diplomatically. Julie Raymond's response is more blunt: "He made up a lot of stories about finding an empty editing office and moving into it. That's a bunch of horseshit."

Spielberg's unpaid clerical job was the humblest, most mundane of beginnings, but it enabled the teenager to roam the lot with a purpose while seeing the inside workings of the studio system. The old-line Hollywood system was then in its last days before splintering in the creative, financial, and political upheavals of the late 1960s. But the Universal lot was the major exception to the rule in that era of studio decline. Still booming when Spielberg went to work there, it would remain so throughout his beginnings in television and features in the late 1960s and early 1970s. Those were the days when Alfred Hitchcock was making his last features on the lot, Universal TV was pioneering the made-for-TV movie format, and as many as two dozen TV series were shooting simultaneously. Spielberg's professional training was much the same as he would have had working his way up the ladder from B pictures to A pictures at MGM or Warner Bros. during the "Golden Age" of Hollywood in the 1930s. While most other filmmakers of his generation know the classic studio system only from history books and old movie footage, Spielberg's precocious start gave him an invaluable firsthand knowledge of how that system functioned.

"I visited every set I could, got to know people, observed techniques, and just generally absorbed the atmosphere," he said in a 1969 interview. "At least I knew where to go when it came time to talk about contracts." There were more tangible benefits as well. Running errands to the Technicolor lab "put him in touch with a lot of people who could get things developed and printed," Silvers recalls. "When Steven moved to L.A., he graduated from 8mm to 16mm, and his dailies [raw film footage for his amateur films] got developed [at Technicolor]. And the paperwork put him in touch with sound people who loaned him equipment."

Extraordinary as it was for a youngster to be allowed such access to a studio lot in those days when Hollywood was resistant to newcomers and had little in the way of formal apprenticeships, Spielberg became "more frustrated watching other directors at work and still not being able to get anybody to look at my movies or even stand still for five minutes to talk to me. I was sitting in an office with a telephone. Nobody to call. Nothing to do. I gave up watching other directors—it's not healthy. They'll take you into their confidence and tell you why they're going to do something. But moviemaking to the casual observer is a long, boring, sometimes cacophonous process. It drove me out of the stages into the cutting rooms. I would hang out with the editors."

He spent more time on sets than those comments would indicate. Julie Raymond says that during those two summers when Spielberg was working with her, she often picked up the office telephone and handed over to him "calls from somebody on set—'We're shooting, come on down.' Almost everybody on the lot would be calling. He was a nice kid then. People would help him. He was ingratiating, and he was talented. He really knew the camera, and he seemed to know how to edit film already. He used to write scripts for his school friends. He couldn't spell worth a damn. I used to read the scripts when he was still in high school and correct the spelling. He was very inventive. He didn't have any money for effects, so he'd make a fade by blowing cigarette smoke into the lens. He didn't have a zoom—I read the script and I asked him, 'How'd you do that?' He told me, 'I put the camera on a skateboard.' He was brilliant."

I F Spielberg felt frustrated at being out of the inner loop at Universal, imagine his frustration when he had to return to high school in northern California following that first tantalizing summer in the Hollywood dream factory. "He was depressed with hanging out in Saratoga, a long way from Universal," says classmate Mike Augustine. "For a seventeen-year-old kid, five hundred miles is a long way. He knew what he wanted to do; he was so confident and sure of himself. At the same time, he was having to live the life of the moment in high school."

"We took typing class together," recalls Spielberg's best friend and neighbor in Saratoga, Don Shull. "He would rattle off the whole time practicing [typing] about Universal Studios and going to the movies, whom he was going to meet. He was so into his movie trip. I always thought this was a kind of dead period for him, but it really wasn't—his mind was already into the next year or two. He had it all prepared."

A R N O L D Spielberg's new job with IBM as technical advisor to the manager of control systems at the company's plant in San Jose was another step upward in his career, placing him in northern California's Silicon Valley, the cutting edge of the burgeoning computer industry. His tasks included designing IBM's new process control computer. "I built that machine, and that was the last machine I ever designed personally," he says. "From there on out, I was up too high to do design work."

The Spielbergs lived briefly in an upscale suburb of San Jose, Los Gatos, where Steven attended the local high school from March 31 through June 12. They then moved to a rambling hillside ranch house in nearby Saratoga, an even more affluent suburb of about 25,000 residents in the foothills of the Santa Cruz Mountains, ten miles from San Jose and fifty miles from San Francisco. There Steven enrolled in the five-year-old Saratoga High School, a sprawling, maze-like complex of cinderblock buildings, an oddly grim and graceless design for such an attractive setting.

Spielberg often has asserted, erroneously, that he spent only the second semester of his senior year at Saratoga High, but the school records show that he started there on September 14, 1964, and after completing the entire school year, he was graduated from Saratoga on June 18, 1965. Spielberg's faulty memory may be the result of a long-standing attempt to repress some of his painful memories of Saratoga High, which he did not discuss publicly in depth until 1993.

Saratoga is an affluent smalltown resort, the second home for many wealthy San Franciscans and a bedroom community for San Jose and other parts of Silicon Valley. The growth of the computer industry and the spread of suburbanization in the fifties and sixties led to the rapid subdivision of most of the town's remaining orchards and vineyards for tract housing, but Saratoga managed to preserve its old-fashioned, rustic qualities. "When you're talking about the 1960s, Saratoga still was almost in a time warp," recalls Hubert E. (Hugh) Roberts, who taught social studies at Saratoga High School when Spielberg was a student. "It looks like a small town, and it looked like a small town then; it's all facade-country. It has a homogeneous, vacuum-packed element to it. Politically, you're in an area that is somewhere to the right of Attila the Hun."

The Spielbergs' ranch house at 21143 Sarahills Drive had a striking view of the Santa Clara Valley. Their next-door neighbors, Don Shull and his family, could hear Leah's piano music drifting down the hill from her sparsely furnished living room. Steven and Don usually walked together to school, about two miles from their homes, although Leah sometimes drove them in her jeep. The gently curving streets and hillsides, hermetically comfortable homes, and blandly conformistic suburban ambience familiar to movie audiences from such Spielberg films as *E.T.* and *Poltergeist* bear more of a resemblance to Saratoga than to any of the other places where the filmmaker lived in his youth. As his classmate Jim Fletcher observes, "Saratoga was gentile. It was as gentile as gentile could be."

Some of the kids at Saratoga High tormented Spielberg for being Jewish. Because of those harrowing experiences, he remembers his senior year in Saratoga as being "Hell on Earth for me."

• • •

T H E issue of Spielberg's treatment at the school did not fully erupt into public consciousness until *Schindler's List* was released. When Spielberg bared his soul to interviewers about his experiences growing up Jewish, speaking with particular passion of his problems at Saratoga, it ignited a firestorm of controversy and soul-searching in the town. "It was such a shock to all of us—our wonder boy, the boy we were all so proud of, actually hated us," says Judith Kreisberg Hamilton, one of several other Jews in Spielberg's graduating class of 290 students.

Recalling his time of "personal horror," Spielberg told interviewers that "to this day, I haven't gotten over it nor have I forgiven any of them." The mistreatment, he said, "consisted of humiliation . . . being hit, being struck, having pennies thrown at me during study hall and name-calling. People coughing 'Jew' into their hand[s] as they walked by me between classes. . . . I felt as alien as I had ever felt in my life. It caused me great fear and an equal amount of shame."

Spielberg remembered daily harassment and physical abuse. He said he was "smacked and kicked to the ground during P.E., in the locker room, in the showers. . . . Like most kids, I had been hit from time to time. But I had never been hit in the face. There's something really humiliating about being punched in the face. My world collapsed. Although I had wanted to be a gentile out of a desire for conformity, the idea that a person would hit me because I was Jewish was startling to me.

"Suddenly, in this affluent, three-cars-to-one-household suburb, these big, macho guys made an event out of my being Jewish. They beat me up regularly after school. I took some pretty good shots. Finally my parents had to pick me up in a car, which was humiliating in itself because we lived close enough for me to walk home. . . . Some of the teachers were aware of what was going on. They showed me no compassion."

In December 1993, the *San Jose Mercury News* reported that Spielberg's former classmates at Saratoga High were "perplexed and disturbed" by his accounts of his experiences "and suggest he may be telling them to hype his new movie about the Holocaust." Class president Philip H. Pennypacker told the paper, "He was a loner, very, very withdrawn, and it was obvious he was going through a bad time in his life. He told kids his home life was tough because his parents were going through a divorce. That's why we figured he put up the barrier, and that's why kids might have done those things to him, not because he was Jewish." Judith Hamilton also had "a difficult time believing" Spielberg's account: "I'm Jewish, too, and I didn't see those kinds of things happening. I would have been upset and I would have been the first to come to his defense. I'm not saying that anti-Semitism didn't exist anywhere, but kids just didn't form cliques based on being Jewish or non-Jewish. I don't think kids knew enough about who was Jewish to be anti-Semitic."

"What he said happened to him happened to him," Spielberg spokesman Marvin Levy responded. ". . . He regrets ever having brought it up, but he couldn't fudge when asked by a reporter where this happened."

THE first friend Spielberg made in Saratoga was his next-door neighbor Don Shull, who also was new to the school, having recently moved from San Jose. "Big Don," as he calls himself, is an affable, gentle man who stands six-feet-eight, a foot taller than Steven. "Steve and I were the odd couple— the Mutt and Jeff of Saratoga High," says Shull, who is now a landscape architect. "I never looked at him as a nerd, just different, offbeat. I think we both felt like fish out of water. It was very difficult being accepted at Saratoga for both of us. I made it passable for him."

Almost everyone who attended Saratoga High or taught there in Spielberg's day uses the same word to describe the student body: "cliqueish." The student body was largely middle-class to upper-middle-class, with only a handful of minority students. "It was not a school to be the new kid in," says Kendra Rosen Hanson, who is also Jewish. "If you stood out, if you were different, it was really tough to get integrated. If you were Jewish, you might have all the more reason for [feeling] different. Spielberg didn't fit in, anyway. It wasn't fashionable to be a nerd, and he was marching to a different drummer. He didn't belong in high school. He was so much more mature than the rest of them."

"Spielberg found himself hung up with this weird social environment," says classmate Jim Fletcher. "It was not a nice place. I remember guys throwing quarters at women who were supposed to be sluts—that's how low it was. It was a very cruel high school in a lot of ways, very white, more like a prep school than anything else—an adolescent, pampered, old-money environment."

In spite of that element, Saratoga High had a reputation for high academic standards. Virtually all the students went on to college, many to nearby Stanford. Although Spielberg applied himself more seriously to his studies than he had in Phoenix, he had a lackluster record of mostly B's and C's at Saratoga. "My most poignant memory of Steven," says his Saratoga neighbor Susan Didinger Hennings, "is that his father would push him to study math, and Steven would say, 'Oh, Dad, leave me alone. I'm going to be a really famous movie director some day. I don't need all this school stuff.' " Describing Steven as "a bright kid who tended not to perform," teacher Hugh Roberts points out, "It was not unusual to have a creative kid falling into that category." His journalism teacher, Bert Pfister, remembers Spielberg as "very capable, a good student, but he very much kept to himself. *One* thing was really unusual—he occasionally wore a fedora similar to the one that Indiana Jones wore. It was something that you'd expect from another generation. He was not part of the high school scene. He was detached and distant—I don't mean to cast any aspersion or criticism, but he had other things that he was occupied with. It's a source of considerable frustration for me that I had this creative genius in my class and I had no inkling of that."

S P I E L B E R G   often went to movies with Don Shull at the Saratoga Theater, the domed Century 25, and the downtown theaters in San Jose. "He would give me a critique afterward," Shull remembers. "He mostly talked in terms of directors more than in terms of movie stars, and I wasn't up on who the director was or who produced the movie. He was always figuring out ways to make that damn movie better. He wore me out.

"His imagination was going all the time. As we walked home up the hill, he would see in his imagination a whole scene in a movie—a movie that had never been filmed but he had the whole scene in his mind—and he'd describe some off-the-wall scene as we would be walking up the hill. One scene I remember had something to do with aliens and the army. It was very similar to *Close Encounters*.

"He told me he'd see big boom tracks along the side of the hill, guys with flying saucers, the whole nine yards. I'd go, 'You gotta be kidding!' It was a steep hill, so it took some engineering—cameras up on a hydraulic boom, helicopters buzzing around, the guys in helmets. I could see it in color! The flying saucer looked like the one in *Firelight*—like two pie plates stuck together, kinda wobbling through the air—but in *Close Encounters* it looked more like a whole city. I saw that whole scene years and years before [on the hillside in Saratoga]—the flying saucer wasn't playing music, it was more in a destruction mode, like in *Firelight,* where he had somebody dressed up as an alien in a silver suit. It was fun. The guy is amazing."

Shull, whose ancestry is Swedish and German, was raised as a Lutheran and a Congregationalist. When the controversy over Spielberg's problems with anti-Semitism broke out, he wrote a letter to the *San Jose Mercury News* insisting, "As for bloody noses, getting beaten up, anti-Jewish slurs, I *never* saw it and I *never* heard a word from Steve on the subject. Furthermore, I don't think anyone knew Steve was Jewish, and I'm sure no one cared if they did know. He kept the thing pretty much under wraps.

"If somebody had beaten up Steve, I would have known, and you can bet I would have had words with that person or persons. I submit to you: *It never happened.* . . .

"So why was Steve so unhappy in Saratoga? It had to do with the breakup of his family and the move from Arizona.

"The whole thing was a nightmare for Steve. . . . No filmmaking. No winning film awards. No future in Saratoga. A very bad divorce rearing its ugly head. A very *mad* mother and two [*sic*] sisters who didn't want to be in Saratoga. And a very unhappy dad, seeing his wife and family slipping from his grasp.

"Sounds like a time of 'personal horror.' But it had *nothing* to do with being Jewish. At least from my angle."

Shull's letter, and others which questioned Spielberg's account of being abused, prompted a response to the *Mercury News* from another classmate who befriended Spielberg at Saratoga High, Gene Ward Smith. Recalling that he and Spielberg often spoke about movies, science-fiction novels, and other subjects while spending study hall time together, Smith wrote, "One subject we discussed was his Jewish background. It is false that he was reticent about this, or that nobody knew of it. . . . It was clear that being Jewish was an important part of his definition of himself.

"Moreover, some people learned of it and used it to tease him. I think some of the boys did this not out of any deep dislike of Jews, but because they knew it bothered Steven. Regardless, it was anti-Semitism; and real hate can grow from such seeds.

"Why didn't Shull see this? I think whether or not he knew it, he was in effect Steven's bodyguard."

Spielberg responded with a letter to the *Mercury News,* published on January 11, 1994: "I read the article from an old friend of mine, Don Shull, who lived down the street from our house in the Saratoga foothills. I was very interested to hear Don's take on my life, because I feel many kids as friends presume to know a lot more about their buddies than they really do.

"When asked the question by countless journalists about anti-Semitism in my past, the grand lie would have been to conceal (as I did from people like Don Shull, other friends of mine and even my family) my experiences in that one semester [*sic*] at Saratoga High School, on weekends, on holidays, and even in San Jose where I had an unfortunate encounter with several seniors from my graduating class. . . .

"I have nice memories of Don Shull, but he certainly did not know very much about what I was going through—he could not have known.

"I actually remember a moment when one of the bullies who had been tormenting me because I was a Jew got into a fight with Don on the basketball court. I remember this because Don stared the boy down. Only one punch was thrown—Don took it, stood his ground, and continued to stare. The boy turned and walked away.

"It was one of the most heroic things I witnessed as a young person, but it made me feel bad about myself—that's the way I wished I could have reacted."

Asked about that incident, Shull says, "I vaguely remember it may have had something to do with Steve being Jewish, but I was reacting to Steve being the little guy being picked on. I didn't stand for that. I remembered my mom telling me never to hit anybody, because I'd take their head off. I just said, 'Buzz off.' No big deal."

As for Steven's recollection that he concealed his problems at Saratoga High from his family, Arnold Spielberg admits, "I never knew he ran into that. I was so damn busy at IBM at that time that I hardly knew anything that was happening. And besides, my marriage was breaking up at that time, so it was a very stressful overall period for me. Our relationship was so sad that

I lost track of the fine-grain stuff. I used to work from seven-thirty in the morning till seven or eight o'clock at night, and I think Leah absorbed all that stuff."

G E N E Ward Smith, now a professor of mathematics, acknowledges that he was even more of a "nerd" than his friend Steven Spielberg. Chubby and bespectacled, Smith was "very much an outsider being picked on by people. All the people who bothered him were the same ones who bothered me." Smith was so advanced in math and science that he was allowed to spend most of his time in the school library studying calculus and general relativity at his own pace. That was where he had most of his contact with Spielberg.

Spielberg impressed Smith because his way of looking at things was so unusual: "He had ideas, he had definitive points of view, and he was creative. He had a terrific influence on how I looked at films. I felt if I talked to him I would learn things; I thought *that* was astounding. I thought of him as a diamond in the rough. I had a kind of project to turn him into more of an intellectual, and a correlative one to make of him a kind of exclusive best friend, of a type that I had had before and would have again. However, he wasn't so easily influenced; he was really an intellectually autonomous person, which was part of the reason he was so interesting. I felt a bit resentful and jealous of Don Shull because of this, and didn't feel as close to Steven later on in the year as I did at first."

Smith had an elitist's attitude toward movies, particularly Hollywood movies. When Spielberg talked about movies being an art form—a notion not yet widespread in the United States—Smith was taken aback. He was all the more surprised to find that, while Spielberg admired the movies of Ingmar Bergman, Federico Fellini, and Orson Welles, the director he "absolutely revered" was Alfred Hitchcock:

"I remember him talking about Hitchcock films all the time—he would go on and on about *North by Northwest,* which I hadn't seen, and *Vertigo*. He would talk about *Psycho* and *Rear Window*. A lot of it went over my head. He read all about Hitchcock, and he would talk about camera movements and all this kind of stuff, but I didn't know what the hell he was talking about. He said, 'I call him the Master.' I thought, 'Wow, that's going pretty far!' I would read *The New Yorker* and *The Saturday Review,* and I would take my opinions from other people. Reviewers were very condescending in praising Hitchcock's mastery of the film art while deriding his subject matter. I thought of him the way people think of Steven Spielberg today—a guy who makes these wonderful, entertaining movies but not with much depth. I don't think Spielberg made up his mind on the basis of what other people said. If he liked Hitchcock, it was because he *liked* him. It made him an original thinker."

While Spielberg talked about his admiration for Hitchcock's enormous technical ability, Smith came to realize that there was a deeper reason for

Spielberg's affinity with Hitchcock, one that suggested the direction and philosophy the younger filmmaker's own career would follow:

"Spielberg said movies were *the* great art form, because they moved the most people. He said movies produce a strong reaction in the average person, the common man, and he was interested in the way Hitchcock would put ordinary people in extraordinary situations. Spielberg wanted to get the entire audience to react. He didn't want to play to an audience of the elite. He seemed terrifically enthralled by the idea of influencing a mass of people. He said, 'The movies reach out and grab you.' That's what he thought was great about Alfred Hitchcock. Spielberg kept saying that the film medium could relate to ordinary people and doesn't rely on some kind of intellectual process to make it work with a broad group. Back then that idea was virtually radical. That was what was thought to be *bad* about movies, this broad appeal, and he thought that was what was *good* about movies.

"Spielberg taught me that you should appreciate movies for what they are, what they try to do, rather than seeing a movie as an inferior version of a book. One thing I keep hearing about Spielberg is that he's always after money, making a buck. But he wasn't going out to reach their pocketbooks, he wanted to reach their hearts."

Spielberg's compulsion to connect with the mass audience was, Smith realized, part of his deep-seated need for acceptance by a society that made him feel an outsider. Those feelings became particularly acute during his time of crisis at Saratoga High.

"I got the impression he wanted to be assimilated and liked by people in general," Smith says. "He liked to be liked, but he was having trouble with that, because people weren't liking him. He didn't like to place himself apart in some sort of snobbish way. That was one of the things that annoyed me. My impression of him was that he was very intelligent but in some sense not an intellectual. He didn't fit my idea of how I divided the human race into two parts—'them' and 'us'—'us' is intellectual, 'them' is non-intellectual. To me, he was an 'us' but he wanted to make himself into a 'them.' "

What they had most in common was their passion for science fiction. Smith remembers Spielberg as "a fiend for science fiction. I'd read everything on the shelf labeled science fiction at the Saratoga library, and he probably had done the same in Phoenix. We'd talk about the big names—Robert Heinlein, Isaac Asimov, Arthur C. Clarke—and even some of the lesser names."

From an early age, Spielberg was particularly fond of Clarke and Ray Bradbury. In his 1968 film *Amblin'*, Spielberg paid homage to Clarke by having the male lead carry a copy of the author's 1953 novel *The City and the Stars* in his guitar case. Spielberg responded to the poetic nature of Bradbury's work, its way of magically transforming reality. When *Close Encounters of the Third Kind* was released, Spielberg asked Bradbury, "How did you like *your* film? *Close Encounters* wouldn't have been born if I hadn't seen *It Came from Outer Space* [1953] six times when I was a kid." Spielberg also admired J. R. R. Tolkien's *The Two Towers* (the second part of the *Lord of the Rings* trilogy) and the work of sci-fi author J. G. Ballard, whose 1984 autobiographical novel, *Empire of the Sun,* he would make into a film.

The teenaged Spielberg "was peculiar in that he was both well read and *not* well read," Smith observes. "Inside the sci-fi, fantasy-adventure field he was well read, but outside that field he wasn't. I would try to get him to read all these books—I would talk about Ralph Ellison's *Invisible Man,* which came up during a discussion of H. G. Wells. I also talked about James Baldwin's essays, *The Fire Next Time,* and probably also *Nobody Knows My Name* and *Notes of a Native Son . . .* I certainly would *not* have mentioned *Giovanni's Room,* despite my particular liking for that book. When I brought up something like *The Brothers Karamazov,* he would respond like he knew what I was talking about, but we would move on to something else; he would burble on about sci-fi books. I kept trying and it was hopeless. I tried to get him to read Joyce, for instance, pushing *Ulysses* as a kind of book which was fantastic without being fantasy, and carefully avoiding any suggestion that it might be difficult reading, but I couldn't sell him on it. Typically, it simply didn't occur to me to bring up a Jewish connection."

"**Y** o u know I am Jewish, don't you?" Spielberg asked Gene Smith one day in the school library.

Smith replied that he didn't know that.

"Didn't you recognize my name was a Jewish name?" Spielberg wondered.

That hadn't occurred to Smith either.

"When Spielberg brought up this whole subject, it was very educational," Smith recalls. "I figured, 'Your parents go to a synagogue on Saturdays. My parents go to Presbyterian church on Sundays. Let's change the subject and talk about something interesting.' [Smith, who is of Swedish descent, was a 'dedicated agnostic at the time.'] But I realized the guy was really interested in the subject. I guess he was doing what everybody was doing in high school—he was questioning what he believed. He didn't know what to make of religion in general, and I got the impression he didn't quite know how seriously to take Judaism. He said his parents weren't very religious anymore and they had to pretend to be. He didn't seem to me to be very religious at the time, but he was very serious about 'Jewish identity.' "

Smith's newfound awareness of Spielberg's ethnic background, and his personal empathy with Spielberg's outsider status in the school, made him more sensitive to the problems his friend began experiencing not long after arriving at Saratoga High, problems to which others were oblivious. Smith remembers Spielberg coming into the school library one Monday morning, looking "so depressed" that another person in the room asked him why he was so glum.

"You look like you just came from your mother's funeral," that person said.

"I had a really horrible experience on Saturday," Spielberg replied.

When pressed about what happened, he offered little more than, "I ran into some guys from school."

This may have been the incident Spielberg identifies in his letter to the *San Jose Mercury News* as "an unfortunate encounter with several seniors from my graduating class." He wrote that it happened in nearby San Jose, but did not go into details; Smith recalls Spielberg mentioning that the place where he ran into the "guys from school" was a shopping center. Perhaps this was the time Spielberg first experienced the abject humiliation of being punched in the face, the time when, as he put it, "My world collapsed."

There were other occasions, Smith remembers, when Spielberg "would say stuff like, 'You know I had a hard time.' He got bothered off campus. People would pester him. It wasn't a major topic [in our conversations]—it was sort of like, 'Oh, these assholes,' and then we'd go on." Smith also remembers Spielberg telling him that students were "giving him a hard time in the locker room"; Spielberg's friend Mike Augustine says people were "being nasty to him in gym class. He was scrawny and awkward, he was not your athletic type, and they related that to being Jewish, which was a thing some people loved to do."

One incident Smith personally witnessed occurred when he was walking a school corridor with Spielberg, "and one of our classmates threw some coins on the ground. He said something [to Spielberg] like, 'Go ahead, pick it up! You want it, don't you? Well, you can have it. I don't want it, it's all yours.' This was all in a nasty, bullying tone.

"I was wondering what this was all about, figuring it must have reference to some private matter or something which had previously happened. He said, 'It's because I'm Jewish.' I, being kind of dense about this sort of thing, asked what did that matter. He said, 'Well, we're supposed to be money-grubbing.' So were Scots, was my way of thinking, but nobody did that sort of thing to them. I asked him how long this had been going on, and he said it had started recently and was the latest idea for how to bug him. . . . If this had happened to a black friend at that time, I would have unhesitatingly put it down to virulent racism. But I had a hard time believing that genuine anti-Semitism could have anything to [do] with Saratoga in the sixties, and since I couldn't recall being exposed to any anti-Semitic ideas when growing up, I assumed other people hadn't either. So I thought of it as phony anti-Semitism, put on to torment Steven. But in retrospect it doesn't really seem like that."

Smith also was with Spielberg when people coughed the word "Jew" at him. As Spielberg passed people in the corridors on the way to class, some would pretend to sneeze "Ahhh . . . *Jew,"* or say things like, "Oh, I think I see . . . [coughing] *'Jew.' "*

What "made an eerie impression on me at the time" Spielberg was undergoing this harassment, recalls Smith, "was the kind of blazing anger and intensity in this boy. It was not just upsetting, but downright creepy, the way he radiated this genuine but seemingly inexplicable rage and disgust. It's creepier thinking back now than it was at the time, in fact, because back then I figured it was something personal, but now I think it was genuine anti-Semitism."

T H E situation became so awful for Spielberg that it colored his view of almost everyone and everything in Saratoga, eating away at his self-esteem. "It wasn't like most people hated Steve," Mike Augustine contends, "but Steve always *felt* as though they did. He came across as attractive—he had a real nice personality, joking and light. When his personality came out, girls liked him, they wouldn't say 'Ugh,' but he didn't understand that they liked him. He was fidgety and self-conscious and nervous about the way he looked. Steve *was* awkward, but he thought he was more awkward than he was."

Smith was disappointed that Spielberg "wouldn't take my advice to stand up to people and push back a little. I had discovered that this actually seemed to reduce your problems, and by my senior year at Saratoga I was happy to note that I seemed to have gotten a real handle on the situation. But he always seemed intent on catching the flies with honey, rather than dosing them with vinegar." Smith also felt that Spielberg may have thought it more prudent to use the hulking Don Shull as his "bodyguard" than to be personally combative.

Spielberg later admitted that he kept most of his anger inside him at Saratoga, "and it's one of the things I'm most ashamed of—I didn't fight back."

O N E of the coping strategies Spielberg developed at Saratoga was humor.

The witty comeback has been used by victims of persecution since time immemorial as a weapon of self-defense. Nowhere has this been seen more clearly than in the rich tradition of Jewish humor, which developed largely in response to prejudice and discrimination, as a means of empowering the powerless. "When the oppressed cannot revolt, he laughs," writes Albert Memmi in *The Liberation of the Jew*. And as Leo Rosten observes in *The Joys of Yiddish*, "Humor also serves the afflicted as compensation for suffering, a token victory of brain over fear. A Jewish aphorism goes: 'When you're hungry, sing; when you're hurt, laugh.' The barbed joke about the strong, the rich, the heartless powers-that-be is the final citadel in which human pride can live." That tradition has greatly influenced American comedy, becoming perhaps its dominant mode in the twentieth century, and it has left a strong (if largely unrecognized) imprint on the personality and art of Steven Spielberg.

Spielberg displayed a "very sharp" tongue during his time in Saratoga, and his "quick wit and quick mouth action" may have exacerbated the abuse he was suffering, Don Shull believes. The superior intelligence and wit of the person being bullied may itself be one of the causes for persecution, inspiring envy and hostility. The dilemma for the person being bullied is whether to suffer in silence and hope the bullying ceases from lack of response, or to stand up and fight back, hoping the bully will be stayed by his own essential cowardice. Spielberg chose to preserve his pride and self-respect by taking the middle ground between silence and physical response, by following the path of verbal resistance.

Mike Augustine, who became close to Spielberg when they both worked on the school paper, recalls, "His sarcastic humor was what I liked about him—'sick' humor—it had that cutting edge, like Lenny Bruce. He liked to surprise people. He was a jokester, mocking guys who were putting him down. It was almost like he *had* to. When they made remarks at him in a violent way, it would be his natural reaction to nervously come back with some kind of statement. Everybody would laugh, and he would disappear."

Although Augustine felt that Spielberg was "depressed" to be in Saratoga rather than in Hollywood, and troubled over his parents' impending divorce, he did not have the impression that Spielberg was terribly unhappy that year: "If he was, he had a shield of humor around him. He didn't appear to be weighed down with remorse. He was a riot."

Spielberg and Augustine became friendly in Bert Pfister's journalism class, which met daily and put out the school paper, *The Falcon.* Augustine, a former football player at the school, was sports editor, and Spielberg, somewhat out of character, soon became his unofficial assistant. They covered varsity football games together, and Spielberg also wrote his own coverage of basketball, baseball, junior varsity teams, and even some sports that previously had not received much coverage in the paper, such as swimming and cross-country.

Although the class prophecy at the end of the school year predicted that Spielberg would join the staff of *The New York Times,* his interest in journalism evidently was more social than professional. By the time Spielberg arrived that September, Augustine points out, "The cliques had been formed. Nothing except journalism class opened up to him. It wasn't that we were into sports, it was that we were into reporting. Steve was able to fill a time and space in his life, and it was a way of being at these events even though he was not good at sports. He was able to feel good about himself being a reporter. He got more into journalism than he did other classes because it brought him more into play with people."

Spielberg's only other extracurricular activity at the school was crew work on the senior play, *Twelve Angry Jurors,* a coeducational version of *Twelve Angry Men,* Sherman L. Sergel's stage adaptation of the television play by Reginald Rose. After trying out unsuccessfully for the cast of the March 1965 production, which was staged in the school cafeteria by English teacher Alden Peterson, Spielberg became involved with the lighting and helped cast members Dan Huboi and Augustine practice their lines.

Spielberg still was "a little weak in the girl department," as Shull puts it, but he came enough out of his shell in Saratoga to go to school dances and to start dating.* One of the girls he dated was Shull's sister Kathy, who was a freshman at the time and later was crowned Miss Saratoga. Recalling Steven as "the class cut-up," she says, "It wasn't any big romance. We necked in the car a couple times. That's why I remember it was winter—we steamed up the windows. I was fourteen and it was experimental dating for me. Mostly we would just talk. He loved telling us stories. He was fun, he was a really loyal good friend, but we weren't really suited to each other. He was short, and I'm five-foot-eleven, so the two of us going out was like Mutt and Jeff. I think he never thought of himself as studly. On a scale of one to ten, he was probably a four."

Most girls at Saratoga High probably agreed with the editor of *The Falcon,* Bonnie Parker, who considered Steven "really nerdy. The gals in the typing department would say he would come in all disheveled and they would give him a comb and tell him to comb his hair. In my crowd [she was also the senior football princess], he wasn't considered someone that anyone even considered going out with. In those days, you were going out with the cutest, most popular guys. The football guys were more attractive. Sometimes you just miss some of the best people that way."

Sportswriting for *The Falcon* was not only Spielberg's way of finding some kind of niche at the school, it also seemed to be a clever form of protective coloration for a boy being harassed by jocks. "They're going to love him," Gene Smith thought. "They're not going to want to annoy him if he writes about them in the school paper." But Smith was troubled and hurt by Spielberg's pragmatic decision to chronicle the exploits of the jock crowd: "It was some of these jock types who were harassing him for being Jewish. I thought, 'Why are you sucking up to them?' In some sense, I felt he was a traitor to our class; he betrayed our intellectual clique. But then I had the impression he wanted not to be isolated and cut off. That's a healthy attitude. I thought the jock clique accepted him after a while. He was having a hard time with these guys and suddenly he was hanging out with them."

Spielberg developed his own idiosyncratic method of covering varsity football for the paper. "I have to film that," he told Augustine, who recalls, "I would be making notes on what they were doing and he would keep track of it on film, running up and down the sidelines with the camera. He

---

* At a Cannes Film Festival press conference for the premiere of *E.T.* in 1982, Spielberg revealed that he had lost his virginity at age seventeen (the girl was not identified). *Variety* reported that Spielberg's sexual initiation took place "at a Holiday Inn motel with a creature that was anything but extraterrestrial."

would show the films to the players and the coach, and we would sit down later and put together the story. He was jazzed about that."*

The Spielberg prose style in *The Falcon*'s sports pages was a blend of energetically marshaled sports clichés, rah-rah school boosterism, and some unsparingly critical judgments about underperforming athletes. A Spielberg article that October about the football junior varsity team began: "As precious seconds ticked away, fingernail fragments flew high into the static-filled air, nerves were on the brink of disaster, hope was everywhere but spirit and determination were not." Spielberg charged that the team's "unnecessary defeat" proved the "flame of determination just wasn't there." And while reporting the following March on a game in which the varsity baseball team blew a ninth-inning lead, Spielberg acidly observed that a "cloud of disgust" hung over the Saratoga players.

The experience of being a reporter, however briefly, helped prepare Spielberg for his dealings with the press in later years. He learned some basic lessons about how reporters put together a story, and, perhaps most importantly, he learned what made a good quote. He also may have learned some lessons about the potential dangers of negative press coverage. Eventually, Spielberg's attempt to ingratiate himself with the jock crowd at Saratoga High painfully backfired, colliding with his sense of journalistic ethics and also, perhaps, with an underlying resentment of athletes. One day he told Gene Smith, "They beat me up because they didn't like something I wrote in the paper."

W H I L E Spielberg was trapped in the "time warp" of Saratoga, the outside world was on the cusp of a momentous transformation. He has recalled being "apathetic" throughout the social upheavals of the late 1960s: "I grew up in the sixties, but I was never into flower power, or Vietnam protests, like all my friends. I was always at the movies." And he said in a 1978 interview with *Rolling Stone,* "I was never part of the drug culture. I never took LSD, mescaline, coke, or anything like that. In my entire life I've probably smoked three joints. But I went through the entire drug period. Several of my friends were heavily into it. I would sit in a room and watch TV while people climbed the walls. I've always been afraid of taking drugs. I've always been afraid of losing control of myself. . . . One of the reasons I never got into drugs is that I felt it would overpower me."

Spielberg's tastes in cinema during the 1960s were more attuned to the classicism of David Lean and Alfred Hitchcock than to the iconoclasm of

---

* While in seventh grade at Ingleside Elementary School in Phoenix, Spielberg had filmed the school's flag football games, touch-football contests in which the players would grab a flag from a rival's uniform instead of tackling him. Steven was "just filming the action," recalls classmate Terry Mechling, but "the coach gave us the films to see how we were doing."

Jean-Luc Godard and Dennis Hopper, and his essentially "unconfrontational" nature kept him from being a social activist in his younger days. Even so, he was more socially aware than his own statements would indicate.

Spielberg and Mike Augustine shared a strong emotional commitment to the civil rights movement, even to the point that, as Augustine recalls, "We wanted to be black. We wanted to be associated with something people didn't like. I felt the old generation had to go, and Steve felt the same." Augustine, who recognized that Steven's Judaism and his minority status in the school made him especially sensitive to discrimination, was one of the few people who was not surprised in 1985 when Spielberg made a film about African Americans, *The Color Purple*. For as their cultural hero, Lenny Bruce, had declared, "Negroes are all Jews." Spielberg and Augustine played Lenny Bruce records—especially his *Togetherness* album—and emulated his hip, iconoclastic attitudes. The new movie that made the greatest impression on them was Stanley Kubrick's groundbreaking 1964 black comedy about the madness of war and nuclear annihilation, *Dr. Strangelove*.

"The thing that attracted me to him, that interested me as a friend," Augustine says of Spielberg, "was that I always had empathy or love for somebody who seemed to have something bothering him. It seemed he needed someone to befriend him and stand up for him. I remember people saying things to him, and I said, 'What are you, a victim?' I got him out of it with humor."

Spielberg has recalled that during his time in Saratoga, "I didn't understand why I was so different from everybody else, and why I was being singled out. And I began to question my Judaism." Augustine remembers "a conversation with Steve about why the Jews were persecuted. He used to ask, 'Why are we persecuted? No one will tell me. I asked my parents, I asked everybody. We must have done something really bad.' Not why am *I* persecuted, but why are *we* persecuted. Steve was very aware of Jewish history, all the way back. He told me the story of Masada, how the Jews at Masada killed themselves by jumping off a cliff [in 73 A.D., to escape Roman persecution]. He said, 'It's true, the Jews did it, and I'm one of them.' I said, 'Come on, Steve, lighten up.' We all were saying, 'Well, far out, Steve. What's been happening *lately?*' He was grappling with [his Jewish identity] by going back thousands of years.

"I asked him what it was like to be Jewish, because I had never known anyone who was Jewish. He invited me to his house at Hanukkah. He was bringing me over to take part in the celebration. After dinner, his mother and father were fighting. I was in the middle. He pointed to them and said, '*That's* what it's like to be Jewish—you have an extra glass of wine a day so you can yell louder at one another.' We left and went outside. I left due to embarrassment on the part of Steve."

Augustine felt Spielberg was deeply troubled by the fact that his parents, in the last stage of their marriage, could be so angry at each other and yet still devoted to each other. Spielberg, according to Augustine, considered his parents' religious beliefs "hypocritical" in that light and as a result wondered if Judaism "was a false religion—[that] maybe it was expressed in talk, in rituals, but not in daily life. That maybe was why he didn't embrace it as a religion. Steve was like me, he was curious about what other religions were. He and I went to Catholic Mass with another guy at school."

Under the influence of Lenny Bruce, Dick Gregory, Stan Freberg, and the ecumenically irreverent *Mad* magazine, Augustine and Spielberg came to believe that mockery was the best antidote to prejudice. Augustine is of Austrian and German descent, and he says that when he and Spielberg joked around together, "Sometimes he would be the Jew and I would be the Nazi. Sometimes *he* would be the Nazi and *I* would be the Jew. He was very good at being 'Herr Steven Spielberg.' He talked with a German accent, as an actor would: 'You swine!' We would do that kind of thing humorously." Don Shull says Spielberg was "fascinated" by the subject of Nazism and had what appeared to be an authentic Nazi helmet amid the clutter in his bedroom.

Spielberg's indulgence in "sick" humor about Nazis in high school appears to have been a vent for his anguish and outrage over his feelings of victimization as a Jew. Flouting a taboo and treating the subject of the Holocaust as black comedy may have relieved some of the pain he was feeling. "A joke," observed Nietzsche, "is an epitaph on an emotion." In flip-flopping between the roles of Jew and Nazi, Spielberg may have been distancing himself psychologically from his predicament at a terrible time of confusion, bitterness, and self-hatred. The boy who admittedly was "so ashamed of being a Jew" and "wanted to be a gentile with the same intensity that I wanted to be a filmmaker" may have felt compelled to put himself into the mind of the enemy.

AFTER he left Phoenix, Spielberg recalled, "[M]y life changed and I went without film for about two years [*sic*] while I was trying to get out of high school, get some decent grades, and find a college. I got serious about studying." Although the stress of his senior year in a new city and school made it impossible for him to undertake anything as ambitious as *Firelight*,* Spielberg was not entirely inactive as a filmmaker during that year in Saratoga. He kept in practice by filming high school football games and by making two other movies, inexpensively but imaginatively.

The murder of President Kennedy, which occurred while Spielberg was a high school junior in Phoenix, was the watershed event for the baby boomer generation, marking the end of its political innocence and the beginning of its distrust of the U.S. government. Spielberg and Augustine, fervent admirers of the late President Kennedy, wanted to find some way of expressing their

---

* "When I make movies," Spielberg told Saratoga neighbor Susie Didinger, "my movies are going to be worth three dollars." He was referring to the admission price in those days for such road-show spectaculars as *Lawrence of Arabia* and *My Fair Lady*.

pain and anger over his death. "I had a wooden Kennedy rocking chair," recalls Augustine. "It was made for the 1964 election and it was put out right after JFK was killed. You wound it up and it would play 'Happy Days Are Here Again.' I showed it to Steve and he thought it was ironic that the thing would have come out after JFK died. He thought people should see that irony."*

With Augustine's help, Spielberg made a three-minute film of the musical rocking chair, turning what could have seemed like a sick joke into an elegy to President Kennedy. "He shot into the sun setting in the wheat outside his house," reports Augustine. "I had a piece of cardboard box or masonite I was waving up and down, blowing on the wheat to create a ripple effect. The rocking chair wound down slowly with this incredible, horrible, tear-wrenching sound and stopped on an off-note."

Spielberg also made a jocular documentary about Senior Sneak Day, the annual outing by Saratoga High's graduating class to the beachfront amusements at nearby Santa Cruz. An elaborately edited series of Mack Sennett-like gags showing the students frolicking in the sand on a chilly day in May, forming pyramids and having a pie-eating contest, it was rounded out with a few scenes shot around the school.

Without explaining why, Spielberg also filmed shots at the beach of several classmates looking up at the sky while flinching and covering their eyes. When he edited the film, the director mischievously spoofed Alfred Hitchcock's *The Birds* by intercutting "dive-bombing" sea gulls with the reaction shots of his classmates cowering in the sand. Among the victims of the gag was one of the bullies who had been tormenting Spielberg. When the movie was shown several times at the all-night graduation party on June 18–19, 1965, at the Bold Knight restaurant in Sunnyvale, Spielberg expected the bully to react angrily to the gag. But after seeing the film, his tormentor "came over a changed person," Spielberg recalled. "He said the movie had made him laugh and that he wished he'd gotten to know me better."

W I T H Vietnam suddenly and unexpectedly looming on the horizon after the U. S. Marines landed in Da Nang on March 8, 1965, the problem of the draft hung like a black cloud over the boys in Spielberg's class. High school seniors graduating that year were forced to confront the question of what to do about the draft, along with the more traditional problem of deciding whether and where to attend college.

The draft law required a young man to register for the draft when he turned eighteen. Spielberg was in the middle of his senior year at Saratoga High School when he turned eighteen in December 1964 and had to register for the draft. With his love of a good story, he has implausibly claimed that

---

* Today Augustine likes to think of himself as another Indiana Jones, traveling the world buying and selling antiques and other rare objects.

his first close encounter with the Selective Service System came several months before that when he was standing in line to see *Dr. Strangelove* the first weekend that film played in San Jose: "[M]y sister pulled up with my father and ran out with the Selective Service envelope, which converted me to 1-A for the first time, eligible for the draft. I was so consumed with [the] possibility of going to Vietnam that I had to see [*Dr. Strangelove*] a second time to really appreciate it, and that's when I realized what a piece of classic, bizarre theater it was."*

Although Spielberg appears to have been relatively uninterested in politics during his senior year in high school, other than in issues involving racial and ethnic discrimination, he clearly had no desire to join the Army. He did not accompany Augustine and other friends to an antiwar protest against Lyndon Johnson in San Francisco during the spring of 1965, but according to Augustine, Spielberg already had antiwar feelings by that time, putting him ahead of many others in his generation in questioning the American involvement in Vietnam. Discussing his decision to attend California State College at Long Beach rather than spending all his time hanging out at Universal, he once said, "I was actually just staying there so I wouldn't have to serve in Vietnam. If the draft had not been after me, I probably wouldn't have gone to college at all."

His first choices were the prestigious film schools at the University of Southern California and the University of California, Los Angeles, but, ironic as it may seem in retrospect, he was rejected at both film schools because of his mediocre academic record. (It didn't help that he failed to take one of his college entrance exams, the ACT, because his friend Dan Huboi's old DeSoto convertible broke down the morning they were to take the test at San Jose State University.) "When Steve's grades didn't muster up, he got bummed out because he didn't go to one of those master classes [at USC or UCLA]," Shull recalls. Even the intervention of Chuck Silvers with both universities was unavailing.

Silvers, who like others in the industry sometimes lectured at USC, recalls, "I called Herb Farmer over at USC. Herb was coordinator of the cinema department for many years, and he was a friend. I explained the situation. I had this kid who was so unbelievable, and I asked if there was some way he could pull a little rank somewhere and get him into the USC cinema department. It didn't work. Everything was filled. It was filled for years to come."

By the spring of 1965, Spielberg "was already working on Plan B," says Shull. That meant using college as a place to hang his hat while he concentrated on breaking into the film industry through his own independent means. "When everybody was running around saying what school they were

* The trouble with the story is that the first weekend *Dr. Strangelove* played in San Jose was March 20–22, 1964. Not only was Spielberg still seventeen at the time, but that was also the last weekend he spent in Phoenix; *Firelight* premiered the following Tuesday, the day before he and his family left for California.

going to," Gene Smith recalls, "Spielberg said, 'I'm going to Long Beach State.' I was taken aback. I thought he was way too smart to go to a state college. He said his grades weren't good enough for USC, and Long Beach State had a great film arts department." In fact, Long Beach State did not even have a film department at the time, although it did have film courses in its Department of Radio and Television. But Long Beach had one crucial attraction for Spielberg: it was in southern California, less than an hour's drive from Universal. Spielberg could maintain a half-hearted presence in school, to avoid the draft and placate his father, while making contacts at the studio and continuing to make his own movies.

Apparently Spielberg wanted additional protection from being drafted, in case he dropped out of college or otherwise lost his student deferment. After interviewing Spielberg for a 1978 *Rolling Stone* profile, Chris Hodenfield wrote: "The psychiatrists kept him out of Vietnam."

"I saw a shrink—primarily to get out of the Army—when I was eighteen," Spielberg told Hodenfield. "I really didn't have a problem that I could articulate, I didn't have a central dilemma that I was trying to get the psychiatrist to help me with. So I would just talk. And I felt at times that the psychiatrist disapproved of the long lapses in conversation, because he would sit there smoking his pipe and I'd sit there with nothing to say. So I remember feeling, even though I was paying the fifty dollars an hour, that I should entertain him. So I would go in, once a week, and for those fifty-five minutes make up stories. And sometimes the stream of consciousness, on the chair in his office, gave me great movie ideas. I would test all these scenarios on him. . . . And I got a feeling that, in all my movies, there's something that came out of those extemporaneous bullshit sessions."

Seeking a draft deferment may not have been his only reason for seeing a psychiatrist. He was under extraordinary psychological stress during the year in Saratoga when he turned eighteen, and one of the things he learned about himself from those sessions was "that I could never lose control. I felt I would never regain it."

E V E N though the topic of Spielberg's family problems was "kind of a hush-hush deal," Shull could tell throughout their senior year that it was "traumatizing the guy. The divorce was looming on the horizon. You could see that coming way off. It was very strained for Arnold and Leah."

The tension continued to manifest itself in Steven's treatment of his sisters. Kathy Shull, who palled around with Anne Spielberg, says Steven gave his sisters "a horrendous time. He was after them incessantly, always terrorizing them. He would want to be in on the girl talk, but he wasn't invited. Anne would tell him where to get off."

Another sign of Steven's inner turmoil was his attitude toward his mother's jeep. "Steve had a serious aversion toward that jeep," Don Shull says. "It got so she'd offer us a ride [on the way to school] and we'd shine her on because of that jeep. It was a symbol of what was to come. I think Steve laid this divorce thing and the breakup of the family on Mom."

Arnold Spielberg moved out of the house on Sarahills Drive and relocated to Los Angeles around the time of Steven's graduation from high school without honors on June 18, 1965. "As soon as the kids were out of school, the whole thing went to hell in a bucket," Shull remembers. "Steve couldn't wait to go down to Universal Studios and get in his groove." Although more firmly set in his career aspirations than the average boy of eighteen, Steven felt an acute sense of anxiety over his future, heightened by the finality of his parents' divorce: "[M]y mom and dad split, and there was no longer a routine to follow. My life changed radically. I left home and went to L.A."

Steven grew closer to his father during the period of the divorce and its aftermath, Shull thought. Arnold, in his view, was "a solid good guy, always there for Steve." That summer, Steven chose to move into his father's apartment in the Brentwood area of Los Angeles. He lived there throughout his first year of college, commuting to Long Beach and Universal City in a gunmetal blue 1962 Pontiac convertible his father had given him for graduation. "It was a beaut," Shull recalls, "but it was a rattletrap, shaking and shimmying at traffic lights, with one of the funkiest engines." While visiting Steven and his father, Shull saw that "things were going pretty well between them, especially that first year in L.A. They were a kind of support group for each other. The family was going separate ways. Steve was clinging to his dad, and his dad was clinging to Steve."

Leah filed for divorce on April 11, 1966, while still living in Saratoga. In a settlement agreement signed ten days earlier, she and Arnold stipulated that he would have custody of Steven, while sixteen-year-old Anne, twelve-year-old Sue, and nine-year-old Nancy would be in Leah's custody. Arnold agreed to support Steven until he reached his twenty-first birthday in December 1967 and to provide $650 per month for the support of Leah and their daughters. The property settlement called for an equal division of proceeds from the sale of the house on Sarahills Drive and of the family's other financial assets, which included three shares of stock in IBM, twenty in GE, and a piece of unimproved land in Cave Creek, Arizona. While most of the household furniture went to Leah, Arnold was allowed to keep such sentimental items as his mother's samovar, his father's silver wine cup, and his World War II mementos, as well as his set of Shakespeare's plays, classical records and balalaika, prayer books and technical books, electronic equipment, and the family "movie equipment, except Ann[e]'s Brownie Movie Camera." All of his son's possessions went with Arnold to Los Angeles, including "Steven's camera 'dolly.' "

The divorce was granted in Santa Clara County Superior Court on April 20, 1966, on the grounds of extreme cruelty. Leah and the girls returned to Phoenix, and after her divorce became final in 1967, Leah married their longtime family friend Bernie Adler.

• • •

L OOKING back on his year of "Hell on Earth" in Saratoga, Steven Spielberg reflected in 1994 that the experience "enlarged me as a person, made me more tolerant toward my fellow man, and perhaps ironically prepared me at the end of that year to leave my family for the first time to go into an uncertain world alone. . . ."

" A H E L L O F A B I G B R E A K "

MY FIRST LOVE, MY MAIN OBJECTIVE IN LIFE, IS MAKING MOVIES. THAT'S MY WHOLE LIFE. EVERYTHING ELSE IS SECONDARY. RIGHT NOW I NEED BOTH FILM EXPERIENCE AND EDUCA-TION. AND I'M GETTING BOTH.

— STEVEN SPIELBERG, 1967

L T H O U G H he often has been described as part of "The Film School Generation," Spielberg never attended film school. Unlike such contemporaries as George Lucas, Francis Ford Coppola, Martin Scorsese, and Brian De Palma, who learned their craft at prestigious film schools in the 1960s, Spielberg remained essentially an autodidact. He took the few rudimentary film and television courses then available at California State College at Long Beach, but as he had done from his boyhood beginnings as a maker of 8mm films, Spielberg followed his own eccentric path to a professional directing career.

Universal Studios, in effect, was Spielberg's film school. But it was a training ground much different from the film schools of USC, UCLA, and New York University, giving him an education that, paradoxically, was both more per-sonal and more conventional than he would have received in an academic environment. Spielberg devised what amounted to his own private tutorial program at Universal, immersing himself in the aspects of filmmaking he found most crucial to his development, both as an observer and, later, as a TV director. Universal had as many as twenty-two series in production during that period, a phenomenal amount of activity, enough to give even a youngster a chance to direct—if that youngster was as promising as Steven Spielberg.

Unusual though Spielberg's apprenticeship was in the Hollywood of the 1960s, it resembled the kind of training he might have received if he had worked his way up through the studio system in the 1930s. Universal was the one studio in the late sixties that still functioned like a studio factory from the "Golden Age" of Hollywood. Both in its production methods and in its choice of material, Universal tended to be a conservative place, institutionally resistant to the cultural and political upheavals that were tearing the country apart. Spielberg's solid grounding in the classical studio system set him apart from most of his contemporaries. While other young filmmakers were trying to change the system, Spielberg was learning to work within it. Spielberg's early years at Universal did much to shape his distinctive personality as a filmmaker, not only by honing his organizational skills and technical exper- tise, but also by strengthening his instinctive affinity for popular filmmaking.

▲ 1968 *Time* magazine article on "The Student Movie Makers" observed that students all over the country were "turning to films as a form of artistic expression. . . . The reason for this celluloid explosion is the widespread conviction among young people that film is the most vital modern art form. Jean Cocteau believed that movies could never become a true art until the materials to make them were as inexpensive as pencil and paper. The era he predicted is rapidly arriving." Spielberg began making films earlier than any of the other famous directors who would emerge from his generation. But he was so far out of the trendy film school loop that he was not mentioned in the otherwise remarkably prescient article, which highlighted the student work of Coppola, Scorsese, Lucas, and John Milius.

At the time "The Film School Generation" came to Hollywood, genera- tions of nepotism had made the studios terminally inbred and unwelcoming to newcomers. The average age of the Hollywood labor force was fifty-five. There was no organized apprenticeship program to train their replacements in an industry that appeared moribund. The studio system, long under siege from television, falling box-office receipts, and skyrocketing costs, was in a state of impending collapse. The movies Hollywood made in the late sixties tended to be bloated, soulless, and increasingly out of step with the cultural and political views of youthful moviegoers. The future seemed daunting for the determined young movie fanatics who came of age in the sixties and for whom film historians Michael Pye and Lynda Myles coined the phrase "The Movie Brats." Spielberg vividly remembers how he and such other "self- starters" as Lucas and Scorsese "had to chisel and dynamite their way into a profession that really never looked to young people, except as actors or possibly as writers. . . . There were no willing producers at the time I was trying to break into the business. My first thrusts were met with a great deal of animosity."

George Lucas, who attended USC, says that "the credo of film school that we had drilled into us every day" was that "nobody would ever get a job in the industry. You'll graduate from film school and become a ticket-taker at Disneyland, or get a job with some industrial outfit in Kansas. But nobody had ever gotten a job in Hollywood making theatrical films."

The "USC Mafia"—who also included such other future Spielberg collaborators as John Milius, Robert Zemeckis, Robert Gale, Hal Barwood, Matthew Robbins, Gloria Katz, and Willard Huyck—were unwilling to settle for such limited dreams. They ate, breathed, and slept movies with a passion earlier generations had brought to writing or painting. The funkier UCLA Film School—whose most prominent students from that period included Coppola, writer-directors Paul Schrader and Colin Higgins, and director Carroll Ballard—encouraged its students to take a more personal approach to filmmaking. USC's Milius defined the difference between the films made at the two schools: "Ours were trying to be professional and imitative of Hollywood. Theirs always had beautiful naked girls running through graveyards. . . . They were, I guess you could say, more left-wing, a little more far-out. They used more powerful chemicals and they smoked stronger things."

Ironically, it took a UCLA student, Coppola, to start breaking down the doors of Hollywood for other film school graduates in the late sixties. He became, as Spielberg put it, "all of our godfathers." Like many UCLA film students, Coppola was as strongly influenced by literature and theater as he was by movies. But he was pragmatic enough to start his professional filmmaking career by making nudie movies and working for *schlockmeister* Roger Corman, the only producer in Hollywood at the time who regularly gave jobs to young filmmakers. Coppola quit school when he was offered a screenwriting contract by Warner–Seven Arts. His Hollywood directing debut, *You're a Big Boy Now* (1967), was not only a Warner–Seven Arts production, it was also his UCLA master of fine arts thesis, a dual achievement that inspired both envy and awe among his contemporaries.

Largely due to Coppola's groundbreaking example, others fresh out of film school began to be given opportunities to tap into the growing youth market, a market little understood by the "suits" in the studio executive suites other than as a welcome source of untapped profit. With the runaway success of Dennis Hopper's 1969 counterculture movie, *Easy Rider,* "A bit of history opened up like a seam," Lucas said, "and as many of us who could crammed in. Then it drifted back closed again."

One day in 1967, Spielberg went to UCLA's Royce Hall to see a festival of student films made at UCLA and USC. The movies included Lucas's futuristic short *THX 1138:4EB (Electronic Labyrinth),* which Lucas later expanded into a Warner Bros. feature, *THX 1138.*

When he saw the short, Spielberg "was jealous to the very marrow of my bones. I was eighteen [actually twenty] years old and had directed fifteen short films by that time, and this little movie was better than all of my little movies combined. No longer were John Ford, Walt Disney, Frank Capra,

Federico Fellini, David Lean, Alfred Hitchcock, or Michael Curtiz my role models. Rather, it was someone nearer my own age, someone I could actually get to know, compete with, draw inspiration from. . . .

"I met George that day, and I realized that there *was* an entire generation coming out of NYU, USC, and UCLA, and I was kind of an orphan abandoned in Long Beach at a college that didn't really have a film program. So I even redoubled my efforts [at] that moment to attend those two [California] universities. And every time I went in with my application for transfer, they kept saying, 'No, your grades aren't high enough.' I remember one teacher at USC said, 'You're probably going to Vietnam anyway.' "*

G O I N G to Long Beach State served its two primary purposes for Spielberg, helping keep him out of Vietnam and keeping his parents relatively pacified. But he later boasted to the school paper, "In college I didn't learn a bloody thing!"

"I didn't think any of us could teach him anything," admits Hugh Morehead, chairman of the Department of Radio and Television when Spielberg was a student. "Steve knew more about cameras than anybody in the department. He could *teach* the department."

The word "Film" was not added to the department's title until after Spielberg left. With film studies in their infancy at most American colleges, Long Beach State, even with its proximity to Hollywood, felt no urgent compulsion to invest the money and manpower to begin competing with USC or UCLA. While Spielberg was there, from September 1965 through January 1969, the department existed mainly to train students for journeyman careers at local TV or radio stations. It offered courses in film appreciation and film production, but there was hardly any budget for filmmaking equipment; the production course used 8mm cameras instructors rented or brought from home. To practice editing, students would buy silent 8mm prints of old Laurel and Hardy movies and recut them. Spielberg was far beyond needing basic training in loading a home-movie camera and putting together a story on film. Acutely frustrated over his rejection by the gilt-edged USC, Spielberg felt being at Long Beach State was a "deterrent" rather than a help in furthering his Hollywood aspirations.

"He was always kind of disenchanted with things," Morehead recalls. "We didn't have the film courses the guy wanted and thought he should be taking. He would drop by my office to talk, and he would say he wished we would get those courses and the equipment he wanted. The kid was absolutely captivated by motion pictures. I never saw him without cameras hanging around his neck. He was always shooting film. College didn't seem to hold

---

* Ironically, when Lucas donated $4.7 million to his alma mater in 1981, he persuaded Spielberg to give USC $500,000. Spielberg received an honorary doctor of fine arts degree from the school in 1994, and two years later was elected to USC's board of trustees.

much interest for him, and quite rightly as it turned out. I felt he was passing through on the way to Hollywood. He should have been at USC. He was marking time [in Long Beach], but he found some people who were helpful to him. He was a very nice boy, the kind of kid you liked and admired."

A s a freshman, Steven commuted from his father's apartment in the posh West Los Angeles community of Brentwood. Their relationship, one of mutual support in the first few months after the family breakup, deteriorated during Steven's college years.

Arnold Spielberg's financial support made it possible for Steven to lead his dual life as a college student and unpaid studio apprentice, but Arnold, who was working for Max Palevsky's computer firm Scientific Data Systems, remained frustrated by Steven's indifference toward education. Steven agreed to attend Long Beach State "just to be close to Hollywood, even though Dad still wanted me to major in computer engineering." Arnold wryly recalls that Steven did do some serious studying during his college years— when it came to the subject of filmmaking: "Once he went to college he started reading up on it. He'd take theater arts, creative writing, anything but science."

Shortly before Steven started college, Arnold made a phone call to Chuck Silvers, Steven's mentor at Universal, who describes their conversation, the only substantial one he and Arnold ever had, as "spirited."

"Steven's going to come and stay in Los Angeles," Arnold told him. "He's going to go to Long Beach State. I'd appreciate it if you would do what you can to make sure he goes to school."

Silvers said he couldn't do that.

"Look, there's something you've got to understand about this motion picture business," he told Steven's father. "For Steven to realize his ambitions he's going to need a hell of a big break. Somebody's going to have to put a lot of faith and a lot of money up so the rest of us can see if Steven is who he appears to be. I'm Steven's friend. If it comes to a choice of Steven having the opportunity to direct something that he could use as a showcase, I will advise Steven to do it, school be damned. Lightning doesn't strike twice in the same place in the industry, so you'd better be ready for it. They don't care whether he's got a degree or not. What they are interested in is what he can put up on screen."

As Silvers recalls, Arnold reiterated that he "wanted him to go to school and get a degree. My reaction was, With talent like Steven Spielberg you don't set that kind of goal. What the hell good is a *degree?* That wasn't Steven. You can tell if somebody is academically inclined or not, and he wasn't. Steven didn't have a whole hell of a lot of support from his father. His father tried to do the right thing. I don't fault Mr. Spielberg. There's no question in my mind, he was a good father. He was doing what a good father would do. I don't agree with him.

"I think Steven thought I was some kind of guru, which I wasn't. I was determined not to be his father, either. Mr. Spielberg made it clear that I should, in effect, be Steven's father. I didn't want to play the part of a father. He had a father. My idea of encouragement [during his college years] was to *be* there. Basically that's the only function I really served. Somehow I always became a listening board every time he got a story idea, every time he shot some film and had dailies."

Asked why he went so far out of his way to help Steven, Silvers replied simply, "I *liked* him. I admired this lump of raw material. When Steven wasn't involved or talking about his involvement in pictures, he really didn't have a whole big personality besides that. There were two Stevens, if you will. There was the one that made the movies and the other one was immature. One of them I knew would grow up and the other one was damn near fully formed."

As it became increasingly clear to Arnold Spielberg that Steven was not concentrating on college but wholeheartedly pursuing a film career, the tension between them grew. "His dad always had the attitude, 'Get a job and get out of the apartment,' " felt Steven's friend Ralph Burris. "Steve was having problems with his dad, who just didn't want him around, basically. I don't think he was all that supportive of Steve. I'm sure he felt Steve wasn't living up to his potential. He [eventually] kicked him out and we ended up living together."

Don Shull, who visited Steven and his father occasionally during Steven's first two years of college, had more sympathy for Arnold's viewpoint: "Steve started out doing the starving-artist routine. He was cutting every corner he could cut to make a go. He wasn't making money and he had to rely on his dad. It was apparent that Steve was just using Dad as a place to hang his hat. The last few times I visited I found myself spending my time with Arnold. I ended up going out to dinner with Arnold and Steve wasn't there. Dad's footing the bill and Steve's too busy to go to dinner with him. He bought him a car, gave him a safe place to live—the mom sure wasn't around."

Leah, who was living in Arizona, shared Arnold's concern about their son's lackluster performance in college. Long Beach State Radio-TV teacher Dan Baker remembers that "Steven's mother would call all the time and she'd get very upset he wasn't paying more attention to his classes. She would call [department chairman] Hugh Morehead and ask, 'How's he doing?' Hugh would tell her, 'Not very well, frankly.' She was very upset he was not going to get a degree. He wasn't interested."

Spielberg did forge a friendship with one of the Radio-TV teachers, a Texan named Billy Joe Langston. The late Joe Langston was "a concerned person" who became "very close" to Spielberg, recalls teacher Howard Martin. Spielberg later paid Langston an affectionate tribute in his 1974 feature, *The Sugarland Express,* which takes place in Texas and revolves around the abduction of an infant known as Baby Langston. But Hugh Morehead felt Spielberg showed more interest in his English classes than in his handful of

beginner-level Radio-TV courses. His embryonic writing talents were stimulated by an English teacher, the late Ronald Foote. Morehead recalls that he
and Foote "used to talk about this unusual and wonderful kid. Steven was
an excellent student in English." "His interest was in writing," Dan Baker
agrees. "He had all these stories running through his head, and he was
always jotting down little story ideas. His TV series *Amazing Stories* is part
of the storehouse [of those ideas]. He was saying that writing was something
he wanted to do as much as anything."

Around the Radio-TV department, Baker says, Spielberg acquired the reputation of "a great talker and a great manipulator, talking his way out of
certain things that were due for school projects. He would come in and out
and he wanted it to go his own way. To me he didn't exemplify responsibility
and sticking to it. I thought he was a young fly-by-night kid who needed to
grow up."

Spielberg has expressed some lingering regrets about not paying more
attention to his college education. "I wanted to direct my first movie the day
I graduated from the university," he said in 1984. "That was the goal: first I'll
do four years of college, make my father very happy. Actually, looking back
now, I wish I hadn't had that attitude, because college could have helped
me. If I'd paid more attention to college and less to motion picture making,
I might have delayed my career by a couple of years, but I think I would
have had a much more well-rounded education."

S PIELBERG arranged his class schedule so that he could spend three
days a week at Universal, watching filmmakers at work and trying to make
useful contacts. He frequently slept overnight in an office at the studio where
he kept two suits so he could emerge onto the bustling lot each morning
looking as if he hadn't slept in an office.

"He just became part of the wallpaper," Shull relates. "Nobody would stop
him. Nobody would ask anything. He would always look presentable. The
gate guards always knew him. He said, 'It was just like I owned the place.'
There was definitely a method to that madness."

A LTHOUGH Spielberg never lived at the frat houses Theta Chi maintained in Seal Beach and later in Long Beach, his limited social life at the
college centered around the frat.* Shull thinks Steven "was always looking
for connections somewhere" and joined the clean-cut brothers of Theta Chi
as another way of advancing himself professionally. Being part of a frat at a

---

* He apparently did not make the acquaintance of the other Long Beach State students of that
era who would go on to notable careers in show business: actor-comedian Steve Martin (a philosophy major in college), sibling pop singers Karen and Richard Carpenter, and future punkish movie
director Penelope Spheeris (whom Spielberg later hired to direct *The Little Rascals*).

large, WASPish commuter college on the border of ultra-conservative Orange County no doubt was a form of protective coloration for the socially insecure Jewish kid from Arizona.

But even though joining Theta Chi was characteristic of Spielberg's youthful desire for assimilation into the American mainstream, it put him somewhat out of step with the changing culture of student life. Fraternities had fallen in disfavor with many students by the time Spielberg entered college. The social values of Greek life seemed hopelessly old-fashioned and reactionary to iconoclastic students galvanized by opposition to the Vietnam War and the incipient hippie movement. The antiquated racial and ethnic exclusionary practices of many fraternities and sororities also inspired a growing antipathy. Some fraternities at Long Beach State were known for excluding Jews, and there was one Jewish fraternity on the campus, Zeta Beta Thi. Theta Chi's Zeta Epsilon chapter, formed only a couple of years before Spielberg's arrival by what Burris calls "all the goofy guys in the dorm," had some members who were "prejudiced against anyone who wasn't white"; there were no blacks among its thirty-four members. But whether a prospective member was Jewish or not was "never really an issue," Burris says.

After Spielberg was brought to rush by Radio-TV student Charles (Butch) Hays in the fall of 1965, Burris quickly forged an enduring friendship with Spielberg, becoming sensitized in the process to Steven's complicated feelings about his ethnic identity.

"If anything, he kind of downplayed being Jewish," Burris recalls. "He never talked about it that much. But his kid sister [Anne] once gave him a small laminated bagel. He wore it around his neck until it turned green. I knew his Hebrew name was Shmuel. I used to call him that. He would go, 'Don't call me that.' One [other] thing bothered him; I didn't understand it then, although I do now. I used to have a striped dark-blue and light-blue bathrobe. He used to cringe when I wore it. He told me his grandfather had been in a concentration camp, and they wore outfits with stripes like that. [Neither of Spielberg's grandfathers was in a concentration camp, but Spielberg might have been referring to one of his other relatives who died in the Holocaust.] It never dawned on me it was such an issue, because I'm not Jewish. At one point he asked me not to wear it. I thought, 'What do I care?' "

When Spielberg met Burris at the rush party, Burris was a senior majoring in English. He had always been interested in show business, and while growing up in San Bernardino, he had his own magic act. He took the film appreciation and TV production courses at Long Beach, but was planning to attend law school. The first words Spielberg spoke to him were enough to make Burris start questioning the course of his life.

"You look like a producer," Spielberg declared.

When Burris asked what he meant, Spielberg said the seersucker jacket he was wearing reminded him of the jackets worn by the production coordinators he knew at Universal.

Burris's first impression of Spielberg was that he was "a nerdy little guy, but something about this guy was unique—the passion he had, the total involvement and interest in films. There was something so charismatic about him you couldn't avoid liking him." His fascination with Spielberg intensified when he began watching Spielberg's amateur films. After only one semester of law school, Burris dropped out to pursue a career in the film industry. "He's really the reason I came to this town," Burris acknowledges. "I don't know whether to thank him or curse him."

In 1967, he and Spielberg moved into a house in the Palms section of West Los Angeles, and they continued living together in West Hollywood and North Hollywood until Spielberg bought his first house in 1971. Aside from their common interest in film, their friendship was a classic case of opposites attracting.

"I was flaky and a dilettante," Burris recalls. "I was kind of the hippie, and he was sort of the straight guy. He was always very straitlaced and driven. Steven was never a drinker. He never used drugs. He was a different kind of guy for the era. He was the nerd who became the king. You couldn't get him laid—then you couldn't get girls off him.

"We had an apartment, but we didn't hang out that much together. The truth is we led separate lives. He was exposed to the hippie movement through me. I think it was a source of constant embarrassment to him when we were living together. I would always bring these chicks to the apartment. He would be going crazy because they would be passing around nude. It may have embarrassed him, but it certainly *intrigued* him. I remember one time when two chicks came down from Canada and they jumped him. They were horny."

D U R I N G his college years, Spielberg recalls with some exaggeration, "I did almost nothing except watch movies and make movies."

The Los Angeles area was a paradise for a film buff in the late sixties. Spielberg watched new movies at art theaters in Long Beach, Seal Beach, and West L.A., and haunted revival theaters such as the Nuart near the UCLA campus and the Vagabond near MacArthur Park. This was a period when his aesthetic horizons were broadened by intensive exposure to foreign films: "Anything that wasn't American impressed me. I went through a period of Bergman. I think I saw every picture Ingmar Bergman made. It was wonderful! You'd go to the theater and see all the Bergman films one week. You'd go to the same theater the next week and see . . . maybe, Jacques Tati. I loved him! Truffaut is probably my favorite director. I saw all the New Wave French films while at school."

But Spielberg had trouble finding people who would take *him* seriously as a filmmaker. When he tried to persuade executives at Universal to watch *Firelight* and his other 8mm movies, they told him they wouldn't be interested unless he could show them something made in 16mm or 35mm. Taking that advice to heart, Spielberg "earned enough money working in the cafeteria and other odd jobs to buy a roll of film, rent a [16mm] camera from Birns & Sawyer, and go out weekends to shoot small, experimental films. . . . I made a film about a man being chased by someone trying to kill him. But running becomes such a spiritual pleasure for him that he forgets who is after him. I did a picture about dreams—how disjointed they are. I made one about what happens to rain when it hits dirt. They were personal little films that represented who I was."

Lacking the resources of a film school, Spielberg relied on Theta Chi to provide most of his cast and crew. "He drew upon us as his slave pool," says Burris. "He had a way of hooking you into what he was doing." Burris was most impressed by *Encounter,* a 16mm, black-and-white film Spielberg made in his freshman year with the help of frat brother Butch Hays. "When I saw it, that's when I really got interested in Spielberg. I could see he had a lot of talent." A *film noir* with existential overtones, *Encounter*—about twenty minutes long—evidently was the film Spielberg had in mind when he talked about running for one's life becoming a "spiritual pleasure." Frat brother Roger Ernest* played a sailor in the merchant marine who is set upon by a mysterious attacker. A knife-and-gun duel on top of a water tower leads to a twist ending akin to an Alfred Hitchcock TV drama, involving a murderer (Theta Chi's Peter Maffia) who, it is revealed, staged the attack to do away with his identical twin.

A much less artsy project brought Spielberg's filmmaking activities to the attention of the school paper. *The Forty-niner* reported in February 1966 that "the starting gun went off last week in the campus cafeteria" on a short comedy called *The Great Race.*† Noting that "Spielberg has been studying directing for one year as an apprentice at Universal Studios," student reporter Bruce Fortune wrote that the Keystone Kops-like farce was being filmed by Spielberg in collaboration with Butch Hays. Roger Ernest and Halina Junyszek, Hays's diminutive Russian girlfriend, played the lead roles. The 16mm black-and-white movie, "complete with sound and musical score," dealt with "a young man who, after an argument with his girl, chases her around the campus. Filming will go on all semester and so, during his chase, Spielberg plans to link events of the college together . . . as Halina and Roger rush through crowded hallways, campus buildings, Pete's Gulch, and the Theta Chi toilet race." Pete's Gulch was the makeshift Western town erected every year by campus social groups for the school's annual 49er Days, a frolicsome charitable fund-raising event. As part of the festivities, Theta Chi staged a race with students riding toilets mounted on soapbox-derby racing cars.

---

* As well as appearing in Spielberg's student films, Ernest had small parts as highway patrolmen in *The Sugarland Express* and *Close Encounters of the Third Kind*.

† The title was borrowed from the previous year's slapstick comedy-to-end-all-slapstick comedies, directed by Blake Edwards.

Spielberg's incorporation of such sophomoric but crowd-pleasing activities into *The Great Race* was, like his filming of Saratoga High's "Senior Sneak Day," a way of ingratiating himself with his fellow students.

N O T H I N G sums up the frustrations of Spielberg's academic experience at Long Beach State better than his record in Howard Martin's TV production course. He received a C. "My particular claim to fame is the grade he got in class, which does not reflect on his visual talents," Martin now says. "I wish it hadn't happened."

The Radio-TV Department boasted a fully equipped TV studio, complete with control booth, suitable for training students in the fundamentals of three-camera production. But Martin came to realize that Spielberg "was not particularly interested in going into a television station and working as a producer-director." Martin gave Spielberg the C because of the youngster's lack of "concentration" on the subject at hand. "In many ways, he was not a beginning student as many students were. I think he was taking television to get some additional experience in another medium. He was concerned to get out of it what he wanted."

Martin did see evidence of Spielberg's talents on one class project, *Ball of Fat,* a live dramatic adaptation of Guy de Maupassant's short story "Boule de Suif," the ironic tale of a prostitute's heroic sacrifice for some hypocritical members of society at a stagecoach station during the Franco-Prussian War (John Ford echoed the story in his 1939 Western classic *Stagecoach*). The one-hour teleplay was produced outside of class time on a voluntary basis, with Martin directing a cast recruited from the college drama department. The production class spent about a month rehearsing blocking and camerawork, then built the set and shot the program over a single weekend.

Spielberg operated one of the three cameras. The large, cumbersome cameras owned by the school did not have zoom lenses. For moving shots, the operator had to push the camera himself, carefully dollying while maintaining focus and composition. With more than a decade of experience as a filmmaker behind him, Spielberg already had acquired considerable facility in the expressive use of the camera. Martin knew little about Spielberg's background, so it came as something of a surprise when the previously inattentive student began to speak up on the studio floor: "Quite frequently he would say, 'I have a suggestion that might work a little better.' His suggestions did make it better, particularly in the third act. We would mark the changes in the script and insert them. They had to do with kinds of framing, where the focus might lie, where the camera moved in and out, or a crossover involving a particular character. He brought a good deal of aplomb to the studio."

Martin may not have appreciated Spielberg's suggestions as much at the time. Perhaps it was because of his extra effort on *Ball of Fat* that Spielberg was surprised to receive a C in the class. "He was terribly upset he couldn't get the grade changed," department chairman Morehead remembers. "He thought he deserved better. That was not my problem. I wish I had known at the time he was going to be so terribly important. I would have paid more attention."

T H E most vivid account Spielberg has given of his time as an observer at Universal is contained in a letter he wrote to Don Shull in June 1965, shortly after his graduation from high school. The letter is jocular and self-deprecating, but it reveals the extent to which Spielberg's precocious combination of charm, *chutzpah,* and unshakable determination enabled him to make the most of his opportunity to roam the studio lot.

Spielberg wrote the stream-of-consciousness letter under the influence of a mixed drink (Scotch and bourbon). He admitted he had been doing some indulging in alcohol of late, a newfound practice that often caused him to throw up. He also alluded somewhat boastfully to one-night stands with girls he picked up on the Sunset Strip, the crowded nightly mecca for the southern California hippie scene. Perhaps it was the pressure of ingratiating himself at Universal that led to these uncharacteristic bouts of hedonism. But he also was reacting to living in Hollywood like the proverbial kid let loose in a candy store. Shull remembers that Spielberg "talked a lot about Hollywood starlets. That was a major forward force in his career. He figured it would be the avenue to meet awesome girls. It worked. I didn't think it was going to work."

The transformation of Spielberg's social life after he came to Hollywood follows a pattern Pauline Kael observed in the lives of young directors of his generation: "A man who was never particularly attractive to women now finds that he's the padrone: everyone is waiting on his word, and women are his for the nod. . . . Directors are easily seduced. They mainline admiration."

But in those early days at Universal, Spielberg had some difficulty keeping up his facade as a Hollywood swinger and mogul-in-the-making. Because he was driving a rattletrap 1962 convertible, he was "kind of embarrassed to go up to the gate of Universal in it," Shull recalls. "That's why he would park it five blocks away."

Nattily attired in a blue sportcoat, black pants, scarf, and sunglasses, Spielberg hiked to the gate one fine morning in the summer of 1965, trying his best to act like he owned the place. But upon discovering that construction trucks had dribbled mud around the gate, Spielberg thought it prudent to take a more circuitous route. As he did so, a passing Lincoln sprayed him with mud from a puddle in the intersection.

Accepting some paternal advice by the gate guard to wash off the mud before going about his daily rounds, Spielberg had the misfortune on his way to the washroom to walk past a tram taking spectators on the Universal Tour. Tram riders snapped pictures of him and mockingly wondered aloud whether he was in makeup for some TV show, perhaps *Alfred Hitchcock*

Presents. Spielberg made a failed attempt to tidy himself up in the washroom before the studio wardrobe department helpfully supplied him with a new outfit.

His agenda that day included an appointment with Sam Spiegel, who failed to show up. The Oscar-winning producer of two of Spielberg's favorite movies, *The Bridge on the River Kwai* and *Lawrence of Arabia,* had not yet returned, as expected, from Europe. But it was a sign of the seriousness with which some people at Universal regarded Spielberg that he was allowed to meet instead with legendary director William Wyler and with Jud Kinberg, one of the producers of Wyler's recently released *The Collector.*

The day at Universal that had started so inauspiciously also included lunch with Charlton Heston. Earlier that year, Spielberg had spent some time watching Heston filming *The War Lord* for director Franklin Schaffner on the Universal back lot. Heston remembered Spielberg as "a determined young man who kept infiltrating the set, only to be ejected again. Frank finally surrendered to his persistence and let him watch." In his letter to Shull, Spielberg indignantly recounted what happened the first time he introduced himself to Heston. The actor snubbed him, failing to acknowledge his presence. But as soon as Heston was informed that the youngster was a promising filmmaker, he turned on the charm and accepted Spielberg's invitation to lunch. When they met at the studio commissary, Heston was flatteringly curious about Spielberg's background. The star even picked up the check. But Spielberg was contemptuous, feeling that Heston was currying favor with *him* and angling for a job in a future Spielberg movie! Spielberg displayed a remarkably well-developed degree of opportunism in eagerly hobnobbing with a veteran star for whom he felt such little regard, but who he thought might also be able to give *his* career a critical boost in the future.

His lunch with Heston was only one of many such opportunities Spielberg created for himself while roaming the studio lot. He told Shull he often walked up to stars and directors and producers on the studio streets and invited them to lunch. Cary Grant and Rock Hudson were among those who accepted; Shull was astonished when Spielberg reported that Hudson was gay. Although impressed by Spielberg's growing list of connections, Shull was hurt that his friend increasingly seemed to prefer the company of Hollywood movers and shakers. "Sonny and Cher were big on his list," Shull remembers. "He was going off to Sonny and Cher's place all the time." Spielberg also made visits with Ralph Burris to the set of the pop-singing couple's TV variety show. Shull finally lost touch with Spielberg around 1967: "When I went down there, he was so busy he just didn't have any time."

O UTSIDERS are seldom welcome when film or television companies are working, and sometimes when Spielberg would show up to kibitz at the back of a soundstage or a scoring stage, people would say things like, "Who's the kid?" or "What the hell is this little kid doing here?" "He never got in the way," the late Universal editor Tony Martinelli, who befriended him, recalled in 1994. "He never bothered anybody. He wasn't shy, but he wasn't pushy, either." Still, some people at the studio were downright hostile. "They would throw me off a set once a day," Spielberg said, "and I'd go back to my office."

He especially remembered the humiliation of being "thrown out of a dubbing room by [veteran producer-director] Mervyn LeRoy and tossed off an Alfred Hitchcock set by an assistant director." Not being able to watch Hitchcock at work on *Torn Curtain,* which was shot at the studio between November 1965 and February 1966, was a terrible disappointment for the young man who called Hitchcock "The Master": "The sad part of the story is you'd think I'd suddenly have this Orson Welles sandbox, this great playpen —and all the opportunity in the world to use it. But it was a very bad experience."

Before he became disenchanted with visiting soundstages, Spielberg established several important personal and professional relationships.

In the fall of 1965, he visited the set of "The Time of the Sharks," an episode of the Ben Gazzara TV series *Run for Your Life.* The director was Leslie H. Martinson, whom Spielberg had watched filming *PT 109* three years earlier. One of the guest stars was a clean-cut, articulate young actor named Tony Bill, who later became a producer and director.* Six years older than Spielberg, Bill had broken into films as Frank Sinatra's kid brother in *Come Blow Your Horn* (1963). In a 1967 interview about Spielberg with the Long Beach State student newspaper, Bill said that when they first met, Spielberg "told me about his films. I saw some of them and told him if he ever needed any help to let me know. I felt he had talent that warranted help—and there's not too many of these people around, you know. Steve is very aware. He has a very original eye—which I think is primary for any director and is something that can't be taught. Either you've got it or you don't . . . and Steve's got it."

When he watched Spielberg's amateur movies, Bill already "was interested in young filmmakers, and I spent a lot of time going to festivals and seeing new filmmakers; it was the heyday of experimental film. I was attracted to people who were of my generation and my personal taste. The search for youth had not occurred by then [in Hollywood]. Youth and originality were looked down upon; movies at the time were not at all addressed to my generation. A movie about young people was a movie with Frankie Avalon and Annette Funicello. Steven was one of the few people I knew who was younger than me. He was open to anything, which appealed to me. Steven wasn't self-conscious and obscure. He was direct and graphic. Compared to a lot of other people—all of whom have fallen by the wayside—he was clear and economical. That's what gave me confidence in his abilities and

---

* His producing credits include *The Sting* and *Taxi Driver.* Among the films he has directed are *My Bodyguard* and the 1994 cable-TV movie *Next Door,* starring Spielberg's wife, Kate Capshaw.

instincts. That basically was my reason for saying, 'Look, if you need help, I'll donate my services.'"

Steven had a more immediate need for help. "He was the literally starving student filmmaker, and he didn't have a social family," Bill recalls. "I was a successful actor, I had a house and a wife who could feed him. We took care of him." Bill also introduced Steven to his informal circle of young maverick filmmakers. "In those days, it seemed the odds were stacked against all of us making headway in the movie business. It was such a closed shop. We were the only ones who could talk to each other. There was a group of us who all tended to know each other and enthuse about each other. Spielberg and Francis Coppola knew each other through me. Steven had the same sense of confidence I felt from Francis at that time."

Another circle Steven joined was what he called a "longhair film society right in the heart of Universal Studios," presided over by writer-producer Jerrold Freedman. Freedman "employed a number of writers, directors, people dealing with esoterica," recalled Spielberg, who eventually worked for him as a director on *The Psychiatrist* TV series and also shared an office with him. Actor Jeff Corey remembered Freedman introducing him to Spielberg in early 1966 during the shooting of another episode of *Run for Your Life*. "Jeff," said Freedman, "I'd like you to meet Stevie Spielberg. Some day he's going to own this company."

Only recently liberated from a long stint on the Hollywood blacklist, Corey ran a prestigious acting studio in a storefront theater on Melrose Avenue in Hollywood. His students in the 1950s and 1960s included James Dean, Jack Nicholson, Richard Chamberlain, and Carol Burnett, and a number of directors and future directors, including Roger Corman, Irvin Kershner, and Robert Towne, who came to learn about directing actors. Tony Bill took Corey's acting classes and brought Spielberg along with him.

"He came for the better part of a year," Corey recalls. "He always avoided acting. He'd sit in the back—very quiet, very attentive. Sometimes he wouldn't sit, he'd *stand* in the back. I would always bug him about bringing in scenes [to perform]. He'd say, 'Yeah,' and he didn't. He was interested in directing. He wanted to watch me work with people and see how performances were altered by me throwing things at people."

What Spielberg absorbed in Corey's class was a playful, improvisatory, daringly unconventional approach to acting, a way of evoking nonclichéd, naturalistic behavior that would help him immensely when faced with the pressures of TV directing. As Patrick McGilligan observes in his biography of Nicholson, Corey taught his students "not to approach a situation head-on, emotionally, but to deal with the content of a scene obliquely." Often, Robert Towne recalled, "the situation that he would give would be totally contrary to the text, and it was the task of the actors, through the interpretation of the various bits of business they could come up with, to suggest the real situation through lines that had no bearing on the situation."

Around the same time he met Corey, Spielberg found another kind of acting teacher when he paid a visit to the set of "Wind Fever," an episode of Universal's TV anthology series *Bob Hope Presents the Chrysler Theater*, directed by Robert Ellis Miller and starring Leo G. Carroll, William Shatner, and John Cassavetes. Spielberg remembers Cassavetes as "one of the first people I met in Hollywood, one of the first people who ever talked to me and gave me the time of day."

When Cassavetes saw Spielberg on the set, "he pulled me aside and he said, 'What do you want to do?' And I said, 'I want to be a director.' He said, 'Okay, after every take, you tell me what I'm doing wrong. And you give me direction.' So here I am, eighteen [actually nineteen] years old, and there's a professional film company at Universal Studios doing this TV episode, and after every take he walks past the other actors, walks past the director, he walks right up to me and says, 'What did you think? How can I improve it? What am I doing wrong?' And I would say, 'Gah, it's too embarrassing . . . Mr. Cassavetes, don't ask me in *front* of everybody, can't we go around the corner and talk?' "

For Cassavetes, acting in Hollywood movies and TV shows was only a day job, supporting his independent filmmaking projects. He invited Spielberg to work on *Faces,* a low-budget movie he had begun directing in January 1965. Cassavetes was not speaking metaphorically when he described *Faces* as "a *home* movie": he filmed it in his own home in the Hollywood Hills and at the home of his mother-in-law. Shot in 16mm black-and-white, it had a small volunteer crew and a cast headed by Gena Rowlands, the director's wife. Released in 1968, *Faces* was an influential piece of American neorealism, a raw, no-holds-barred "view of a culture run psychologically amok," as Ray Carney describes it in *The Films of John Cassavetes*.

Although he received no credit, Spielberg recalled that Cassavetes "made me a production assistant on *Faces* for a couple of weeks, and I hung around and watched him shoot that movie. John was much more interested in the story and the actors than he was [in] the camera. He loved his cast. He treated his cast like they had been a part of his family for many years. And so I really got off on the right foot, learning about how to deal with actors as I watched Cassavetes dealing with his repertory company. . . . I've thought that one of the best ways of being a director was to, as John did, scrounge around for the cast, promise them anything but give them quality, and look with great poignance and attitude at your cast and your crew up through your eyebrows, your nose facing the ground! That's something else I learned from John."

M U C H of his time at Universal, Spielberg "would hang out with the editors. I spent a year with them at Universal. They loved having me around. I'd sit with them and they'd show me how and why they were making a cut. I even cut a few *Wagon Trains*, you know—cuts and trims which I wasn't supposed to do because I didn't have a union card. That was the raw beginning."*

One of the editors Spielberg spent the most time with at Universal was Tony Martinelli, an amiable old pro who had started in the industry in 1925. "He was just sixteen when he came into my cutting room—he was still going to school," Martinelli recalled. "We had cutting rooms in the old Universal lab building, and Chuck Silvers asked if he could send Steven up to my room. He was a personable young man, very friendly. There wasn't a conceited bone in his body. He had an 8mm film, a version of *Close Encounters of the Third Kind* [i.e., *Firelight*]. He had a projector, and we ran it on the wall. He had sound, but he couldn't get it to sync. It was quite a piece. Very, very well done. He had angles that were very interesting for an amateur— he *was* no amateur at the time. I knew he had it on the ball, from his 8mm film. He knew where he was going, and he was going in the right direction."

When Spielberg was honored by the American Cinema Editors in 1990 as a director who "respects the editors he works with and appreciates what they do," Martinelli took the occasion to reminisce with him about their first meeting: "I mentioned that I had always enjoyed the 8mm film. He said I was the only one [aside from Silvers] who would look at it. Everybody else turned him down. He mentioned that I was one of the few men who let him in the cutting room. Most of the fellas dusted him off—'I'm busy'—they frowned on it. I never closed the door on anybody. My room was always open to him. He was just a young boy, but if you asked him something he would answer. He was very hep, very sharp. He came up to the cutting room to learn from me, and I stood by and I learned from him."

While some editors may indeed have dusted Spielberg off, he was more welcome in the editing rooms than he recalled in expressing gratitude to Martinelli. Richard Belding, who succeeded Dave O'Connell as head of the TV editing department during the time Spielberg was an observer at Universal, recalls that Spielberg "hung around editorial quite a lot. He would go into the editors' rooms and look over their shoulders all the time." Spielberg "asked a million questions" of the editors, Silvers says. "It was a process of absolute technical application. He worked out his own curriculum. It was the real world. There's no school you can really go to learn to be a filmmaker. That's not what they teach."

• • •

* In his 1983 biography of Spielberg, Tony Crawley questions whether Spielberg could have worked on *Wagon Train*, which Crawley incorrectly claims had finished production before Spielberg came to the studio. Production on *Wagon Train* lasted until 1965, and the Universal TV editing department continued reediting episodes for reruns and syndication for some time after that. Chuck Silvers thinks it's "very possible" Spielberg worked on the series when editors shortened episodes so stations could play more commercials and made the shows less violent, in response to changing standards and practices.

AT the end of his first semester of law school, in early 1967, Ralph Burris picked up the phone and told Spielberg, "Let's go make this movie." "This movie" was a Spielberg project called *Slipstream,* about high-speed bicycle racers. He wanted to make *Slipstream* in the standard theatrical film gauge, 35mm, as his first professional-quality short film. "Steven was a real hustler," Burris says. "He not only knew how to make movies, he knew how to get the money to make them."

Burris dropped out of school and, in hopes of launching his own career as a producer, persuaded his parents, Ben and Thirza, to invest $3,000 in Spielberg's movie. Another Theta Chi, Andre (Andy) Oveido, who had a newspaper distribution business, agreed to kick in $1,000. Oveido was given a part in the film, along with other college friends of Spielberg's, including Roger Ernest, Peter Maffia, and Jim Baxes. Through Silvers and other people at Universal, Spielberg acquired, without cost, "short ends" of film reels, scraps of unexposed footage he used to shoot much of the movie.

Production began on weekends during the spring of 1967 in and around Long Beach. The film was credited to Playmount Productions, a company formed by Arnold and Steven Spielberg. "I did it because nobody would give him credit," Arnold says. "He was a kid. So when we'd go to CFI [Consolidated Film Industries] to rent movie equipment, I signed for it. And I paid some of the bills. Sometimes he paid me back, sometimes not, but it didn't make any difference. I just recently turned over to him all the books that we had. 'Hey, Dad,' he said, 'you really *did* help me out with my career.' " Steven's eyes proved bigger than his wallet. "We essentially underestimated what it would cost," Burris admits. "We were very naive. Steven thought we could do it for less than $4,000, in 35mm color, with a Chapman crane [a large mobile camera platform]."

Spielberg's choice of a sports subject for *Slipstream,* like his sportswriting in high school, seemed a calculated attempt to ingratiate himself with an aspect of mainstream American culture from which he otherwise felt excluded. If *Slipstream* was a relatively impersonal project, particularly for a debut film, Spielberg may have felt that a film more closely reflecting his own personality would not appeal enough to the booming youth market. The hero of *Slipstream* was no Spielbergian nerd, but a handsome jock whose obsession with bicycle racing probably was borrowed from the personality of Don Shull.

When Spielberg was living in Saratoga, Shull and four of his jock friends would race their high-speed, $1,500 European bikes all around Santa Clara County (Steven was not included). "We used to tear up those hills," Shull recalls. "We were animals. I think Steve would have been dusted on the first turn, maybe; he was kind of a small guy. Some of the crashes we had, I know he filed those in the back of his mind. He claimed he took some of my bicycle shenanigans and incorporated them in that movie. I never saw it."

A "slipstream" is defined as "the region of reduced air pressure and forward suction produced by and just behind a fast-moving ground vehicle."

Thrill-seeking bicycle riders sometimes risk their lives to speed up close behind a truck and ride in its slipstream. *Slipstream* was to feature a bravura action sequence of bicyclists racing down a steep hill. The hero, riding in the slipstream of a truck, is pursued by his rival, a dirty-trickster who wants to knock him off the road. But when the hero swerves around the truck, the other racer's momentum pulls him headlong into the back of the truck, knocking him bloody and throwing him off the road.

Roger Ernest, who helped Spielberg with the script, was cast as the dirty-trickster, a character somewhat reminiscent of the bullies who had tormented Spielberg in Phoenix and Saratoga. The good guy was played by Tony Bill, who, like everyone else involved in the production, gladly donated his services to the twenty-year-old director.

While looking for a cameraman, Spielberg met Allen Daviau, a young film buff and beginning cinematographer. Daviau, who served as a camera operator on *Slipstream,* later became one of Hollywood's most distinguished cinematographers, working with Spielberg on several of his most lyrically shot films, including *E.T., The Color Purple,* and *Empire of the Sun.* "Nobody who knew Steven back in '67 is in the least surprised by his success," Daviau once said. ". . . But nobody [then] would give him a job. He was growing old —he was all of nineteen [actually twenty]—and he was feeling that time was weighing down on him and he had to get something made."

When asked in 1995 what made him recognize Spielberg's talent, Daviau replied, "I think it is that rare quality of possessing both the artistic sensitivity and the passion for the medium, with being a hard-as-nails producer at the same time and knowing how to get what he wants done and how to deal with the harder-than-nails money people to get it. Even from the beginning, he could get people to put up money!

"For *Slipstream,* he had done this incredible sales job. They had gone out and gotten all these European-style bicycle racing groups in southern California to haul themselves and their bicycles, with no payment for gas or anything else, in the total darkness to some godforsaken spot in the desert, so that when the sun started to rise on the highway, these guys would be in full gear roaring toward us down the street. These people would do it over and over for this kid, for nothing, because he was inspiring."

Spielberg asked Daviau to be director of photography on *Slipstream,* but Daviau explained that he "had only shot 35mm one time, some titles and pickup shots for Roger Corman's [1967 LSD movie] *The Trip.* I said, 'I really don't think I've had enough experience to be the cameraman on this, but I know a wonderful French cameraman named Serge Haignere.' " Haignere, who had come to Hollywood just before the *Nouvelle Vague* started, was working as an assistant cameraman on studio pictures. "When I first saw Steve," he said during the making of *Slipstream,* "I saw a young kid—a scared young kid—and I remember thinking, Oh no, here comes another one who wants to invent movies! But I find out he is very creative, very talented. I wouldn't work with him if he wasn't. We make a very good team."

After visiting the location of *Slipstream* for the Long Beach State paper, *The Forty-Niner,* feature writer Ron Thronson presciently observed that Spielberg already was "carving his own place" alongside leading contemporary directors. With *Firelight,* Spielberg had "evidently impressed enough people in Hollywood, so that he is now given the run of a major studio lot as an observer, a privilege that is given to few men, young or old. . . . He is well regarded by his peers, a fact that stands by itself in consideration of the professional people who work with him and hold him high in their regard. . . ."

"Why do such men want to cast their lot with a young man who is working on his own, with his own production company? Why are they willing to do this work for nothing? Because they feel that Steve Spielberg has the ability to become an important and noticed director, and because they want to help him. . . . Steve looks more like a college cheerleader than an experienced film director, but he is impressive to watch, and might be on his way somewhere."

"Every film is an experience," Spielberg told Thronson. "I'll be learning when I'm sixty years old. I've learned more out on my own than I'll ever learn inside a studio."

The sheer professionalism of Spielberg's approach to filmmaking impressed the student reporter: "At one point in the proceedings, the company spent almost two hours on eight takes of a sequence that is approximately thirty seconds in length and requires one actor to approach a group of his fellows and say, 'Any of you guys want a Coke?' He pauses to follow with, 'Well, I only thought I'd ask.' Through this brief sequence, the camera is moving rapidly, dollying in, swiveling around, and zooming in on the subject. If the director is a good one, he won't let the scene end until it is right, and sometimes that takes a while."

But it was not long before the production came to an abrupt halt. The shooting of the beginning and ending sequences—the start and finish of the race—was scheduled over a weekend near the ocean. Spielberg and Burris had recruited a sizable turnout of bicycle riders and spectators. "They bet the farm on the last weekend of shooting," Daviau remembers, "and it didn't just rain, it *monsooned* that weekend."

"We basically ran out of money," Burris says. "We were dead in the water. I've got pictures of our Chapman crane sitting in the rain. It cost $750 a day, including the driver. We got some pretty good footage [before that weekend] —it was all terrific, but we didn't get enough. We got all the establishing stuff, the racing stuff, six thousand to seven thousand feet of film [a little more than an hour of film], but we never really got into the dramatic stuff."

"When that money was gone, Steven was very depressed," Daviau says. "After *Slipstream,* he tried to do a little 16mm project with dolls that Serge was shooting. I just knew he had to get *something* off the ground."

Citizen Steve, a biographical film his wife, Amy Irving, made as a surprise present for Spielberg's birthday in 1987, includes a forty-five-second montage of shots from *Slipstream,* which it half-jokingly calls "the Mozart angle" in Spielberg's life, "the unfinished symphony, the unfinished film." The laboratory that Spielberg and Burris used for *Slipstream,* Consolidated Film Industries (CFI), took a lien on the footage because the filmmakers couldn't make their payments, and in 1987 the footage still was sitting on a shelf at the lab in Hollywood. It since has been bought back by Spielberg. Unhappy as the fate of *Slipstream* was, the dynamic and lyrical scenes of bicycle racing assembled by Daviau give tantalizing glimpses of Spielberg's youthful promise.

Before the project fell apart, Spielberg gave a characteristically unpretentious and self-aware statement about his filmmaking philosophy to student reporter Jo Marie Bagala: "I don't want to make films like Antonioni or Fellini. I don't want just the elite. I want everybody to enjoy my films. For instance, if an Antonioni film played in Sioux City, Iowa, the people would flock to see [Disney's 1967 fantasy] *The Gnome-Mobile.* But I do want my films to have a purpose! I just want to make pictures in which I say something, something I am close to and can convey to the audience. If, in doing so, I create a style, then that's my style. I'm trying to be original, but at times, even originality tends to become stylized. I feel that right now the worst thing for me to do at twenty is to develop a style."

S HORTLY after Robert Kennedy was assassinated in June 1968, the networks sent out an urgent directive to their suppliers to cut back on violence in TV shows. Spielberg happened to drop in on Chuck Silvers when Silvers was frantically trying to deal with the problem.

"He came into the office and he was all charged up talking about something he was doing," Silvers recalls. "I cut him short. I told him, 'Steven, I'm in the middle of something here. I don't have any time, because this [program] is going on the air in a couple of days. I have to remove all this stuff.' I won't say I blew up or hollered at him. I did it with a kind of biting tone. I said, 'I have a big problem I have to solve *now. I don't have time to listen, Steven.* I don't want to see any more of your dailies. I don't want to hear your stories. I don't want to see your assemblies.' The look on his face was like I'd hit him or something. 'Steven, the next thing I look at from you is going to be a 35mm color composite film'—which means a finished film. 'When you have that, you call me.'

"I didn't see him for a few months. Then I got a call from him on a Sunday. He said, 'I've got something for you to look at.' I asked him, 'How long is it?' 'Twenty-six minutes.' 'OK, I'll book a room this afternoon.' I suppose I felt guilty. He wouldn't go into the projection room. He was too nervous, or he didn't want any questions thrown at him. I went into the projection room alone and I viewed *Amblin'.* I looked at what I still feel is the perfect motion picture."

• • •

EVEN though Spielberg was far from a beginner—after all, he had been making films for half of his twenty-two years—*Amblin'* became its young director's official "debut" film when it was released theatrically in December 1968. Eloquently wordless, this short film tells the bittersweet story of a girl and boy who come together but ultimately drift apart while hitchhiking from the desert to the sea in southern California.

The uncredited godmother of *Amblin'* was Julie Raymond, who put Spielberg together with aspiring producer Denis Hoffman, with whom she had worked at Pacific Title. Nine years older than Spielberg, Hoffman was running the optical and title company Cinefx. He also managed a rock group called October Country and was looking for a film project that could feature their music. Early in 1968, shortly after Spielberg's twenty-first birthday, Raymond took Hoffman to lunch with the young filmmaker.

Hoffman's first impression of Spielberg was that he was "very aggressive, charming, and dedicated. He ate, breathed, and slept film. His dream was to be a director, plain and simple. He said he'd do anything if I'd put up the money. Steve was a disarming person. He had a kind of childlike quality about him, a naïveté. You wanted to help him. It's not an accident Spielberg is where he is, it's not luck, it's all a plan he had. He's not only a genius in filmmaking, he's a genius in promoting himself. He and I had a great ambition to make films. The truth is I helped him out because *I* wanted to get someplace. I wanted to get into production. And I did it as a friend to help *him* out, because I liked him and he needed help."

The first project they discussed was *Slipstream*.

"He needed about $5,000 to finish it. He'd gone to his dad and his dad had not given him the money. The photography was gorgeous, but what I recollect of it was boring—a lot of people riding on a lot of bicycles. It went on forever and it didn't excite me. Probably because of my ego, I told him, 'I'm really not interested in completing something.'

"I told Steve I wanted to see something in writing. I wanted to see a treatment or a script. He presented me with two or three different projects, three- or four-page treatments. He first proposed a short film about a drive-in movie theater. It took place at nighttime. People left their cars to get candy, and it was about what they saw along the way. When they came back, they couldn't find their cars—the cars were all Volkswagens. It was a cute premise, but it cost too much, and my music group couldn't fit into it. I thought he would have an easier time as a first-time director if he did not have to handle dialogue. I told him, 'Let's do something that doesn't require so many sets, so many people. Let's do something without sound, with no dialogue. We're going to be on location, without a lot of equipment. It will be easier. And let's do something that could use my music.'

"The next script was tailor-made. I picked *Amblin'* because it did not have any dialogue and the premise was very timely. Steve was not a rock 'n' roll fan, but he went off and wrote it to our specifications. He did the story, but I set the guidelines. We had several meetings; it was a cooperative effort.

Amblin' was not done as a labor of love for him. *Amblin'* was done because he needed a vehicle to become a director."

Spielberg has described *Amblin'* as "an attack of crass commercialism. I had made a lot of little films in 16mm that were getting me nowhere. They were very esoteric. I wanted to shoot something that could prove to people who finance movies that I could certainly look like a professional movie-maker. *Amblin'* was a conscious effort to break into the business and become successful by proving to people I could move a camera and compose nicely and deal with lighting and performances. The only challenge that's close to my heart about *Amblin'* is I was able to tell a story about a boy and a girl with no dialogue. That was something I set out to do before I found out I couldn't afford sound even if I wanted it."

B U R R I S and Spielberg had learned a great deal about economizing from their sorry experience with *Slipstream*. Or at least they had learned how to manipulate an inexperienced would-be producer. "The original budget they made up [for *Amblin'*] was for $3,000 or $4,000," Hoffman recalled. "They were cutting a lot of corners." Realizing that figure was unrealistically low, Hoffman authorized further expenditures until his total outlay reached about $20,000, including costs for lab work at Cinefx, CFI, and Ryder Sound Service; 35mm release prints by Technicolor; and several thousand dollars' worth of advertising and publicity.

Amblin' was shot almost entirely on natural locations in southern California, but Hoffman also wangled the use of Jack Palance's beach house at Malibu for the ending sequence and supplied his own small soundstage at Cinefx for the filming of a night exterior scene. That scene of the two characters making love in a sleeping bag by the light of a campfire was done in the studio to cut down on location expenses and so cinematographer Allen Daviau could better control the lighting conditions.

Everyone involved in the film, including Spielberg, worked for nothing but screen credit; it was a showcase film for all twenty-five of them, including the five members of October Country. Spielberg found the lead actress, redheaded gamine Pamela McMyler, in the *Academy Players Directory*. A graduate of the Pasadena Playhouse, she had played a small part in *The Boston Strangler*. The male lead, Richard Levin, was working as a librarian at the Beverly Hills Public Library. He bore a striking resemblance to the director, which helped underscore the autobiographical undertones of the character.

Spielberg has claimed Hoffman "wanted the possessory credit. That means the film said: Denis Hoffman's *Amblin'*. I said, 'Fine!' I took the money and I made the film." But there is no possessory credit on *Amblin'*, which bills Hoffman as producer and Burris as "in charge of production," while listing as its final credit: "written and directed by Steven Spielberg." Hoffman felt people who wrote about the film unfairly emphasized only Spielberg's creative contribution and "made me out to be a guy with more money than brains. I discovered Spielberg. I put up the money for his movie. I took care of the cast and crew. I paid all those bills. And when all was said and done, I was forgotten about. I was the producer."

O N the first day of filming *Amblin'*, July 6, 1968, Burris became alarmed when he found Spielberg on the Cinefx soundstage "shooting a long tracking shot of matches going up to a campfire. It made sense in terms of the story, but he wouldn't tell us what he was doing. I knew that film was our most expensive commodity, and I thought if the whole film goes like this, we're going to use ten thousand feet of film. I hollered, 'Cut!' Steve started going crazy: 'Nobody says "Cut" on *my* set!' I learned my lesson. I've never yelled 'Cut' on a set since. I don't think he has ever forgiven me."

"The first weekend, Denis almost canceled the whole project," Daviau reports. "We shot the campfire scene that Saturday and Sunday, and by the end of Saturday we shot I think three or four times our promised allotment of film for that day. Denis said, 'This is it. We're going to pull the plug right here. I can't afford this.' We said, 'All right, we'll be good, we'll be good!' And the next day we were very careful and shot very little film so we could get out to the desert and start shooting the real thing."

Once those tests of his directorial authority were out of the way, Spielberg seemed to be in his element. For the next eight days, filming shifted to locations in the desert near Pearblossom, north of Los Angeles. "It was a hundred and five degrees in July in Pearblossom," Daviau recalls. "It was not meant for human beings to be out there with film cameras." Despite that physical ordeal, Spielberg was "wonderful" with everyone involved in the production, Hoffman said: "These were a bunch of kids, absolute amateurs. Steven works with people extremely well. He has an immediate rapport with anybody. It doesn't matter who you are, he'll direct you. Also, he does his homework and his preparation." Spielberg even documented the making of *Amblin'* with his own 8mm camera.

"People say, 'How did you get to know Spielberg?' " Daviau relates with a laugh. "I got to really know Spielberg because I shot sunrise and sunset every day for *eight straight days,* with Steven Spielberg in high gear. Every morning he wanted to get up and shoot the sunrise. 'Steven, we got a *great* sunrise yesterday.' 'Yeah, but this one might be better!' It was very loosely structured, and Steven was making it up as he went along. So we would do sunrise and then we'd shoot all day and we would get a sunset shot. *Then* we would drive in to town, to Technicolor, and see our rushes from the day before. Steven was just doing it to get an idea of how we could reshoot that one little shot that we could do better. We'd drive all the way back, get to bed, and *bang!* Five A.M., Steven would be up, going, 'Up! *Up!* '"

Other *Amblin'* crew members who went on to careers in Hollywood included composer Michael Lloyd; Spielberg's teenaged sister Anne, who served as continuity supervisor and prepared the food; production assistant Thom Eberhardt, a Long Beach State student who is now a director; production assistant Robin C. Chamberlin, who later produced the TV series *Wings;* and assistant cameraman Donald E. Heitzer, a UCLA film school graduate who also worked with Daviau on rock 'n' roll shorts and eventually became an associate producer and production manager.

Hoffman remembered the picture as "a labor of love" for everyone concerned, but for some it was just labor, and unpaid labor at that. After toiling from early morning to late evening on the grueling locations, the crew would return to their little desert motel "beat to shit," Heitzer says. Burris recalls that the crew kept changing because "Guys would say, 'Fuck this, I'm leaving.' " "The hours were hard," admits Heitzer, one of those who left Pearblossom before the film finished shooting. "It was tough. It was very strenuous. It was hot. It was the middle of nowhere. We would climb up a hillside and set up the camera. We didn't have the normal amenities."

Heitzer soon discovered Spielberg was not as relaxed as he appeared: "We would leave early in the morning for location, and Spielberg said he would vomit every morning before he came out. It's understandable—every director is nervous, and he was a young kid. But still, he was the leader. He was serious. When you take somebody's dough and you're making something there probably isn't a market for, you'd *better* be serious."

S P I E L B E R G found the editing process on *Amblin'* "cathartic, since the editing was crucial to the story." He shot more than three hours of film for a twenty-six-minute short, and by the time he was ready to start editing, his producer had little money left to hire an editing room. Once again, Julie Raymond came to the rescue: "I got him an editing room in Hollywood where he could cut the film—Hal Mann Laboratories. I had known Hal; he had been head of the lab for Pacific Title."

"Julie Raymond called me and recommended Spielberg," Mann recalls. "We had worked with him before at Pacific Title. He had done some 16mm work and he brought it to be developed. Larry Glickman [the company's owner] did a lot of work with students. He was very kind, giving, and understanding. We gave them the [film] stock for the cost of the stock plus five percent. At that time Spielberg was another student. I semi-remembered him. He was working with an [assistant] editor [Burris] on *Amblin',* and he had just gotten to the point of doing special effects. I guess he ran out of money. He needed a place to edit and stay all kinds of hours. He came in and we spoke. We were impressed with him and said we would give him help. He seemed like a nice kid, very polite and respectful. Everybody was 'sir.' He conducted himself in a businesslike way. We had one spare editing room we let him use; we told him he could have the room for free if he worked late."

Spielberg spent six weeks huddled over Mann's Moviola, editing the picture and the soundtrack, which included Michael Lloyd's music, a wistful title song performed by October Country lead singer Carole Camacho, and the only other human sounds in the film, Pamela McMyler giggling during a pot-smoking sequence. Spielberg's editing was bold, elliptical, and propulsive, with a jazzy, New Wave–like fondness for sudden, offbeat jump cuts and freeze-frames. He worked on the editing seven days a week, from about four each afternoon until four each morning, with only a single crewman in the building with him and Burris during the night hours. Spielberg was determined to have the film ready for release by the end of the year, the deadline for Academy Award consideration in the live-action short subject category.

Spielberg "lived on pizza and night air," Mann recalls. "He spent close to two weeks, day and night, just listening to film scores [to guide him in editing the film]. He had a record player, and he had brought all these 33 rpm records. He was walking around all night listening to them in conjunction with his film. He was quite a perfectionist. He wanted to know everything about everything. He wanted to know how our lab worked, how our special-effects machine worked. We had two or three special-effects operators, and he wanted to know what they did. He got advice from a lot of good people. Very few people begrudged him the time or the knowledge. People wanted to help him. He was a very forceful person in a quiet way. He didn't sound like a know-it-all; he was eager to learn. We got a kick out of it. Every once in a while someone comes along you want to go all the way for. We all thought he would go places. Film was his life."*

IN later years, Spielberg dismissed *Amblin'* as "a great Pepsi commercial" with "as much soul and content as a piece of driftwood." Since buying his debut movie from Hoffman in 1977, Spielberg has not seen fit to reissue it. "Steven was reluctant to have people see that film for many years," Daviau says, "because he felt that it was so obviously calculated to do what it did, that is, convince a group of executives at Universal to put their money on this guy who's a twenty-one-year-old director. It was so obviously aimed at that kind of an audience, with enough of a flash of the new, but it was a very old-fashioned movie in a lot of other ways. I think it's fair to say he was a little embarrassed by it."

"I can't look at it now," Spielberg admitted in 1978. "It really proved how

---

* Spielberg found time to strike up a relationship with Mann's daughter Devorah, who was there to learn the family business (now Devorah Hardberger, she is supervisor of the laboratory at Cinema Research Corp.). Besides watching *Amblin'* footage if Spielberg "needed an extra ear or an extra eye," Devorah also began dating the young filmmaker.

apathetic I was during the sixties. When I look back at that film, I can easily say, 'No wonder I didn't go to Kent State,' or 'No wonder I didn't go to Vietnam or I wasn't protesting when all my friends were carrying signs and getting clubbed in Century City.' I was off making movies, and *Amblin'* is the slick by-product of a kid immersed up to his nose in film."

Spielberg is underrating his own movie. The visual precocity of *Amblin'* still has the power to astonish after all these years, and despite its obviously calculated attentiveness to the demands of the marketplace, the film is much more than a mere director's showcase or a soulless piece of sixties youth-market exploitation. The simplicity and charm of its storytelling are affecting, and Spielberg's microcosmic treatment of that era's cultural divisions, as represented in the contrasting personalities of the hitchhiking couple, is shrewd and surprisingly complex. The film's ambivalent perspective on hippiedom, which reflected the director's own personality as a maverick working within the establishment, also demonstrated Spielberg's canny career instincts. While satisfying his ostensible target audience of young moviegoers, Spielberg simultaneously was pitching the film to his real, and more limited, target audience of middle-aged Hollywood executives who viewed the emerging youth culture with a mixture of wariness and fascination. In so doing, he made a film that managed to be both commercial in its broadly based appeal and surreptitiously personal in its underlying feelings—a combination that would become a hallmark of Spielberg's career.

With his guitar case, Army fatigue hat, and casual clothing, the Richard Levin character in *Amblin'* appears to be a hippie, or at least a middle-class Jewish kid trying his best to be a hippie. His shyness and sexual awkwardness appeal to the Pamela McMyler character, whose pretty but funky, fragile but weatherbeaten appearance stamps her as a drifter bruised by experience. As she takes the lead in initiating him into pot-smoking and lovemaking, her playfulness seems to loosen him up, but his underlying uptightness becomes more pronounced as the wordless story progresses.

The boy's anxious refusal to let his traveling companion look inside his guitar case, at first a seemingly harmless quirk, gradually alerts her to a secretive side of his personality. When they finally reach the Pacific Ocean, he frolics in the surf, fully clothed, as she rocks morosely in a beach swing, sensing that their brief journey together has no future. In a series of time-compressing jump-cuts, Spielberg brings her closer and closer to the guitar case lying in the sand. When she opens it, with a touching smile of mingled chagrin and amusement, she finds the emblems of the boy's true personality —a business suit and tie, brown wing-tipped shoes, toothpaste and mouthwash, a roll of toilet paper—along with a paperback copy of Arthur C. Clarke's *The City and the Stars,* a seemingly incongruous inclusion that helps alert the knowledgeable viewer to the extent of Spielberg's personal identification with the character.

The boy is not only a *faux* hippie, a closet square, but a rather unpleasant user to boot, despite his seeming social maladroitness. Initially unable to get a ride on the highway while traveling alone, he latches onto the girl as bait for unsuspecting drivers, a stratagem that backfires in a series of amusing sight-gags as drivers catch on to their game. On a more serious dramatic level, subtly conveyed by Spielberg's intricate direction of the couple's wary glances toward each other, the boy callously allows the girl to become closer to him emotionally than he is able to be toward her. She comes to the unhappy realization that the (unstated) goal he is pursuing in southern California leaves no room for the feelings of a rootless, less socially ambitious vagabond. Viewing his male protagonist critically, through the eyes of a more sensitive and more clear-minded female character, Spielberg provides an implicit critique of male ambition and emotional aloofness. Although it may not have appeared so to audiences at the time, Spielberg is also giving us a surprisingly harsh and objective portrait of the artist as a young man. The Levin character takes much the same attitude toward the girl that the strait-laced Spielberg did toward his hippie roommate Ralph Burris—he is embarrassed yet intrigued by her sexual and emotional openness. The director's poignant portrayal of McMyler's character is a gesture of respect toward the counterculture from a filmmaker self-aware enough to know that he could never truly belong to it.

While not overtly politically conscious, *Amblin'* is hardly the work of an "apathetic" filmmaker, but that of a deeply *feeling* filmmaker who captures the disaffected mood of his generation with both fidelity and artful understatement. Spielberg described *Amblin'* in 1968 as "hopefully standing for everything that's happening today. It takes no position on marijuana or sex, just simply presents them." He could have phrased that better, for while *Amblin'* may not take a "position" in the sense of preaching about changing social mores, it examines them concretely, passionately, and without resorting to caricature. Spielberg's deft and witty use of the camera, the vigorous and unexpected rhythms of his compositions and editing, and the engaging naturalism of the performances he draws from his actors give *Amblin'* a sense of emotional spontaneity and freshness within the framework of a mature, highly controlled, even classical visual style. Compared to some of the better-known youth pictures of the sixties, which are so hysterically overstated as to be virtually unwatchable today, *Amblin'* is an elegant and unpretentious miniature, a time capsule of the period that transcends cliché and requires no apology from its director.

"W H E N I saw *Amblin',"* Chuck Silvers reports, "I've got to be honest with you, I cried. It was everything it should have been. It was perfect. Certain things he did with the camera were fun, but they weren't *just* for fun —he was telling a story. It was such a simple story, so well told, and it was a silent motion picture. Steven Spielberg is as close to a natural-born cameraman as anybody I've ever known of; he knows what he has in mind has to be conveyed visually. I don't want to cast myself in any way as his teacher. I wish to hell I *had* been. How the hell do you teach Maria Callas how to sing? Who taught Da Vinci? You can *expose* people to things, but they have to have it in themselves. As far as I'm concerned he's the most gifted person in motion pictures. Not just today—*ever*.

"I didn't trust my own reaction to *Amblin'*. I thought maybe I wasn't being as objective as I could be. I saw it again, and I looked at it in a more professional sense. I didn't find anything I would change, and that's very unusual for me. I ran it for some of the editors I was close to. One of the guys even cried—Carl Pingitore. Carl was a gruff bear. He said, 'That's the most beautiful thing I've ever seen.' When I had shown *Amblin'* to three or four editors, I knew I had available to me Steven's showcase."

The "hell of a big break" Silvers had wished for Steven now was about to come to pass. As Spielberg has said, what happened next was "truly a Cinderella story." Although others who worked at Universal at the time have tried to take credit for bringing *Amblin'* to the attention of Universal's top brass, Silvers was the person who did so first.

"It took me three days to figure out what to do with *Amblin'*," he recalls. "It was pretty obvious that television was the way to go for Steven. I was in television, and the people I knew were in television. That would be Steven's first exposure. I thought, 'What the hell could I do? Call the guy who's in charge.' "

T H E guy in charge was Sidney J. Sheinberg. The tall, imposing, thirty-three-year-old Texan was vice-president of production for Universal TV.

"My feeling about the future of television," he said shortly after hiring Spielberg, "is that there are no rules." Sid Sheinberg came to California in 1958 to teach law at UCLA and was hired the following year by the legal department of Revue Productions, the television production arm of MCA, then a leading Hollywood talent agency. After helping negotiate MCA's purchase of Universal in 1962, Sheinberg began climbing the corporate ladder as a TV business affairs executive. He started a new era in television in 1964 when he came up with the idea for the made-for-TV movie (then known as the NBC "World Premiere"). As Universal's TV division thrived, Sheinberg soon became the favored son and heir apparent of MCA president Lew Wasserman.

Remembering Sheinberg's days in TV, writer-producer William Link says that he "would give you a decision within seconds. There was no stall; there wasn't that famous Hollywood 'slow no.' There was none of that. He has a lawyer's mind, and story conferences were great with Sid. He would make [creative] suggestions, which was rare [for an executive]. Sid would re-plot, he could restructure, and it was a two-way street. He was a sophisticated man." Martin Hornstein, an assistant director who worked on Universal TV shows with Spielberg, remembers Sheinberg as "a visionary. He wasn't afraid to try new things."

It was shortly before 9:00 on a rainy night in the fall of 1968 when Silvers made his call about *Amblin'* to Sheinberg's office in MCA's executive headquarters, the Black Tower. "He's in a meeting with some NBC people," Sheinberg's secretary told Silvers. "I'll try and get him to take your call."

Sheinberg came on the line and barked, "Jesus Christ, I'm in the middle of a goddam meeting, arguing with these people."

Silvers gamely pushed ahead, "Sid, I've got something I want you to see."

"I've got a whole goddam pile of film here [to look at]," Sheinberg replied. "I'm going to be here half of the night. I'll be lucky to get out of here by midnight."

"I'm going to put this [film] in the pile for the projection booth. You really should look at it tonight."

"You think it's that goddam important?"

"*Yes,* I think it's that goddam important. If you don't look at this, somebody else will."

Taking no chances about Sheinberg changing his mind, Silvers told Sheinberg's projectionist, "If he says, 'That's all,' put it up and run it anyway."

"Now, the projectionist isn't going to do that," Silvers explains, "but I wanted to impress on him how important it was. Sometime in that night, Sheinberg took the half hour and watched it. The next morning I got in early and there were about five or six messages. George Santoro had been calling. George was Sid's right-hand man. I returned the call to George. George said, 'Who is Steven Spielberg?' "

"He's a young man that we know," replied Silvers, who remembers thinking, "Aha! He's hooked! Got him!"

"Can we talk to him?" Santoro asked.

"I think I can arrange that."

Sheinberg later recalled his initial reaction to *Amblin'* and to the phone call from Silvers that alerted him to it: "He said there's this guy who's been hanging around the place who's made a short film. So I watched it and I thought it was terrific. I liked the way he selected the performers, the relationships, the maturity and the warmth that was in that short. I told Chuck to have the guy come see me."

SILVERS immediately called Spielberg: "They want to talk to you. When can you be over here?"

"I'll leave right now."

"Fine, you come over here to the office. I need to talk to you first."

When Spielberg arrived shortly thereafter, Silvers told him, "Look, whatever the hell you do up there, remember, they're talking business and you're talking opportunity. The best thing to do is a lot of listening. And don't sign anything, for Chrissake."*

Spielberg recalled what happened in Sheinberg's office: "He's a very nice man, Sid. Very austere. He sat there in his French [provincial] office, overlooking Universal. Like a scene out of *The Fountainhead*. He always calls people 'sir.' He said, 'Sir, I liked your work. How would you like to go to work professionally?' And . . . well, what are you gonna say to that! He laid out the whole program. 'You sign the contract and start in television. If you do a few shows and other producers like your work, you can—maybe— branch out into feature films.' It was a dream contract come true. I mean, it was all very vague. But it *sounded* great."

Sheinberg recalled being so convinced of Spielberg's precocious talent that he unhesitantly took a chance on "this nerdlike, scrawny character. . . . I said, 'You should be a director.' And Steven said, 'I think so, too.' Steven was very much a young boy."

"Sid was really the fairy godfather," Silvers says, "because he had the ability to make it happen. He's the one who saw it and reacted. What a lucky phone call that was! But without any question in my mind, if it had not been through the aegis of Universal, it would have been somebody else. Steven would have gone on to be exactly what he is now. That kind of talent is bigger than life. That talent could not have gone unrecognized."

W H E N his meeting with Sheinberg ended, Spielberg went straight back to Silvers's office.

"They offered me a contract," Spielberg said.

"You didn't sign anything?"

"No."

Spielberg then "asked me if I would be his manager," Silvers relates. "I said, 'Steven, you need someone who knows a hell of a lot more about the business than I do. I'm not the right person.' He asked me what I wanted [for helping him]. I said, 'Well, Steven, by the time you really make it big, I'll probably be too goddam old for you to do me any good.' If I had known then what I know now, I would have given him a completely different answer. In effect, what I told him was, 'When you can, pass it on. When you make it big, you can be nice to young people. I learned from people I had no way of thanking. You learned it here, and you can, in effect, pay off the people. You can pass it on.'

"Steven made a promise and he's kept it. He has a hospital wing with

* Shortly before his meeting with Sheinberg, Spielberg used *Amblin'* to sign with his first agent, Mike Medavoy of General Artists Corp., which was acquired soon after that by Creative Management Associates, a partnership of Freddie Fields and David Begelman. Medavoy did not accompany Spielberg to the meeting, but the agency subsequently negotiated his deal with Universal.

his name on it [the Steven Spielberg Pediatric Medicine Research Center at Cedars-Sinai Medical Center in West Hollywood]. At USC there's a Steven Spielberg scoring stage. You look at the list of first-time directors and new writers and first-time producers he has made an opportunity for—he puts his money and he puts his business personality on the line.

"He's kept the other promise to me. He said, 'How about something personal? What do *you* want?' I said, 'Every time we meet I would like a hug.' Whenever I see him, he gives me a hug."

EIGHT

"THIS TREMENDOUS MEATGRINDER"

I'VE ALWAYS RESENTED THE TELEVISION MEDIUM, EVEN THOUGH IT WAS THROUGH TV THAT I
FOUND AN INROAD TO THEATRICAL FILMS.

— STEVEN SPIELBERG, 1974

THEY just signed me and told me to imagine up something, which to me is proof that the old Hollywood way of doing things is breaking up a bit," Spielberg said in a December 1968 interview with the *Los Angeles Times*. His studio contract felt "like a dream come true," he later recalled. "At last I had the means to show what I could do. But it was not something I wanted to do for the benefit of others. No, I wanted to do it for myself, for everything I had believed in since I was a child. I could finally bring to life all those stories I had in my head."

But his elation was tempered by the anxiety he felt as a young amateur filmmaker suddenly thrust into a professional director's chair. Even before he started directing his first television program at Universal, he told *The Hollywood Reporter*, "Now I'm caught up in this tremendous meatgrinder. *Amblin'* is the only film I will ever make with so much freedom."

AMBLIN' had its world premiere on December 18, 1968, in a one-week Academy Award–qualifying engagement at Loew's Crest Theater in Westwood. Spielberg's short was ill-matched with Otto Preminger's misfired comedy about hippies and gangsters, *Skidoo*. The newspaper ads barely squeezed in a minuscule mention of *Amblin'*: "It Packs the Wallop of a Rock Concert!" But *Los Angeles Times* feature writer Wayne Warga called it "a splendid film to watch."

On the night of the premiere, producer Denis Hoffman threw a party at a screening room on Sunset Boulevard, and Spielberg showed up looking self-consciously hip in a Nehru jacket. By a happy coincidence, it was also Spielberg's birthday. His twenty-*second* birthday, even though the*Times* reported the following day that he was twenty-one. As part of the Oscar campaign conducted by publicist Jerry Pam, Hoffman held another screening party for *Amblin'* that month at the Directors Guild of America Theater and took out ads in the trade papers. Spielberg also was invited to screen *Amblin'* before a USC directing class taught by Jerry Lewis, who told his students, "That's what filmmaking is all about."

Despite all the ballyhoo, *Amblin'* proved a difficult sell to theaters. "The problem was it was too long," Hoffman recalled. "The theater people didn't like it, because it caused them to give up one screening per day. They would play a seven-minute short, but this was twenty-six minutes. We had a terrible time trying to get them to play it."

The first distributor Hoffman approached, in the fall of 1968, was Universal, a logical choice since it was in the process of signing not only Spielberg but also Pamela McMyler to a contract.* But the studio seemed to regard *Amblin'* itself as an afterthought, making an offer of only $2,000 for the world rights, which Hoffman indignantly refused. After being rejected by United Artists, Hoffman made a temporary releasing deal with Sigma III to split the proceeds from the Crest engagement, but the distributor chose not to exercise its right of first refusal for a national release. Hoffman contracted instead on June 15, 1970, with Four Star Excelsior Releasing Co., which found the film occasional playdates around the country for about a year (Four Star later released the film in the United Kingdom as well). Although Hoffman said in 1994 that *Amblin'* barely returned its costs overall, it did better in its nontheatrical release by UPA, which rented and sold 16mm prints for several years to such outlets as schools, libraries, and military bases.

Spielberg also managed to place *Amblin'* in the June 1969 Atlanta and Venice Film Festivals. When Hoffman wasn't able to pay Spielberg's way to Atlanta, Spielberg persuaded Universal to pick up his travel expenses. *Amblin'* was chosen best live-action short subject by the festival, whose program described it as "a solid contender for an Academy Award nomination." "Everybody said we were going to get the nomination," Hoffman remembered. "Everybody believed it was a shoo-in."

But when the nominations were announced on February 18, *Amblin'* failed to make the list. Hoffman and Spielberg were "devastated" that *Am-*

---

* The studio cast McMyler immediately in a *Dragnet* episode. *Amblin'* also led to her casting in Warner Bros.' 1970 John Wayne movie *Chisum*. She appeared in several other films but never reached stardom.

blin' wasn't nominated. The Oscar winner in the live-action short-subject category was Charles Guggenheim's *Robert Kennedy Remembered,* the kind of sober, traditional filmmaking the Academy has always favored over more adventurous, groundbreaking work. Hoffman said he was told by members of the Academy's Short Subjects Awards Nominating Committee that *Amblin'* "was not nominated because people at the Academy did not like the reference to drugs in the movie. In a little segment, we portrayed marijuana as a fun thing." (In addition, one of the trade ads promoting *Amblin'* for Oscar consideration prominently featured a smoking joint and a bag of marijuana.)

This was the first snub of a Spielberg film by the Academy, but it was not to be the last.

S PIELBERG had one bit of unfinished business before he could start directing at Universal—college. When Sheinberg offered him a seven-year contract, with a starting salary of $275 a week, Spielberg hesitated for a moment, evidently thinking of what his father's reaction would be.

"Well," said Spielberg, "I haven't graduated yet."

To which Sheinberg impatiently replied, "Do you wanna graduate college or do you wanna be a film director?"

"I signed the papers a week later," Spielberg says. "I quit college so fast I didn't even clean out my locker. I went from Cal State at Long Beach to Stage 15 at Universal—where Joan Crawford met me at the door."

That's only a slight exaggeration. Spielberg completed the first semester of his junior year at Long Beach State, officially dropping out of college on January 31, 1969, the day before he began rehearsals with Crawford on *Night Gallery,* his first TV show for Universal. He said later, "I began directing a year shy of graduation, which my father will *never* forgive me for."

A MEASURE of the faith Universal had in Spielberg came when the actress originally cast in *Night Gallery* balked at being directed by a twenty-two-year-old. Rather than changing directors, Universal fired Bette Davis and replaced her with Joan Crawford. During the show's filming, Crawford was asked by a journalist how she felt about working with such a young director. She replied, "They told me when I signed to do this that he was twenty-three!"

Following the tempestuous teaming of Davis and Crawford in Robert Aldrich's 1962 Grand Guignol classic *What Ever Happened to Baby Jane?,* the two legendary actresses were reduced in the late sixties to competing for increasingly tacky roles as geriatric horror queens. When Crawford accepted a $50,000 offer from Universal to star in one episode of the three-part NBC "World Premiere" TV movie *Night Gallery,* she was not in a position to be choosy about her director. She needed the money, and she was well aware of what had happened to Davis.

Written by Rod Serling in the waning, sadly derivative days of his career, and originally pitched as a theatrical feature, *Night Gallery* served as the pilot for a series of supernatural tales that vainly attempted to recapture the eerie magic of *The Twilight Zone.* Spielberg, who had been deeply influenced by that series while growing up in Arizona, was assigned to direct "Eyes," the middle episode in the *Night Gallery* anthology movie.*

Adapted from a story published in Serling's 1967 collection, *The Season to Be Wary,* "Eyes" is the lurid tale of Claudia Menlo, a wealthy blind woman who blackmails her doctor (Barry Sullivan) into removing the eyes of a desperately impoverished small-time gambler (Tom Bosley) and transplanting them into her so she can have a few hours of sight. When she removes her bandages, she finds that the world is still mysteriously dark— the lights of New York City have been extinguished by the great blackout of 1965. A massive suspension of disbelief is required to go along with even the secondary devices of the gimmicky yarn: Why wouldn't the victim simply skip town before the operation, after taking Miss Menlo's money to cover his gambling debt? Why would she want the removal of her bandages to take place at night? When she stumbles outside in the dark, why can't she see the headlights of cars jamming the street outside her building?

But "Eyes" was enlivened by Spielberg's energetic and inventive visual style, and by a credibly monstrous performance by Crawford. "It was a trick piece," the producer of *Night Gallery,* William Sackheim, says of Spielberg's episode. "It's not going down in the history of film as one of the greatest things ever done, but it's a showy piece that worked well."

SPIELBERG claimed that after signing his contract with Universal, he was left to molder in an office with "Nobody to call. Nothing to do. No producer on the lot was going to give me a break." His first assignment for the studio was "to escort this tall young man and give him a tour of Universal Studios because he'd just sold the novel *The Andromeda Strain* to [director] Robert Wise and Universal." The tall young man was Michael Crichton, who later would write the novel on which Spielberg based *Jurassic Park.* Despite his characteristic impatience, Spielberg actually had little time to feel neglected by the Black Tower, for his assignment to direct "Eyes" was reported in *Daily Variety* on January 23, 1969, less than six weeks after the announcement of his signing by the studio.

Spielberg had the impression that Sheinberg "twisted somebody's arm— or broke it off!" to get him his maiden assignment. But Sackheim, a veteran of many successful TV productions, insists that Sheinberg "never called me and said, 'Put Steven Spielberg on it.' I didn't know Steven, but Steven, I guess, was kind of a legend even then. A legend in the sense that he just kind of climbed over the fence and plunked himself in a trailer—at least that

---

* The other two parts were directed by TV journeymen Boris Sagal and Barry Shear.

was the story I heard. Sheinberg called me one day and said, 'Sir, I have something I want you to see. Have you ever heard of Steven Spielberg?' I said, 'The legend, the kid?' He set up a screening of *Amblin'*. It was an incredible piece of work, a very professional job. I said to Sheinberg, 'I wonder if Steven Spielberg might be a good director for this. I think it might be an interesting idea.' Sheinberg said, 'I think it would be a *great* idea. Let's go with it.' "

But Sheinberg then had to sell Spielberg on the idea. The problem, unbeknown to Sackheim, was the script.

"The script was terrible," Spielberg said later. "It was by a very good writer, Rod Serling. But the story was not one of his best. . . . I really didn't want to do the show. I said to Sid Sheinberg, 'Jesus, can I do something about *young* people?' He said, 'I'd take this opportunity if I were you.' . . . And, of course, I took it. I would have done anything. I would have shot . . . I dunno . . . the Universal directory if I had to. Just to get on a soundstage. I began rereading the macabre script, trying to make it interesting visually; and it turned out to be the most visually blatant movie I've ever made, which goes to show how much the script inspired me."

Despite his low opinion of the script, Spielberg found Serling "the most positive guy in the entire production company. He was a great, energetic, slaphappy guy who gave me a fantastic pep talk about how he predicted that the entire movie industry was about to change because of young people like myself getting the breaks."

W H E N Spielberg was told that Joan Crawford had been cast in "Eyes," "That's when the cold sweat began." It was on a Sunday, shortly before the start of filming, that he had his first meeting with the legendary star, who was sixty-two years old and had been working in Hollywood since 1925. Spielberg called Chuck Silvers and said anxiously, "They've told me I've gotta go and talk to her today. Tell me what's going to happen."

"How are you dressed?" asked Silvers.

"Jeans."

"Fine, don't try to be anybody but yourself."

"They're going to send a limousine for·me!" Spielberg said excitedly.

"Make sure you allow the chauffeur to do his job. Make sure he opens the door for you. Make sure you sit down until he opens the door to you."

(Silvers says that the message he was trying to convey to Spielberg was, "Be yourself, but let's start being the director.")

"Just remember she's a very, very famous lady," Silvers continued. "Before you're picked up, sit down and write down a number of names of pictures she was in that you remember."

("Because I knew he was nervous," Silvers explains, "I wanted to give him something to do while he was waiting.")

Spielberg was familiar only with Crawford's work in *Baby Jane* and *Mil-*

dred Pierce. So he went out and bought a copy of Lawrence J. Quirk's book *The Films of Joan Crawford*. Before his 8:00 P.M. appointment with Crawford at her Hollywood apartment, he gave himself a crash course in her career.

As Spielberg told the story to Crawford biographer Bob Thomas, when he arrived at her apartment, he heard her call out in a warm voice, "Come in, Steven," but at first he didn't see her. Then, wrote Thomas, Spielberg "was startled to find her standing behind the couch with a mask covering her eyes. He watched in astonishment as she stumbled about the room, bumping into furniture, holding out a protective hand as she moved."

"This is how a blind person walks through a room," she told him. "I'm practicing for the role. How difficult it is without the benefit of sight. You feel lost in a world of blackness. I've got to do this on the set, Steven. I need to practice with the furniture two days before we shoot so I'll be able to let my eyes go blank and still find my way around like a blind person."

At that point, Thomas related, "She removed the blindfold. Her huge eyes blinked in bewilderment as they gazed for the first time on the man who would be her director. Her smile froze as she studied the smooth, beardless face. 'Hello, Steven,' she said, offering a brave hand. 'Hello . . . Joan,' he replied, wishing that he could escape."

"Goodness," she told him, "you certainly must have done something important to get where you are so soon. What films have you directed?"

"Uh, none."

"No films at the studio?"

"No, ma'am."

"Then . . . ?"

"Well, I did make a movie that the studio liked. That's why they signed me."

"Oh? And what was that?"

"It was, uh, a twenty-minute short I made at Cal State Long Beach."

"At school."

"Yes."

"Do you happen to be the son of anybody in the Black Tower?"

"No, ma'am. I'm just working my way through Universal."

"Steven," she laughed, "you and I both made it on our own. We're going to get along just fine! C'mon, let's go to dinner."

While they dined on Polynesian food at the Luau, a campy Beverly Hills hangout popular with movie people, Crawford drank vodka while Spielberg sipped a non-alcoholic fruit punch. She pumped him on his background, and he told her about his aspirations to make films. She spoke about her life with her late husband, Alfred Steele, president of the Pepsi-Cola Company; she had remained involved with the company as a board member and spokeswoman. She laughed uproariously when Spielberg said, "I guess about the only thing we have in common is that we're both members of the Pepsi generation."

By the end of the evening, their unlikely camaraderie had progressed to the point that she said, "Now, I know what television schedules are, and I know the pressure that will be on you to finish the show on time. You'll want your first work as a director to be something you can be proud of, and I'll break my ass to help you. Don't let any executive bug you because the picture's not on schedule. If you have any problems with the Black Tower, let me take care of it. I'll be your guardian angel. Okay?"

"Okay," said Spielberg, smiling with relief.

The next day he told Chuck Silvers, "I was on cloud nine all the way home." He had passed his first test as a professional director.

"It was a quantum leap," he said later. "I never got over the idea of directing *Joan Crawford!!* But she was great. . . . She took pity on me, this little kid with acne all over my face. She must have been expecting George Stevens or George Cukor to direct her first TV show."

Contrary to Spielberg's belief, *Night Gallery* was not Crawford's first acting job on television. She had done nine previous TV shows, the first in 1953 and the most recent a 1968 episode of Lucille Ball's sitcom *The Lucy Show*. But Crawford *"was* a little apprehensive" about the television medium, Sackheim says. "You're talking about a woman who probably never shot more than two pages of dialogue a day in her life. Now you're shooting *eight* pages. She had difficulty remembering her lines. Ultimately we had cue cards made up. I remember she apologized to Steven. She was very upset about her own inability to provide what he needed."

Spielberg remembered, "I was so frightened that even now the whole period is a bit of a blank. I was walking on eggs. . . . I don't know if you've ever not been to bed for four days in a row? Shooting *Night Gallery* was like that. I don't take drugs. I never have. Or I would have used every drug under and over the counter at that time. That show put me through dire straits. It was good discipline but a very bad experience."

Joan Crawford remained true to her word, however, treating him "like I had been working fifty years. . . . Once she knew I had done my homework —I had my storyboards right there with me every minute—she treated me as if I was The Director. Which, of course, I was. But at that time she knew a helluva lot more about directing than I did."

But as cast member Barry Sullivan recalled shortly before his death in 1994, Spielberg also "handled her very nicely. He was very flattering. He used the right butter-up words, not the words he would have used normally. She had fallen in love with him, but she didn't trust herself, that was my interpretation. She was very impressed with him, but she didn't know why. She thought he was some kind of nut."

T H E first day of shooting, February 3, "was frightening because I hadn't met the crew before," Spielberg recalled at a 1973 American Film Institute seminar. "I came on the set and they thought it was a joke. They really thought it was a publicity stunt and I really couldn't get anybody to take me seriously for two days. It was very embarrassing. . . . I set up a shot in *Night Gallery*—I shot through a bauble [in a chandelier], just a real gimmicky shot—and I remember seeing people titter and say, 'He doesn't have long to go.' "

Barry Sullivan realized what Spielberg was feeling. He took the director aside and told him, "Life is short. Don't put yourself through this if you don't have to." That advice, Spielberg recalled, "has stayed with me, although it's an old cliché."

Spielberg came to *Night Gallery* with a precociously well-developed sense of his own visual style. He disdained the usual TV method of mechanically "covering" scenes with master shots, medium shots, and close-ups. He had an instinctive aversion to the over-the-shoulder shooting style TV editors favor for ease in linking shots, and with his passion for control and his fondness for the moving camera already strongly in evidence, he preferred whenever possible to stage a scene in a single flowing master shot. Because of his unorthodox shooting methods and Crawford's difficulty remembering her lines, the first two days went slowly. As Bob Thomas reported, Spielberg "knew that his bosses in the Black Tower were more interested in maintaining the schedule than in achieving quality, and he feared that both would elude him. If he failed on his first assignment, would he ever have another?"

Spielberg's visual flamboyance also caused friction with his producer. As film editor Edward M. Abroms recalls, "The first day we went to dailies [the screening of footage shot the previous day], the first scene up was Barry Sullivan coming into [Crawford's] suite, seen through a chandelier. Steven put the camera close to the chandelier, and I remember Bill Sackheim going, 'Oh, my God, what an arty-farty shot! Jesus Christ!' " Hearing such remarks, Spielberg said later, was "really a disturbing experience." But his crew soon became "very sympathetic," doing their best to help him get the shots he wanted.

When Bob Hull of *The Hollywood Reporter* interviewed the "long-haired, very youthful-appearing tyro" on the final day of shooting, Spielberg stressed his willingness to work within the system: "I'm trying to show that it's possible to be both commercial and, well, artful. People my age in this business are malleable, you know, not merely one-way, their way. We can learn from the past." Diplomatically glossing over his early difficulties with the crew, he said, "I expected hostility when I started on this. But no one seemed to think it was unusual. Nobody called me 'Hey, kid.' As a matter of fact, the older people on the set were the first to accept me. I guess they figured that if someone up there thought I was good enough for the job, then that was good enough for them."

"From the time he'd holler 'Action!' 'Cut!,' he was the director," Chuck Silvers says. "It was a totally professional operation. On most sets there's a lot of grab-ass, cardplaying, jokes, and lightness. You don't see that on a Spielberg set. By showing respect he engenders respect."

• • •

O N the third day of shooting, there was another crisis. Joan Crawford became ill. She was diagnosed with an inner-ear infection and given a day to rest. Spielberg's efforts to keep up with the schedule seemed doomed.

At the end of her first day back, a shaky Crawford told Spielberg, "Tomorrow I really need your help, Steven. That scene where I take off the bandages and see for the first time. It scares the hell out of me. That may be the most important shot in the picture, and I simply don't know how to do it."

"We'll work it out, Joan, don't worry," he promised. But the following day he was under intense pressure from the production office to complete his work on the apartment set so that the stage could be turned over to another production. He was almost done when the assistant director, Ralph Ferrin, said Crawford needed to speak with him.

"Later," said Spielberg. "I've got to finish with this set by six."

"I think you'd better talk with Joan," Ferrin said, "or else you may not be able to finish with the show."

Spielberg found Crawford weeping in her dressing room.

"You have let me down," she told him. "I rarely ask anyone for help, but this time I needed it—badly. I asked you last night if you could spare some time today to help me with the scene where I am able to see. Now, here it is, the end of the day, and you haven't talked to me."

Spielberg canceled shooting for the day, even though he hadn't finished with the set. For the next hour he went over the scene with Crawford in her dressing room, promising, "I don't care what the production office says. I'll give you any number of takes until we get it on film just the way you and I believe it should be."

Spielberg "was painstaking the next day, calling for take after take until Joan was satisfied," Bob Thomas reported. "The shot lasted less than five seconds in the film, but the experience proved an invaluable lesson for the young man—the director's responsibility for his actors."

On the last day and night of shooting, Spielberg filmed the finale of Miss Menlo, her sight fading at sunrise, crashing through the window of her penthouse as she cries out, "I want it! *I want the sun!*"

"We were thinking of using a stock shot of the sun," editor Abroms recalls. "She had a problem, being the actress that she was, with, 'How am I going to be motivated to feel this heat on my face? And how am I supposed to go here when there's no glass?' Because of Steven's immaturity at the time, he could not quite reason with her. He said, 'We'll have some padding on the other side, and we're going to catch you.' But she just couldn't work up enough inner motivation. Bill Sackheim took her aside and she did it."

"Miss Crawford and I just had our first argument," Spielberg told *The Hollywood Reporter* at the end of shooting. "It wasn't really much of a disagreement, a little thing over punching up a scene. It's a pleasure discussing such a thing with a woman like that."

When Crawford died in 1977, Spielberg was the youngest speaker at a Hollywood memorial tribute organized by George Cukor. He recalled that during the shooting of *Night Gallery,* "She treated me like I knew what I was doing, and I didn't. I loved her for that."

S P I E L B E R G ' S episode finished shooting two days behind its seven-day schedule, a development frowned upon in assembly-line TV production, even if the director was not entirely responsible. Spielberg then took such pains with the editing that he eventually was barred from the cutting room. He later claimed that editor Ed Abroms "threw me bodily out of his cutting room, and called the producer to complain. I think he threw something heavy at me, too, but missed." Asked about Spielberg's removal from the show, Abroms replied that he was "a little hesitant" to discuss the circumstances, but Sackheim insists, "Nobody threw him out." The producer does admit that they had "a little problem trying to get the film away from him. He shot some really wild, wacky stuff. In the operation scene of Tom Bosley losing his eyes, we were having trouble putting it together." "There was virtually no operation [scene], no footage," Abroms says. "Steven shot the two of them on gurneys going into the operating room, and down shots on their faces—how do we put across that the eyes are being taken out? I had to pull a few tricks, some manipulation of film and some opticals." The special-effects finale of Miss Menlo falling to her death also required some reshooting during postproduction, without Spielberg's involvement.

"I put the show together and didn't work [as a director] for a year after that," Spielberg recalls. "Because I was disillusioned with Hollywood, with show business. . . . I was so traumatized. The pressure of that show was too much for me. . . . I really felt this wasn't the business I wanted to be in."

Veteran *Daily Variety* television reviewer Dave Kaufman had a different opinion. After the show aired November 8 on NBC, Kaufman wrote: "Steve Spielberg's direction of the Crawford seg is topnotch." He praised Crawford for a "superb" performance and described the episode as "highly imaginative and gripping." But in *The Hollywood Reporter,* John Mahoney wrote condescendingly: "The second episode was directed by twenty-two-year-old Steven Spielberg, who employed such new techniques as the spiral wipe. The episode featured Joan Crawford in a showy fourth-gear performance, [and] looked as if it hadn't been completed." Forgetting Kaufman's praise in *Daily Variety,* Spielberg later recalled the reviews of *Night Gallery* as "awful. Some critics said I shouldn't have done it—because of my age. All of a sudden, the age factor began to plague me."

Despite surprisingly strong ratings, which led to a three-year run for the series, the *Night Gallery* pilot gave Spielberg the unwelcome reputation around Universal of being "avant-garde," Sid Sheinberg said. "So many people take bows for his success now, but at the time, they complained because he wanted to put the camera on the floor." Spielberg's agent at the time, Mike Medavoy, recalls, "After the first *Night Gallery,* while they thought he had some talent, they had all those episodic guys working, and he wasn't like Michael Ritchie, whom they thought the world of, and a lot of other people. There were young guys working all the time, but Steven was *really* young. He looked like he was fifteen years old."

"I spent eight months on the lot then," Spielberg told *The Hollywood Reporter* in 1971, "and now that I was officially there I got a Rolodex and a charge number and I was forgotten except for the one segment of *Night Gallery* I directed starring Joan Crawford. I submitted three properties to people and was turned down on all of them."

O N his final day of shooting the *Night Gallery* episode, Spielberg announced his next project, *Snow White,* to *The Hollywood Reporter:* "It's the story of seven guys in San Francisco who run this Chinese food factory." He was not kidding.

Planned as a feature film for Universal, *Snow White* was a cynical update of the beloved fairy tale to the swinging sixties, based on a Donald Barthelme novella first published in a February 1967 issue of *The New Yorker.* The straitlaced Spielberg would have had to strain to find anything congenial to his talents in this protracted dirty joke, in which the heroine cheerlessly dispenses her sexual favors among her seven randy roommates. Barthelme's rambling, pretentiously obscure story has minimal character or plot development. Although intended as a satire, it has little humor, a confused attitude toward the free-love movement's effect on women, and a dismal finale: Snow White's false "prince" winds up dead of poisoning, and one of her seven roommates is hanged. On February 23, 1969, *The New York Times* reported that producer Dick Berg, impressed with Spielberg's work on *Amblin',* had hired him and TV writer Larry Grusin to give *Snow White* the "youth treatment."

Universal's grasp of the youth market was, to say the least, rather shaky. "Universal at the time was a disaster," recalls Medavoy, who brought the *Snow White* project to Spielberg. "The only picture they had was *Airport."* A frenzy of misguided would-be with-it-ness soon led the studio to plunge recklessly into the counterculture with Monte Hellman's terminally arty *Two-Lane Blacktop,* Peter Fonda's torpid Western *The Hired Hand,* and Dennis Hopper's incomprehensible *The Last Movie,* all released in 1971. Even if Spielberg relished the idea of paying back Disney's *Snow White and the Seven Dwarfs* for terrifying him as a child, he can be grateful in retrospect that the Black Tower finally had sense enough to scuttle the notion of making a bawdy lampoon of an animated classic that has captivated audiences since 1937.

In May 1969, Spielberg came up with a much better idea for a movie, one that he later described as "a tragic fairytale." The banner headline in the May 2 issue of the *Hollywood Citizen–News* would have grabbed any young filmmaker's attention, for it read like a Hollywood story pitch: NEW BONNIE 'N [*sic*] CLYDE.

Although the movie Spielberg finally made more than four years later— *The Sugarland Express*—departed considerably from the facts of the original incident, its emotional core was clear to him from the opening paragraph of the article: "An ex-convict, freed just two weeks ago and willing to do anything 'to talk to my kids and love them,' kidnapped a Texas highway patrolman in his squad car today in a high-speed c[h]ase that ended seven hours later in a gunfight with lawmen." The article reported that Robert Samuel (Bobby) Dent and his wife, Ila Faye, had taken hostage a highway patrolman named J. Kenneth Crone. Threatening to kill him with a shotgun, the Dents drove several hundred miles across southeast Texas in Crone's patrol car, followed by a posse of more than a hundred cars. Eventually, Texas Department of Public Safety Captain Jerry Miller struck a deal with Dent, who agreed to free Crone unharmed if Miller would let him see his two children, a boy and a girl, at the home of Dent's father-in-law in Wheelock. "I want ten or fifteen minutes to talk to my kids and love them and I don't think they'll be seeing us again," Dent told the lawman. But when he entered the house, Dent's children were nowhere to be seen, and he was shot to death.

It was only later that Spielberg learned the full story of the bizarre incident and the comedy of errors leading up to it. While driving with his wife between Beaumont and Port Arthur, Dent had failed to dim his headlights to a passing police car. When the cop tried to pull him over, the ex-con drove off in a panic. After a pursuit by several patrol cars, including one driven by Crone, the fleeing couple abandoned their car and sought help from a farmer. Thinking the Dents had been beaten by robbers, the farmer called the local sheriff. Crone heard the radio report and went to the farmhouse, only to be taken hostage. Rather than dying in a "gunfight," Bobby Dent was gunned down by Robertson County Sheriff E. T. Elliott and FBI agent Bob Wyatt after hostage Crone dove for cover and Dent, in the confusion, failed to obey a command to drop his gun.*

When *The Sugarland Express* was released in 1974, it was generally assumed that what primarily interested Spielberg about the saga of Bobby and Ila Faye Dent was the opportunity to stage the biggest car chase ever put on film. Although the director was intrigued by the circuslike spectacle surrounding the chase, he said in 1974 that "there is very little to directing automobiles. . . . The human drama . . . inspired me long before I was visually wooed by the thought of all those cars." What undoubtedly struck the deepest emotional chord in Spielberg was Bobby Dent's fatal desire to see

---

* Spielberg echoed the name of E. T. Elliott in the names of both the title character of *E.T.* and Elliott, the boy who protects him.

his children. Spielberg was the same age as Dent (twenty-two) when the events occurred. His own family's breakup was still a raw wound for the young filmmaker as he began his professional directing career in 1969. Even though he later learned that the chain of events was not entirely set in motion from the outset by Dent's desire to see his children, Spielberg kept to the spirit of the original article by making the attempt to reconstitute a broken family the primary dramatic focus of *The Sugarland Express*.

When he proposed the story to Universal in 1969, the studio was not interested. The story was too somber, too downbeat, they told him. It wouldn't make any money. Youth movies that *were* making money in the late sixties, even tragic road movies like *Bonnie and Clyde* and *Easy Rider,* allowed their characters an intoxicating sense of rebellious freedom before they met their ultimate fate. There wasn't much exhilaration to the story of Bobby and Ila Faye Dent; those two hopeless losers hardly fit the popular mold of romantic outlaws. Spielberg reluctantly filed away the clipping from the *Hollywood Citizen–News,* letting the story germinate in his mind.

Not only had he failed to interest Universal in letting him "bring to life all those stories I had in my head," but no one even was offering him TV episodes to direct. "I was in a despondent, comatose state and told Sheinberg I wanted a leave of absence. I got it."

D U R I N G the months he spent away from the studio from the summer of 1969 into the early part of 1970, Spielberg tried to raise money to make low-budget independent films in 16mm. If he had been able to do so, he said later, "I might have made underground movies first: I might have been like Brian De Palma and made nine films before breaking into the Establishment." But once he had become a professional filmmaker, there was no turning back. He was chagrined to find that he could not even raise $1,000 to make a short.

At the same time, Spielberg set out to develop feature-length screenplays with other writers. He began to approach other studios with projects during his informal leave of absence from Universal, with his agent's help and encouragement. Although Universal had an exclusive contract with Spielberg, Medavoy says that "I felt that if I could get someone to buy him, I could go to Universal and ask them for a loanout. I never asked Sid for his blessing. I figured, Steven wasn't working, so why did they have to know?"

A future studio executive, Spielberg's agent had been born Morris Medavoy in 1941 to Russian Jewish parents in Shanghai, where they lived in the British Protectorate before emigrating to Chile in 1947 and the United States ten years later.* After his graduation from UCLA in 1963, Medavoy earned a

---

* Unlike the young hero of Spielberg's 1987 film *Empire of the Sun,* which is set in Shanghai during World War II, Medavoy was not separated from his parents during the war. When Spielberg made the film, Medavoy assisted his research by supplying him with family photographs.

reputation as an aggressive, literate young agent of rare taste and sophistication. In 1968, the same year he signed Spielberg, Medavoy also signed such director clients as George Lucas, Francis Coppola, John Milius, Terrence Malick, Michael Ritchie, Philip Kaufman, Monte Hellman, and Michelangelo Antonioni. His hot new clients at CMA became known collectively as his "Class of '68"; to Spielberg, he was affectionately known as "The Czar."

"We were quite close when we first got started," Medavoy recalls. "We spent a lot of time together. We ate a lot of peanut-butter sandwiches together. We knew some of the same women. But it's funny, just to show you how wrong I was, I thought the real successes would be Monte Hellman, Terry Malick, John Milius, Phil Kaufman—I never expected any of the others. I never knew whether Steven was going to [be a great success]. I always thought he was extraordinarily talented, and I knew that he was ambitious. But, at first, I thought he was a guy who was going to emulate and copy as opposed to being original. And what he did was, he emulated and copied the best of them, and he *became* an original."

One of the projects Spielberg shopped around was a World War II aviation "dogfight film" he was planning with a Medavoy client named Carl Gottlieb. A young TV comedy writer and actor, Gottlieb later played small parts for Spielberg and wrote the final shooting script for *Jaws*. Spielberg's interest in airplanes and in World War II had already been abundantly demonstrated in his amateur films, notably *Fighter Squad*. The dogfight project attracted interest from Warner Bros., but Spielberg's desire to direct the film was, according to Gottlieb, "the rock on which the project foundered, despite his clearly evident talent." Spielberg and Gottlieb also tried to rouse studio interest in "a comedy about life in the Catskills," but "the deals kept falling apart because of Spielberg being locked in as director."*

Undeterred, Spielberg began work on another idea for a flying movie, in collaboration with a young screenwriter named Claudia Salter, whom he also met through Medavoy. *Ace Eli and Rodger of the Skies,* the first Hollywood feature to bear Spielberg's name (he received story credit), was set in rural Kansas in the 1920s and dealt with the troubled relationship between a barnstorming pilot, Eli (Cliff Robertson), and his son, Rodger (Eric Shea). As the characters appeared on screen, the father is a drunken, abusive, pathological lout who carouses from town to town, exploiting his false romantic image as a dashing flier and great ladies' man, while his embittered twelve-year-old son tends to his dissipated needs, pays his bills, and flirts pathetically with his women. In the first scene, Eli crashes his plane, killing Rodger's mother before his eyes; at the end, his sense of manhood shattered, the

---

* Spielberg lobbied unsuccessfully in 1969 to direct *The Christian Licorice Store,* an offbeat tale of a young tennis player searching for the meaning of life. The job went instead to James Frawley, who had worked on *The Monkees* TV series. With Beau Bridges in the lead, the film received only a brief release in 1971.

despondent Eli rejects Rodger's declarations of love and jumps from the plane, leaving the boy an orphan.

Although Spielberg disowned the film made from his story, *Ace Eli* appeared to have been his way of working out some of his confused adolescent feelings about manhood, in a plotline that pointedly reversed the psychological roles of father and son. This bizarre project combined Spielberg's fascination with flying—as symbol of both the exhilaration and dangers of escape —with another theme close to his heart as a filmmaker, that of the irresponsible father figure. It is a theme with personal resonance (however oblique) from his difficult relationship with his own father, whose experiences as a radio operator on B-25 bombers in World War II gave Steven his lifelong interest in aviation.

In 1969, Spielberg had taken the script to Twentieth Century–Fox president Richard D. Zanuck, then in his last year as head of the studio. This was Spielberg's first encounter with Zanuck, who after leaving Fox would produce *The Sugarland Express* and *Jaws* for Universal with David Brown. "I liked the [*Ace Eli*] script and I wanted to buy it," Zanuck recalls. "One of the conditions of buying the script was that [Spielberg] wanted to direct it. I said [to his agents at CMA], 'That's very, very unlikely.' He was trying to get his feature break; it didn't matter where. It wasn't likely because we were looking for experienced, front-ranked directors for our project. They said, 'OK, would you at least meet him and consider him?'

"So he came into my office at Fox. We chatted for a few minutes. For me, it was just kind of a mandatory thing to get out of the way. Little did I know I would work with him so closely, and little did I know that he would turn out to be the Walt Disney–Cecil B. DeMille–D. W. Griffith of our time, all rolled into one. He looked even younger than he was, and he was pretty damn young! He looked about fifteen. I went through this obligatory meeting so I could make the deal to buy the script. He struck me as nice and intelligent, a bit shy, but I didn't see any signs of greatness out of that first meeting. I was meeting a lot of young directors. There *were* many young directors getting work then, but he seemed to be younger than *any* of those directors."

Zanuck agreed to look at Spielberg's *Night Gallery* episode, but it did not change his mind. However, on January 6, 1970, not long after Zanuck left the studio, Fox announced that Spielberg would direct *Ace Eli,* with Joe Wizan producing. Shooting was scheduled for that summer on midwestern locations. Cliff Robertson, a pilot in his offscreen life, met with Spielberg and Salter and contributed ideas to the script. But the plan to have Spielberg direct fell through when producers Robert Fryer and James Cresson took over the project. Aghast at the way the young British director Michael Sarne had just run amok at Fox on their appalling film version of Gore Vidal's *Myra Breckenridge,* Fryer declared, "I don't want any directors under thirty-five ever again!"

Spielberg returned to Universal early that year to resume directing television programs. *Ace Eli* went into production in the summer of 1971 with John Erman directing. As Zanuck says, it "turned out to be a terrible film."* What seems most grotesque about the film is its schizoid presentation of the seamy subject matter, larding over the pain with jaunty visuals mindlessly celebrating the romance of barnstorming. After Fox gave *Ace Eli* a belated release in the spring of 1973, Spielberg publicly charged that his story had been "turned into a really sick film. They should bury it."

"**A** s soon as [Spielberg] was seeing action at other studios, he was called back to Universal," Sue Cameron of *The Hollywood Reporter* wrote after interviewing him in April 1971. Spielberg later claimed that it was the other way around: he was so fed up with freelancing that he begged Sheinberg to let him come back. There was truth in both accounts. Sheinberg had not lost faith in his future, and Medavoy confirms that Universal "perked up" when Spielberg found nibbles elsewhere: "They demanded he come back and do episodic [i.e., series television]." But Spielberg was desperate to get back to work as a director. "I'll do anything," he said. He also promised to be less avant-garde with his camerawork, agreeing "to shoot six inches below the nostrils instead of from a hole in the ground."

Medavoy was vehemently opposed to his young client's return to episodic television. "I said to Steven, 'Look, it's time for you to get out of there. You can't be under contract and do television. I don't want to handle you if you're going to do that.' He said, 'Well, I feel a loyalty to Sid. Besides that, I'm getting a check every week.' I said, 'You're going to have to trust me that I'll be able to get you a movie and get you away from here, because this place is not going to make the kind of movies you want to make. Let me go ask permission.' And he said, 'I can't do it.' I said, 'Well, then, you've got to get another agent. I don't want to represent you if you're going to be doing that.' He said, 'You can't do that to me.' I said, 'I can.'

"I walked him over to Dick Shepherd, who was the head of the motion picture department then. I said, 'Dick, here's your new client, Steven Spielberg. Steve, here's your new agent, Dick Shepherd. I'm outta here.' And I walked away, hoping that he would come back and say, 'OK, let's get outta here.' But he didn't. Guy McElwaine took over [as Spielberg's agent] with Shepherd, but he gravitated toward McElwaine, and that was the end of it.

"He had a lot of loyalty to Universal, and that's where he stayed. I think in part it was the security. Steven always felt at that moment that the world was going to collapse from under him. Most creative people are insecure, and there was an enormous amount of insecurity in him."

By the end of his apprenticeship in television, Spielberg would come to

---

* As a result of studio recutting, Salter and Erman had their credits replaced with pseudonyms (Chips Rosen and Bill Sampson), and Fryer and Cresson also had their names removed (the producing credit went to the nonexistent Boris Wilson).

regard his seven-year contract with Universal as "the biggest mistake of my life." Medavoy came to that conclusion first: "I told him that, and I put my whole relationship with him on the line on that basis. It wound up being *my* biggest mistake, and in the final analysis, staying at Universal wound up being the thing that saved him. Because he wound up directing *Jaws.*"

A M B L I N ' cinematographer Allen Daviau remained in touch with Spielberg throughout the director's early days in episodic television. "He's never given enough credit for the battles he fought at Universal Television," Daviau says, "because they were trying to mold him into a Universal television director, even though when he went in there he stated very firmly he wanted to do feature films and that he wasn't interested in television. They told him, 'Just a little television to warm you up.' Well, of course, they intended to absolutely enslave him.

"There was probably no worse preparation for feature films than the episodic television of that era. Because that was really just 'Bang it out and get it done.' There was another director at Universal who came in at about the same time—I'll not name him—and [in discussions with that director], they were always pointing to Steven as somebody who was doing it the bad way: 'Oh, he'll come to no good end. Now, you listen to us, and you'll have a great career here.' Of course, it was the exact opposite, because Steven knew he had to fight in that atmosphere. And I mean to the extent that he had to literally put it on the line to walk out. They'd be yelling at him, 'You'll never work again in this town' type of stuff. He stood up for it, because he didn't want to get trapped in the episodic thing."

Spielberg's first assignment on his return to Universal was "The Daredevil Gesture," a youth-oriented episode of *Marcus Welby, M.D.,* the popular new series starring veteran actor Robert Young. After that program, which aired in March 1970, Spielberg directed six shows for other series, airing between January and September of 1971. In order of shooting, they were another *Night Gallery* segment, the lackluster "Make Me Laugh" with Godfrey Cambridge;* two episodes of *The Psychiatrist;* single episodes of *The Name of the Game* and *Owen Marshall, Counselor at Law;* and the first regular-season *Columbo.* Despite his frustrations, Spielberg learned to play the studio game, working efficiently under the intense pressures of TV shooting schedules. While acquiring more confidence and finesse as a professional director, he had increasing success in using the medium of episodic television to express his own creative vision and to advance his career as a would-be feature filmmaker.

When Spielberg was assigned to *Marcus Welby,* assistant director Joseph E. Boston recalls, "The word came down to the set that he had only done a student film" (the crew evidently didn't realize that he had directed part of

* Partially reshot by director Jeannot Szwarc.

Night Gallery). "There must have been a dozen first assistant directors on the lot who had ambitions to direct, and many had been working for years as ADs trying to make the transition. Here's a young lad, fresh out of college, who was not going to be coming up through the ranks, but was going to start at the top. So nobody could understand what was coming down! I do remember he was on the phone a lot, and I got the impression he was usually talking about other projects. But he was accepted right away—a nice guy, no pretensions, fast and decisive, who got along."

The "daredevil gesture" of the title is made by teenage hemophiliac Larry Bellows (Frank Webb), who insists on making a high school field trip in defiance of his overly protective mother (Marsha Hunt) but with the support of Dr. Welby. Larry, who also suffers from the trauma of divorce, "has spent most of his life in a padded nursery," but his greatest wish is to "try to act normal, be normal." Spielberg's empathy with Larry's feelings of being an outcast helped the director evoke a performance of seething, manic energy from Webb, a fellow graduate of Phoenix's Arcadia High School.

On a visual level, the *Welby* episode is the least flamboyant of Spielberg's episodic work. Like most TV series, *Welby* tended to look "very formulaic, because of the time pressure," says Marty Hornstein, production manager on Spielberg's episode. "But Spielberg's stuff *did* look a little different. There would always be something a bit extra." Spielberg's fondness for compositions with an extreme foreground-background tension helps energize the character relationships, particularly the flatly written mother-son relationship. The director's characteristically intricate choreography of actors and moving camera can be seen fully developed in a tracking shot in the high school locker room, filmed on the first day of shooting. Assistant director Boston remembers "being impressed by a lovely, flowing master shot he devised that encompassed over-shoulders and close-ups, with split-second cast movements, that enabled the camera to be in a unique position at just the right place and the right moment. After Steven turned it over to the DP [director of photography Walter Strenge] for lighting, I remember coming up to him and asking if he worked on that shot all night. He laughed and said he had just made it up!"

"Of course, they were all freaking out because it was the first day's work and he didn't get a shot by eleven or so," Allen Daviau relates. "He goes in and pulls off this incredible master with zooms and dollies and tracks and rises and falls, and does it all in one shot. He's got the day's work done. Steven said, 'OK, Walter, now let me get a shot with the 18mm [wide-angle lens] by the piano over here,' and Walter Strenge goes, 'Kid, on this show we don't take the zoom off the camera.' Steven loved to tell that story."

ONCE Sheinberg started getting him regular assignments, Spielberg stopped complaining—for a while—about being under contract to the studio. "Universal has done an about-face," he told *The Hollywood Reporter*.

"Thanks to [senior TV and film executives] Jennings Lang and Ned Tanen, they are not treating filmmakers as threats anymore, but as assets. I realize that Sid was up against a lot of the corporate stuff when he first got to Universal. Once he waded through that stuff, he proved to be a guy with a lot of good ideas and he will do a great job for Universal."

The Sheinberg-Spielberg relationship has endured over the years as Spielberg's longest and most important professional loyalty. Early on, they developed "a father and son relationship, even though Sid wasn't that much older than Steve," says *Columbo* writer-producer William Link. "Sid was very responsible for him," recalls TV editorial chief Richard Belding. "Nobody said, 'I don't want him,' but I think it took convincing."

"During Steven's early career, I was his agent," Sheinberg said in a 1988 interview. ". . . He didn't just go from *Night Gallery* to *Jaws*. His career stalled at a number of occasions, and I had to restart it. I've been involved in starting or stimulating the careers of a significant number of directors, but it was different with Steven, because it wasn't just getting the first job. It was having to get a number of jobs. To the point where more than one person wondered, 'What the hell is it with Sheinberg? Why am I being leaned on so much to use this kid?' "

Shortly after signing Spielberg to a contract, Sheinberg began the selling process by arranging a screening of *Amblin'* for some of the studio executives and the entire publicity staff. "They wanted us to realize that this young man was an important asset to the studio," recalls publicist Orin Borsten, who worked regularly on Alfred Hitchcock films. "Of course, we were deeply impressed. There was a very great belief in him. He was anointed. He was the young golden boy, the successor to the great directors." After that, the process by which Sheinberg went about finding television jobs for Spielberg fell "somewhere between selling and ordering," Sheinberg wryly explained. Exactly where on that scale each job offer fell depended on the individual producer, not all of whom had the same degree of autonomy.

One of those who hired Spielberg was Richard Irving, executive producer of *The Name of the Game* (and uncle of actress Amy Irving, whom Spielberg later married). When Dick Irving was looking for a director in the fall of 1970 for "LA 2017," a futuristic episode dealing with ecological catastrophe, Sheinberg told him in no uncertain terms, "I've got just the guy to do this. Use Steven."

The episode's producer, Dean Hargrove, had seen *Amblin'* at one of Sheinberg's screenings. "I thought it was very imaginative, and very impressive relative to his age and resources," says Hargrove, "but I didn't infer from that film the scope of this guy's talent." After Irving passed the word from Sheinberg, Hargrove watched a rough cut of "Par for the Course," Spielberg's episode of *The Psychiatrist* with Clu Gulager as a professional golfer coming to terms with dying of cancer, and Joan Darling as his anguished wife. The show had not yet aired, but it was enough to convince Hargrove of Spielberg's talents: "It had such a distinctive look to it, and it wasn't a particularly exotic show, it was a medical show. There was something about his imprimatur that was discernible even then, the visualization that he brought to it, the staging. He had a very interesting way of moving the camera and moving the actors. He shot some of the most interesting masters I'd seen.* I thought he had an incredible filmic sense that was distinctive from all other directors'."

S HEINBERG took a more soft-sell approach in offering Spielberg's services to Richard Levinson and William Link, the creator-producers of *Columbo*. By the time the series began filming in the summer of 1971, Levinson and Link already had made a pair of TV movies featuring Peter Falk's rumpled but wily detective. The studio was accustomed to treating the literate and successful producers with uncommon deference and respect, and when it came to hiring Spielberg, "There were never any orders from the Black Tower, 'You must use the kid,' " Link recalls. "You had to be impressed with his work, and it had to be your decision. It was the first year of *Columbo*, and we were looking not only for the tried and true, dependable television directors who could do mysteries, but we were also looking for some young blood, some new blood that could add some excitement to the show."

However, TV producers naturally were reluctant to take a chance on an inexperienced director, because, as Link explains, "In television you shoot six or seven pages a day—it's Mack Sennett time. It's not like features, where you have $60 million, and Brian De Palma shoots five-eighths of a page a day. Television is the salt mines of the entertainment field. There is never enough money, never enough time. It wasn't an easy task for Steve to get assignments in television, because he didn't have the credits."

Levinson and Link had seen *Amblin'* at a private screening in the company of Sheinberg and Lew Wasserman. Link considered it "a terrific audition film. *Amblin'* had film techniques that were prevalent in those days, like rack focusing, which came to be a real cliché. But he was more than a remarkable talent. I mean, you didn't *see* things that burnished from a kid." But what finally "sold Dick and me that the kid really had something," Link says, was the same sample of Spielberg's work that had earlier convinced Hargrove: a rough cut of "Par for the Course."† "Then we had to sell him to Falk," Levinson recalled. "People were saying then that Steve was a technical director, that he could handle cameras but not actors. We knew that wasn't true, but we had to convince Peter." "Peter preferred to go with the tried and true, and Spielberg was a wild card," adds Link. "It wasn't just verbal encomiums that would sell Mr. Falk. Peter is very bright, and it was hard to pull the wool over his one eye. We had to show him film. We showed him the Clu Gulager–Joan Darling *Psychiatrist,* and he was very impressed."

Even after that, Spielberg had to pass another formidable hurdle. The

---

* A master is a full scene, or part of a scene, filmed in a single uninterrupted shot.
† Levinson and Link created *The Psychiatrist* series, but were not involved in producing it.

cinematographer for his *Columbo* episode, "Murder by the Book," was Russell L. Metty, who had won an Oscar for Stanley Kubrick's *Spartacus* and had worked on four films with Orson Welles. After meeting Spielberg, Metty told the producers, "He's a kid! Does he get a milk and cookie break? Is the diaper truck going to interfere with my generator?" "Metty was a crusty old guy, with barnacles all over him—he would always refer to Orson Welles as 'The Kid,' " Link recalls. "Russ was a guy in his sixties, and here's this twenty-one-year-old kid [Spielberg was actually twenty-four at the time]— it's not a generation gap, it's a generation *chasm.*"

The cameraman initially complained about Spielberg's unorthodox techniques, telling the producers, "Your hot-shot director has me in this room down on Sunset Boulevard which is four walls of glass. Where the hell do you expect me to put my lights?" "We didn't know what he was talking about," Levinson admitted. "We didn't know anything about lights. And to our eternal credit, we said, 'He's the director. Do what he says.' "

But during the shooting, Link says, "Steve used to call us from the set and say, 'Come on down.' We said, 'Steve, we've got six more shows to write and produce. You're doing a great job. The dailies are wonderful.' He'd say, 'Come on down.' We finally figured out he had nobody to talk to. He was the youngest person on the set. While waiting for setups, he was lonely. I don't think there was anybody he could bond with on those sets. We would go down on the set or go to our own bungalow and schmooze with him."

THAT same summer, Spielberg was hired to direct an episode of the new *Owen Marshall* lawyer series. "We were handed him," admits Jerry McNeely, its cocreator and executive story consultant. "The Black Tower wanted him working. My first inkling that this was somebody out of the ordinary was the producer, Jon Epstein, telling me how pleased he was we were getting Spielberg. He was just a kid, but he had done *Night Gallery, Marcus Welby,* and *The Psychiatrist* with Joan Darling. My memory is literally that he did not have a beard. I don't mean he wasn't *wearing* a beard—I mean he looked too young to have *grown* a beard yet. He looked like he was maybe fifteen or sixteen years old. That was a startling thing, right off the bat. I was goggle-eyed: 'Here's a director! And it's The Kid!' By the time we started, I realized that this was *not* a fuzzy-cheeked kid. He knew what he was doing.

"What's really remarkable is that the genius was visible that soon. For people like Sheinberg to take a chance on him, it's one thing to give him a TV show to direct, but it's another to let him be the star warming up in the bullpen. There was definitely that feeling at the time. Jon Epstein said, 'We got this kid genius.' I don't think Jon meant it literally—I don't think he knew the *size* of it. But those were the terms they were throwing around."

• • •

"**T** E L E V I S I O N is basically a producer's medium," notes *Name of the Game* producer Dean Hargrove. "The producer is the one who makes the final decisions on casting and editing. In films the director is everything, but in television, directors tend to be more of an employee." But even though Spielberg made no major changes in novelist Philip Wylie's script for "LA 2017," the young director "clearly made [the show] reflect his sensibilities," Hargrove says. "He brought his own imagination not only to the visuals in the piece, but in the way he played it. It had a consistent acting style—a little more than real but not unreal. Steven was shrewd in casting—we did it together—and he got along with the actors very well."

Spielberg's most expressionistic work for episodic TV, with its vision of a future so polluted that Angelenos have to live underground, "LA 2017" allowed the director wide latitude for nightmarish visuals. Anticipating Ridley Scott's apocalyptic images of 21st-century Los Angeles in *Blade Runner,* Spielberg used red and orange filters and fire-blackened Calabasas landscapes to represent the bleak, deserted surface of southern California. His sinuous tracking shots through the city's subterranean living quarters (filmed at the Hyperion sewage treatment plant), populated by a frenetically choreographed cast, convey the feverish, claustrophobic sense of hell on Earth. Although the storyline is fairly standard sci-fi melodrama about rebels trying to overthrow a fascistic ruling class, led by the suave Barry Sullivan (the whole cautionary tale turns out to be a hallucination by series regular Gene Barry), Spielberg makes his most telling points about environmental pollution without resorting unduly to verbal rhetoric. His ability to conjure up such a compelling futuristic vision is especially remarkable given his twelve-day shooting schedule and $375,000 budget for what amounted to his first feature-length film in Hollywood. One of four series rotating under Universal's "Four-in-One" umbrella on NBC, *The Name of the Game* ran in a ninety-minute time slot, which, after commercials, left seventy-four minutes of film to tell the story.

"Steven had a very short schedule for such an ambitious show," Hargrove says. "He was loyal to the schedule, and he was very prepared. He would show me his shot list in the morning before he would shoot. He didn't operate off a literal storyboard, but I think he had it in his mind. There was no guesswork. Some directors would start with watching the rehearsal and then see how to shoot it. Steven worked the other way around. He would tend to start with his particular vision of how a scene was physically, like Hitchcock would do. He stayed with the picture through the dubbing process, which was something directors didn't normally do."

"Some directors put in token appearances [in the editing room], and some were into their work enough to want to be sure it was done as well as it could be," says "LA 2017" film editor Frank Morriss. "Steve was one of those. He had his hand in as much as he could get it in. He was very inventive and amazingly knowledgeable about editing. He was just a little punk, but [his personality] was like a fountain. I learned a *ton* from Steve. My relationship with Steve never seemed like work to me. It was all so much fun."

When "LA 2017" aired on January 15, 1971, NBC gave it unusually vigorous promotion because of its offbeat qualities and the timeliness of its subject matter. *Daily Variety* reviewer Jack Hellman found the program "a dramatic thunderbolt on ecology. . . . Unlike other shows dealing with ecology in documentary form, this bizarre concoction had all the feel of high drama with all the stops out. . . . Steven Spielberg directed with firm strokes."

"That show opened a lot of doors for me," Spielberg said.

I F "LA 2017" prefigured the flamboyantly visual filmmaking style for which Spielberg would soon become famous, his *Owen Marshall* episode, "Eulogy for a Wide Receiver," showcased another side of his talents, the more low-key humanism that would become predominant in such films as *The Color Purple* and *Schindler's List*. Though it could have been just another clichéd TV message-melodrama, "Eulogy" proved affecting in its three-dimensional portrait of high school football coach Dave Butler (Stephen Young), whose pressure tactics prove fatal to his star player, Steve Baggett (Anson Williams), a boy with a concealed rheumatic heart condition.

When he was assigned to *Owen Marshall,* Spielberg was offered a script about a young opera singer. "Steve just hated it," recalls story consultant Jerry McNeely. "Today I see why, but at the time we all thought he was a spoiled brat. It was a very talky, quiet, involved, plotty kind of thing, and obviously Steve was looking for a way to do *his* things. He asked, 'Do you have anything else?' So we looked around and found 'Eulogy for a Wide Receiver' [written by Richard Bluel]. Steve said, 'God, I would rather do this, but it needs work.' So I spent a weekend and put it through a heavy rewrite."

Spielberg brought to the project not only his practical experience filming grade school and high school football games, but also a sharply critical perspective on school athletics. The wimp who was bullied by the jocks he wrote about for his school paper responded viscerally to the script's attack on the paramilitary nature of high school football and to the torment of the player who literally kills himself for his Vince Lombardi–like coach.

"The day before we were supposed to start," McNeely remembers, "Steve came in and said, 'Oh, God, I'm depressed. I went to see *Pretty Maids All in a Row.'** Steve said *Pretty Maids* did a lot of the things filmically that he was planning to do. He thought he was in fresh territory with the high school football setting. It was a minor glitch. There was never any sense of his having gotten lost. On the football field, Steve had a long boom and dolly

---

* The 1971 Roger Vadim black comedy starred Rock Hudson as a high school football coach who sleeps with female students and turns out to be a murderer; it also featured one of Spielberg's *Owen Marshall* cast members, John David Carson.

shot—it starts in the stands and comes down, trucks along with the actors, and fellows them onto the field. There's nothing unusual about that today with the Steadicam, but in those days that kind of shot could have taken a day or two. Steve had stuff like that in our one-hour television movie. Moves that you'd take a day or two to get, he'd get in an hour and a half!"

The second half of the show took place on the courtroom set. "On a lawyer show, you're stuck in that set," McNeely notes. "Every week you're shooting fifteen pages on that courtroom set. Everybody's going to be sitting down except one person. They're not fun to shoot. We had seen good, solid TV directors on *Owen Marshall,* but right off the bat with Steve, we sat down and watched and said, 'Man, this is different!' They were running a projector in the courtroom [showing football footage], and he had shot through the spokes of the projector. He switched focus from the projector to a kid sitting on the other side. I hadn't *seen* that shot."

Spielberg also showed precocity in working with the actors. The star of the series, Arthur Hill, was an actor whose distinguished stage career had included a Tony Award for the creation of the role of George in Edward Albee's *Who's Afraid of Virginia Woolf?* Shortly after he began working with Spielberg, Hill told McNeely, "This kid is really something."

"I was astonished, first of all, at the ability of someone so young to be able to handle people," Hill remembers. "I was even more astonished at his eye for the camera. He seemed to be able to *see* more than other people saw. He didn't seem to waste any time. He didn't seem to get caught up in what directors often do when shooting courtroom dramas—eating up camera time, eating up miles and miles of film. He seemed to cut on the floor. We knew that this boy knew about the camera. But to find that he really knew what to do with actors! He had a nice manner, which is very helpful for a director. That gets you a long way. When a director has the attitude, 'I don't know everything about this, but would you like to try something?,' you're willing to knock yourself out for the director."

S PIELBERG once recalled that he "had some bad experiences with TV stars," although he did not specify which actors he meant. On the first day of shooting his *Columbo* episode, "Murder by the Book," Spielberg and series star Peter Falk found themselves faced with the unpleasant task of shooting a scene with a supporting cast member who was "not sober and was stumbling around," Link reports. "Steve was crushed by this. The show was going to be important to him, and he had set up an elaborate master. He had this whole thing worked out.

"That was the thing that impressed Dick and me about Spielberg: Here's this kid who could stage a master. Most directors can't do it; they don't have a clue. With most directors, it's all talking heads. Spielberg could stage it like theater. His setups were always beautiful. His shots were never boring. He would avoid dead-on shots. He would come at you with interesting angles."

When the actor showed up incapacitated, Spielberg quickly had to rethink his approach to the scene. "On a feature you can shoot around" such a problem, Link notes, "but here you can't. You *go*. Unfortunately, what he had to do was break down his master; he had to do coverage. He was very disappointed, but we were impressed because he was resilient."

But by that stage in his career, Spielberg has recalled, "I was already saying, 'Life's too short to worry about the size of someone's trailer. Or the fact that they don't like the hairdresser because the hairdresser has coffee breath.' Little petty things used to make me crazy. Actors not wanting to hit a mark, wanting to stage themselves, wanting to give themselves direction, not wanting to hear any of my ideas. I only had a few negative experiences in TV, but it kind of soured me along those lines." After he started directing theatrical features, Spielberg tended to avoid working with major stars. He usually casts character actors rather than superstars in lead roles, which not only has made his life easier on the set but also befits his overriding thematic interest in "Mr. Everyday Regular Fella."

The casting of Peter Falk as Columbo, the Everyman detective, was what Link calls "one of those marriages made in television heaven." But the perfectionistic Falk's battles for creative control of *Columbo* were legendary. Spielberg considers the seventy-six-minute "Murder by the Book" one of his two best TV episodes, along with the "Par for the Course" episode of *The Psychiatrist*. Of the seven initial *Columbo* episodes filmed in the summer of 1971, "Murder by the Book" was the second to go before the cameras, but it was chosen to inaugurate the regular run of the series on September 15, and it remained the creators' favorite episode of that long-running series. Nevertheless, the director's diplomatic comments on working with Falk suggest he did not feel entirely in charge of the situation.

"The *Columbo* was fun," Spielberg said in 1977, "because *Columbo* was an experience in helping, but mostly watching, Peter Falk find this terrific character. . . . Peter was still finding things. I was able to discover 'Columboisms' along with Peter that he's kept in his repertoire." However, Link disputes the notion that Spielberg added anything to the character of Columbo, which was "fully formed when Spielberg came in. We had done two pilots with [Falk as] Columbo. We had all the kinks out when we did the series."

"Let's face it, we had some good fortune at the beginning," Falk recalled. "Our debut episode, in 1971, was directed by this young kid named Steven Spielberg. I told the producers, Link and Levinson, 'This guy is too good for *Columbo.*' Let me tell you the thing I most appreciated about Steven. I'm rehearsing a scene where I'm walking up a street talking to a guy, and it suddenly dawns on me: there's no camera around that I can see. Steven was shooting me with a long lens from across the street. That wasn't common, twenty years ago. The comfort level it gave me as an actor, besides its great look, artistically—well, it told you this wasn't any ordinary director."

Spielberg's elegant but relatively unobtrusive direction of "Murder by the Book" reflected his growing maturation as a professional filmmaker. The droll teleplay about an untalented mystery writer (the magnificently unctuous Jack Cassidy) with a homicidal envy of his partner (Martin Milner) was credited to the series's story editor Steven Bochco, later the successful producer of such series as *NYPD Blue* and *L. A. Law*. Unlike in "Eyes" or "LA 2017," Spielberg did not need to resort to showy visual flourishes to energize a clichéd storyline. "When I was first starting out, I used a lot of fancy shots," he recalled. "Some of the compositions were very nice, but I'd usually be shooting through somebody's armpit or angling past someone's nose. I got a lot of that out of my system and became less preoccupied with mechanics and began to search more for the literary quality in the scripts I was reading."

From the opening shot of "Murder by the Book," which begins on an extreme overhead view of the murderer's Mercedes driving along Sunset Boulevard and glides back from an office window to show his unsuspecting partner working at the typewriter, Spielberg gracefully uses the camera to create suspense and involve the viewer's emotions. His unconventional use of sound helps conjure up an ominous, unsettling mood: throughout the opening sequence, the car is eerily silent, and we hear only the sound of the clattering typewriter. Spielberg suggested the use of this motif to composer Billy Goldenberg, who synthesized typewriter sounds as part of the musical score.

When it came to mixing the sound for another murder scene, Spielberg and Link came up with a chilling editing device, perhaps inspired by a similar touch in Alfred Hitchcock's 1929 *Blackmail*. "Usually the producer or associate producer mixes the picture," Link says. "Usually your director goes on to something else. Not Spielberg. Spielberg was right there. The cliché [in showing a woman being attacked] was a big scream. Spielberg and I both decided we were going to cut out the scream and go to black [using only music over the image]. My partner hated it. To the day Dick died, he hated it. It was an abstract thing we were doing." That was the only creative disagreement Spielberg encountered with Levinson or Link. "This is the only picture I produced," Link says, "where Dick and I saw the director's cut and said, 'Freeze it.' Steve was annoyed. He said, 'There is twenty feet I want to get rid of.' We said, 'Steve, be our guest, shake out your twenty feet.' "

Reviewing "Murder by the Book," Tony Scott of *Daily Variety* had some reservations about the script but commented that the program "moves expertly along at [the] hands of director Steven Spielberg." Spielberg had gone from "tyro" to "expert" in the Hollywood trade press in only two and a half years!

"W E are very proud of this one," Spielberg and his collaborators on "Par for the Course" proclaimed in a trade advertisement when NBC aired the program Spielberg considers "my best work in television."

Filmed in the fall of 1970 and aired the following March 15, that episode of *The Psychiatrist,* with Clu Gulager as the dying golf pro, was "one of the most brilliantly directed shows I've ever seen," Sid Sheinberg told an interviewer shortly after shooting was completed. Sheinberg's opinion was widely shared at the studio. After the show received its first internal screening, recalls TV editorial supervisor Richard Belding, "There wasn't a word. Everybody had tears in their eyes. It was just a hell of a show. *That* was the starting of Steve."

The feeling of something extraordinary in the air had begun to get around the lot when the show was still shooting. "Steven shot so much film on that they could have made a feature," Chuck Silvers remembers. "One day, I happened to pass Bill Wade, the head of the camera department, on the street. He told me, 'You've got to go down to the soundstage. It's something you'll never see again. Your friend Spielberg is directing.' I said, 'I've seen people directing before.' He said, 'You've never seen a crew stand there and *cry.*' They were shooting Clu Gulager's death scene. I didn't go down there, but a couple of other guys did, and they said it was dead quiet at the end of the scene. Spielberg said, 'Cut,' and it still remained dead quiet *between* shots."

Spielberg attributed the intensely personal qualities of "Par for the Course" and his other *Psychiatrist* episode, "The Private World of Martin Dalton," largely to the fact that producer Jerrold Freedman allowed him to have "a lot of input into the writing of the shows. So it was a real challenge." In "Private World," scriptwriter Bo May created a protagonist with strong resonances of Spielberg himself: a child (Stephen Hudis) who escapes from his troubled family life into a world of fantasy and comic books. "Several elements of this sensitive show point to Spielberg's excellent rapport with children," Marc Wielage wrote in a 1982 article on Spielberg's TV work. ". . . Both episodes of *The Psychiatrist* are marked by fascinating Daliesque dream sequences, with excellent cinematography by Lloyd Ahern. These TV shows are closer to the heart of Spielberg's current work than any of his other programs, with unusually sensitive, three-dimensional characters caught up in crises that challenge their everyday lives."*

"Par for the Course" (based on a story by Thomas Y. Drake, with a script by Drake, Freedman, May, and Herb Bermann) seemed unexpected terrain for such a young director, with its intimate portrait of a man coming to terms with his impending death. But the story, and the unusual creative freedom he was given by the producer, enabled Spielberg to draw on previously unexplored emotional depths from his own childhood experience. The filming of that program, Spielberg said, was "the first time since my 8mm days when I could have an idea at nine o'clock in the morning and incorporate that idea into the show at two o'clock in the afternoon."

---

* Using "The Private World of Martin Dalton" as flashback fodder for another *Psychiatrist* episode directed by Jeff Corey, Universal cobbled them together into a feature titled *Whispering Death,* which played in Europe and had its American premiere on CBS-TV in 1980.

He gave as an example a scene in which two of Gulager's golf partners visit him in the hospital: "As it was written, they're so uncomfortable: Gulager has faced his death many times, but these two men can't face it along with him. They can't share his acceptance, and eventually they have to leave. I thought it would be very moving—it was just an idea I had in the morning—if these two golf partners went out to the eighteenth hole with a shovel and dug out the entire eighteenth hole, put it in a shoebox, stuck in the flag, brought it to the hospital room, and laid this thing on him. So in the scene he gets the gift, opens it up, and here's the dirt and the grass and the flag. It was wonderful. Clu began to cry—as a person and as an actor. His immediate response when the camera was rolling was to burst into tears. He tore the grass out of the hole and he squeezed the dirt all over himself and he thanked them for bringing him this gift, the greatest gift he had ever received. It was just a very moving moment that came out of being loose with an idea. Everything didn't have to be locked down because of so many hours in the day and so much film in the camera and so much money in the budget."

The best-remembered scene in "Par for the Course" involves Joan Darling, who plays Gulager's wife. Chuck Silvers gives a vivid recollection of the unusual way Spielberg shot the scene: When she learns from a doctor that her husband has only a few days to live, "she goes into his room knowing this and she puts on a bright face. She comes out in the hallway, and all of a sudden you know from the look on her face and from her body language that she's just barely hanging on. She sees a pay phone at the end of the hallway. She gets on the phone and she's trying to put through a long-distance call to her mother. She has a terrible time handling the conversation. My God, it was truly great acting.

"She turned sideways to the phone, the camera was in very close. I thought, Here it comes, she's going to come totally unglued. You hear the phone pick up, and she turns her back to the camera. No director in his right mind is going to leave her face! But the camera starts to pull back and you hear her say one word: 'Mama.' Steven is able to present intimacy by doing the opposite thing—the opposite of what anybody else would have done. The whole thing was like that. He broke all the rules and did better by breaking them."

When she was offered the role in "Par for the Course," Darling "was living on Cape Cod and trying to decide whether to retire from the business. I got a call from my agent, 'Can you be on the set at Universal at ten in the morning?' Some girl fell out, and the producers remembered me from *Marcus Welby*. I told them, 'I can't get there till noon.' They picked me up at the airport and took me straight to wardrobe. I hadn't met Steven Spielberg yet. When I come on the set for the first time, I always case the director to see how he works. I was looking around for the director, and I see this kid in a cowboy hat. I went over and eavesdropped. He said a couple of things to Clu and I thought, Oh, my God, this is a real director!

"Later that day we still hadn't met, and I was sitting under a tree. Steven came up to me and said, 'You know, when Jack Kennedy was shot, Jackie Kennedy—' I said, 'Don't say a word. I know exactly what you mean.' We had an immediate, nonverbal communication. It was the beginning of trust between us. I knew that he wanted my best stuff and that he would be receptive. When he said, 'like Jackie Kennedy,' I knew what he meant. It was her way of placing her manners, her way to behave out in front of abject terror. I understood that and knew how to do that. He trusted me that I understood it. That is the absolute good direction—you drop an analogy that feels yummy to the actor, but doesn't dictate.

"I realized right away that his understanding of psychology is as complex as mine. We both have an incredible enthusiasm, an unsullied childlike enthusiasm for the world and for being in it. We both have a curiosity, a sophisticated interest in human behavior. He has an enormous soul. He *sees* so much. I'm not talking visually—he sees the details, he sees the dynamic of a person. I have to reach to catch up with him. 'Par for the Course' is an astounding piece of work. This piece was all adult content. I was so impressed with his adult understanding of the world. I don't think since this piece did he really show the world what he was capable of in this area until he made *Schindler's List.*"

Darling later became a film and television director herself, and directed two episodes of Spielberg's TV series *Amazing Stories,* including his sister Anne's haunting tale of childhood, "What If . . . ?" "When I first started directing," Darling remembers, "I called him up and asked him, 'What should I do?' He said, 'Get a real good pair of shoes.' I said, 'OK.' The second time I got a feature, I called him, and he was on the set of *Close Encounters of the Third Kind.* He said, 'Don't shoot a lot of people going in and out of doors.' I literally asked him, 'Steven, when the archivists come and ask me what kind of advice you gave me, do you want me to tell them you said—' He said, 'Well, it really doesn't work.' I told him, 'I don't know anything about the camera. How should I decide where to put the camera?' He said, 'Notice where you're standing when you watch the rehearsal and put the camera there.' That's so profound a statement, because it focused me on, 'What kind of story am I telling?' "

Daily Variety reviewer Tony Scott praised "Par for the Course" as "magnificently" directed. "Gulager's powerful interpretation of the dying golfer, railing against fate, is an unsettling reminder of the frailty of life. Miss Darling deserves special attention as the wife who lives with life-in-death, and in the scene where she calls her mother long-distance, she creates a poignant portrait of what can happen when too much accumulates. . . . The Gulager-Darling relationship is beautifully rendered."

"Young Steve Spielberg from his direction of that small film was firmly established as one of the most exciting talents in town," Cecil Smith of the *Los Angeles Times* wrote in 1973. Smith added that he had been Darling's "profound admirer" ever since seeing "that gut-wrenching performance."

Chuck Silvers was so moved by Spielberg's direction of "Par for the

Course" that he made a point of asking his protégé, "Steven, how the hell do you know what pain is? In your young life, how do you know about pain?"

Spielberg told him, "Every week I used to go visit my grandfather in the nursing home [when Fievel Posner was living near the Spielbergs in Arizona]. I just watched him. I'd just play, and I'd watch him and I'd watch my mom and I'd watch people in the hospital."

"What he obviously observed was not what was going on on the surface, but what was important," Silvers realized. "The little kid was standing back and observing. I think he's been watching people for as long as he's been able to see. He somehow is able to see what's behind the surface."

SINCE 1968, Spielberg had been living with Ralph Burris in an old two-bedroom writers' bungalow at 3649½ Regal Place across from Universal, a small but convenient San Fernando Valley dwelling whose only distinction was that Bobby Darin had written his hit song "Splish Splash" while living there.

"We didn't hang out that much together," Burris remembers. "He had a couple of different girlfriends; one was an agent. We tried to do things together, but the truth is we led separate lives."

Their parting as roommates was precipitated by two upheavals in their lives. One was natural and the other was economic.

"Steve rescued me from the earthquake of '71," Burris recalls. "It happened at six A.M. [on February 9, with the worst damage located in the San Fernando Valley]. I had been out partying the night before and I was pretty wasted. When the earthquake hit, I woke up and envisioned a tidal wave coming over the mountains. So I threw a cover over my head and started chanting—I was into that shit in those days. My room was in the back of this little house, and Steve's was in the middle. Steve came running in and said, 'It's an earthquake! Get out!' We went running through the living room— stereos were falling down, but the place didn't fall down. We were on a hill, out by the swimming pool, and we could look out on the mountains. We could see the earthquake coming—the hills were rolling, and we could see transformers exploding. The whole valley turned to liquid. We had a lot of damage, but we didn't own that much. I freaked out and went to Hawaii. He signed [a new contract] with Universal and bought a house."

Spielberg's deal, signed in December 1970, was described by the director as "a more liberal amendment" to the exclusive seven-year contract he had signed two years earlier. *Daily Variety* reported Spielberg now had "a five-year exclusive pact as a producer and a six-year nonexclusive contract as a director for feature films, vidpix and [episodic] TV." The new deal gave him just enough freedom to keep him from wanting to leave Universal for greener pastures and never return, but it still gave Universal first call on his services. It also allowed Spielberg to put down modest roots in Hollywood, enabling him to make a downpayment on a small house in casual but fashionable Laurel Canyon, which he bought for $50,000. Shared with a cocker spaniel named Elmer, the house was decorated largely with movie posters, in a style Spielberg described as "bachelor funky."

After producing the 1971 feature *The Second Coming of Suzanne,* Burris tried unsuccessfully to produce another film. He then embarked on a busy career as a production manager, but he has not worked with Spielberg since they made *Amblin'* together. "We went our separate ways," Burris says. "I see him occasionally. I have a signed poster of *E.T.* at home: 'To the longest friendship I've ever had.' "

S PIELBERG'S social life after he moved to Laurel Canyon revolved around moviegoing or small gatherings at home to watch movies and TV shows with his friends. He tended to avoid large Hollywood parties, but when he went to them, he was all business. Joan Darling marvels at "how incredibly smart Steven was about the things that needed to be done socially to be successful in the business." But he also found pleasure in the social advantages of being a successful Hollywood director. "There was no way any woman was going to think of him as a nerd," Darling says. "It was fun for him to date and have pretty women go out with him. I always thought he was a really attractive guy. His sense of humor, his playfulness—he's my kind of man." Even in his early twenties, she felt, Spielberg had an unsatisfied urge to settle down with the right woman and have a family: "Family was really important to him."

Darling and her husband, Bill Svanoe, a singer and screenwriter, became part of Spielberg's circle. "We would go out to a movie and get a bite to eat and talk about the movie afterward," she recalls. "We would lie around on the floor and laugh. We would write three-page movies together. I have one we wrote about a lobster. We would just laugh until we would make ourselves silly. Steven and Bill and I went out to the Riverside Raceway. I had a Super-8 camera. I handed it to Steven and he shot a whole film. He and Bill were interested in gadgets—not just movie gadgets, but all kinds of gadgets. One time Steven called us and said, 'You've gotta come over to this bowling alley at the corner of La Cienega and Santa Monica.' It had the first video games, fighter-pilot story-type games, and he was just overwhelmed with fascination. He's an extraordinarily curious person.

"We were all ambitious and wanting work and none of us was getting the kind of work we wanted to do. Steven knew he wanted to do features. We would talk about what we wished to do [in features], if Steven could get a directing job. I remember saying to my husband, when Steven was very discouraged trying to sell a script and break in, that he always had a positive, forward motion, whatever he may have been suffering inside."

Not everybody sympathized with Spielberg's frustration. Jerry McNeely, the story consultant on *Owen Marshall,* remembers an incident shortly after

Spielberg directed his show for that series. McNeely and the producer, Jon Epstein, were walking on the Universal lot when "Steve drove up in a nice little green Mercedes convertible and stopped. He had a gripe about something, I can't remember what it was. Steve drove off and Jon said, 'Yeah, kid, how many kids your age have a Mercedes convertible? Be happy you're working.' "

"TV for me wasn't an art form. It was a job," Spielberg recalled in 1995. "I actually, because of television, didn't know for a while there whether or not I wanted to continue making film, because I felt that it was like working in a sweatshop and I wasn't getting any of that stimulation, that gratification that I even got making 8mm war movies when I was twelve years old. I didn't have that passion, because television sort of smothered the passion. It's only when I got into feature films—actually when I got into TV movies and made *Duel*—that I kind of rediscovered the fun about making films."

N I N E

" T H E

S T E V E N   S P I E L B E R G

B U S I N E S S "

O N November 22, 1963, the fantasy and science-fiction writer Richard Matheson was playing golf in Simi Valley, California, when he heard the news that President Kennedy had been assassinated. Matheson and his golfing partner, writer Jerry Sohl, stopped playing and headed back toward Los Angeles. Matheson recalls that as Sohl drove through a narrow canyon, a truck began tailgating them at a dangerously high rate of speed: "I'm sure the emotion with which I reacted to that experience was so much more extreme because we were going through the trauma of the Kennedy assassination. Partially we were terrified, and partially infuriated, turning our rage about the Kennedy assassination into rage at the truck driver. We were screaming out the window, but the truck driver's window was closed and he couldn't hear it. My friend had to pull up, skidding onto one of these dirt places [turnouts] in the road. In the writer's mind, once you survive death, you start thinking of a story. The story idea occurred to me and I jotted it down on the back of an envelope. I tried to sell it to *The Fugitive* and several other TV series. They thought, 'There's not enough there.' So I thought, 'Guess I've got to write it as a story.' "

Matheson's gripping short story about a battle to the death between a truck and a car, "Duel," was not written until seven years later. The author,

whose scriptwriting credits also include several classic *Twilight Zone* episodes, adapted "Duel" for Spielberg's TV movie version, which aired on
November 13, 1971, as ABC's Saturday night Movie of the Weekend. The
critical praise and the reaction from those in the industry who saw *Duel*
vaulted the director, a month before his twenty-fifth birthday, into the leading
ranks of Hollywood filmmakers.

Stephen King has given a vivid appreciation of the electrifying visual and
aural qualities Spielberg brought to Matheson's story: "In this film, a psychotic trucker in a big ten-wheeler pursues Dennis Weaver over what seems
to be at least a million miles of California highways. We never actually see
the trucker (although we do see a beefy arm cocked out of the cab window
once, and at another point we see a pair of pointy-toed cowboy boots on
the far side of the truck), and ultimately it is the truck itself, with its huge
wheels, its dirty windshield like an idiot's stare, and its somehow hungry
bumpers, which becomes the monster—and when Weaver is finally able to
lead it to an embankment and lure it over the edge, the noise of its 'death'
becomes a series of chilling Jurassic roars . . . the sound, we think, a *Tyrannosaurus rex* would make going slowly down into a tar pit. And Weaver's
response is that of any self-respecting caveman: he screams, shrieks, cuts
capers, literally dances for joy. *Duel* is a gripping, almost painfully sus-
penseful rocket ride of a movie."

D U E L was a perfect match of story and director. Spielberg has always
tended to place his protagonist—"Mr. Everyday Regular Fella"—in an extraordinary situation testing his abilities to survive and overcome the tedium
and terror of mundane reality. Spielberg remembered his reaction when his
secretary, Nona Tyson, showed him Matheson's story in the April 1971 issue
of *Playboy:* "I was just knocked out by it. And I wanted to make it into a
feature film."

By the time Spielberg read "Duel," Universal already had bought the film
rights for George Eckstein, a producer on the Robert Stack segments of *The
Name of the Game* TV series. Matheson's magazine story was brought to
Eckstein by Steven Bochco, the young writer and future TV producer credited with writing Spielberg's *Columbo* episode. "I hired Dick Matheson to do
a script," adds Eckstein. "He and I developed the script together." Matheson
at first resisted Universal's offer, "Because I didn't see how you could get a
whole movie out of it—it was just one guy in a car. At one point I suggested
having his wife aboard so he would have somebody to talk to. Thank God
they paid me no attention."

"We were all facing deadlines," Eckstein relates. "I was looking for a
director. The script was floating around. Steven Spielberg got ahold of the
script and came in my office and said he wanted to do it. I knew Sid [Shein-
berg] was very high on him, and I had seen *Amblin';* Sid had shown it to all
the producers on the lot. It was charming, and it was wonderful that a

twenty-one-year-old kid had directed this, but it was just a nice little picture. There were no hints of genius.

"What most impressed me about Spielberg was that his idea of how to do *Duel* was very much in sync with my idea of how to do it, which was to shoot primarily from the point of view of the driver, to keep the camera inside the car and not drop back, or to drop back as seldom as possible. I also was impressed with Steven's eagerness to do the project. You work with a lot of directors, it's a job, but he was *excited*. His enthusiasm was infectious for everybody who worked with him. And he did his homework. He was a young director you knew could shoot a show in the time he was given."

Some consideration was given to making *Duel* as a theatrical film, but that proved a hard sell both to the studio and to creative talent. Universal told Spielberg he could make it as a feature if Gregory Peck would agree to play the lead, but the veteran actor refused. Matheson considers that fortunate, because making *Duel* at theatrical length "wouldn't have worked. Even extending this, as they did later, to a theatrical didn't work. They had to add a lot, [eighteen] minutes. It was so tight at seventy-three minutes, it was perfect. You can't expand perfection."*

After being rebuffed by Peck, Eckstein took the project to Barry Diller, ABC's vice president in charge of movies for television (Diller later became a prominent film studio executive). At first, recalls Eckstein, "Barry felt it wouldn't sustain a ninety-minute time slot, which equaled seventy-three minutes of film." But then Diller watched Spielberg's *Psychiatrist* episode "Par for the Course," and that convinced him Spielberg could make *Duel* work as a Movie of the Week.

THE greatest directorial challenge Spielberg faced in preparing *Duel* was to avoid visual repetition, because the film is essentially one long chase. The problem was exacerbated by the tight shooting schedule (sixteen days) and the budgetary necessity of shooting much of the film on a fifteen-mile stretch of road winding through six arid canyons along Highway 14, thirty to forty miles north of Los Angeles (near the stretch of desert highway where Spielberg shot *Amblin'*). But the young director of *Duel* proved to be "an incredibly inventive guy," says the film's editor, Frank Morriss. "Many sequences were shot in the same area, going around the same turns, the same hills, the

---

* Four sequences (two written by Spielberg and two by Eckstein) were added in 1972 for the theatrical version, released overseas. Spielberg's were entirely visual: the opening from the point of view of Weaver's car as it leaves his garage and heads out onto the highway (the TV version started with the car on the open road), and the truck's attempt to push the car into a train. The other added sequences were those of the truck coming to the aid of a stalled school bus, and Weaver on the telephone arguing with his wife (Jacqueline Scott), who is shown at home as their two sons play with a toy robot (a Spielberg touch). Although Eckstein says Spielberg made no objection at the time to the husband-wife exchange, the director later regretted shooting the scene, which Matheson considers "so soap-opera-ish and unnecessary."

same road. It was never apparent in the picture. We were able to use fifteen different angles of the truck going around a curve and you do not notice it."

Already accustomed to using storyboards to preplan his episodic TV shows, Spielberg went one step further with his innovative storyboard for *Duel:* "I had an artist paint an entire map, as if a helicopter camera had photographed the entire road where the chase was taking place. And then that entire map had little sentences—like, 'This is where the car passes the truck,' or 'This is where the truck passes the car and then the car passes the truck.' And I was able to wrap this map around the motel room [in Lancaster where he stayed during location shooting], and I just crossed things off. When we were shooting, I'd try to progress eight or ten inches on the map —sometimes two feet if we had an exceptionally good day—until the entire map was shot. That overview gave *me* a geographical sense, a lot of help in knowing where to spend the time, where to do the most coverage, where to make a scene really sing out." Spielberg also had storyboard drawings of every shot on IBM computer cards, pinned to a bulletin board in his motel room. Each day he took his quota of cards for reference while shooting, tearing them up when the shots were completed.

Filmed between September 13 and October 4, 1971, and rushed to air only five weeks later, *Duel* had a production cost of about $750,000, according to Eckstein, not the $425,000 Spielberg has claimed.* The young director was surrounded by a highly experienced crew, including cinematographer Jack A. Marta (who received *Duel*'s only Emmy nomination), first assistant director Jim Fargo (who later became a director), stunt coordinator Carey Loftin, and unit production manager Wallace Worsley. "Steven was wonderful to work with," says Eckstein. "He was very firm in his opinions. He had very few doubts. He commanded respect in everybody, which was rare in a twenty-three-year-old [sic]. He was not deferential, but he was respectful of the Jack Martas, the people with a lot of experience. And the people around him had as much respect for him. They respected him and they were a little bit in awe of him."

A dissenting view on Spielberg's talents and his relationship with the crew was offered by Carey Loftin, who also drove the truck in *Duel*. The crusty action-movie veteran was not terribly impressed by the young director. "At that point, I don't think he had any strong points," Loftin recalls. "He was a kid. To be honest, I thought anybody could have done it better. *I* could have done better. I'm too old to lie. I disagreed with quite a few things on it."

One of the most chilling aspects of *Duel* is that the driver's face is never seen. We see only his sinister-looking cowboy boots and his arm, disingenuously waving Weaver into the path of an oncoming car. Spielberg followed Matheson's lead in declining to psychoanalyze the truck driver, understanding that it is more frightening to contemplate the existence of unmotivated

---

* Universal invested an additional $100,000 in three days of shooting by Spielberg for the theatrical version.

evil than to ascribe it to some mundane cause. The truck and its driver are as enigmatic in their fathomless malevolence as the shark in *Jaws* or the *Tyrannosaurus rex* in *Jurassic Park*. But Loftin thought, "To do all this for no reason, it didn't make sense. If you have action, you gotta have a reason, or that's a stunt show."

During the first day of shooting, Loftin approached Spielberg and suggested that a scene be added to give the truck driver a clear motivation for seeking revenge. "Look at the truck," Spielberg told him. "It's beat up. It's terrible-looking. It's painted to look worse than it is. You're a dirty, rotten, no-good son of a bitch."

"Kid," replied Loftin, "you hired the right man."

In what Eckstein remembers as "the casting session with the truck," production manager Wally Worsley "brought a bunch of trucks for Steve and me to look at on the back lot. Some looked new, but Steve wanted a truck that looked like it had been around, a street-smart truck." Spielberg chose a battered Peterbilt gasoline tanker truck, which he described as "the smallest one, but the only one that had a great snout. I thought that with some remodeling we could really get it to look human. I had the art director add two tanks to both sides of the doors—they're hydraulic tanks, but you ordinarily wouldn't have two. They were like the ears of the truck. Then I put dead bugs all over the windshield so you'd have a tougher time seeing the driver. Dead grasshoppers in the grille. And I gave the truck a bubble bath of motor oil and chunky-black and crud-brown paint."

Casting the lead human character in *Duel* proved far more difficult. Besides Peck, at least three other actors turned down the role of David Mann, including David Janssen, star of TV's *The Fugitive*. Also considered was Dustin Hoffman, the young star of *The Graduate* and *Midnight Cowboy*. "We were going after feature people," Eckstein says. "We were turned down 'because I don't do television.' We went through name after name. We wanted Everyman, with a vulnerable quality. We were very lucky to wind up with Dennis Weaver." Matheson reports that Universal "finally had to shut down [its TV series] *McCloud* to get Weaver."

Spielberg was delighted at the chance to work with the actor who had delivered such a memorably quirky performance as the cowering, sex-crazed motel clerk in Orson Welles's *Touch of Evil*. In *Duel*, Weaver perfectly embodies an Everyman for the Age of Anxiety, a tremulous worm who turns "Valiant" (as the model of his little red car is ironically named) and hysterically accepts the challenge of an irrational highway duel to prove his dubious manhood.* One of the few major flaws in *Duel* is that David Mann's emasculation is laid out verbally in such a heavy-handed fashion, through voiceovers and other dramatic devices. There is no need to refer to his home life, since the theme is implicit in the action. The problem was exacerbated when the scene was added for the expanded version showing the henpecked Mann

---

* Dale Van Sickle did the stunt driving in the Valiant, with Weaver doing mostly the closeups.

arguing with his unhappy wife about another man's display of sexual interest
in her at a party the night before.

If he were to remake *Duel,* Spielberg acknowledged in 1982, "I'd make it
a little tougher, I'd take all the narration out, all of Dennis Weaver's inner
monologues and probably most of the dialogue. . . . I objected to the amount
of dialogue the network imposed on the show. They forced the producer,
George Eckstein, and the writer, Richard Matheson, to keep adding narration
internalizing Dennis Weaver so the audience would understand his deepest
fears. I don't believe you need that."*

S PIELBERG'S dynamic compositions in *Duel* reflect his awareness of
the importance of point of view in visual storytelling, with the camera alter-
nating between the vantage points of the truck and David Mann inside his
car. Some of the most powerful shots were taken from a camera with a
fish-eye lens mounted on top of the truck as it bears down upon the tiny
automobile, and from a low-slung platform mounted on the front of a camera
car traveling up to 135 miles per hour as it filmed the back of the Valiant
from the angle of the truck's bumper. The upward angle from the camera car
to the hurtling truck made the truck assume what Spielberg called "Godzilla
proportions."

Spielberg and cinematographer Jack Marta also heightened the visual tension by their use of wide-angle lenses, artificially shortening the distance
between the truck and the car. The close-ups of the frantic Mann are so tight
that he often appears to be on the verge of bumping into the camera. Some
were taken from a fixed camera-mount outside the car, but many were shot
with a handheld camera by an operator on the seat or the floor of the car.
The quarters became so cramped that in one accident of framing visible only
in the theatrical version, Spielberg can be glimpsed for a moment in Mann's
rearview mirror, sitting in the back seat.

"When [the studio] saw Steven's dailies the first few days, they were thinking of pulling the rug, it looked so unusual," Matheson reports. But Eckstein
maintains that Spielberg was never in danger of being taken off the picture,
and that Sid Sheinberg was "ecstatic" when he saw the rough cut. "I think
there were some excesses in *Duel,*" the producer adds, "but they were so
much balanced by the excitement or the energy of the piece. Sometimes
with Steven you want to yell, 'Less is more.' That's about his only flaw."

The agonizing slow-motion demise of the truck as it tumbles off the hillside, lured by Mann's driverless automobile, provoked strong opposition
from the network, although it was one of the film's most memorable images.

---

* Spielberg suggested cutting all the voiceovers for the international theatrical version, keeping
only the dialogue in Weaver's interactions with other people, but the distributor (Cinema International Corporation), would not go along with such a radical idea. Eckstein says he and Spielberg
still managed to remove "a lot" of narration and other dialogue for that version.

"In the script, the truck explodes. I thought that was too easy," Spielberg recalled. ". . . I thought it would be much more interesting to show the truck expiring, slowly ticking away—the truck's a nasty guy, you want to see him twisting slowly, a cruel death. I just took it upon myself. I thought, 'I'm the director, so I can change the script. I just won't blow the truck up.' Well, when the network saw the film, all they kept saying was, 'It's in your contract to blow the truck up, *read* your contract.'" Eckstein finally persuaded network executives not to force Spielberg to blow up the truck.

Staging the climactic scene required the rigging of a spring-loaded hand throttle attached to the steering wheel of the truck, so that Carey Loftin could keep the truck going in the direction of the hillside after climbing outside the cab and jumping off at the last minute. Spielberg had six cameras set up at various spots around the cliff to record the scene late in the afternoon on the last day of shooting, October 4.

"I damn near went over the cliff myself," Loftin remembers. "I pulled the throttle and the whole damn thing fell off. I got out and realized the truck was slowing down. I thought, 'I gotta get my right foot on the throttle.' I tried to get the speed up. I shouldn't have done it."

As the truck raced toward the edge of the cliff, all Loftin could think about was that he was due at the opening of Florida's Walt Disney World the following day to perform an automobile stunt.

"I could have turned the truck and just called it off, but I had to go to Florida. I rolled and wound up right on the edge of the cliff myself. It was over three hundred feet down. The truck wound up at the bottom and the little car was on *top* of the truck."

"The scissors in my editing room came down just a frame after Carey's butt is out of the frame," Spielberg said. "He's at the beginning of the shot. Leaping for his life."

"I remember sitting in dailies watching the crash," Eckstein says. "It was the last day. It *had* to be the last day. The first five cameras really didn't have it. We were afraid we were going to have to piece it together. I remember that terrible moment sitting there. Finally the last camera got it. The relief in that room was palpable."

To create the death cry of the truck, Spielberg first thought of mixing truck noises with the distorted sound of a woman's scream. "So I went into the studio and screamed," recalls Joan Darling. "He wanted a death-of-the-monster sound." In the end, however, Spielberg decided not to use Darling's scream, but the sound of a famous monster of filmland. One of the sound editors came up with the idea of distorting the roar of the prehistoric Gill-Man from Universal's 1954 horror movie *The Creature from the Black Lagoon—* the chilling sound Stephen King recognized as a "Jurassic roar."

Postproduction on *Duel* had to be rushed to make the November airdate. Because of Spielberg's frequent use of multiple cameras, there was so much film to edit (95,000 feet, a shooting ratio of twelve to one) that Frank Morriss had to bring in four other editors and several sound editors to help him assemble different sequences. For thirteen days, Morriss recalls, Spielberg kept "roller-skating from editing room to editing room" to supervise their work.

" I S A W the rough cut of *Duel,*" Barry Diller recalled, "and I remember thinking, This guy is going to be out of television so fast because his work is so good. It was sad because I thought I'd never see him again. It was a director's film, and TV is not a director's medium."

In a promotional move that was unusual for a TV movie and reflected the studio's high degree of pride in *Duel* and in Steven Spielberg, Universal threw a press preview party on the lot, showing the film simultaneously in several screening rooms. The first public indication that something extraordinary was about to appear on the nation's television screens came from *Los Angeles Times* TV columnist Cecil Smith. On November 8, Smith reported on another advance screening held at Universal by Spielberg and Eckstein for film students from Claremont College, some of whom were older than the director. Asked by Professor Michael Riley how he would have approached *Duel* differently if it had been made for the big screen, Spielberg replied, "Time. I took sixteen days shooting . . . I would have liked fifty. Time to try things." Smith hailed *Duel* as a "unique" TV movie, because it was virtually a silent movie and "so totally a cinematic experience." He added, "Steve Spielberg is really the *wunderkind* of the film business. At twenty-four, he looks fourteen and talks film like a contemporary of John Ford. He's been making movies all his life."

That article prompted many people in the film industry to stay home and watch *Duel* the following Saturday night. They were alerted further by a full-page ad placed in the Hollywood trade papers that Friday by Spielberg, Eckstein, Matheson, and composer Billy Goldenberg. Over a picture of the truck bearing down upon the helpless Weaver standing in the road, the ad said simply: "We invite you to a unique television experience."

In the following Monday's *Daily Variety,* TV reviewer Tony Scott wrote, "Film buffs rightfully will be studying and referring to 'The Duel' [*sic*] for some time. Finest so far of the ABC Movies of the Weekend, [the] film belongs on the classic shelf reserved for top suspensers. Director Steven Spielberg builds step by logical step towards the exquisitely controlled climax and symbolic conclusion of Richard Matheson's teleplay. Anyone switching channels after the first five-minute hooker is in need of whole blood."

That week, Spielberg received about a dozen offers to direct feature films. "I visited Steven in his office," Matheson recalls, "and the walls were plastered with letters of congratulations from people in the business."

Although it performed only moderately well in the TV ratings, *Duel* became Spielberg's first feature-length film released theatrically (aside from the single theatrical screening of *Firelight)* when the expanded version was distributed in Europe, Australia, and Japan. A sleeper success at the box office, grossing $8 million, it established Spielberg's reputation with international critics and won the grand prize at the Festival de Cinema Fantastique in Avoriaz, France, as well as the prize for best first film at Italy's Taormina Film Festival.*

The veteran critic of *The Sunday Times* of London, Dilys Powell, "kicked off my career," Spielberg once declared. Before the film's international debut in England in November 1972, "She saw *Duel* and then arranged for another screening in London for the critics. As a result, the film company spent more money than they'd intended on the film's promotion."

"You would hardly think that so slight, indeed so seemingly motiveless a plot (the script is by Richard Matheson) would be enough for a film of ninety minutes," Powell wrote. "It is plenty. It is plenty because the increase in tension is so subtly maintained, because the rhythm and the pace of movement is so subtly varied, because the action, the anonymous enemy attacking or lying in wait, is shot with such feeling for dramatic effect. . . . Mr. Spielberg comes from television (*Duel* was made for television); he is only twenty-five. No prophecies; but somehow I fancy this is another name to look out for."

Traveling to Europe to promote the film (his first trip abroad), Spielberg found that with his new artistic status, people expected him to pontificate on weighty issues. In Rome, the young director "tried to steer clear of politics during his first European news conference, despite efforts by Italian journalists to politicize his 'social comment' film," *Variety* reported in September 1973. "While expressing certain dissatisfaction with American politics, Spielberg said he intended the film as an 'indictment of machines' and a fight for survival between man and machine-made danger, denying contentions by journalists that the danger is the Establishment or the struggle between two Americas." When Spielberg would not agree that the truck and the car symbolized the upper class and the working class, four journalists walked out on him.

For some of the leading international directors, *Duel* marked Spielberg's seemingly overnight arrival as one of their peers. François Truffaut, Fred Zinnemann, and Spielberg's idol, David Lean, were among those expressing admiration for the film. "I knew that here was a very bright new director," Lean said later. "Steven takes real pleasure in the sensuality of forming action scenes—wonderful flowing movements. He has this extraordinary size of vision, a sweep that illuminates his films. But then, Steven is the way the movies used to be."

• • •

---

* When it received a belated U.S. theatrical release in 1983, *Duel* did little business, because it had been so widely seen on television, where it still is shown frequently in its longer version. The original TV version is no longer in release.

"U NTIL *Duel,* I thought maybe I'd made the wrong decision signing that seven-year Universal contract," Spielberg reflected in a 1977 interview. ". . . After *Duel,* everything fell into place and made perfect sense."

Even though he suddenly found himself a hot director, Spielberg still remained bound by that onerous contract. He was more eager than ever to make features now that he had demonstrated his talent so spectacularly in television. Shortly after the end of production on *Duel,* Spielberg began shooting *Something Evil,* a stylish but predictable horror film for CBS-TV. "Universal had nothing for me," Spielberg recalled, "and rather than watch me sit in my office and kill time, they said, 'Go ahead.' " Spielberg's subsequent TV movie for Universal, *Savage* (1973), was "an assignment bordering on *force majeure. Savage* was the first and last time the studio ordered me to do something."

Something Evil, written by Robert Clouse, starred Sandy Dennis and Darren McGavin as a couple who escape city life for a Pennsylvania farmhouse only to find that the house is inhabited by a demon seeking to possess their adolescent son (Johnny Whitaker). Echoing William Peter Blatty's 1971 novel *The Exorcist* (the film version of which was released in 1973), *Something Evil* allowed Spielberg and cinematographer Bill Butler room for some flamboyantly surrealistic visual imagery of the family's battle with the demon, but the formulaic plot made the film seem a bit of a comedown after the freshness of *Duel.*

Spielberg remembers *Something Evil* primarily as a technical exercise, and Butler responded enthusiastically to Spielberg's "desire to experiment . . . the newness of his thinking." "I loved Steve's tenacity," says his acting teacher Jeff Corey, who played a possessed Pennsylvania Dutch farmer in the TV movie. "I remember him spending a whole day on one shot. He covered a whole party, starting from exterior to interior, going through the living room and the kitchen, in one shot. He wouldn't let go until he had it. I was a little more pliable [as a director], but he certainly had guts."

When *Something Evil* aired on January 21, 1972, as the CBS Friday Night Movie, *Daily Variety* reviewer Dave Kaufman wrote, "Clouse engages in a good deal of hokum in his teleplay, stressing weird special effects more than characterization, and director Steven Spielberg does the same. Thus Sandy Dennis, as the femme driven into hysteria, begins her performance on a high key and never wavers. There is no shading for real impact. . . . Spielberg displays a keen awareness of numerous techniques, but not of [the] importance of vivid emotional involvement."

Still stymied in his efforts to persuade Universal to let him make *The Sugarland Express,* Spielberg continued to look elsewhere for his opportunity to break out of television. Following his abortive attempt to direct *Ace Eli* for Fox, the next film announced as Spielberg's feature "debut" was *McKlusky,* a Burt Reynolds car-chase picture written by William W. Norton Sr. for United Artists. Already in danger of being typecast, the director of *Duel* began preproduction on *McKlusky* in February 1972. Spielberg met with Reynolds, started casting other parts, and scouted locations in the South, but then "realized it wasn't something that I wanted to do for a first film. I didn't want to start my career as a hard-hat, journeyman director. I wanted to do something that was a little more personal." By April, Joseph Sargent had signed on to replace Spielberg as director of *McKlusky,* released in 1973 as *White Lightning.*

The next, and last, TV movie Spielberg directed was *The Savage Report,* which aired as *Savage* on March 31, 1973.* Dealing with what later would become known as "tabloid television," Spielberg's NBC World Premiere movie starred Martin Landau as crusading TV political journalist Paul Savage and Barbara Bain (Landau's wife and *Mission: Impossible* costar) as Savage's producer. The teleplay by Mark Rodgers, William Link, and Richard Levinson revolved around the blackmailing of a nominee to the U.S. Supreme Court (Barry Sullivan). "Universal had a commitment to do a replacement series, and NBC was in bed with Universal—anything Sheinberg wanted to do got on the air, in most cases," Link says. "Sheinberg came to Dick and me and said, 'I've got an old script [by Rodgers] you might be able to adapt. Let's do it as a pilot.' We didn't like that script. We rewrote it, but there's just so much you can do—it was sow's purse time. We told Sid, 'The only way we can make this is if we have a brilliant director. Get Spielberg.'

"Steve reads the script and agrees with us—it stinks. We called Sid and said, 'Why don't you call Steve and hotbox him. Get him to do it.' We never told Steve. I remember it was on a Sunday, a rainy day, and Steve had a meeting on the twelfth floor [with Sheinberg]. Dick and I crossed our fingers. Steve came back almost in tears. We asked, 'What happened?' We were playing dumb because we had set this up. He said Sheinberg gave him a big hype, bending his arm that he had to do the script. Steve had made the mistake of saying that he wasn't in the Universal business, he was in the Steven Spielberg business. Maybe he got a little angry. Sheinberg hit the roof and threatened to put him on suspension. They had a very good relationship, but Steve was hurt by that. We told him, 'You ought to do it, Steve. You don't want to be on suspension.' I don't think we admitted to him that we had Sheinberg sell him on it. In a way he was right—the script is not very good, but he did a brilliant job."

Martin Landau considered the show "ahead of its time" as a critique of TV news, and claimed it never led to a series because "we got shot down for the wrong reasons. It was clearly political. The network news department took exception to our show. I got a call from Sid Sheinberg and he said, 'It's the best thing we've got, NBC is crazy about it, it's on the air.' And it went from there to being buried in a week's time." *Daily Variety* reviewer Tony Scott, on the other hand, felt the seventy-two-minute movie would have trouble

---

* That was the night Spielberg joined much of Hollywood's elite and President Richard Nixon to honor the dying director John Ford at the first American Film Institute Life Achievement Award dinner in Beverly Hills.

generating a series because it "barely scrapes by in [the] plot department." But he added that *Savage* "generates interest thanks to Steven Spielberg's superior and often inventive direction, and character studies."

RENEWING his campaign to make a feature at Universal, Spielberg shifted some of his focus from Sid Sheinberg to another executive, Jennings Lang. Spielberg shrewdly courted Lang, who helped him make the transition to features. "When Sid was bringing Steven along, Jennings was the patriarch," says Peter Saphier, Lang's assistant at the time. "After all, Jennings was a mentor to Sid, and he felt a real connection to Steven."

The roguish, coarse-talking Lang was a legend in Hollywood circles. A former agent whose clients included Joan Crawford and Joan Bennett, he carried on an affair with Bennett that in 1951 provoked the actress's estranged husband, producer Walter Wanger, to shoot him in the groin. Subsequently joining MCA when it was still a talent agency, Lang was largely responsible for building MCA's Revue Productions, and then Universal TV, into a powerhouse of production and syndication. By the time Spielberg came to the studio, Lang was a senior vice-president of Universal Pictures, outranked in the MCA hierarchy only by board chairman Jules Stein and president Lew Wasserman. Lang's title carried with it the rare power to approve and supervise a slate of theatrical films.

While directing TV shows in the early 1970s, Spielberg began spending time at Lang's home, also befriending the executive's wife, singer Monica Lewis, and their adolescent son Jennings Rockwell (Rocky) Lang. "My father was involved in nurturing and advising Steven," Rocky says. "I recall Steven being around a lot when *Sugarland* started. His girlfriends would come over to dinner with him. Through my eyes, my parents were sort of surrogate parents to Steven, and I looked at Steven as an older brother."

Now a director and producer himself, Rocky already was trying his hand at filmmaking by the time he was in eighth grade and met Spielberg. "Steven sent me a clapper board for elementary school graduation, and he put 'Congratulations' on the clapper board," he recalls. "After Steven looked at my Super-8 movies, he put the curse on me. He sent me a photo of himself when he was younger and told me I was more advanced than him at the same age. It put tremendous pressure on me. My sister-in-law is a psychologist, and she said she knows a lot of young filmmakers who are afflicted with 'Steven Spielberg disease'—all these kids set their sights on being the next Steven Spielberg, and they get depressed when they aren't as successful as he was at an early age. It's created this sort of neurotic behavior around him."

But Spielberg was "great with kids, a really accessible person," Rocky says. "My conversations with Steven were about my girlfriend problems, my tennis, my school, and the movies I was making—he made me feel I was on the right track. The only advice Steven gave me was to be passionate about what I wanted to do. That was something I needed to learn, because I viewed the business from very early on as a commercial enterprise, like any business; I wanted to be a success and have the perks of it. He told me, 'Take a project you really love and take it all the way,' making a statement and leaving something behind, looking at it more seriously."

Spielberg's relationship with the Langs paid off when Jennings Lang agreed to let him work with screenwriters Hal Barwood and Matthew Robbins to develop the screenplay that became *The Sugarland Express*.* The project's working title, *Carte Blanche,* was an obscure reference to the seemingly unlimited freedom enjoyed by Spielberg's young fugitive couple driving through Texas with their hapless hostage from the Texas Department of Public Safety. Around the time Spielberg bowed out of United Artists' *McKlusky* in the spring of 1972, he had pitched *Carte Blanche* to the young writers by reading them the Associated Press article about the 1969 Texas incident. After talking over the story with the director for a couple of days, Barwood and Robbins wrote an outline, which UA agreed to let them develop into a screenplay. But UA soon had second thoughts, and Spielberg took *Carte Blanche* back to Universal, which had rejected the story three years earlier.

This time "it happened fast," said Spielberg. "And everything was done just as I wanted to do it." On April 11, 1972, the director showed the outline to Lang, who put the project into development that very afternoon. The following day, Spielberg and his writers flew to Texas for a week of research. Barwood and Robbins wrote the first draft in thirteen days, but Universal once again decided not to make the movie; in Hollywood jargon, the studio put the script "in turnaround." Only a few weeks later, however, it was revived by Richard D. Zanuck and David Brown when they signed an exclusive, multipicture production deal with Universal. Lang had given Spielberg's career a critical boost by agreeing to finance the writing of the script, but he was eased out of the production when the studio agreed to let Zanuck and Brown make the picture. "Jennings got very, very upset about *Sugarland Express*—he felt the studio had taken it away from him," his assistant Peter Saphier reports. "He had a 'cerebral incident.' He passed out in the commissary over *Sugarland*. He went home for several months."

During the filming of *Sugarland,* Lang was the executive supervising the project, but that was a largely meaningless task since, as Saphier notes, "The deal with Zanuck/Brown was that they had no one supervising them while shooting." Lang later became involved in the studio's decision to purchase the film rights to Peter Benchley's *Jaws,* the novel that served as the basis for Spielberg's 1975 commercial breakthrough film. But that project also wound up as a Zanuck/Brown production, and Lang unhappily became just another

---

* Barwood and Robbins previously had written seven unfilmed scripts, including *Clearwater,* a futuristic tale set in the Pacific Northwest. It was announced by Universal as a Spielberg/Lang project in October 1973.

Universal producer, making the Sensurround spectacles *Earthquake* and *Rollercoaster* and other even more forgettable pictures.

After Lang suffered a debilitating stroke in 1983, few Hollywood people visited him. In 1994, two years before his father's death, Rocky Lang said, "It's brutal—if you can't help them, your best friends are not there. Steven is still there. He's been terrific with my parents. He's never forgotten them. He sends them presents for their birthdays, he sends them presents on their anniversaries, he sends his movies for them to watch. He's been over as much to see my dad as some people who owe him more."

Speaking of his own relationship with Spielberg, however, Rocky admitted, "I lost touch with him after *Jaws,* when he and my father stopped working together. I have very little contact with him now. We're in touch maybe once a year. I don't know Steven the person anymore. His standing socially has grown to the point where he spends the night at the White House. When you get to that status, everybody wants something from you. I wish he would help [me] out more than he does, but I don't call him, because I don't want to fall into that category. I have a very warm spot for Steven, and I feel a tremendous loss that I don't have a relationship with him now."

N O T long after turning down the opportunity to hire Spielberg as a director at Twentieth Century–Fox, Richard Zanuck was fired as head of the financially troubled studio by his legendary father, Darryl F. Zanuck. Following a brief interlude as executives at Warner Bros., Zanuck and David Brown, his former right-hand man at Fox, formed their own production company in 1972, signing with Universal shortly thereafter. It was a coup for Universal to have such prominent executives come aboard as producers, and Lew Wasserman's respect for their abilities ensured Zanuck/Brown an enviable, but not unlimited, degree of creative freedom.

"Before signing on at Universal, in the six to seven weeks when Mr. Brown and I were deciding where to go, we were reading scripts," Zanuck recalls. "Guy McElwaine [Spielberg's agent] gave me the script of *The Sugarland Express,* which Steven wanted to direct. I sent it to Mr. Brown and he liked it. I told Steven, 'I'll tell you a secret. We're going to make a deal at Universal.' He said, 'Oh, no, it's in turnaround from Universal.' I said, 'That makes it a little harder, but doesn't knock it out of competition.' "

At that point, Zanuck and Brown met with Wasserman, who told them, "This picture's a downer, and audiences won't respond to it. It will play to empty houses, but what do I know? You're the guys who make the picture. If you want to make it, make it." Wasserman "turned out to be right with that evaluation," Zanuck admits, "but his belief in us also led to *The Sting* and *Jaws,* where the [MCA] stock quadrupled. Frankly, I wish more studio executives operated today like Lew Wasserman. He backed people he had a belief in, instead of bringing them in and telling them what to do. He was always looking down the road.

"Universal had a very high respect for Steven, and I think they had plans to have him direct something. Steven was surprised we were making *The Sugarland Express* at Universal. We had a meeting in the commissary. He slid into the booth and said, 'God, I can't believe it! Are you going to be my producer?' I was known as a studio head. He said, 'Who's actually going to do the line-producing work?' I said I was. He said, 'That's great. Are you going to be there every day?' I told him I was. I had a very close working relationship and friendship with Steven."

"*Sugarland* was basically Steven's film, one that he had developed with Matt and Hal, and the studio, recognizing the inexperience of the three of them, wanted to have a strong producer involved," says William S. Gilmore Jr., the Zanuck/Brown production executive who served as the film's unit production manager. "Steven had a wonderful ability to play to people older than him, as if saying 'Help me, I'm just feeling my way,' when in fact he had tremendous talent. It seemed like everybody in the unit had something to prove. Steven had to prove he could direct a feature as opposed to television. Zanuck had to prove he could produce films instead of being just the production manager for his father. There was such an *esprit de corps*. We all loved the idea, and we were doing a picture in a non-studio way, with a small, handpicked crew moving like greased lightning."

"Producing is an Excedrin headache job," Spielberg told *The Hollywood Reporter* shortly after the film was released. "If I can avoid it, I will. Zanuck and Brown served the picture well and gave me total freedom, the kind of [freedom from] controls I never had in television. Dick Zanuck backed me all the way. . . . In our few disagreements, he was right and I was wrong."

The third time proved lucky when Spielberg's feature directing "debut" on *Carte Blanche* was announced in the Hollywood trade papers on October 17, 1972. The next day, Barwood and Robbins turned in the second draft of their novelistically nuanced screenplay, which underwent further revisions throughout the filming (Spielberg shared story credit with the two screenwriters). The title became *The Sugarland Express* that November, although for a while the filmmakers considered simply calling the movie *Sugarland,* the name of the small town where the "tragic fairytale" comes to an end.*

In adapting the saga of Bobby Dent for the screen, Spielberg turned Dent's wife, Ila Faye, into the movie's central character, Lou Jean Poplin. In *Sugarland,* the couple's two-year-old son has been removed to a foster home, and it is Lou Jean who persuades her convict husband, Clovis, to break out of a prerelease center—with only four months left on his sentence—to retrieve the child. The young mother's desperation over being separated from her baby, and the tragedy-of-the-absurd that results from it, provided fertile ground for a working-out of Spielberg's complex feelings about his own family. Spielberg conceived Lou Jean as behaving like a spoiled child,

---

* The town where the climactic events actually took place was Wheelock, but the filmmakers borrowed the name of the town of Sugar Land and then filmed those scenes in Floresville.

sexually manipulating Clovis to go along with her whims and finally throwing an infantile tantrum that causes him to walk into the fatal ambush. Lou Jean's reckless need for her child is less an expression of mother love than an irresponsible prolongation of her own childhood.

Universal insisted that Spielberg and the producers provide commercial insurance for the offbeat film by signing a major female star to play Lou Jean. After meeting with several female stars, who all passed on the script, Spielberg became convinced that Goldie Hawn, best known as the giggling blond sexpot of the *Laugh-In* TV series, had the blend of scatterbrained charm and underlying mulish obstinancy the part required. "I always thought she *was* a dramatic actress, for she took her comedy very seriously," Spielberg recalled. "So I met with her—we had a great afternoon—and you could tell she was thousands of kilowatts smarter than the people of *Laugh-In* had ever allowed her to demonstrate." Winner of an Oscar as Best Supporting Actress for *Cactus Flower* (1969), Hawn had her own production deal at Universal, and she had been turning down scripts for a year before agreeing to star in *The Sugarland Express*. She was paid $300,000 on a film that, according to Gilmore, cost about $3 million.

Spielberg and Universal hoped the public's affection for Hawn would help them accept a character whose actions worked against audience sympathy. The filmmakers also thought that in the wake of her Oscar, audiences would be intrigued to see Hawn in a demanding, three-dimensional role that was more dramatic than comedic. Spielberg said in 1974 that her Lou Jean would come as "a real surprise to those who only see her as a pie-in-the-face type. She takes herself seriously as a person and is mostly concerned with how far to reach inside a character."

For Hawn, the "most exciting" aspect of the project was the director. "Think of the career Steven's got ahead of him," she said.

W HEN he rolled the cameras on January 15, 1973, Spielberg had just passed his twenty-sixth birthday, making him a year older than Orson Welles was when he began shooting his first feature, *Citizen Kane*. Zanuck vividly remembers Spielberg's first day of shooting on location in Texas:

"I had told the production people, 'It's his first day. Let's start him off slow. Do something relatively simple until he breaks in.' He'd never worked with a crew this big. I didn't want to be there for the first shot; I wanted him to think he was running the show. So I deliberately took my time getting there. I got there about eight-thirty. Jesus, by the time I'd gotten out there, he had already laid out the most complex shot I've ever seen in my life! I walked up to the production manager and said, 'What is this? We're supposed to be starting him off with something simple!'

"By then I had run *Duel* a couple of times, and something with Joan Crawford ['Eyes'], and I had been with him for three or four months on a daily basis, but it was a small body of work, and you never do know until that day, standing there with a hundred people doing things, whether a guy has it or not. I knew right then and there, when I saw him in action, that he knew what he was doing. He was very definite in his opinions. He was in command. I could sense it, because I had been around long enough with a lot of great directors—the Robert Wises, the William Wylers, the John Hustons—and I knew almost immediately that he had knowledge and command and ability, and an innate, intimate sense of the visual mechanics of how you put all these pieces together so that the final result is very striking.

"I *still* don't think anyone I've ever worked with knows the mechanics as well as he does. It's like trying to read the mind of a master chess champion who's got all the moves. Like an old-time director did, he knew the capacity of all the lenses and equipment. He knew how to move the camera, when to move it, when not to move it, how to have it move in different ways, how to move people around—he just *knew* it."

"*Sugarland* was his first real location shoot," recalls art director Joseph Alves Jr., who had worked with Spielberg on *The Psychiatrist* and *Night Gallery*. "Steven didn't realize how much other departments could do for him, that he didn't have to do all the visual things himself. When you're young, especially when you do your first little films, you have to do everything yourself. But to rely on others gives you choices. That was something he discovered on *Sugarland,* as opposed to television, when we didn't spend much time together.

"On *Sugarland,* Steven and Bill Gilmore and I went to Texas and drove around together on the initial scout, [four] weeks before we began shooting. I remember when we came back from scouting one day having solved a lot of problems. Within a thirty-mile radius [of San Antonio], we found a number of locations that all sort of fit together. To have that change of topography and less travel time allowed him to have more time to work with his actors and more time to work visually. He said, 'Gosh, you guys are doing a lot of work for me.' We told him, 'Well, that's what we're *supposed* to do. That's what we're hired for.' He said, 'Oh. OK.' He realized that if people do these things, it could relieve the pressure he was under."

Vilmos Zsigmond, the Hungarian-born cinematographer who shot *Sugarland,* says it was "probably the only time when Steven worked as a director that he worked as a conductor and was relying on the expertise of his collaborators. He knew what he wanted, and still he was open—if there was a better way to do it, he would listen. He didn't seem like a novice—he already knew the business, he knew a lot—but I could still help him. He was not experienced enough to know everything. I caught him during *Sugarland Express* when he was just learning—I think he learned more on *Jaws,* and by the time we did *Close Encounters* he knew *everything*. On *Sugarland,* Steven gave a one hundred percent chance to collaborate. Everybody had a good relationship with Steven. He asked the impossible with a smile on his face. How could you say no?"

"Vilmos and I were almost brothers on our movie," Spielberg said at the time. "I'd heard about this crazy Hungarian who lights with six foot-candles [an extremely low level of light] and who'll try absolutely everything. . . . It's an enormous help when egos don't clash and you can creatively exchange thoughts—not on just the momentary problems, but on conceptual ideas as well. Vilmos is the kind of cameraman whom I'd invite into the cutting room, because he would have something to contribute. I would never do that with any other cameraman that I know."

Spielberg and Zsigmond usually ate breakfast and dinner together on location, energetically discussing their plans for the day. One morning when they were having breakfast at The Greenhouse along the Riverwalk in downtown San Antonio, Zsigmond introduced Spielberg to a pretty young waitress. "I wanted to take her out," Zsigmond recalls, "but she was only interested in Steven. She told me, 'I want to meet your friend.' I said to Steven, 'This girl's in love with you.' It became a friendship, and he took her to Hawaii [after the filming]. She came to Hollywood, and he dated her for a long time. He was surprised, actually, that this girl really liked him. It was something new in his life. He was shy in those days." Years later, when San Antonio film critic Bob Polunsky asked him about his memories of making *The Sugarland Express,* Spielberg replied with a smile, "I fell in love in San Antonio once, on the Riverwalk."*

Before shooting began, Spielberg spent many hours with his cinematographer comparing their tastes in movies. "We both liked *Citizen Kane,* we both liked European movies, we liked Fellini," Zsigmond found. Spielberg greatly admired Zsigmond's daringly offbeat work with director Robert Altman on such films as *McCabe and Mrs. Miller* and *The Long Goodbye.* The impressionistic visual style of those films, which freely used natural source lighting, diffusion, extreme variations in light intensity, and long lenses to compress spatial planes, was a major influence on *The Sugarland Express.*

Freeing himself from the visual constraints of television, Spielberg shot for the first time in the Panavision wide-screen format, composing richly textured, multilayered images. But he strove for a grittier, less self-consciously stylized look than Altman's, telling Zsigmond that what he wanted was "European lighting" with "a documentary feeling." He and Zsigmond watched documentaries together, examining them for creative solutions to the problems of location shooting. They agreed to shoot as much as possible with natural lighting and live sound, and to avoid using process photography† for the many scenes inside cars. Spielberg hoped to encounter plenty of rain and to shoot scenes through moving windshield wipers, trying everything

* Besides his new girlfriend, Spielberg brought back two other mementos from the location, the revolving neon chicken sign from the scene at Dybala's Golden Fryers drive-in and the bullet-riddled police car, Car 2311. Spielberg installed the chicken sign in his quarters at Universal and drove Car 2311 around Hollywood before donating it to a museum.

† Rear-projected scenes shot separately from the actors, who are then filmed in front of the "process screen" backgrounds to create the illusion of their presence in those scenes.

to remove Goldie Hawn's "Tinkerbell" aura. Little rain materialized, but the wintry conditions in Texas gave the film a suitably overcast look.

"We considered it an art piece," says Zsigmond.

THE Texas Department of Public Safety, understandably concerned about how its image would withstand a movie about the Bobby Dent affair, initially refused to cooperate with the filmmakers. While location sites in Louisiana and other states were considered, Bill Gilmore eventually persuaded DPS officials that the film "wouldn't portray their people in a bad light. I'm sure I said whatever I had to." That half-truth enabled the filming to proceed along Texas roads, but the film company still had to assemble its own fleet of vehicles for the pursuit of the police car in which Lou Jean and Clovis (William Atherton) are traveling with their hostage, Officer Maxwell Slide (Michael Sacks). Gilmore bought 23 cars at a police auction and rented 17 others from non-DPS sources (the original chase involved more than a hundred police and civilian vehicles). After the film was released, DPS director Colonel Wilson Speir reacted with outrage, insisting that "no law enforcement officer of this department or any other police agency in Texas would conduct himself in such an unprofessional manner."

Both *Duel* and *The Sugarland Express* are road movies, constantly in motion, but in contrast to the earlier film's elemental simplicity, *Sugarland* is almost baroque in its logistical complications. "What is surprising," wrote *Newsweek* reviewer Paul D. Zimmerman, "is Spielberg's breathtaking command of action, the visual sweep he achieves with cinematographer Vilmos Zsigmond, the vision, satiric but strangely beautiful, of an America on wheels." To help keep his bearings, Spielberg, as he had done on *Duel*, had a mural made showing the progress of the chase. He also had Joe Alves storyboard some of the scenes, although much of the action was improvised on location, again with the expert help of stunt coordinator Carey Loftin.

For filming in and around Officer Slide's patrol car, the wheels were removed from a vehicle and it was mounted close to the ground on a flatbed trailer. Not content to shoot only with locked-down or handheld cameras, Spielberg and Zsigmond set up tracks on a platform attached to the vehicle, using a small dolly to film tracking shots alongside the car in motion. They went even further with the help of the newly manufactured, highly compact Panaflex camera, which was so mobile and quiet that it allowed for shots of astonishing dexterity inside the car, with the camera mounted on a sliding board that served as a makeshift tracking device. The Panaflex arrived during the last two weeks of shooting after the Panavision Corp. chose the *Sugarland* company over a hundred and thirty other applicants to give the camera its "acid test" under production conditions. Although he shot the film largely in continuity, Spielberg saved some of the most complex highway shots until the end of filming in order to use the Panaflex.

"We did things on *Sugarland* that had never been done before," marvels Gilmore. "We shot a 360-degree pan inside a car with dialogue. That had never been done before. It was the first film that had a dolly shot *inside* a car, [moving] from the front to the back seat. We did a dolly shot into the back seat at thirty-five miles per hour! We were awed by Steven's knowledge and his basic instincts when it came to doing things with a camera."

"I don't know where Steven got the ideas he tried to do, because I had never seen shots like that," Zsigmond says. "Steven realizes the moving camera is essential for movies. I feel the same way. That's what gives you the third dimension, which is the way movies should be. If you lock down the camera, it's like seeing everything with one eye. It's like shooting in a theater. Movies should be untheatrical. The first time when the camera approaches the police car, we found two roads that converged. With me in the camera car paralleling, getting closer and closer, we go into a close shot. It was a very difficult shot to do, and it was fun to do."

Spielberg and Zsigmond shared a dislike for the crudely obvious use of the zoom lens that was then in fashion, so they frequently employed the Altmanesque device of zooming and panning simultaneously, a fluid technique that disguises the fact that the camera is zooming, yet allows the camera to change perspectives rapidly and with a more subtly disorienting effect on the audience. Spielberg also made striking use of a combined zoom and dolly movement near the end of the film, when the car with the principal characters slowly approaches the house of the baby's foster parents. The camera dollies forward, toward the window and over the shoulder of a sharpshooter, while simultaneously zooming back from the car coming from the distance, framed by the window curtains. This was the technique Hitchcock had used to create James Stewart's subjective "vertigo effect" in *Vertigo,* and which Spielberg later would use to create a celebrated moment of terror in *Jaws.*

At that critical moment before the climax of *Sugarland,* Spielberg's use of that camera technique "suspended animation for fifteen seconds," Gilmore notes. "As Steven moved in, he zoomed out, so the foreground and background were juxtaposed, with the people in the car and the sharpshooter all in the same relation to each other. With two tools fighting against each other, he literally froze time. To this day, I am absolutely in awe of that shot."

Spielberg already seemed to have "the experience of a man forty years old," Zsigmond said in a location interview with *American Cinematographer.* "The way he directs a film makes you think that he must have many features behind him. . . . I can only compare him to Orson Welles, who was a very talented director when he was very young. . . . Most young directors, when they get their first film, somehow get timid; they pull back; they try to play it safe, because they are afraid that they will never get another chance to make a feature. Not Steve. He really gets right into the middle. He really tries to do the craziest things. Most of the shots he gets he could only dream about doing, up until now."

• • •

P E R H A P S the most impressive achievement of Spielberg's direction is that it never lets the spectacle of the chase overwhelm the personal drama inside the car involving Lou Jean, Clovis, and Officer Slide. It was the depth of his feelings about the characters, particularly about Lou Jean, that kept Spielberg plugging away for four years to make something "a little more personal" than the other, less commercially risky projects he was being offered at that formative stage of his professional career.

"A lot of Steven was in that movie, more than in some of his other movies," Zsigmond believes. "He didn't think about commercializing *The Sugarland Express*. He just wanted to make a good movie with good characters. I think Steven has never been better."

Although the fugitive's wife was only mentioned in passing in the newspaper article that triggered Spielberg's interest in the Dent affair, she became his central dramatic focus in the film, emerging as a largely unsympathetic character, a symbol of mother love gone berserk. The film reveals, if not a streak of latent misogyny, a fear of women in the youthful Spielberg, and a deep ambivalence about mothers. It also introduces a recurring theme of Spielberg's films, that of the irresponsible parent. Lou Jean and Clovis, petty criminals both, behave so desperately to get Baby Langston back because they know they have failed so miserably in their parental obligations.

The DPS officer leading the pursuit, Captain Tanner (Ben Johnson), recognizes that Lou Jean and Clovis are not hardened criminals but "just kids." Tanner is more mature and a benevolent father figure, but he too is a failure, abandoning his principled attempt to avoid violence. Most painfully, after giving his personal word of honor to trade Baby Langston for Officer Slide, Tanner has to go back on his word to bring the chase to an end. A familiar face from John Ford Westerns, the weatherbeaten Johnson embodies the rectitude of a nineteenth-century lawman, but in the debased environment of this contemporary Western-on-wheels, he also represents the obsolescence of the cowboy code of honor.

In a 1993 essay on Spielberg's films, "A Father Runs from It," Henry Sheehan observed that "at the bottom of many of the movies lies a dark and forbidding desire to be rid once and for all of one's responsibilities, one's family, one's children. It is that keenly felt urge, usually buried deep within the movies, that gives Spielberg's films their anxious drive and the climaxes their sense of overwhelming relief." Lou Jean's compulsive need to reunite her family at all costs expresses the childlike pain Spielberg continued to feel over his own family breakup, for which, at the time it occurred, he primarily blamed his mother. In his depiction of Lou Jean as a child-woman can perhaps be seen his boyhood recognition that his own mother was "just like a little girl who never grew out of her pinafore." His depiction of the disastrous results of Lou Jean's impulsive, deluded behavior reflects a level of mature understanding in the twenty-seven-year-old filmmaker—his recognition of the impossibility of putting the pieces of a shattered family back together. Spielberg's examination of irresponsible parent figures and broken families, from *The Sugarland Express* to *Schindler's List,* has led him to film terrifying images of the primal trauma of children being separated from their parents, and to explore the unbearable grief on both sides. The irrational behavior, even madness, that can result from such trauma is the profoundly unsettling emotional core of *The Sugarland Express.*

"Every film I find out a little more about myself," Spielberg said after completing *Sugarland.* "I've discovered I've got this preoccupation with ordinary people pursued by large forces. A personal movie for me is one about people with obsessions."

For a director who so often has been accused of sentimentality, Spielberg started his feature career with a remarkably unsentimental character study, as well as an unsparing mockery of what Vincent Canby in his *New York Times* review called "the American public's insatiable appetite for sentimental nonsense." Lou Jean and Clovis are lionized as folk heroes by people in towns they pass along the way, who line the roads, waving at them and shoving presents into the car, mistaking these two dimwits for genuine symbols of rebellion against an authoritarian state.* In satirizing the carnival-like atmosphere surrounding the Texas chase, partially whipped up by media sensationalists, Spielberg said he was inspired by Billy Wilder's vitriolic 1951 film *Ace in the Hole,* about an unscrupulous reporter (Kirk Douglas) who keeps a man trapped in a cave to turn his plight into a media event.

To screenwriter Hal Barwood, *The Sugarland Express* is about "how Americans find it very easy to confuse notoriety with fame." Such a confused sense of values was a symptom of the major social issues of the time—the social disintegration caused by the war in Vietnam, the loss of respect for authority, the breakdown of the family, and the widespread recourse to violence—and while *Sugarland* does not address the root causes directly, it is a vivid metaphor for the chaos resulting from those problems. But *Sugarland*'s critique of American society is not easily classifiable politically. Spielberg's relatively isolated personal and artistic development tended to keep him out of step with his generation's rebelliousness, and led him to make a withering critique of the romantic, anarchic excesses of the road movie. His film, in which the young couple on the run is less sympathetic than the lawman directing the chase, would not appeal to left-leaning viewers expecting to have their antiauthoritarianism pandered to and their own social prejudices unexamined. Yet it also would alienate right-leaning viewers with its equally scathing critique of the other trigger-happy lawmen and their gun-crazed vigilante followers.

Although he had been uncomfortable with European critics' attempts to read social meanings into the more clearly allegorical *Duel,* Spielberg strove

---

* The low-speed police pursuit of O. J. Simpson in 1994, with members of the public cheering and waving at him from the sides of Los Angeles freeways, made *Sugarland* seem prophetic.

more consciously for social meaning with *The Sugarland Express*. Generally allowing his themes to emerge organically from the action rather than from verbal rhetoric, Spielberg was less successful when he tried to explain his intentions to the press: "I wanted to make *Sugarland* because it made an important statement about the Great American Dream Machine. . . . And it was meant to say something about the human condition which, obviously, isn't terribly optimistic."

Because the theme was so downbeat, Matthew Robbins said that he and Barwood consciously strove for "distancing" effects in their screenplay. They employed a "kaleidoscopic" viewpoint so the audience would not experience Clovis's death as a "shattering event. . . . There were still other figures who were sympathetic in the movie to cling to."

Spielberg's compassionate direction of the actors tended to downplay the comic aspects of the script and heighten the dramatic aspects; contrary to what the writers intended, Clovis's death is indeed a "shattering event" for the audience. Spielberg also carried the script's "kaleidoscopic" approach even farther, not so much for distancing purposes but to heighten the complexity of the film's perspective, through his daring multiplicity of visual points of view and the resulting audience empathy with various secondary characters, including Officer Slide and Captain Tanner, compensating for the audience's distancing from the central character, Lou Jean. The emotional residue from his parents' divorce may have prevented Spielberg from viewing Lou Jean's motherly impulses as anything but destructive, and led him to look more kindly on the well-intentioned but essentially impotent males she has under her control.

Viewers accustomed to films that ask them to identify with a single character—in Hollywood parlance, to "root" for a hero or heroine—inevitably were confused and upset by the complexity of tone in *The Sugarland Express*. Spielberg himself seemed to have second thoughts about his approach after the film's commercial failure, sketching out in 1977 how "if I had it to do all over again I'd make *Sugarland Express* in a completely different fashion." He said he wished he had done the first half of the film entirely from the viewpoint of Captain Tanner, "from behind the police barricades, from inside his patrol cruiser. I would never see the fugitive kids, only hear their voices over the police radio, maybe see three heads in the distance through binoculars. Because I don't think the authorities got a fair shake in *Sugarland*. . . . Then [in] the second half of the movie I would have told the entire story inside the car and how really naive and backwoodsy these people are and how frivolous and really stupid their goals were."

That simplistic remake might have been more successful at the box office, but it is not the film Spielberg actually made. The director's multifaceted point of view makes it possible to experience an unusually wide and subtly inflected range of human emotion.

• • •

SPIELBERG finished shooting in late March 1973, five days over his fifty-five-day schedule; production manager Bill Gilmore says the delays were all attributable to the weather and the shortness of the winter days, which caused them to lose the light early. After editing the film that summer with Edward Abroms and Verna Fields, Spielberg completed postproduction on September 10. *Sugarland*'s musical score was the first composed for Spielberg by John Williams, who became a regular member of the director's creative team. Spielberg had greatly admired Williams's "wonderful Americana scores" for two Mark Rydell films, *The Reivers* and *The Cowboys:* "When I heard both scores I had to meet this modern relic from a lost era of film symphonies. . . . I wanted a real Aaron Copland sound for my first movie. I wanted eighty instruments, a colossal string section. But John politely said no, this was for the harmonica—and a very small string ensemble."

In the fall of 1973, the film was ready for its first public preview. "The studio was very pleased with *The Sugarland Express,*" veteran Universal publicist Orin Borsten recalls. "He wasn't sharpening his talent on it—he was a *full-blown* talent." "You cannot believe the excitement [there was] within our ranks over *Sugarland,*" says production executive Bill Gilmore. "It was so innovative for its time, so exciting, we thought it was going to win the Academy Award for best *everything.*"

Sugarland was previewed on a double bill with Peter Bogdanovich's Depression-era comedy *Paper Moon* in San Jose, the northern California city adjacent to Spielberg's former hometown of Saratoga. Spielberg attended with Zanuck, Brown, Gilmore, Barwood, Robbins, and a delegation of Universal executives.

"The audience loved the first half," Gilmore recalls. "Goldie Hawn was a piece of fluff and she was involved with two nincompoops [Clovis and Officer Slide]; it was all a romp. But when the two sharpshooters came on the scene—we cast two real Texas Rangers [Jim Harrell and Frank Steggall] as sharpshooters—I can remember the audience gasping, 'Oh my God, this is life and death, real flesh and blood.'

"From that moment on, we lost them. I think the mistake was that the audience perceived the film to be another Goldie Hawn piece of fluff, and she brought with her that goodwill. When we became deadly serious, about three-fifths of the way through the film, they sat there in stunned silence. They didn't know what they were looking at. They didn't want to hear about it. That taught me a lesson. We should deliver what they think they are going to see."

Some of the audience members left in tears. And there were some, Barwood recalled, who "walked out with blue murder in their eyes."

Zanuck and Brown wanted to leave the film as it was, but Spielberg persuaded them to let him cut it from 121 to 108 minutes and recut some of the intended moments of comedy in the first half of the film, when he had held for laughs that hadn't come. With the new version, the reaction was dramatically different at film industry preview screenings in the fall and winter. As a result of those screenings, according to *The Hollywood Reporter,* "word went around the Hollywood circuit that a major new director and film were on the horizon."

But with its fears of the film's lack of commercial appeal confirmed by the disastrous San Jose preview, Universal changed the release plans. Originally scheduled for Thanksgiving release, *Sugarland* was delayed to avoid competing with such major commercial entries as *The Sting* (a Zanuck/Brown production for Universal) and Warner Bros.' *The Exorcist.* The plan then was to open *Sugarland* in February at one theater in Los Angeles and one in New York, but Spielberg already was worried that Universal would quickly go wider if the openings weren't successful. At that time, films with any kind of prestige usually were opened in a few theaters in major cities before being released gradually across the country, in what was known as a "platforming" release strategy. Opening a film unusually wide (a "saturation" release) tended to indicate that the studio had little regard for its quality and wanted to get its money quickly, before negative word of mouth could spread. Universal finally decided to forego showcase runs for *Sugarland,* opening it in 250 theaters across the country on April 5. Box-office results predictably were disappointing, a modest $7.5 million gross in the United States and Canada, and an additional $5.3 million overseas. The film eventually made a small profit after being sold to television.

In an interview with *The Hollywood Reporter* three weeks after *Sugarland* opened, Spielberg complained that Universal had failed to capitalize on the Hollywood screenings. "There was a huge four-month gap between those initial screenings and the release," he said. "The immediacy of the word of mouth wore off." But it is unlikely that opening any earlier would have helped, for Hollywood's appreciation of Spielberg's directorial talents wouldn't have translated to the mass audience, and hosannas from leading American and British reviewers made little impression on the public.

S PIELBERG "could be that rarity among directors, a born entertainer —perhaps a new generation's Howard Hawks," Pauline Kael proclaimed in *The New Yorker.* "In terms of the pleasure that technical assurance gives an audience, this film is one of the most phenomenal debut films in the history of movies."

Combining his review with a profile of the director, *Newsweek*'s Paul D. Zimmerman also heralded "the arrival of an extraordinarily talented new filmmaker." Dilys Powell of the London *Times,* who had spotted Spielberg's talent when *Duel* played in overseas theaters, wrote, "One is apt to fear for the second film of a promising young director, but for once anxiety was unnecessary." While noting thematic similarities between *Duel* and *Sugarland,* Powell was pleased to find that this time, "The human element has pushed into the foreground."

Dissenting critics were outnumbered, but Stephen Farber's vituperative commentary on the film in *The New York Times* helped set the tone for subsequent critical attacks on the director. "Kael and some other gullible critics have probably been intimidated by Spielberg's youth, and by his technical facility," wrote Farber. ". . . *The Sugarland Express* is a prime example of the new-style factory movie: slick, cynical, mechanical, empty. . . . Everything is underlined; Spielberg sacrifices narrative logic and character consistency for quick thrills and easy laughs. . . . *The Sugarland Express* is a 'social statement' whose only commitment is to the box office."

Even Kael's review expressed some concern about Spielberg's future development: "Maybe Spielberg loves action and comedy and speed so much that he really doesn't care if a movie has anything else in it. . . . I can't tell if he has any mind, or even a strong personality, but then a lot of good moviemakers have got by without being profound."

"**I**T did get good reviews," Spielberg said of *The Sugarland Express,* "but I would have given away all those reviews for a bigger audience." That disappointment left Spielberg somewhat wary of overtly "personal" filmmaking and more dedicated than ever to surefire crowd-pleasing entertainment.

Internal postmortems by the filmmakers pointed to several reasons why the public rejected the movie. "Bad title" was the diagnosis of Universal publicist Orin Borsten. "So many pictures are ruined by a bad title." Although intended ironically, the title unfortunately played into the Goldie Hawn image that Spielberg otherwise had worked so hard to avoid. Perhaps the commercial fate of the film was inevitable once the decision was made to cast Hawn. "It wasn't a happy picture, and people didn't want to see her in a serious role—they wanted to see her as a goofy gal," Richard Zanuck concludes. Stubbornly loyal to his star, Spielberg said in September 1974 that the film's box-office failure "was not due to the presentation of Goldie as an anti-*Laugh-In* character, but to the promotional campaign, timing, release pattern, and appreciation of the film by the studio. It had nothing to do with Goldie being rejected by audiences."

Not known for sophisticated ad campaigns during the early 1970s, Universal seemed to have even more trouble than usual when it came to selling *Sugarland*. The trailer and the print ads vacillated between portraying it as a shoot-'em-up melodrama and emphasizing Hawn's cuter, more comedic moments. But Spielberg was being a bit disingenuous in pinning all the blame on the studio. As David Brown recalled, "Universal gave Spielberg and us carte blanche in developing advertising and getting outside creative shops, to avoid that studio look. Our early ads were our own; Spielberg himself shot one of them. Our campaigns didn't work." "I now think the right graphics campaign and a plan of attack for releasing a picture are as important as finding a good script and making a good movie," Spielberg told *The Hollywood Reporter* in retrospect. But he admitted, "There's nobody to accuse. This is an immensely difficult picture to sell." It was an especially hard sell to the youth market because of its harshly critical view of its young female protagonist and its more sympathetic portraits of lawmen. Nor was its frontal attack on the public's sentimental gullibility calculated to endear the film to the majority of American moviegoers. In the final analysis, the public's rejection of *The Sugarland Express* probably stemmed from the single overriding fact that, as Lew Wasserman had warned, it was too much of a "downer" for the mass audience.

But as Vilmos Zsigmond says, "It's a shame that Steven doesn't make people remember more of *Sugarland Express*. He just wants to forget it, because he thinks of it as a failure. *I* don't think of it as a failure. It's an artistic triumph."

W H E N he received the bad news about *Sugarland* in April 1974, Spielberg did not have much time to sit around engaging in second-guessing or nursing his wounds. He was on the Massachusetts island of Martha's Vineyard, immersed in preparations to make another film for Zanuck/Brown and Universal. This was no "art piece," but a genre film aimed squarely at pleasing the mass audience.

It was a modestly budgeted thriller called *Jaws*.

" A P R I M A L S C R E A M M O V I E "

WHO WANTS TO BE KNOWN AS A SHARK-AND-TRUCK DIRECTOR?

— STEVEN SPIELBERG, 1973

IN November 1973, with *The Sugarland Express* completed and awaiting release, Spielberg told an American Film Institute seminar that "when you make your first feature in this town, you're incredibly hot, and if you have a good agent, he'll make your next three deals—before your film comes out. Then, if your film comes out and it crashes . . . you've got three films in which to redeem yourself. I have a terrific agent [Guy McElwaine], and he has created the greatest hype. . . . At four studios, he's got me carte blanche to do whatever I want for a reasonable sum of money."

"Carte blanche" was something of an exaggeration. Spielberg was eager to direct Peter Stone's screenplay *The Taking of Pelham One Two Three*, from the thriller novel by John Godey about the hijacking of a New York subway train. After a rough-cut screening of *Sugarland,* United Artists production chief David Picker acknowledged Spielberg's promise. But Picker considered *Pelham* "director-proof" and opted instead for the journeyman Joseph Sargent, who had succeeded Spielberg on UA's *White Lightning.* Then Spielberg passed up another picture that Sargent went on to direct. Richard Zanuck and David Brown offered him *MacArthur,* a screenplay by Hal Barwood and Matthew Robbins about the controversial career of General Douglas MacArthur. Spielberg claimed he rejected the film because he was wary of the logistical problems involved in staging World War II and the Korean War, but Zanuck thinks he "just didn't care for the subject."

Spielberg knew how important it was to choose his projects with care in that formative period of his feature career. On the heels of *Sugarland,* another failure, particularly an artistic as well as a financial failure, could have been a catastrophic setback for the young director. It was around this time that, according to Brown, Spielberg "turned down a script given to him by one of the biggest stars in the world because he didn't think the star was right for the role. In explanation, the young director said, 'Look, if I ever make a picture again, I'm not going to make those kinds of compromises or I will have a very short career.' "

Spielberg's choosiness paid off when he made a development deal for his dream project. An unofficial remake of his 8mm sci-fi feature *Firelight* on a far grander scale, the film that would become *Close Encounters of the Third Kind* was even more deeply personal to Spielberg than *The Sugarland Express*. "I would have gone to great lengths to make it—whether I did it here in this country, or elsewhere," he said. "Somehow I would have found the money. It's a movie I'd wanted to make for over ten years."

He first considered making a documentary about people who believe in UFOs, or a low-budget feature, before realizing that "a picture that depended a great deal on state-of-the-art technology couldn't be made for $2.5 million." *Close Encounters* evolved from a short story he wrote in 1970 called "Experiences," about a "lovers' lane in a small midwestern town and a light show in the sky overhead that these kids see from inside their cars." Borrowing a famous phrase from the ending of the 1951 movie *The Thing from Another World,* Spielberg retitled the project *Watch the Skies* before making a development deal with Columbia Pictures in the fall of 1973.

D U R I N G postproduction on *Sugarland,* Spielberg had become friendly with the young producer Michael Phillips, who was at Universal producing *The Sting* for Zanuck/Brown along with his wife, Julia, and Spielberg's friend Tony Bill. Michael Phillips found Spielberg "an eager kid who continually bubbled with enthusiasm. He was interested in everything, not just films, he wasn't one-dimensional. He was always interested in new technologies, and he was one of the first people to get hooked on video games; he was the first filmmaker to install a *Pong* game or a *Tank* game on his dubbing stage. He was full of genuine love of movies, and he didn't seem to have much competitiveness with other filmmakers; this distinguished him from the group. And he had this incredible film under his belt called *Duel.*

"We became friends by having lunch every day at the Universal commissary and talking about our favorite science-fiction films, such as *The Day the Earth Stood Still.* He said, 'I want to invite myself over for dinner and pitch you a story.' All he said was that it was about 'UFOs and Watergate.' It focused on the cover-up of the truth that the government was hiding from the citizenry about UFOs and Project Blue Book [the long-classified U.S. Air Force study of UFOs]. It was very, very different from what we wound up making, and I don't think it was anywhere near as good as it wound up being."

Screenwriter-director Paul Schrader remembers the summer of 1973 as "very heady, because every weekend a lot of people would assemble at Michael and Julia's house" at Trancas Beach in Malibu. "We used to have a continual open house," says Michael Phillips. "It was a place where all of us in the film community of roughly the same age would have a barbecue, swim, lie in the sun, listen to music, and talk about movies. A lot of these writers and directors helped each other. They worked on each other's films, they would contribute scenes or dialogue, and help on the rough cuts. It was a wonderful community at that time."

The group included Spielberg, Martin Scorsese, Robert De Niro, John Milius, Joan Didion and John Gregory Dunne, Blythe Danner and her producer husband, Bruce Paltrow, Margot Kidder, Janet Margolin, attorney Tom Pollock (later an executive with MCA and Universal), screenwriter David Ward (an Oscar winner for *The Sting*), and the married screenwriters Gloria Katz and Willard Huyck (George Lucas's collaborators on the script of *American Graffiti*). "Even though we were relatively unknown," Schrader recalled, "there was a real feeling that the world was our oyster."

After meeting the Huycks at one of those gatherings, Spielberg asked them to write a screenplay based on what Katz calls a "little weird pink book. It was a biography of the inventor of the toilet, Thomas Crapper. It was titled *Flushed with Pride: The Story of Thomas Crapper* [by Wallace Reyburn, 1969]. We came up with the great idea of doing it as *Young Tom Edison*." "But like *Little Big Man*," adds Huyck. The book that so tickled Spielberg's fancy begins (quite earnestly) with these words about the British inventor: "Never has the saying 'A prophet is without honour in his own land' been more true than in the case of Thomas Crapper. Here was a man whose foresight, ingenuity and perseverance brought to perfection one of the great boons to mankind. But is his name revered in the same way as, for example, that of the Earl of Sandwich? . . . It was left to the Americans to give the man his due."

"We wrote a treatment," Huyck relates, "and we gave it to our [mutual] agent, Guy McElwaine, who said, 'Steve, if this is the kind of movie you want to do, I don't want to be your agent.' "

That bizarre excursion into bad-taste humor made the Huycks more skeptical when Spielberg pitched another movie idea. "Steve took us to dinner and told us he had this story he wanted us to write about things from outer space landing on Robertson Boulevard [in West Hollywood]," says Katz. "I go, 'Steve, that's the worst idea I ever heard. I don't want to be told an idea about a spaceship. It's very strange.' He had Paul Schrader write it."

The troubled but brilliant Schrader, who was in rebellion from a strict Dutch Calvinist upbringing in Michigan, explored his religious preoccupations in his 1972 book *Transcendental Style in Film: Ozu, Bresson, Dreyer.* Spielberg briefly expressed interest in directing Schrader's dark, semiautobiographical screenplay *Taxi Driver,* which became the controversial 1976 Robert De Niro film directed by Martin Scorsese and produced by the Phillipses for Columbia. Spielberg agreed to serve as a back-up director on the film, a condition Columbia insisted upon before allowing Scorsese to begin shooting; Spielberg's only other involvement was to make suggestions on the rough cut.

Spielberg chose not to offer *Watch the Skies* to Universal. "He wanted to get away from Universal a little bit," Michael Phillips explains. "He didn't want to be a captive of Universal. He's been consistent with this—he's been incredibly loyal [to Universal], but he makes movies with all the studios, he works with everybody. He had other people in town that he was friendly with. He used to play cards every week with Alan Ladd Jr. [Twentieth Century–Fox's feature-division executive in charge of creative affairs], and that's why we started to go to Fox first [with *Watch the Skies*]." In her waspish Hollywood memoir *You'll Never Eat Lunch in This Town Again,* Julia Phillips took a more jaundiced view of Spielberg's first steps at becoming a mogul: "Steven was hanging out with men who were too old for him. Who bet and drank and watched football games on Sunday. Who ran studios and agencies. . . . We got Steven outta Guy [McElwaine]'s house in the Bev Hills flats, and on to the beach, where people were still discussing art and greatness, and were occasionally smoking a joint."

After initial discussions with Fox, Spielberg and the Phillipses concluded that the studio had insufficient enthusiasm for *Watch the Skies.* The producers suggested offering the project to an executive with whom they all had a friendly relationship, David Begelman, the recently hired president of financially shaky Columbia Pictures.* "We went with Columbia because David was ready and able and willing to step up at a level of a commitment that made us think he was going to stand behind the film," Michael Phillips says. "It was a big bet, and he took it. David was a believer in Steven from *Duel.*"

In the two decades since *Star Wars* and *Close Encounters* were released, science-fiction films have accounted for half of the top twenty box-office hits. But before George Lucas and Spielberg revived the genre, "There was no real appetite at the studios for science fiction—it was a B genre," Phillips recalls. "The conventional wisdom was, 'Science-fiction films never make more than $4 million, except for *2001,* and that's an exception.' But Columbia needed a hit. Had they not been in such desperate financial condition,

---

* Begelman had been a principal in Creative Management Associates, the agency that represented Spielberg. CMA merged with International Famous Artists (IFA) in 1975 to form International Creative Management (ICM).

maybe they would have been less needy, less aggressive, but here they had a shot. They could see that if it all worked out well, they had a chance for a big, big hit."

Intrigued by the unorthodox spiritual overtones implicit in mankind's yearning for contact with extraterrestrial life, Paul Schrader was hired by Columbia on December 12, 1973, to write the screenplay of Spielberg's UFO project, for which the writer was to receive $35,000 and 2.5 percent of the net profits. *Watch the Skies* originally was scheduled to begin shooting in the fall of 1974. But as Phillips recalls, "We went through a lot of trouble getting the script in its final form. We were struggling with it for a couple of years. Steven came to us one day [in 1973] and said, 'Listen, would you mind terribly, I really need the money, this picture's being delayed and I've got an offer to do a movie about a shark. It will take me six months. Then I'll get back and finish *Watch the Skies.*' We said, 'Oh, no, that'll be fine, we're stuck here anyway.' "

S HORTLY after Spielberg returned from the Texas locations of *The Sugarland Express,* he spotted a copy of an unpublished novel in his producers' office and "stole the galley proofs off Dick Zanuck's desk! I said, 'I can make something of this. It'll be fun.' " But for Zanuck, Brown, and Universal, Spielberg was not the first choice to direct *Jaws,* the film that would become the biggest moneymaker in motion picture history.

The idea for the novel began germinating in the mind of author Peter Benchley during the summer of 1964, when he read a small item in the New York *Daily News* about Long Island shark fisherman Frank Mundus, who had harpooned a giant shark weighing an estimated 4,500 pounds. Mundus would become the prototype for Captain Quint, the obsessed shark-hunter in *Jaws.* As a youth, Peter Benchley, the grandson of humorist Robert Benchley and son of novelist Nathaniel Benchley, had spent summers in Nantucket going on shark-fishing expeditions with his father and brother. His awareness of the power of sharks to strike awe and terror into movie audiences was heightened by his viewing of Peter Gimbel's 1971 documentary *Blue Water, White Death.* That same year, Benchley, who was working as an associate editor at *Newsweek,* accepted the first $1,000 of a $7,500 advance from Doubleday and began writing his first novel, a thriller about a great white shark feeding on human prey off the coast of Long Island.

Before the galley proofs reached Universal and several other movie studios in 1973, *Jaws* had been turned down by ABC as a TV movie, because the network figured it would cost too much to produce. That decision was made before the book stirred a feeding frenzy in the publishing industry with its paperback auction: Bantam Books bought the paperback rights for a staggering $575,000. "There was a lot of heat around town on this book," recalls Peter Saphier, who was Jennings Lang's right-hand man at Universal. "It was given to me on a Wednesday [April 11, 1973] by Benchley's agent

[John Ptak of International Famous Artists], and I read it over the weekend. I thought, This is going to be a smash movie—send it to Lew Wasserman. We had to move quickly. Jennings was a consummate packager, and when I gave him the report on Monday, he said, 'I'll call Lew. I'll call Leonard Hirshan [a William Morris agent] and send it to him for Paul Newman.' I wrote a note to Lew and—thinking of the old man and the sea—I suggested Alfred Hitchcock to direct."

On April 17, the Universal story department, which generated a reader's report on every property offered to the studio, rendered its opinion. To Saphier's astonishment, "They didn't like it! If the story department liked a property, they would stamp on the first page 'Recommend,' or they would stamp 'Possibility.' If they didn't like it they wouldn't stamp it at all. They didn't stamp it at all. I thought, Oh, God, they're killing me." But by the following day, Zanuck and Brown had read the synopsis by studio reader Dennis McCarthy, and they called Wasserman to express their strong interest in the project.

They soon found themselves in what Zanuck remembers as "a fierce bidding contest." Columbia expressed interest on behalf of veteran producer-director Stanley Kramer, but the final bidding came down to Warner Bros. and Universal. "We did everything," Zanuck said. "We got down on bended knee. We made a lot of promises that, happily, we lived up to. . . . The other people had as much money as we did. It got down to who was going to make the better picture. We convinced [Benchley] that we would." In a deal concluded on May 1 between Ptak and Universal, Zanuck/Brown agreed to pay the author $150,000 and 10 percent of the net profits for the book and $25,000 for his screenplay adaptation.* "Jennings, frankly, erupted when that happened," Saphier says. "He felt it should have been our picture, under our wing."

A few days later, when Saphier was having lunch in the studio commissary, Zanuck and Brown thanked him for finding *Jaws*. "We figure on making it as a low-budget picture for about $750,000," they said. Saphier expressed skepticism that a film made on the water—traditionally regarded as a nightmarish environment for filmmakers—could be shot so cheaply. The producers thought for a moment and replied, "Maybe a million." Brown later admitted that after acquiring the book, he and Zanuck "experienced a panic of unpreparedness. If we had read *Jaws* twice, we might never have made the movie. Careful analysis could have convinced us that it was too difficult to make."

Z ANUCK and Brown initially thought the best way to ensure themselves against the production problems posed by *Jaws* was to hire an experi-

---

* Benchley also received a $70,000 licensing fee for each sequel and a $50,000 bonus keyed to his book's lengthy stay on *The New York Times* best-seller list.

enced action director. The first director with whom they discussed the picture was John Sturges, whose films included not only the classics *Bad Day at Black Rock* and *The Great Escape* but also *The Old Man and the Sea,* a travesty of the Hemingway novel filmed mostly in a studio tank, with Spencer Tracy sitting in front of a process screen. That was exactly the kind of film the producers came to realize they did *not* want to make of *Jaws.* They decided to offer the job instead to Dick Richards, who was in his late thirties and had made his feature debut at Fox in 1972 with a Western about a teenaged cowboy, *The Culpepper Cattle Company.*

"Part of the deal, if we were to buy this book, was that it would be much appreciated if we took an IFA director," Zanuck recalls. "We had a gentleman's agreement with Mike Medavoy [Spielberg's former agent, then head of the motion picture department of IFA]. They came up with several names. We went back [to New York] to meet with Benchley, and we brought this director [Richards] with us to lunch at '21.' The director kept referring to this thing as 'the whale.' After he'd done it three times, I said, 'For God's sake, this is a fucking shark!' As we walked back to the office after this disastrous lunch, I said to Mr. Brown, 'We gotta renege. No way this guy who thinks a shark's a whale is going to direct this picture.' I called Mike. It was a tough call. Mike said, 'This is a big renege. I'm going to lose the client.' I said, 'Your client should know the difference between a whale and a shark. I can't go out to sea with this man.' "

Spielberg by then had made his interest known, and the producers, delighted by his work on *The Sugarland Express,* were beginning to think it might be better *not* to work with a more experienced Hollywood hand. "The studio visualized having one of those guys out there," Zanuck says. "It probably would have made more sense from an economic standpoint, and we would sleep better at night, but we wanted to make something that would knock everybody's socks off." "We were looking for a film as well as a movie," said Brown, "and that's why we selected Steven Spielberg."

His signing was announced on June 21, 1973. But not before Spielberg, too, began having second thoughts. "Steven got very excited about it, and then got very scared," Zanuck says. "It became a question of 'How do you *make* the son of a bitch?' It's one thing to read the book and another to build the shark." *Jaws* co-screenwriter Carl Gottlieb reported that Spielberg also was "afraid of being typed as an action director who specialized in contests between brave men and insensate killers. 'Who wants to be known as a shark-and-truck director?' was his complaint." Spielberg "was reluctant to take on *Jaws* because he recognized it would be primarily a commercial movie and not necessarily a distinguished film, and he is a serious filmmaker," Brown said shortly before *Jaws* was released in 1975. "Dick and I convinced him, and I think he now realizes he did make a film as well as a movie—not that he doesn't respect the big commercial movie and regard it as a necessary part of his career."

All of Spielberg's instincts from childhood had driven him to seek acceptance and approval from the majority. Being a marginal artist rather than a popular filmmaker was psychologically unacceptable to him. And after the *succès d'estime* of *The Sugarland Express,* it was vital for him to prove to Hollywood that he was more than an art-house *auteur.* So he swallowed his doubts and agreed to make "the big commercial movie."

"We went to Wasserman and Sheinberg," Zanuck recalls, "and it's hard to imagine now, but at the time you're talking about a guy's second picture. He hadn't proved himself. Even though Wasserman was very impressed by the kid—in those days we referred to him many times as 'the kid'—Wasserman thought he was a strange choice."

"Jesus, Dick, the kid's great and everything," Wasserman said, "but remember you're going to be out there, it's going to be a big production, and it can get out of control. Wouldn't you be better off with one of the sure-handed guys who's done this kind of picture before?"

Zanuck replied, "That's exactly what we *don't* want. We don't want to do *Moby-Dick* again. The kid can bring visual excitement to it. We'll give him the support he needs."

TWENTY years after the making of *Jaws,* Zanuck/Brown production executive Bill Gilmore described it as "the most difficult film ever made, to this day." Soon after principal photography began on May 2, 1974, on Martha's Vineyard, it became apparent that the star of the film, the mechanical shark, was refusing to cooperate. "Around August 1, when the movie was in terrible jeopardy, with the shark not working," Gilmore relates, "I came back to the hotel and I was agonized. My wife said to me, 'Who was the guy that told 'em the movie could be done in the first place?' I took a big Scotch. We were all heroes in retrospect, but we all thought we had failed because we'd gone double the budget and double the schedule." In fact, *Jaws* went almost *triple* the schedule, with its planned 55 days of shooting ballooning to 159.

At the beginning, when Zanuck gave Gilmore the galleys of the book, wanting his ideas about how to make the movie and how much it would cost, Gilmore "read it as being sort of a Hollywood shark, a supershark that could do everything but fly. Benchley wrote, 'Towering overhead, it blocked out the light.' Dick Zanuck said, 'Can we do it?' I said, 'Yes, we can do it.' I was speaking out of all the arrogance of somebody who had grown up in the business and felt Hollywood could do anything—Gene Kelly could dance with a mouse, we could put people into orbit. We accepted and believed that we could build a mechanical shark and we could shoot over the head of the victim toward the shark and over the head of the shark toward the victim. It had never been done before.

"And we took on the Atlantic Ocean. Nobody had ever done a movie at sea with a small boat. Every movie that was shot at sea, they always wound up shooting in a tank with a process screen, and it looked like it. From the beginning, Steven and [production designer] Joe Alves and myself and

Zanuck agreed we would shoot on a real sea. I can't tell you how many times that came back and bit us in the ass. But despite all the problems it caused us, ultimately it's why the picture was so incredibly successful, because everybody was *there*. It was a real sea and a real boat."

Gilmore's belief that a mechanical "supershark" could be built by Hollywood special-effects wizards began to focus the producers on the realities involved. Gottlieb reported that Zanuck and Brown "had innocently assumed that they could get a shark trainer somewhere, who, with enough money, could get a great white shark to perform a few simple stunts on cue in long shots with a dummy in the water, after which they could cut to miniatures or something for the close-up stuff." Spielberg laughed when he remembered those discussions: "Sure, yeah, they'd train a great white, put it in front of the camera, with me in a cage. They tried to convince me that this was the way to go. I was yelling: 'Disney!' The minute I read the script, I was yelling, 'Disney! We've gotta get the guy who did the squid in *20,000 Leagues Under the Sea!*' . . . I didn't know who he was at the time. It turned out to be Bob Mattey and we hired him to build us a shark. But they still wanted me to experiment with live sharks."

While Mattey, who had been lured out of retirement, started to work on three twenty-five-foot mechanical sharks to perform various functions in the film, Zanuck and Brown hired the husband-and-wife team of Ron and Valerie Taylor to shoot live shark footage off Dangerous Reef on the coast of South Australia. The producers felt that whatever wonders Mattey might be able to perform, it was important to see an actual shark in the film and to be able to publicize that fact. The Taylors were renowned for their intrepid underwater photography on *Blue Water, White Death*. When Gilmore met them in Australia, he "was nervous, because I felt here are the greatest shark experts in the world. I said, 'How did you like the book?' Ron Taylor said, 'I don't know who Mr. Benchley is, but whoever he is, he knows the great white. Because everything he writes about could happen.' The hair went up on the back of my neck. Being a cynical Hollywood type, I was stunned that a great white shark really *could* do all this. From that moment on, I knew we had a chance."

Spielberg made a wish list of sixteen shots he wanted from the Taylors, including footage of a shark circling a man in an underwater cage. Later, close shots of Richard Dreyfuss in a wet suit would be filmed in a studio tank to match their footage. To make the real shark look even larger, a midget stuntman, an ex-jockey named Carl Rizzo, was sent down as Dreyfuss's underwater double. "When we were shooting the live shark footage," Valerie Taylor recalled, "none of us had any idea that the film would be such a tremendous success. To Ron and me it was just another filming job, our eighth at that time, involving great white sharks. It was the first time that Ron had to work to a script." But the shark did not follow the script.

The Taylors put out to sea with shark expert Rodney Fox on February 16, 1974. After ten days, they managed to get footage of a shark circling a cage.

Then they readied Rizzo for a dive in his cage, which was five-eighths scale. He was about to be lowered from a nineteen-foot fiberglass auxiliary boat, the *Skippy,* when the shark suddenly attacked the boat. "The *Skippy* rolled onto her side, dragged down by a half a ton of fighting fish," Valerie Taylor wrote in her diary of the filming. "A huge head rose above the spray twisting and turning, black maw gaping in a frenzy of rage and pain. Triangular teeth splintered as they tore the restricting metal. The brute dove, his cycle tail whipping the air six feet above the surface.

"Carl stood frozen with shock. As Rodney pulled him back, the tail brushed Carl's face. Had Rodney been two seconds slower, the little stunt-man would have been killed, his head crushed into pulp. . . . The great white shark's body crashed into the hull. The noise was incredible, splitting wood, thrashing water, cage against boat, shark against boat. . . . A last mighty splash, then shark, cage, winch, and deck vanished in a boiling, foaming swirl. Had Carl been in the cage, he too would have vanished with no possible chance of survival."

What happened next was related by Spielberg: "Immediately, our stunt-man turned around and quite calmly walked to the hold of the ship and locked himself in the head [the toilet]! And they tried to get him out of there with a butter knife and he was holding the door closed and he would not move!"

The next day, Gilmore received a phone call from Ron Taylor on the coast of Australia. "He was so excited on the phone he was interrupting himself," Gilmore says. "He went on to tell us he had just shot the most spectacular shark footage he had ever seen in his professional life. I said, 'Ron, that's great. Was the little guy in the cage?' He said no. My heart sank. I said, 'It's unusable.' They sent the film; it was the most spectacular footage. [Film editor] Verna Fields and Steven and I were all so bummed by the fact that it was unusable until we decided it was so good we had to have it in the movie. In the book, the Dreyfuss character goes down in the cage, the shark comes over and takes his cage on—it's the end of Dreyfuss, the shark eats him. We had Dreyfuss drop his gun, the shark would go on, and Dreyfuss would get out of the cage, swim down, and hide in the rocks. Can you imagine *Jaws* without Dreyfuss's character? He was the most likable character. The shark down in Australia rewrote the script and saved Dreyfuss's character."

W H E N Spielberg approached Dreyfuss to play the outspoken ichthyologist Matt Hooper,* the actor said, "I would go to see this movie in a minute. I don't want to do it."

"Why?" asked Spielberg.

"Because, as an actor, it doesn't do a thing for me."

---

* Spielberg had first met Dreyfuss when the actor turned down a role in his TV movie *Savage.*

After completing the movie, Dreyfuss explained, "The character, as it existed, was just there to give out shark information. . . . Boring, boring, boring. But then I had no money, everybody said there was going to be an actors' strike, everyone I trust as an advisor said, 'Do it.' So we constructed a character over three days and finally I said OK, I gave in, I surrendered, I was a prostitute."

Dreyfuss was not cast until shortly before the start of principal photography. Spielberg's first choice for Hooper, Jon Voight, had turned down the part; the director also considered Timothy Bottoms, Jeff Bridges, and Joel Grey. In casting the young actor he came to view as "my alter ego," Spielberg was reshaping the character and the film to reflect his own sensibilities. Besides being short and full of what Spielberg called "kinetic energy," Dreyfuss has other traits in common with the director. As the actor's longtime friend Carl Gottlieb observed, "When his speech exceeds rationality, it is only because his fast-moving mouth has not caught up with his even faster-racing brain." Dreyfuss is "not an intellectual man. His college education is incomplete, and he can be surprisingly naive on certain issues. . . . [But he] can easily grasp a complex problem, reduce its conflicts and ambiguities to a few broad generalities, and then set a course of action that enables him to deal specifically with those large assumptions."

To Spielberg, Dreyfuss also "represents the underdog in all of us." Using him as a mouthpiece, Spielberg and Gottlieb were able to elevate *Jaws* from a formulaic monster melodrama to a film with a modestly stated, yet clearly defined social perspective. As "an American Jew with clearly defined ethnic roots," Dreyfuss exemplifies what Gottlieb defined as "a tradition of intellectual inquiry, respect for learning, and intense involvement with morality and law." Those qualities are abundantly present in the film's Matt Hooper, the voice of scientific reason and civic responsibility against a town whose leaders initially are more concerned with tourist dollars than with protecting their citizens against harm. In taking a principled stand against official hypocrisy, Hooper helps awaken the conscience of Roy Scheider's police chief Martin Brody. After an initial display of cowardice, Brody risks his career to defy the venal mayor (Murray Hamilton), the toadying newspaper editor (Gottlieb), and the town's short-sighted merchants.

Despite his disdain for the movie, which lasted throughout the shooting process, Dreyfuss responded enthusiastically to his collaboration with Spielberg: "Steve's not what you'd call an actor's director in the classical sense. But he's relaxed and open in the way he communicates what he wants, and he helps you to get there. In his philosophy, the actors serve the story. But this doesn't eliminate improvisation—not at all."

Spielberg's shrewd, offbeat casting sense also was evident in his rejection of Universal stalwart Charlton Heston, who made it known that he wanted to play Chief Brody. No doubt recalling his unfavorable impression of Heston from their meeting when Spielberg was serving his apprenticeship at the studio, the director realized that Heston's stentorian, larger-than-life persona would make it hard for the audience to see him as a small-town police chief, particularly one with such unheroic, all-too-human failings. After trying to persuade Zanuck and Sheinberg to let him cast the little-known Joseph Bologna, Spielberg offered the part to Robert Duvall, but Duvall wanted to play Captain Quint, and Spielberg had trouble envisaging him in such a flamboyant role (a decision the director later regretted). According to Brown, Spielberg was "slow to come around" on the decision to cast Roy Scheider as Brody. The actor was best known at the time as the hard-boiled New York cop in *The French Connection,* and Spielberg did not want Brody to be played as a tough guy. But Scheider proved highly credible in a low-key performance as Spielberg's "Mr. Everyday Regular Fella."

Lee Marvin turned down the role of Quint, and Sterling Hayden was unable to appear in the film because of his ongoing tax problems. Spielberg turned to Robert Shaw, the colorful British actor, playwright, and novelist who had worked for Zanuck and Brown in *The Sting.* Although worrying that Shaw's film performances were always "over the top," Spielberg rationalized that Quint should be played larger than life. Shaw came to admire Spielberg once they started working together, but the actor initially approached the project with cynicism. He told *Time* magazine, "*Jaws* was not a novel. It was a story written by a committee, a piece of shit."

"PETER Benchley's view of his book was not my view of the movie I wanted to make from his book," Spielberg told *Newsweek* reporter Henry McGee in an unguarded moment on location in Martha's Vineyard. "Peter didn't like any of his characters, so none of them were very likable. He put them in a situation where you were rooting for the shark to eat the people —in alphabetical order."

Although an efficient page-turner, Benchley's first novel is peopled with cardboard characters and bogged down by a pulpish subplot Spielberg aptly described as "too much like *Peyton Place"*—the shark action is repeatedly and distractingly interrupted by the couplings of the police chief's wife with the visiting ichthyologist. Spielberg insisted on doing away with the book's sexual and Mafia subplots and minimizing its *Moby-Dick* parallels. Sid Sheinberg concurred, suggesting, "Why don't we simply make *Duel* with a shark?"

Benchley wrote two screenplay drafts, one in consultation with Spielberg. Although the structure of the film follows Benchley's second draft fairly closely, most of his dialogue was rewritten and the action scenes became far more exciting as Spielberg reimagined them, often improvising to deal with problems posed by the sea and the mechanical sharks. "I was not a competent screenwriter," concedes Benchley, who says he failed to grasp how much a book has to be changed in the transition from script to screen. "The only argument Steven and I had was over the ending," the novelist adds. "He said, 'The ending of the book is a downer,' and he told me what he wanted to do." In the book, Hooper and Quint are killed by the shark, and the shark escapes. But in the film, Hooper survives and Chief Brody kills the shark by ramming a tank of compressed air into its mouth and firing a bullet into the tank. Benchley told Spielberg, "That is incredible. The audience will never believe it." Spielberg replied, "If I have them for two hours, they'll believe it. I want them to go out of the theater screaming." Benchley concedes that the director "absolutely pulled it off."

Looking for new writers, Spielberg first turned to Richard Levinson and William Link, as he previously had done on *The Sugarland Express,* but received the same answer they had given him before. "We were not interested at all," Link says of *Jaws.* "We hated the whole idea. We were doing important television like *The Execution of Private Slovik* and *That Certain Summer*—we were the social-issue boys. We, idiots that we were, tried to talk him out of it. We said, 'Why do you want to do a dumb horror film? It's like a Hammer film. You're so talented, what do you want to do a dumb thing about a shark for?' He wasn't too all fired up about it, and he hated the first half of the book. He said, 'I'm going to make it on Cape Cod. You can come there with your wives. You'll have a good time.' We said, 'No, no, Steve. Why would you approve meretricious material like this?' As we all know, *Jaws* turned out to be a brilliant thriller. He invited us to see it about two months before it came out. We said, 'Gotta buy MCA.' We bought thousands of shares, and it was very lucrative for us. The woman who became my wife saw the film and said, 'Never turn that kid down again!' "

Howard Sackler, the playwright and screenwriter who had won a Pulitzer Prize for his play *The Great White Hope,* was brought in to tackle the great white shark. An experienced scuba diver, Sackler spent five weeks rewriting the script of *Jaws* but requested no credit. One of his most significant contributions was the story of the 1945 sinking of the USS *Indianapolis* in shark-infested waters. As a monologue for Quint, the haunting tale gives the grizzled shark-hunter a reason for his obsessive hatred of sharks. Spielberg thought Sackler's speech needed to be expanded, so he enlisted the help of John Milius, a World War II buff who "really wanted me to cast him as Quint all along and wrote the speech as only John Milius would say it." The final version was revised by Shaw, who "was a brilliant writer and ad-libbed," Zanuck says. "He was half drunk at the time."

Spielberg felt Sackler helped refocus the script on "the four or five elements that made the book so enthralling—especially the last hundred pages," but the director was far from satisfied with Sackler's draft and his own subsequent attempt to rewrite it. "I knew what I needed to do was cast the movie and do something that is very frightening to me—which I understand Bob Altman does quite a lot—you subjugate absolute control to meaningful collaboration; everybody gets into a room to determine jointly what kind of movie we are going to make here. Is it going to be a picture about the shark—or about the heroes who kill the shark? I hired a man named Carl Gottlieb, who was an old friend of mine, and he came with me to Martha's

Vineyard essentially to polish the script as the actors sat with me every night —often only twenty-four hours before the shot—and *improvise*. . . . I dealt with the actors in *Jaws* as intensely as I dealt with the special effects."

To facilitate their work on the script, Gottlieb and Spielberg shared a house on location, with Gottlieb continuing to work on the revisions after Spielberg went to sleep. Each morning, Gottlieb would give new pages to the company typist, and by 8:30 A.M. they would be approved and ready for filming. "It made for incredible tension on the location, because of changes in props," Gottlieb said in a 1975 interview. "Some days the production manager, William Gilmore, and Spielberg wouldn't even talk."

FURTHER tension arose when Benchley visited the location. Spielberg asked him to play a TV reporter broadcasting a report from the beach about shark attacks. As it happened, the day Benchley arrived on Martha's Vineyard was the day the *Newsweek* article hit the stands with Spielberg's bad-mouthing of the novel. When Benchley stepped off the plane at the local airport, he was met by unit publicist Al Ebner and *Los Angeles Times* reporter Gregg Kilday, who was there to do a feature on the filming. As Benchley recalls, Kilday announced: "Spielberg says your book is a piece of shit."

"You must understand," Benchley shot back to the reporter, "there has never been a question of controversy. I understood what they had to take out. When I finished my version of the screenplay, Brown said it was won-derful. Zanuck said it was OK. Spielberg didn't say anything. After Howard Sackler did his rewrite, I sent an angry letter to David Brown. I accused one of the characters, the oceanographer [Hooper], of being an insufferable, pedantic little schmuck. I think Spielberg took it to mean him. [*Benchley laughed.*] But that is *not* what the letter said.

"Spielberg needs to work on character. He knows, flatly, zero. Consider: He is a twenty-six-year-old [actually twenty-seven] who grew up with mov-ies. He has no knowledge of reality but the movies. He is B-movie literate. When he must make decisions about the small ways people behave, he reaches for movie clichés of the forties and fifties."

With what Kilday described as "a certain sardonic pleasure," Benchley concluded: "Wait and see. Spielberg will one day be known as the greatest second-unit director in America."

Recalling that outburst twenty years later, Benchley said, "In the great catalogue of stupid things one says in life, that ranks high on the list. It was an extremely unfortunate bit of anger. We had both been manipulated by the press. We were both extremely naive. I regretted my petulant response immediately and I tried to take it back [Kilday reported both versions in his July 7 article]. Universal was getting upset we were pissing all over each other in public. They said, 'Please stop this.' After that, the two of us got together and told each other we were really sorry. In a way, my remark was a cleansing."

Spielberg claimed *Newsweek* had misrepresented his comments. He explained to Benchley that what he *really* felt was, "The book is not a good book as a film." Benchley took that convoluted statement to mean: "You couldn't just shoot the book." Nevertheless, Benchley laments, "Steven had an unfortunate tendency to denigrate the book in public." Three months before *Jaws* was released, the film magazine *Millimeter* published an interview Spielberg had given on Martha's Vineyard. This time the director was quoted as saying, "If we don't succeed in making this picture better than the book, we're in real trouble."

Spielberg sent Benchley a letter of apology, to which the beleaguered author responded: "Thanks for your letter, I don't see *Millimeter* (in fact, your mention of it was the first I'd ever heard), so whatever vicious, putrid, scabrous, scurrilous, subversive slime you ladled on me would probably have escaped my view. Nevertheless, forewarned is . . . etc. You were thoughtful to write.

"In fairness, though, you should know that I have employed mercenaries to prepare a broadside about you, revealing, at last, the sordid truth about your personal life. It'll all be there—whips, leather sneakers, shorty-nighties and crunchy peanut butter. I'm aiming for the June issue of *Jack & Jill*. . . ."

"LOOK, *Jaws* could have turned out to be the laugh riot of '75," Spielberg said later. "I made it to entertain myself, then I tried to get off it three times."

In the months before shooting began, Spielberg gave serious consideration to quitting *Jaws* to direct *Lucky Lady* for Twentieth Century–Fox. An original screenplay by Willard Huyck and Gloria Katz, *Lucky Lady* was a romantic comedy/action melodrama about 1930s rum-runners involved in a *ménage à trois*. Paul Newman wanted Spielberg to direct him in it. "I was offered a film that I very much wanted to direct at Fox," Spielberg said at his November 1973 AFI seminar, "and Universal had a preemption right in [my contract], so they exercised their preemption right against the Fox project for a film [*Jaws*] that I had committed to do but wasn't going into production for at least eight months. Universal is a corporation, and they don't treat you like an individual. . . . [Y]ou reach a certain high point in your career and you really want out bad. They make you pay the piper again and again." After shooting *Jaws,* which he considered "the worst experience of my life," he told studio publicist Orin Borsten, "I will never do another picture for Universal."

When Jennings Lang heard that Spielberg wanted out of *Jaws,* he yelled at Spielberg over the telephone (in a conversation overheard by Lang's teen-aged son Rocky): "You're going to stay with this movie. You're going to do a great job. It's going to be great. What do you want to go to Fox and do *Lucky Lady* for? It's going to be a disaster." The savvy Jennings Lang was right on both counts. With Stanley Donen directing Burt Reynolds, Gene Hackman, and Liza Minnelli, *Lucky Lady* became, as Gloria Katz put it, "an appalling movie."

Sid Sheinberg also had words with Spielberg over *Jaws*. "It was one of the few disagreements that Steven and I had," the MCA president said in a 1988 interview. "I literally forced him to do it. . . . I think he was upset for a while. He turned to me and said, 'Why are you making me do this B movie?' "

"I was tipped off that Steven was going to come in my office and resign," Zanuck recalls. "This was about three months before the picture started. He was scared, and I think he felt overwhelmed. He wasn't sure he was the right guy for it, and he was being tempted by offers to do other things. When I made the deal with him at Fox [for the script of *Ace Eli and Rodger of the Skies*], we included two cheap directorial options at $50,000 each. They had *Lucky Lady*, and I didn't think much of it. I told him, 'You're well off not getting involved.' I would have said that about *Gone With the Wind*, because I wanted him to stay on this project. We were under deadline to get started and finished before an actors' strike.* Wasserman had told us we would have to start before a certain date or we couldn't start. We had a lot of people involved in building the shark. It was a nightmare.

"Steven had made up some *Jaws* T-shirts, and when I was told he was coming in to resign, I hurriedly took off my shirt and put on the *Jaws* shirt and sat behind my desk. It threw him, because he had made a big deal of giving out these shirts. He had a real hard time getting words out of his mouth, but all the difficulties and concerns poured out. This picture was important to him, vitally important. There were such huge professional stakes, and he said, 'Jesus Christ, we're going off half-cocked.'

"I laid a giant guilt trip on him. I laid it right on the line that this was a great opportunity, and we were going to make a successful picture; he couldn't even *think* not to be part of it. I told him we were backing him all the way. It was one of those things where I myself was shitting in my pants, because I didn't know how the hell we were going to start the picture. Nothing was ready. It was, at that stage, completely out of control, as it was during most of the shooting."

J A W S ran into so many production problems that exasperated crew members began referring to the movie as *Flaws*. "[F]our days out of seven we were making it," Spielberg later admitted, "I thought it would be a turkey."

The changing weather was a constant headache, and filming at sea caused enormous logistical difficulties. But the biggest culprits were Bob Mattey's three mechanical sharks—collectively named "Bruce," after Spielberg's lawyer, Bruce Ramer. Bruce had not been tested in ocean water before being trucked from Universal to Martha's Vineyard, and no one had anticipated the

---

* The Screen Actors Guild was threatening to strike on July 1, 1974, but the strike did not take place.

corrosive effects of saltwater electrolysis on his complex substructure. For most scenes, the shark was to ride on an underwater crane, moving along a track on a submersible platform, controlled by pneumatic hoses operated by men at a floating console. The entire apparatus, which had to be towed out to sea each day, weighed twelve tons.* For weeks after shooting started, Bruce simply refused to work. After Spielberg watched the first rushes of the shark, the atmosphere was "like a wake," recalled director Brian De Palma, who was visiting the location. "Bruce's eyes crossed, and his jaws wouldn't close right." That night, Dreyfuss declared, "If any of us had any sense, we'd all bail out now."

At a makeshift workshop dubbed "Shark City," Mattey, production designer Joe Alves, and their staff kept tinkering frantically with the machinery while Spielberg anxiously shot around the star of the movie. Picking up on a device in Howard Sackler's screenplay draft, Spielberg, out of desperation, began shooting barrels instead of the shark; in the movie, the barrels are affixed to the shark by harpoon and they cruise the ocean surface as a stand-in for the submerged creature. It was not until late summer that the shark itself was ready for action, and then only intermittently.

"The shark was a disaster," Zanuck says. "It let us down tremendously. We were starting to lose confidence in Mattey. We were very scared. Quite frankly, I didn't know whether any of us could do it. We thought, Jesus Christ, we're making a picture called *Jaws,* and we don't have the fucking shark. Today, with computer stuff, you could put the shark in, like Steven did with dinosaurs in *Jurassic Park.* In those days, it was a strictly mechanical thing. We had a platform with thirteen guys sitting at a console—one guy would control the dorsal fin, one guy would control the eyes . . . it was like an orchestra. It was the goddamnedest thing to watch. The tail would be going right, but the head would be cockeyed. It was really painful. It took all of Steven's skill as a filmmaker to make it look like it worked. When it did work, by a miracle, it worked so *great.*"

"We shot when the shark was working," Spielberg recalled. "It didn't matter what the light was doing, whether the actor had the right shirt on—if the shark worked, roll! You know the shark on the Universal tour? Well, that thing works ten times better than the one we had on the movie!"

The pressure on the twenty-seven-year-old director was enormous. "I thought my career as a filmmaker was over," Spielberg admitted in a 1995 interview. "I heard rumors from back in Hollywood that I would never work again because no one had ever taken a film a hundred days over schedule —let alone a director whose first picture had failed at the box office. . . . There were moments of solitude, sitting on the boat waiting for a shot, thinking, This can't be done. It was stupid to begin it, we'll never finish it.

---

* One of the three sharks was not attached to the platform, but rode a mechanized sled controlled by scuba divers.

No one is ever going to see this picture, and I'm never going to work in this town again."

Coping with the recalcitrant shark was hard enough, but Spielberg also had to deal with unrelenting pressure from Gilmore and the producers to keep shooting . . . *something*. Because of the shark and the weather, there were days when Spielberg could manage to complete only a few seconds of footage, or none at all. But with the film looming as a potential disaster, Spielberg did not want to start compromising on quality on the rare occasions when he was able to shoot. "There were times early in the picture when we felt we had made a mistake [in hiring him] because Steven was maddeningly perfectionistic," Brown wrote. "Yeah, he was a perfectionist," agrees Zanuck. "And I have to hand it to him for sticking to his guns. The situation was very agitating. By the same token, when he knew there were no solutions, he would find solutions. He had to prove himself to a lot of the crew members. Steven can be rough on a crew. He's very demanding. He does some very unorthodox things. Everybody was older than Steven, and a lot of them were very skeptical of him. They weren't seeing the dailies."

"The entire company had developed a foxhole mentality, behaving like troops in the line, experiencing battle fatigue, nervous exhaustion, and incipient alcoholism," screenwriter Gottlieb recalled. ". . . [T]he cast was going quietly insane, along with their director, who could not reveal the fact. Steven would keep his cool, wait patiently for setups, work with his actors, and listen as they babbled hysterically of other projects, pictures they were missing, home and family, and Robert Shaw's income taxes." At one point, Gottlieb reported, Roy Scheider became fed up with the catered food they were served on the boat. The actor "threw the tray on the deck, and screamed at the AD [assistant director], and shouted at Steven, and then unburdened himself of all the frustrations and observations that had been bubbling inside him for the preceding months. It was probably a Primal release, and it took hours for Steven to calm him down and walk it off, which isn't easy on a small boat."

Joan Darling spent a day with Spielberg on location and witnessed his frustration when technical problems made filming impossible in the morning and excruciatingly slow in the afternoon. "It was hard for him to sit around," she realized. "He has incredible courage and endurance as a director. Beat by beat, shot by shot, he was going to get that movie, not in an unpleasant way, but with an inner quiet. Even though inside he may have been going through agony, that never pulls him away from his target."

A major source of delay and conflict was Spielberg's insistence that the horizon be kept clear in scenes involving the shark-hunting boat, the *Orca*. If the audience was to believe that the *Orca* was out on the ocean alone, far from any possible help and with a broken radio to boot, it was crucial that they not see a pleasure boat drifting by in the distance. But as the summer months wore on, the waters around Martha's Vineyard became crowded with sailboats. If a boat appeared in the background of a shot, the company would dispatch a crew member in a motorboat to ask the boater to stay away while they were filming. "Some people were nice about it," Zanuck recalls, "but other people wanted to see the filming and said, 'Fuck you. You can't tell me to get off the ocean.' " In such instances, it could take as long as an hour for the horizon to clear. Sometimes Bill Gilmore had to resort to paying a boater a couple of hundred dollars to move away.

"I was amazed at how unrattled Steven would get, at that young age," comments production designer Joe Alves. "Steven's idea was to have *nothing* on the horizon. He wanted to get this vulnerability of three men out there on their boat—and the shark. The studio kept saying, 'Couldn't you shoot if there was just *one* boat?' But he was relentless about it. There was a *lot* of pressure from the studio. Any lesser director might have given in, but he stuck to his guns about that."

"Steven will never know the severe beating we would take every night when we would report the day's activities [to Universal]," Zanuck has said, "and that's where the buffer comes in." The studio was "anxious for us to get out of there. There's always a very tough and fine line that has to be danced around between the production manager and the director, because the production manager's looking at his watch all the time. Sure, he wants to get it right, but he also wants to move on. He's the guy who's talking to the studio every night, and there was a lot of tension there. We backed [Spielberg] up whenever we could. Some things he wanted to do we thought were unreasonable—some suggestions to do further shooting—and we couldn't.

"He would jump on an idea with great enthusiasm and take it a little step further until it became unreal. *Nobody* has energy and enthusiasm like he has; it's a wonderful trait. But if you said, 'I think the family should have a dog,' next day you'd see *three* dogs there. We would reel him back in, because he does have a bit of a propensity to go over the top. His idea for the final shot of *Jaws*—I don't know how serious he was about it—was to have a lot of [shark] fins on the horizon, coming to the island. He thought it would be a great irony that when they had killed the shark, more sharks arrive. We said that was not a good idea. We talked him out of it."

Spielberg has said that, during the desperate period that summer when the shark would not work, Universal was thinking of canceling the picture —in Hollywood parlance, "pulling the plug"—or firing him. Sheinberg, however, insisted, "No one ever contemplated doing anything of that sort," and Zanuck and Gilmore also contend that pulling the plug was not an option. But Zanuck admits *Jaws* "was in intensive care. The studio at one point was talking about shutting down and coming back and trying to figure out the mystery of the shark here [in Hollywood], without two hundred and fifty people standing around." The idea of delaying the picture a year and coming back to Martha's Vineyard the following summer to finish shooting also was considered, but that "would have ruined all the momentum the film had going," Zanuck felt.

"We listened and agonized," Brown recalled, "but finally concluded it was wiser to keep on going, however slow the process. . . . Our budget for the film was about four and a half million dollars, which we exceeded by one hundred percent [including studio overhead, the total production cost was about $10 million]. How could we anticipate costs? We were budgeting a production unlike any previous production. Nobody had ever budgeted a shark."

Sheinberg and Marshall Green, Universal's executive production manager, visited the location to decide what needed to be done. Gilmore recalls that Green, "who was such an old pro, took one look at what we were doing and said, 'Keep up the good work.' " "To Wasserman's credit, and Sheinberg's, they didn't put any pressure on us," Zanuck adds. "They were concerned, because they were putting up the money, but they never considered taking the cameras away. They were very supportive."

When a studio executive urged Wasserman to have the production brought back to the studio for completion there, Wasserman asked, "Do we know how to make it better than they do?"

"No," admitted the executive.

"Then," said Wasserman, "let them keep going."

Sheinberg's wife, TV actress Lorraine Gary, was making her first feature-film appearance as Ellen Brody, the wife of Roy Scheider's Chief Brody. Her casting in *Jaws* and two of its three sequels inevitably led to charges of nepotism against her husband, but those charges were unfounded, because the decision to cast her in *Jaws* was Spielberg's. When Zanuck suggested casting his own wife, actress Linda Harrison, not realizing Spielberg already had offered the part to Gary, Spielberg exclaimed, *"Oy vey!"* Casting Gary was "a very shrewd political move" on Spielberg's part, William Link observes. "Zanuck and Brown would say, 'The kid is waiting for the sky, watching for the boats to leave the horizon,' and Sid would talk to Lorraine, who'd say to him, 'He's a brilliant director.' Steve wasn't using Lorraine as a favor to Sheinberg, she was very good for the part, but it was a little dividend. Steve knew at that early age that filmmaking is not just filmmaking—it's a people game. And he played it well."

When Sheinberg visited Martha's Vineyard, he had dinner with Spielberg at the house the director shared with Gottlieb. At the end of dinner, Sheinberg recalled, Spielberg and Gottlieb "excused themselves and went into a corner and started typing, started preparing the next day's work. It was an absolutely terrifying experience. 'My God! This is the way this is being done?' The thought went through my mind that we may have footage that would never be assembled into a movie."

After watching attempts to shoot at sea the following day, Sheinberg asked the director whether it would be possible to make the movie in a studio tank. Spielberg replied, "Well, I wanted to shoot this in the ocean for reality."

"Reality is costing us a lot of money," Sheinberg said.

"I understand that, but I really believe in this movie."

"Well, I believe in you. If you want to quit now, we will find a way to make our money back. If you want to stay and finish the movie, you can do that."

"I want to stay and finish the movie," Spielberg said.

"Fine," said Sheinberg.

As Universal feature production chief Ned Tanen recalled, "[W]hen it got ugly and tough—and it got ugly and tough—Sheinberg wouldn't turn his back on Steven. That is really where this relationship comes from. Sheinberg was the president of Universal, but had not been so for very long, so it was a very dicey moment for him."

F R O M childhood, Spielberg has used moviemaking as a way of exorcising his fears. "Fear is a very real thing for me," he once said while talking about *Jaws*. "One of the best ways to cope with it is to turn it around and put it out to others. I mean, if you are afraid of the dark, you put the audience in a dark theater. I had a great fear of the ocean."

When he read Benchley's book, Spielberg instantly recognized a subject that would grip his audience on a deep, visceral level: "I wanted to do *Jaws* for hostile reasons. I read it and felt that I had been attacked. It terrified me, and I wanted to strike back. . . . I knew I would be happy making a film like that, because it somehow appealed to my baser instincts. . . . I didn't have any fun making it. But I had a *great* time planning it, going tee-hee-hee! . . . In fact, I thought *Jaws* was a comedy."

Watching swimmers being menaced by the shark—from camera angles on shore, bobbing on the surface of the water, or from below—puts the viewer into a position of extreme childlike vulnerability. That strategy is implicit in Spielberg's description of *Jaws* as "a primal scream movie." The reason it "hit a nerve" with audiences, he felt, was "maybe because it's basically Freudian. We have been taught to suppress our fears, [with] the macho cover. But *Jaws* makes it safe to express fear in public. Then there's the theory of its relationship to our prenatal hours, because people are little sharks at one point; they know how to survive in water for a while." At the same time, Spielberg's frequent employment of the shark's menacing point of view, seen from the safely vicarious perspective of the theater seat, perversely encourages the viewer to revel in hostility toward its human prey. "You will root for the shark as you rooted for King Kong," Spielberg promised. The director's indulgence in his "baser instincts" accounted for some of the film's extraordinary commercial success with mid-1970s audiences seeking new levels of violent stimulus, but it troubled the director in retrospect. "*Jaws* is almost like I'm directing the audience with an electric cattle prod," he admitted in a 1977 interview with the British film magazine *Sight and Sound*. "I have very mixed feelings about my work on that picture, and two or three pictures from now I'm going to be able to look back on it and see what I've done. I saw it again and realized it was the simplest movie I had ever seen in my life. It was just the essential moving, working parts of suspense and terror. . . . I could have made that a very subtle movie if I wanted to."

A particularly disturbing aspect of *Jaws* is its mingling of sexuality and violence in the opening sequence, in which the naked limbs of a voluptuous young female swimmer (Susan Backlinie) dangle alluringly in the water before she is torn to pieces (the same sexually charged image was used to advertise the book and the movie). Like the slasher movies that became popular later in the 1970s, the sequence seems to punish the woman for being sexually aggressive; she enters the water to entice a drunken young man into skinnydipping with her, but he sprawls impotently in the sand, unable to respond as she is attacked. In a 1978 essay, *"Jaws* as Patriarchal Myth,"* Jane E. Caputi argued that the scene is "a carefully constructed form of subliminal cinematic rape," with the shark as a rampaging phallic symbol. Caputi's analogy is somewhat muddied, however, by the fact that the rest of the shark's victims are males, and by her argument that the shark also represents "the mythological motif of the *vagina dentata* (the toothed, i.e., castrating vagina)." Still, there is no doubt that *Jaws* is swimming in some treacherous psychological waters. That streak of misogyny is an attitude *Jaws* shared with other American films made during the period when the women's liberation movement was threatening traditional male prerogatives. Film editor Verna Fields admitted she "came very close to not doing *Jaws"* because of her concerns over whether it would exploit sex and violence: "Steve told me about *Jaws,* and it just sounded awful. The only thing he could promise me was that the picture was going to be in good taste."

An even more pervasive sexual overtone is the theme of male impotence, as seen in Chief Brody's initial failure to protect his community, and his own son, from the shark. Brody's weakness is typical of Spielberg's thematic preoccupation with flawed father figures. In one of the film's most memorable scenes, Spielberg visually conveys Brody's helpless anguish by using the *"Vertigo* effect" (the combination of forward tracking shot and reverse zoom) as Brody sits on the beach watching a small boy being torn apart by the shark. Brody's reassertion of his fragile manhood in hunting and killing the shark, with the help of Hooper and Quint, is the dominant theme of the last third of the film. For Caputi, this is simply Spielberg's "ritual retelling of an essential patriarchal myth." But her reading of *Jaws* fails to take into account Spielberg's explicit critique throughout the film of patriarchal and macho behavior traits.

Dreyfuss's Hooper, a bearded, bespectacled, deceptively nerdy-looking intellectual, uses brains (and technology) more than brawn to hunt the shark, but summons up the courage to descend in an underwater cage with a poison-dart gun when there seems no other alternative. The offbeat, sarcastic Hooper serves as a Spielbergian foil for the traditional hero figure, Shaw's swaggeringly macho, Ahab-like Quint. Pauline Kael observed, "When the three protagonists are in their tiny boat, you feel that Robert Shaw, the malevolent old shark hunter, is so manly that he wants to get them all killed; he's so manly he's homicidal. . . . When Shaw squeezes an empty beer can flat, Dreyfuss satirizes him by crumpling a Styrofoam cup. The director, identifying with the Dreyfuss character, sets up bare-chested heroism as a joke and scores off it all through the movie." (The joke with the Styrofoam cup came out of a bull session Spielberg and Gottlieb had over coffee with Dreyfuss in a Boston hotel room, when they were trying to coax the reluctant actor into agreeing to do the picture.)

Equally crucial to the film's nuanced portrayal of contemporary masculinity is Spielberg's depiction of the vulnerabilities of Chief Brody, who, like the director himself, is deathly afraid of water. Spielberg was determined to "take the edge off Roy Scheider as the hotshot masculine leading man . . . and let him have all the problems, all the faults of a human being. And let him have fears and phobias, and bring all these fears and phobias out in the picture, and then not resolve all of them. Because you can't. That's why a person spends all his life learning about himself."

"**J** A W S M A N I A" was the word the press used to describe the public reaction to the movie, an "epidemic of shark fever" that gave swimmers everywhere a serious case of the jitters and severely depressed beach attendance. In fact, the danger of being attacked by any kind of shark, let alone a great white shark, is extremely remote. But the rarity of shark attacks has done little to dampen the fear that sharks have always provoked in the public imagination, a fear greatly heightened by *Jaws* and its sequels.

Spielberg's great white shark is as relentless and implacable as the truck in *Duel*.* But unlike that truck, whose malevolence was due to the irrationality of its unseen driver, the shark in *Jaws* is inherently destructive, and therefore even more frightening. It attacks people because that is part of its *raison d'être*, not because it is "a sea beast slightly influenced by the occult," as Spielberg fancifully put it. Despite its seemingly supernatural destructiveness, the great white is depicted in the film with scientific understanding and even a degree of admiration. As Dreyfuss's Matt Hooper tells the mayor, "What we are dealing with here is a perfect engine—an eating machine. It's really a miracle of evolution. All this machine does is swim and eat and make little sharks." Hooper's respect for the great white has been echoed in the recent work of real-life scientists, who have increasingly come to regard sharks as an endangered species. The worldwide impact of *"Jaws*mania" exacerbated the vulnerability of what Richard Ellis and John E. McCosker, in their 1991

---

* When the shark dies, Spielberg uses the same sound effect he used for the death cry of the truck in *Duel,* the "Jurassic roar" of the prehistoric *Creature from the Black Lagoon*.

book *Great White Shark,* call "this unreasonably maligned and misunder-stood creature . . . a powerful, magnificently adapted creature of ancient lin-eage that has resisted our understanding and control, mindless of our attempts to eradicate it." Benchley acknowledges he couldn't write *Jaws* the same way today, "because all the information on sharks has changed so radically since then. I couldn't show him as being the bad guy, as I did then."

Ironically, a large part of Spielberg's success in creating terror stemmed from the problems he was having with the mechanical shark. A portfolio of storyboarded scenes Universal distributed to the press when the film began shooting shows the shark acrobatically performing a number of stunts that aren't contained in the finished film. But because the director had to shoot around the recalcitrant shark, he had to suggest its presence more than showing it: "I thought that what could really be scary was *not* seeing the shark." As a result, *Jaws* "went from a Japanese Saturday-matinee horror flick to more of a Hitchcock, the less-you-see-the-more-you-get thriller." Roy Scheider felt that from the actors' point of view, while the malfunction-ing shark "drove everybody crazy, it was also a key element in making the movie much better. There was so much time for the actors to get to know each other, to improvise and evolve as a team. . . . So it's ironic that the very problem that stalled the production was the one that cemented the movie."

What Spielberg referred to as his "documentary style" on *Jaws* also was dictated by necessity. "This film required a straightforward photographic style," David Brown said in 1975. ". . . We did not want what was done brilliantly and appropriately by Vilmos Zsigmond in *The Sugarland Express.* This was a different kind of story." Zsigmond, however, says he turned down an offer from Spielberg to photograph *Jaws* because he considered it "just a suspense story. I didn't think I could contribute anything."

Bill Butler, who took the assignment, recalled that Spielberg initially "in-sisted that we would not handhold it, that we would have everything on a tripod. I told Steve Spielberg, 'You've never shot on water before, have you? You have no idea how seasick the audience would become if you did that.' And he had to be convinced. We had to shoot some footage and show him what we meant. He soon came to love the idea." "One of the unsung heroes of the movie," Gilmore says, was Michael Chapman, a distinguished cinema-tographer in his own right who did the graceful and unobtrusive camera operating. "Every shot at sea, every shot in the last thirty minutes, was handheld. Chapman had to compensate with his legs for the pitch and roll. I don't know how many times I saw him in incredibly difficult conditions, and you'd see the dailies and the horizon was rock-solid." To *American Cinematographer* magazine, Spielberg described *Jaws* as "the most expen-sive handheld movie ever made."

Spielberg's frustrations were epitomized by what happened during the filming of what Gilmore says was intended to be "the majestic shot of the picture," when the shark jumps out of the water onto the boat before sinking it and eating Robert Shaw. "We shot it and we were so disappointed," Gilmore remembers. "The shark was supposed to come out of the water with tremendous energy. Take one was no good. The shark came out of the water kind of like a dolphin walking along the water and fell on the boat. We assumed it was a rehearsal and that the second take was going to be better. It wasn't. The shark sort of came up like a limp dick, skidded along the water, and fell onto the boat.

"I went to Bob Mattey and I said, 'Bob, the shark looks like shit.' He mumbled something about 'We don't have enough power.' I got into it, and it turned out that a year earlier when he was putting this whole million-dollar package together, the motor that we needed—the motor that drove the thing out of the water—cost $27,000. And without talking to me or anybody, he bought one for $9,000. I said, 'Are you telling me for the $18,000 we saved that we can't make this shot? It's the *movie!*' Bob said, 'Sorry.' I told Spielberg, 'We'll have to print what we've got and move on.' He went bananas. I told him, 'Steven, it will never be any better.' I knew a lot better than he did. He could be there till *today* and it would never be any better. It's done in cuts, we change the angle; Steven didn't want to break it up. My mother will never know the difference, but all of us film people wanted it to be in one shot. I think Steven will agree it was the only compromised shot in the picture."

Spielberg's unwillingness to compromise not only estranged him from Gilmore but also made him unpopular with many other men in the crew. "I'm glad I got out of Martha's Vineyard alive," Spielberg recalled. "The morale was my responsibility, and it was important to keep people from losing their minds. . . . I was really afraid of half the guys in the crew. They regarded me as a nice kind of Captain Bligh. They didn't have scurvy or anything, but I wouldn't let them go home." According to Spielberg, there was a rumor on the set that when the film finished shooting on Martha's Vineyard, the crew was planning to drown him: "They were going to hold me underwater as long as they could and still avoid a homicide rap." Carl Gottlieb put a more benign construction on the rumor: "Steven had heard that they were going to throw him over the side to celebrate." Whatever the case, Spielberg took the precaution of preplanning the final shot with Butler the night before, and secretly arranging to have a speedboat waiting to spirit him away from the location as soon as the shot was ready for filming. Speeding off for the island, where a car was waiting for him, Spielberg shouted, "I shall *not* return!"

"On the road to Boston," reported Gottlieb, "Steven started blinking and twitching, reacting to a whole new set of visual stimuli. Billboards. Traffic. Highways. Lots of cars and people. The closer the car got to Boston, the crazier he felt. It was like coming down off a five-and-a-half-month psyche-delic experience, and he wasn't used to it. That night, sitting in the bar of the hotel, he and a hyperkinetic Rick Dreyfuss made a spectacle of themselves, mostly by screaming 'Motherfucker, it's over! It's over! Motherfucker!' (That's Rick's influence. Steven is not so outspoken.)

"That night, staying in Boston to catch the morning flight to Los Angeles, Steven couldn't sleep, jolting upright in bed with a sensation of being shocked with electricity. A full anxiety attack overwhelmed him, complete with sweaty palms, tachycardia, difficulty breathing, and vomiting. When he did sleep, he dreamed he was still filming. Repetitive dreams of Martha's Vineyard kept assaulting his unconscious, and it persisted for three months after he left the island."

"W H E N we came back [to Universal], no one loved us," Joe Alves remembers. "We were really looked down upon as 'those guys out there making this dumb shark movie.' "

Undaunted, Spielberg pushed ahead with three weeks of additional shooting at Universal, in the MGM tank, and off Catalina Island. Verna Fields had been editing the film throughout the shooting on Martha's Vineyard, commuting to location sites on a bicycle and consulting with Spielberg at sea by walkie-talkie, as well as participating in the nightly script discussions. Along with Alves, she even did some second-unit filming. Affectionately known as "Mother Cutter" to the young directors with whom she preferred to work, Fields also served as a "terrific diplomat" when friction would arise on the island, Bill Gilmore said. "She would get people to kiss and make up. She was very maternal. Steven loved Verna. She was like another mother to him." By the time they left the island, Fields had a rough cut of the first two-thirds of the picture, up to the shark hunt. During months of arduous postproduction, she remained intimately involved in Spielberg's creative decisions as he fine-tuned and restructured the film in the editing room at her Van Nuys home.

Just how much credit Fields (who died in 1982) deserves for the success of *Jaws* has been the subject of heated debate since the film's release. Hollywood gossip claimed that she "saved" the picture. As recently as 1995, when the issue was raised in *The New York Times,* Carl Gottlieb replied, "Speaking from firsthand knowledge and without denigrating Verna Fields's enormous contribution to *Jaws,* that film didn't need saving." Shortly before the film's release, however, the studio tacitly acknowledged Fields's crucial role in its completion by naming her an executive consultant on all Universal films, and the following year she became feature-production vice president. "A skillful film editor can make all the difference between a movie that doesn't work and a movie that does," Mary Murphy pointedly observed in a 1975 *Los Angeles Times* profile of Fields. Others, including Spielberg, have felt that Fields was given, or took, too much credit at his expense—a feeling that intensified after she won an Academy Award for *Jaws* and he didn't. Fields diplomatically stated that Spielberg "delivered so much good foot-

age that it became an editor's dream," but she did not discourage the speculation with her Delphic utterance, "I got a lot of credit for *Jaws,* rightly or
wrongly."

On Spielberg's next film, *Close Encounters,* Fields was to be both editor
and either a producer or associate producer, but, reported Julia Phillips,
"Steven started to resent all the credit she was giving herself for [the] success
[of *Jaws*] and asked me to kill her off." Paul Schrader—who had his own
falling-out with Spielberg over his uncredited draft of *Close Encounters*—
said that after various people connnected with *Jaws* gave interviews about
their contributions to the film, Spielberg "felt they had all conspired to take
away his credit. . . . He seemed to resent the fact that *anyone* has ever helped
him, whether they be Verna Fields, Zanuck and Brown, Peter Benchley, Carl
Gottlieb, Mike and Julia Phillips. That's Steve's problem."

Fields "didn't rescue the film—it's Steven," Zanuck comments. "But Verna
Fields did a hell of a lot. She was really brilliant. She actually came in and
reconstructed some scenes that Steven had constructed for comedy and
made them terrifying, and some scenes he shot to be terrifying and made
them comedy scenes. I'm not saying that Steven didn't partake in it, but it
was her idea to reconstruct it." Although "Verna's contribution was fantastic,"
Gilmore points out, "she was not out there on the boat. She wasn't in the
heat of battle. Steven has a very good editing sense. In the end, we had the
film. If we didn't have the film, it wouldn't matter how good Steven was or
Verna was."

In working with Spielberg on *Jaws,* Fields explained, she tried to "get
inside his head and know what he was aiming for. Steve is a good sport, a
mature young man who is open, does not mind contributions, but has a clear
picture of what he wants. . . . There was a lot of talk on the set that if *Jaws*
ever got put together it would be a miracle, and the picture would never get
to the screen unless Verna was a genius. It isn't true. But no one really knew
what pieces were going to be put in where; it was so mixed up because they
were so dependent on weather and special effects and whether the shots
worked that day. . . . There were enormous problems with matching the look
of water, sky, things like that. But we suddenly realized that the picture really
worked. There were some cuts I would have liked to make that we didn't,
because the continuity just looked too bad, but if we managed to distract the
eye for a moment with action we could make it work."

A F T E R Sid Sheinberg saw a rough cut of *Jaws* in a Universal screening
room, the lights came on and the MCA president displayed no reaction.
"Well, Sid," asked an anxious David Brown, "what do you think?" "It's OK,"
Sheinberg said. Hearing that remark "was like being given one-half a star,"
Brown remembered. " *'OK'* for a hundred and fifty-nine days? Well, *of course*
it was only OK. It didn't have Johnny Williams's music. It didn't have some

major underwater stuff that we filmed in the tank at MGM Studios. . . . So the reaction was, 'Go get the rest of the movie.' "

Even people who had worked on the film had serious doubts about how it would play with audiences. As Joe Alves recalls, "When I saw pieces of it —cut, assembled footage—the color wasn't corrected, it didn't have music, the shark just made funny sounds splashing through the water. You'd hear pneumatic rams, hoses whipping through the water. The color would jump radically. I was just afraid that people were going to laugh at the shark." As the film neared the date of its first public preview, Alves worried that if the public thought the shark was phony and ridiculous, "We're dead."

John Williams's celebrated musical score—his pulsating, heart-stopping, four-note motif, primitive in its force and simplicity—signals the unseen presence of the shark and viscerally establishes a mood of abject terror. The first time Williams played the theme for Spielberg, the director began to laugh. "Oh, no, this is serious," insisted Williams. "I mean it. This is *Jaws*." "At first I thought it was too primitive," Spielberg admitted. "I wanted something a little more melodic for the shark, and then Johnny said, 'What you *don't* have here is *The L-Shaped Room* . . . you have made yourself a popcorn movie.' And he was absolutely right."

With the addition of the music, it no longer mattered that the mechanical shark had such a limited repertoire or that when it emerges from the sea to gobble up Robert Shaw in the climactic scene it looks like a performer on the Universal Studios tour. *Jaws* "was a good picture before it was scored," said Fields, "but [the] score did tremendous things for it."[*]

T H E first sneak preview of *Jaws* at Dallas's Medallion Theater on March 26, 1975, was advertised without the title but with a drawing of a shark menacing a swimmer, lifted from the cover of the paperback edition. Zanuck and Brown drove from their hotel at three in the afternoon to check out the theater. "There was a huge line," recalls Zanuck. "We asked each other, 'What's playing here?' Then it dawned on us."

The landlocked Texans greeted the movie with a gratifying cacophony of screams, cheers, and applause. Not only that, they laughed in all the right places and didn't laugh at the shark. There was so much demand to see *Jaws* that a second screening had to be added that night. The producers celebrated with champagne in a penthouse of the Registry Hotel until four in the morning with Spielberg, Sheinberg, Gilmore, Fields, and Williams.

"When we heard that first scream, David and I nudged each other—we were in," Zanuck says. "A lot of doomsayers had pronounced the picture terrible and in trouble. We ourselves had some concerns. We were so accus-

---

[*] On another movie, when cinematographer Allen Daviau worried about a technical glitch, Spielberg told him, "John Williams will put some cellos in there and you'll look like a genius."

tomed to the shark being a failure that until we had heard that first scream in the theater, we didn't know whether it was going to be a scream or a failure or a [Bronx cheer]. The word got out immediately to Wall Street." The morning after the preview, while preparing to leave Dallas, Brown received a call from his stockbroker in New York, who "told *me* that we had had two previews, the exact card count at both, and gave me the comments of leading exhibitors who were in the audience. The stock of MCA/Universal went up several points."

The reaction was confirmed at another preview at the Lakewood Theater in Long Beach, California, on March 28. The audience in the seaside city where Spielberg had attended college gave *Jaws* a standing ovation. One member of the public wrote on a preview card, "This is a great film. Now don't fuck it up by trying to make it better." But they *did* make it better. "There were certain things we did not know were going to be big laughs," Fields said. "Nobody knew that Roy Scheider saying, after the shark jumps, '[You'll] need a bigger boat' was going to be an enormous laugh. As a matter of fact, we went back and looped it to try to raise the volume. Nobody ever hears that line thoroughly because they're still mumbling from the scream. I have tapes of the preview that are incredible because that audience not only went out of their seats, they carried on and talked for a full minute."

A more substantial change was made in the underwater scene of Dreyfuss exploring the wreckage of a boat and coming upon the body of a man killed by a shark. "I have a four-scream movie," Spielberg said. "I think I can get it up to a five-scream." Spielberg had a dummy head constructed and, using camera equipment surreptitiously borrowed from the studio, shot new footage in Verna Fields's backyard swimming pool, punching up the moment when Dreyfuss discovers the head popping out of a hole in the boat. The footage was inserted in time for the final preview at Hollywood's Cinerama Dome on April 24, and it became one of the movie's two biggest screams, along with the scene of the shark jumping out of the water at Roy Scheider.

O N its fourteenth day of release following its opening on June 20, 1975, *Jaws* turned a profit. Sixty-four days later, on September 5, it surpassed Francis Ford Coppola's *The Godfather* to become the most successful film in motion picture history to that date.

Jaws held that distinction until November 1977, when it was dethroned by George Lucas's *Star Wars*. Spielberg took out an ad in the Hollywood trade press showing the little robot from *Star Wars,* R2D2, catching Bruce the shark in his jaws with a fishing hook. Congratulating Lucas for capturing the box-office title, Spielberg wrote, "Wear it well. Your pal, Steven." Inflated ticket prices would help push several other movies—including Spielberg's own blockbusters *E.T.* and *Jurassic Park*—ahead of *Jaws* on the list of the top box-office hits. But with its $458 million in world box-office gross, *Jaws* remains one of Hollywood's most phenomenal successes, all the more re-markable in light of its calamitous production history.*

"IT'S A MOVIE, TOO!" Universal reminded readers of *The Wall Street Journal* in a July 10 advertisement. By then, the iconography of the shark and his naked female prey had become ubiquitous. The ad reprinted several editorial cartoons, including one showing the shark with its teeth shaped like a ham-mer and sickle, attacking Uncle Sam, and another showing the shark as the CIA, attacking the Statue of Liberty. The public frenzy landed Bruce on the cover of *Time* and prompted the opening of a "Jaws" discotheque in the Hamptons. Ice-cream stands began selling such flavors as "sharklate," "finilla," and "jawberry," and a Maryland entrepreneur with a macabre sense of humor began marketing strap-on Styrofoam shark fins. Although Universal was not prepared for the full extent of the demand, it hurriedly licensed a wide variety of product tie-ins, including T-shirts, beach towels, inflatable sharks, and shark's tooth jewelry; animal-rights activists managed to stop the studio tour's souvenir shop from selling bottles of formaldehyde containing actual shark fetuses. (Months before *Jaws* opened, Spielberg proposed that the studio sell little chocolate sharks which, when bitten, would squirt cherry juice. "We'll clean up," he said, but Universal vetoed the idea.)

Universal spent $1.8 million, an extraordinary amount at that time, for pre-opening advertising on the film, including $700,000 for TV commercials. But no amount of ballyhoo could account for the way that *Jaws,* as *Newsweek* put it, appealed to "primal fears buried deep in the collective unconscious of all mankind." The magazine also suggested an underlying political reason for the film's runaway success, quoting psychiatrist Alfred Messer, who "viewed the film as a metaphor for the 'helplessness and powerlessness' ordinary folk in the United States feel in their everyday lives—just this once with a happy ending." Fidel Castro offered a Marxist interpretation of *Jaws,* seeing it as an indictment of greedy capitalists willing to sacrifice people's lives to protect their investments. "Wonderful!" exclaimed Spielberg when he heard Castro's remark. "That's the whole *Enemy of the People* question."

Critical opinion on the film was widely divergent, showing that the battle lines were beginning to be drawn on Spielberg.

"*Jaws* is an artistic and commercial smash," wrote *Daily Variety* reviewer Art Murphy, calling it "a film of consummate suspense, tension, and terror."

---

* While MCA stock skyrocketed, Alfred Hitchcock was shooting his last film, *Family Plot,* at Universal. He gleefully received daily reports on the box-office performance of *Jaws* and its effect on his sizable stock holdings. Spielberg had been thrown off the set of Hitchcock's *Torn Curtain* ten years earlier, but he still wanted to see the man he considered "The Master" at work, so after *Jaws* was released, he crashed the *Family Plot* soundstage. "Hitchcock was sitting with his back to me watching the action," he recalled. "All of a sudden it was as if he sensed an intruder in his reverse vision. He couldn't have seen me, but he leaned over to an assistant director and whispered something. A few moments passed and the AD came over to me and said, 'Sir, this is a closed set.' I was escorted off the set and it was actually quite thrilling. That was the closest I came to Hitchcock. I learned that he had eyes in the back of his head."

Time's anonymous cover story described *Jaws* as "technically intricate and wonderfully crafted, a movie whose every shock is a devastating surprise." Frank Rich proclaimed in *New Times* that "Spielberg is blessed with a talent that is absurdly absent from most American filmmakers these days: this man actually knows how to tell a story on screen. . . . It speaks well of this director's gifts that some of the most frightening sequences in *Jaws* are those where we don't even see the shark."

But William S. Pechter confessed in *Commentary* that he could not "warm very much to filmmaking of this essentially manipulative sort, whose sole aim is systematically to reduce one to a quivering mass of ectoplasm. *Jaws* is the very essence of what Brecht characterized as the 'culinary' element in modern art, high and low—a mind-numbing repast for sense-sated gluttons." While grudgingly admitting that *Jaws* was "a scare machine that works with computer-like precision," Molly Haskell told the readers of *The Village Voice* that she did not feel "compelled to give it a rave review because I jumped out of my seat. . . . You feel like a rat, being given shock treatment."

When *Jaws* broke the box-office record, Universal took out an eight-page ad in *Variety* quoting dozens of positive snippets from reviews and claiming hyperbolically, "The most popular movie of all time is also the most acclaimed film of our time." Sid Sheinberg told the *Los Angeles Times* that July, "I want to be the first to predict that Steve will win the best-director Oscar this year." But as Spielberg noted, "For the first twelve weeks of *Jaws,* people were thrilled by it. Six months later they were saying that no film that made that amount of money could be that good."

In February 1976, Spielberg blithely ushered a camera crew from a Los Angeles TV station into his office to record his reactions as he watched the Oscar nominations being announced on television. "*Jaws* is about to be nominated in eleven categories," he declared. "You're about to see a sweep of the nominations. We're very confident." But as the last name was read from the list of directing nominations, the TV crew captured Spielberg's astonishment: "Oh, I didn't get it!" he moaned, clenching his fists against his cheeks. "I didn't get it! I wasn't *nominated!* I got beaten out by Fellini."* That slap in the face was given an added sting when *Jaws* received a Best Picture nomination. Told that his film also had been nominated for music, editing, and sound, Spielberg said, "That's *it?* Best screenplay, we didn't—? Not even *special effects?*" Regaining his composure somewhat, he picked up his own video camera and taped himself saying in a jocular tone of voice, "For *my* record, I am outraged that I wasn't nominated for best director for *Jaws.*" He added, "This is called 'commercial backlash.' . . . [W]hen a film makes a lot of money, people resent it. Everybody loves a winner. But nobody loves a *WINNER.*" Although *Jaws* went on to win the three craft

---

* Federico Fellini was nominated for *Amarcord*. The other nominees were Robert Altman, for *Nashville;* Milos Forman, *One Flew Over the Cuckoo's Nest;* Stanley Kubrick, *Barry Lyndon;* and Sidney Lumet, *Dog Day Afternoon.*

"Scouting gave me my start," Steven Spielberg once said. He began making story films as a Boy Scout in Phoenix, Arizona. Filmmaking allowed him to express his feelings in "a place where I felt safer: in front of my camera." He is shown outside Ingleside Elementary School in July 1961 with fellow Scouts Ray Chenhall and Bill Hoffman as their troop prepares to leave for its annual summer camping trip. (Photo by Richard Y. Hoffman Jr.)

I hereby certify this to be a true certified copy of the certificate on file with the Cincinnati Board of Health.   Date Issued: FEB 17 1994

Richard G. Howard M.B.A.
Local Registrar, City of Cincinnati
Assistant Commissioner of Health

OHIO DEPARTMENT OF HEALTH
COLUMBUS
CERTIFICATE OF LIVE BIRTH   State File No. 1547

1. PLACE OF BIRTH:	2. USUAL RESIDENCE OF MOTHER: 66
(a) County Hamilton	(a) State
(b) Cincinnati	(b) County
(c) Name of hospital or institution Jewish Hospital	(c) City or village (If outside city or village, write RURAL)
(d) Mother's stay before delivery 5hrs. In this community 26yrs	(d) Street No. 817 Lexington Ave.

| 3. FULL NAME OF CHILD Steven Allan Spielberg | 4. DATE OF BIRTH: Dec. 18, 1946 |

9. Full name Arnold Spielberg
10. Color or race White 11. Age at time of this birth 29 yrs.
12. Birthplace Cincinnati, Ohio
13. Usual occupation Student
14. Industry or business University of Cincinnati

15. Full maiden name Leah Posner
16. Color or race White Age at this time 26
18. Birthplace Cincinnati, Ohio
19. Usual occupation Housewife

24. I hereby certify that I attended the birth of this child who was born alive at the hour of 6:16 P M and that the information given was furnished Leah Spielberg related to this child as Mother

25. Registrar's signature Grace LePoria, Dep.
26. Date received by local registrar JAN 13 1947

Signature F.A.S.Kautz, MD.
Address 19 W.7th St.
Date signed 12/16/46

For years, Spielberg claimed he was born on December 18, 1947, but his birth certificate shows the date to be one year earlier. (Cincinnati Board of Health, Office of Vital Statistics)

Steven's parents, Leah and Arnold, were delighted and somewhat bewildered by the unusual creature they had brought into the world. "When he was growing up, I didn't know he was a genius," his mother later admitted. "Frankly, I didn't know what the hell he was."

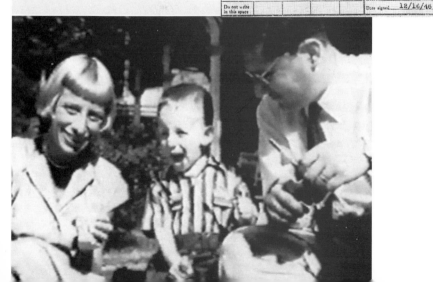

When Spielberg received his Life Achievement Award from the American Film Institute on March 2, 1995, his divorced parents were reunited. Paying tribute to them in his acceptance speech, he said, "Growing up was frustrating for me. . . . But I thank you for letting me own that experience. Thanks for giving me the chance to answer some of my own questions, for not panicking and trying to spoonfeed me all the answers." (American Film Institute/NBC-TV)

"Just as I'd become accustomed to a school and a teacher and a best friend, the FOR SALE sign would dig into the front lawn"—as it did in front of the Spielberg home at 267 Crystal Terrace in Haddon Township, New Jersey, on December 16, 1956, shortly before the family left for Arizona. (Loretta Knoblach)

On the rare occasions when his "workaholic" father accompanied him on Boy Scout camping trips near Phoenix, "We became our closest," Steve remembered. This was November 1958, shortly before his twelfth birthday. Bill Hoffman is at right. (Photo by Richard Y. Hoffman Jr.)

STEVE HOLDING THE FLAMING ARROW PATROL FLAG OF INGLESIDE'S TROOP 294 IN THE FALL OF 1960. HE THOUGHT OF THE BOY SCOUTS AS BEING "LIKE A SURROGATE DAD." (PHOTO BY RICHARD Y. HOFFMAN JR.)

INFATUATED WITH THE SIXTEEN-YEAR-OLD SPIELBERG, HIGH SCHOOL CLASSMATE SUE ROPER, WHILE BABY-SITTING FOR HIS SISTERS, SKETCHED THIS SOULFUL POSE AS STEVE WATCHED TELEVISION ON THE COUCH OF HIS HOME IN PHOENIX. (SUSAN ROPER ARNDT, 1963)

THIS HANDMADE CREDIT EMBLAZONED SPIELBERG'S 1960 WORLD WAR II FLYING MOVIE, FIGHTER SQUAD.

SPIELBERG ALREADY HAD VISIONS OF BECOMING ANOTHER DAVID LEAN WHEN HE RE-CREATED WORLD WAR II IN *ESCAPE TO NOWHERE* (1959–62), HIS 8MM EPIC SET IN NORTH AFRICA. THIS BATTLE SCENE WAS SHOT ON CAMELBACK MOUNTAIN, STEVE'S ALL-PURPOSE LOCATION NEAR HIS HOME IN PHOENIX. *(BARRY SOLLENBERGER)*

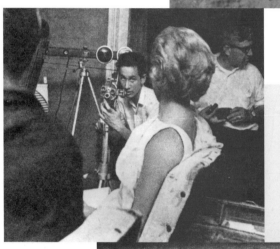

BY THE END OF HIS YEARS IN PHOENIX, SPIELBERG HAD BECOME SUCH A HOMETOWN CELEBRITY THAT *THE ARIZONA REPUBLIC* SENT PHOTOGRAPHER RALPH CAMPING TO DOCUMENT THE MAKING OF HIS FIRST FEATURE, *FIRELIGHT*, IN 1963. STEVE IS SHOWN BEHIND HIS BOLEX 8MM CAMERA, FILMING ACTRESS CAROL STROMME, WITH HIS FATHER AS A CREW MEMBER, AND SHOOTING THE OPENING SEQUENCE INSIDE THE FAMILY CARPORT, USING HIS MOTHER'S JEEP TO SIMULATE A DRIVE THROUGH THE DESERT NIGHT. *(PHOENIX NEWSPAPERS, INC.)*

American Artist Productions
presents

World Première
OF THE MOTION PICTURE

FIRELIGHT

Phoenix Little Theatre

MARCH 24, 1964
8:00 P.M.

THE PREMIERE OF *FIRELIGHT* IN PHOENIX WAS COM-
MEMORATED WITH A MIMEOGRAPHED PROGRAM.
(SUSAN ROPER ARNDT)

CONFERRING WITH CAMERAMAN SERGE HAIGNERE, SPIELBERG SHOWS CONCERN ABOUT THE SHOOTING SCHEDULE DURING THE
1967 FILMING OF HIS UNFINISHED BICYCLE MOVIE, *SLIPSTREAM*. BECAUSE THE DIRECTORS HE WATCHED AT UNIVERSAL WORE TIES
AND SWEATERS, THE ASPIRING YOUNG DIRECTOR DID TOO. *(© RALPH BURRIS)*

THE FIRST FILM SPIELBERG COMPLETED IN 35MM, *AMBLIN'* (1968) WAS A SHORT SUBJECT DESIGNED TO PROVE HE COULD MAKE A PROFESSIONAL-LOOKING MOVIE. HE BEGAN FILMING THIS BITTERSWEET TALE ABOUT A YOUNG HITCHHIKING COUPLE THAT JULY ON A SOUNDSTAGE IN HOLLYWOOD. *AMBLIN'* WON SPIELBERG A SEVEN-YEAR CONTRACT AS A UNIVERSAL TV DIRECTOR. (© RALPH BURRIS)

THE END OF THE ROAD IN *AMBLIN'*: FORESHADOWING THE MATURE SPIELBERG VISUAL STYLE, THIS COMPOSITION REVEALS THE CONTRASTING MOODS OF PAMELA MCMYLER AND RICHARD LEVIN AS THEY REACH THE PACIFIC OCEAN. ALLEN DAVIAU, WHO LATER PHOTOGRAPHED *E.T.* AND OTHER SPIELBERG FEATURES, WAS THE CINEMATOGRAPHER.

PRODUCER DENIS C. HOFFMAN ACCEPTING AN AWARD FOR *AMBLIN'* WITH SPIELBERG AT THE 1969 ATLANTA FILM FESTIVAL. TWENTY-SIX YEARS LATER, THE FORMER PARTNERS SUED EACH OTHER OVER THE OPTION CLAUSE IN THEIR CONTRACT. (*DENIS C. HOFFMAN*)

JOAN CRAWFORD WAS TAKEN ABACK BY SPIELBERG'S YOUTH, BUT THE LEGENDARY STAR BEHAVED LIKE A TROUPER WHEN HE DIRECTED HER IN HIS FIRST PROFESSIONAL ASSIGNMENT, THE "EYES" SEGMENT OF ROD SERLING'S 1969 TV MOVIE NIGHT GALLERY. (PHOTOFEST/UNIVERSAL TELEVISION)

THE LANDMARK 1971 TV MOVIE *DUEL*, WITH DENNIS WEAVER, VAULTED SPIELBERG INTO THE LEADING RANKS OF HOLLYWOOD FILM-MAKERS. "I KNEW THAT HERE WAS A VERY BRIGHT NEW DIRECTOR," PROCLAIMED DAVID LEAN AFTER *DUEL* PLAYED IN THEATERS OUT-SIDE THE UNITED STATES. (*THE ACADEMY OF MOTION PICTURE ARTS AND SCIENCES/ UNIVERSAL PICTURES*)

A PORTRAIT OF THE ARTIST AS A YOUNG MAN, CIRCA 1976. (*COLUMBIA PICTURES*)

THE FIRST SPIELBERG FEATURE RE-LEASED TO AMERICAN THEATERS, *THE SUGARLAND EXPRESS* (1974), WAS HAILED BY *NEW YORKER* REVIEWER PAULINE KAEL AS "ONE OF THE MOST PHENOMENAL DEBUT FILMS IN THE HISTORY OF MOVIES." SPIELBERG SHARES A LIGHT MOMENT WITH GOLDIE HAWN, WILLIAM ATHERTON, AND MICHAEL SACKS ON LOCATION IN TEXAS. (*UNIVERSAL PICTURES*)

AN UNFORGETTABLE MOMENT OF MOVIE TERROR—THE OPENING OF *JAWS* (1975), WITH SUSAN BACK-LINIE AS THE SKINNY-DIPPING SWIMMER ATTACKED BY AN UNSEEN SHARK. FOR SPIELBERG, CLAD IN A WET SUIT AS HE DIRECTED THE YOUNG STUNTWOMAN OFF MARTHA'S VINEYARD, THE FILMING WAS AN EXCRUCI-ATING ORDEAL HE FEARED MIGHT RUIN HIS PROMISING CAREER. BUT *JAWS* WENT ON TO BREAK ALL BOX-OFFICE RECORDS. *(UNIVERSAL PICTURES)*

CLOSE ENCOUNTERS OF THE THIRD KIND (1977) WAS SPIELBERG'S DREAM PROJECT, HIS $19-MILLION "REMAKE" OF *FIRELIGHT*. THE UFO LANDING SITE IN SPIELBERG'S SCIENCE-FICTION MASTERPIECE WAS DEVIL'S TOWER NATIONAL MONUMENT IN WYOMING. *(COLUMBIA PICTURES)*

SPIELBERG SELECTED THIS SCENE WHEN ASKED TO IDENTIFY A SINGLE "MASTER IMAGE" THAT SUMS UP HIS WORK — THE LITTLE BOY IN *CLOSE ENCOUNTERS* (CARY GUFFEY) OPENS HIS LIVING-ROOM DOOR TO SEE THE "BEAUTIFUL BUT AWFUL LIGHT" EMANATING FROM A UFO. "AND HE'S VERY SMALL, AND IT'S A VERY LARGE DOOR, AND THERE'S A LOT OF PROMISE OR DANGER OUTSIDE THAT DOOR." *(COLUMBIA PICTURES)*

AMY IRVING WITH SPIELBERG AT THE GOLDEN GLOBES CEREMONY IN 1989, IN THE FINAL MONTHS OF THEIR MARRIAGE. *(COLLECTORS BOOKSTORE)*

REHEARSING THE CLIFFHANGER OPENING SEQUENCE OF THE FIRST INDIANA JONES MOVIE, *RAIDERS OF THE LOST ARK* (1981), SPIELBERG DEMONSTRATES TO HARRISON FORD WHY HE GAVE UP ACTING FOR DIRECTING. *(PARAMOUNT PICTURES)*

SPIELBERG'S SECRET IN ELICITING SUCH EXTRAORDINARY PERFORMANCES FROM CHILDREN IS SIMPLE—HE TREATS THEM AS EQUALS. SPEAKING QUIETLY TO HENRY THOMAS BEFORE THEY SHOOT THE SCENE OF ELLIOTT WATCHING HIS ALIEN FRIEND DYING IN *E.T. THE EXTRA-TERRESTRIAL*, THE DIRECTOR IS TELLING THE YOUNG ACTOR, "IT'LL BE SADDER IF IT'S HAPPY-SAD, YOU KNOW WHAT I'M SAYING? I THINK *YOU'LL* FEEL SADDER IF IT'S MORE YOU'RE TRYING TO COVER THAT UP, TRYING TO COVER THE SADNESS WITH SOME HAPPY TALK TO E.T." *(UNIVERSAL PICTURES)*

MAKING *E.T.* LEFT SPIELBERG WITH A "DEEP YEARNING" TO BECOME A FATHER. HERE HE DIRECTS THE IRREPRESSIBLE DREW BARRYMORE AS ELLIOTT'S LITTLE SISTER, GERTIE. *(UNIVERSAL PICTURES)*

Inspired by the nursery rhyme "The cow jumped over the Moon," this famous Spielberg image from *E.T.* later became the logo of his production company, Amblin Entertainment. (*Universal Pictures*)

During the making of *Twilight Zone — The Movie* on July 23, 1982, veteran actor Vic Morrow struggles to cross a river carrying seven-year-old My-Ca Dinh Le (left) and six-year-old Renee Shin-Yi Chen (right), at Indian Dunes Park north of Los Angeles. Moments later, the three were killed by a crashing helicopter. This footage was not included in the film but became an exhibit in the trial of director John Landis and four others involved in the filming. Spielberg, who produced the film with Landis, was not charged.

Kate Capshaw as she appeared in *Indiana Jones and the Temple of Doom* (1984), five years before becoming the director's second wife. (*Paramount Pictures*)

SPIELBERG'S DECISION TO FILM *THE COLOR PURPLE*, ALICE WALKER'S NOVEL ABOUT A BATTERED AFRICAN AMERICAN WOMAN, BAFFLED MANY OBSERVERS AND ANGERED SOME. BUT THE DIRECTOR FELT A DEEP PERSONAL KINSHIP WITH THE EMOTIONALLY RESILIENT CELIE, PLAYED BY COMEDIENNE WHOOPI GOLDBERG IN HER HEARTRENDING 1985 FILM DEBUT. *(WARNER BROS.)*

SPIELBERG'S FILM OF J. G. BALLARD'S *EMPIRE OF THE SUN* (1987) LOOKS AT WORLD WAR II THROUGH THE EYES OF JIM GRAHAM (CHRISTIAN BALE), A BRITISH ADOLESCENT INTERNED IN A JAPANESE PRISON CAMP IN CHINA. BALE, WHOSE PERFORMANCE IS THE FINEST SPIELBERG HAS DRAWN FROM A CHILD ACTOR, IS SEEN ON THE SET IN SPAIN WITH SPIELBERG AND JOHN MALKOVICH. *(WARNER BROS.)*

SPIELBERG AT WORK ON *INDIANA JONES AND THE LAST CRUSADE* (1989) WITH PRODUCER FRANK MARSHALL (FAR LEFT) AND EXECUTIVE PRODUCER GEORGE LUCAS, TWO OF HIS MOST IMPORTANT COLLABORATORS THROUGHOUT THE 1980s; BRITISH CINEMATOGRAPHER DOUGLAS SLOCOMBE IS AT FAR RIGHT. *(PARAMOUNT PICTURES)*

One reason *Jurassic Park* became the highest-grossing film ever made is that Spielberg so effectively tapped into primal fears about children in jeopardy. In the film's most bravura set piece, child-hating paleontologist Grant (Sam Neill) is forced to protect young Arianna Richards from the rampaging *T. rex*. *(Universal Pictures)*

"The critics in awe of how much I've stretched just don't know me," Spielberg said after filming Thomas Keneally's *Schindler's List* in 1993. ". . . I had to tell the story." With Liam Neeson playing Oskar Schindler, the German industrialist who rescued eleven hundred Jews from the Holocaust, Spielberg filmed this scene outside the Auschwitz death camp in Poland. *(Universal Pictures)*

In *Schindler's List*, the irresponsible father figure familiar from so many Spielberg films gradually comes to accept his responsibility. *(Universal Pictures)*

Spielberg considers his work as founder of the Survivors of the Shoah Visual History Foundation "the most important job I've ever done." In the foundation's 1996 documentary *Survivors of the Holocaust*, Sol Liber concludes his testimony by saying, "I cheated Hitler and his henchmen, and this is what I got right here—a lovely family, my wife and my kids. And this is the happiest moment of my life, because I loaded everything on tape. Maybe I'm not gonna be so crazy anymore." *(Turner Home Entertainment)*

Sol Liber and Family

"I feel I have a responsibility," Spielberg said while directing *Jurassic Park* (left). "And I want to go back and forth from entertainment to socially conscious movies." The film project he chose to follow *Schindler's List* was *The Lost World*, his 1997 sequel to *Jurassic Park*. *(Universal Pictures/ Amblin Entertainment)*

Oscars at the March 29 ceremony, it lost in the top category to *One Flew Over the Cuckoo's Nest,* whose director, Milos Forman, also received an Oscar.

Richard Zanuck later commented that Spielberg "made a terrible mistake having a television crew with him when they read the names." The humiliating experience evidently taught Spielberg not to wear his heart so publicly on his sleeve about the Oscars and other sensitive subjects. His youthful candor to interviewers gradually gave way to far more circumspect public utterances, such as his remark a few years later, "I think my films are too, umm, popular for the Academy."

NEVERTHELESS, *Jaws* had a profound and lasting influence on Hollywood and the way it does business. The most obvious impact was the most superficial: the plethora of cheesy *Jaws* sequels and rip-offs that followed in its wake, such as *Orca, Grizzly, Alligator, Day of the Animals, Eaten Alive, Tentacles, Great White, The Jaws of Death, Jaws of Satan,* and *Piranha.* Spielberg considered the low-budget, tongue-in-cheek *Piranha* "the best of the *Jaws* ripoffs." The film's director, Joe Dante, learned later that Universal was "less than thrilled *Piranha* was coming out at the same time [in 1978] as *Jaws 2*. They wanted to take out an injunction. Steven saw it and said, 'This picture's OK. Leave them alone.' "

Spielberg initially did not want anything to do with Universal's inevitable attempt to capitalize further on the success of *Jaws*. While being honored with a somewhat premature retrospective at the San Francisco Film Festival in October 1975, he told the audience that "making a sequel to anything is just a cheap carny trick." Universal, he said, "offered me the opportunity to direct the sequel, but I didn't even answer them. I didn't call or write or anything." Despite those harsh words, his attitude changed in June 1977, when *Jaws 2* director John Hancock was fired in the early days of shooting. Universal then offered the job to its feature-production vice president, Verna Fields. Because Spielberg felt Fields had received too much credit for the success of *Jaws,* it may have been the prospect of her directing the sequel that briefly caused him to reconsider his opposition.

David Brown recalled that while he and Zanuck were negotiating with Fields, Spielberg (then in postproduction on *Close Encounters*) "called Dick and me in Martha's Vineyard and said he would like to be of any help he could. He felt allegiance to the project. We said, 'Do you think you could do it?' And he said, 'Let me think about it.' At this point I said to Verna, 'How would you feel if we could get Steve? We feel we should take him, don't you?' And she said, 'I would insist upon it.' Steve also called Sid Sheinberg. . . . We finally had another telephone call from Steve, who said he would definitely like to do it. And negotiations were undertaken. However, because of his contract with *Close Encounters,* he couldn't undertake the contract for a year. Furthermore, he wanted to make radical revisions on the script."

Spielberg offered a somewhat different account: "I said I'd spend the July Fourth weekend trying to find the solution to a sequel and that if I could write it and Zanuck and Brown would push the production to the spring of '78, I'd do it. I spent three days at the typewriter and wrote seven or eight schematic breakdowns. I kept the Dreyfuss and Scheider characters in it. Then I finally said to myself, 'I can't, I can't.' For me, a sequel becomes a real fish story. I called Sid back and said I couldn't do it. . . . I decided a sequel would not be an exercise in expanding my own horizons. It would be corporate business."

According to Joe Alves, Spielberg had proposed scrapping the existing script for *Jaws 2* and dealing with the mass attack by sharks in 1945 on sailors from the USS *Indianapolis,* the story recounted by Robert Shaw in *Jaws.* Howard Sackler, who wrote *Jaws 2* with Carl Gottlieb, previously had suggested basing it on the *Indianapolis* incident, but was overruled by Sheinberg, who said, "That's a different kind of shirt than we want to wear."* Whether or not Spielberg would have been able to change Sheinberg's mind, it was the director's scheduling demand that proved decisive. "[W]e couldn't wait that long," Brown explained. "We had a cast and crew and contracts and a release date." Universal reapproached Fields, but the Directors Guild of America would not give her a waiver to direct the film, so the job went to Jeannot Szwarc. *Jaws 2* ran into many of the same production problems as the original, but its commercial success in 1978 led to two even tackier, more pointless sequels, *Jaws 3-D* (directed by Alves, 1983) and *Jaws: The Revenge* (directed by Joseph Sargent, 1987).

The most lasting impact of *Jaws* on Hollywood was in helping bring about what has been called "the blockbuster mentality." Before *Jaws,* it was rare for an important film to open in several hundred theaters simultaneously. But that was what Universal originally planned to do with it. "Universal had planned a mass-saturation blitzkrieg campaign in more than 1,000 theaters," Spielberg told *The Hollywood Reporter* in the week after the opening. "I don't think then that Universal knew what it had on its hands." But after the second preview in Long Beach, Universal scaled back the planned initial break to 409 theaters and "began handling the film with kid gloves," Spielberg said. The publicity and word of mouth had a steamroller effect, making *Jaws* not only a national fad, like hula hoops in the 1950s, but a national event. As a result, studios began opening films more and more widely, and eventually it was not unusual for a potential blockbuster to open simultaneously on two thousand or even three thousand screens, backed by advertising expenditures of commensurately gargantuan proportions.

The blockbuster mentality made Hollywood concentrate its resources on fewer and more expensive films. Most film critics and historians believe that trend has had a serious impact on the overall quality of films made in Hollywood in the last twenty years. Spielberg and George Lucas, whose films

---

* The *Indianapolis* incident served as the basis for a 1991 TV movie, *Mission of the Shark.*

have dominated the list of biggest box-office hits, have seen their critical reputations suffer as a result. In part, Spielberg and Lucas were simply being blamed for their popularity, for in America's traditionally puritanical dichotomy between art and entertainment, a popular artist is automatically and unfairly suspected of not being an artist. But more serious questions, ones that would haunt Spielberg's career after *Jaws,* were posed by film historian Peter Biskind in his 1990 essay "Blockbuster: The Last Crusade." Biskind argued that Spielberg and Lucas, with their high-tech, massively popular "aesthetic of awe," had helped "reduce an entire culture to childishness. . . . To infantilize the audience of the sixties and empower the audience of the seventies, to reconstitute the spectator as child, Lucas and Spielberg had to obliterate years of sophisticated, adult moviegoing habits. . . . The blockbuster syndrome probably started with *The Godfather* in 1972 and got an added boost from *Jaws* in 1975 but really took off with *Star Wars.* Once it became clear that certain kinds of films could reap immeasurably greater returns on investment than had ever been seen before, studios naturally wanted to turn the trick again, and again, and again: enter the Roman-numeral movie, product of the obsession with surefire hits. Blockbusters were expensive to make, and the more they cost, the safer and blander they became, while the smaller, riskier, innovative projects fell by the wayside."

S PIELBERG'S own personal fortunes were greatly changed by *Jaws.* His directing fee under his Universal contract was "very meager" compared to what another director might have been paid for the film, Zanuck says, and the studio initially "refused to give him any percentage at all," but before the film was released Spielberg was granted 2.5 percent of the net profits. Spielberg's agent at ICM, Guy McElwaine, also renegotiated his contract with Universal in July 1975. The new four-picture contract for Spielberg and his Amblin' production company* obligated Spielberg to direct two more films for the studio by 1981, but provided that he also would receive a share of the profits.

With each point of *Jaws* worth more than a million dollars, Spielberg became a wealthy man at the age of twenty-eight, though not on the scale of Zanuck and Brown, who shared about forty points in the film; Zanuck said he made more money from *Jaws* than his father, Darryl, made in his entire career in the movie business. *Close Encounters* producer Michael Phillips says Spielberg "still feels that, in principle, two [and a half] percent was too little for his contribution [to *Jaws*]."

More important to Spielberg than the money he made for *Jaws,* however, was the creative freedom the movie bought him: "It was a free ticket for half a dozen rides." The immediate leverage it gave him was to convince Columbia Pictures to keep increasing the budget on *Close Encounters* at a time when

---

* The first mention of the name Amblin' in that context, with the apostrophe temporarily intact.

that studio was in precarious financial condition. "After *Jaws,*" recalls Phillips, "the money spigots opened."

Spielberg's newfound success also brought with it a new level of anxiety, for he found that people kept asking him, "How are you going to top *Jaws?*" But, said Phillips in 1977, "Steven is a *mensch*. The only change in him is that he's stronger now and better able to get what he wants. His values are the same. He could have had his head turned by the success of *Jaws,* but all it did was give him more toys to play with. The interesting thing now is that he's still maturing as a person. He's mastered his craft. I think his films will change now as his experience deepens. In other words, he's only going to get better."

ELEVEN

WATCH THE SKIES

"IT IS GOOD TO RENEW ONE'S WONDER," SAID THE PHILOSOPHER. "SPACE TRAVEL HAS AGAIN MADE CHILDREN OF US ALL."

— RAY BRADBURY, *THE MARTIAN CHRONICLES*

UNLIKE most of the science-fiction movies Spielberg grew up watching, *Close Encounters of the Third Kind* takes a benign view of human contact with extraterrestrials. The aliens in Spielberg's film don't carry ray guns or threaten to blow up the Planet Earth. They aren't fire-breathing creatures with horns and tentacles, but childlike figures with spindly limbs, large craniums, and shy, beatific smiles. They are emissaries of goodwill, communicating through a dazzling display of light and music. And they are received in similar spirit. Spielberg's optimistic vision of interplanetary contact marked a radical departure from the Cold War xenophobia that characterized most sci-fi movies in the 1950s, when fear of space aliens served as a metaphor for America's phobia about Communism.

The Jewish filmmaker who grew up thinking of himself as an "alien" in Middle America, and whose family was not far removed from its immigrant roots, gravitated toward the point of view of the outsiders in *Close Encounters,* seeing their arrival and influence in only the most positive, transforming light. Spielberg often has been accused of romanticizing suburban conformity, but *Close Encounters* paints a harsh picture of the dull, repressive midwestern community where the UFOs make their first appearance. Municipal power repairman Roy Neary (Richard Dreyfuss)* yearns to escape from his Muncie, Indiana, surroundings to share the company of fellow "aliens." Roy's "whole belief structure is shattered," Spielberg commented. ". . . He had to go through . . . I guess you could call it a 'socially dislocating awakening'; and without this cultural shock there is no way he would have been ready or capable or willing to step on that ship and leave the parameters of our astronomy."

Close Encounters and *Schindler's List* form contrasting yet complementary thematic bookends in the trajectory of Spielberg's career to date. *Schindler's List,* Spielberg's most powerful confrontation with reality, depicts the cruelty with which the world too often treats those it considers "alien," and yet, while facing this bitter fact, the film still manages to find a solitary ray of hope. *Close Encounters,* Spielberg's most spellbinding dream of the transcendence of mundane reality, celebrates the potential for universal brotherhood, while offering in its purest form what the director called "my vision, my hope and philosophy."

T H E origins of *Close Encounters* trace back to Spielberg's experiences watching a wondrous meteor shower with his father as a young boy in Phoenix. The film germinated in his mind throughout his adolescence, when he absorbed vast quantities of science-fiction books, movies, and TV shows, and watched the desert skies over Camelback Mountain through his front-yard telescope.

Two seminal cinematic memories from childhood stood out in Spielberg's mind when he began work on *Close Encounters* in the 1970s. The first was the image of the mountain from the terrifying "Night on Bald Mountain" sequence in *Fantasia.* The second was a soothing memory from another Disney movie: the song "When You Wish Upon a Star," performed in *Pinocchio* by Cliff (Ukulele Ike) Edwards as Jiminy Cricket. "I pretty much hung my story on the mood the song created, the way it affected me emotionally," Spielberg said. "The mountain became the symbolic end zone of the movie, and everything danced around that."

His 1964 rough draft for *Close Encounters, Firelight,* seemed to vacillate on the question of whether a meeting with alien kidnappers was something to be feared or something to be welcomed. Perhaps it was Spielberg's youthful ambivalence toward his own ethnic identity, and his resulting tendency to identify more with the dominant culture, that was keeping him from fully accepting the "alien" within him. According to producer Michael Phillips,

---

* Spielberg originally wanted Jack Nicholson to play the lead role in *Close Encounters,* but Nicholson's schedule would have required a two-year delay in the start of production. "I wrote *Close Encounters* for a forty-five-year-old man," Spielberg said, "but Dreyfuss talked me into casting him in the film. . . . Richard heard me talking about *Close Encounters* all through *Jaws.* . . . He had to listen to about 155 days' worth of *Close Encounters.* He contributed ideas, and finally he said, 'Look, turkey, cast me in this thing!' "

Spielberg still seemed somewhat conflicted on the subject in the preliminary stages of work on *Close Encounters:* "I think my biggest contribution was to convince Steven that the aliens would be friendly. He wasn't sure that, dramatically, you could have a climax of the meeting of these two species based on the sense of wonder alone. I remember arguing a great deal, saying, 'If they were this advanced, they wouldn't come to squash us. Would *we?* If we found lower life on Mars, would we enslave it or would we give help to it?' But he got into it, and went beyond it, and came up with this cornucopia at the end. That's why I think *Close Encounters* is like *The Day the Earth Stood Still.*" Historian Arthur Schlesinger Jr., on the other hand, questioned the innocent optimism of *Close Encounters:* "[H]ow can we be so sure that a civilization sufficiently in advance of our own to put its spaceship on Earth will regard us with any more consideration than white intruders from Europe regarded the Indians of the American continent, the blacks of Africa, or the primitive peoples of the South Pacific? . . . Let us pray that the future dreamed of in this humane, attractive, brilliant movie turns out to be right."

Like *Firelight,* but on a far more sophisticated level, *Close Encounters* is an eclectic compendium of sci-fi movie motifs and archetypes. Its closest affinities are with the handful of movies that departed from the Cold War norm by depicting space aliens as relatively benign, including *The Day the Earth Stood Still* and *It Came from Outer Space.* One of Spielberg's favorite sci-fi writers, Arthur C. Clarke, also was a major influence; both Clarke's 1953 novel *Childhood's End* and his story "The Sentinel," the source of Stanley Kubrick's 1968 classic film *2001: A Space Odyssey,* deal with aliens helping earthlings reach a higher plane of spiritual evolution. Somewhat more covertly, Spielberg also drew from his favorite films in other genres. Although he credits Hal Barwood and Matthew Robbins with suggesting the plot about a kidnapped child, Spielberg evidently was inspired by the treatment of that theme and some visual elements in John Ford's Western *The Searchers,* which he watched twice while on location for *Close Encounters.* Spielberg also echoed the scenes of family tension in Frank Capra's *It's a Wonderful Life.* He has noted that the theme of "ordinary people in extraordinary circumstances" (as François Truffaut's ufologist character puts it in the film) gives *Close Encounters* affinities with both Capra and Hitchcock.

"During *Close Encounters,* Steven used to see one or two movies every night," cinematographer Vilmos Zsigmond recalls. "Every night he was watching movies and getting more ideas. They had storyboarded everything; we had four sketches to do every day. Then Steven would see a movie and we would add sketches—suddenly four sketches became five we had to do, and five became six. One day Steven was complaining to the crew, 'Gotta shoot fast.' Earl Gilbert, an old, experienced gaffer [head electrician], said, 'Steven, if you would stop watching those fucking movies every night, we would be on schedule.' "

• • •

C L O S E Encounters melds such purely fictional storytelling elements with the extensive post–World War II reports and folklore about UFO sightings. The modern "flying saucer" phenomenon dates from Spielberg's infancy, when Kenneth Arnold reported sighting nine bright saucerlike objects over the Pacific Northwest in June 1947. The possibility of visitors from other planets stimulated an extraordinary mixture of fear and anticipation, especially among baby boomer children prone to fantasizing.

Spielberg's desire to escape into otherworldly fantasy was especially acute. In his 1959 book *Flying Saucers: A Modern Myth of Things Seen in the Skies,* Carl Jung suggested that a belief in UFOs stems from "an *emotional tension* having its cause in a situation of collective distress or danger, or in a vital psychic need." The Cold War and collective anxieties about the dangers of nuclear war helped stimulate that tension in Spielberg's formative years. It may not have been coincidental that the widespread revival of interest in UFOs during the early 1970s occurred at a time when the Vietnam War and the Watergate scandal were causing an unusually high degree of "collective distress" in the American psyche; Spielberg's 1973 pitch of *Close Encounters* as dealing with "UFOs and Watergate" suggests that such a connection existed in his mind. His family problems during adolescence and difficulties finding social acceptance among his peers also stimulated his fantasies of extraterrestrial contact. Another psychiatrist who has studied the UFO phenomenon, Kenneth Ring, noted that when a child from a dysfunctional family learns "to dissociate in response to the trauma," he is "much more likely to become sensitive to alternate realities."

Although Spielberg was careful to call himself an "agnostic" on the subject, the fact that his interest in UFOs only increased as he reached adulthood suggests that his "vital psychic need" to believe in such phenomena was still intact and undiminished. And he realized that he was not alone in having such a need: "I knew that if this film was to be popular it wouldn't be because people were afraid of the phenomena, but because the UFOs are a seductive alternative for a lot of people who no longer have faith in anything." In his *"Close Encounters of the Third Kind" Diary,* cast member Bob Balaban reported that on the night of July 22, 1976, during location shooting in Alabama, "some people thought they saw a UFO over the hangar. By the time Spielberg and the rest of us ran outside to look, the lights had disappeared." Spielberg, however, recalled initially being convinced that he *had* seen his first UFO that night. "When I found out later that it was only an Echo satellite," he said, "I was as depressed as I've ever been."

Soon after Spielberg finished shooting the film, John Milius took him to actor Robert Stack's duck-hunting lodge near Colusa in northern California. There had been reports for months of UFOs being sighted in the nearby buttes, and Spielberg, Stack recalls, was eager to see one. Late one night, when they were all in the cabin, Milius reported seeing a UFO outside. Spielberg stayed up the rest of the night with Milius, hoping for an encore. The caretaker on Stack's property, Bill Duffey, later told them brilliant lights had flown over that night and "lit up the entire orchard, sixty-five to seventy acres. They hung there and dropped pieces like tinfoil." Duffey said that he had jumped into his car to pursue the UFOs, which he claimed made chugging sounds, like a washing machine. "I've done research," Spielberg replied, "and that's not the sound they're supposed to make. It should be a solid humming sound."

Continuing to hope for a sign of extraterrestrial life, Spielberg donated $100,000 to The Planetary Society in 1985 to make possible its META (Megachannel Extraterrestrial Assay) system using a Harvard telescope to scan the skies for possible radio signals from distant civilizations. After throwing the switch while holding his infant son, Max, Spielberg said, "I just hope that there is more floating around up there than just old reruns of *The Jackie Gleason Show.*"

S P I E L B E R G ' S technical advisor on *Close Encounters* was the prominent ufologist Dr. J. Allen Hynek. For many years, Hynek was scientific consultant to the U.S. Air Force and its Project Blue Book on Unidentified Flying Objects. A professional astronomer, he initially was asked by the Air Force "to weed out obvious cases of astronomical phenomena—meteors, planets, twinkling stars, and other natural occurrences that could give rise to the flying saucer reports then being received. . . . For years I could not accept the idea that a genuine UFO phenomenon might exist, preferring to hold that it was all a craze based on hoaxes and misperceptions. As my review of UFO reports continued, and as the reports grew in number to be of statistical significance, I became concerned that the whole subject didn't evaporate as one would expect a craze or fad to do."

Considered a professional debunker by UFO believers, Hynek later admitted, "To put it bluntly, the Air Force was under orders from the Pentagon to debunk UFOs." Hynek broke with the Air Force in the late 1960s because he "could no longer, in good conscience, keep calling everything 'swamp gas.' " Founding the Center for UFO Studies in Evanston, Illinois, he cautiously emerged as an agnostic, if not a true believer, on the subject of UFOs and extraterrestrial contact.

It was in his 1972 book, *The UFO Experience: A Scientific Inquiry,* that Hynek originated the term "Close Encounters." He defined Close Encounters of the First Kind as those in which "the reported UFO is seen at close range but there is no interaction with the environment (other than trauma on the part of the observer)." In Close Encounters of the Second Kind, "physical effects on both animate and inanimate material are noted." Close Encounters of the Third Kind are those in which "the presence of 'occupants' in or about the UFO is reported." People who report such encounters, he wrote, "are in no way 'special.' They are not religious fanatics; they are more apt to be policemen, businessmen, schoolteachers, and other respectable citizens."

After playing a scientist in the final sequence of *Close Encounters,* Hynek said, "Even though the film is fiction, it's based for the most part on the known facts of the UFO mystery, and it certainly catches the flavor of the phenomenon. What impressed me was that Spielberg was under enormous pressure to produce another blockbuster after *Jaws,* and he decided to do a UFO movie. He's putting his reputation on the line."

Although Spielberg's first proposal for *Close Encounters* explicitly linked belief in UFOs with the public's loss of faith in the American political system, the political implications became less overt as the screenplay gradually evolved. The film takes only a mildly critical view of the military's use of a cover story (a phony nerve gas spillage) to evacuate a Wyoming site for the UFO rendezvous. Explaining his decision to downplay the military cover-up aspect, Spielberg told a European interviewer in 1978, "I didn't want to beat it to death because in the U.S. it's passé. We have lived through Watergate, the CIA, and people already find them redundant."

Close Encounters was filmed under conditions of extreme secrecy. Spielberg was determined to retain the element of surprise and concerned that the story might be ripped off for a quickie TV movie before he could complete his lengthy shooting and postproduction schedule. Most of the film was shot in an abandoned U.S. government dirigible hangar in Mobile, Alabama, and security was so tight that even Spielberg was denied admission to the set one day because he had forgotten to wear his plastic ID card.

The clandestine goings-on, which included a virtual blackout on press coverage, helped give rise to a strange rumor. As Balaban reported, the story went around that the film was "part of the necessary training that the human race must go through in order to accept an actual landing, and is being secretly sponsored by a government UFO agency." In fact, both NASA and the Air Force refused to cooperate with the film, fearing that it would inflame public hysteria about UFOs, just as *Jaws* had terrified people about sharks. "I really found my faith when I heard that the government was opposed to the film," Spielberg said. "If NASA took the time to write me a twenty-page letter, then I knew there must be something happening."

Even though the director had to forge ahead on his own, the rumor about the film's secret sponsorship continued to live long after its release, and Spielberg found his 1982 film *E.T. The Extra-Terrestrial* accused of being part of the same sinister plot to indoctrinate the public. The tale also circulated among ufologists that when Spielberg visited the White House to screen *E.T.,* President Ronald Reagan confided to the filmmaker, "You know, there are fewer than six people in this room who know the real story."

S P I E L B E R G receives sole screenplay credit for *Close Encounters,* but he was not the only writer who worked on the film. He has acknowledged Paul Schrader's early involvement in the writing, but only to disparage Schrader's work as "one of the most embarrassing screenplays ever professionally turned in to a major studio or director. . . . Actually, it was fortunate that Paul went so far away on his own tangent, a terribly guilt-ridden story, not about UFOs at all."

"The only thing I deserve a credit for," Schrader said, "is changing Steve's mind about doing the film as a UFO Watergate. I thought it ought to be about a spiritual encounter. That idea stayed and germinated." In Schrader's draft, which the writer titled *Kingdom Come,* the protagonist whose life is transformed by an encounter with a UFO on a deserted country road was not the film's common-man hero Roy Neary, a thirtyish, lower-middle-class working stiff from Indiana. The original protagonist was a forty-five-year-old Air Force officer whose story bore an unmistakable resemblance to that of Dr. Hynek. Both Spielberg and Schrader have claimed authorship of that character.*

Spielberg said he changed the protagonist to a civilian "because I find it very hard to identify with anybody in uniform. . . . A favorite theme of mine has always been the ultimate glorification of the common man. . . . A typical guy—nothing ever happens to him. Then, all of a sudden, he encounters something extraordinary and has to change his entire life in order to measure up to the task of either defeating it or understanding it. So that was my theme in *Close Encounters."*

Schrader's account was that after he wrote his draft, he and Spielberg "had a falling-out along strictly ideological lines, which was quite an instructive disagreement—it says a lot about him and it says a lot about me. My script centered on the idea of a modern-day St. Paul, a guy named Paul Van Owen, whose job for the government is to ridicule and debunk flying saucers. But then one day, like St. Paul, he has his road to Damascus—he has an encounter. Then he goes to the government; he's going to blow the lid off the whole thing, but instead the government offer him unlimited funds to pursue contact clandestinely, so he spends the next fifteen years trying to do that. But eventually he discovers that the key to making contact isn't out there in the universe, but implanted inside him.

"About the only thing that was left of all that when Steven finally made the film was the idea of the archetypal site, the mountain that's planted in his mind, and some of the ending. What I had done was to write this character with resonances of Lear and St. Paul, a kind of Shakespearean tragic hero, and Steve just could not get behind that, and it became clear that our collaboration had to end. It came down to this. I said, 'I refuse to send off to another world, as the first example of Earth's intelligence, a man who wants to go and set up a McDonald's franchise,' and Steven said, 'That's exactly the guy I want to send.' Steven's Capra-like infatuation with the common man was diametrically opposed to my religious infatuation with the redeeming hero —I wanted a biblical character to carry the message to the outer spheres, I

---

* The 1977 release version of the film contains a scene with George DiCenzo playing a vestigial version of the character, an Air Force officer in charge of misleading a group of UFO witnesses (he is named Major Benchley, after *Jaws* author Peter Benchley). Spielberg eliminated the scene from the 1980 *Special Edition* of *Close Encounters.*

wanted to form missions again. Fortunately, Steven was smart enough to realize that I was an intractable character, and he was right to make the film that he was comfortable with."

When asked by *Cinefantastique* magazine interviewer Don Shay in 1978 whether anyone else besides Schrader had worked on the script, Spielberg replied, "No. There was just me." Later in the same interview, however, the director admitted that he had received help with the story from his frequent collaborators Hal Barwood and Matthew Robbins, who also play two of the returning airmen who emerge from the spaceship at the end of the film. Other writers who contributed to *Close Encounters* included John Hill, who wrote the second draft after Schrader left; David Giler; and Jerry Belson, a TV comedy writer who polished the script with Spielberg at New York's Sherry-Netherland Hotel shortly before shooting began and also on location in Mobile. Julia Phillips reported that Columbia paid for "one under-the-table rewrite after another."

Spielberg's conceptual work during preproduction began with a year of exchanging visual ideas with a production illustrator, George Jensen, who made thousands of scene drawings and color sketches as a result of those discussions. Spielberg recalled that "together we plotted seven major sequences—including the last thirty minutes of the movie, which is all phantasmagoria." After rejecting the Schrader and Hill screenplays, Spielberg wrote his own draft during the period when he was editing and promoting *Jaws*. His script, he felt, "had a pretty good structure, but I wasn't crazy about some of the characters. . . . I find writing to be the most difficult thing I've ever done. I find it much more difficult than directing, because it requires a lot of concentration and I'm not the most concentrated of people. . . . Essentially I'm not a writer and I don't enjoy writing. I'd much rather collaborate. I need fresh ideas coming to me."

However, Spielberg was so possessive about the genesis of his magnum opus that he wanted the final credit to read simply "Written and Directed by Steven Spielberg," as if sharing credit with anyone else for the story or screenplay would have diminished his own creativity in the eyes of the public, and perhaps in his own eyes as well. His need to insist on sole writing credit may have stemmed not only from the project's deeply personal nature but also from an anxiety that others involved in the film would try to appropriate credit to themselves that he felt belonged more properly to him, as he thought had happened with *Jaws*. Such anxiety tends to be an occupational hazard for directors, particularly for young directors who have had a major hit and suddenly find themselves in a position of great power. The success of *Jaws*, Spielberg admitted in 1982, initially had "a very negative effect on me. I thought it was a fluke. . . . I began believing it was some kind of freak and agreeing when people said it could never happen again. They were saying it was the timing and the climate that created the success of *Jaws* more than what I had done to make the movie a success." A typical defense mechanism against such feelings of insecurity is to exaggerate a genuine achievement or credit into a claim of omnipotence.

Julia Phillips wrote in *You'll Never Eat Lunch in This Town Again* that Spielberg "made me pressure every writer who made a contribution to the script. When the Writers' Guild insists on an arbitration, I get Schrader and Grady [her pseudonym for one of the other writers] to back off their right to credits." (In a 1991 interview with *Los Angeles* magazine, Phillips, who had fallen out with the director during the making of *Close Encounters,* called Spielberg "the ultimate writer fucker.") Schrader recalled that "at Steven's request I withdrew from the credit arbitration, which is something I've come to regret in later years, because I had [2.5 profit-participation] points tied to credit. So I gave up maybe a couple of million dollars that way, but that's the way it happens."

Michael Phillips believes that Spielberg's sole writing credit is appropriate: "Paul Schrader wrote a different film. Paul's was a much more serious quest, a religious transformation of a doubter into a believer. It wasn't a surprise to us, because we talked it out first, and it sounded like a good idea. But when it came in, it just wasn't a Steven Spielberg film; it wasn't a joyous roller-coaster. *Close Encounters* is really Steven's script. It was a project that he had started in his childhood and had always wanted to do. He got help from his friends and colleagues here and there, but 99.9 percent is Steven Spielberg. There was not really a basis for a credit for Paul except that the first writer on a project usually gets the benefit of the doubt, but in this case, since Steven really started over, I think that it would have been wrong to put it into an arbitration. Jerry Belson made a contribution that was appreciated, but he did not in any way author the story."

W H I L E in the throes of making *Jaws,* Spielberg was sure he would never face a more difficult filmmaking experience. But he found *Close Encounters* "twice as bad—and twice as expensive, as well."

It was a two-year ordeal of trying to realize a vision of mind-boggling technical and artistic complexity, while at the same time having to coax more and more money out of financially strapped Columbia Pictures. "Poor Steven was involved in a terrible battle with the studio," cinematographer Vilmos Zsigmond recalls. "He was not used to it. It was not pleasant." At one point, when the studio refused to pay several thousand dollars for a special effect involving shattering glass, Spielberg paid for it out of his own pocket. As François Truffaut observed, "In [the] face of overwhelming hardships and in-numerable complications that would, I suspect, have discouraged most direc-tors, Steven Spielberg's perseverance and fortitude were simply amazing."

Perhaps the hardest part for a director who acknowledges being a control freak was having to shoot scenes without knowing exactly how Douglas Trumbull's elaborate visual effects would look when they were added months later in postproduction. "The difference between *Jaws* and *Close Encounters*," Spielberg later reflected, "is that *Jaws* was a physical effects movie and *Close Encounters* was an optical-effects movie. It meant that for *Jaws* I had to shed blood six days a week—from eight in the morning to eight at night—and for *Close Encounters* I had to shed blood seven nights a week, from eight at night to eight in the morning, because of the laboratory turnover time. But the problems were exactly the same between the studio and myself, and between the cast and the script."

"I saw Steve more frustrated on *Close Encounters*," says production designer Joe Alves. "It was unlike *Jaws,* where he was dealing with concrete objects. You go out on the water, it gets too rough to shoot, you say, 'OK, we couldn't do it, the shark didn't work.' It's *real.* You have *things* to get upset with. The shooting of *Close Encounters* was more questionable [because of the visual effects]. It's hard for a director—you have to have a lot of confidence that the stuff's going to happen. So there was tension on the set."

"If I were Steven, I would have been terrified," Trumbull says. "I'll never be able to thank him enough for having the confidence and the patience to see it through and not panic. There was enormous pressure on the production all the time from the studio to keep moving on."

Columbia had been near collapse in the early 1970s, amassing more than $220 million in bank debt. The First National Bank of Boston had veto power over any Columbia film budgeted at more than $3 million. By the mid-1970s, the studio had begun a partial recovery under the leadership of Alan Hirschfield, president and chief executive officer of Columbia Pictures Industries, and studio president David Begelman. But the studio's financial health was still marginal when Spielberg began shooting his commercially dicey sci-fi movie.

More than half of Columbia's film production funding was derived from tax-shelter sources, a short-term strategy that helped the studio remain functional but necessitated the sharing of film-rental income with outside investors. When *Close Encounter of the Third Kind* (as it was then titled) began shooting on December 29, 1975, at an air-traffic control center in Palmdale, California, the company filmed for only two days to qualify for tax-shelter provisions before resuming the following May. Budget escalations caused a string of crises during production, and further anxiety arose during the final stages of postproduction in 1977 when Begelman was suspended from his job (he was later forced to resign) for forgery and embezzlement, in one of Hollywood's most widely reported financial scandals. Although Columbia eventually laid off about $7 million of *Close Encounters'* $19,400,870 production cost on outside investors,* it was not journalistic hyperbole when it was

---

* The British entertainment conglomerate EMI, Time Inc., and a group of German tax-shelter investors. The last official budget for the film, formally agreed upon by the Phillipses and Columbia during production, was $15,942,296. The final production cost was $3,458,574 over that figure, and the producers' contract called for an additional penalty of the same amount to be included in the final break-even accounting figure of $22,859,444.

said that the future of the studio was riding on the film. Shortly before the film's opening, *Variety* calculated that *Close Encounters* had to be among the top eighteen moneymakers in film history simply to break even.

"I just didn't expect to have two [blockbusters] in a row," Spielberg later admitted. "Nobody expects one mega-hit, let alone two. So I was not one of those running around saying *Close Encounters* would be a big hit. I was just running around saying, 'I hope Columbia can get their money out of it.' . . . [Columbia's executives] were too frightened to share my pessimism—they had more to lose than I did. I would just go on and direct another movie, but they would go down with the lady who holds the torch [on the Columbia logo]."

"If we knew going in that the picture was going to cost $19 million, we wouldn't have made it, because we didn't have the money," admits John Veitch, the Columbia production executive who supervised *Close Encounters*. "No Columbia picture, at that time, had cost that kind of money."

Michael Phillips recalls that at the meeting in the fall of 1973 when they pitched the project to Begelman, "David asked Steven, 'How much will this cost?' Steven said, '$2.7 million.' Julia and I looked at him, we didn't say anything—[but we thought,] 'How could he have the *temerity* to come out with the figure?' As soon as we got out the door, we said, 'What were you doing?' He said, 'I just had an instinct that that was as high a number I could mention.' . . . Then, due to the problems of getting a script developed that we really liked, we were delayed and Steven was offered the opportunity to do *Jaws*. When he came back it was a whole new ballgame. Suddenly he was a much better risk from the studio's point of view and he was given free rein to come up with the best that his imagination could conjure. . . . He was in a position for the studio to really invest, to bet the farm. They needed to; Columbia was teetering on the brink of insolvency, and here they had the hottest director in town and a subject matter that seemed a natural fit for him. So they did bet the farm."

Spielberg's wishes did not come true all at once. With the nightmarish filming of *Jaws* still fresh in his mind, Spielberg told the producers, "I never want to do a location picture again." He was thinking in terms of making *Close Encounters* in and around the Burbank Studios, which Columbia shared with Warner Bros.; the budget was set at $4.1 million. As Spielberg's plans became more grandiose, the memory of Martha's Vineyard receded, and he became convinced that he needed to make much of the movie away from Hollywood. Convincing Columbia was not so easy.

Early in preproduction, Spielberg sent Alves "to scour America for a place that only my imagination told me existed," the mountain chosen by extraterrestrials for their landing on Earth. "Steven was off doing promotion on *Jaws*," Alves relates, "so I reported to John Veitch. He told me, 'Steven wants you to find a mountain. This is a $4 million picture. We're going to do one day on location and the rest on the back lot.' I said, 'Are you sure?' We were starting *Close Encounters* as another small science-fiction film, like we were starting *Jaws* as a little horror picture. We couldn't get a handle on *Close Encounters* visually—the visual effects, the scope of it. I remember John Veitch taking me to Warner Bros. Stages 15 and 16 and saying, 'This is where we're going to put the big [Box Canyon] set.' I said, 'It's not big enough.' He felt maybe we were feeling our oats from *Jaws*. He said, 'My God, they did *Camelot* on this!' "

Before principal photography began in earnest on May 16, 1976, the budget already had risen in stages to $5.5 million, $7 million, $9 million, and $11.5 million. The cost kept climbing as Spielberg gradually convinced Columbia to let him expand the scope of the movie. "We had six wrap parties on *Close Encounters,*" Michael Phillips recalls. "We popped the champagne six times. Each time we thought we were finished, he would come up with a great idea that warranted going out and picking up something else. Steven always comes up with new ideas that make the movie better."

In order to find Spielberg a mountain, Alves drove through 2,700 miles of western scenery before suggesting Devil's Tower National Monument near Gillette, Wyoming. An imposing granite landmark with long jagged serrations up and down its front and back aspects, Devil's Tower closely resembles Mitchell Butte, one of the most prominent features of Monument Valley, where John Ford filmed *The Searchers* and other classic Westerns. Devil's Tower had the advantage of being less familiar to movie audiences, and perhaps more eerie in its solitary, abrupt emergence from a wooded landscape.

Alves and Spielberg considered building the Box Canyon landing site in Monument Valley before deciding it would be too difficult to control weather and lighting conditions for a special-effects movie on a remote outdoor location. Even so, Spielberg found himself facing "horrendous" technical problems shooting in the Mobile, Alabama, hangar housing the enormous Box Canyon set, which was built by Alves at a cost of $700,000. The hangar was bigger than a football field and six times the size of Hollywood's largest soundstage. The humidity inside sometimes caused artificial clouds and drizzle during filming, and rigging the set with dozens of huge lights while choreographing the movements of two hundred extras led to seemingly endless delays and expense. Even though the scenes filmed on the set accounted for only about one-fifth of the running time, they consumed about half the shooting schedule. "That set," lamented Spielberg, "became our 'shark' on this picture."

The initially cost-conscious John Veitch eventually became Spielberg's staunch ally in what the executive remembers as "a labor of love" for both of them. Spielberg said that Veitch's "understanding of our enormous logistics" made him "sometimes a not very popular guy with the other Columbia executives." The late studio president David Begelman, despite his many failings in a tragically self-destructive career, also deserves a lion's share of the credit for enabling Spielberg to make the film he envisioned. "David was fiercely loyal to me throughout *Close Encounters,*" Spielberg said after

Begelman's suicide in 1995. "When I needed something from the studio, he was there to give it. I think we had faith in each other."

The problems Columbia had in trying to budget the film, Veitch says, arose from the impossibility of predicting how much the special effects would cost, particularly in the early stages when the script was constantly being rewritten: "It was no one's fault, because we were experimenting. From the beginning, Steven always wanted to go one step further as far as visual effects were concerned, and it was time-consuming. It's not that Steven is not a dedicated individual. He was cost-conscious, but he wanted everything to be just right." But the man in charge of special effects, Douglas Trumbull, has a different perspective: "When I put in the effects budget at a fairly early phase, with my partner Richard Yuricich, we estimated the effects to be about $3 million. That news never got to upper management until much later. I have no idea what they said to upper management, but it was just too scary a number. Nobody had ever heard of a number like that for effects. It was right on— [the final cost] was maybe $3.2 million or $3.3 million.

"I think there was a lot of avoidance of facing the realities of what the movie was going to cost. Everybody was trying to make himself believe it was going to be a less expensive movie than it ultimately was. It took on a bigger and bigger scope at every turn, not just in terms of special effects but in terms of the scale of the sets and a lot of complicated production out on location. Nobody at the beginning of that movie knew what it had to look like or how ultimately to achieve the goal."

REJOINING Spielberg after passing up the opportunity to shoot *Jaws,* cinematographer Vilmos Zsigmond missed the close creative partnership he had shared with Spielberg on *The Sugarland Express.* As a result of his triumph over enormous technical odds on *Jaws,* "Steven started to know all the answers," Zsigmond felt. "He was sort of telling me things rather than discussing things." But Zsigmond was excited about working on *Close Encounters* because it "had the smell of a great movie. We fell into sandtraps not because anybody made mistakes, but because we were making things that had never been done before."

Zsigmond's conflicts with line producer Julia Phillips and with Columbia, however, almost led to his firing in the midst of the Mobile location shoot. The trouble began when he said he needed time to prelight the massive set rather than simply start filming cold. The studio was so worried about the shooting schedule that it had not allotted any time for prelighting, and it objected when Zsigmond insisted on a minimum of one day for the task. A compromise was reached in which second-unit cameraman Steven Poster spent a day shooting exterior scenes while Zsigmond stayed behind to prelight.

"It was a nightmare from that point on," Zsigmond says. "There was a lot of pressure from the studio. Nobody could even conceive how much light we needed. I never gave in to the pressure to use less light, to do things that

I knew were not right. Doug Trumbull stood behind me. He kept saying, 'Vilmos is doing the right thing. We *need* a lot of lights,' because he had to match the scenes with the special effects. Everybody was trapped into that situation. Steven stood behind me, but he was battling the studio and battling Julia Phillips. The budget kept going up. Poor Julia Phillips in her book blames me for many things. I was the scapegoat for many, many things."

After the first two months of shooting, when nervous studio executives and bankers were beginning to show up in Mobile, Phillips wanted to bring in a replacement cameraman. But, she wrote, "Steven refuses to fire Vilmos, and by now we have shot enough to have to be committed to him." Exasperated over the memory of "Vilmos fiddling with the lights on every shot" (a singularly odd complaint to make about a cinematographer), she wrote that "on a bad night, I can still see a scene being shot, with Vilmos walking into it, and telling his crew that we just need 'vun leetle inky-dinky over here.' "

"I guess she had to blame it on somebody," Zsigmond responds. "It would have been the easy solution to tell the studio to fire me. There was tension for a couple of days when this happened. They called four or five people [including John A. Alonzo and Laszlo Kovacs]. Most of those people were friends of mine, and they all came back to me. When I told them our problems, they all said, 'If you can't do it, nobody can.' The only one who was going to possibly take over was Ernest Laszlo. He had done *Fantastic Voyage,* and they thought he could do it. But this was 1976, and he was in Montreal. Ernest Laszlo called back and said, 'You guys crazy? I'm going to the Olympics.' "

After that, Spielberg continued to let Zsigmond "do what I had to do," and the director's support helped make *Close Encounters* a "very rewarding" creative experience. But when additional sequences and pickup shots were filmed after the company's return from Alabama, Zsigmond was not asked to shoot them. "Unfortunately, because of the studio and Julia Phillips, Steven could not hire me anymore," Zsigmond says. "He told me I was going to shoot the India sequence, and he sent me to get [inoculation] shots. I found out later that Dougie [Douglas] Slocombe was going to do the India sequence, which hurt my feelings very much." Although Zsigmond says he shot about 90 percent of the film, William A. Fraker shot the majority of the added material, notably the opening sequence of a lost squadron of World War II airplanes discovered in the Mexican desert. Fraker, Slocombe, Alonzo, and Kovacs were given prominent credit as additional directors of photography.* Phillips admitted in her book that she did "everything in my power to let the world know how [Zsigmond] sandbagged us, by the credits."

"I'm glad she wrote exactly how it was," Zsigmond comments, "because I always felt bad that they gave these people credit to diminish my credit. I don't think Steven was really that vicious to do this. I think it came mostly from the studio and Julia Phillips, because they were so mad at me. It hurt

---

* Frank Stanley also shot two days on the film, without credit.

my credit so badly, because some of the reviewers wrote [that *Close Encounters* was shot by] 'Vilmos Zsigmond and all the great cameramen.' They don't realize I'm the only one who got the Academy Award. That was a vindication, but it was not really a pleasant vindication. I was so bitter at the whole thing that I didn't thank 'Steven Spielberg and Julia Phillips who gave me the opportunity to do this picture'; I thanked a couple of teachers I had in Hungary, and I thanked America for giving me a new life. It was not politically correct for me [to avoid thanking the director and producer]; I never shot a picture for Steven again. But we've talked a lot since, and we've gotten together many times. I still think he's the greatest."

C O N S T A N T time and budget overruns during the Mobile filming and during a year of postproduction caused the beleaguered studio to become increasingly impatient with all the filmmakers, but especially with the stressed-out line producer. Because of her cocaine problem (exhaustively documented in her 1991 memoir), Julia Phillips was forced off the picture by Columbia during postproduction in the summer of 1977.

She felt "betrayed by the only partners who have mattered: Michael. Steven. Begelman." Her ex-husband* takes strong exception to that statement: "There was no conspiracy to do her in. That was complete nonsense. She had a drug problem and she was really out of it. At that point she was not helping, but she was in the way of the picture getting done. Her authority was removed. She went off to Hawaii when that happened and we didn't really communicate. Her perceptions were, at the time, not really accurate. It was a lot of pressure because it was a high-profile film with budget problems, and the press and everybody kind of rooting against it. But I don't think that's what the problem was for her. It was a serious chapter of substance abuse that made her not capable of functioning the way she would normally have functioned."

Julia Phillips claimed in a 1991 interview that cocaine "had never been a problem" for her before *Close Encounters:* "It was only after I started working with Steven. He was such a perfectionist." In her book, she attacks Spielberg as "the little prick . . . a precocious seven-year-old" with "a childish self-preoccupation." At the time of the book's publication, a spokesman for Spielberg told the press that the director was busy shooting *Hook* and would have nothing to say about *You'll Never Eat Lunch in This Town Again*. To this day, he has made no public comment about it.

S o much of the imagery of *Close Encounters* was added in postproduction that the actors had to spend most of their time staring into lights passing

---

* The Phillipses were divorced in 1974 but continued working together as producing partners on *Close Encounters* until her firing.

overhead, trying to imagine sights they could not see. "There's no way to work with effects," said Melinda Dillon. ". . . For weeks we were just sitting on a rock, shifting positions, pretending to look at the landing site and the sky. Steven would say to us, 'There's a light going by you. Oh, but there's an *extraordinary* light going by you.' It was a great acting exercise." François Truffaut, however, found the experience unnerving: "I never had the impression of playing a role, only of lending my carnal envelope. Spielberg had shown me the two thousand sketches of his storyboard, so I knew that what he was after was a grand cartoon strip and that I could put back in my suitcase the book by Stanislavsky that I had bought for the occasion."

Richard Dreyfuss was "very upset with several moments in his performance," Spielberg recalled, "because he feels that had he seen the effects, he might have reacted differently." Dreyfuss admitted being depressed the first time he saw the film, because "I didn't like my work. And it took me a long time to recontact that feeling in me of why I made the film. . . . I didn't do it because it was a Spielberg movie, because they didn't exist as such yet, or because it was a great role. I did it because I knew that they would show that film in the Museum of Modern Art in the year 2030, that . . . this movie would be potentially the most important film ever made, and I wanted desperately to be a part of that experience."

More than two hundred shots in *Close Encounters* involved special effects, and some shots contained as many as eighteen separate visual elements. Dozens of matte paintings by Matthew Yuricich rounded out the design, which also employed miniature outdoor settings for some of the Indiana and Devil's Tower landscapes. The film's night imagery was augmented with artificial stars and cloud formations, and animation was used for sequences showing the Big Dipper and a meteor appearing above Devil's Tower. Spielberg commissioned tests of computer-generated imagery (CGI), a technique then in its embryonic stages, but concluded it did not look believable enough and would be prohibitively expensive (seventeen years later, Spielberg would help pioneer the combined use of live action and CGI in *Jurassic Park*).

Admitting he had "no savvy about optical and miniaturized special effects," Spielberg interviewed various effects technicians but felt he needed "one enthusiastic, driving 'wilderness guide' who would take me where nobody else had gone before." He found that person in Douglas Trumbull, who had played a crucial role in helping Kubrick realize his vision on *2001*. "If Trumbull hadn't accepted the job," Spielberg acknowledged in his 1978 article on the filming in *American Cinematographer*, "I'd still be on the Columbia back lot trying to get a cloud to materialize from thin air."

After making his feature directing debut with the sci-fi movie *Silent Running* in 1971, Trumbull was resistant to doing special effects for another director; he was working on innovative projection systems with his Future General Corporation and had turned down an offer from George Lucas to work on *Star Wars,* which was in production at the same time as *Close*

Encounters. "I didn't have any adverse reaction to *Star Wars* per se, but I felt I was space-movied-out," Trumbull recalls. "When Steven came along, I was hunting for ways to put together 65mm camera equipment to develop the Showscan process, and that was part of the deal with Steven, to put together this 65mm facility I needed. I was very impressed with *Jaws,* and I thought, This is going to be a really interesting filmmaker to work with, and an opportunity to push the envelope."

The guiding principle of the special effects in the first two-thirds of *Close Encounters* was to bring about a seamless integration of fantasy elements into a mundane, Middle-American setting. That would help the audience accept the UFOs as real and prepare them for the rhapsodic, almost avant-garde spectacle of the last forty minutes when the mother ship lands. Spielberg's UFOs announce their presence by activating a toddler's toys, turning out the Muncie municipal light grid, vibrating a railroad crossing sign, and illuminating a McDonald's billboard. Manipulating those familiar sights and sounds makes the film's most extravagant phantasmagoria—clouds turning into strange shapes and colors, a dazzling orange light flooding through the door of a farmhouse—seem natural occurrences.

"I believe that the success of *Close Encounters of the Third Kind* comes from Steven's very special gift for giving plausibility to the extraordinary," Truffaut wrote. "If you analyze *Close Encounters,* you will find that Spielberg has taken care in shooting all the scenes of everyday life to give them a slightly fantastic aspect, while also, as a form of balance, giving the most everyday possible quality to the scenes of fantasy."

What made it possible to blend all the elements so smoothly was the innovative Electronic Motion Control System, a digital, electronic system that recorded and programmed camera motions so they could be duplicated later when matching miniature effects were composited with the live-action photography. The system allowed all the visuals to move in harmony, adding an almost subconscious sense of credibility to the many composite images in *Close Encounters.* "Our plan," explained Trumbull, "was that even though the UFOs wouldn't be shot until postproduction, any live-action scene in which they appeared had to include the apparent illumination created by them, complete with flared-out overexposure, shifting shadows, and correct color." To that end, dozens of sweltering electricians spent twelve hours a day manipulating lights from catwalks and cranes above the actors, who, Truffaut punned, felt "im-Mobilised . . . everything seems to take forever."

The film's single most spectacular effect, the mother ship, did not take on final form until late in the production. It was originally conceived by Spielberg and Alves as a "horrifyingly huge" black shape blotting out stars and emitting light from an opening in its underbelly. The massive shadows seen in the film as the mother ship passes overhead are remnants of that design. But given Spielberg's preoccupation with childhood motifs, it is fitting that the overwhelmingly large object transporting Roy Neary to a womblike state of bliss is called the mother ship and filled with childlike inhabitants. "My first concept," Trumbull said, "was that the mother ship underbelly—this big thing that hung down from there—should look like a giant breast with a nipple." That concept reflected psychological studies of the human longing for contact with UFOs, which link the phenomenon to the recall of infantile perceptions, especially the approach (both frightening and comforting) of the mother's breast.

Spielberg's ideas for the mother ship evolved further when he visited India for location shooting (his first outside the United States) in February 1977. For six days, coming and going to a village outside Bombay, Spielberg passed a gigantic oil refinery lit by thousands of small lights and festooned with pipes, tubing, and walkways. Upon his return to Los Angeles, Spielberg had illustrator George Jensen draw a new ship from that description. "[T]hat very same night," Spielberg related, "I was up on Mulholland Drive—a little stoned—and I got on my head on the hood of my car and looked out at all the lights from the San Fernando Valley upside down. And I thought that would be incredible as the underbelly of this oil refinery from Bombay." Combining both elements into what Trumbull described as a "City of Light . . . like the Manhattan skyline at night," the ship for the film was designed by Ralph McQuarrie and built by Greg Jein. When shooting was completed, Spielberg took the mother ship home as a keepsake.

TRUMBULL and Kubrick experimented with concepts of alien beings for the finale of *2001,* but the tests proved too costly and time-consuming, and Kubrick finally decided not to risk losing credibility by showing aliens on screen. The film's elliptical approach befitted Kubrick's detached, cerebral view of mankind's first contact with extraterrestrials, but for the warmer, more emotional Spielberg, showing communion between humans and aliens was a *sine qua non.* "I also knew that it was the most dangerous move I could possibly make with this movie," he admitted. Coming up with believable aliens was such a problem that the final shots of the lead alien, nicknamed "Puck" by the director, were not filmed until three weeks before the first preview.

"The first thing I did was go in search for the perfect E.T.," Spielberg recalled. "I had the strange idea that they shouldn't be people in costume; they had done that from the dawn of time in Hollywood. So what I did was, I had a chimpanzee brought to the set. We put the chimpanzee in an E.T. suit and further complicated the test by putting rollerskates on him, because I didn't want the chimpanzee to walk simian-like, but I wanted him to glide smoothly down a ramp. You can imagine the test . . . a chimpanzee with a large rubber latex head and a little kind of flimsy ballerina costume and large rollerskates, disguised with a kind of dust ruffle so you couldn't see the actual wheels. We put the chimpanzee on a ramp and the first thing that happened, of course, was the chimpanzee fell and slid down the ramp . . . and it kept making these rather remarkable Charlie Chaplin pratfalls . . . the chimpanzee was laughing like he had a great time doing this. . . . At one point the chimpanzee did pull off his head and throw it at the crew. That was his way of telling me, 'Find another way.' "

Because people who report encounters with aliens usually describe them as short, childlike creatures with spindly limbs and large heads, most of the aliens were played by six-year-old girls from dance classes, wearing over-sized heads and gloves. But Spielberg found Tom Burman's alien design "a complete disaster." "He thought they looked too scary," Burman recalled, "and he wanted something softer and more gentle-looking." Burman revised his design and Spielberg spent several days shooting scenes of aliens, most of which did not wind up in the finished film. "Spielberg was changing his mind drastically all the time," noted Burman assistant David Ayres. "But he had guts. He'd try *anything* to see if it would work on film. . . . At one point, the camera was on a dolly mount and Spielberg went running around with it, in and out of this whole crowd of technicians, and people would be jumping away—like a subjective point-of-view for the aliens. And he had them open a can of [Coca-Cola] and it fizzed all over. He had a whole lot of wild, crazy ideas."

The script called for the aliens to behave "like children let loose in a toy factory," flying through the crowd of scientists and curiously stroking Drey-fuss, Truffaut, Hynek, and others with their long, willowy fingers. Judging from Jensen's production drawings, those scenes might have appeared too bizarre or frightening for a movie portraying aliens as benign, ethereal crea-tures. But Spielberg's biggest concern was that such extended scenes with aliens "bordered on the ridiculous" and "would destroy the credibility that I had hopefully achieved."

"Unfortunately, the aliens didn't look real," Zsigmond says. "Steven told me, 'The only way we can do this is to overexpose them, so we can hardly see them.' I overexposed two and a half stops, but the lab screwed up the dailies and printed the whole scene with nothing in it—white, no details. Julia Phillips came down to me, panicking: 'Vilmos, you ruined it. We have to shoot it again.' I was really insulted that they went to see dailies without me. I said, 'Show me the dailies.' I saw from the lab information that they didn't print it right. I said, 'Tell the lab to print it eight points darker.' We had to wait twenty-four hours. The next day the dailies came back, and it was just perfect. Steven said, 'Thank you.' "

After Spielberg returned to Hollywood, he turned his attention to "Puck." The full-body figure was created by marionette maker Bob Baker and the upper torso and head (for close-ups) by Carlo Rambaldi, an Italian craftsman who came to Spielberg's attention with his facially expressive animatronic title character in the remake of *King Kong*. Eight people operated the cable mechanisms controlling Rambaldi's Puck. Spielberg was so pleased with the creature that "he spent a lot of time playing with it," Rambaldi recalled. "He especially liked the smile; and during the filming, it was he who operated the levers controlling it." The joyous exchange of smiles between Puck and

Truffaut, Spielberg's representative of mankind at its most humane, is the film's emotional climax. "The audience's reactions to the extraterrestrials will be largely determined by Truffaut's reactions," Bob Balaban, who played Truffaut's English interpreter, observed in his diary. "[Spielberg] wants Truffaut to think of the extraterrestrials as little children. He knows how Truffaut likes little children." The French filmmaker became so enchanted with Rambaldi's creation that each day when he arrived on the set and saw Puck, Truffaut would go over and shake the alien's hand, saying, *"Bonjour! Ça va?"*

"DIRECTING a movie with Truffaut on the set," Spielberg said, "is like having Renoir around when you're still painting by numbers."

Truffaut was one of the directors Spielberg most admired when he was breaking into the movie business. The French filmmaker left perhaps an even more lasting and pervasive imprint on Spielberg's work than had his boyhood masters Alfred Hitchcock and David Lean. While attending Cal State Long Beach, Spielberg studied such Truffaut films as *Shoot the Piano Player, Jules and Jim,* and *Stolen Kisses* at art theaters, drawing inspiration from their romantic lyricism, their visual *frissons,* and their graceful blend of playful humor and emotional gravity. Truffaut's celebration of the communal process of moviemaking in *Day for Night* made it "the closest to home for me of Truffaut's films," Spielberg recalled. ". . . *Day for Night* brought you into what Truffaut was. And he was the movies." Their deepest temperamental affinity, Spielberg felt, was their mutual fondness for "working with children, and with adults who act like children. . . . There was a child inside François Truffaut. Watching him perform in his films *The Wild Child* and *Day for Night,* I saw that child. . . . That was the spirit I wanted for Lacombe."

Even so, Spielberg hesitated to approach him. "I didn't want Truffaut to say no to me," he explained. "I didn't want to insult him by saying, 'I'd like you to be an actor.' " But after considering such European actors as Gérard Depardieu, Philippe Noiret, Jean-Louis Trintignant, and Lino Ventura, Spielberg finally summoned up the courage to call Truffaut at his home in Paris.

"Steven attracted me," Truffaut recalled. "I knew his work. I had confidence in him. When he called me in France and said he had written the role especially for me, I didn't think he was serious. I assumed he thought I spoke English."

Truffaut protested, "I am not an actor. I can only play myself."

"But that's what I want," Spielberg assured him.

After reading the script, Truffaut accepted an offer of $75,000 to play a character he described as *"un savant français."* He had no particular interest in the subject matter. When asked if he believed in UFOs, Truffaut replied, "I believe in the cinema." On other occasions, he declared, "When people talk about UFOs, I tune out," and "The only close encounters I ever have are with women, children, or books." Until he arrived in Mobile, Truffaut did not admit to Spielberg that he had ulterior motives for wanting to be in *Close Encounters*. He planned to use the experience as research for a book called *The Actor* (a project he later abandoned), and he used his spare time on location to write the screenplay for *The Man Who Loved Women*.

The endless waiting on the set of *Close Encounters* exasperated Truffaut, who felt himself losing interest and growing impatient to shoot his own movie. One day during the filming in Wyoming he exclaimed to actress Teri Garr, "It cost $250,000 for that shot they just did with the helicopters. I could make a movie for that. *And they did two takes!*" But the experience also helped him understand why "the atmosphere becomes so passionate and intimate" for actors working on a film. With all the fussing and coddling he experienced between shots from wardrobe, hair, and makeup people, the actor becomes "like a little baby again," he mused. A more sobering discovery was that "everybody says many nasty things behind the director's back."

Truffaut was not entirely immune to that temptation. In one of the many letters he wrote from Mobile to friends in France, Truffaut reported, "Like every actor in every film ever made, I'll find myself saying, 'He never directed me, no one ever told me what to do,' and, in fact, it's both true and false. In any event, I find it very amusing to watch another director at work, and despite the huge differences (to give you an idea, his favorite French directors are [Robert] Enrico and [Claude] Lelouch), to discover all kinds of points in common, or rather reactions in common. In any case, he really isn't pretentious, he doesn't behave like the director of the most successful film in the history of the cinema (*Jaws*), he's calm (outwardly so), very even-tempered, very patient and good-humored. This film of flying saucers means a great deal to him, it's a childhood dream come true."

At first Spielberg felt "intimidated" having Truffaut in his movie. Truffaut reassured him, "I will be the easiest person you've ever worked with—either in the cast or on the crew. This actor will not have ideas. I will perform your ideas." Truffaut not only was true to his word, but often seemed to know what Spielberg wanted without being told. Sometimes Spielberg deliberately refrained from giving Truffaut any direction at all, such as in the sublime moment when Lacombe says good-bye to Puck with hand signs and "that expression on his face when he almost laughs at the gentleness of it all." Truffaut's personality also made the character "much more intense than he was originally written," Spielberg acknowledged. "He's still a man of peace . . . still a man-child, but he has a great deal of cunning and enthusiasm."

Although he had warned Spielberg that he could not be asked "to laugh or cry on command like a professional actor," Truffaut found that "several times during the shooting he made me surpass myself. He directed me so as to make me come out of myself. Thanks to that, I discovered a real pleasure as an actor. I behaved like every actor in the world who, as soon as the take has been shot, turns to the director to find out if he is satisfied. And every time I achieved the result Spielberg expected, I was satisfied."

Truffaut's benign facade concealed a sly and sometimes waspish guile. He finally let his frustration boil over in rage against Julia Phillips, telling *The New York Times,* "The picture started with a budget of $11 million and now I think it is up to $15 million, but that is not Spielberg's fault. It is the fault of the producer, Julia Phillips. She is incompetent. Unprofessional. You can write that. She knows I feel this way. Sometimes it was so disorganized that they had me show up and then do nothing for five days." At the behest of the furious Phillips—who seethes in her book, "Of all the dead people I know François Truffaut wins the prick award hands down"—Spielberg played the good soldier, writing a letter to the *Times* expressing his disbelief that Truffaut could have made those "rather unkind remarks." Implausibly arguing that the highly experienced and sophisticated French director must have been ignorant of the production's unique technical challenges, Spielberg went on to claim, "I've never had such constructive and consistent support from a producer as I have had from Julia Phillips, and I know that Columbia Pictures concurs." Rather than being grateful, Phillips complained that Spielberg's letter was "weaker than I would have hoped."

Truffaut expressed contrition of a sort in an interview with *The New Yorker:* "Jeanne Moreau once told me, 'On every picture, you must love everybody except the one who becomes the scapegoat.' I followed Jeanne Moreau's advice. I made Julia Phillips, the producer, my scapegoat. Every time I find something not to my liking, I say I am sure it is the fault of Julia Phillips."

W I T H *Close Encounters of the Third Kind,* Spielberg pulled off the remarkable feat of making a deeply personal film on a grand scale within the Hollywood studio system. Even more remarkably, he was able to communicate his personal vision to a huge worldwide audience. "This is probably the most collaborative art form in the world," he wrote in an *American Cinematographer* article paying tribute to his crew on *Close Encounters.* "There is no such thing as [an] *Auteur.* Without all these people movies simply are not made." And yet Spielberg managed to use the talents of all those people to realize the dream implanted in his mind as a boy in Phoenix when his father roused him from bed in the middle of the night to watch a meteor shower.

That incident was adapted by Spielberg for the scene of Roy Neary, fresh from his first UFO sighting, excitedly awakening his family and taking them on a (futile) nocturnal quest to share his otherworldly encounter. Spielberg's depiction of the Nearys' dysfunctional family life also is filled with echoes of his childhood experiences. Far from celebrating suburban conformity, as his detractors often accuse him of doing, Spielberg offers a bleak view of suburban life in *Close Encounters,* depicting it as a place of quiet desperation, a plastic purgatory from which Roy Neary longs to escape. Roy's unimaginative wife, Ronnie, reacts to his interest in UFOs with hostility, thinking he has gone mad. Her incomprehension and abandonment of Roy, while an understandable reaction under the circumstances, helps the audience sympathize with Roy's decision to leave his family behind for a new life in outer space. Along the way, Roy forms a temporary new "family" allegiance with fellow UFO believer Jillian Guiler (Melinda Dillon). The anguish Jillian experiences over the extraterrestrials' abduction of her small son, Barry (Cary Guffey), makes her kin to all the other Spielbergian mothers forcibly separated from their children, from Lou Jean Poplin in *The Sugarland Express* to the Plaszów forced-labor camp inmates in *Schindler's List.*

Ronnie, who mockingly addresses her husband as "Jiminy Cricket," is an unhappy homemaker whose emotional and intellectual horizons are bounded by the walls of her messy tract house. Spielberg's depiction of Ronnie is no mere plot expediency, but a reflection of his youthful animosity toward mother figures. In a 1990 documentary on the making of *Close Encounters,* Spielberg expressed second thoughts about his depiction of Ronnie, recalling that he cast Teri Garr after seeing her in a coffee commercial: "I said, 'A homemaker—makes great coffee!' I was young, naive, and chauvinistic. . . . She was the bad guy in the movie, in a sense. She's not *really* a bad guy, she's somebody who's trying to preserve her family and save her family from the kind of insanity she's assuming Dreyfuss is experiencing, and doesn't want her family to be tainted by this."

While a more emotionally mature Spielberg might have had more empathy with Ronnie, the raw pain suffusing his depiction of the Nearys' chaotic household might have been diluted as well. As played by the "alter ego" of the thirty-year-old bachelor filmmaker, Roy is a child-man unprepared for the responsibilities of marriage or fatherhood. It is not until he drives his family away by symbolically regressing to an infantile state—shaping a mountain out of mud in his living room like a toddler playing with his own waste—that Roy finds a way to escape from his oppressive surroundings. When his Disneyish dreams of "wishing upon a star" are fulfilled by his ascension into the womb of the mother ship, Roy is symbolically reborn, like the astronaut at the end of *2001.* Escorted aboard by the tiny childlike aliens to whom he seems both brother and father, Roy, in Spielberg's description, "becomes a real person. He loses his strings, his wooden joints, and . . . he makes the most important decision in the history of the world."

With Roy Neary, the "Peter Pan Syndrome" takes on cosmic dimensions. Some of the film's detractors argued that Spielberg is simply glorifying the abandonment of a family by an irresponsible father. Calling the film "a hymn to regression and emotional retardation," Stephen Farber wrote in *New West* that "if the ordinary world had some attractions, if Roy's family had a strong emotional hold on him, the ending would have been richer and more meaningful." While that argument is true enough as far as it goes—"I couldn't have made *Close Encounters* today," a more paternal Spielberg said in 1994, "because I would never leave my family"—such criticism tends to reduce the film to a mundane level of meaning and underestimates the degree to which Spielberg succeeds in convincing us that Roy's alienation is justified.

Farber himself points out that *Close Encounters* reworks an archetypal American myth defined by literary critic Leslie Fiedler as "The flight of the dreamer from the shrew—into the mountains and out of time, away from the drab duties of home and town." The existential dreariness of Roy's Middle-American life, and his family's utter inability to comprehend his spiritual yearning for a more beautiful and fulfilling existence, are conveyed with considerable emotional force.

Befitting a film with so many overt and covert autobiographical overtones for its director, not only do the extraterrestrials communicate by putting on a spectacular light and music show, with François Truffaut "directing" the human response, but Roy and Jillian cope with, and compound, their alienation from society by turning to artistic expression. When Truffaut's Lacombe meets Neary, he asks, "Mr. Neary, are you an artist or a painter?" In an extended sequence derived from Schrader's original draft, Roy (following Barry's lead) obsessively sculpts a model of the mountain, an image implanted in his consciousness by the extraterrestrials (the sculpture is literally a "Play Mountain," the meaning of Spielberg's family name in German). Jillian compulsively churns out sketches and paintings of the same mysterious shape, which she and Roy later discover (via television) to be the Devil's Tower landing site.

What Roy considers "art," conventional society considers "madness." Spielberg knows this dilemma well, having been stigmatized as "kind of nuts" and "the strange kid on the block" for his early filmmaking activities in suburban Arizona. Roy's emotional breakdown at the family dinner table while sculpting the mountain out of mashed potatoes ("Well, I guess you've noticed there's something a little strange with Dad") is the most moving moment in Dreyfuss's performance. When the mud-streaked Roy piles together his massive artwork, alarming his neighbors and almost wrecking his own home in the process, he exhibits the frenzied, furious passion of a demented sculptor. These dark-humored scenes are so disturbing that many audience members and reviewers had a visceral reaction against watching the protagonist going "mad," a virtual taboo for a father/hero figure in mainstream American filmmaking. Spielberg caved in to that negative response by drastically abridging the scenes for his *Special Edition*. That unfortunate decision diminished the psychological impact of Roy's experience, tacitly accepting the misunderstanding that his obsession with UFOs is merely a cop-out from social responsibility, rather than a matter of overwhelming spiritual urgency.

"I used the Van Gogh analogy to Richard many times," Spielberg said in a 1978 interview. "When I justified the psychotic behavior in building the mountain in the den, I used the Van Gogh madness parallels several times. A person who is an artist—and Neary is an artist—probably all the people who wound up there are artists of some sort, even if they had no external ability, they certainly had something inside of them that made them worthy."

While the artistic impulse is falsely equated with madness, its true source, for Spielberg, is the "naive wonderment" of childhood, a quality represented at various levels of consciousness by Roy, Lacombe, and little Barry Guiler. Lacking the cultural conditioning that leads adults to xenophobic reactions, Barry accepts the aliens (whom, at first, only he can see) as "friends" beckoning him, like Peter Pan, to a great adventure. Spielberg underscores their kinship by casting an angelic-looking toddler whose soft, round, wide-eyed features and beatific smile give him a family resemblance to the Casper the Ghost–like aliens. "I really wanted to take a child's point of view," Spielberg said. "The uneducated innocence that allows a person to take this kind of quantum jump and . . . go abroad, if you will. A conscientious, responsible adult human being probably wouldn't."

In the marvelous scene of Barry discovering the aliens disrupting his mother's kitchen, Spielberg evoked an extraordinarily spontaneous and affecting series of expressions from the untrained child actor. As the pajama-clad Barry stands in the shadowy doorway, his expression changes in a single close-up from initial trepidation to quizzical amusement and, finally, to an almost rapturous joy.

Spielberg's instinctive affinity with children manifested itself in the magical means he used to direct Cary Guffey in that scene: "I had to the left of the camera a cardboard partition, and to the right of the camera a second cardboard partition. To the left of the camera, I put Bob Westmoreland, our makeup man, in a gorilla suit—the full mask and hands and hairy body. To the right of the camera, I dressed myself up as an Easter Bunny, with the ears and the nose and the whiskers painted on my face. Cary Guffey didn't know what to expect. He didn't know what he was gonna react to. His job was to come into the kitchen, stop at the door, and just have a good time. . . . And just as he came into the kitchen, I had the cardboard partition dropped and Bob Westmoreland was there as the gorilla. Cary froze, like a deer caught in car headlights. . . . I dropped my partition, and he looked over at me, and there was the Easter Bunny smiling at him. He was torn. He began to smile at me—he was still afraid of that thing. Then I had Bob—I said, 'Take off your head.' Bob took off his mask, and when Cary saw it was the man that put his makeup on in the morning, Cary began to laugh. Even though it was a trick, the reaction was pure and honest."*

Spielberg's employment of the "child's point of view" in presenting Trumbull's luminous, multicolored space vehicles (Barry calls them "Toys!") gives the audience the same awestruck feeling reported by those who claim to have experienced close encounters. One does not have to be a believer in UFOs to share Spielberg's sense of wonder about the possibility of an en-

---

* Spielberg was not always able to work such magic with Cary Guffey. "One time, God bless him, the little boy was tired, and we were filming at night," production executive John Veitch recalls. "He said to his mother, 'I'm not working tonight. I want to go to sleep.' Steven and all of us said to him, 'We'll give you any kind of a toy, anything you want.' 'I don't want anything. I want to go home, Mom.' And he did. We lost about $100,000, because that was the big set with all the people and the mother ship."

counter with higher forms of life. In proposing "a seductive alternative for a lot of people who no longer have faith in anything," Spielberg countered the growing cynicism of the post-Vietnam, post-Watergate era with a myth of transcendence, expressed in the secular idiom of the modern world. Skeptical of organized religion, Spielberg expresses his hope for social harmony in a high-tech, quasi-spiritual vision of an alternate reality.

"The present world situation is calculated as never before to arouse expectations of a redeeming, supernatural event," Jung wrote in his 1959 book on flying saucers. ". . . We have indeed strayed far from the metaphysical certainties of the Middle Ages, but not so far that our historical and psychological background is empty of all metaphysical hope. . . . It is characteristic of our time that, in contrast to its previous expressions, the archetype should now take the form of an object, a technological construction, in order to avoid the odiousness of a mythological personification. Anything that looks technological goes down without difficulty with modern man. The possibility of space travel makes the unpopular idea of a metaphysical intervention much more acceptable."

Spielberg's visual style in *Close Encounters* is characterized by shots of people gazing in wonderment at something bigger than life, in images flooded with what he calls " 'God light,' shafts coming out of the sky, or out of a spaceship, or coming through a doorway." Such images would become Spielberg's cinematic signature, his way of conveying the sentiment expressed by his grandfather Fievel: "How wondrous are Thy works."

E A R L Y in 1977, when *Close Encounters* was still months away from completion, George Lucas showed a rough cut of *Star Wars* (without John Williams's rousing musical score) at his San Anselmo home, in northern California. The audience included executives of Twentieth Century–Fox; Gloria Katz and Willard Huyck, who had worked on the script; and several of Lucas's other filmmaker friends, among them Brian De Palma, John Milius, Hal Barwood, Matthew Robbins, and Spielberg.

"It was the first time the executives from Fox had seen it," Katz recalls. "It had no special effects; the battles were scenes from old World War II movies. Afterward, there was stunned silence. George's then-wife [Marcia] broke into tears. I told her, 'Don't cry when there are people from the studio there.' She said, 'It's the *At Long Last Love* of sci-fi.' Brian De Palma said, 'What *is* this shit?' "

But while Lucas, Spielberg, and the writers were driving to a restaurant after the screening, Spielberg piped up, *"I* liked it. I think this movie's going to make a hundred million dollars."

Lucas was pessimistic, predicting that his offbeat sci-fi epic would do about as well as an average Disney film. When *Star Wars* opened that May, Lucas escaped to the Hawaiian island of Maui to recuperate from the editing process and to avoid dealing with the anxiety of the opening. He invited

Spielberg to join him at the Mauna Kea Hotel. The two filmmakers were on the beach building a sand castle for good luck when Lucas excused himself to take a call from Los Angeles. Learning that *Star Wars* was selling out at every theater it was playing in the United States, Lucas returned in what Spielberg described as "a state of euphoria."

As they continued sculpting their sand castle, Lucas asked Spielberg what he wanted to do after *Close Encounters*. "I said I wanted to do a James Bond film," Spielberg recalled. "United Artists approached me after *Sugarland Express* and asked me to do a film for them. I said, 'Sure, give me the next James Bond film.' But they said they couldn't do that. Then George said he had a film that was even better than a James Bond. It was called *Raiders of the Lost Ark*, and it was about this archeologist-adventurer who goes search-ing for the Ark of the Covenant. When he mentioned that it would be like the old serials and that the guy would wear a soft fedora and carry a bullwhip, I was completely hooked. George said, 'Are you interested?' and I said, 'I want to direct it,' and he said, 'It's yours.' "

Star Wars exceeded even Spielberg's optimistic box-office prediction, passing the hundred-million mark in only three months and eventually gross-ing more than half a billion dollars. Spielberg's gracious advertisement in the trade press congratulating Lucas after *Star Wars* broke the box-office record of *Jaws* did not tell the whole story of his reaction. *"Star Wars* was our rival," says *Close Encounters* producer Michael Phillips. "Steven felt really upset about the fact that they were coming out ahead of us." Not only was Spiel-berg disappointed to see his record surpassed, he worried that *Star Wars* would steal much of *Close Encounters'* box-office potential.

Those fears were exacerbated after Columbia held sneak previews of *Close Encounters* at Dallas's Medallion Theater on October 19 and 20. Spielberg felt he needed seven more weeks of postproduction to finish the movie properly for a mid-December release, but Columbia was pushing for a November 1 opening. As a result of that pressure, Spielberg considered the initial release version a "work in progress that had never been finished." One decision he left up to the preview audiences was whether they wanted to hear Jiminy Cricket singing "When You Wish Upon a Star" under the end credits as the mother ship ascends into the heavens with Roy Neary aboard. After pre-viewing the film both with and without the song, Spielberg realized that the song seemed to imply "everything up until the last thirty minutes was a fantasy. Audience response to it was somewhat fifty-fifty. The people who liked it didn't *love* it—they *liked* it. The people who didn't like it were *adamant."* "It diminished the film," Douglas Trumbull felt. "It was too corn-ball and too referential to something else that took you out of the mood that had been created for the film." Although the song had helped inspire the movie, Spielberg reluctantly excised it. But he retained two instrumental quotations of the tune in John Williams's score, and vowed as early as 1978 that he would put back the song when the movie was reissued (the 1980 *Special Edition* used an instrumental version over the end credits). While a previously scheduled international press junket to Los Angeles and bicoastal press previews were delayed following the Dallas previews, Spielberg also trimmed the movie by seven and a half minutes.

The most dramatic fallout from those previews was a premature review by *New York* magazine financial writer William Flanagan. By offering a $25 bribe to someone who resembled him, Flanagan made his way past security guards checking driver's license photographs of the preselected test audience. Flanagan's scathingly negative article, which hit the streets on October 31, noted that Columbia's stock had risen from $8 to $17 a share over the past few months in anticipation of the release of *Close Encounters,* but that the studio still seemed unusually anxious to keep the film under wraps. "I can understand all the apprehension," Flanagan wrote. "In my opinion, the picture will be a colossal flop. It lacks the dazzle, charm, wit, imagination, and broad audience appeal of *Star Wars*—the film Wall Street insists it measure up to, despite author/director Steven Spielberg's artistic protestations."

Flanagan's piece triggered panic selling on Wall Street, causing Columbia to issue a statement reaffirming its "faith in backing Steven Spielberg" and attacking Flanagan's supposed bias "because he was denied access to the film and saw it at a preview to which he was not invited. In fact, no member of the press was invited to the preview." Nevertheless, Frank Rich of *Time* magazine also managed to see the film in Dallas and ran a glowing review at the same time as Flanagan's pan. "Although the movie is not a sure blockbuster—it lacks the simplicity of effect that characterizes most all-time box-office champs—it will certainly be a big enough hit to keep Columbia's stockholders happy," wrote Rich, while failing to mention that Time Inc. was a silent investor in the movie. To the relief of Columbia, which did not criticize *Time* for jumping the review date, Rich continued, "More important, *Close Encounters* offers proof, if any were needed, that Spielberg's reputation is no accident. His new movie is richer and more ambitious than *Jaws,* and it reaches the viewer at a far more profound level than *Star Wars.*"

That was enough to reverse the stock slide, although *The Hollywood Reporter* noted that "tension concerning the public's response to the film was running sufficiently high to keep director Steve Spielberg ensconced in his hotel room, unwilling to attend [November 6] screenings" for media and financial analysts at New York's Ziegfeld Theatre.

After opening on November 16, *Close Encounters* easily reached the box-office stratosphere, with its worldwide box-office gross eventually totalling almost $270 million.* But Spielberg always regretted that his many production delays had forced him to miss the originally planned spring release date, thereby enabling *Star Wars* to beat *Close Encounters* into the marketplace.

---

* According to a 1994 *Forbes* magazine profile of Spielberg, while his contract for *Close Encounters* called for him to receive 17.5 percent of the profits, he "ended up with about $5 million. Spielberg was discovering the first rule of Hollywood accounting: Even the biggest hits show very little 'profit' after overhead, interest and distribution fees are generously factored in."

Although Michael Phillips feels that by reviving the appeal of the dormant sci-fi genre, *Star Wars* may have helped *Close Encounters* at the box office, Spielberg could not help thinking that his movie would have been a bigger hit if only it had opened earlier. Nevertheless, *Close Encounters* proved that *Jaws* was no fluke. Sending Columbia profits soaring to record levels, it sealed Spielberg's commercial clout within the industry as a filmmaker with a seemingly magical box-office touch. He and Lucas now found themselves with virtually unlimited power to choose their subject matter and dictate the terms of their deals with studios. Their unprecedented levels of success would embolden them to demand a degree of independence within the Hollywood system that few filmmakers had ever been granted.

S P I E L B E R G received his first Oscar nomination as director of *Close Encounters,* one of eight nominations the film received. But in the impenetrable wisdom of the Academy's overall membership, Spielberg's film was not worthy of a nomination for Best Picture. Richard Dreyfuss's eminently forgettable comedy vehicle *The Goodbye Girl* (for which he won an Oscar) took what should have been the *Close Encounters* slot on the list of nominees for Best Picture, which otherwise matched up with the directing nominations. *Close Encounters* won two Oscars, for Zsigmond's cinematography and a special achievement Oscar for Frank Warner's sound effects editing. Woody Allen's *Annie Hall* was the winner for Best Picture and Director, so at least Spielberg could take the consolation that his movie was passed over for another that has become a modern classic.

Critical opinion on Spielberg, which had begun to diverge as a result of *Jaws,* was polarized further by *Close Encounters*. Some reviewers mocked Spielberg for making what Molly Haskell, in *New York* magazine, called "children's films that parents can love without shame"; her review was headlined "The Dumbest Story Ever Told." Reviewers who responded favorably to *Close Encounters* were willing to partake in what Frank Rich called "a celebration not only of children's dreams but also of the movies that help fuel those dreams." *Newsweek*'s Jack Kroll compared Spielberg to Walt Disney, "with his metamorphic genius, sentimental idealism and his feeling for the technical magic of movies as a paradigm for technological utopia." But Kroll also understood the darker side of Spielberg, finding the much-maligned imagery of Roy Neary building the mountain in his den "a crazy, funny, touching scene . . . it seems to come from something deeply personal in Spielberg."

Praise for Spielberg's technical wizardry was nearly unanimous, but Charles Champlin of the *Los Angeles Times* was among those for whom this "magic set with dramatic interludes" nevertheless confirmed a suspicion that Spielberg was a director of "effects rather than characters or relationships." In the same paper, however, Ray Bradbury described *Close Encounters* as "the most important film of our time. . . . For this is a religious film, in all the great good senses, the right senses, of that much-battered word. . . . Spielberg has made a film that can open in New Delhi, Tokyo, Berlin, Moscow, Johannesburg, Paris, London, New York, and Rio de Janeiro on the same day to mobs and throngs and crowds that will never stop coming because for the first time someone has treated all of us as if we really did belong to one race."

Perhaps the most fitting comment on *Close Encounters* came from the great filmmaker Jean Renoir. In a March 1978 letter to François Truffaut, Renoir reported from Beverly Hills, "We have finally seen *Close Encounters*. It is a very good film, and I regret it was not made in France. This type of popular science would be most appropriate for the compatriots of Jules Verne and Méliès. . . . You are excellent in it, because you're not quite real. There is more than a grain of eccentricity in this adventure. The author is a poet. In the South of France one would say he is a bit *fada*. He brings to mind the exact meaning of this word in Provence: the village *fada* is the one possessed by the fairies."

U N F O R T U N A T E L Y, Spielberg could not let go of his masterpiece. *The Special Edition of Close Encounters of the Third Kind* went before the cameras in 1979, on weekends over a nineteen-week period while he was otherwise occupied with filming *1941*. Columbia let him spend $2 million to reedit *Close Encounters* and shoot additional scenes he had been unable to film for the original version, when "certain compromises had to be made as a result of budget and schedule. . . . I've had the opportunity to see how the film plays for audiences. Film is not necessarily a dry-cement process. I have the luxury of retouching the painting."

But Columbia exacted a heavy aesthetic price. "I never really wanted to show the inside of the mother ship," Spielberg admitted in the 1990 documentary about the making of *Close Encounters*. "That was, in a way, how I got the money to fix the movie." Michael Butler was enlisted to photograph the scene of Roy Neary entering the mother ship, on a newly built set at the Burbank Studios, with added special effects by Robert Swarthe (Douglas Trumbull says he passed up the opportunity to work on the *Special Edition* because Columbia expected him to do it without pay).

Although the expanded ending was the major selling gimmick in Columbia's ad campaign—"NOW, FOR THE FIRST TIME, FILMGOERS WILL BE ABLE TO SHARE THE ULTIMATE EXPERIENCE OF BEING *INSIDE*"—the scene proved to be a terrible letdown from the phantasmagoria preceding it. Little happens except for Neary gaping around inside an essentially empty, plastic-looking environment bearing a distinct resemblance to the lobby of a Hyatt hotel. By preventing the viewer from simply imagining what happens to Neary, the ending squandered much of the film's sense of wonder and magic.

That commercial compromise alone would have been a fatal miscalculation, but Spielberg, as he later put it, also "added some *gestalt* and took out some *kitsch* and reshaped the movie." His cuts amounted to sixteen minutes of footage. His additions included six minutes of newly shot scenes and seven minutes of footage shot for the original version but previously unseen by the public; the *Special Edition* runs three minutes shorter than the original's 135-minute length. The *"gestalt"* Spielberg added included the scene of a cargo ship, lost in the Bermuda Triangle, turning up in the Gobi Desert (photographed by Allen Daviau). Although it expands the story's geographical scope, that scene is superfluous because it serves the same function as the opening scene of airplanes turning up in the Mexican desert. What Spielberg considered *"kitsch"* was much of the heart of the story involving Roy's estrangement from his family, notably a large chunk of the mountain-building sequence. In partial compensation, Spielberg added a harrowing scene of Ronnie discovering a freaked-out Roy huddled in the bathtub under a steaming shower. He had not used it in the original because it was "so powerful, it was almost another movie." But for the 1980 edition Spielberg also cut another pivotal scene of Neary and other UFO witnesses being publicly belittled by mendacious Air Force personnel. The net effect of the changes was a diminution of Roy's personal story in favor of special effects.

Rather than confirming critical reservations about Spielberg, as one might have thought, this change of emphasis was greeted with uncritical praise when the *Special Edition* debuted in theaters on July 31, 1980. (The public response, on the other hand, was unspectacular, and one patron actually sued Columbia, claiming that fraudulent advertising had led her to expect a new movie.) In part, the critics' response to the retooling reflected gratification that Spielberg had listened to their advice about how to downplay Roy's mental problems. But it also indicated that, even in its bastardized form, *Close Encounters* had become a consensus classic and its director a cultural icon. "What has happened is a phenomenon in the annals of film," Arthur Knight proclaimed in *The Hollywood Reporter.* "Director Steven Spielberg has taken his 1977 flawed masterpiece and, by judicious editing and addition of several scenes, has turned his work into an authentic masterpiece."

At the time Spielberg issued his *Special Edition,* Michael Phillips, who had no involvement with it, presciently raised a note of caution: "I just hope it doesn't lead to a trend in which filmmakers 'redo' their movies. That would simply be dreadful. Some filmmakers might start withholding a few minutes from the first release so they could add this material in the reissue and get people to spend their five dollars again."

That is just what has happened in recent years. The release of revised "directors' cuts" too often has become a dubious exercise in historical revisionism, undertaken largely to gratify egos and obtain additional revenues from the home-video and laserdisc market. While the restoration of such classic films as *Lawrence of Arabia,* which Spielberg helped sponsor, has been a more positive trend, the continual metamorphosis of film history *Close Encounters* helped inaugurate raises disturbing questions about the legacy filmmakers are leaving for future generations. When Columbia announced in 1980 that the original version of *Close Encounters* was being "retired" from the marketplace, Spielberg publicly objected, insisting, "There will be two versions of *Close Encounters* showing for the next one hundred years, as far as I'm concerned." Videotapes of the film in distribution today, however, are of the *Special Edition*. The original version sometimes airs on television in a pan-and-scan format, but it can be seen in its proper wide-screen aspect ratio only on the 1990 Criterion laserdisc edition. Spielberg's involvement with that third edition of the film, which includes the added scenes as a supplement, seemed a tacit admission that his original cut should be regarded as the true version.

Expressing hope that the *Special Edition* would not replace the original, Pauline Kael wrote in 1980, "I want to be able to hear the true believer Roberts Blossom tell people that he has seen Bigfoot as well as flying saucers. It may not seem like a big loss, but when you remember something in a movie with pleasure and it's gone, you feel as if your memories had been mugged."

" R E H A B "

IN EVERY FILMMAKER'S LIFE, A *1941* INVARIABLY COMES ALONG. I CAN SEE *1941* MORE AS
A CLEANSING EXPERIENCE, THE ONE POSSIBLE WAY I CAN MAKE YOU FORGET ALL THE GOOD
THINGS I'VE DONE IN MOTION PICTURES.

— STEVEN SPIELBERG, SEPTEMBER 1979

M E T a real heartbreaker
last night," Spielberg told Julia Phillips while they were working on *Close
Encounters*. The "heartbreaker" was Amy Irving.

The twenty-two-year-old actress, whose curly-brown-haired, sloe-eyed,
high-cheekboned beauty masked an intense and fiercely ambitious nature,
had recently returned to California from dramatic studies in London when
she met Spielberg in 1976. The daughter of TV producer-director Jules Irving,
former artistic director of New York's Repertory Theatre of Lincoln Center,
and actress Priscilla Pointer, Amy was of Russian-Jewish ancestry on her
father's side and Welsh-Cherokee on her mother's, but she was raised as a
Christian Scientist. She was the niece of Universal TV executive producer
Richard Irving, who had worked with Spielberg on *The Name of the Game*.
Amy grew up on the stage in San Francisco and New York and felt somewhat
alienated when she followed her parents to Hollywood. "When we were in
San Francisco, Los Angeles was a dirty word to us," she admitted. "I never in
a million years thought I'd ever be in television or films. I always thought I
was going to be a struggling stage actress."

But with her three-year stint completed at the London Academy of Music
and Dramatic Arts, Amy found herself unexpectedly in demand in Holly-

wood. After playing a few TV roles, she tried out for the part of Princess Leia in George Lucas's *Star Wars*. Although she was passed over for the more hard-edged Carrie Fisher, Amy caught the attention of director Brian De Palma, who was conducting the audition jointly with Lucas in order to find actresses for *his* next movie. De Palma offered Amy her first movie role, as the sweet-natured high school girl Sue Snell in *Carrie*. Since he "had a feeling Amy and Steven would like each other," De Palma also sent her to audition for the role of Richard Dreyfuss's wife in *Close Encounters*.

"I was much too young [for the role], and Steven said so right away," Amy recalled three years later. "We just sat and talked for a while. It was a month before I saw him again. That encouraged me, however. If he'd been one of those directors who immediately asked an actress out for a date I'd be very worried today; in fact, I'd probably insist on sitting in on all his auditions."

Their second meeting came at a small dinner party arranged by De Palma during the shooting of *Carrie*. Steven reminded Amy of her father, who was also a "wonderful, boyish man, a real hard worker—gifted with a silly sense of humor." She soon moved out of her Laurel Canyon house and into Steven's "bachelor funky" digs nearby. Later described by director Robert Markowitz as having "an icy exterior but a high degree of sexuality teeming beneath the surface," Amy would spend the next four years living with Spielberg in a passionate but often turbulent relationship.

A few months after they began living together, they moved into a lavish new home Steven bought in Coldwater Canyon, close to the Beverly Hills Hotel. "The house that *Jaws* built," as they called it, marked a considerable step up the social ladder for Spielberg. "Steven had this huge, huge house— eight or nine thousand square feet, it must have been," screenwriter Bob Gale recalls. "He was proud and embarrassed at the same time to have a five- or six-bedroom house. What was he going to do with all this? He said, 'You know, I thought about it. I could either take my money and have it invested and every month I could look at numbers in a book or on a sheet, or I could live in it. So I decided I should live in it.' "

Steven and Amy shared the house with a cook and a cocker spaniel, Elmer; two parrots, named Schmuck I and II after Steven's boyhood pets in Arizona; and, briefly, a monkey who could not be housebroken. Elmer made appearances in *The Sugarland Express, Jaws, Close Encounters,* and *1941,* and one of the parrots was trained to croak the five-note interplanetary signal from *Close Encounters*.

Spielberg worked at an elaborate customized desk with built-in telephone, radio, tape recorder, and (befitting his growing sense of privacy) a security television monitor and a paper shredder. The five-year-old house had a fancy screening room where Spielberg, Amy, and their friends watched 35mm prints of movies borrowed from the studios. He also relaxed by listening to his collection of movie soundtrack albums and by playing *Space Invaders* and other state-of-the-art video games.

If all that wasn't enough to keep him occupied, "There was a television in just about every room of that house, and there was always a television on," reports Gale. "He'd have a conversation, and out of the corner of his eye he'd be watching television and see something and get excited about it. He'd make a note, 'Find out the name of this actor or who directed this commercial.' He was always thinking about what he was seeing and filing it away."

Amy did not find it easy to accommodate to Steven's hyperkinetic, high-powered lifestyle or to the publicity spotlight that went with it. Since she was just at the beginning of her career, and he was already phenomenally successful, she naturally felt in his shadow. While growing up, she had become tired of hearing herself described as "Jules Irving's daughter," resenting people's assumptions that whenever she won a part, it was because of her father. Now she faced the same problem all over again, but on a much bigger stage. "I don't want to be known as Steven's girlfriend," she already was telling the press in 1978. They did not work together during their first four years as a couple, in part because Amy wanted to ensure that whatever success she attained was her own.

She felt overwhelmed, at first, by Steven's creative abilities. When she saw *Close Encounters,* she was moved to tears, both by the beauty of the images and, she said, "by the beauty of Steve Spielberg's soul. He disclosed things none of us ever imagined." But by 1979 she had developed more mixed feelings about his work. "I know he's an incredible moviemaker," she said, "but the kind of films he makes aren't necessarily the kind I want to be in."

During that period, De Palma put Amy into another surreal horror film, *The Fury,* and Robert Markowitz directed her in *Voices,* a love story in which she played a deaf woman who teaches hearing-impaired children. *Voices* was not a commercial success, and while her reviews were respectful, they did not win her the separate identity she craved. She suffered because she "wasn't secure enough to have some people think I owed my career to Steven." Steven, for his part, still had to overcome his lingering resistance to growing up and assuming the responsibilities of a husband and father.

Amy felt herself treated as a "second-class citizen" in a status-conscious industry town consumed with talk about moviemaking and box-office grosses. "Our social life was going out to dinner with studio heads," she complained. Like Steven's former girlfriend who met him during the making of *Sugarland Express* but ultimately went back to Texas because she couldn't share his obsession with movies, Amy quickly became frustrated by Steven's single-minded absorption in his career. "Steven has trouble with a level of intimacy," his longtime producer Kathleen Kennedy has said. "He gets close to people to a point, and then it begins to break down, because I don't think Steven is always comfortable communicating his feelings. His inability to trust very many people creates a certain amount of personal loneliness for him. But I also think it comes from just wanting to be by himself and be close to some creative, inanimate world he can live within, rather than deal with the real world and real people."

While making *Close Encounters,* Steven publicly admitted he had no time to do anything but "eat, shoot your movie, plan your shots for the next day, sleep, and forget women." When Amy visited him on the Mobile location that summer, he confided to Julia Phillips, "I wish she hadn't come. She keeps crying and I keep wanting to say, 'Don't you understand, I'm fucking my movie.' "

T o follow the personal epiphany of *Close Encounters,* Spielberg considered several projects, including a pirate movie he had been developing for Twentieth Century–Fox with screenwriter Jeffrey Fiskin. Spielberg described it as a sixteenth-century action yarn "in the old Errol Flynn tradition," about a love triangle involving a woman and two half-brothers, a peasant and an aristocrat. He dropped the project after Universal's 1976 pirate movie *Swashbuckler* sank without a trace.

Spielberg came much closer to directing a comedy-drama about Negro leagues baseball players, *The Bingo Long Traveling All-Stars and Motor Kings.* The Motown-Universal film was based on the 1973 novel by William Brashler and adapted by *Sugarland Express* writers Hal Barwood and Matthew Robbins. When the director originally hired for *Bingo Long,* Mark Rydell, dropped out because of a disagreement over budget limitations, Universal offered Motown the services of Spielberg, then in postproduction on *Jaws.* Spielberg was enthusiastic about the project, but as producer Rob Cohen explained, "The trouble was that as *Jaws'* opening got nearer and nearer, Steve became less and less available. We were set to begin shooting within about a month of that, and there were a million things to be done. We couldn't postpone production because we had a play-or-pay deal with James Earl Jones, so we simply had to have another director." Spielberg was succeeded by another former Universal TV director, John Badham.

Spielberg's youthful fondness for *The Twilight Zone* was reflected in his interest in William Goldman's novel *Magic,* a spooky tale about a ventriloquist controlled by his dummy. Reminiscent of the 1962 *Twilight Zone* program "The Dummy" with Cliff Robertson, as well as the Michael Redgrave episode in the 1945 British thriller *Dead of Night, Magic* was a project Spielberg coveted before Richard Attenborough was hired to direct the United Artists release. "I had talked to Robert De Niro about playing the part that Anthony Hopkins wound up playing," Spielberg recalled. ". . . I had it in my mind how I would have made that film, and I thought it would have been pretty good. After a year had gone by, and Dickie's film opened in theaters [in 1978], I went to see the picture and realized that it was a hell of a lot better than what I would have done."

Spielberg also considered directing a live network TV production of Reginald Rose's teleplay *Twelve Angry Men* with a cast of both men and women. In his senior year at Saratoga High, Spielberg had worked on a stage production of the jury drama, which was first presented on CBS's live *Studio One* series in 1954 and was made into a 1957 film (titled *12 Angry Men*) by director Sidney Lumet. In the end, however, Spielberg was seduced by the prospect of working with two young comedy writers whose motto was "Social Irresponsibility."

I N 1973, a USC film school class visited Universal for a prerelease screening of *The Sugarland Express*. Afterward, student filmmaker Robert Zemeckis asked Spielberg to watch his black comedy *A Field of Honor*, about a newly discharged mental patient driven to a murderous rampage by exposure to the everyday violence of American society. "[M]y God, it was spectacular for a film student in his early twenties to have made such a picture with no money, with police cars and a riot and a lot of crazy characters . . . all dubbed to Elmer Bernstein's score for *The Great Escape*," Spielberg said later. "I saw that picture and I said, 'This man is worth watching.' "

Following their graduation from USC, Zemeckis and writing partner Bob Gale wrote TV scripts for Universal and collaborated on two unproduced feature screenplays. One was *Tank*, about a group of dissidents who steal a Sherman tank from a National Guard Armory and threaten to blow up a Chicago building to protest the actions of oil companies. *Tank* tickled the fancy of writer-director John Milius, who recalled that Zemeckis and Gale "came in my office at Goldwyn, and they were just crazy, they were just raving wild men."

"Boys," growled Milius, "this script has a healthy sense of social irresponsibility. I applaud that."

The burly, bombastic, yet genial Milius was an unabashed war freak who loved to goad Hollywood liberals with his retro politics, which were somewhere to the right of John Wayne's. "I just absolutely hate liberals and people who are civilized," Milius proclaimed in a 1975 *Daily Variety* interview with the author of this book. Spielberg had a clipping of the article delivered to Milius's office, attached to a wooden carving board with a hunting knife stuck through a piece of raw, bloody meat.

Milius's A-Team Productions had a deal to produce movies for MGM, and Zemeckis and Gale were hired to write a World War II movie titled *The Night the Japs Attacked*. Although objections from Japanese-Americans forced Milius to change the title (temporarily) to *The Night the Japanese Attacked*, the script offered something to offend virtually everyone in its broad lampooning of anti-Japanese hysteria among Los Angeles residents in the early days of the war. Spielberg changed the title to *The Rising Sun* and, finally, *1941*.

The two Bobs began hanging out with Spielberg and Milius on Thursday nights at the Oak Tree Gun Club in the Newhall Pass north of Los Angeles. Milius had introduced Spielberg to the sport of skeet shooting, a male-bonding ritual for Milius and his fellow Hollywood gun enthusiasts. "There are numbers of gun owners—collectors, hunters, sport shooters—in the film community, plus many more who keep firearms for protection," National Rifle Association spokesman Charlton Heston, also a friend of Milius's, wrote in his 1995 autobiography, *In the Arena*. "I suspect, in fact, that there are more filmmakers who are closet gun enthusiasts than there are closet homosexuals. Steven Spielberg has one of the finest gun collections in California, but never refers to it, and never shoots publicly. Can you imagine the most famous filmmaker in town worried about his reputation?"

Spielberg, who had learned to shoot from his father while growing up in Arizona, still visits the Oak Tree Gun Club. "He's a darn good shot," says club member Robert Stack, himself a world-class target shooter. "He has terrific reactions. Clay target shooting is a very subtle, highly sophisticated sport; it takes a lot of nerve. He shot some very good scores."

Evenings with the boys at the Oak Tree Gun Club also involved a stop along the way at a hamburger joint called Tommie's. "Steven had this cheap Super-8 camera," Milius recalled, "and he had all these films of us eating at Tommie's and covering ourselves in chili and throwing up on the car, doing Bigfoot imitations, wonderful stuff. Great howling mad evenings out there at the range, out of which came *1941*."

In his only partly tongue-in-cheek introduction to a comic-book version of the movie, Spielberg wrote, "I was immediately attracted to [the script] because of its highly illiterate nature—it appeared to have been written by two guys whose only excursions into literature had been classic comics. My initial instincts were not far off: I subsequently learned that the sole writing experiences of the authors had been spray-painting the walls of public buildings with profanity and ethnic slurs. I continued to read their first-draft screenplay at a local junk-burger dive in the San Fernando Valley. Moments of the script were so funny that I vomited from laughter. It was this feeling of nausea that I felt moved to translate into cinematic imagery."

R E T U R N I N G to Los Angeles from five weeks of rewriting *1941* on the Mobile location of *Close Encounters,* the two Bobs began work on a script satirizing Beatlemania. The first of many films Spielberg has produced without directing, *I Wanna Hold Your Hand* follows six New Jersey teenagers journeying to New York City in February 1964 to take part in the frenzy surrounding the American TV debut of the Beatles on *The Ed Sullivan Show*. While borrowing unabashedly from *A Hard Day's Night* and *American Graffiti,* Zemeckis and Gale tempered their nostalgia with sly insinuations about the repressed sexual hysteria underlying American teenagers' obsession with the long-haired Liverpudlians.

Spielberg set up the movie with Sid Sheinberg, who agreed to let Zemeckis make his directorial debut at Universal. *I Wanna Hold Your Hand* was filmed on studio back lots for a modest $1.6 million in late 1977, with a cast of mostly unknown young actors and with doubles used to stand in for the Beatles. "Steven would come down to the set a lot when we were shooting," Gale says, "and he'd make suggestions to Bob about how to block the scene. He'd say, 'Here's how you can play all this in one shot.' Boy, it was great, because Steven was so good at that. He would quietly make a suggestion to Bob, or Bob would say, 'Steven, help me out here.' "

In those days, Spielberg disclaimed any ambitious plans to act like a mogul or to supervise his own slate of projects with other directors. "My own theory about producing is, I'll produce films that I would have otherwise directed," he said in 1980. ". . . Movies slip away—you can't do everything. But I like to *think* I can do everything, I *want* to do everything."

The production of the charming, energetic *I Wanna Hold Your Hand* went smoothly, and though it was not a box-office success, the film gave Spielberg the gratifying experience of testing his hand as a producer while giving a break to another young director. Spielberg's first mentor, Chuck Silvers, had asked him to remember to put something back into the industry once he became successful. Spielberg was doing just that.

S P I E L B E R G planned to take a few weeks from preproduction on *1941* to knock off a low-budget comedy about children, *After School,* from yet another script by Zemeckis and Gale. The impetus for the project (sometimes referred to by Spielberg as *Growing Up*) came from François Truffaut, whose view of Spielberg's true talents was diametrically opposed to the conventional Hollywood wisdom. Truffaut was celebrated for his films with children, including *The Four Hundred Blows* and *Small Change*. While acting in *Close Encounters,* Truffaut frequently urged Spielberg to make an American equivalent of *Small Change:* "You must make a movie about keeds. You must stop all this big stuff and make a movie about keeds! If it's the last thing you do!"

Summoning the two Bobs, Spielberg said, "I want you guys to write a movie I'm really passionate about—about kids."

"Great, Steven," they replied. "What about 'em?"

"That's it," Spielberg said. "Kids."

According to Gale, that was the extent of the guidance they received on the subject from Spielberg.

After talking with Spielberg in February 1978, *Variety* claimed that the film would be "a personal story of his own young adulthood." In fact, Zemeckis and Gale were drawing from *their* adolescent experiences. "Zemeckis and I being the renegades we are—certainly we were more so then—we thought that to make it really interesting, it should be rated R, and we wrote it that way," Gale says. "We swore like truckdrivers when we were twelve. A lot of kids do that, and we thought that would be the way to go. It was the classic nerds-against-jocks story. The nerds had a dogshit bomb on a radio-controlled car." Spielberg found their concept amusing and provocative. "I don't want to make a movie about children that's dimples or cuteness," he said. ". . . It's my first vendetta film: I'm going to get back at about twenty people I've always wanted to get back at."

Shooting was to begin that May for Universal, with a budget of only $1.5

million. Spielberg planned to use a cast of unknowns between the ages of eight and fourteen, shooting in a semi-improvisatory fashion and letting the kids contribute their own experiences to the screenplay. The writers set *After School* in Zemeckis's hometown of Chicago, but Spielberg shifted the locale to his far more sedate hometown of Phoenix. Before preproduction could begin in earnest, Spielberg got cold feet about the screenplay. "I think it was a little too much for Steven," says Gale. The turning point came when Spielberg asked cinematographer Caleb Deschanel to shoot *After School*. Deschanel "read it and hated it. He said, 'This is disgusting.' Steven didn't really have a focus on what *After School* was going to be. The movie that he really wanted to make about kids turned out to be *E.T.*"

Spielberg explained his decision to drop the earlier movie about kids by saying, "I hadn't grown up enough to make *Growing Up.*" But he ruefully admitted a few years later, "I wanted to do a little film—not *Annie Hall,* because I haven't met my Annie Hall yet, but a small film, an intimate film. They said, Anyone can make a little film, we want you to make big films. It was capricious of me, but I agreed. . . . I plunged into [*1941*] with such wild abandon that I didn't really focus on the story I was telling, to know whether it was funny or simply stupid or whether the film was getting too overblown. . . . On about the hundred and forty-fifth day of shooting, I realized that the film was directing me, I wasn't directing it."

"**W**E realize now that no one in his right mind would have tackled our story," Zemeckis said after *1941* finished shooting. "But we didn't reckon on Steve." Outwardly, at least, Spielberg seemed like one of the sanest young filmmakers in Hollywood of the late seventies, even one of the squarest. Yet part of him wanted to fit in with that era's "wild and crazy" humor, typified by John Belushi, Dan Aykroyd, and the rest of the *Saturday Night Live* crowd. "I must say that there's a part of me, in my nice, conservative life, that is probably as crazy and insane as Milius and the two guys who wrote that script," Spielberg said in a 1996 documentary about the making of *1941*. ". . . I really thought it would be a great opportunity to break a lot of furniture and see a lot of glass shattering. It was basically written and directed as one would perform in a demolition derby."

Much as Spielberg would like to claim a truly anarchic spirit, more likely it was his lifelong need to seek protective coloration through conformity that resulted in what he acknowledged was the "total conceptual disaster" of *1941*. While not about to surrender enough of his self-control to embrace the self-destructive drug lifestyle of Belushi and so many other young people in show business during the 1970s, Spielberg nevertheless was uncomfortable seeming too far out of step with his generation. *Time* magazine aptly summarized *1941* as "Animal House Goes to War." An elephantine postmodernist farce about World War II whose large cast featured Belushi and Aykroyd, it broadly satirized anti-Japanese hysteria in Los Angeles during the week following Pearl Harbor. Spielberg borrowed Belushi and Tim Matheson from director John Landis's 1978 *National Lampoon's Animal House,* and Landis himself played a small part as a motorcycle messenger in *1941.* With its crude sexual innuendos and equally witless attempts at social satire, *1941,* as Ron Pennington of *The Hollywood Reporter* observed, "makes *Animal House* look like a highly sophisticated comedy."*

The clash of styles and sensibilities was obvious from the first day of shooting. "This is not a Spielberg movie," the director kept saying to himself. "What am I doing here?"

Zemeckis and Gale had come across the little-known story of "The Great Los Angeles Air Raid" and the events leading up to it while doing research for *Tank* at the downtown Los Angeles public library. "Although *1941* is based on actual incidents that took place in southern California during World War II," Gale wrote in his novelization of the screenplay, "in many cases the truth has been modified, embellished, or completely thrown out the window in the interests of drama, entertainment, cheap sensationalism, and getting a few laughs."

The facts were these: On the night of February 22, 1942, a Japanese submarine lobbed about twenty shells at the oil fields on the coast of southern California, twelve miles north of Santa Barbara. The shells did little damage. One hit an oil well derrick a quarter mile from the beach, and a fuse from an unexploded shell injured an Army officer trying to disarm it a few days later. Nevertheless, the attack was the first on the American mainland by a foreign enemy since the War of 1812. Nearby Los Angeles went into a heightened stage of alert. Two nights later, shortly after 3:00 A.M., the sky over the city was filled with ack-ack rounds from antiaircraft guns for forty-five minutes when unidentified enemy planes were thought to be spotted over the coastline. L.A. AREA RAIDED! screamed the *Los Angeles Times* in an extra edition on February 25.

Although it never was determined exactly what set off the initial barrage —probably an errant weather balloon—Angelenos reacted in an orgy of unrestrained panic. All over the city there were phantom enemy aircraft sightings, and it was incorrectly reported that four enemy planes were shot down over the city. Exploding shrapnel from 1,440 rounds of antiaircraft ammunition rained down on houses as people cowered inside for shelter or dashed madly around the darkened streets. One man was injured by an exploding shell, and five people died of heart attacks or traffic injuries during the blackout resulting from the imaginary "air raid."

William A. Fraker, Spielberg's cinematographer on *1941,* witnessed the event as a young signalman on a Coast Guard transport ship in San Pedro Harbor. To Fraker's eyes, "It was all so exquisite. My mouth hung open for

---

* The Landis-Spielberg mutual admiration society continued when Landis cast Spielberg in a bit part as a geeky Chicago bureaucrat in the wildly overblown Belushi-Aykroyd comedy *The Blues Brothers* (1980).

the entire time. We couldn't believe it was happening. From San Pedro to Malibu it looked like the Fourth of July. We didn't think the war could have come this far."

This bizarre event might have provided the framework for a corrosive satire of wartime jitters and racist anxieties on the homefront. One can easily imagine what Preston Sturges might have done with the story, lampooning the sheltered gullibility of ordinary Americans in the trenchant manner of his wartime comedies *The Miracle of Morgan's Creek* and *Hail the Conquering Hero*. But social satire, however farcical in spirit, cannot depart so far from reality that it turns into outright fantasy, or much of the satirical sting is lost. Having an aerial dogfight take place over Hollywood Boulevard, to cite the most egregious example, lends visual excitement to *1941,* but only adds to its unbelievability.

The film's most pervasive credibility problem is that the writers divorced the Los Angeles "air raid" from much of the social context that would have made it meaningful. While the characters' hysterical fear of "Japs" is exploited for what Milius gleefully referred to as "politically incorrect" farce, the most significant omission is any mention of the rounding-up of Japanese-American residents of Los Angeles and their deportation to internment camps, a process that was beginning in earnest during the week the actual shelling took place. The movie was backdated to the day and night of December 13, 1941, to heighten the proximity to Pearl Harbor. Purely for comic effect, the screenwriters took the license of throwing in Los Angeles's 1943 zoot-suit riots, while barely alluding to the anti-Hispanic bias that led to those riots. Acknowledging the true extent of the racist paranoia in wartime California would have made the film's satire of war hysteria much more troubling and incisive.

But Spielberg admitted, "I really didn't have a vision for *1941.*" It would have been a better film, he now thinks, if it had been directed by Zemeckis, who has described his own vision of *1941* as "very dark and very cynical." Indeed, if Zemeckis had prevailed, the film's ending would have written a new chapter in the annals of darkness and cynicism: Jitterbugging delinquent Wally Stephans (Bobby Di Cicco), having become the bombardier on the *Enola Gay,* drops the atomic bomb on Hiroshima as revenge for losing a USO dance contest. That ending was "too outrageous for everyone," Zemeckis regretted. "No one would listen to me."

T HE screenwriters' reckless conflation of historical events undermines the memorable scene of Major General Joseph W. Stilwell (Robert Stack) watching Walt Disney's *Dumbo* in a movie theater on Hollywood Boulevard. This scene was inspired by a letter Stilwell wrote to his wife from Washington, D.C., about his activities with his personal aide on December 25, 1941: "[W]e had Christmas dinner—and a good one—at a restaurant—and dissipated further by seeing *Dumbo*. I nearly fell off my chair when the elephant pyramid toppled over. We sat through the film twice."

Stilwell at the time was based in Monterey, California, as commander of the Third Army Corps, with responsibility for California coastal defenses from San Luis Obispo south to San Diego. He was in the Los Angeles area briefly in December, and though he encountered "strange cases of jitters" and some "wild, farcical and fantastic" rumors of imminent danger, no civil unrest occurred during his visit, nor was there any outside the Washington theater where the real-life general watched *Dumbo*. Considered in isolation, the scene in *1941* of Stilwell tearfully watching the baby elephant being caressed by its imprisoned mother is a strangely charming expression of childlike tenderness, evoking the power of entertainment to provide solace in time of war. But the unspoken (and no doubt unintended) implication that Stilwell is criminally oblivious to his duties makes nonsense of the historical character and undercuts Stack's dignified portrayal of Stilwell as one of the few sane individuals in the movie.

The role originally was offered to John Wayne, who read the script and "spent an hour trying to persuade me not to direct it," Spielberg recalled. "I'm so surprised at you," Wayne told him. "I thought you were an American, and I thought you were going to make a movie to honor the memory of World War II. But this dishonors the memory of what happened." Another conservative icon, Charlton Heston, passed on the part for the same reason. "I never saw it as an anti-American film," Spielberg insisted. ". . . What's wrong about sticking a pie in the face of the Statue of Liberty from time to time, if it's in the spirit of humor?"

Spielberg also offered the role to the legendary B-movie director Samuel Fuller, a former World War II infantryman, but Fuller objected that he bore no physical resemblance to Stilwell. Casting Fuller instead as the cigar-chomping commanding officer of the Southern California Interceptor Command, Spielberg finally turned to his shooting buddy from the Oak Tree Gun Club. With a military haircut, wire-rimmed glasses, and a minimal amount of makeup, Robert Stack bore an uncanny resemblance to "Vinegar Joe."

When they went on location at the downtown Los Angeles Theatre to shoot the scene of Stilwell watching *Dumbo,* Spielberg asked Stack if he wanted drops for his eyes to help himself cry.

"If I remember *Dumbo,* it was a great scene," Stack replied. "If I look at *Dumbo,* I can do it without acting."

"I want the scene run for Bob!" Spielberg said. "Roll it!"

"He made sure I had the setting all around me," Stack remembers. "He didn't say, 'OK, you're reacting to . . .' When I made my first picture, with Deanna Durbin, they had a blackboard and they pointed to it and said, 'There she is, she's beautiful!' As I was watching the scene in *Dumbo,* tears were starting to come. This guy was shooting with a massive camera and all that incredible equipment, but he didn't get overpowered with the camera.

Steven shot that in one take! I couldn't believe it. He has incredible confidence. I've never done anything like that before, without coverage or protection. I thought, 'This guy knows what he wants. That's class!' "

Stack adds, "But if you want the truth, I never fully understood the script. It was a strange script. Just plain strange."

SPIELBERG'S fondness for *Mad* magazine's "Scenes We'd Like to See" was gratified by *1941*'s irreverent riffs on the patriotic fervor of vintage World War II movies. On a deeper thematic level, the script offered him a demented comic inversion of *Close Encounters*. Its satiric portrayal of a narrow-minded American populace overcome with exaggerated fear of alien invasion and unidentified flying objects allowed Spielberg license for his hitherto submerged sense of comic invective.

Although Spielberg rather foolishly described *1941* at the time of its release as "a celebration of paranoia"—an indication of how confused his conscious intentions were in approaching the subject—his deepest and most truly subversive sympathy is, as always, with the outsiders. While Japanese-Americans are conspicuous by their absence, the commander of the Japanese submarine, Mitamura (Toshiro Mifune, hero of *The Seven Samurai* and other Akira Kurosawa classics), is portrayed as a man of fierce dignity and stature, if a bit blinkered in his idea of military "honor." (It's fortunate that Spielberg had second thoughts about the propriety of casting John Belushi in the role.) In one of the few genuinely funny scenes in the movie, Mitamura, searching for a way to "destroy something honorable on the American mainland," brushes off the skepticism of a subordinate who asks, "Is there anything honorable to destroy in Los Angeles?" To which the boyish navigator brightly suggests, "Hollywood!"

Mitamura's decision to shell Hollywood to "demoralize the Americans' will to fight" gives Spielberg the opportunity to trash the Los Angeles basin from the Santa Monica Pier to the La Brea Tar Pits and Hollywood Boulevard. Far removed in spirit from the apocalyptic vision of "The Burning of Los Angeles" in Nathanael West's *The Day of the Locust,* this gleeful fantasy of destruction is sheer juvenile indulgence on Spielberg's part. The lovingly and lavishly rendered mayhem of riots, plane crashes, and explosions, along with the wholesale trashing of any available prop, became the movie's mindless *raison d'être*. The Three Stooges served as the screenwriters' inspiration for much of the film's infantile humor. The director, reports Gale, was also "a big Stooges fan."

Spielberg's need to unwind from the pressures of filming *Close Encounters* led him to dream up all sorts of zany, outrageous gags for *1941,* such as the self-referential opening sequence of a naked female swimmer encountering a Japanese submarine off the fog-shrouded coast of northern California. Parodying the opening of *Jaws,* Spielberg cast the same shapely young woman (Susan Backlinie) who had been attacked by the shark and had John

Williams repeat his ominous musical theme. While mildly amusing, the scene went on far too long, and it was a bit early for Spielberg to begin paying homage to his own movies. "We wouldn't have had the audacity to propose that," Gale admits. "And we have a lot of audacity."*

Spielberg's impulses toward self-conscious stylization made him flirt with an even more radical notion. "In the back of my mind," he said, "I always saw *1941* as an old-fashioned Hollywood musical," with big-band numbers written by Williams. ". . . I just didn't have the courage at that time in my life to tackle a musical." The film's excitingly staged jitterbug contest was described by the director as "a fragment of what I wanted to do . . . [and] the most satisfying experience for me in making *1941.*"

T H R E E months before the cameras rolled, Spielberg vowed, "I will not make this movie if it costs a penny over $12 million." As the budget escalated well beyond that figure, Zemeckis and Gale had the quotation bound into their revised drafts of the screenplay, and Spielberg's vow also mysteriously appeared on gag T-shirts distributed to the crew. Another T-shirt, made up by the crew members themselves during the 247 days of shooting, contained the weary sentiment, *"1941* Forever . . . and ever . . . and ever."

Although initially developed under Milius's deal at MGM, *1941* was made as an unusual joint venture of Columbia and Universal. "Spielberg didn't want to make the movie at MGM," Gale explains. "He had just made *Close Encounters* for Columbia. Steven had an interesting theory, which was to make your next picture for the same studio you were working on your current picture for, because that would keep them honest about wanting to promote it. Dan Melnick was running MGM at the time we developed *1941;* Melnick didn't like the script at all—he didn't get it. Then Melnick ended up at Columbia; after [David] Begelman left, he was running the store [as head of worldwide production]. I remember Melnick saying, 'I don't understand this script, I don't think it's funny, but I guess if both Milius and Spielberg say this is gonna be a good picture, we'll do it.' So that's how it got to Columbia. At the same time, Sid Sheinberg was putting a tremendous amount of pressure on Steven to do his next picture at Universal: 'You gotta make another picture for me, Steven. You owe me.' "†

The two studios shared all costs and proceeds on *1941,* with Universal handling U.S. and Canadian distribution and Columbia distributing the film overseas. Completed at a cost of $31.5 million, *1941* was one of the most expensive films made up until that time, more than $5 million over its $26 million budget (and a whopping $20 million over its original cost estimate).

---

* Spielberg also alluded to *Duel* in the scene of Belushi refueling his plane at a desert gas station. Shot on the same location in Agua Dulce where the truck attacked Dennis Weaver, the scene in *1941* also brought back Lucille Benson as the station owner.

† Spielberg still owed Universal two pictures under his 1975 contract.

Although *1941* had an executive producer, John Milius, and a producer, Buzz Feitshans, Spielberg admitted *1941* went "capriciously and lavishly over-budget and over-schedule, which was all my fault. . . . We would have been better off with $10 million less, because we went from one plot to seven subplots. But at the time, I wanted it—the bigness, the power, hundreds of people at my beck and call, millions of dollars at my disposal, and everybody saying, Yes, yes, yes. . . . *1941* was my Little General period." *1941* became a textbook example of what can happen when a director coming off two successive hits (both of which had gone well over budget) has no one willing or able to say "no" to him.

Columbia's production president John Veitch, the executive directly responsible for the film, told Zemeckis and Gale he would let Spielberg do whatever he wanted because he was a "genius." Although Veitch's faith in Spielberg's creative instincts had been triumphantly borne out by the artistic and commercial success of *Close Encounters,* such license allowed the misconceived *1941* to spiral out of control, giving free rein to Spielberg's worst instincts. "If you're going to go over budget, you want to go over budget with someone like Steven," Veitch contends. "He's not going over budget because he's being careless or because he's going to get a scene no matter how much it costs or how long it takes. Steven's dedication is to getting the finest picture possible."

The runaway atmosphere of the production was exacerbated by factors beyond Spielberg's control, including the fact that Belushi and Aykroyd could only work three days a week because they were commuting to New York for *Saturday Night Live.* Rampant cocaine use also was a major problem. According to Bob Woodward's book *Wired: The Short Life and Fast Times of John Belushi,* the actor's heavy use of cocaine often made it hard for him to remember lines and forced him to work in short, unpredictable bursts of energy. On one occasion, Belushi arrived on the set an hour and a half late, "so drugged up that he nearly rolled out of the car onto the ground." Angrily confronting Belushi in the star's trailer, Spielberg told him, "You can do this to anyone else, but you can't do it to me. For $350,000 [Belushi's salary] you're going to show up." Spielberg delegated associate producer Janet Healy to watch over Belushi, but as Woodward reported, "Healy didn't find John's drug use unusual compared to that of some other members of the cast and production crew. She counted twenty-five people on the set who used cocaine at times."

Spielberg may have been one of the soberest members of the *1941* company, but his "dedication to getting the finest picture possible" escalated into a near-addiction during the eighteen months of production, with more than a million feet of film cascading through his cameras. This time he did not rely on an extensive use of optical effects to help create his grandiose illusions. "I had it, waiting half a year to see film on *Close Encounters,* so I decided to make a picture the way they used to make 'em," Spielberg explained. ". . . I've had it with matte work and motion-control cameras. Everything here is done the way it would have been done by D. W. Griffith. . . . I'm going to make this one as physical as possible." As a result of that questionable decision, the largely studio-bound production ran up extraordinary expenses for the staging of full-scale gags and the construction of elaborate miniature sets.

At a cost of almost $400,000, two takes were filmed of a full-sized P-40 fighter plane crashing at sixty miles an hour onto a street at the Burbank Studios decorated to resemble Hollywood Boulevard during the 1941 Christmas season. The master shot of the riot sequence involved numerous crashing vehicles, stuntmen doubling as zoot-suiters, and several hundred extras in period costumes, including 650 in military uniforms, stampeding on cue when Milius fired a rifle into the air. For the film's ending, Spielberg had an actual full-sized house built at a cost of $260,000 and dropped off a beachfront hillside, with seven cameras capturing its descent.

The spectacularly detailed miniatures built by *Close Encounters* modelmaker Gregory Jein included a panoramic aerial view of the San Fernando Valley; the Hollywood Boulevard canyon where the dogfight occurs; and Ocean Park in Santa Monica, where a Ferris wheel blasted free by Japanese shells rolls into the ocean. Impressive as the miniatures are on screen, they required extensive use of fog effects to make them believable. That meant smoke had to be used in all the other scenes for matching purposes. Although cinematographer William A. Fraker created a subtly fantastic mood in the scenes involving miniatures, his lighting in other scenes sometimes appeared fuzzy and overexposed.*

The entire first month after filming began on October 23, 1978, was spent working on the miniature set featuring the Ferris wheel. Shooting on miniatures went for weeks following the conclusion of principal photography on May 16, 1979. "Steven fell in love with his miniature footage, which, in my opinion, is the best miniature stuff ever filmed," Gale says. "But he used every single shot he did of the dogfight, in some way, shape, or form, and I think that sequence is probably about 30 percent too long. How many times can you watch the planes go up and down the street? Sometimes you can't see the forest for the trees, and I think that's what happened in *1941*."

S PIELBERG'S disenchantment with *1941* was evident long before its first exposure to an audience. "Comedy is not my forte," he admitted during the shooting. While editing the film, he bluntly called it an "utter horror. . . . I can't correct the overall conceptual disasters about *1941*, but I can fix little pieces here and there that I think will help speed the pace. If you can't do anything about it, then you're at the mercy of what comics call 'the death silence': you expected a laugh and all there is is a hole."

---

* Fraker received two Oscar nominations, for his cinematography and as part of the special visual effects team; the film also was nominated for sound.

Following the first preview on October 19, 1979, at the Medallion Theater in Dallas—where Spielberg had had such success previewing *Jaws* and *Close Encounters*—the opening was delayed from November 16 until December 14 while *1941* underwent what *Daily Variety* called "surgery." "When we opened with that sub surfacing and the [*Jaws*] music and so forth, the people started to applaud, they flipped," Veitch recalls. "Leo Jaffe [Columbia's chairman of the board] was sitting next to me; we thought we had something very special. Then it started to dissipate. By the time the picture ended, we knew we were having some problems with it. They applauded, but it was not the thunderous applause that you were hoping to get after a Steven picture. I think the audience expected a lot more than what was on the screen."

In the lobby after the preview, Sid Sheinberg put his arm around Spielberg and said, "I think there's a movie somewhere in this mess. There's a really good movie, and we should go off and find it." "The rest of the executives from Columbia and Universal," Spielberg remembered, "didn't even want to talk to me." The angry director said at the time that the preview had taught him one important lesson: "I learned not to invite Universal and Columbia executives and sales people to previews anymore. Let them stay home and watch *Laverne and Shirley* on TV. I'll preview my pictures and make the changes."

A second preview was held in Denver, where the film played "a little better," says Veitch, "but still by that time the word was out." Spielberg and editor Michael Kahn finally emerged from the cutting room with a 118-minute release version of *1941,* 17 minutes shorter than the version previewed in Dallas. Many of the discarded scenes turned up later in the expanded ABC-TV version and in the restored 1996 laserdisc version released by MCA Universal Home Video, which runs 146 minutes. Although the restoration is somewhat less frenetic and more coherent than the theatrical version, the essential foolishness of the concept remains impervious to change. But Gale was correct in observing that the director's prerelease editing tended to sacrifice character development for spectacle: "Steven got scared of the movie. Steven had a certain amount of impatience about not wanting to take the time to set things up. When he got nervous that it was taking too long to get to be night in *1941,* he'd start lopping out chunks of exposition, not realizing how important some of the stuff was. Bobby Di Cicco is not in the movie enough, and he was intended to be the central character. Steven played against the wrong-side-of-the-tracks aspect of his character. Steven was always afraid of those kind of guys; they were the ones who used to pick on him. So he was afraid about how to make that kind of character into a hero."

Knowing that critics and his Hollywood colleagues were "just waiting in ambush to tear me apart," Spielberg chose not to attend the film's predictably deadly premiere at the Cinerama Dome in Hollywood. Instead he took Amy Irving on a vacation to Japan, where he wouldn't have to face the first batch of devastating reviews, such as Charles Champlin's in the *Los Angeles Times,* which was headlined "Spielberg's Pearl Harbor." Describing *1941* as "the most conspicuous waste since the last major oil spill, which it somewhat resembles," the usually benevolent Champlin was provoked into a rare display of wrath: "What characterizes *1941* is its abiding cynicism, which arises, however, not in a considered contempt for the world's follies but out of an apparent indifference to and withdrawal from anything but spliced celluloid. It offers a nihilism based not on a rejecting rage but on an arrogant indifference to values." Michael Sragow of the *Los Angeles Herald-Examiner* used even harsher rhetoric, calling it "a movie that will live in infamy. . . . *1941* isn't simply a silly slur against any particular race, sex, or generation—it makes war against all humanity."

Spielberg later complained that "it was like the critics thought I was Adolf Eichmann." By almost any standard of critical taste and judgment, the attacks on the film were richly deserved. But the unusually hostile reaction of some critics also may have reflected a gleeful desire to see its precociously successful young director receive his comeuppance. "Maybe *1941* will finally force a few reevaluations of this *wunderkind*," wrote Stephen Farber of *New West*. In the "cult of puerility" that had taken over Hollywood in the 1970s, Farber declared, *1941* stood alone as "the most appalling piece of juvenilia yet foisted on the public." Spielberg could not resist the director's favorite dodge of passing the blame to his writers, who, he told *The New York Times,* "caught me at a weak moment. . . . I'll spend the rest of my life disowning this movie." As he had done after publicly disparaging Peter Benchley's source material for *Jaws,* Spielberg "came to us and asked us to forgive him," Gale recalls. "He'd given an interview to some magazine and he said he'd blamed the whole movie on us—[implying,] 'These writers just kinda buffaloed me into doing it.' "

1941 was not the box-office disaster its reputation might suggest. With a worldwide gross of $90 million, it actually turned a profit, and it found somewhat more favor among viewers in other countries who enjoyed its jibes at American jingoism, a response that caused Spielberg some discomfort. While the film's alarming extravagance gave Hollywood serious concern about Spielberg's reliability, the damage it did to his critical reputation would have a far more long-lasting effect. Its failure cast a retrospective cloud over the childlike vision of *Close Encounters* and the technical cunning of *Jaws,* encouraging critics who harbored lingering doubts about those aspects of his earlier films to castigate Spielberg as emotionally arrested and overly infatuated with technique for its own sake.

W H E N George Lucas, in 1977, first told him the story of an intrepid, somewhat disreputable archeologist searching for the lost Ark of the Covenant, Spielberg was intrigued by the sheer fun of it, the opportunity to do "a James Bond film without the hardware." But by the time he began shooting *Raiders of the Lost Ark* in June 1980, Spielberg had a more urgent agenda.

Hoping to "make some amends for going way over on *1941, Close Encounters,* and *Jaws,*" he had to prove he could "make a movie responsibly for a relatively medium budget that would appear to be something more expensive." Michael Finnell, a producer who later made three films for Amblin Entertainment, recalls that Spielberg "used to say he was born again after *1941.*"

Working as a hired hand for Lucas, a conservative and highly disciplined producer, Spielberg used *Raiders of the Lost Ark* as a form of professional "rehab," veteran film business analyst A. D. Murphy wryly observes. At the time preproduction began on *Raiders* in the fall of 1979, Lucas was riding the crest of *Star Wars* and finishing work on its sequel, *The Empire Strikes Back.* Joining forces with Lucas and his production company, Lucasfilm, enabled Spielberg to assuage Hollywood's fears that *Raiders* would turn out to be another *1941.* But several studios still passed on the opportunity to become involved, despite the fact that Lucas and Spielberg were responsible for four of the top ten box-office hits at that point in film history. The problem was that the two filmmakers were demanding what Spielberg called an "unprecedented profit definition" for their joint venture.

"I hate to talk like a mercenary," Spielberg said at the time of the film's release in 1981, "but George came over to my house when we decided to make the picture and he said, 'Let's make the best deal they've ever made in Hollywood. And let's do it without the agents, just you and me.' We wrote it out on lined note paper and shook hands over the table. And then we presented that to our agencies and said, 'This is the deal we want. Now, fellows, go try to make it.' "

The Lucas-Spielberg proposal was presented to the studios not by their agents but by their lawyer, Tom Pollock (who later became the head of Universal Pictures), Lucasfilm president Charles Weber, and Howard Kazanjian, who was executive producer with Lucas on *Raiders.* The proposal dared to assault standard Hollywood financial practices at several especially sensitive points. Chief among them was that while the distributor would be expected to put up the movie's budgeted $20 million negative cost, it would receive no distribution fee and take no overhead charge. Those items usually accounted for more than 50 percent of the gross film rentals (the amount returned to the studio after exhibitors take their share). Besides demanding large sums of money up front, Lucas and Spielberg also wanted enormous shares of the distributor's gross, a demand that was especially unusual for a director in that era. And while the distributor would be allowed to recover the entire negative cost of *Raiders* from gross film rentals before Lucas and Spielberg started to receive their shares of the gross, Lucasfilm eventually would assume full ownership of the movie.

Not only were the studios taken aback by such *chutzpah,* they were dubious about the apparent cost of shooting the film. Lawrence Kasdan's flamboyant screenplay paid homage to grade-Z serials on a spectacular scale more in keeping with the grandiose fantasies of *Star Wars* and *Close Encoun-*

ters. "A lot of people looked at that first scene with the huge rock and thought it would cost $40 million just by itself," said then Paramount president Michael D. Eisner.

Such were the filmmakers' track records, however, that when the proposal was circulated, Paramount, Warner Bros., Columbia, and Disney expressed interest (Fox, which had made *Star Wars* under the previous regime of Alan Ladd Jr., passed on *Raiders,* as did Universal's Ned Tanen). Frank Price, president of Columbia's film division, was eager to establish a working relationship with Lucasfilm, "but Columbia did not have a strong distribution system," Kazanjian says. "We knew we could make a deal somewhere, or we knew we could sell financing, or we knew we could make the picture. What we couldn't do was distribute the picture, and we wanted the best distributor." Closing the deal with Paramount took a year of contentious negotiations. Some at the studio "thought Michael Eisner was crazy," Kazanjian remembers. "Barry Diller [Paramount's board chairman and chief executive officer] thought he was crazy. But he did it. And they made a ton of money on it."

Paramount insisted on taking distribution and overhead fees, but those reportedly amounted to only about half of the industry standard, and the studio agreed to assume the entire negative cost, as well as letting Lucasfilm own the negative. Paramount wanted outright ownership of sequel rights but finally agreed that Lucasfilm would have to be involved in the making of four possible sequels.* Spielberg received a $1 million directing fee for *Raiders* and a sizable percentage of the gross; Lucas personally received a $1 million fee for serving as executive producer, in addition to his company's large share of the gross. Lucas and Spielberg also received "very handsome" bonuses for completing the film just under the $20 million budget, Kazanjian says. "It was George's bonus, but he split that with Steven as an incentive, and said, 'Half of it is yours if you bring this in on budget.' "

"We built in tremendous penalties if they went over, and they agreed without hesitation," Eisner said. "I figured either they don't care or they've got this thing figured out. . . . You don't make standard deals with these kinds of people. . . . If we got shafted on this agreement, we would like to be shafted two or three times a year in this way."

Despite their triumphant dealmaking, Spielberg was not entirely enthusiastic about making the film. It took so long to put the deal together that by the time *Raiders* was a "go" project, he had lost a certain amount of interest in it and "wanted to move on to smaller, more personal projects." "George and I would go down and visit Steven on the set of *1941,"* Kazanjian recalls, "and we would discuss *Raiders.* And we weren't really getting a firm commitment out of him that he would direct it. We started even looking at, or thinking about, other directors, because Steven had not committed. We never

---

* As of 1996, only two feature sequels have been made, but another has been under discussion. Lucasfilm also has made *The Young Indiana Jones Chronicles* as movies for television.

got a firm commitment until almost the very end, when we said, 'OK, folks, in about three weeks we're going to start preproduction and we're ready to go. Yes or no?' Steven loved the project, but he had a lot of things going.

"One of the challenges we had was that Steven owed one picture to Universal, and [Sid] Sheinberg kept saying, 'You can't do *Raiders of the Lost Ark,* you owe a picture to me.' Also at that time, there was a lawsuit over *Battlestar Galactica* [Fox, at Lucas's urging, sued Universal for copyright infringement over the TV series, claiming it was a copy of *Star Wars*]. So that even angered Sid more. Universal passed on *Raiders:* that wasn't a Steven picture, that was a George Lucas picture. It was only at the last minute that Sid released Steven and said, 'OK, you can do it.' "

"**I** F I could be a dream figure," Lucas once declared, "I'd be Indy." The character of Indiana Jones, an improbable amalgam of archeologist, soldier of fortune, and playboy, was the kind of heroic surrogate a bright, nerdy kid would create after watching a Saturday matinee program of cliffhanger serials.

Lucas and Spielberg decided to collaborate on *Raiders of the Lost Ark* after discovering that they shared a nostalgia for the serials of the 1930s and 1940s. Among the serials they cited as inspirations were *Flash Gordon Conquers the Universe, Don Winslow of the Coast Guard, Blackhawk,* and *Commando Cody.* Those two-fisted adventure yarns depicted a world in which good and evil were clearly distinguishable and virtually nonstop action took the place of the more emotionally complicated dialogue and "mushy stuff" that dominated movies made for adult audiences. For two filmmakers who clung stubbornly to boyish behavior and preoccupations but were uncomfortably aware that they were no longer boys, such regression was a tempting response to the increasingly vexatious responsibilities of adulthood.

In the early 1970s, Lucas began outlining four stories featuring "a shady archeologist" who wears a 1930s-style fedora and carries a bullwhip, like Zorro or Lash La Rue. The character was named Indiana after a female Alaskan malamute owned by Lucas's wife, Marcia. Indy also had what Lucas called his "Cary Grant side," a fondness for wearing top hat and tails and lounging around drinking champagne with slinky blondes. The first director Lucas approached to work on the project, fellow Bay Area filmmaker Philip Kaufman, added a weightier theme. He proposed that Indy search for the lost Ark of the Covenant of Hebraic Law, the sacred cabinet in which the broken tablets containing the Ten Commandments were stored. "There was an old doctor I went to [as a boy] in Chicago who was obsessed with the lost ark's legendary powers," recalled Kaufman. "And books have been written about Hitler's search for occult artifacts, which he thought would make him omnipotent."

Lucas's own passionate interest in mythology and the supernatural, which is also at the heart of his *Star Wars* saga, was stimulated by the notion of sending Indy on a quest for a legendary object with transcendent spiritual significance. But the element of Jewish mysticism in *Raiders* probably never would have occurred to Lucas, who was raised as both a Methodist and a Lutheran. Kaufman put *Raiders* aside in 1974 to work on another movie, and Lucas bought him out after Spielberg expressed interest in the dormant idea three years later; Kaufman's lawyers had to insist on their client sharing a story credit with Lucas, over Lucas's initial objections.

Raiders is by no means a simple pastiche of old serials. "When George and I first began talking about this project," Spielberg recalled, "we sat in a screening room at Universal and saw *Don Winslow of the Navy*—all fifteen episodes—and we were bored out of our minds. I'd already said, yes, I'd do this for George. But I was so depressed that I walked out of the theater thinking, 'How can I get out of this?' "

"These things sure don't hold up after twenty-five years," Lucas remarked as they left the screening room.

Then his commercial pragmatism quickly reasserted itself: "I was appalled at how I could have been so enthralled with something so bad. And I said, 'Holy smokes, if I got this excited about this stuff, it's going to be easy for me to get kids excited about the same thing, only better.' "

LAWRENCE Kasdan was writing TV commercials for a Los Angeles advertising agency when Universal bought his original screenplay *Continental Divide* for Spielberg in late 1977. An aficionado of the films of Howard Hawks, Kasdan conceived *Continental Divide* in the spirit of Hawks's smart, sassy, unsentimental romantic comedies such as *Bringing Up Baby* or *His Girl Friday*. Kasdan's script paired a rumpled big-city newspaper columnist with a reclusive ornithologist he tracks down in the wilderness for a personality profile. Spielberg said he bought the script with plans to direct it, but as Kasdan puts it, "Steven buys everything and he owns everything. The first thing he says is always, 'I might direct.' He talked about it for about ten minutes."

Spielberg's interest helped trigger a bidding war that saw the final purchase price of the script escalate to $250,000. "He wanted me to write *Raiders of the Lost Ark,* and *Continental Divide* was a kind of carrot," Kasdan says. "When I met Steven for the first time before he bought it, they were shooting *I Wanna Hold Your Hand* at Universal, and Steven was hanging around. We sat down on a curb. He said, 'I really like your script. I don't know who's going to do the movie, but the person I really want to talk to you is George Lucas. He and I are going to do this adventure film, and you are the perfect guy to write it. But I want to warn you, he's excited about you, and he's going to want you to write *More American Graffiti*. Don't do that.' These guys were desperate for writers—two months ago I had been an advertising writer!"

What Spielberg and Lucas were looking for, Kasdan realized, was "someone who could write *Raiders* in the same way that Hawks would have someone write a movie for him—a strong woman character, a certain kind of hero. So that's what got me the job."

Continental Divide did not turn out well. Kasdan's script was reworked by Hal Barwood, Matthew Robbins, and Jack Rosenthal. After casting diffi-culties and tense arguments between Spielberg and Universal production chief Ned Tanen, the studio refused to let Robbins direct, continuing to hold out hope that Spielberg would take over the reins. But Spielberg washed his hands of the project, selling his right to direct for $100,000 and 5 percent of the profits. He took an executive producer credit on the 1981 release along with Bernie Brillstein, manager of the male lead, John Belushi. Under the lugubrious direction of Englishman Michael Apted, the romantic chemistry between Belushi and leading lady Blair Brown not only failed to reach combustion, but seemed virtually nonexistent.

K A S D A N , Lucas, and Spielberg met for story conferences on *Raiders of the Lost Ark* from January 23 to 27, 1978. Their nine-hour daily brainstorm-ing sessions at the Sherman Oaks home of Lucas's assistant Jane Bay were tape-recorded and formed the basis for Kasdan's six months of work on the first-draft screenplay.

Spielberg and Lucas had clear visual ideas for some scenes they wanted to see. "We want to have the boulder" was one of their instructions to Kasdan: for the thrill-packed opening sequence of Indy fleeing a booby-trapped cave, Spielberg invented the memorable image of the hero being pursued by a giant boulder. Lucas's wish list included a submarine, a monkey giving the Hitler salute, and a girl slugging Indiana Jones in a bar in Nepal. Out of the story conferences also came a hair-raising chase through a moun-tain in a mine train and an elaborate sequence of Indy escaping from a Shanghai palace with a precious artifact, jumping from an airplane in an inflatable rubber raft, and making his way down a river. Eventually elimi-nated in preproduction for budgetary reasons, those two sequences wound up being adapted for use in the 1984 sequel, *Indiana Jones and the Temple of Doom*.

While Lucas and Spielberg dwelled on gags and set-pieces, Kasdan em-phasized the need to round out Indy's personality. "I became worried that the thing was becoming a straight action piece, which is probably the way it turned out," the writer said in 1981. Spielberg acknowledged that Kasdan "didn't stick with our story outline a hundred percent. . . . Larry essentially did all the characters and tied the story together, made this story work from just a bare outline, and gave it color and some direction."

Kasdan turned in his first draft in August 1978, but before even reading it, Lucas assigned him to do an emergency rewrite of *The Empire Strikes Back*. When Lucas eventually found time to turn his attention to the *Raiders* script, he told Kasdan, "It's too expensive and too long. Go back and take out everything that isn't the main bones of the story." "I hated doing it," the writer admits, "but after I was done I realized it was very muscular and fast-paced." Spielberg did not have time to begin working with Kasdan on screenplay revisions until he returned from his vacation to Japan in December 1979.

A F T E R four years of living together and three months of being engaged, Spielberg and Amy Irving decided to get married in Japan on what was planned as a three-week honeymoon. "I'll be pregnant by April," Amy told friends. "We can't wait to start a family." Exactly what happened on the trip has never been revealed by either party, but while they were traveling, the marriage plans were called off for the time being. "We weren't ready," was all Amy would say publicly.

There had been rumors that while shooting *Honeysuckle Rose* earlier that year in Texas, Amy had had an affair with her romantic partner in the movie, grizzled country singer Willie Nelson. Although she denied the rumors, she did say, "When I was in Texas, I suddenly met all these people who really just loved you for being yourself. They were more honest than people I'd met in Los Angeles, and that appealed to me." To explore her own identity in a more private setting, she moved to Santa Fe, New Mexico. "Having come from a relationship with a very public man, I needed to go and find out what my life on my own was about."

Whether or not Steven still felt he was not ready for marriage, his breakup with Amy was a traumatic event, his worst emotional experience since his parents' divorce. But he admitted it was a necessary lesson in helping him reach emotional adulthood. "Life has finally caught up with me," he said. "I've spent so many years hiding from pain and fear behind a camera. I avoided all the growing-up pains by being too busy making movies. I lost myself to the world of film. So right now, in my early thirties, I'm experiencing delayed adolescence. I suffer like I'm sixteen. It's a miracle I haven't sprouted acne again. The point is, I didn't escape suffering. I only delayed it."

One of the immediate consequences of their breakup was that Amy lost the part of Marion Ravenwood, Indiana Jones's love interest in *Raiders*. Amy's previous resolve not to mix romance and work apparently had weakened long enough to let her convince Steven she should play the part. After their split, Spielberg told Lucas, "Let me cast Marion." That seemed equitable, for Marion was only to appear in the first of the three Indiana Jones movies, and Lucas and Spielberg jointly decided on the casting of Indy. After screen-testing many candidates for Indy, including some unknowns, they first offered the part to Tom Selleck, who was prevented from playing it when CBS-TV exercised its option for the series *Magnum P.I.* Less than six weeks before shooting began, Spielberg and Lucas spotted Indy right under their noses and cast Harrison Ford, who had played the hard-boiled but lovable pilot Han Solo in *Star Wars*.

Spielberg offered Marion to Debra Winger, the sultry star of 1980's *Urban Cowboy*, with whom he later would be romantically linked in the press.* But Winger also had a scheduling conflict, so he turned to Karen Allen, a winsome alumna of *Animal House*. In the boys' fantasy world of Spielberg and Lucas, Allen's Marion behaved less like Lauren Bacall than like an overage tomboy. As critic Molly Haskell put it, Marion "has lived a little, talks tough, can drink men under the table, but she has neither a nose for danger nor the guile to get out of it. In other words, she has the failings of both sexes and none of their virtues."

S P I E L B E R G "was in a strange state" when he returned from his ill-fated trip to Japan, Kasdan recalls. "He had just had *1941* coming out, and I think his personal life was in turmoil. He had done some storyboards, and he was full of ideas about how to improve the script. Some of them were great, and others just seemed crazy to me. He wanted the guy with the monocle† to have a light in his head coming from his eye wherever he looked. I thought if we have a guy with a light in his head, that broke the conventions of the story we were telling, which was a 1930s serial.

"I reacted badly, I think. I had worked hard on the script, and I had not had this experience before. I don't like rewriting, and I'm not one of these guys who can write for other people's whims. I went to George and said, 'I think you need somebody else for this job. These ideas are too crazy for me. It's not the story we set out to make.' George told me, 'Steve's always full of ideas at this stage, but a lot of them will fall away before you get to the movie. Just ride it out.' Some of his ideas I wrote into the script, and some I was able to argue him out of. They were always kidding me, 'Oh, you won't write it, but we'll do it when we make the movie.' When they were in North Africa, they sent me a picture they had taken of Steven, Karen Allen, and Harrison Ford all sitting at a typewriter."

The most serious disagreements came over Ford's character. Lucas's initial concept of Indy as a James Bondian playboy who uses archeological expeditions to fund his expensive lifestyle met resistance from Spielberg, Kasdan, and Ford. "My feeling," said Kasdan, "was that Indiana Jones's two sides (professor and adventurer) made him complicated enough without adding the playboy element." At Lucas's insistence, Kasdan wrote a scene involving

---

* During preproduction on *Raiders*, Spielberg also dated nineteen-year-old TV actress Valerie Bertinelli and began a three-year, live-in relationship with Kathleen Carey, a thirty-one-year-old talent scout for Warner Bros. Music who joined him on location in Tunisia. Spielberg said Carey "taught me that there's a life after movies."

† Toht, a particularly fiendish Nazi played by Paul Lacey, who wears wire-rimmed glasses in the film.

a tuxedo-clad Jones at home with a blonde, but Spielberg successfully argued against filming it.* Spielberg wanted to go to the opposite extreme. Thinking of Indy as resembling Humphrey Bogart's unscrupulous bum Fred C. Dobbs in John Huston's *The Treasure of the Sierra Madre,* the director suggested making Indy a seedy alcoholic. Lucas vehemently resisted the idea, but Spielberg felt he still managed to insinuate enough grittiness into the character to provide an intriguing contrast with Indy's tweedy, academic side.

"The original idea," Kasdan says, "was to have him be a little more tortured about what he does, about having fallen from the pure faith of archeology into this graverobber status. It was George's idea—George said the guy who is going after the ark is 'sort of a dark figure'—and it was in the first draft even more. Steven liked it too, but as we did more drafts that sort of fell away, and he became more of a standard action type of guy."

Commercial expediency no doubt was the principal reason for the failure to create a three-dimensional character. Lucas and Spielberg wanted to make a film of nonstop, unreflective derring-do, the kind that takes no time to grapple with moral ambiguities. But since *Raiders* is not a 1930s serial but a film made with a postmodernist sensibility, there had to be at least a nod in the direction of complexity. Spielberg claimed that Indy is "not a cardboard hero but rather a human being with ordinary frailties." But despite Ford's valiant attempt to suggest those frailties with his brooding, world-weary demeanor, Indy remains peculiarly unformed, hardly less artificial a character than any tough-guy hero in the old serials.

I N D Y ' S two sides never add up to a coherent whole. A scholar who loves adventure and physical danger, he behaves in a casually amoral and brutal way whenever it suits his purposes. He loots Third World cultures and slaughters the natives with the abandon of a mercenary from colonial days. And yet the contemporary audience throughout the world was skillfully manipulated into identifying with this ruthless figure and finding him heroic. Cynically exploited for purely visceral thrills, Indy's violence and greed is presented in a winking, tongue-in-cheek style to anesthetize the audience's moral sense. The scene of Indy pulling out his pistol to mow down a sword-wielding Arab—a gag Spielberg and Ford improvised on location to shorten the shooting schedule—"was very popular, but it disturbed me," Kasdan says. "I thought that was brutal in a way the rest of the movie wasn't. I'm never happy about making jokes out of killing people. Steven is more in touch with popular taste than I am."

Spielberg seemed eager to pass the blame to Lucas for Indy's violent behavior: *"Raiders* is more in George's vein; it's the only film of mine [until that time] in which scores of people are violently eliminated. But George's

* That aspect of the character surfaces briefly in *Temple of Doom,* which opens with Indy, in white tuxedo, hooking up with blond singer Kate Capshaw in a Shanghai nightclub.

violence is kids' violence; it's intentionally scary-funny. . . . I took the movie as seriously as I took a barrel of buttered popcorn." While conceding that the "concepts in *Raiders* were extremely violent," Lucas insisted "the treatment was not repulsive. For one thing, we were back to good guys beating bad guys. Steven actually got carried away in a couple of places, but we cut back on the blood."

To help make its violence seem acceptable and amusing, *Raiders* recruits its legions of "bad guys" from groups the audience is expected to hate at first sight. Nazis satisfied that requirement so perfectly in *Raiders* that Spielberg pressed them into service as cartoon heavies again in *Indiana Jones and the Last Crusade* (1989). But as *New York* magazine's David Denby wrote in his review of *Raiders,* Spielberg used Nazis "for a thrill of evil, for graphic and even comic possibilities, not because he has anything to say about Nazism. In pop filmmaking, neither death nor history ever matters. Only thrills matter." The Third World villains in the Indiana Jones movies tend to be drawn from racial stereotypes, a mindless carryover from the mentality of old-style adventure movies made in a less enlightened age when colonial attitudes still prevailed. *Raiders* has hordes of caricatured Arab and South American bad guys, while *Temple of Doom* employs Indians and Chinese as the evil antagonists of the square-jawed white American hero.

Because of modern ethnic sensitivities and the controversy that often results from ethnic stereotyping in movies, "When you pick villains, you get into trouble," notes *Temple of Doom* cowriter Willard Huyck. One of Lucas's suggested storylines for the third Indiana Jones film was set in Africa. Locations were scouted, and Chris Columbus* wrote a screenplay, but it was rejected because, as Charles Champlin reported in his book on Lucas, "neither Lucas nor Spielberg was comfortable with the story." "I knew there was no way they were going to make the movie in Africa," says Huyck. "Natives were going to be a real problem if any of them were foolish or villainous. They couldn't do it, and they went back again to Nazis."

In their portraits of Third World heavies, Spielberg and Lucas fell into the trap of uncritically imitating antiquated Hollywood conventions. But the absence of malicious intent hardly excuses the presence of such stereotypes in movies made in the 1980s; indeed, one can argue that their unthinking perpetuation for the purposes of mass entertainment constitutes a far more insidious form of racial insult. With its revival of previously discredited fantasies of American cultural dominance over Third World primitives and cartoonish villains from an evil empire, *Raiders of the Lost Ark* was the perfect film to mark the beginning of the Reagan era.

* * *

---

* Columbus wrote the scripts for the Spielberg productions *Gremlins* (1984), *The Goonies* (1985), and *Young Sherlock Holmes* (also 1985), before becoming a director himself on such films as *Adventures in Babysitting* and *Home Alone.*

I⟶T was a measure of Spielberg's emotional distance from *Raiders of the Lost Ark* that he so willingly surrendered his independence to work as an employee of Lucas. Spielberg's pragmatic decision to prove that he could toe the budgetary line by turning out a piece of unabashed commercial entertainment was only possible, however, because of the mutual respect he and Lucas shared. "I generally let Steven do whatever he wants to do," Lucas said. "I'm very sensitive to the director and what his problems are because I've been a director. And Steven takes suggestions. I mean, I offer lots of suggestions and he takes some of them and some he doesn't take. . . . Steven does a great deal of homework when he goes into a picture. He's very organized."

Lucas was present "to troubleshoot" for five of the sixteen weeks of filming. Though he directed some second-unit footage on location in Tunisia, his influence was unobtrusive, leaving no doubt that Spielberg was in command. Most of Lucas's efforts as an executive producer were concentrated on preproduction and postproduction. Lucas believed Spielberg's tendency toward excess could be kept in check with careful preplanning and a solid screenplay. "He got a lot of bad press for *1941,*" Lucas said, "but his direction was brilliant—the *idea* was terrible."

Lucas could say no to Spielberg, and Spielberg, humbled by his experiences on *1941,* would listen. When they disagreed, Lucas would say, "Well, it's your movie. If the audience doesn't like it, they're going to blame you." Giving in, Spielberg would joke, "Okay, but I'm going to tell them that *you* made me do it."

Lucas also provided Spielberg with a first-rate British crew and support staff, many of whom had worked on *Star Wars* and *The Empire Strikes Back.* Most of *Raiders* was filmed in places where Lucas had shot the earlier films, including the so-called *"Star Wars* canyon" in Tunisia and EMI-Elstree Studios in Borehamwood, England. Additional filming took place in France, Hawaii, and Long Beach, California. The London area was chosen as the film's base of operations both for cost reasons and because its distance from Hollywood enabled the filmmakers to keep a lid of secrecy on the project, as Spielberg had done in Alabama on *Close Encounters.*

Spielberg requested that Frank Marshall be hired as producer of *Raiders.* Marshall had met Spielberg through Verna Fields in 1974, when he was working as an associate producer for Peter Bogdanovich. Skilled at the art of bringing in films economically while serving the director's needs, Marshall recalled that Spielberg was "looking for someone who would protect him from a studio situation . . . someone to sort of be on his side and work with him, rather than *against* him. . . . He wanted a producer who could actually get the movie made for a price, keep the momentum going on set . . . which is the way I like to do things."

Marshall's future wife, Kathleen Kennedy, worked closely with him on *Raiders.* Kennedy and Marshall went on to be Spielberg's most important professional collaborators throughout the 1980s. They produced most of his films in that period and were his partners in Amblin Entertainment, the production company they founded together in 1984.

Previously a TV talk show producer in San Diego, Kennedy entered the film industry as an assistant to John Milius during preproduction on *1941*. After three weeks, she was asked to help Spielberg organize the film's special effects. Arriving at the director's home, she found he "had little pieces of paper, backs of envelopes, tops of newspapers, anything he could get his hands on, on which he had written these notes and camera shots, drawn little figures. And he said, 'Can you take these and make some sense of it?' . . . The only thing going through my mind was, I can't work here because he'll figure out I don't know how to type. So I gathered everything together and headed back to the office. I poured myself into this, all day, all night, going through, redrawing the little drawings, calling him a few times to clarify things I didn't understand. And I made these little booklets, which I had stacked up on his desk when he came in.

"He was blown away. It seemed to me a certain amount of common sense, but for whatever reason, he had never had anyone organize things for him in that way before. From that point on, he gave me little jobs to do, things he wanted me to take care of." While working on *Raiders,* she "didn't think about where it was leading. When Steven asked me to produce his next film, which later turned out to be *E.T.,* I was shocked. It seemed to come from out of the blue, but I think it was because he felt confident about the way I got things done for him. He had come to rely on me to get things done. And that is basically what a producer does."

Lucas's right-hand man on *Raiders,* executive producer Howard Kazanjian, had known him since film school at USC.* Kazanjian was given authority to crack the whip on budget and scheduling. "Part of my job was to say no to Steven," he recalls, "and I never said no to Steven. There are ways—and you had to work at it—for Steven to say no to himself. You present the two sides, especially if it's monetary, and let Steven say no. I guess *occasionally* I said no, but I didn't like doing that, I liked to have Steven come to a decision on his own.

"We knew that we were making a B picture. We knew we had to compromise. There were some moments where it would go to take two or take three and take four, and something wasn't working. Steven would say, 'That's it, let's move on. We'll figure out another way to do it.' He was very, very good in that respect. *Raiders* was his first picture he brought in on budget. I heard Steven say that all his friends were doing smaller pictures than him, less expensive pictures than him, coming in on budget, and they were able to see more money on the back end. Steven rarely had that opportunity, so he

---

* Kazanjian began as an assistant director at Universal, working with such veteran filmmakers as Alfred Hitchcock, Billy Wilder, and Robert Wise, as well as for one day with Spielberg on studio pickup shots for *The Sugarland Express*. He was elevated to producer on Lucas's *More American Graffiti* (1979).

was bound and determined to bring a picture in on budget, so he could see back-end. Steven said, 'If we had spent another dollar, we wouldn't have gotten another dollar at the box office.' "

Working with four illustrators, Spielberg storyboarded *Raiders* more fully than any of his previous films. He initially succumbed to the temptation of planning elaborate compositions full of *film noir* shadow effects. "I orgasmed in the first two months of my preparation," he said, "and then I essentially tore it up and just told the story." For the first time in his career, Spielberg also made use of the services of a second-unit director, action veteran Michael (Mickey) Moore, who spent three weeks shooting the truck chase from Spielberg's storyboards. "Steve wasn't always going for 100 percent, sometimes he was going for 50 percent," Lucas said. "But my theory is that a director as talented as Steve going at 50 percent is better than most people giving their all. When he goes at 100 percent it can get out of hand."

Raiders officially was scheduled for eighty-five days of shooting, but Lucas and Spielberg had a secret plan to make it in only seventy-three days. Kazanjian explains that this was done "to challenge Steven to do it on schedule and budget" and to minimize studio interference: "There are times when you're over a day, but you know you can pick it up somewhere, and the pressure is so great from the studio. George didn't want that. George had been successful in being able to make his pictures without studios; that was one of the reasons why *Raiders* and *Star Wars* were [based] in Europe, because they were farther away from studio control. [Spielberg's] taste was richer in the shooting than it had been in preparation, but if Steven wanted something else, we took it from someplace else.

"We had a model of the Flying Wing [a futuristic airplane for transporting the ark to Hitler]. I said to George, 'It just is too big. We can't build this thing. It's going to cost about a million dollars, and we need to make it smaller. We need to do *something.*' I had already gone to Steven on that and was vetoed. So I went to George, and George walked into this conference room we were in, I'll never forget it, and said [*sotto voce*], 'OK, listen to what I'm going to do.' There was the model. He said, 'Oh, what's *this?*' He picked up the model of the Flying Wing, like he didn't know that this is the Flying Wing. It had four engines, two on each side. He said, 'Terrific'—George always talks in short sentences—'It's great. Looks super.' And he broke the ends of the two wings off, taking two of the motors away. He said, 'How much money do we save if it's only *this* big?' "

With that one gesture, they saved $250,000. The film was completed just under its final budget figure of $20.4 million ($400,000 had been added after Harrison Ford was cast) and exactly on its clandestine seventy-three-day schedule.

H O W E V E R lively and entertaining *Raiders* proved to be, the price Spielberg paid for his "rehab" was a soulless and impersonal film. Reestablishing his professional credentials meant taking a step back artistically, a run for cover rewarded handsomely by Hollywood and the public. With a worldwide gross of $363 million, *Raiders* became the runaway box-office champion of 1981 as well as the highest-grossing film in the history of Paramount Pictures.* Spielberg received his second Oscar nomination for directing the film, one of its eight nominations; although he did not win, the film received five Oscars, all in technical categories.

Spielberg's anxiety over the possibility of commercial failure and his need to please the widest possible audience would continue to motivate him throughout much of the 1980s. His intermittent forays into new creative territory often were followed by retreats into safer, more derivative material. When those formulaic efforts were rewarded with great commercial success, Spielberg found himself increasingly trapped in a need to follow narrowly defined audience expectations. The critical reception for some of his more ambitious, problematical works would, in turn, be colored by those expectations. When he was being praised for the wrong reasons, he also tended not to be praised for the right reasons.

Many reviewers welcomed what they saw as Spielberg's return to form with *Raiders,* a film that encouraged a retreat from complexity and a revival of simple, old-fashioned Hollywood pleasures. "It's hats-in-the-air, heart-in-the-mouth time at the movies again," wrote Sheila Benson of the *Los Angeles Times,* praising the film for having "no pretensions to importance." But the implications of its success were troubling to some critics. Robert Asahina observed in *The New Leader,* "*Raiders* tells us less about society as a whole, I'm afraid, than about Hollywood, which of late seems to be laboring under the illusion that today's moviegoers are subliterate teenagers unable to distinguish between good and bad comic books. Or worse, perhaps films are now made by people who are no brighter than the dullest members of the audience they have in mind."

Spielberg felt he was "playing a role" in directing *Raiders of the Lost Ark.* "I was the Indiana Jones behind the camera. I felt I didn't have to shoot for a masterpiece. Every shot didn't have to be something David Lean would be proud of." That melancholy admission seemed to reveal Spielberg's awareness of "the perils of facility . . . the journeyman-for-hire aspect of his collaboration on *Raiders,*" Victoria Geng wrote in *Film Comment.* "Indy the hack adventurer is a bit of a self-portrait, with touches of both vanity and self-loathing. . . . But if *Raiders* represents his approach to this material, only a miracle can save him now."

---

* A title it finally surrendered in 1994 to Robert Zemeckis's *Forrest Gump.*

THIRTEEN

"ECSTASY AND GRIEF"

I TOLD KATHY KENNEDY BEFORE I STARTED SHOOTING *E.T.* AND *POLTERGEIST* THAT THE SUM-
MER [OF 1981] WOULD TELL ME ONCE AND FOR ALL IF I WAS SUITED TO BEING A FATHER. IT
WAS GOING TO GO ONE OF TWO WAYS: I WAS GOING TO COME OUT OF IT EITHER PREG-
NANT OR LIKE W. C. FIELDS.

— STEVEN SPIELBERG, 1982

URROUNDED by
thousands of snakes on a British soundstage, Steven Spielberg was becoming
depressed about the movie he was making. *Raiders of the Lost Ark* was a
mechanical job of work offering few opportunities to express his personal
feelings. "Action is wonderful," he said later, "but while I was doing *Raiders*
I felt I was losing touch with the reason I became a moviemaker—to make
stories about people and relationships." Feeling lonely far away from home
and his girlfriend Kathleen Carey, Spielberg yearned to escape into a world
of the imagination where he could express the sense of wonder that had
sustained him since childhood:

"I remember saying to myself, 'What I really need is a friend I can talk to
—somebody who can give me *all* the answers.' It was like when you were
a kid and had grown out of dolls or teddy bears or Winnie the Pooh, you
just wanted a little voice in your mind to talk to. I began concocting this
imaginary creature, partially from the guys who stepped out of the mother
ship for ninety seconds in *Close Encounters* and then went back in, never to
be seen again. Then I thought, What if I were ten years old again—where
I've sort of been for thirty-four years anyway—and what if he needed me as
much as I needed him? Wouldn't that be a great love story?"

Luckily for Spielberg, he had somebody on hand who could help realize his fantasy. Melissa Mathison was a thirty-year-old screenwriter with only one credit, a rewrite on *The Black Stallion*. Mathison accompanied her boyfriend, Harrison Ford, during the shooting of *Raiders,* and Spielberg found himself "pouring my heart out to Melissa all the time." He told her his idea for a movie about a lonely little boy and his friend from outer space, an idea he later claimed he had been harboring as a fantasy since childhood. Mathison said her interest in the story was "not on any sort of sci-fi level. It was the idea of an alien creature who was benevolent, tender, emotional, and sweet that appealed to me. And the idea of the creature's striking up a relationship with a child who came from a broken home was very affecting."

A beautifully simple and lyrical parable of interplanetary friendship, *E.T. The Extra-Terrestrial* was also the little movie about "keeds" François Truffaut had been urging Spielberg to make since 1976.* Produced for Universal by Spielberg and Kathleen Kennedy, *E.T.* was made for a comparatively low production cost (about $10 million) and with few of the elaborate visual effects that accompanied the aliens' visit to earth in *Close Encounters*. But, ironically, it was in finally delivering the "little movie" he had promised himself and the public that Spielberg made the film that still holds the record for the highest domestic box-office gross in motion picture history.† What touched the hearts of more than two hundred million moviegoers throughout the world in the film's first year of release was a disguised emotional autobiography of Steven Spielberg.

Perversely, the immediate origins of *E.T.* were not in Spielberg's Disneyish fantasies but in the darker side of his personality. The idea mutated from *Night Skies,* a screenplay John Sayles wrote for him about a band of extraterrestrials terrorizing a farm family. The leader of the band of eleven aliens was an evil creature called Scar, after the Comanche villain in John Ford's *The Searchers*. In the opening scene of Sayles's script, Scar killed farm animals simply by touching them with his long bony finger. Only one of Scar's followers was benevolent, an alien called Buddy who befriended an autistic child. Buddy, of course, turned into E.T. Spielberg later mused that he "might have taken leave of my senses" in developing the xenophobic *Night Skies*. But its evolution into *E.T.* paralleled the process by which the sinister aliens of *Firelight* gradually evolved into the benign visitors of *Close Encounters*.

E.T. can be read as a fable of immigration, but with a bittersweet ending in which the unassimilated alien, after almost dying of homesickness, decides to leave American suburbia and return to his homeland. Spielberg saw *E.T.* as "a broad-based story about an ugly duckling, someone who didn't belong. Someone who wasn't like everyone else. And because E.T. wasn't like every-

---

* When the author of this book informed Truffaut that Spielberg's movie about children also would feature an extraterrestrial, Truffaut laughed uproariously.

† $399 million in 1980s dollars, not adjusted for inflation. Spielberg's 1993 *Jurassic Park* broke *E.T.*'s worldwide record gross of $701 million.

one else, he was picked apart and made very sick and almost died. I always felt *E.T.* was a minority story . . . that stands for every minority in this country." As a pencil-necked geek with a huge head, big eyes and nose, and protruding ears, the younger Spielberg could have passed as a human cousin to E.T., whom he described as "a creature that only a mother could love."

Spielberg's relatively impersonal involvement in *Night Skies* was evident from the fact that he was only planning to produce it, with cartoonist Ron Cobb making his directing debut on the $10 million film.* *Night Skies* began preproduction at Columbia in April 1980, while Spielberg was in England preparing *Raiders*. Reflecting a lingering anxiety in Hollywood over the *1941* debacle, John Veitch, who had become Columbia's president of worldwide production, pointedly told *Daily Variety* that "Steven is not a one-man show" and vowed that studio executives would be working closely with him on *Night Skies*. "We had a meeting or two with Steven on it," Veitch recalls. "Steven wasn't quite positive that he wanted to do that particular story. The more he thought about it, I guess, and with Melissa getting involved, it changed [and Spielberg decided he wanted to direct]. Then when we got the script, the script was the one that they filmed, with the little creature."

Before pitching his new concept to Mathison, Spielberg asked Sayles if he would be interested in trying a fresh draft. But the novelist and screenwriter, who had made his directing debut with *The Return of the Secaucus Seven* (1978), was about to begin directing another movie of his own. In any event, Sayles had little interest in writing a movie about a sweet-natured alien. "The *last* scene of *Night Skies*," Sayles noted, "is of the nice E.T. being marooned on Earth by his peers" (the scene that became the opening of *E.T.*). Sayles did not pursue screen credit, considering his script "more of a jumping-off point than something that was raided for material. I thought [Mathison] had done a great job."

Mathison's collaboration with Spielberg was harmonious, and she received the sole writing credit on *E.T.* However, a public dispute arose in 1989 when she won a Writers Guild of America arbitration award giving her a share of the lucrative merchandising revenues, on the grounds that the first written description of the alien character was in her screenplay.

Arbitrator Sol Rosenthal found that Mathison had "extensively detailed her main character in her first two working drafts, before Carlo Rambaldi's model was done."† Universal argued that the character had been described by Spielberg and Sayles for *Night Skies,* but Rosenthal concluded that while there were "some similar references to the extraterrestrial in the earlier material . . . a review of Sayles' description (of a character with a beaklike mouth

---

* Cobb had been a designer on several films, including *Star Wars* and the *Special Edition* of *Close Encounters*.

† Rambaldi, who designed the alien Puck for *Close Encounters*, built the two marvelously supple animatronic creatures used for 90 percent of the shots involving E.T. The rest of the scenes were performed by little people inside a Rambaldi-designed E.T. costume. Rambaldi's screen credit reads simply, "E.T. Created by Carlo Rambaldi."

and eyes like a grasshopper's) demonstrates that E.T. was not copied from Sayles' script. . . . Mathison did not stop at writing only that E.T.'s finger glowed. She described his unique hands and fingers. Mathison did not only write that E.T. was three-and-a-half-feet tall; she created short squashed legs, a telescopic neck, a protruding belly, long, thin arms and a glowing heart. She did not simply write that E.T.'s face was round, but detailed his wide head, the softness in his face, his large, round eyes, the leathery creases and furrows in his brow."

Spielberg's lawyer, Bruce Ramer, subsequently wrote in a letter published in *Daily Variety,* "That determination does not justify, by any stretch of the imagination, the implication that Mr. Spielberg had little or nothing to do with the birth and shaping of the character and concept central to the most successful motion picture in history. As Ms. Mathison would unquestionably confirm to you, Mr. Spielberg conveyed his views and concepts to her respecting *E.T.* in the most minute detail, both before and during the writing process."*

I N C R E D I B L E as it seems in retrospect, Columbia passed on the opportunity to make *E.T.*

After running demographic surveys on *E.T. and Me* (as Mathison's screenplay was then titled), Columbia's marketing and research department, headed by Marvin Antonowsky, concluded that it had limited commercial potential. Antonowsky thought *E.T. and Me* would appeal mostly to juvenile audiences; the word around Hollywood was that the studio considered it "a wimpy Walt Disney movie." Columbia president Frank Price took the advice seriously and put Mathison's script into turnaround, allowing the project to escape to Universal. Spielberg reportedly was so angered at Price that when the executive later shifted to Universal himself, Spielberg insisted that in any dealings with the studio, he would not have to talk to Price.

Price publicly blamed Universal for his decision to put *E.T.* into turnaround, claiming Universal had exercised a contractual hold on Spielberg for another picture. "I could have told Steven to go direct a picture for Universal and then come back and do *E.T.* here," Price said. "But this was the project he wanted to do next." Sid Sheinberg denied that account, saying, "Steven had no compulsion to deliver that project to us—contractual or otherwise. It is very simple. Steven brought us the script and said he thought we could acquire it from Columbia."

Columbia "had a million dollars into [*Night Skies/E.T.*] for development before we let it go," Veitch recalls. "I talked to Sid Sheinberg about it, and they were willing to go partners with us, but [Columbia] for whatever reason didn't want to do that. [Price simply explained, 'I don't do co-ventures.'] But

---

* Mathison made no public response to that letter, and she did not respond to requests to be interviewed for this book.

we kept a little piece of *E.T.* [5 percent of the net profits], and I think that year we made more on that picture than any we did on any of *our* films."

Before taking *E.T.* to Sheinberg, Spielberg tried to sell Universal on letting him make a musical, *Reel to Reel,* which he had been developing with writer Gary David Goldberg. *Daily Variety* columnist Army Archerd described *Reel to Reel* as "a semi-autobiographical original story by Steven Spielberg . . . about a young director making his first movie—a sci-fi musical!" One of the principal characters was based on Sheinberg. While in London working on *Raiders,* Spielberg had Goldberg ensconced in the same hotel, writing the script for the musical.

"Many days while we were in Europe shooting *Raiders,"* recalls executive producer Howard Kazanjian, "Steven and I, and sometimes Kathy [Kathleen] Kennedy, would ride out together or ride back to the studio, and Steven was talking about a musical, *Reel to Reel,* that he wanted to direct next. At one time he flew home to make the presentation to Sid. Sheinberg didn't want to do it. When Sid said no on this musical, Steven kinda said, 'OK, I'll quickly do this other little picture, *E.T.,* to get my obligation out of the way.' I think that's why he really did it, just to fulfill that last-picture deal with Sid."*

S P I E L B E R G ' S description of *E.T.* as "a very personal story . . . about the divorce of my parents, how I felt when my parents broke up" helps account for his film's extraordinary ability to touch deep emotional chords in the mass audience.

By the early 1980s, divorce and single-parent families were becoming the norm in America. The 1950s model of the ideal nuclear family survived largely on sitcoms and in Disney movies. As *Daily Variety* critic Art Murphy observed at the time, one of the reasons *E.T.* succeeded while Disney films were failing was that Spielberg was willing to acknowledge the harsh reality of divorce and incorporate it into his fantasy. Disney's misguided executives, on the other hand, were trying to replicate the kind of movies their founder had made in the fifties. What they failed to understand, in Murphy's view, was that if Walt Disney himself were still alive, *he* would have changed with the times. The reason Spielberg and Disney became such enormously popular artists was that they were such representative figures, their personal obsessions coinciding with major underlying currents in their society.

As a child of divorce and suburban anomie, Spielberg grew up learning not to idealize family life. But in the emotional void left by his family's dissolution, he could not help yearning for a substitute father figure. In his adulthood, that led him to seek father/mentors in such powerful figures as Sheinberg and Time Warner's Steve Ross. It was an emotional need that loomed large in Spielberg's conception of *E.T.* "When I was a kid," he

---

* Spielberg announced *Reel to Reel* as a Columbia project in 1983, but by then he only planned to produce it, with Michael Cimino directing. That odd pairing never materialized.

recalled, "I used to imagine strange creatures lurking outside my bedroom window, and I'd wish that they'd come into my life and magically change it."

Elliott's father is absent from the film—on vacation in Mexico with his new girlfriend—and in one bittersweet scene, Elliott and his brother Michael (Robert Macnaughton) ruefully examine a shirt their father has left behind in the garage, trying to recall what brand of aftershave lotion he used. The boys' emotionally bereft mother (Dee Wallace) is so distracted that for much of the film she does not even notice an extraterrestrial is living in her house. The absent father and the childishly vulnerable, scatterbrained mother are a reflection (albeit somewhat exaggerated) of Spielberg's ambivalent feelings about his own parents. The wise and wizened E.T. takes the emotional place of Elliott's father, while Elliott, in a touching reversal of roles, serves as the protector of the homesick little creature, trying to keep him safe from the world of adults.

As a way of compensating for the pain of E.T.'s departure, Spielberg introduces another surrogate father figure, the government scientist played by Peter Coyote, who initially appears menacing but eventually becomes Elliott's ally in helping E.T. return home. Like Truffaut's Lacombe in *Close Encounters,* the scientist is a sympathetic figure because he remains in touch with his childhood feelings. He says of E.T., "Elliott, he came to me too. I've been wishing for this since I was ten years old." In the credits, the character is referred to as "Keys," because in the early part of the film he is seen mostly from waist-level, visually identified by the set of keys dangling from his belt. As critic Andrew Sarris observed, Spielberg in the final sequence subtly implies a romantic pairing of Keys with Elliott's mother by linking them together in two-shots as they watch the spaceship depart. By suggesting the relationship visually rather than verbally, Sarris wrote, Spielberg ensured that "only children and Freudians can make the crucial connections between the telltale keys fondled near the crotch of the potential father figure and the displaced phallus represented by E.T. himself."

Like so many other children in Spielberg films, Elliott is mature beyond his years. He has been forced by his parents' separation to act more like an adult than like a child. Elliott's protectiveness toward E.T. stemmed from "a situation in my life," Spielberg said. "When my father left, I went from tormentor to protector with my family. . . . I had to become the man of the house."

Eleven-year-old Henry Thomas plays Spielberg's adolescent alter ego with a gravity and reserve that helps keep the movie from becoming cutesy or cloying. When Thomas auditioned for the role, Spielberg was intrigued by that quality, yet worried that "Henry was too serious. But then I introduced him to E.T. and he burst out laughing. . . . I felt the best way to work with Henry in *E.T.* was not to be his director but his buddy. It was easy because we both like *Pac-Man* [a popular video game]." Spielberg and Thomas spent every lunch hour during the making of the film playing video games together. That was an example of what the director has called his "intuitive" approach to directing children, finding a shared interest with them and communicating his feelings about the movie by osmosis, much as E.T. does in his telepathic communication with Elliott. Never talking down to children, but dealing with them as equals, Spielberg makes them feel like teammates in the marvelous game of moviemaking. In Thomas's case, Spielberg's unusually close personal rapport with both the actor and the character was what made the performance seem so effortlessly affecting.

"The friendship that E.T. and Elliott find and hold on to—clinging to each other desperately—is sort of what I went through in four moves from the ages of four to sixteen [actually two to seventeen]," Spielberg said. "I wished I had had a best friend. . . . My feeling about the whole story is that if E.T. had not come into Elliott's life and without Elliott having a father around, Elliott would have gone down a dark road. E.T. filled the gap left by the father who flew to Mexico with another woman, and then transforms the father-son relationship into something much more cosmic. That's probably the most important aspect of the movie for me, personally. I think it's critical for our understanding of the movie that we realize that Elliott, without a dad, will go in a very rebellious direction."

Spielberg's fascination with outer space again provides him with an alluring visual metaphor for escape from an intolerable family situation. But there is an important difference between the ways the protagonists deal with space creatures in *E.T.* and *Close Encounters*. While Roy Neary was perfectly willing to leave wife and children behind to sail off into space, Elliott finally is unwilling to abandon his family to go off with E.T. In part, this is because he is not a grown man desperate to escape a dead-end marriage, but a child with strong emotional ties to his mother and siblings. While acknowledging the bitter aftereffects of divorce, *E.T.* also reflects a growing recognition by Spielberg of the importance of family responsibility.

In a 1996 documentary on the making of *E.T.*, Spielberg recalled, "I didn't have children back in the early eighties, and suddenly I was becoming a father! Every single day I felt like I was Drew [Barrymore]'s father, Henry's father, and Robert [Macnaughton]'s father, and, you know, it felt good. And I think I have a big family now because it felt pretty good having three kids back then."

Spielberg also attributed this development to his newfound emotional openness in his relationships with women, declaring after making *E.T.* that he had a "deep yearning now to become a father. I think Kathleen [Carey] and I will have kids. . . . I think I've opened up more in the last three or four years than I had ever before. I allowed myself to be hurt. I'd never really allowed anything to reach me before . . . and I think that now that I'm starting to deal with just basic things in a relationship with Kathleen, I'm able to turn around and be a little more open through movies about how I feel. . . . Five years ago, I think I would probably have been too embarrassed about what people might think of me to make *E.T.*"

Opening himself up to those feelings meant exposing himself again to something he had tried to banish from his life: the possibility of losing someone he loved. Spielberg relived his inner feelings about separation in the film's most moving scene, the final interchange between Elliott and E.T. as the spaceship prepares to depart. E.T. says simply, "Come." Ellliott replies, "Stay." Has any exchange of dialogue in movies ever been so eloquent in its simplicity? Embracing, the extraterrestrial and the boy (who is looking over E.T.'s shoulder at his mother) come to the mutual recognition that either of the two alternatives is impossible. E.T. utters the word he has learned to equate with suffering: *"Ouch."*

"When I did the good-bye scene," Henry Thomas said, "I couldn't stop crying because I worked with E.T. every day and he was real to me." The close-up of Elliott watching the spaceship depart carries an emotional power similar to that of the famous ending of George Stevens's *Shane*—the boy shouting "Shane, come back!" and then watching silently in a tearful close-up as his hero rides out of his life forever. Critic Donald Richie described the boy's words as "the cry of innocence in pain. The boy is calling for the return of his own pristine state, and he will never be the same." In *E.T.*, as in *Shane*, though we are witnessing the traumatic end of boyhood innocence, we are also witnessing the beginning of maturity.

"It's the most emotionally complicated film I've ever made and the least technically complicated, which for me was a breath of fresh air," Spielberg said. "The equivalent of the mother ship landing in *Close Encounters* is, in *E.T.*, perhaps a tear out of Henry Thomas's eye. That was my equivalent of a super-colossal special effect, and it was nice to be able to scale down to where everything rested on how people felt about people."

E.T. marked the first time in Spielberg's career in feature films that he decided to do without storyboards (except for the shots involving special effects). For a director accustomed to elaborate preplanning, that was the creative equivalent of working without a net. "I decided that storyboards might smother the spontaneous reaction that young children might have to a sequence," he explained. "So I purposely didn't do any storyboards and just came onto the set and winged it every day and made the movie as close to my own sensibilities and instincts as I possibly could."

Faced with the self-imposed discipline of a tight budget and a brisk sixty-five-day shooting schedule (which he bettered by four days), Spielberg decided to take another creative chance by hiring a cameraman who not only could work fast but was also "a little hungry, hadn't done a [major] theatrical feature before, [and] was going to make an audacious first impression." However, he came to that decision only after offering the job to two well-known cameramen, William A. Fraker, the cinematographer of *1941,* and Italian cinematographer Vittorio Storaro, celebrated for his work with Bernardo Bertolucci; both were unavailable. The cameraman he finally turned to was his old friend Allen Daviau, who had photographed *Amblin'*.

After winning entry into the cameramen's union through a protracted lawsuit, Daviau shot a sequence for Spielberg on the *Special Edition* of *Close Encounters* and made a modest breakthrough in TV movies. Spielberg saw his work on *The Boy Who Drank Too Much* and "did something that I rarely do. I didn't think twice: I picked up the telephone that night and phoned Allen and said, 'Would you photograph my next feature?' There was a rather stunned pause on the other end of the phone and Allen said, 'Why?' I said, 'I just saw something on television which knocked me out and I'd love for you to work on this.' "

Daviau's delicately lyrical lighting for *E.T.* proved crucial to the film's success. As the cameraman puts it, "I remember saying from the very beginning when I read the script, 'It's got to be so real. The whole world around has got to be absolutely realistic, so that the magic that happens isn't hokey, so that the whole thing isn't *intentionally* magical. The magic *comes out of* this incredible situation.' "

Location scenes were filmed in the southern California suburban communities of Northridge and Tujunga, in a redwood forest near Crescent City in northern California, and at a Culver City high school. But most of the movie was shot in the fall of 1981 on three small soundstages at Laird International Studios in Culver City. "Steven wanted to be away from the Universal lot," Daviau explains. "He wanted secrecy, and he felt he could maintain his secrecy a lot better if he wasn't on a major lot." Fearing a TV movie ripoff, Spielberg shot *E.T.* under a phony title, *A Boy's Life.* Deliberately causing confusion with Spielberg's previously announced project *Growing Up,* the company simply described *A Boy's Life* as a "Comedy about antics and lifestyles of boys living in southern California today." Everyone working on the movie was required to sign an agreement not to talk about it. Leading lady Dee Wallace thought the secrecy "almost got to the point of ridiculousness." She was so intimidated that she felt she had to ask permission to discuss the movie with her own husband. Even Spielberg's cocker spaniel, Willie, wore a photo ID badge on his collar while visiting the set.

Shooting many of the exterior scenes on sets designed by James D. Bissell helped Spielberg and Daviau control and stylize *E.T.*'s environment, as did the film's extensive use of fog effects and backlighting, by now a trademark of Spielberg pictures. Since the director was making an unusually small-scale movie, much of it taking place in the cramped quarters of Elliott's bedroom closet, those limitations "suddenly got me thinking we don't have a thousand extras to paint my canvas with, but we do have light, we do have the sun, and we do have a kind of color texture to work with, [so] let's let the lighting give the movie the production value," Spielberg told *American Cinematographer* in 1982. "I think as a director I was more conscious of lighting on *E.T.* than I have been on any other movie before."

The director gave Daviau an endless series of creative challenges. As the cameraman recalled, "One time he told me, 'Allen, if you blow a scene because you went too far, I won't be half as mad at you as I would be if you blew it because you played it too safe.' For instance, one time he asked, 'How would it look if we overexposed somebody's face five stops?' I wasn't sure, but I gave it a try and held my breath throughout. It was when the boys were searching the garage for objects to build the communicator. The extreme contrast made a dramatic effect and the scene is in the picture.

"Steven will say two things that may appear contradictory. That means he wants you to work toward incorporating both. For example, he wanted E.T.'s skin to glisten, but wanted him to stay indistinct. Another time he said, 'I don't want to see his face, but I want to see *just enough.'* Challenges like that make for distinctive photography."

Daviau's photographic magic convinced the audience that Rambaldi's alien creature was *not* made of plastic and rubber. "E.T. could not only look sad, but he could look curiously sad," Spielberg marveled. "Not by the way we controlled E.T. mechanically but by the way Allen shifted light."

"If you got one iota too much light on him, particularly in the early scenes, it was a disaster," Daviau explains. "One iota too little, and there was nothing there. So it was all like riding that knife edge; it was very tricky stuff. And the pressure on every department to move so fast! TV schedule–type pressure, *beyond* TV schedule, and yet trying for this incredible, special, magical quality. People go, 'Oh, *E.T.*—it must have been wonderful.' No, it was hell! It was so nerve-wracking because you didn't have time to reshoot anything, and yet you were riding this knife edge.

"*E.T.* was so tough because Steven had made a bet with Universal that he could do this thing for $10 million. [Completing *E.T.* within that budget enabled him to satisfy his obligation for the final remaining film in his 1975 contract with Universal.] In the initial stages, they never expected him to do it. I think they saw how serious he was once he started shooting. He would make speeches to us, 'This isn't just about money. It's about my freedom. But they'll come after my money, they'll make me pay for any overages. Or I'll have to work for them and do terrible pictures for years.' If he went over on it, oh, he'd owe them! He'd still be doing *Jaws 5* or something.

"I oftentimes say to film students, 'There are times you do things because you're too dumb to know they can't be done.' One of the great things about Steven is that he demands not just your best, but he demands you do things you don't think you can do. Just because of the way he inspires you to do them, you pull amazing rabbits out of hats. That's what this whole picture was like for every department."

I N the first weeks after the film's release on June 11, 1982, Spielberg personally was earning as much as half a million dollars *per day* as his share of the profits. He found several new places to plant his money that year. He spent several million dollars on real estate, including a four-acre spread in Long Island's fashionable East Hampton, with a transplanted 1790s Pennsylvania Dutch barn renovated by architect Charles Gwathmey and puckishly dubbed "Quelle Barn"; a parcel of land in the posh Bel Air section of Los Angeles; and an apartment on the West Side of Manhattan. The week *E.T.* opened, "Citizen Spielberg" (as he was dubbed in the press) treated himself to one of the original balsa wood "Rosebud" sleds from *Citizen Kane* (cost at Sotheby's auction: $60,500).

The steady, unrelenting box-office performance of *E.T.* dethroned *Star Wars* as the record-holder. Spielberg's film played in theaters for an entire year before the studio pulled it from the market for a two-year rest. It was not its revenues but the overwhelming outpouring of emotion *E.T.* engendered in both young and old alike that made it instantly recognizable as a film classic of the magnitude of *The Wizard of Oz* and *It's a Wonderful Life.* Sid Sheinberg and Lew Wasserman flew down to join Spielberg for the first preview in Houston. "That first screening of *E.T.*—I don't think there's ever been an experience like it," Sheinberg remarked in a 1988 interview. "I surely will never have another one like it in film. I don't think anyone will ever have another one like it in film. It truly was like a religious experience. It must be a little bit like the way people feel if they feel they've seen God.

"The lights go on, and Steven Spielberg is sobbing."

Describing the film's premiere in May 1982 at the closing-night gala of the Cannes Film Festival, critic Roger Ebert rhapsodized, "This is not simply a good movie. It is one of the rare movies that brush away our cautions and win our hearts. . . . When the film is over, the audience rises en masse and turns and shouts its approval and cheers Spielberg, who sits in the front row of the balcony and stands up with a silly grin on his face." Spielberg found the experience "very humbling."

Not every review of *E.T.* was favorable. Curmudgeonly conservative George F. Will wrote a *Newsweek* column entitled, "Well, *I* Don't Love You, E.T.," claiming with a straight face that the movie spread "subversive" notions about childhood and science. But most critics agreed with *Rolling Stone's* Michael Sragow that Spielberg "shows himself to be a personal artist with all the uncanny intuitive force of a space-age Jean Renoir. Watching this vibrantly comic, boundlessly touching fantasy, you feel that Spielberg has, for the first time, put his breathtaking technical skills at the service of his deepest feelings."

E.T. brought its director an unprecedented and somewhat troublesome new level of worldwide fame and adulation. His life story was celebrated and mythologized in countless newspaper and magazine profiles, notably in *Time,* whose lengthy encomium began: "Once upon a time there was a little boy named Steven, who lived in a mythical land called Suburbia . . ."* Many of Spielberg's childhood acquaintances did not know what had become of him until the summer of *E.T.* Spielberg found he had become so recognizable, at least in New York and Los Angeles, that "I often run into mommies

---

* Spielberg was slated to appear on the cover of that issue before being bumped by war in the Falkland Islands. His first appearance on the cover of *Time* did not come until 1985.

who immediately throw their six-year-olds at me." Another unnerving price
of success was having to deal with allegations that *E.T.* was plagiarized
from an unproduced screenplay, *The Alien,* by the celebrated Indian director
Satyajit Ray, or from the 1978 one-act play *Lokey from Maldemar* by Lisa
Litchfield, who filed an unsuccessful $750 million lawsuit. "It's the people
you've never heard of who crawl out of the woodwork like cockroaches to
sue you," Spielberg commented.

On June 27, 1982, Spielberg was invited to show *E.T.* at the White House
to Ronald and Nancy Reagan and a handful of guests, including Supreme
Court Justice Sandra Day O'Connor. "Nancy Reagan was crying toward the
end," Spielberg reported, "and the President looked like a ten-year-old kid."
On September 17, the director showed his film to the staff of the United
Nations, where he was introduced by Secretary General Javier Pérez de
Cuéllar and received the UN Peace Medal. And on December 9, Spielberg
was presented to Queen Elizabeth II at a royal benefit premiere in London,
leading *The Hollywood Reporter* to quip, "Steven Spielberg may yet be
knighted."

The reflected glory of *E.T.* even made Spielberg's mother a celebrity,
when the effervescent Leah appeared on *The Tonight Show* to reminisce with
Johnny Carson about her son's precocious childhood. E.T. himself appeared
on the cover of *Rolling Stone,* reading a copy of *Variety* bearing the headline
THE SPACEMAN THAT SAVED H'WOOD. In 1985, Spielberg filed an indignant protest
in E.T.'s name after the *Los Angeles Times* ran a caricature of the alien as a
decadent Hollywood hipster wearing a glittering pinkie ring, with a coke
spoon and razor blade dangling from his neck.

The first biographies of Spielberg appeared in the year following *E.T.*'s
release: British author Tony Crawley's *The Steven Spielberg Story: The Man
Behind the Movies* and Tom Collins's children's biography *Steven Spielberg:
Creator of E.T.* The *E.T.* marketing blitz also spawned a book of *Letters to
E.T.,* introduced by Spielberg; a novelization by the noted science-fiction
writer William Kotzwinkle, *E.T. The Extra-Terrestrial in His Adventure on
Earth;* and, for younger readers, Kotzwinkle's illustrated *E.T. The Extra-
Terrestrial Storybook.* Each of Kotzwinkle's books sold more than a million
copies.

Although Kotzwinkle wrote a 1985 sequel, *E.T.: The Book of the Green
Planet,* based on a story by Spielberg, the director has staunchly resisted
public and industry pressure to make a filmed sequel, feeling it "would do
nothing but rob the original of its virginity." But Spielberg was tempted
enough in July 1982 to write a treatment with Mathison, "E.T. II: Nocturnal

---

* Since then, five more children's biographies of Spielberg have been published, as well as
three other adult biographies, Philip M. Taylor's *Steven Spielberg: The Man, His Movies, and Their
Meaning* (1992); Frank Sanello's *Spielberg: The Man, The Movies, The Mythology* (1996); and John
Baxter's *The Unauthorised Biography: Steven Spielberg* (1996).

Fears," in which Elliott and friends are kidnapped by evil extraterrestrials (perhaps refugees from *Night Skies*) and must contact E.T. to rescue them. Spielberg also was involved in the planning of Universal Studios' exhilarating *E.T.* ride, a $40 million attraction that opened in 1991. A live-action sequel to the movie, preceded by a filmed introduction by Spielberg and E.T., the ride whisks the audience to E.T.'s planet on flying bicycles.

Spielberg initially said he didn't want to "flood the market" with *E.T.* product tie-ins and that he wanted any products to be designed in the spirit of the film, but MCA/Universal eventually licensed more than two hundred products in a belated attempt to capitalize on the film's unexpected box-office performance. MCA spent more than $2 million pursuing rip-off items, filing more than two hundred lawsuits. Perhaps the most egregious unauthorized product was a recording entitled "I Had Sex with E.T." Some of the authorized products were in little better taste, ranging from E.T. dolls and costumes to ice cream, chocolate-flavored cereal, and women's undergarments with E.T.'s face stitched on the leg. Reese's Pieces, the candy Elliott uses to lure E.T. out of hiding, saw its business climb by 65 percent after Hershey agreed to spend $1 million for advertising tie-ins.* But most companies selling *E.T.*-related products failed to reap the marketing bonanza of the *Star Wars* films, whose products had grossed an astonishing $1.5 billion by 1982. An "E.T. Earth Center" toy store at Universal Studios closed after only five weeks.

The commercial exploitation of *E.T.* was so blatant and crass that it began to tarnish many people's images of the movie. "Spielberg—who had personal control over merchandising—turned his film into a toy factory, trivializing the movie almost beyond recognition," Michael Ventura observed in *L.A. Weekly*. ". . . Gorged with greed, he sells and sells and sells, until the name *E.T.* no longer conjures a marvelous surprise that uplifted us in a huge dark room, but a lot of dolls and bumper stickers and Michael Jackson records and games and candy bars, all sticky with sentimentality. . . . It's as though Spielberg needs *not* to believe in these images he creates."

Nevertheless, all the huckstering failed to discourage the most remarkable aspect of the *E.T.* phenomenon, its widespread embrace as a quasi-religious parable. The spiritual dimension that was only implied in *Close Encounters* was foregrounded unmistakably in *E.T.* Stanley Kauffmann's *New Republic* review dubbed it "The Gospel According to St. Steven." English professor Al Millar, who published a pamphlet entitled *E.T.—You're More Than a Movie Star,* was among those pointing out parallels between Spielberg's creature and Jesus Christ, including the mysterious stranger's arrival in a shed, his glowing heart, power to work miracles, healing touch, spiritual teachings,

---

* That became a major embarrassment for another candymaker, Mars, which had turned down an opportunity to have its M&M's used in the movie. Mars thought E.T. was an ugly creature that would frighten children.

persecution by civil authorities, death and resurrection, and climactic ascent into the heavens after bidding farewell to his disciples.*

At Christmas 1982, Universal made the religious overtones even more explicit, with ads showing E.T.'s glowing finger touching the hand of a child, evoking Michelangelo's Sistine Chapel image of God's finger touching the hand of Adam. The ad logo read simply, "Peace." Spielberg seemed somewhat embarrassed by such religiosity, insisting he had not intended *E.T.* as a spiritual parable. But he admitted that "the only time Melissa and I sort of looked at each other and said, 'Gee, are we getting into a possibly sticky area here?' was when E.T. is revealed to the boys on the bicycles and he's wearing a white hospital robe and his 'immaculate heart' is glowing. We looked at each other at that point and said, 'This might trigger a lot of speculation.' We already knew that his coming back to life was a form of resurrection. But I'm a nice Jewish boy from Phoenix, Arizona. If I ever went to my mother and said, 'Mom, I've made this movie that's a Christian parable,' what do you think she'd say? She has a kosher restaurant on Pico and Doheny in Los Angeles."

A L T H O U G H he had banished the evil extraterrestrials of *Night Skies* from his more benign conception of *E.T.,* Spielberg's fascination with ghoulish morbidity and wanton destructiveness was given free rein in his production of *Poltergeist,* a horror movie about ghosts invading a suburban California tract home built over an Indian burial site. The making of *Poltergeist* overlapped with that of *E.T.,* and the two films were released virtually simultaneously in the summer of 1982.

"*Poltergeist* is what I fear and *E.T.* is what I love," explained Spielberg, relishing the opportunity to display both sides of his creative personality on adjoining screens in shopping malls. "One is about suburban evil, and the other is about suburban good. . . . *Poltergeist* is the darker side of my nature —it's me when I was scaring my younger sisters half to death when we were growing up."

His involvement on *Poltergeist* was unusually intense for a producer and writer. He was on the set for all but three days of the film's twelve-week shooting schedule, and he, not director Tobe Hooper, often appeared to be calling the shots. The issue of the film's authorship leaked into the press and gave rise to an acrimonious controversy over whether Spielberg was the *de facto* director of *Poltergeist.* It was generally believed in Hollywood that Spielberg simply moved in and took over the film creatively, just as producer Howard Hawks had done with Christian Nyby, the credited director of the 1951 science-fiction/horror film *The Thing from Another World.*

A mild-mannered, bearded Texan with a quirky sense of humor and a gift

* On the other hand, televangelist Jimmy Swaggart, in 1985, denounced E.T. as "a beast from Hell" and accused Spielberg of being an "agent of Satan."

for cinematic Grand Guignol, Hooper came to Spielberg's attention with *The Texas Chain Saw Massacre,* a low-budget 1974 horror film that became a cult classic. Spielberg found it "one of the most truly visceral movies ever made. Essentially it starts inside the stomach and ends in the heart. . . . I loved it." When he suggested to Hooper that they make a movie together, Hooper said he had always wanted to make a ghost story.

By 1981, Spielberg had come up with a story he thought could serve as the basis for a mutually stimulating creative collaboration. Taking story credit as well as joint screenplay credit with Michael Grais and Mark Victor, Spielberg combined horror genre elements with his own suburban milieu of hilly, winding streets and cookie-cutter homes. In a malevolent twist on *Close Encounters,* the spectral title characters (*poltergeist* is German for "noisy ghost") kidnap the small daughter of a white-bread WASP family called the Freelings.* "I really based the neighborhood on suburban Scottsdale, Arizona, where I grew up," Spielberg said, though his home was actually in neighboring Phoenix. ". . . The Freeling family in *Poltergeist* is not atypical of the people I knew and grew up with."

A soulless technical exercise in scaring the wits out of the audience, *Poltergeist* is a feature-film equivalent of the gross-out pranks little Stevie pulled on his sisters and neighbors. Its *pièce de résistance* is a grisly sequence of revengeful corpses rising out of the Freelings' muddy backyard swimming hole. *Poltergeist* may have been payback time for Spielberg, who seemed to take a sadistic relish in putting his complacent WASP neighbors through Hell. Most of the thinly plotted movie is taken up with elaborately horrific (if occasionally cheesy) visual effects by George Lucas's northern California company Industrial Light & Magic, as Steve and Diane Freeling (Craig T. Nelson and JoBeth Williams) battle ghosts to rescue their angelic little daughter, Carol Anne (Heather O'Rourke). Because the Freelings are such plastic Middle-American clichés, *Poltergeist* fails to arouse much empathy for the beleaguered family. Spielberg's familiar thematic obsession with a child's separation from his/her parents serves as little more than a plot device.†

S P I E L B E R G and Hooper at first appeared to be a good match. "We sit around and talk about movies almost like Huey and Duey [Donald Duck's nephews]," Hooper said. "Half of a piece of construction would be suggested

---

* The name may be a sly nod to Warner Bros. cartoon director Friz Freleng.

† The story bears a striking similarity to "Little Girl Lost," a 1962 *Twilight Zone* program written by Richard B. Matheson, who based it on his own short story about a six-year-old girl who rolls under her bed and disappears into another dimension. "That was based on an occurrence that happened to our daughter," Matheson said. "She didn't go into the fourth dimension, but she cried one night and I went to where she was and couldn't find her anywhere. I couldn't find her on the bed, I couldn't find her on the ground. She had fallen off and rolled all the way under the bed against the wall. At first, even when I felt under the bed, I couldn't reach her. . . . After the shock is over, as with *Duel,* you start to come up with a story." Matheson says that before making *Poltergeist,* Spielberg asked him for a videotape of "Little Girl Lost."

by one of us, and the other half would be completed by the other." But it was not long before Spielberg came to the disenchanted conclusion that "Tobe isn't what you'd call a take-charge sort of guy."

Making the film for MGM, where David Begelman, the fallen champion of *Close Encounters,* was now in charge, Spielberg was concerned about making good on his promise to deliver the film at no more than 10 percent over its $9.5 million budget. The final cost of $10.8 million was 12 percent over the budget, although the movie (which Spielberg produced with Frank Marshall) finished shooting two days ahead of schedule. JoBeth Williams commented that Spielberg "drove us all like racehorses . . . I think that since making *1941* he's acutely conscious of time and money."

A number of practical problems prevented Spielberg from personally replacing Hooper as director. *Poltergeist* started shooting in May 1981, while *E.T.* was in active preproduction, requiring Spielberg's daily attention to a myriad of technical and conceptual details. Although *E.T.* wound up being pushed back a month, it originally was scheduled to begin shooting that August, the same month *Poltergeist* finished shooting. Even if Spielberg could have found a way to juggle his schedule and give his full attention to both movies, his contract with Universal prevented him from directing another movie while making *E.T.,* and Directors Guild of America rules prohibited the producer from taking over the job of the director.

"My enthusiasm for wanting to make *Poltergeist* would have been difficult for any director I would have hired," Spielberg later admitted. "It derived from *my* imagination and *my* experiences, and it came [partly] out of *my* typewriter. I felt a proprietary interest in this project that was stronger than if I was just an executive producer. I thought I'd be able to turn *Poltergeist* over to a director and walk away. I was wrong."

Being hired to direct *Poltergeist* was a quantum jump in Hollywood prestige for Hooper, since it was his first theatrical feature for a major studio and made him the latest protégé of Hollywood's most successful filmmaker. That may have been why he paid the price of acceding to Spielberg's constant presence on the set and turning over the last few months of postproduction to his writer-producer. "Tobe seemed to resolve Steven's participation in his mind," felt production manager Dennis E. Jones. "But I'm sure inside he was hurting."* Less than a month into shooting, Jeff Silverman of the *Los Angeles Herald-Examiner* reported Hollywood gossip that Hooper was *"not* really directing the pic anymore." That prompted a response from Hooper that Spielberg's "involvement spans all aspects of this film and does not differ from those functions normally performed by the executive producer. He is on the set when I specifically request it and this is becoming increasingly less as he prepares for an upcoming picture which he will direct beginning in August."

Other observers did not see it that way. Screenwriter Bob Gale, who made

* Hooper did not respond to a request to be interviewed for this book.

two visits to the MGM soundstage where *Poltergeist* was filming, found it an "uncomfortable set," because whenever Hooper gave an instruction to cinematographer Matthew F. Leonetti, Leonetti would look over his shoulder at Spielberg, who would nod or shake his head. Screenwriter David Giler and Spielberg's agent, Guy McElwaine, spent a day acting in the film as part of a group of men watching football on television, an inside joke about the male-bonding parties Spielberg attended at McElwaine's house. Giler recalls, "My partner, Walter Hill, and I were working on *Southern Comfort* in a cutting room right across the way. When I came back from the set, I said, 'Well, now I know what the executive producer does. I've always wondered. He sets up the camera, tells the actors what to do, stands back, and lets the director say, 'Action!' "

Hooper made no public objection when the ads for the film treated him as a virtual nonperson, relegating his name to small type while proclaiming, "Steven Spielberg has fascinated, mystified and scared audiences with *Jaws, Close Encounters of the Third Kind* and *Raiders of the Lost Ark*. Now, he takes you into a world of terrifying forces that defy reason . . ." But Hooper finally had enough when he saw the trailer, in which the line "A Steven Spielberg Production" was twice as large as "A Tobe Hooper Film." That was a violation of Directors Guild rules. Arbitrator Edward Mosk awarded Hooper $15,000 in damages, finding the trailer "denigrated the role of the director." Mosk noted that "broader issues of dispute exist between the producer-writer and the director which seem to have exacerbated the current dispute over the trailer credit." Ordering MGM to redo trailers running in New York and Los Angeles, Mosk also directed the studio to take full-page advertisements in three trade publications apologizing to Hooper and the DGA. The ads called the credit error "inadvertent" and said it "was not intended to diminish Mr. Hooper's creative achievement as the director of the film."

Spielberg took out his own double-edged ad in the trades, in the form of a letter addressed to Hooper: "Regrettably, some of the press has misunderstood the rather unique, creative relationship which you and I shared throughout the making of *Poltergeist*. I enjoyed your openness in allowing me, as a producer and a writer, a wide berth for creative involvement, just as I know you were happy with the freedom you had to direct *Poltergeist* so wonderfully. Through the screenplay you accepted a vision of this very intense movie from the start, and as the director, you delivered the goods."

While the advertisements by MGM and Spielberg may have helped salve Hooper's wounded pride, the brouhaha was a setback to his career, negating any positive effect the film's box-office success otherwise would have had on his future in Hollywood. Generally treating *Poltergeist* as an efficient but uninspired genre piece, reviewers knew where the true credit lay. Pauline Kael wrote in *The New Yorker*, "Whatever the credits say, [Spielberg] was certainly the guiding intelligence of *Poltergeist*—which isn't a high compliment." David Ehrenstein commented in the *L.A. Reader* that if only Hooper had been given free rein, he would have been "the ideal person to tear this vision of domestic bliss limb from limb." But Spielberg wanted a family audience for the PG-rated film, and Ehrenstein accused him of wanting "to play with horror, but not for keeps. . . . You don't have to be a dedicated follower of the *politique des auteurs* to recognize that *Poltergeist* owes a lot more to the creator of *Close Encounters of the Third Kind* than it does to the perpetrator of *The Texas Chain Saw Massacre.*"

Despite his insistence on claiming credit in the press ("I designed the film. . . . I was the David O. Selznick of this movie"), Spielberg seemed somewhat uncomfortable with the public scrutiny of his role as shadow director of *Poltergeist.* Coming at the same time *E.T.* was making him (in the words of *Rolling Stone's* Michael Sragow) "the most successful movie director in Hollywood, America, the Occident, the planet Earth, the solar system and the galaxy," Spielberg's treatment of Hooper looked like a symptom of incipient megalomania. Spielberg told the *Los Angeles Times* he had learned a lesson from the experience: "If I write it myself, I'll direct it myself. I won't put someone else through what I put Tobe through, and I'll be more honest in my contributions to a film."

A N O T H E R   low-budget moviemaker whose work Spielberg admired was Joe Dante. After making *Piranha,* Dante directed *The Howling,* a 1981 black comedy about werewolves. Spielberg cast its leading lady, Dee Wallace, in *E.T.,* and hung a poster from the movie on the wall of his production office. A few months later, Dante and producing partner Michael Finnell were struggling to put together projects from their small Hollywood office, a dump they called "Cockroach Palace," when a script arrived unannounced from Steven Spielberg.

Gremlins was a horror yarn by the then-unknown young writer Chris Columbus. Dante remembers thinking the script "must have come to the wrong address. I thought, This is incredible—this guy [Spielberg] doesn't know I'm alive! It came at a time when I was dead broke. *The Howling* was a big hit, but it wasn't for me. My career seemed pretty much stalled. If it wasn't for Steven, I probably would have made twenty-seven more low-budget movies. I think he has a genuine desire to be able to give directors a chance. He loves being the mentor and having protégés." Explaining why that is so, Spielberg reflected in 1986, "I have instant recall about how I felt when I wanted to be a movie director and there was nobody around who wanted me to be one. . . . All people see a reflection of themselves when they're helping other people. I can't deny, and no one can, that there is vanity involved in helping a young person achieve his goal. The vanity is a chance to get started a second time, to project oneself into the young filmmaker's own career and to feel what it was like to get that first break all over again."

Despite his elation at being tapped for stardom by Spielberg, Dante was aware of all the "negative publicity about Steven being responsible" for the direction of *Poltergeist*. "I have no idea how true that was, but it was certainly something that was in the back of my mind: 'Am I going to be making my picture or somebody else's picture?' Steven was very sensitive about those allegations. He said, 'I can't do that, because if I do that, nobody will want to work here.'"

Gremlins dealt with little furry creatures going on a rampage in a Capraesque small town, and it has been interpreted as Dante's sly parody of Spielbergian cuddliness gone amok, "E.T. with teeth." Asked if that was intentional, Dante replied, "Yes, and Steven cooperated entirely with it. He got the joke right away." Many people were surprised to find Spielberg's name attached to a movie about vicious little monsters, but those who knew him personally recognized that he secretly shared Dante's gleeful, boyish penchant for that kind of ghoulish comedy. *Gremlins* represented "something Steven would like to do—get that side of his E.T. personality out—except he doesn't really want to do it himself," Dante observed. ". . . He once said he wanted to make movies he didn't want to direct, to express different sides of his personality without having to invest a year in them. But I don't think he was quite prepared for *how* wacky *Gremlins* was. I remember sitting with him in a Warner Bros. screening room, and I saw him in the row behind me hitting his head [again and again] while he was watching the movie."

Spielberg originally conceived *Gremlins* as a low-budget movie, made outside the studio system, "which is why he came to me," says Dante. "He really wanted to do it down-and-dirty." But it soon became apparent that filming scenes involving elaborate puppetry would be expensive and time-consuming, and *Gremlins* escalated into a major Warner Bros. production, costing $11 million by the time of its release in 1984. With little to do while Chris Walas was busy on the nine-month job of designing the gremlins, Dante and Finnell found themselves diverted onto a more imminent project Spielberg was developing at Warners, *Twilight Zone—The Movie*.

W H E N Rod Serling sold the syndication rights to his *Twilight Zone* series —a decision he later regretted, since the show has never stopped running— he kept the right to make a feature film version of the series. Inspired by the 1945 British anthology film *Dead of Night,* Serling first pitched studio executives the idea of making a *Twilight Zone* "trilogy" he would host. His outline said that it would be "shot in black & white for a budget of under a million dollars. The stories are separate and distinct, but have a background thread that moves one into the other." At one time, Serling planned to include "Eyes," the story Spielberg eventually filmed for Serling's *Night Gallery* pilot in 1969. Serling also tried a different approach, taking one of the most memorable *Twilight Zone* programs, "It's a Good Life" (based on a Jerome Bixby story about a little boy with sinister powers), and expanding it into a feature-length screenplay.

But Serling found no takers for a *Twilight Zone* movie before his death in 1975, and it was not until several years later that Warner Bros. chairman Ted Ashley revived the idea of a multipart *Twilight Zone* feature, acquiring the rights from Serling's widow, Carol. Fruitless attempts were made at the studio to develop the project until Ashley's successor, Terry Semel, mentioned the idea to Spielberg, whom he was trying to lure into a long-term, nonexclusive relationship with Warners, similar to Spielberg's long-standing relationship with Universal. Spielberg responded with immediate enthusiasm to the prospect of paying homage to a TV series that had been one of the formative influences on his youthful imagination.

Spielberg thought a big-screen *Twilight Zone* anthology would not only appeal to baby boomers and the many other fans of the series, but that it also would be a perfect opportunity for a collaboration with his friend John Landis, the irreverent director of *Animal House* and *The Blues Brothers*. In April 1982, Spielberg and Landis agreed to produce *Twilight Zone—The Movie* together (each taking 5 percent of the gross profits) and to direct separate segments of what ultimately became a five-part feature, costing a total of about $10 million. Landis planned to write original scripts for his own two segments (including a brief prologue featuring Dan Aykroyd and Albert Brooks). To write the rest of the film, Spielberg brought in Richard B. Matheson, the author of *Duel* and one of the principal writers of Serling's TV series.

The first script Matheson wrote for the *Twilight Zone* movie was based on a Halloween story Spielberg had been planning to direct for MGM. Matheson described it as the story of "a bully who's mistreating all these young trick-or-treating kids, and the supernatural world gets him for it. Creatures—real live monsters—start chasing him around." Eventually, the bully finds that his monster mask cannot be removed from his own face. This revenge fantasy was put aside when Spielberg decided to remake a 1960 *Twilight Zone* program, "The Monsters Are Due on Maple Street," about neighbors consumed with the paranoid fear that one of them may be an alien infiltrator in human guise. Serling's nightmarish fable of prejudice and xenophobia offered Spielberg an opportunity to explore in far more serious form the feelings of scapegoating and exclusion he had felt while growing up Jewish in mostly WASP suburbia.

"The concept was that all the stories were going to connect," explains Joe Dante, who was brought aboard after Landis. "Characters were going to recur in various segments, so it would seem like one movie, not an anthology. One of the mistakes I thought they were making was that they were remaking old episodes. Everybody knew the shows, and the shows depended on these O. Henry twist endings, so everybody knew how they were going to come out. But that was the concept, take it or leave it. My idea was a different take on the short story 'It's a Good Life' was based on. I didn't want people to be able to recognize, at first, what episode it was based on."

In Dante's brilliantly stylized version, one of the most surreal pieces of filmmaking ever released by a major studio, the little boy (Jeremy Licht) "wishes" people he doesn't like into "cartoonland," literally turning them into cartoon characters. The house he rules is a cockeyed vision reminiscent of a Looney Tunes cartoon, and his family behaves in the frenzied, goofy manner of Warner Bros. animated characters. "When the picture came out," Dante says, "people were constantly saying to me, 'Your picture is about Steven,' because it's about this little kid who's always getting everything he wants. I suppose you could read it that way, but that wasn't the intention."

The fourth director was chosen in very off-the-cuff fashion. Australian filmmaker George Miller, visiting Warner Bros. to oversee the U.S. release of his futuristic fantasy *Mad Max 2 (The Road Warrior),* dropped into Spielberg's office, where he found "they were having a meeting to discuss *The Twilight Zone.* I remember Steven was there, Kathy Kennedy, and a few others, and they invited me to sit down. Up to that time, it had been planned to do three stories [not including the prologue], and now they'd decided to do a fourth. 'Why don't *you* do one?' someone said. I wasn't sure they weren't having me on at the time." Miller found himself directing John Lithgow in "Nightmare at 20,000 Feet," Matheson's story about a neurotic man whose terror of flying escalates when he sees a monster crouched on the wing of the plane. Although a *tour de force* of visual storytelling, Miller's segment focused so squarely on the physical details of the man's anxiety attack that it jettisoned the original version's ambiguity, a suggestion that the monster may exist only in the man's disturbed mind.

Landis's main segment was the story of a bigot named Bill Connor (Vic Morrow), who, to his horror, finds himself successively in the place of a German Jew persecuted by Nazis in occupied France, a southern black lynched by the Ku Klux Klan, and a Vietnamese fired upon by American troops. After Terry Semel and another Warner Bros. executive, Lucy Fisher, urged Landis to find a way of redeeming the mean-spirited character, he wrote a scene in which Morrow would rescue two Vietnamese children from their firebombed village. Landis's script for what he considered "the only political or moral episode in the film" was reminiscent of Serling at his preachiest and most heavy-handedly ironic.

B E F O R E dawn on July 23, 1982, George Folsey Jr., associate producer of the *Twilight Zone* movie, telephoned his production secretary, Donna Schuman. "There has been an accident," he told her. "Actually, the worst possible thing has happened: Vic and the kids have been killed. A helicopter fell on them."

Veteran actor Vic Morrow, six-year-old Renee Shin-Yi Chen, and seven-year-old My-Ca Dinh Le had been killed instantly at 2:20 A.M., during the filming of the firebombing of the Vietnamese village. The gruesome accident, which occurred at the Indian Dunes Park location site near Saugus, forty miles north of Los Angeles, led to the filing of criminal charges of involuntary manslaughter against director Landis, Folsey, and three others involved in the filming, unit production manager Dan Allingham, special-effects coordinator Paul Stewart, and helicopter pilot Dorcey Wingo. Landis, Folsey, and Allingham were each charged with two counts of involuntary manslaughter, resulting from child endangerment, and three additional manslaughter charges were filed against Landis, Stewart, and Wingo, resulting from their "gross negligence" on the set.

It was the first time in the history of Hollywood that a director had ever been charged with a criminal act because of a fatality on his set. If convicted, Landis could have faced up to six years in prison, and the others faced up to five years. Landis, Allingham, and Folsey offered in 1985 to plead guilty to charges of conspiracy to illegally employ the children, in exchange for dropping the manslaughter charges against them and dropping all charges against Stewart and Wingo, but that plea bargain was rejected by the Los Angeles County district attorney's office. After a long, controversial, and bitterly divisive trial on the manslaughter charges, Landis and his fellow defendants were acquitted on May 29, 1987. In January 1988, however, the national board of directors of the Directors Guild of America reprimanded Landis, Allingham, and the movie's first assistant director, Elie Cohn, for conduct "unprofessional, inconsistent with their responsibilities, and extremely prejudicial to the welfare of the DGA."

Because the two nonprofessional child performers had been hired illegally and were used in violation of child-safety laws, fines were levied against Warner Bros. and the defendants by the California Labor Commission and the state Division of Occupational Safety and Health. The families of the three victims collected multimilllion-dollar settlements of their civil lawsuits against the studio and the filmmakers (including Spielberg). Warners also paid several million dollars in legal fees to the defendants' attorneys.

The accident had a sobering effect on many people in Hollywood, making the industry somewhat more safety-conscious, if still less than entirely responsible about putting performers and crew members at risk. The accident has had little dampening effect, however, on the career of John Landis, who has worked virtually nonstop in films and television ever since the accident. In striking contrast, Stephen Lydecker, a camera operator on the *Twilight Zone* movie who testified against Landis, found himself "tagged as a troublemaker" and blacklisted after twenty-six years in the film business (he turned to a career in real estate). Much of the industry did not want to deal with the disturbing allegations about Landis's behavior on the *Twilight Zone* set, because to do so honestly would have meant changing some of Hollywood's basic attitudes about the license it grants to money-making directors.

◗ N E of the pre-dawn telephone calls Landis made after the crash was to his fellow producer on the film, Steven Spielberg. According to Landis, the first question Spielberg asked him was, "Do you have a press agent?"

Although there were far more important issues at stake than anyone's public image, Spielberg soon had reason for serious concern about how the public would view *his* involvement in *Twilight Zone—The Movie*. Some initial news reports of the accident prominently identified *Twilight Zone* as a Spielberg movie, with the name of the lesser-known Landis appearing farther down in the stories. Coming only six weeks after the opening of *E.T.,* the appalling event at Indian Dunes had the potential to undo much of the goodwill Spielberg had accumulated with his previous films. If he were held responsible in any way for the deaths—particularly those of the two children—his reputation as a maker of heartwarming family movies, often featuring children as protagonists, would have been irreparably harmed. If he were found to have been involved with the hiring of the children, his own permit to work with children could have been denied.

"It was a very emotional time for Steven," Dante recalls. "Steven was very affected by the accident. Then he felt somewhat betrayed by it. He felt he couldn't understand what happened, and he suddenly became the brunt [of bad publicity]. I think he deeply resented it."

On November 5, 1982, Carl Pittman, a Teamster who drove the special-effects truck on the movie, told the National Transportation Safety Board (NTSB) and the Los Angeles County Sheriff's Department that he had seen Spielberg at the filming site on the night of the accident. In sworn testimony, Pittman said that after the accident occurred, while he was helping Landis and the parents of the dead children into cars, "Mr. Spielberg requested a car, so I got him a car—he needed to go to the phone, and I was mad enough at him that I had to walk away from him." When asked by the investigators what caused him to say he was "mad" at Spielberg, Pittman replied, "He was too cold about it. . . . In fact, I didn't want him to have the car; I wanted to keep it there in case anyone else [needed the car]—at this point, no one knew how many people were injured." None of the thirty-one other people involved in the production who had been interviewed by the NTSB placed Spielberg on the set, however, and Landis called Pittman's allegation "preposterous." Pittman later admitted he probably had confused Spielberg with Frank Marshall, the film's executive producer. The NTSB nevertheless decided to send a written inquiry to Spielberg, asking if he had any relevant information about the accident. That resulted in Spielberg's only sworn declaration on the subject, a letter stating in its entirety:

"In response to your request, I was never at the Indian Dunes location of *Twilight Zone* on the night of the accident or at any other time.

"I declare under penalty of perjury that the foregoing is true and correct, executed at Los Angeles, California, this first day of December, 1982."

Throughout the five-year investigation and ten-month trial, no evidence was ever found or presented directly linking Spielberg to any criminal act relating to the accident. But despite the fact that he produced the *Twilight Zone* movie with Landis, Spielberg was never interviewed about the accident by any governmental agency, he was not called to testify at the trial, and he did not even have to give a deposition in the civil suits resulting from the accident. Explaining the seeming lack of interest in Spielberg displayed by the Sheriff's Department, the lead homicide detective investigating the case, Sergeant Tom Budds, said, "There is no indication that Spielberg even knew anything about the hiring of the children."

Spielberg's ability to distance himself from the case, and his almost total public silence on the accident, were enough to raise lingering questions in some people's minds. "Was the NTSB following commands from Washington in order to protect some powerful individual in Hollywood?" Stephen Farber and Marc Green asked in their 1988 book *Outrageous Conduct: Art, Ego, and the "Twilight Zone" Case.* "Rumors to that effect were bandied about when it was learned that Steven Spielberg had managed to avoid being questioned by the Safety Board."

The fact that some of Spielberg's closest associates—including his right-hand man, Frank Marshall—were involved with the hiring of the children was the principal reason such questions continued to be raised. In 1985, Landis's defense attorney Harland Braun publicly demanded that the district attorney's office investigate Spielberg's possible involvement in the hiring of the children, even though the statute of limitations had expired on that matter. Charging that the office's investigation of the crash was "consciously truncated," Braun wrote in a November 20, 1985, letter to chief deputy district attorney Gilbert Garcetti that Spielberg "was able to deflect the investigation away from himself by simply submitting a letter stating that he was not on the set the night of the accident. His full and complete knowledge and approval of what was to take place must be assumed and never has been disputed.

"What other major witness could avoid questioning by signing a piece of paper? Your office never asked Spielberg a single question about the accident or the hiring of the children. Your claim that Spielberg was 'unavailable' is simply false."

Braun later declared, "If Frank Marshall went out on a Spielberg movie and hired kids illegally who ended up being killed, and Spielberg didn't know about it, he would can Marshall immediately. It's clear that Marshall and [Kathleen] Kennedy [who was associate producer on Spielberg's segment] told Spielberg." Folsey, Landis's associate producer and codefendant, similarly insisted, "We wouldn't have hired the kids on a Spielberg picture unless either Spielberg or his people knew it. I mean, that would have been a terrible thing to do, put them in that position. The fact that Frank agreed to do it made me feel that it was OK, that it was really his responsibility, too."

The complicated hiring process began five weeks before the accident, when Landis and Folsey described the scene involving the children to casting directors Mike Fenton and Marci Liroff. Liroff, who had worked on *E.T.* and *Poltergeist,* told the filmmakers that working children late at night was illegal under California labor laws. She added that the scene "sounded kind of dangerous." Since the children did not have speaking parts, Fenton told

Landis and Folsey, "Then they're extras, and our office doesn't hire extras." "The hell with you guys," Landis gruffly replied. "We don't need you. We'll get them off the streets ourselves." Liroff subsequently repeated her objections to Marshall, who told her, "I will check it out."

According to Folsey, Kennedy, at Marshall's request, called the state labor commission and asked if waivers could be issued for children to work at night. She was told children that young would not be allowed to work late at night. As a result, Landis admitted in court, "We decided to break the law. We decided, wrongly, to violate the labor code. . . . I thought, and we discussed, that we would honor not the letter of the law but the spirit of the law. And I thought, and we discussed, that we would find children whose parents—we would explain to them that we were doing a technical violation, that we were working them without a teacher on the set—explain to them what we were going to do." The parents, he said, would "be the guardians, be there with them on the set. . . . Frank and George volunteered to try and find people."

Three days before the accident, Marshall's accountant, Bonne Radford, who worked out of Spielberg's offices, asked veteran Warner Bros. production manager James Henderling if child extras could be hired outside of the auspices of the Screen Extras Guild. Henderling said any children hired, whether through the guild or not, would require work permits from the labor commission. After speaking to Marshall, Radford told Henderling no children were going to be hired after all.

The two children, who had no acting experience, were recruited through Dr. Harold Schuman, the psychiatrist husband of Folsey's production secretary, Donna Schuman. The money to pay the children's parents came from the production's petty cash funds, on a check made payable to Folsey and cosigned by Marshall and Henderling. Henderling later said he had suspicions about what the money might be used for, but was told by his superior, Edward Morey, to sign the check on the grounds that a producer could not be refused petty cash. The check was cashed by Radford (a longtime Spielberg aide, she still works for him today). A sealed envelope containing twenty $100 bills was picked up at Spielberg's offices by a Landis assistant, Carolyn Epstein, who passed it to Folsey for payment to the children's parents.

The parents testified that they were not told work permits for their children were required by law and that they were not informed how dangerous the scene might be. That did not stop defense attorneys from trying to shift part of the blame for the accident onto the children's parents for allowing the youngsters to participate in the scene. In response to a wrongful-death suit filed against Spielberg and others by the parents of Renee Chen, Spielberg's attorneys filed a legal brief stating:

"Spielberg is informed and believes and thereon alleges that at the time and place of the events complained of, plaintiffs [the Chen and Le families] and each of them were not exercising ordinary care, caution or prudence to prevent the injuries sustained by them or by decedent and that, therefore, the injuries alleged were proximately caused by the negligence or comparative negligence of the plaintiffs."

In its response to the suit filed by the parents of the same six-year-old victim, Warner Bros. Inc. went even farther, arguing with stunning callousness, "That if the plaintiffs suffered or sustained any loss, damage or injury . . . the risk, if any risk there was, was knowingly assumed by the decedent, Renee Shin-Yi Chen."

As the circuitous trail of responsibility for the hiring of the children shows, although the money for their payment was routed through Spielberg's office, and although some of his closest aides were involved in the hiring, no direct involvement by Spielberg was found in those processes. That still left open the key question posed by Farber and Green: As one of the movie's producers, *"shouldn't* Spielberg have known that his associates were planning to violate the child labor laws? Whether Spielberg intentionally turned a blind eye to the illegal hiring of children or was too busy to keep himself informed, his behavior did not reflect well on him."

The *Los Angeles Times* reported in 1985 that according to Gary Kesselman, the first prosecutor assigned to the case, "Investigators attempted to interview Marshall and Spielberg but were unsuccessful because the men were either unavailable or out of the country when the grand jury was conducting its deliberations." The investigation was hampered by Marshall's repeated evasion of attempts by Budds to question him about the hiring process and about what he had seen as an eyewitness to the accident. During much of the investigation, Marshall was out of the country producing the next movie Spielberg directed, *Indiana Jones and the Temple of Doom,* and the Amblin Entertainment production *Who Framed Roger Rabbit.* While the trial was underway, Marshall was out of the country with Spielberg, making *Empire of the Sun* in China, Spain, and England.

In June 1986, Detective Budds traveled to London to arrange for Marshall to be served with a subpoena at the St. James Club, where the producer was staying during the preproduction of *Roger Rabbit.* When an employee of the U.S. embassy went to the club to deliver the subpoena, Marshall said he was not receiving visitors that morning, but would see her if she came back later in the day. In less than half an hour, he checked out of the club and left for Paris on a private jet operated by Spielberg's film company, Amblin Entertainment.

Marshall made no public comment on the *Twilight Zone* accident until he told the *Los Angeles Times* in 1990 it was "terrible and horrible for everybody. But it was an accident. Which is eventually what the jury decided." He also said he had been in Los Angeles for two years after the accident, "and nobody ever talked to me." After that, he said, he was "inaccessible" making movies abroad, "And I didn't really feel that I had anything to add that wasn't already out there [other] than what had already been revealed."* Marshall's evasiveness during the *Twilight Zone* investigation, Farber and Green wrote, "was not illegal. But, as [sheriff's detective] Tom Budds says, 'it certainly is less than meeting your civic responsibility.' The actions of Frank Marshall and Steven Spielberg lent credence to what cynics have long suspected, and what the *Twilight Zone* trial would attempt to refute: Some people in Hollywood may indeed be above the law."

T H E acquittals in the criminal cases against Landis and the others came as a shock to many observers. In media postmortems, prosecutor Lea Purwin D'Agostino was singled out for heavy criticism. A lengthy analysis by Gay Jervey in *The American Lawyer,* "Misfire in the Twilight Zone," carried the subhead, "How the Los Angeles D.A.'s office—and prosecutor Lea D'Agostino—blew the case against John Landis." D'Agostino's flamboyant, often abrasive courtroom style was considered a liability by many observers, as was her tendency to make provocative statements to reporters. She was accused of overtrying the case by calling too many witnesses, muddying the impact of the basic allegations, and acting as if she were prosecuting a murder case, not a manslaughter case. The district attorney's office was faulted for what Jervey called its "critical decision . . . not to charge the defendants with the one crime of which they were indisputably guilty: illegally hiring the children." One of the jurors, Lauretta Hudson, commented, "I still say and will always say that their asses could have been in jail, and should have, but not for what they were accused of."

Shortly after the verdict, D'Agostino said, "You've got a situation where three people died because they were placed twenty-four feet under a helicopter which has a main rotor blade that's four feet longer than the courtroom, forty-four feet, with gigantic bombs going off a hundred and fifty or two hundred feet in the air at 2:20 in the morning. How can anyone tell me that it is not reckless? If I live to be a thousand years old, I will not accept that."

In the final analysis, however, the case may have been decided by the testimony of James Camomile, the special-effects technician who set off the explosive charges. Under a grant of immunity that backfired against the prosecution, Camomile testified he was wearing a welder's hood at the time of the accident and did not look up at the low-flying helicopter just before he detonated an explosive underneath it in the set of the Vietnamese

---

* The author of this book, who has known Marshall since working with him in the early 1970s on Orson Welles's still uncompleted film *The Other Side of the Wind,* encountered Marshall at a film screening in October 1995 and requested an interview about his association with Spielberg. Marshall agreed. But after repeated attempts in the following months to set an appointment with Marshall and his wife and producing partner, Kathleen Kennedy, the author was informed that they had decided not to be interviewed.

village. The resulting explosion hurled debris from the set and sent a fireball into the path of the helicopter; according to differing theories of the accident, either the debris or the fireball could have caused the helicopter to crash.

Camomile's immunized testimony made him a handy scapegoat, enabling Landis to blame him for the crash. The jury was not swayed by testimony by crew members that Landis, in staging the scene, had behaved in reckless disregard of safety considerations. Crew members testified Landis had joked before the accident, "Well, we may lose the helicopter," and that during the scene he had shouted over a bullhorn to the helicopter pilot, "Lower! Lower! Lower!"

Reaching for a cinematic comparison to describe the jury's action in acquitting him, Landis told the press it was "like a Frank Capra movie." But he added more soberly that the crash "changed everyone's life connected with it. No deceptions, no lies, no overt chicanery is going to change the fact that three people died in a terrible accident."

Although Spielberg and Landis had to confer occasionally during postproduction on the *Twilight Zone* movie, it became increasingly obvious as time went on that Spielberg wanted to distance himself as much as possible from Landis.

When Landis made a public appearance in December 1995 to autograph copies of his movies at a Los Angeles area laserdisc store, the author approached him with tape recorder in hand, seeking an interview for this book. All Landis would say about Spielberg was, "I haven't talked to Steve in years." Landis heatedly refused to answer questions posed to him about *Twilight Zone—The Movie*.

Spielberg made a rare public statement on the accident in an April 1983 interview with Dale Pollock of the *Los Angeles Times*. "This has been the most interesting year of my film career," Spielberg reflected. "It has mixed the best, the success of *E.T.*, with the worst, the *Twilight Zone* tragedy. A mixture of ecstasy and grief. It's made me grow up a little more. The accident cast a pall on all 150 people who worked on this production. We are still just sick to the center of our souls. I don't know anybody who it *hasn't* affected."

Spielberg summed up the lessons of the accident with a philosophical observation that, while not referring by name to Landis, seemed a pointed criticism of his former friend and colleague:

"A movie is a fantasy—it's light and shadow flickering on a screen. No movie is worth dying for. I think people are standing up much more now than ever before to producers and directors who ask too much. If something isn't safe, it's the right and responsibility of every actor or crew member to yell, 'Cut!' "

AFTER the accident, Spielberg lost interest in making his own segment of the movie. "His heart just wasn't in it anymore," said his first assistant director, Patrick Kehoe. Indeed, Spielberg tried to abandon the entire project, but Warner Bros. lawyers, fearing that cancellation of the film could be construed as an admission of guilt, insisted he fulfill his contract.

Feeling there was "something odd about proceeding" under the circumstances, Joe Dante was the first director to film a segment following the accident. "When the accident happened, everybody became very scarce. George [Miller] and I, whose first studio filmmaking experience this was, were given a lot of autonomy. I was amazed that they went ahead with it." Dante remembers being anxious to do as good a job as possible on his contribution, because he knew there would be "a lot of people looking to justify that movie. It's not *Schindler's List*—it's not worth dying for. *No* movie is worth that."

Dante's "It's a Good Life" began filming on September 28, 1982, and was followed before the cameras by Miller's "Nightmare at 20,000 Feet" and then by Spielberg's segment (Dante later filmed a new ending for the film, a gag taking the movie full circle back to Landis's prologue). The story Spielberg originally planned to film, "The Monsters Are Due on Maple Street," would have required a permit for a prominently featured child actor to work outdoors at night, in frightening scenes involving special effects. Spielberg switched to a simpler, less disturbing story from the TV series, "Kick the Can," which also had scenes taking place at night involving children but was filmed mostly on a soundstage during normal daytime working hours.

As a boy living on Crystal Terrace in New Jersey's Haddon Township, Spielberg had played kick the can, a simple game requiring only a tin can and some imagination. His remake of George Clayton Johnson's ethereal, sweet-natured fantasy about old people reverting to childhood centers on an itinerant miracle worker, Mr. Bloom, played by Scatman Crothers, whom the director called "the black E.T."* After Mr. Bloom's magical game of kick the can turns them into children, all but one of the old folks of the Sunnyvale retirement home decide to go back to being old, realizing that they value their adult memories and accumulated wisdom too much to start over. That poignant addition to the original story reflects the complexity of Spielberg's view of childhood—not a simple nostalgia, by any means, but the acknowledgment of an unfulfilled wish for a state of innocence that perhaps never really existed. Mr. Bloom's gentle influence has taught them that "fresh young minds" do not require young bodies. The defiant exception is a Peter Pan–like character who emulates the swashbuckling fantasy life of his movie idol, Douglas Fairbanks Sr. Part of Spielberg could not surrender that dream of escapism, which he had inherited from his own father, a boyhood admirer of Fairbanks.

"Kick the Can" began shooting the day after Thanksgiving 1982 and finished only six days later. "It seemed like he was just going through the

---

* For "Kick the Can," Spielberg brought back both the writer (Melissa Mathison) and the cinematographer (Allen Daviau) of *E.T.* After rewriting earlier drafts by Johnson and Richard Matheson, Mathison was credited under the pseudonym Josh Rogan.

motions," said Spielberg's secretary, Kathy Switzer. Although filmed in an excessively whimsical manner that blunts some of its emotional potential, "Kick the Can" represents a further step in Spielberg's maturation process. Under the sobering influence of the events of the previous summer, he made a bittersweet film about the need to turn one's back on childhood and accept the coming of age.

D E S P I T E opening on June 24, 1983, the same day the indictments were handed down in the criminal case, *Twilight Zone—The Movie* was not a total failure at the box office, grossing $42 million worldwide. It even received a few good reviews, mostly for the Miller and Dante segments, but some of the critical response was vitriolic.

"A lot of money and several lives might have been saved if the producers had just rereleased the original programs," Vincent Canby wrote in *The New York Times*. The critics for both *Time* and *Newsweek* seemed almost as outraged at Landis for the aesthetic shortcomings of his segment as for what took place on his set. "Even with the helicopter sequence mercifully cut," wrote Richard Corliss of *Time,* "the story hardly looks worth shooting, let alone dying for." David Ansen of *Newsweek* judged that the segment's "poor quality and moralizing tone make that tragedy doubly obscene."

Spielberg's contribution, which might have seemed innocuous enough in another context, came in for some remarkably vicious attacks, of which J. Hoberman's in *The Village Voice* perhaps was the most extreme: "In terms of pathology, . . . Landis is easily eclipsed by the project's *capo di tutti capi,* Steven Spielberg, whose remake of the 1961 *Zone* episode 'Kick the Can' is a lugubrious self-parody set to a raging torrent of sappy music. . . . Spielberg has become the King Midas of Candyland—from space monsters to senility, everything he touches turns to icky goo."

I N what may have been partly an expression of disgust over the events surrounding the making of *Twilight Zone—The Movie,* as well as a more obvious backlash against the runaway success of *E.T.,* the Academy of Motion Picture Arts and Sciences again snubbed Spielberg in the Oscar competition. Although nominated as Best Director for *E.T.,* Spielberg lost to Richard Attenborough, director of *Gandhi.** Attenborough's victory did not come as a surprise, for he earlier won the Directors Guild of America award, traditionally a harbinger of things to come at the Oscars.

At the DGA dinner, Attenborough "went out of his way to embrace me before going up onto the podium to collect the award," Spielberg recalled in 1994. "That meant a great deal to me then, as it does now." Attenborough

---

* *E.T.* won four Oscars, for Best Music, Sound, Special Visual Effects, and Sound Effects Editing. It also was nominated for Best Picture, Screenplay, Cinematography, and Film Editing.

explained, "I thought *E.T.* was the more exciting, wonderful, innovative piece of film, as against *Gandhi,* which fitted into the David Lean mold in terms not of cinematic execution but of concept and sweep. . . . Steven and I were at opposite sides of the room, and when the winner's name was announced after all the speeches and such, I literally had to be nudged. I couldn't believe it. I got up from the table and it was a sort of knee-jerk actor's reaction. I didn't go to the podium, I went over to Spielberg. He got up, I put my arms round him, and I said, 'This isn't right, this should be yours,' and then I went to collect the award."

Although he regarded Attenborough's gesture as "an honorary Oscar," Spielberg reflected a few hours before the Academy Awards ceremony, "I've been around long enough to know that people who deserve Oscars don't always win them. . . . If the Academy decides to give me an Oscar someday, I'll be glad to accept it. But I don't think I'll get it for a film that I really care about. *E.T.* is my favorite movie, although it's not my best-directed film. That's *Close Encounters of the Third Kind.*"

P ERHAPS it was just a coincidence that Spielberg's next film after *Twilight Zone—The Movie* featured a twelve-year-old Asian boy and dealt with the rescue of a village of lost children. Perhaps the horrifying images that filled *Indiana Jones and the Temple of Doom*—images of enslaved Indian children, people being burned alive by an evil cult, a man's heart being ripped from his chest—were not a reflection of any inner turmoil on the part of the director. Perhaps the film's nightmarish sequence depicting a drugged Indiana Jones as an evil, menacing father figure was nothing but a plot device. Perhaps *Temple of Doom* was just what Spielberg said it was, a "popcorn adventure with a lot of butter."

But the film's unusually gruesome and disturbing imagery, coming in the wake of the *Twilight Zone* tragedy, gives cause to wonder what was going on in Spielberg's subconscious while he made his return to feature-length filmmaking following the event he said made him "sick to the center of his soul." Spielberg himself added the character of Short Round to the story as Harrison Ford's sidekick, casting the Chinese/Vietnamese child actor Ke Huy Quan. "I wanted a kid in this movie," the director explained. ". . . I wanted this mission to come from Indiana's heart."

The film's screenwriters, Gloria Katz and Willard Huyck, insist they did not find Spielberg in a dark mood when they spent five days blocking out the storyline with him and George Lucas at Lucas's home in northern California. Any personal obsessions of Spielberg's that can be found in the movie are "unconscious," Katz feels. As well as recycling unused ideas from the scripts of *Raiders of the Lost Ark* (the escape from the airplane, the mine chase sequence) and Lucas's then-unfilmed project *Radioland Murders* (the opening musical number), *Temple of Doom* borrows liberally from old movies. The idea of the kidnapped children emerged at the story meeting when someone suggested, "What's weird about the village? No children. It's like *Village of the Damned."* The writers attribute the morbidity of *Temple of Doom* to the desire of both Spielberg and Lucas to do "something very different" from the sunlit derring-do of *Raiders.*

"I had some worries about making the same film, only trying to do it better—I didn't want to spin my wheels," Spielberg said. "I had to make this film different enough to make it worth doing, yet similar enough so it would attract the same audience. I had to satisfy myself creatively."

The sequel (on which Lucas gets story credit) originally was titled *Indiana Jones and the Temple of Death,* until it was decided that *Temple of Doom* would sound less of a "downer." "Steve wanted to do a very dark movie," Huyck recalls. "This was going to be his nightmare movie." Publicly, Spielberg attributed that to his producer: "When George Lucas came to me with the story, it was about black magic, voodoo, and a temple of doom. My job and my challenge was to balance the dark side of this Indiana Jones saga with as much comedy as I could afford."

But even the comedy in *Temple of Doom* is the stuff of nightmares, from the early sequence of Indy, Short Round, and Indy's blond girlfriend Willie Scott (Kate Capshaw) plunging in a rubber raft from a pilotless airplane to the squirmy scenes of Willie covered with crawling bugs and being served a revolting dinner of "Eyeball Soup" and "Snake Surprise." Katz considers the movie "boy's adventure time. We didn't see it as being that realistic. We saw it as being sort of funny. We had a lot of fun sitting around thinking of the most disgusting meal you could eat—monkey brains." Forced into the same helpless, bullied position occupied by Spielberg's kid sisters when he was tormenting them in childhood, the audience may giggle uncomfortably at such sights and feel relieved when the ordeals of *Temple of Doom* are over, but it is a strange kind of "fun" Spielberg is inflicting on his paying public. If the imagery of a film serves as a window into the soul of the filmmaker, then what was filling Spielberg's soul in 1983 was (in his words) "torchlight and long shadows and red lava light . . . a lot of spooky, creepy, crawly, nocturnal imagery. . . . I always try to bring my own terrors and fantasies to a film."

If such a thing is possible, *Temple of Doom* could be described as an impersonal personal film. While tapping into Spielberg's subconscious, it does so in the slick, mechanical manner he adopts when he wants to skate lightly over the surface of his material and avoid dealing consciously with its implications. It is Spielberg in his theme park mode, using a plot as merely a springboard for a safe, enjoyable thrill ride, without genuine danger or emotional involvement. After the dazzling panache of the opening in a Shanghai nightclub, a wide-screen homage to Busby Berkeley in which Kate Capshaw sings Cole Porter's "Anything Goes" in Chinese, the film soon degenerates into lurid, melodramatic claptrap, stirring little emotional involvement other than a frequent sense of disgust. While touching on some of Spielberg's personal obsessions, it does only to trivialize them; one need only compare the glibly picturesque treatment of child slavery in *Temple of Doom* with the angry passion that suffuses every frame of the forced-labor camp scenes in *Schindler's List*.

"I wasn't happy with [*Temple of Doom*] at all," Spielberg said in 1989. "It was too dark, too subterranean, and much too horrific. I thought it out-poltered *Poltergeist*. There's not an ounce of my own personal feeling in *Temple of Doom*."

T H E first negative reaction came even before shooting began, when Spielberg and Lucas were refused permission to shoot location scenes in India. Indian government officials, Katz recalls, were offended by the sto-ryline because they "thought it was racist." With its stereotypical Indian villains and its lurid relish in depicting bloodthirsty Thuggee rituals, *Temple of Doom* went far beyond the casual racism of *Raiders of the Lost Ark*, paying mindless homage to the worst aspects of *Gunga Din* and other past examples of Hollywood cultural imperialism. As a result, most of the location work had to be done in Sri Lanka, with matte paintings and miniatures filling in for the village, the temple, and the palace of the boy maharajah. Other location shooting took place on the island of Macao, in Hong Kong, and in northern California, Arizona, Idaho, and Florida, but 80 percent of *Temple of Doom* was shot on soundstages at EMI-Elstree Studios in London.

Principal photography on *Temple of Doom* began in April 1983 and fin-ished a week behind schedule in September, because Harrison Ford had to return to the U.S. for treatment for a previously sustained back injury. Despite budgetary inflation, which made the sequel cost $28 million, almost $8 mil-lion more than the original, Spielberg continued to take pride in his frugal and often ingenious shooting methods. When scenes inside a moving car were shot at Lucas's Industrial Light & Magic (ILM) for a car-chase sequence set in China, it turned out that the background plates filmed earlier in Hong Kong by the second unit had been shot at the wrong angle. Assistant director Louis B. Race recalls that Spielberg "came up with an idea he said he'd used on a film as a kid [*Firelight*]. He'd taken Christmas tree lights and put them on a clothesline and run them through the background. It's what's known as 'poor man's process.' So at ILM we built a tubular metal lazy Susan and put the car in front of it. We hung pieces of cardboard cutout for the window. We had beer signs in the background modified to look Chinese, and we spun the lights around on the lazy Susan behind the window. The location man-ager, Dick Vane, turned to me and said, 'You ever get the feeling that you're making films in somebody's garage?' "

With the *Twilight Zone* crash fresh in his mind and a child actor involved in many of the action sequences, filming most of the film in controlled studio conditions made Spielberg feel more confident about safety concerns. Discussing the underground-mine chase sequence in an interview with *American Cinematographer,* Spielberg stressed that he had achieved its sense of danger and speed through various forms of cinematic illusion.

"What we actually did," he said, "was build a roller-coaster ride on the soundstage. And it really worked. It was safe. It was electrically driven. You could take rides in it." Some of the shots involved miniature mine cars with puppets standing in for the actors. "Movies are unharnessed dreams," Spielberg reflected, "but if they become too costly, or if danger is a factor, or it will take ten years to get there, you have to pull back on the tack and compromise your dream."

W H E N *Temple of Doom* was screened internally, "Everybody was appalled" by its violence, screenwriter Gloria Katz recalls. "Everybody was saying, 'Steve, let's take it down,' " adds Willard Huyck. "At such a late point, it was very difficult to make changes. There were some changes having to do with the intensity of the violence."

Ever since the institution of the Motion Picture Association of America rating system in 1968, there had been controversy over the MPAA's lenience toward violence in films, particularly in those released by major studios. *Jaws* and *Poltergeist,* which received PG ratings, often were cited as examples of films that were too violent for young children. "I don't make R movies! I make PG movies!" Spielberg declared while making a successful personal plea to the MPAA's Classification & Rating Appeals Board in May 1982 to overturn the R rating originally assigned to *Poltergeist*. Despite the opposition of the MPAA toward changing the system, there was increasing support in the industry for an intermediate rating between PG (parental guidance) and R (restricted for children unless they attend with a parent or an adult guardian).

"I've been advocating a fifth rating for a long time, along with many other filmmakers and studio executives," a more subdued Spielberg said in 1984. "But we just don't have the strength to get it through. . . . The responsibility to the children of this country is worth any loss at the box office." When *Temple of Doom* and *Gremlins* received PG ratings around the same time, both movies became battlegrounds in the debate about cinematic violence, all the more so because of their commercial success. In another rash of bad publicity, Spielberg came in for some harshly personal attacks in the press.

Part of the outcry against *Gremlins* was the false expectation, encouraged by the advertising campaign, that the movie was another feel-good children's fantasy like *E.T.* The most notorious scene in *Gremlins* shows a housewife chopping up gremlins in a blender and exploding them in a microwave oven. Joe Dante remembers getting "vitriolic" letters from people whose "big worry was that somebody was going to put his little brother or his poodle in the microwave. I think people are smarter than that. It didn't happen." But before the film's release, Spielberg persuaded the director to tone down some of the bloodier scenes of humans attacking gremlins, telling him, "I don't know if they've done anything bad enough to deserve this."

Spielberg also publicly admitted that he would be inclined to put his own hand over the eyes of a ten-year-old child during the lengthy passage in

Temple of Doom depicting torture and human sacrifice. *Temple of Doom* was denounced by *People* magazine film critic Ralph Novak as "an astonishing violation of the trust" audiences placed in Spielberg and Lucas as makers of family entertainment. "The ads that say 'this film may be too intense for younger children' are fraudulent," Novak complained. "No parent should allow a young child to see this traumatizing movie; it would be a cinematic form of child abuse. Even Ford is required to slap Quan and abuse Capshaw. But then there are no heroes connected with this film, only two villains; their names are Spielberg and Lucas."

It can be argued, on the other hand, that subteens are the natural audience for the outlandish violence and gore of *Temple of Doom,* just as they were for the horror comics that provoked such overwrought outrage in the 1950s. Spielberg often is mistakenly accused of having an overly sunny view of life, but the phobias he has wrestled with since childhood have deeply affected his work. Whether children are traumatized by nightmarish imagery when it is presented in an unrealistic context or whether they find it cathartic in helping them deal with their own fears, as they do with the gruesome violence in fairy tales, is a matter on which child psychologists sharply disagree.

In *The Uses of Enchantment,* his 1976 book on the psychological implications of children's fairy tales, Bruno Bettelheim observed that "the dominant culture wishes to pretend, particularly where children are concerned, that the dark side of man does not exist. . . . [and] the prevalent parental belief is that a child must be diverted from what troubles him most: his formless, nameless anxieties, and his chaotic, angry, and even violent fantasies. Many parents believe that only conscious reality or pleasant and wish-fulfilling images should be presented to the child—that he should be exposed only to the sunny side of things. But such one-sided fare nourishes the mind in a one-sided way, and real life is not all sunny."

The uproar resulting from *Temple of Doom* and *Gremlins* led in short order to the MPAA's creation of the PG-13 rating, which cautions parents that "some material may be inappropriate for children under 13." The PG-13 rating has helped filmmakers avoid the stark editing choices previously dictated by the lack of an intermediate rating between PG and R, and it has helped ease some of the pressure on Hollywood from groups calling for greater censorship of sex and violence on screen.

M A K I N G *Indiana Jones and the Temple of Doom* may have been a cathartic experience for Spielberg personally. Although he paid a price in public opprobrium for making such a grisly film, it may have helped him deal with the living nightmare of *Twilight Zone—The Movie.*

Like so many other irresponsible father figures in Spielberg's work, Indiana Jones in *Temple of Doom* must exorcise his adult weaknesses and undergo a purifying test of character in order to be worthy of his fatherly responsibilities. Before he can rescue the lost children, Indy must be freed from his murderous trance, brought on by the forced drinking of blood during the ritual of human sacrifice. "Tempted by the violent cruelty of adulthood, Indiana is called back to childhood's innocence by his surrogate son [Short Round]," observed critic Henry Sheehan in *Film Comment*. What is crucial for Indy "is that he abandon the corrupt world of adults and once again affirm his essential child-ness. The film even closes with a shot of Indiana and Willie—happy, it seems, at being a mom—being engulfed by a tide of laughing children."

At age thirty-seven, Steven Spielberg finally was ready to become a father.

" A D U L T   T R U T H S "

BEFORE I HAD MAX, I MADE FILMS ABOUT KIDS; NOW THAT I HAVE ONE, I'LL PROBABLY START MAKING FILMS ABOUT ADULTS.

— S TEVEN S PIELBERG, 1 9 8 5

E S C R I B I N G   the kind of woman he liked to cast in his movies, Spielberg once said, "Maybe I've been searching for the ultimate *shiksa.*"* He found her when Kate Capshaw walked into his office to read for *Indiana Jones and the Temple of Doom*. He was captivated with Kate's finely sculpted model's features, lissome figure, and midwestern emotional bluntness. She resembled a corn-fed, all-American, more innocent-seeming version of Julie Christie. Though not a natural blonde, Kate was willing to dye her brown tresses to conform to Spielberg's fantasy image of a *shiksa* heroine. Sending her audition tape to *Temple of Doom* screenwriters Gloria Katz and Willard Huyck, he said, "I really liked this girl Kate. Could you say something good about her to George?"

Spielberg may not have recognized the element of calculation behind his future wife's wholesome facade. "I read an article [about him] when *E.T.* came out," she recalled in 1996. "I knew that I had a love connection." When she went for her audition, she "wasn't that interested in getting the job. I still

---

* In *The Joys of Yiddish*, Leo Rosten defines a *shiksa* as "A non-Jewish woman, especially a young one. . . . Pronounced SHIK-*seh,* to rhyme with 'pick the.' "

had those young notions of being an artist, doing only the sorts of movies that Meryl Streep would do. I couldn't imagine *her* doing a sequel to *Raiders of the Lost Ark."* As a result, she concentrated her entire attention on Spielberg himself.

Entering his office at Warner Bros., she was told to sit facing him, but sidled alongside and turned on the charm. "The minute I met him," she recalled, "I sensed he was a sweet, shy guy who was kind of wondering, 'How did I get here?' I love that in men, that shyness and humility." She was careful not to gush over his movies, as most young actresses would have done in that situation. As she left, he told her, "Thanks for not saying anything about *E.T."* On their next meeting, he offered an unmistakable sign of his affection, inviting her to play a video game.

Kate had "an immediate, full-throttle reaction" to meeting Spielberg. "I went home and I said, 'I think I'm in really big trouble here.' " Although she has not disguised the fact that she campaigned fiercely to marry him, Capshaw portrayed her romantic attraction to Spielberg as instinctive, if somewhat maternal: "What attracted me was the way he smelled. Like babies when they are born, like he was mine. They say if you blindfold a mom and present her with twenty babies, she'll be able to pick hers out because of the smell. It was like that."

B O R N Kathy Sue Nail in Fort Worth, Texas, in 1953, Kate Capshaw was raised in the St. Louis suburb of Florissant, the daughter of a beautician and an airline operations manager. Her family was Methodist, middle-class, and Middle-American to its core. "My parents were the first generation to leave the farm," she said in 1984. "I looked very WASPy, but I wanted to look ethnic. I wanted to be a Jewish intellectual. I also wanted to be an actress, but I didn't know to study to be one. 'What can I do in Missouri?' I asked myself. . . . Teaching was a very socially acceptable, respectable position, so I became a teacher." Earning a master's degree in learning disabilities at the University of Missouri, she spent two years teaching in a rural Missouri school district but was "not really very happy with what I was doing. It was what everyone else thought I should do, not what *I* thought I should do."

Kate married her college sweetheart, Robert Capshaw, who became a high school principal. They had a daughter, Jessica, in 1977. Bob accompanied Kate to New York so she could pursue her dream of becoming a professional actress, but the marriage soon became a casualty of her ambition. She raised her daughter while modeling, appearing in TV commercials, and acting in soap operas. Her movie debut as the girlfriend of womanizer Tim Matheson in *A Little Sex* (1982) led to her casting in another box-office dud, *Windy City* (1984), written and directed by Armyan Bernstein. Capshaw was living in Los Angeles with Bernstein when she was cast in *Temple of Doom.*

Willie Scott, her character in Spielberg's film, proved to be a dreary role—

in Kate's own words, "not much more than a dumb, screaming blonde." A spoiled nightclub singer, Willie looks ravishing in the slinky red dress she wears in the opening scene, but becomes bedraggled and whiny while tagging along on Indy's adventures. Spielberg's adolescent relish in putting Indy's girlfriends through physical ordeals made the filming a trying experience for Kate, who reluctantly allowed bugs to meander over her body but drew the line at taking a bath with a fourteen-foot boa constrictor. "I felt that some days all I did was shriek, and it was exhausting," she admitted. "It wasn't hard to play Willie Scott, who is always bitching about things, because it *was* hot, the bugs *were* disgusting, and the elephant was a pain in the butt." Seeing how gleefully Spielberg tortures, mocks, and humiliates her character, one wonders whether he was expressing the kind of ambivalence insecure adolescent boys feel in the presence of the prettiest girl in school. Coming at such a vulnerable time in his life, Spielberg's attraction to the dazzling, aggressive *shiksa* may have shaken him emotionally and found perverse expression in juvenile teasing and hostility.

The film's blatant sexism deprived Capshaw of even the tomboy gutsiness Karen Allen was allowed to display in *Raiders*. Rather than blaming the writers and the director for creating and molding the character, reviewers were merciless toward Capshaw for playing what Gene Siskel called a "whining deadhead. . . . When we see Willie dangling over molten lava, frankly, we wish she would fall in." Capshaw was so upset by the hostility of the press that she cut short her publicity tour for the movie: "I was getting absolutely killed, and finally said, Relax, will you? You're wasting your breath on a B movie. It's an adventure, it's popcorn, it's for Saturday afternoon."*

She initially had "difficulty understanding Steven" because she was not a movie buff. "He talks in movie language, you see. He'd say, 'Remember that scene in *It Happened One Night*—the one where Claudette Colbert did such-and-such? That's what I want here.' And I'd say, 'Steven, I never saw that movie.' And he'd groan and reply, 'Kate, how can I possibly communicate with you?' " Still, she found him so personally agreeable to work with that she could later say, "I fell in love with him watching him direct a movie."

Their early relationship, however, amounted to little more than what she called a "flirtation." Determined on something more serious, she was pained that Spielberg did not reciprocate her feelings: "I felt, this is a man who must get everything he wants. What if I'm just one more flavor of ice cream? I knew if I became involved with him he wouldn't take my feelings as seriously as they needed to be taken care of. I also felt there was something unfinished with Amy. And I knew who would lose in that one."

· · ·

---

* She did not make another film for Spielberg until his 1995 production of *How to Make an American Quilt*, directed by Jocelyn Moorhouse.

A M Y was playing an Indian princess in the cable TV miniseries *The Far Pavilions* when she learned that Spielberg was en route to India to scout locations for *Temple of Doom*. As his plane touched down at the airport, she was there to surprise him with a reunion. "We saw each other across the runway," she recalled, "and by the time we came together, I *knew*." Spielberg remembered it somewhat differently: "Love in her eyes, and anger and resentment in mine. But we fell in love again."

Following their breakup in 1979, Amy had found her elusive professional identity on the New York stage, giving well-received performances in such plays as *Amadeus* and *Heartbreak House*. She received an Oscar nomination for her supporting role in Barbra Streisand's 1983 musical version of Isaac Bashevis Singer's *Yentl*, playing Hadass, the softly feminine young woman who marries Streisand's cross-dressing title character. Although Amy's father was Jewish, she had been raised by her mother as a Christian Scientist, so Streisand had to give her books about Judaism to study as background for playing a traditional Jewish wife.

Streisand herself was rumored in the press to have been romantically involved with Spielberg in the early 1980s. Streisand "pitched *Yentl* to him" in 1979, Amy recalled, and while editing the film, Streisand showed him some assembled footage. He told her, "Don't change a frame." But when it was reported that he was giving her advice about the editing, Streisand took umbrage: "That's like saying this woman, this actress, could not make the movie without the help of a man. . . . Do you know how repulsive that is to me? I hate it. It's like they're already taking my film away from me!" After seeing the completed film, Spielberg told her, "This is the greatest directorial debut since *Citizen Kane*."

Amy, with acclaimed film and stage performances in her résumé and a career full of promise ahead of her, began to lose the "chip on my shoulder" about being considered "the little girlfriend that Steven brought along. I've earned my wings." That self-confidence made her less obsessed with her career and enabled her to reestablish a romantic relationship with Spielberg, with whom she had remained on friendly terms. His bond with Amy was strong enough to survive their painful breakup and their subsequent relationships with other people. He also had begun to show greater interest in her work, often going east to watch her onstage.

After Kate Capshaw appeared in *Temple of Doom*, she was cast in *Best Defense*, a comedy directed by Willard Huyck and produced by Gloria Katz. "Steven and Kate got into an enormous fight," Katz recalls. "They were not speaking. Amy had come back into his life." Kate was in a studio relooping lines for *Best Defense* while Steven was on an adjoining stage mixing *Temple of Doom*. Informed by the Huycks that Steven was next door, Kate replied, "I don't want to talk to him. He's so immature."

On Amy's thirty-first birthday, September 10, 1984, she and Steven celebrated with a dinner by candlelight. It was on that night that Amy became pregnant. "This pregnancy," she said, "is something Steven and I have wanted for a long time."

Steven was so delighted at the prospect of fatherhood that he became upset when Amy picked out maternity clothes without him. When she reported hearing their child's heartbeat for the first time in her doctor's office, Steven insisted on taking her back to the doctor so he could have the same experience. "When the baby comes," Amy said only half-jokingly, "Steven will have somebody to share his toys with." He even started cutting back a bit on his work schedule to be closer to his new family. But Amy and Steven saw no reason to get married before their child was born. "We're so married in our hearts," said Amy, "it seems *redundant* to think of a wedding now." Steven did, however, sign an agreement formally assuming all the rights and responsibilities of fatherhood.

"For the first time in my life," he said of Amy, "I'm committed to another person." But he admitted that commitment was difficult for him, "since I have a tendency to dramatize real life. . . . I often want to direct reality, to direct the scene, to say, 'Stay in your frame. I'll deal with it, but stay there.' When I commit to a movie, it's like . . . marriage. I'm hoping it's the same in real life."

Steven and Amy were married on November 27, 1985, at a private ceremony before Judge Thomas A. Donnelly at the courthouse in Santa Fe, New Mexico. By then their son, Max, was five months old. "We got married like the characters in a Frank Capra film, before a wise old judge," Steven said. He had proposed to Amy while "sitting in a bubble bath. Max was crawling on the floor. Amy had stuff on her face. It wasn't very romantic. . . . I knew she'd say yes because she'd already asked me to marry her seven or eight times."

I N 1984, the year he formed Amblin Entertainment with Frank Marshall and Kathleen Kennedy, Spielberg moved from his offices at Warner Bros. into lavish new headquarters on a quiet corner of the Universal back lot.

In a move Sid Sheinberg engineered to keep Spielberg underfoot, the studio absorbed the entire $3.5 million cost of building him a Santa Fe–style adobe office compound, later adding a postproduction annex across the road. "There are very few things Steven could ask of us that he would not get," said Sheinberg. Sheinberg had earlier offered him the more modest-sized bungalow long occupied by the late Alfred Hitchcock, but Spielberg rejected the idea as "sacrilegious." Spielberg did not even have to sign an exclusive production agreement with Universal to receive the extraordinary largesse of his own office complex. Determined not to be bound to any one company, he insisted on remaining in frequent business with Warner Bros. and its chairman, Steve Ross, whom he came to regard as a second father.

Spielberg's headquarters was officially known as Bungalow 477, although the entranceway sported the new Amblin logo, the image from *E.T.* of a boy flying a bicycle past the moon. The compound included a forty-five-seat screening room, two cutting rooms, a video arcade, a kitchen with a professional chef, a gym, an outdoor spa, gardens, and a wishing well with a miniature *Jaws* shark. Spielberg decorated the offices with his favorite movie posters and Norman Rockwell paintings, as well as Indian blankets, rugs, and pottery. While the southwestern ambience of Spielberg's "home away from home" served as a comforting reminder of his boyhood roots in Arizona, and, for Amy, of her home in New Mexico, Hollywood wags quickly began referring to the hideaway as Spielberg's "Taco Bell."

Writer Richard Christian Matheson* recalls a bizarre experience when he visited the high-tech, high-security Amblin complex with a screenwriting partner in 1987. As they strolled through the gardens with Spielberg, discussing film and TV projects, "Every once in a while, from a rock or a tree, you'd hear, 'Steven, your two-thirty is here.' Obviously there were microphones among the rocks that talk, because you'd hear a voice saying, 'Steven, do you want something?' He'd say, 'Guys, do you want some Popsicles?' And then he would say to nobody, 'Bring us three root-beer Popsicles.' The whole place was obviously tracking his whereabouts."

The palatial Pacific Palisades estate Steven and Amy bought in early 1985 from singer Bobby Vinton—situated on an isolated hilltop overlooking Malibu and bordering on Will Rogers State Park—was similarly redecorated in the southwestern style. "The only difference between redoing the house and making a film is that I paid for it," quipped Spielberg, who added, "The history of the house attracted me instinctively. It was important for me to know that David Selznick had lived there during the time he produced *Gone With the Wind.*"† The remodeled house had more than its share of idiosyncratic Spielbergian touches, including "the Hobbit room," a family room with a retractable television set and mushroom-shaped fireplace and windows. "Hobbits were part of my personal mythology growing up," said Spielberg. "I wanted to have the TV room, where I spend most of my life, to have a Hobbit feel."

With the turmoil of recent years subsided, Spielberg was happy to be a homebody, boasting of his very un-Hollywood squareness: "I don't live on the French Riviera with seven women feeding me while I sit in the sun with a reflector under my chin. I'm proud that I go home at night and watch TV until I fall asleep, and then wake up the next morning to go to work."

M A X Samuel Spielberg was born on June 13, 1985, at Santa Monica Hospital. The exultant father described Max as "my best production yet."

---

* The son of Richard B. Matheson, the author of *Duel*.

† Other owners of the home, which Spielberg still occupies, had included Cary Grant and Barbara Hutton, and Douglas Fairbanks Jr.

The baby's middle name was chosen in honor of Steven's grandfather. Amy said they had no particular reason for choosing the name Max, a popular name with baby boomer parents in the 1980s. But it was a fitting (if unintended) reminiscence of Max Chase, the Spielberg relative who gave Arnold Spielberg his first movie camera.

During her pregnancy, Amy played one of the two women Dudley Moore impregnates in Blake Edwards's farce *Micki and Maude*. Since she was nearing delivery when Spielberg's film version of Alice Walker's *The Color Purple* began shooting, he arranged to film the studio interiors at Universal before the company departed for the location site near Monroe, North Carolina. "We had to wait for Max to arrive," recalled the film's cinematographer, Allen Daviau, "and we want to thank him—he showed up on schedule, bless him." The timing of Max's arrival was uncanny, for Spielberg was shooting the childbirth scene on June 12 when Amy "called Steven on the set to let him know I was in labor. He ran to the phone from the middle of filming a dramatic childbirth, and I told him very calmly, 'Honey, now come and direct my delivery.' "

The baby's cries in the film were those of Max Spielberg, recorded by his father at home one night while Max was taking a bath.

W H A T was a white male director doing making a movie of *The Color Purple?* What, of all people, was Steven Spielberg doing making *The Color Purple?*

Those questions were asked by many people when Spielberg filmed Walker's passionately feminist novel about a black woman in the Deep South of the early 1900s. Celie Johnson—played as an adolescent by Desreta Jackson and as an adult by Whoopi Goldberg, in her film debut—suffers decades of abuse, first from her incestuous stepfather and later from the violent, chauvinistic husband she calls simply "Mister." Although he came to respect "the genuine sweetness of Spielberg's regard for his characters," *Newsweek* reviewer David Ansen initially considered the conjunction of director and material "as improbable as, say, Antonioni directing a James Bond movie. . . . Early on I had the disorienting sensation that I was watching the first Disney movie about incest."

Many people assumed Spielberg could only have made *The Color Purple* in a calculated and cynical attempt to win an Academy Award. There was no doubt he was impatient with the widespread perception of his work as juvenile escapism, and that he was seeking greater respect by making an "adult" film from a Pulitzer Prize–winning novel dealing with the kinds of themes that often impress Academy voters. The director spoke frankly of wanting "to challenge myself with something that was not stereotypically a Spielberg movie. Not to try to prove anything, or to show off—but just to try to use a different set of muscles." The lingering shadow of the *Twilight Zone* court case, which was in the headlines throughout this period, also may have played a role in Spielberg's need for greater respect from the Hollywood community.

But there was something profoundly cynical in his critics' suggestion that winning an Oscar was all that motivated Spielberg to make *The Color Purple*. That argument assumed a white director could not *really* be interested in a story about black characters without having some kind of ulterior motive. To Peter Rainer of the *Los Angeles Herald-Examiner,* the movie was "ostensibly about the ordeal of being black and poor* and a woman in the South in the first half of this century. But the movie is really about winning awards." Sneered *Time*'s Richard Corliss: "[F]rom the geriatric elite of Hollywood, Spielberg got no respect—no Oscars, that is. So here comes Steven the Nice, with his first 'respectable' motion picture." Hollywood wags referred to the movie as Spielberg's *Close Encounters with the Third World*.

Because of Spielberg's habitual reticence on the subject of his Jewish heritage and his experiences with anti-Semitism—a subject he did not discuss publicly with complete candor until he made *Schindler's List*—few people seemed to realize how personally he empathized with the plight of Walker's abused heroine. "Someone someday will write a Spielberg psychobiography which will tackle the particular significance this project has for him," J. Hoberman wrote in his largely negative *Village Voice* review. While recognizing that Spielberg's decision to make *The Color Purple* stemmed from his long-standing concern with "the healing of wounded families" and the celebration of "a kind of ambiguous matriarchy," Hoberman speculated that the film was "Spielberg's apology for the rampant white male supremacism of *Indiana Jones and the Temple of Doom.*"

Celie's determination to survive the twin burdens of racism and sexism made her kin to Spielberg because it touched a secret place in his heart that had never healed. "Spielberg shares the torment with us," said Quincy Jones, the black composer who was one of the producers of *The Color Purple*. "He cares. . . . He cares about fighting prejudice." As a high school senior living through his own "Hell on Earth" of ethnic prejudice, Spielberg had shown a passionate interest in the civil rights movement. His instinctive feelings of solidarity with members of another oppressed ethnic group, like those of many other Jews who supported the civil rights movement in that era, bore out the observation of Spielberg's 1960s icon Lenny Bruce: "Negroes are all Jews." Spielberg dates his acceptance of his Jewish heritage to the birth of his son, and that event's occurrence during the filming of Celie's

---

* This is a fundamental misunderstanding of the story. As the film's cinematographer, Allen Daviau, noted in a 1991 interview, "Alice Walker made it very clear in her depiction of Mister and his family, his house and so on, that this was *not* a poor black man, this was a well-to-do, middle-class to upper-middle-class, landowning black family. This was to be extremely apparent in the house itself, the way the house was furnished, the tableware, the linen. These people shopped in Atlanta. She was very specific about this, and said, 'I don't want it misinterpreted. These people were well off. They had money.' The instructions were followed to show it this way, and Steven was *personally attacked* because he 'failed to depict the poverty.' "

childbirth scene intensified Spielberg's emotional identification with her character.

Some journalists writing about *The Color Purple* questioned Spielberg's sincerity by claiming that his previous work had not shown much interest in African Americans. But *The Color Purple* was not the first time Spielberg had told a story with a black protagonist, even if the two earlier instances were minor efforts. His 1970 *Night Gallery* segment "Make Me Laugh" starred Godfrey Cambridge as an unhappy nightclub comedian, and his "Kick the Can" segment of *Twilight Zone—The Movie* featured Scatman Crothers as the elderly miracle worker. And after seeing *E.T.*, Alice Walker observed, "From the very beginning of the film, I recognized E.T. as a Being of Color."

It was Kathleen Kennedy who brought *The Color Purple* to Spielberg's attention, telling him, "Here's something you might enjoy reading." One of the few people in whom he had confided about his persecution as a youth in Saratoga, Kennedy recognized that Spielberg and *The Color Purple* might make a good emotional match, however unlikely it may have seemed on the surface. "You know, it's a black story," she told him. "But that shouldn't bother you, because you're Jewish and essentially you share similarities in your upbringing and your heritage." Kennedy also understood his yearnings to expand his artistic horizons. "I always believed he would feel confident at some point to do other things," she recalled in 1993. "That's why I brought him *The Color Purple.* After he read it, he said, 'I love this, because I'm scared to do it.'"

Even after he agreed to become involved with the Warner Bros. project under his Amblin Entertainment banner, Spielberg kept it gingerly at arm's length for a while. "I didn't really think I was going to direct the movie until much later, into the development of the second-draft screenplay. To me it was a wonderful diversion from all the Saturday matinee kidflicks I was executive producing [including the 1985 releases *The Goonies, Back to the Future,* and *Young Sherlock Holmes*]. . . . With open arms and great hosannas I would sit with Menno Meyjes, the writer [of the *Color Purple* screenplay], and we'd spend a lot of time dealing with adult truths. Then we'd finish something and I'd go back and put on my waders and go into five feet of water on the *Goonies* set and shoot an insert for [director] Dick Donner." While on location for *The Color Purple,* Spielberg said the principal reason he took so long to commit to directing it was that he was accustomed to making "big movies. Movies about out there. I didn't know if the time was right to do a movie about in here [tapping his chest]."

Another reason he hesitated was that he anticipated the kneejerk reaction many critics would have to his involvement in the project. "I don't know that I'm the filmmaker for this," he told Quincy Jones. "Don't you want to find a black director or a woman?" Jones replied, "You didn't have to come from Mars to do *E.T.*, did you?"

• • •

B E F O R E the cameras could roll, Spielberg had to pass an interview with Alice Walker. It was the first time in eleven years that he found himself in the position of being interviewed for a job.

The author had misgivings about letting Hollywood film her epistolary novel, written largely in a southern black-English idiom of the period. Hollywood's record of dealing with African Americans generally had been dismal, and the book presented minefields for any moviemaker with its stylistic audacity, its fiercely feminist themes, and its explicit treatment of incest, domestic violence, and lesbianism. Her respect for Jones helped overcome her qualms, but when Spielberg was proposed as director, she at first did not recognize his name. Later, however, she would recall having seen part of *The Sugarland Express,* whose "passionate intensity and sense of caring" made her realize he had an affinity for *The Color Purple*.

Following his visit to her home in San Francisco with Jones on February 20, 1984, Walker wrote in her journal, "Quincy had talked so positively about him I was almost dreading his appearance—but then, after a moment of near I don't know what, uneasiness, he came in and sat down and started right in showing how closely he had read the book. And making really intelligent comments." Spielberg's "absolute grasp of the essentials of the book, the feeling, the spirit," was what convinced her to trust him with the project.

Walker sensed that Spielberg, for all his worldly success, remained a minority person. She recognized that his sensitivity enabled him to share the feelings of characters of another race and another gender. For a filmmaker whose own feelings about the pain of childhood were still raw, it was no emotional stretch to empathize with Celie's suffering at the hands of her father and her tyrannical husband. "I saw Alice Walker's book as a Dickens piece," said Spielberg, whose idea it was to have Celie reading *Oliver Twist*. As a child of a broken family, Spielberg empathized instinctively with Celie's pain at being forcibly separated from her sister and her two children. Nor was it difficult for Spielberg, who knew what it was like to be physically mistreated by bigots, to enter into the agony of Sofia (Oprah Winfrey), the strong, defiant black woman who loses her children by refusing to submit to white racist authority. Perhaps with his difficult relationship with his own father in mind, Spielberg also heightened the story's emphasis on the estrangement of blues singer Shug Avery (played by actress Margaret Avery) from her father, a puritanical Baptist preacher. As Susan Dworkin reported in her *Ms.* magazine article about the film, Walker "saw that these women and their breaking hearts and soaring spirits did not feel strange to Spielberg."

On the other hand, it proved even harder for Spielberg than it had for Walker to get inside the skin of Mister (Danny Glover), that embodiment of patriarchal insensitivity whose two-dimensionality on screen evoked a firestorm of protest. Spielberg's visceral revulsion toward bullies left him little room for understanding how someone becomes a bully, particularly someone from such a vastly different social background. When Mister finally redeems himself, Spielberg musters up far less sympathy and forgiveness than the novelist feels for the character, whom she based on her own grandfather. Spielberg cannot help keeping the repentant Mister at a wary distance, treating him as a solitary and pathetic figure bereft of the mature companionship he shared with Celie in the latter parts of the book.

Ironically, the white male director's reworking of Walker's novel sees the relationship between Celie and Mister from a viewpoint that is even *more* onesidedly feminist. But as the novelist pointedly observed, people who most vehemently objected to the characterization of Mister often displayed a selective sense of outrage: "[W]hen *The Color Purple* was published, and later filmed, it was a rare critic who showed any compassion for, or even noted, the suffering of the women and children explored in the book, while I was called a liar [as was Spielberg] for showing that black men sometimes perpetuate domestic violence."

Walker exercised an unusual degree of influence over the filming of her book. She consulted on the casting and had a clause inserted in her contract providing that half the crew members would be "women or blacks or Third World people." Using photographs of her grandparents' home to indicate how Mister's home should look, she convinced production designer J. Michael Riva that not all southern blacks lived in abject poverty during the early 1900s. Riva admitted that "to do justice to this film, I had to confront my own prejudices." Walker also wrote her own screenplay, which was rejected in favor of one written by Menno Meyjes, a Dutch immigrant who had impressed Spielberg with his script about the Children's Crusade, *Lionheart*.* The author was present for much of the production, working closely with Meyjes and the cast to ensure that the dialogue sounded true to the period and did not violate the spirit of the book.

There were moments of anxiety for Walker when she questioned the depth of Spielberg's understanding of racial issues. One such occasion was the day "Steven referred to *Gone With the Wind* as 'the greatest movie ever made' and said his favorite character was Prissy [the childlike slave played by Butterfly McQueen]. . . . I slept little for several nights after his comment, as I thought of all I would have to relay to him, busy as he was directing our film, to make him understand what a nightmare *Gone With the Wind* was to me." Spielberg's naïveté about some aspects of the black American experience also showed through in a poignant moment of mutual misunderstanding. At a preproduction meeting, Spielberg and his colleagues were discussing how they could make cameo appearances in the movie (the director eventually dubbed in the forlorn whistling of Willard Pugh's Harpo when

---

* Walker vetoed Spielberg's choice of Melissa Mathison as screenwriter, finding no "chemistry" with her. The author's own adaptation, which dealt far more explicitly than the film with the sexual nature of Celie's love for Shug Avery, was published in her 1996 book about her experiences with the filming, *The Same River Twice: Honoring the Difficult*.

his wife, Sofia, leaves him). In what he undoubtedly intended as a heartfelt gesture of solidarity, Spielberg asked the novelist if she would appear in a scene holding his infant son, Max.

"I was upset by your question, because of course I could not," Walker wrote Spielberg in 1989. "There is just too much history for that to have been possible. It's a very long Southern/South African tradition, after all—black women holding white babies. And yet, I felt so sad for us all, that this should be so. And especially moved by you, who had this history as no part of your consciousness."

F o r the first day of shooting, Spielberg scheduled the scene of Shug Avery serenading Celie in Harpo's rowdy "jook joint." In a happy confluence of milestones, this also was Whoopi Goldberg's first day before a movie camera, and her shy, elated look of surprise represents the beginning of her character's sensual awakening.

As the scene was described by cinematographer Allen Daviau, "We have this tiny, scared woman, who has barely been off her farm in over a decade, yet there she is in a nightclub, a 'jook joint,' seeing a life she didn't know existed, as a churchgoing woman of that time. Here she was, almost hiding, in this marvelous old hat that Aggie Rodgers, the costume designer, gave her, as all the action of the 'jook joint' happens around her." With Celie's face softly caressed by a tiny light hidden on the table, but seemingly by the glow from a kerosene lantern, "This shot is when we first realized the magic of Whoopi Goldberg's eyes," Daviau recalled. "It was one of those wonderful moments when you're working on a movie and you realize something special is really happening. You feel that you've just seen a character *live* on screen and you really know where the movie is going.

"Even though it might've been done for logistical reasons, it was a stroke of real genius by Steven to choose to start in the 'jook joint.' I think he knew in his heart that a lot of things would come together in this scene. It was one of those magic decisions that sets the tone for the film in all aspects."

The performance Spielberg evoked from Goldberg has few, if any, equals in the director's body of work. Perhaps only Ben Kingsley's Itzhak Stern in *Schindler's List* has a similar degree of richness and complexity, expressed with such eloquent economy of gesture and intonation. But while Kingsley's Stern is ever a man of infinite subtlety and shrewdness, Celie's character is formed before our eyes, year by year, look by look, word by word. She begins as a helpless girl of seemingly artless simplicity, only gradually acquiring the fiercely self-protective survival skills that, in the end, give her a transcendent strength and wisdom.

Goldberg came to Spielberg's attention with her acclaimed one-woman show, in which she played several offbeat characters. The comedienne (whose real name is Caryn Johnson) read *The Color Purple* and, like many other female readers of the book, felt a personal emotional connection with it. She wrote Alice Walker asking to play Sofia in the movie, adding that just to be part of it, she would be willing to "play a venetian blind, if necessary." Walker caught Goldberg's show in San Francisco and recommended her to Spielberg for the part of Celie.

Spielberg asked Goldberg if she would perform her act for him and "a couple of friends." She was stunned to find Spielberg's screening room filled with people, including Walker, Quincy Jones, Michael Jackson, and Lionel Richie. She cheekily included in that performance "a piece I'd been asked not to do by other people": a parody of *E.T.* in which the alien winds up on dope in an Oakland jail. Although Spielberg later expressed outrage when the *Los Angeles Times* pictured E.T. wearing a coke spoon, he "loved" her privately performed parody, Goldberg reported. He asked her to play Celie, but she wanted to play Sofia, a character she felt "had more spirit, more heart. . . . And then I realized that Steven Spielberg's sitting there trying to convince me to be in his movie. And it was like, 'Wake up, stupid. Say *yes.*' "

During rehearsals, Spielberg felt Goldberg "didn't interact with the other cast members very well—she was intimidated by the professionalism of Danny Glover and the spontaneity of Oprah Winfrey. I got very worried about her because she wasn't part of that cast. Then once she got on the set she essentially gave herself over to me, and just said, 'Listen, you're going to have to help me because I don't know what the hell I'm doing!' That performance came out of her soul."

Spielberg patiently taught her the basic lesson of movie acting, which is to work from within, letting the camera observe the character's thought processes rather than projecting the character as one would do on the stage. "In that camera are a million people," Spielberg told her. "They can see everything you do."

"The cat just gave me all kinds of faith," Goldberg recalled. "Plus, we had a lingo because he's a movie fanatic like me. He would say something like, 'Okay, Whoopi, do Boo Radley right after the door opens in *To Kill a Mockingbird.*' Or he'd say, 'You know the scene where Indiana Jones finally finds the girl at the end? That kind of relief he has? That's what I want.' . . . When I had a terribly wrenching scene with Danny Glover, he'd say, 'OK, it's *Gaslight* time,' and I'd crack up."

Oprah Winfrey, who at the time was the host of a local TV talk-show, *AM Chicago,* also made a spectacular film debut in *The Color Purple.* The role of Sofia introduced her to the nationwide audience that soon would make her a TV superstar. Winfrey was cast in the film after Quincy Jones, on a visit to Chicago, saw her on his hotel TV. Immediately recognizing her similarity to the stout, outspoken, defiantly self-respecting Sofia, he suggested her to Spielberg.

"Terrified" to be acting in her first film, Winfrey also felt intimidated by the director. When she had difficulty crying on her first day of shooting, she thought, "I'm gonna go down in history as the actress who couldn't cry in a Spielberg movie." Spielberg "didn't seem upset but said we'd get it another day. I left the set and cried all afternoon because I couldn't cry for him." With some pointers from veteran actor Adolph Caesar (who played Danny Glover's father), she finally managed to cry on cue, but continued working in a constant state of insecurity. In the journal she kept during the filming, she wrote of Spielberg, "I know he hates me. I know he must be sorry he ever cast me, a non-actor, in this movie. If I don't get better soon he's probably going to ask me to leave. Or maybe we've shot too much already. O God, why didn't I take an acting class?" After she criticized a fight scene between Sofia and her husband, Harpo, as being "too slapsticky," the director told her, "You're being too analytical, and you can't watch the dailies anymore." But she felt vindicated when he eventually dropped the scene from the movie. Spielberg admitted being "a little frustrated" at first with her inexperience, but his respect for her acting ability grew and he enlarged her role as filming progressed.

When Winfrey played Sofia's reawakening scene at Celie's dinner table toward the end of location shooting in North Carolina, it became an emotional epiphany for both the character and the actress. That scene also is a major turning point for Celie, in which she finally gives liberating vent to all her pent-up rage against Mister. Spielberg's usual method of shooting underwent a dramatic change when it was filmed.

"That was a tough scene," Allen Daviau recalls. "We were in a real house in North Carolina, not on a stage, and the *heat!* We were filling the room with smoke; we had a lot of people crowded in. They were seemingly simple setups, but when you're dealing with that many people, every time you shifted a setup, a whole bunch of things had to shift. And he wanted every reaction there was. He went by the book in covering that scene. He had different [image] sizes, he had different looks, he just had it every way you could possibly look. I kidded him, 'This is George Stevens' kind of coverage.' Very unusual for him. Most of the time you know he's got exactly in his head what he's going to do. He generally does not shoot a lot of takes. A lot of it had to do with Oprah's character being very, very lost, showing all of her pain and then having a recovery, and how this was going to be achieved."

Winfrey recalled that Spielberg encouraged her to improvise much of her dialogue in that scene, "like when I started to rock in my chair, and I said to Whoopi, 'I want to thank you, Miss Celie, for everything you've done for me.' And then Sofia started to cry—I started to cry. When Steven yelled 'Cut,' I looked up, and there he was, giving me a great big hug. . . . Whoopi stood up and said, 'My sister today became an actress!' "

The Color Purple marked "only the second time I didn't storyboard the whole picture," Spielberg said. "The first time was *E.T.,* because it was an emotional journey. I felt that *The Color Purple* was even more of an emotional journey, and I wanted to surprise myself through the process of discovery every day during the making of the movie.* I was afraid the storyboards would tie me down to preconceived ideas that would no longer be relevant once the cast got together and began performing their hearts out. . . . Allen and I were very gentle to everybody. On *E.T.*, we were yelling and screaming all the time, but on this picture we were a lot more mellow. I was never more relaxed while making a picture."

Alice Walker carries a lasting impression of "the feeling of love that was palpable daily on the set. . . . 'What makes this Jewish boy think he can direct a movie about black people?' critics fumed. Well, what did, exactly? It was this that I wanted to know. I thought it might be love. I thought it might be courage. I thought it might be the most wonderful thing of all: Steven had outgrown being a stranger."

H o w disheartening it was, then, for Spielberg when his labor of love was met with a hostile response from critics who were not content to attack his work but also tried to put him in his place with venomous personal insults. The majority of the film's reviews actually were positive—thirty-three reviewers put it on their 1985 top-ten lists—and the public warmly embraced it. Opening on Spielberg's thirty-ninth birthday, December 18, 1985, *The Color Purple* grossed a remarkable $142.7 million in worldwide box office, with a production cost of only $15 million. But its popular success only served to heighten the contempt of Spielberg's detractors. The negative reviews left a lasting sting, as did the angry reaction in some segments of the black community.

"This film's total inauthenticity proves that [Spielberg] finds it harder to imagine black people than spacemen, and suggests that his gifts have been wholly corrupted: He can't make an honest film if he tries," wrote John Powers of *L.A. Weekly*. Spielberg's "suburban background shows all over the place," claimed Rita Kempley of *The Washington Post,* mocking the director's vision of rural Georgia as "a pastoral paradise that makes Dorothy Gale's Kansas farm look like a slum." Other reviewers compared the movie to *Amos 'n' Andy,* Disney's *Song of the South,* MGM's all-black musical *Cabin in the Sky,* and even D. W. Griffith's infamous paean to the Ku Klux Klan, *The Birth of a Nation*.

Favorable reviews, such as Gene Siskel's in *The Chicago Tribune,* could barely be heard over all the commotion. Calling the film "triumphantly emotional and brave," Siskel wrote, "Nothing in the book appears to have been soft-pedaled in the film, and yet *The Color Purple* couldn't have a sweeter, more uplifting tone. The director who tugged at our hearts with the rubber

---

* Only the scenes set in Africa were storyboarded. Some were filmed by Spielberg in a village built in Newhall, California; the rest were filmed by producer and second-unit director Frank Marshall on location in Kenya.

alien E.T. works at an even deeper emotional level with flesh-and-blood characters this time. . . . [and] to its everlasting credit, *The Color Purple* is also a film that takes risks. Specifically, it takes an incredibly strong stand against the way black men treat black women."

That strong stand was what caused the angriest backlash against the film, although Spielberg was faulted as well by Walker and other feminists for downplaying the novel's lesbian themes. The backlash started even before filming began, when the announcement that Spielberg was to direct the movie brought objections from some African Americans. "These people bitch and moan that you never see a black face in the movies," Whoopi Goldberg responded during the shooting, "and as soon as there's a movie with a black cast that is not singin' and dancin', they bitch and moan about it. . . . I say to people, cool the fuck out, and see what this man does with the movie."

The most vocal opposition came from a twenty-member Los Angeles group calling itself the Coalition Against Black Exploitation, whose persistent attacks on the film helped set the tone for media coverage (as well as a similar protest by the Hollywood branch of the NAACP). One member of the coalition, Kwazi Geiggar, accused the movie of portraying black men as "absolute savages" and depicting all blacks "in an extremely negative light. It degrades the black man, it degrades black children, it degrades the black family."

While his detractors' rhetoric often distorted the film out of recognition, certainly Spielberg is most vulnerable to the charge of using one-dimensional depictions of the black male characters. Alice Walker often has been attacked as anti-male, but she was able to find more forgiveness in her heart than Spielberg does for Mister. Spielberg's black male characters are defined by their mostly unnuanced roles as rapist (Celie's "Pa"), tyrannical patriarch (the fathers of Mister and Shug), philandering abuser (Mister), or henpecked buffoon (Harpo). The fact that the characters' given names are so seldom heard on screen underscores their archetypal status, which the film's detractors have viewed as racial stereotyping.

Walker defended herself and Spielberg by writing in 1986, "A book and movie that urged us to look at the oppression of women and children by men (and to a lesser degree, women) became the opportunity by which many black men drew attention to themselves—not in an effort to rid themselves of the desire or tendency to oppress women and children, but instead to claim that inasmuch as a 'negative' picture of them was presented to the world, they were, in fact, the ones *being* oppressed." And yet Walker also tried to justify the depiction of black men in *The Color Purple* by explaining their behavior in light of their oppression: "In the novel and in the movie (even more in the movie because you can *see* what color people are) it is clear that Mister's father is part white; this is how Mister comes by his run-down plantation house. It belonged to his grandfather, a white man and a slave owner. Mister learns how to treat women and children from his father,

Old Mister. Who did Old Mister learn from? Well, from Old *Master,* his slave-owning father . . ."

These subtleties may be read into the film by readers knowledgeable about the history and sociology of the post-Reconstruction South, but Spielberg and screenwriter Menno Meyjes make no attempt to deal with them dramatically or otherwise explain them to the audience. Spielberg may have blundered into the appearance of racial stereotyping because of a limited ability to relate to male authority figures and an inadequate understanding of the film's sociohistorical background.

If the director had more carefully situated the characters in terms of their time and place, uncomprehending white viewers also might have understood more easily why the characters live in what some felt were incongruously comfortable, even luxurious, surroundings. Whether that kind of explanation *should* have been necessary is another matter. "I knew I had a responsibility to *The Color Purple,*" Spielberg said, "and yet I didn't want to make the kind of movie from the novel that some people wanted me to. . . . I think some people had a kind of *Uncle Tom's Cabin* view of what the picture should be, which is wrong. And, ironically, it pointed out their own inclination for racial stereotyping, which is what some of the same people said *we* were guilty of."

"Every time there is a play or movie with white people in it," Winfrey pointed out, "they don't expect them to represent the history or culture of the race. We aren't trying to depict the history of black people. It's one woman's story, that's all." On the other hand, Margaret Avery, who played Shug, says, "I did understand the black reaction. It was the first [major] black film in years, since *Sounder,* and the black community I feel was just so needy of a film that when they had one, they wanted it to represent themselves. No one film can do that."

The controversial love scene between Celie and Shug is one of the film's most affecting scenes. When Shug gently kisses her, the shy, self-effacing Celie, for the first time in the film, breaks into a broad, beaming grin, delighted at her own effrontery in feeling pleasure; it is like watching a flower opening in magical stop-motion photography. Spielberg's delicacy in directing the scene keeps the emphasis not on voyeuristic physical details of lovemaking but on the transforming power of love itself. And yet the scene became a focus of some of the most heated criticism of the film, both from black males who felt threatened by it and from feminists who felt the male director was too timid to explore the full dimensions of Celie's lesbianism. The film elides the development of the women's intimate relationship after they move together to Memphis, and some critics contended that this diminishes the motivation for Celie's rebellion against Mister, as if her virtual enslavement were not ample motivation.

Walker, who proudly proclaims her bisexuality, regrets that in the film, "Shug and Celie don't have the erotic, sensuous relationship they deserve. . . . It took a bit of gentle insistence, in talks with Menno, Steven, and Quincy, simply to include 'the kiss,' chaste and soon over as it is. However, I was aware, because Quincy Jones sent copies of some of the letters he received, that there were people in the black community who adamantly opposed any display of sexual affection between Celie and Shug."

Admitting that he "downplayed the lesbian scenes," Spielberg explained, "I confined them to just a series of kisses; I wasn't comfortable going beyond that. In the book, which handles the scenes beautifully, Shug actually holds up a mirror to Celie's private parts. But a scene like that plays at least 150 times bigger on the screen, and I just couldn't do it. Marty Scorsese could do it; not me." He insisted it was "an artistic decision" simply to suggest the relationship with the kissing scene: "No one had ever loved Celie other than God and her sister. And here Celie is being introduced to the human race by a person full of love. I didn't think a full-out love scene would say it any better."

What Spielberg's harshest critics may find most offensive about his style of filmmaking, in the last analysis, is simply that he expresses deep emotion and does so without embarrassment. His full-throated romantic mode of visual storytelling is not fashionable by the postmodernist standards of contemporary film criticism. That may explain the gap between the mass audience's often tearful enjoyment of a film such as *The Color Purple* and the distaste of critics who view *any* evocation of strong emotion as a form of directorial "manipulation," to use a word often applied disparagingly to Spielberg.

But as the African American critic Armond White observed in 1994, "Spielberg attempted a first—applying Hollywood's entire fictional apparatus to create a romance about African Americans, all the while adhering to the pop-feminist politics that marked Alice Walker's novel as a modern work. *The Color Purple* is the most successful example of the eighties' interest in cultural signs and signifiers of African American and Hollywood history that there is in mainstream American cinema, and is the quintessential example of Spielberg's sophistication."

T H E loudest slap in the face Spielberg received over *The Color Purple* came from the Academy of Motion Picture Arts and Sciences. When Oscar nominations were announced on February 5, 1986, the film was named in eleven categories, including Best Picture, Best Actress, and two nominations for Best Supporting Actress (Avery and Winfrey). Although Spielberg was nominated as one of the film's producers, he conspicuously was *not* nominated for his work as director.

Warner Bros. took the unusual step of issuing a statement congratulating its nominees but adding, "At the same time, the company is shocked and dismayed that the movie's primary creative force—Steven Spielberg—was not recognized." Only once before, when journeyman director Sam Wood was ignored in the eleven nominations for his 1942 film *Pride of the Yankees,* had such an egregious snub been made by the Academy. Veteran *Daily Variety* columnist Army Archerd reported the day after the nominations were announced that "all the nominees we spoke to were shocked, surprised, disappointed, [and] amazed" by the Academy's latest insult to Spielberg. George Perry of the London *Sunday Times* speculated that as a result of Spielberg's unprecedented success, envious Hollywood colleagues believed "he must have some knowledge denied lesser mortals. They cannot understand how he does it, but shamelessly imitate his work, and feign indifference to his achievements by signally not awarding him Oscars." Others suggested Spielberg's chances for a directing nomination were hurt by the controversy surrounding the film and by what some perceived as his pandering for an Oscar. The ongoing *Twilight Zone* case perhaps added to the anti-Spielberg backlash.

Defenders of the Academy were quick to point out that under Oscar nominating rules, it was not the entire voting membership that overlooked Spielberg for the directing nomination, but only the membership of its directors' branch, an elitist group totaling only 231 at the time. One of those members, the self-financed boutique filmmaker Henry Jaglom, said, "None of the directors I know think[s] the movie is good. The picture is a sentimental cartoon. It's as if Walt Disney decided to direct *The Grapes of Wrath*. Spielberg means well. But there's a lesson here. People should direct what they know about." But veteran director Richard Brooks, who voted for Spielberg, said, "I feel badly that he didn't get a nomination. He's the most successful director in the world. I guess when you get up that high, you're bound to find people who will throw stones at you."

The Directors Guild of America, a much more broadly based organization of eight thousand voting members, including assistants and production managers, subsequently gave Spielberg its award for Best Director. Only twice in the previous forty years had the DGA winner not gone on to win the directing Oscar. "I am floored by this," Spielberg said as he accepted the award on March 8. "If some of you are making a statement, thank God, and I love you for it." Asked by the press backstage to comment on the Oscar brouhaha, Spielberg, who had not been talking publicly about the subject until then, said, "I'm a moviemaker and not a bellyacher. . . . Certainly, anybody would feel hurt to be left out of a category of richly deserved nominations, but I'm not bitter or angry about it. I've gotten so many letters and [so much] support from the public, I feel like Jimmy Stewart at the end of *It's a Wonderful Life*." (It was not until 1996, appearing on Oprah Winfrey's TV talk show, that Spielberg admitted he was "real pissed off" not to have been nominated.)

Stung by what Academy president Robert Wise called the questioning of "the integrity of the Academy" with "this overkill in the media," the organization compounded the insult by not giving a single Oscar to *The Color Purple*. Winfrey said she "could not go through the night [of the March 24 ceremony] pretending that it was okay that *Color Purple* did not win an Oscar. I was pissed and I was stunned." But in retrospect she thought it was "a greater statement that [the film] won no awards than if it had won one or two. It put the whole Oscar in perspective for me, which is not to say I wouldn't want to win one now. It would be great, but it would never mean the same thing, because for *The Color Purple* to be totally excluded says to me the Oscar isn't what I thought it was."

Shortly after the Oscar ceremony, Spielberg left for Israel to join Amy Irving on location for *Rumpelstiltskin,* a film in which she was being directed by her brother, David. Speaking to a reporter from an Israeli newspaper, Spielberg attributed his snubbing by the Academy to the box-office success of his movies. Then he added:

"When I'm sixty, Hollywood will forgive me—I don't know for what, but they'll forgive."

" A N   A W F U L L Y   B I G   A D V E N T U R E "

IF HE COULD GET THE HANG OF THE THING HIS CRY MIGHT BECOME "TO LIVE WOULD BE AN AWFULLY BIG ADVENTURE!" BUT HE CAN NEVER QUITE GET THE HANG OF IT . . .

— J A M E S   M .   B A R R I E ,   *P E T E R   P A N*

W E E K   before Max was born in 1985, Spielberg vowed that "the child is going to change my life. . . . I want to be like most parents. I want to drive home in bumper-to-bumper commuter traffic, which means I've got to leave the office by five-thirty to hit the peak traffic hours. And that's going to change everything I do." Fatherhood did bring profound changes to his life. "Steven's a great father—I sometimes can't get him to go back to work!" Amy said when Max was a year old. "He's cut his work week to four days; he doesn't want to miss anything at home. He changes dirty diapers, which he vowed he'd never do, and he gets up in the night with the baby."

Those habits have persisted. He said in 1994, "I've grown up more because I have kids, because my kids don't *want* me to be a kid. *They* want to be a kid, and in a sense they have directed me to be more of an adult than I probably ever could do for myself." Being a father deepened Spielberg's work as a filmmaker, teaching him to accept adult responsibilities in every aspect of his life. But his final passage from boy to man was not smooth or easy.

•   •   •

S P I E L B E R G ' S sideline as a producer of other directors' movies kept his workload heavy following his founding of Amblin Entertainment. From 1984 through 1990, when he began cutting back on his producing chores, his name appeared on nineteen feature films as producer or executive producer, other than the films he directed. In that same period, he produced an ambitious but unsuccessful sci-fi/fantasy series for Universal TV and NBC, *Amazing Stories* (1985–87), and started his long-running Warner Bros. TV animated series *Tiny Toon Adventures* (1990–present).*

Spielberg began conceiving grandiose plans of running his own Hollywood production company as early as the 1970s. "He said he wanted to do what Walt Disney had done, except that he would do it for all audiences," recalled Warner Bros. president Terry Semel. After *E.T.,* Spielberg rejected offers to run Disney and three other major studios, preferring to be what *The Wall Street Journal* described as a "one-man entertainment conglomerate." "After Max was born," he explained, "the ambition wasn't there as much. It became, in some ways, a real choice. I realized that I could be a Disney, but that I would be a terrible father, or I could forget Disney and be a great father."

Whether it was wise to spread himself even as thin as he did with Amblin was debatable. In addition to taking up time he could have devoted to directing, his work as a producer has often exhibited dubious artistic taste along with uneven commercial results. How he fares as a partner with Jeffrey Katzenberg and David Geffen in his own fully fledged studio, DreamWorks SKG, which they founded in 1994, and how that ambitious venture will affect his directing career, remains to be seen.

Art Murphy of *Daily Variety* warned in the early 1980s that by attaching his name to films he did not direct, Spielberg ran the risk of confusing the public and cheapening his reputation. Since many people outside the industry are unclear about the difference between what a producer does and what a director does, they might assume Spielberg had as much to do with such stinkers as *The Goonies* (1985), *The Money Pit* (1986), *Joe Versus the Volcano* (1990), and *The Flintstones* (1994) as he did with such classics as *Close Encounters, E.T.,* and *Schindler's List,* and wonder why his work has seemed to fluctuate so widely in quality. But by and large, as far as the public is concerned, Murphy's dire prediction does not seem to have been borne out. The public is more intuitive and discriminating (as well as more forgiving) than Hollywood tends to recognize, and Spielberg's box-office appeal as a director has not been tarnished appreciably by his association with many mediocre or downright awful films as a producer or executive producer. The better films bearing his name, such as Robert Zemeckis's *Back to the Future*

---

* Aside from the phenomenally successful *ER* (NBC-TV, 1994–present) and his animated series for children (which also include the droll and sophisticated *Animaniacs*), Spielberg's record as a TV producer has been disappointing. Such prime-time series as *seaQuest DSV, Earth 2,* and *Champs* have not added to his luster.

(1985) and *Who Framed Roger Rabbit* (1988), have helped enhance his image. Such smaller-scale, quietly affecting Amblin films as Gary David Goldberg's *Dad* (1989), Jocelyn Moorhouse's *How to Make an American Quilt* (1995), and Don Bluth's animated feature *An American Tail* (1986) have broadened Spielberg's image and made the public more receptive to his own ventures into more challenging emotional material.

There can be little doubt, however, that Spielberg's critical reputation, which became increasingly problematical when he started directing more "adult" movies in the 1980s, suffered as a result of his producing sideline. Critics' fixation on the image of Spielberg as an emotionally arrested film-maker, despite mounting evidence to the contrary in recent years, is not easily dispelled when the title "Steven Spielberg Presents" precedes such movies as *Young Sherlock Holmes* (1985), *Harry and the Hendersons* (1987), *The Little Rascals* (1994), and *Casper* (also 1994), the kind of derivative, assembly-line product that gives family entertainment a bad name. Much of Spielberg's producing output has been aimed at teenagers or subteens, and most of his protégés, who tend to ape his style shamelessly, find it next to impossible to duplicate his knack for visual and emotional wonderment. *Young Sherlock Holmes,* an uncharacteristically formulaic early effort from director Barry Levinson, was so derivative of other Spielberg special-effects extravaganzas that one reviewer called it *Indiana Holmes and the Temple of the Goonies.* "It used to be that when a director's hits were copied he was far from happy about it; he understood that his pictures were being devalued —cheapened," Pauline Kael wrote in *The New Yorker.* "But Steven Spielberg 'presents' *Young Sherlock Holmes. . . .* Spielberg has said that he had 'virtually nothing to do' with this movie except to offer some advice on the special effects, and there's no reason to doubt that. But didn't he even look at the script?"

Another unfortunate side effect of such mediocre Spielberg movies is that they and their often offensively crass merchandising have helped foster a perception that Spielberg is not only a commercially minded filmmaker but a greedy one as well. Why else would he want to waste his time making such a lumbering, unfunny dinosaur of a comedy as *The Flintstones?* Spielberg may have been trying to signal his disdain for the work of director Brian Levant by jokingly changing his own screen credit to "Steven Spielrock Presents," but with all of his vast wealth, does he really need more money badly enough to make such a movie? Or, as Kael wrote of George Lucas when they made *Raiders of the Lost Ark,* is Spielberg still so "hooked on the crap of his childhood" that he feels a compulsion to keep replicating it on the big screen, in all its unalloyed dreckiness?

As an executive producer, Spielberg is motivated largely by the fact that he "just likes movies and wants to make movies he would like to see, movies he doesn't want to spend a year of his life on," says Michael Finnell, who has produced three films for Amblin. Spielberg's ability to spawn so many productions while still managing to focus on his own personal projects is a byproduct of his remarkably overactive metabolism. His Amblin partner Frank Marshall, who served as line producer on many of the company's films along with his wife, Kathleen Kennedy, once said of Spielberg, "He has an idea every thirteen seconds. I have to figure out how serious they are. If he wants to do something, I figure out how to make it possible financially. Steven doesn't think in monetary terms."

But that image is somewhat illusory, a bit of Spielbergian public relations to distract the paying customers from the fact that, as Sid Sheinberg once told *The Wall Street Journal,* "Steven's as good a businessman as he is a director." Spielberg is renowned—and sometimes deplored—in Hollywood for driving hard bargains with everyone from technicians to actors to studio chiefs. In recent years, his standard deal has been a remarkable 50 percent of the distributor's gross on his pictures (compared with the 5–to–15 percent even major stars can command, with only a few going higher). The studios also fully finance Spielberg's films, even though the copyright is owned or shared by Amblin or one of its subsidiaries. "Steven gets the studios to carry the risk and he takes in the money," observed Jeffrey Berg, chairman of International Creative Management.*

From the time he worked his way out of his remaining obligations to Universal in the early eighties, Spielberg has taken care to avoid being pinned down to any one studio. Even his own DreamWorks allows him to take directing jobs elsewhere. While ensconced for many years in his cozy headquarters on the Universal lot, Spielberg freelanced projects all over town, but concentrated his work at two studios, Universal and Warner Bros.

T H E Warners connection came through his close friendship with Steve Ross, the late chairman of the board of Time Warner. Ross was the most colorful, and controversial, of the film industry mentors to whom Spielberg has attached himself. There can be little doubt that Spielberg's growing interest in becoming a movie mogul during the eighties was largely a result of their mutually enriching friendship. And if Spielberg imbibed some of Ross's piratical attitudes along with his largesse, that would hardly have been surprising.

From their first meeting in 1981 until Ross's death in 1992, Ross carefully cultivated his and Time Warner's relationships with Spielberg, whose association with the company became a crucial element in its success and stability. Biographer Connie Bruck reported that Ross "was determined to find a

---

* When he was a teenager, Spielberg talked his way into an interview with one of his idols, John Ford. After showing the nervous youngster his collection of Western prints and growling, "When you understand what makes a great Western painting, you'll be a great Western director," Ford ended the brief meeting with a succinct piece of advice: "And never spend your own money to make a movie. Now get the hell out of here." That advice governed Spielberg's career until the founding of DreamWorks, but it's worth noting that even before he met Ford, Spielberg spent his parents' money to make *Firelight*.

means to loosen the Universal-Spielberg bond and bring Spielberg to Warner Bros. Spielberg would have been an alluring asset for the Warner studio at any time, but the early eighties were especially fallow."

"I had typecast what a CEO was—I'd never met one before, and I wasn't far off, because I've met them since—and in my mind, they looked like J. C. Penney," Spielberg recalled. "And suddenly here was this older movie star. We quickly found out what we had in common: my favorite movies were made between 1932 and 1952 and those were his favorites, too. Steve to me was a blast from the past. He had silver-screen charisma, much like an older Cary Grant, or a Walter Pidgeon. He had style in a tradition that seems to have bred itself out of society. He had flash. He was a magnetic host —eventually, that became his calling card. And at Acapulco, he *was* the weekend."

Assuming the roles of Spielberg's best friend and idealized father-figure, as well as business mentor, Ross began educating Spielberg in the finer aspects of life as a Hollywood mogul. Studio president Terry Semel recalled that when he introduced them, Spielberg "was a young man, in his early thirties, with no business sophistication. He found Steve, who was much older, so fascinating. Steve Ross was into things we knew only a little about —art, planes, homes." Wooing Spielberg with lavish gifts and hospitality (he once sent the company plane to fly Spielberg's dogs from California to New York), Ross went so far as to insist that Spielberg become his neighbor in East Hampton, setting the real-estate deal in motion almost before Spielberg knew what was happening.

The Spielberg-Ross relationship resulted in Spielberg making eleven feature films for Warners during the executive's tenure, including *The Color Purple* and *Empire of the Sun,* as well as the studio's TV series *Tiny Toon Adventures* and *Animaniacs* (the latter began airing after Ross's death). Spielberg also lent his name and talents to more ephemeral projects aimed unabashedly at glorifying the house of Ross. When the executive's wife, Courtney Sale Ross, produced *Strokes of Genius,* a 1984 TV series of documentaries on artists, Spielberg donated his services as director for the introductions, hosted by Dustin Hoffman. Spielberg himself was one of the hosts of the 1991 TV special *Here's Looking at You, Warner Bros.* And when Columbia Pictures vacated the former Burbank Studios in 1990 and Warners reclaimed sole ownership of the lot, Ross tapped Spielberg to serve as an executive producer for a "Celebration of Tradition," an outlandishly decadent super-A-list party costing $3 million. While being driven through the lot on trams, guests watched spectacular musical numbers being performed in the studio streets before arriving at a soundstage transformed into Rick's Café Américain from *Casablanca,* with the added attraction of bathing beauties diving into a swimming pool for a Busby Berkeley–style homage.

Ross rewarded Spielberg's professional favors with unusually generous film deals and stock options. The other stockholders did not complain about this special treatment. Explaining the hidden benefits of letting Spielberg use the company's Acapulco villa, Ross once said, "Look, Spielberg goes down there on the company plane and wakes up in the middle of the night after a nightmare. He can't sleep, and in the morning he gets up and writes the script for *The Goonies*.* That's worth tens of millions to us."

Perhaps even more important to Ross, Spielberg threw his power and prestige behind the executive during periods of upheaval at Warner Communications Inc. and its successor, Time Warner. At a WCI shareholders meeting in 1987, Spielberg said, "I am too secure in my line of work, and too fat as a result of it, to be seduced by deals and perks and promises. I have settled down to live and work in only two houses. . . . MCA and WCI." He said he had decided to do so because of his "respect and admiration . . . for two people in particular, Sidney J. Sheinberg and Steven J. Ross."

S P I E L B E R G ' S involvement as producer has varied greatly from film to film, ranging from his virtual takeover of the directing of *Poltergeist* to his far more tangential involvement as executive producer on movies with strong directors he respects, such as Robert Zemeckis, Joe Dante, Don Bluth, Martin Scorsese, and Clint Eastwood. On their movies, Spielberg has regarded himself largely as the filmmakers' advocate, protecting them against studio interference. Describing Spielberg as "a perfect executive producer" on *Back to the Future*, Zemeckis said, "The most important thing he does is create an atmosphere for you to comfortably create a movie. He says, 'It's your movie —but if you need me, I'm here.' He respects the filmmaker's vision. He lets you do the movie the way you see it."

Spielberg's reluctance to play the heavy with other filmmakers, even mediocre ones, sometimes has led him to be too much of a hands-off executive, when a firmer hand might have been more advisable. "The worst thing about working at Amblin," Richard Benjamin said while directing *The Money Pit*, "is that one day I'm going to have to leave it and go back to the real world." That film's screenwriter-producer, David Giler, says Spielberg's greatest strength as an executive producer is that "he's got final say. He doesn't really have to ask anybody else. You convince him, it stops there."

Spielberg's popular instincts enabled him to go against conventional Hollywood wisdom when he produced the original *Back to the Future*. The biggest hit Amblin has produced, other than the films Spielberg himself has directed, it grossed $211 million in domestic box office. But the rest of Hollywood had turned thumbs down on the script by Zemeckis and Gale, believing that movies about time travel never make money. "Steven was the only guy who said, 'I want to do this,'" Zemeckis recalled. "And I said, 'Steven, if I do another movie with you that fails, the reality of the situation

---

* Spielberg was an executive producer on *The Goonies* and received story credit for the Amblin production, with Chris Columbus receiving screenplay credit.

is that I will never work again.' And he said, 'You're probably right.' A lot of lean years went by because I had done two movies that he executive-produced [*I Wanna Hold Your Hand* and the 1980 black comedy *Used Cars*] and they did no business. The word was getting around town: Bob Zemeckis can't get work unless Steven Spielberg is the executive producer." After Zemeckis finally directed a hit movie away from Spielberg's company, *Romancing the Stone*, he took *Back to the Future* back to Spielberg, who set up the deal with Sid Sheinberg at Universal.

Spielberg also participated in the painful decision to replace the star of the movie (Eric Stoltz) with Michael J. Fox after five weeks of shooting, a decision that necessitated the scrapping of $4 million in footage and proved a serious setback to Stoltz's career, but added a crucial element to the picture's box-office chemistry. "We've got to do something drastic, because this isn't funny," Spielberg said after the worried director showed him the Stoltz footage. Spielberg blamed himself for not voicing his reservations earlier, "but I didn't do anything about it [at first] because I thought it was up to Bob to make his movie."

"I'll tell you a great story about how Steven earned his executive-producer fee on *Back to the Future* [a reported $20 million]," adds Gale. "Sid Sheinberg will deny this story, because he doesn't remember it, but it's a true story. Sid Sheinberg didn't like the title *Back to the Future*. Every other executive at Universal thought it was a great title, as did Steven, as did we. And Sheinberg would not get off [the idea] that *Back to the Future* was a bad title. He said, 'It's not hip, like *Ghostbusters* was hip.' So he sent us a memo and he said, 'My suggestion for the new title of this movie is *Spaceman from Pluto*. Here are some notes I have regarding the script and how we can make reference to this in the movie.'

"There's a scene in the movie when the DeLorean is in the barn and the kid has a comic book, and it's called *Space Zombies from Pluto*. Sheinberg said, 'Change that to *Spaceman from Pluto*, and have the kid say, "Look, it's a spaceman from Pluto!" And in the scene when Marty intimidates George McFly by saying, "My name is Darth Vader—I'm an extraterrestrial from the Planet Vulcan," have him say that he's a spaceman from Pluto.' We were saying, 'He's serious about this, Steven. What do we do? We don't want to change the title of this movie.' Steven said, 'OK, I know what to do.' So Steven dictated a memo back to Sid, and the memo said something like this: 'Dear Sid, Thank you for your most humorous memo of such-and-such a date. We all got a big laugh out of it. Keep 'em coming.' Steven said, 'Sheinberg will be so embarrassed to tell us that he was serious about this that we'll never hear from him about it again.' And he was right."*

Spielberg has admitted that in his relationships with directors, he has "found out that not everyone is like Bob Zemeckis." As a result, he said in

---

* Sheinberg did not respond to requests to be interviewed for this book.

1992, "Producing has been the least fulfilling aspect of what I've done in the last decade." He began scaling back his producing in the nineties partly for that reason and also because he finally recognized that his name was appearing on too many inferior movies. Furthermore, Frank Marshall and Kathleen Kennedy were becoming restless and wanted to start their own independent company; Marshall also was branching out into directing, starting with second-unit work for Spielberg before making his solo debut in 1990 with Amblin's horror comedy *Arachnophobia.*

The Academy of Motion Picture Arts and Sciences gave Spielberg its Irving G. Thalberg Memorial Award in 1987, an honor given to "creative producers whose bodies of work reflect a consistently high quality of motion picture production." That award was generally regarded as more a gesture of apology by the Academy for past slights of his work as a director than a genuine measure of his highly uneven track record as a producer.* Far too willing to encourage his many protégés to make *faux* Spielberg movies rather than express their own individual visions, he has not been responsible for developing even half as many first-rate talents as B-movie *meister* Roger Corman. Spielberg may have given the world at least one genuine original, Zemeckis, and elevated Dante to A-picture status, but he has given his imprimatur to a host of forgettable talents as well. Could it be that he has a problem fostering genuine competition? The occasional films Amblin has made with major directors, such as Martin Scorsese's *Cape Fear* (1991), Peter Bogdanovich's *Noises Off* (1992), and Clint Eastwood's *The Bridges of Madison County* (1995), have been solid pieces of craftsmanship but not among those directors' most important work. In some cases, including *Cape Fear* and *Madison County,* Amblin's productions have been projects Spielberg seriously considered directing before losing interest.

Spielberg occasionally has reached out to help one of the legendary directors whose work has given him inspiration. He and George Lucas found financing and distribution from Warner Bros. for a 1990 film by Japanese master Akira Kurosawa, *Dreams.* But no such support was forthcoming when Orson Welles, near the end of his life in 1985, invited Spielberg and Amy Irving to lunch at the West Hollywood bistro Ma Maison. Welles hoped Spielberg would finance his stalled project *The Cradle Will Rock,* in which Irving had agreed to play Welles's first wife. Just a few months earlier, Spielberg had spent $60,500 to buy a Rosebud sled from *Citizen Kane* as "a symbolic medallion of quality in movies. When you look at Rosebud, you don't think of fast dollars, fast sequels, and remakes. This to me says that movies of my generation had better be good." But rather than offering to help Welles with *The Cradle Will Rock,* Spielberg spent most of their luncheon asking questions about *Citizen Kane.*

---

* He said in his acceptance speech, "I'm resisting like crazy to use Sally Field's line from two years ago" ("I can't deny the fact you like me. Right now, you *like* me!").

"Why can't I direct an *Amazing Stories?*" Welles later wondered. "Everybody else is doing *Amazing Stories."**

AMAZING *Stories* was Spielberg's "elephant burial ground for ideas that will never make it to the movie screen because they are just too short-form. And if I didn't exorcise them in one form or the other, they would just float around in my head and mess me up later in my life."

"This man is a fountain of story ideas," says Peter Z. Orton, story editor during the series' second season. "When I first got on the show, they gave me a looseleaf binder of story ideas. I realized when I got a quarter of the way through that they were all by Steven. That notebook I saw was about three inches thick. When people ask me to describe Steven, I say, 'He's a guy you'd swear had just drunk four cups of coffee, but that's just him.' He gets his enjoyment out of his work. He's there at seven in the morning making matzohs and he's there until nine or ten at night. Ten to fifteen percent of what he says is way over the top, about fifty percent makes you think, and twenty percent is absolutely great. If you wait long enough, he'll have a genius idea."

Launched with loud fanfare and great expectations by NBC-TV in the fall of 1985, *Amazing Stories* was touted as a blend of *The Twilight Zone* and *Alfred Hitchcock Presents,* filtered through the visionary talents of Steven Spielberg. But Spielberg's anthology series, a highly uneven mixture of fantasy with often leaden doses of whimsy, soon proved an expensive, embarrassing dud, like most of his TV ventures before he finally managed to strike gold in 1994 with the hyperkinetic medical series *ER.*

Speculating on the failure of *Amazing Stories* to find an audience, Orton offers the theory "that when people watch television, what they're looking for are continuing characters. The anthology shows that succeeded had a modicum of continuity. They had the same host, Walt Disney or Rod Serling, who would be there at the beginning of every show. At the time there was some discussion of Steven Spielberg hosting *Amazing Stories.* He nixed that idea. He felt, 'I don't want to be mobbed every time I go out.' He tends to be a behind-the-scenes kind of guy. He likes to let the work speak for itself." Spielberg also vetoed the network's suggestion of calling it *Steven Spielberg's Amazing Stories,* saying, "I don't want my name to give it that false continuity." He might not have the same qualms today, since he has become increasingly comfortable over the years appearing in public and promoting his work.

Amazing Stories never lived up to the grandiose promise of its title, borrowed from the venerable pulp magazine that inspired Arnold Spielberg's

---

* Spielberg may have been miffed over Welles's mischievous comment to the press that "the sled he bought was a fake."

boyhood interest in science fiction. "I like stories that were the sort told to me when I was sitting on my father's knee at four or five years old," Steven said. But TV critics were quick to seize on the title as a handy battering ram against Spielberg. Tom Shales of *The Washington Post* wrote in his review of the first program, "I hear America asking, what was so Amazing about *that?*" Indeed, the sense of wonder that Spielberg conjures up so naturally in his best theatrical films was largely absent from the overly literal-minded, often fatally hokey series. Ironically enough, it was the stories themselves (many of them credited to Spielberg) that constituted the weakest element of *Amazing Stories*. Even so, it was hard to shake the suspicion that in writing off the series as hastily and completely as they did, the critics were betraying an eagerness to see the cocky, fabulously wealthy *wunderkind* fall flat on his face.

That was especially unfortunate because the opening program was the underrated "Ghost Train," an eerie and poignant vignette directed by Spielberg and photographed by Allen Daviau. Inspired by Spielberg's childhood memory of hearing an unseen train speeding each night through his neighborhood in New Jersey, as well as by his love for his Grandpa Fievel, "Ghost Train" (written by Frank Deese) tells the story of a seemingly blinkered elderly man (Roberts Blossom) who tenderly convinces his grandson (Lukas Haas) that he must board the ancient express taking him to his rendezvous with death.

"The most amazing thing about the first episode, in fact, was that Steven Spielberg directed it," wrote David Blum in *New York* magazine. *Amazing Stories* proved that "the emperor is naked," *L.A. Reader* television critic Michael Kaplan charged just a few weeks after the premiere. Kaplan claimed Spielberg had already "squandered a once-in-a-lifetime opportunity: to reshape a commercial medium that has opened itself up completely to one man's artistic vision."

Spielberg was his own series's worst enemy, feeding the press's antagonism with what was widely perceived as an arrogant approach to publicity. Not only did Spielberg follow his habitual practice of keeping sets off-limits to virtually all members of the media—with the exception of two reporters from *Time* preparing that magazine's Spielberg cover story—but he even refused to allow NBC to preview *Amazing Stories* programs for TV reporters and reviewers, claiming that to do so would rob the series of its ability to surprise the audience. The network later persuaded him that he had made a serious mistake.

His secretiveness provoked an all-out attack profile by Richard Turner in the August 2, 1986, issue of *TV Guide,* perhaps the single most negative piece of writing ever published on Spielberg. Turner, then the Hollywood bureau chief of the nation's most widely distributed magazine, painted Spielberg as autocratic, paranoid, and stingy in his dealings with employees and the press, and as a "consummate Hollywood insider" who bullied network executives into acceding to his demands. "Spielberg tends his public image carefully," Turner wrote, "and it's no coincidence that stories about him are almost universally positive." The reality, charged Turner, was that people who worked with him "were *scared*. Scared? Of Steven Spielberg? That beneficent troll, that kindly gremlin whose gentle fantasies transport millions? Scared? They were terrified." Sid Sheinberg told the *Los Angeles Times* he had to read Turner's article two or three times because "at first, I couldn't believe what I was reading. . . . It characterized Steven as being greedy, cold, and selfish. But that's not the Steven Spielberg I know. You're talking about someone I've known for seventeen or eighteen years."

Spielberg's remarkable deal with NBC helped bring about the resentment in Hollywood, particularly after Brandon Tartikoff, president of NBC Entertainment, described Spielberg as behaving like an "800-pound gorilla." Without even having to make a pilot, Spielberg was guaranteed a two-year commitment for *Amazing Stories,* ensuring that forty-four shows would be broadcast no matter how the series performed in the ratings. He was granted creative carte blanche, having to conform only to network standards and practices, which in his case were relaxed considerably. The average budget for each half-hour program was a lavish $1 million, as much as the average hour-long dramatic program on television at that time; NBC put up $750,000 per show, with Universal making up the difference.

Many *Amazing Stories* directors were Spielberg protégés, such as Joe Dante, Phil Joanou, Kevin Reynolds, and Lesli Linka Glatter. The unusually generous budgets and shooting schedules helped attract such major feature directors as Scorsese, Eastwood, Zemeckis, and Irvin Kershner. While directing "Ghost Train," Spielberg invited his idol, David Lean, to visit the set. The famously perfectionistic Lean could not resist the temptation to offer a suggestion: "Don't you think on the next take that it would be absolutely marvelous if the debris fell a beat sooner than it had on the first two takes?" "Absolutely!" said Spielberg, yelling to his special-effects crew. "Drop the *day-bree* a beat sooner!" Then he asked Lean, "Would you like to do one of these?"

"Well, dear boy," Lean replied, "how many days do you give a director?"

"Between six and eight," said Spielberg.

"Oh, my," said Lean. "Well, if you perhaps add a zero after the six or the eight, I'll consider."

Some *Amazing Stories* directors, mostly those who came from features, nevertheless managed to exceed their budgets and schedules. The series "was impeccably produced—*too* impeccably produced," Dante feels. "And because the shows were so overproduced, it diminished the series." The second show Spielberg directed, a thinly plotted World War II fantasy titled "The Mission," was padded to fill an hour slot when his first cut clocked in eight minutes too long.

Such disparities between the elaborate scale of production and the tongue-in-cheek wispiness of the storylines were a recurring problem. As far as *Amazing Stories* had any particular formula, Orton says, it was to introduce "one drop of magic" into a dramatic setting and then "develop it in a realistic way." On rare occasions, the magic worked, such as in the haunting "What If . . . ?," directed by Joan Darling from a script by Spielberg's sister Anne. This show has what most other *Amazing Stories* programs lack—a powerful emotional situation leading to a satisfying fantasy presented with conviction and a minimum of gimmickry. The tale of a small boy who suffers from parental neglect and is granted his wish to be reborn as the child of a kindly female stranger, "What If . . . ?" touches the heart much like *E.T.,* by providing a delicate fable of childhood pain, but it does so with a freshness and originality that never seems imitative of Steven Spielberg. On too many other *Amazing Stories* programs, "Steven would come up with the ideas and the people who wrote the shows would be afraid to deviate from them," Dante observes. "They would do slavish versions of his ideas." While lambasting Spielberg for encouraging "an infantilization of the culture" through the work of his imitators, Pauline Kael added caustically of *Amazing Stories,* "I can't think of any other director who's started paying homage to himself so early."

After the series finished its first season a disastrous thirty-fifth in the ratings, one of its producers, David E. Vogel, said that "the spectacular visual effects for which Mr. Spielberg is renowned didn't work on television," such as the locomotive crashing through the living room of a suburban ranch-house in "Ghost Train." Tartikoff thought the series was too childish, and Spielberg vowed that in the second season, "The silly factor will be seriously minimalized," but the series played out its run to diminishing audiences.

Spielberg's "The Mission" was a perfect exemplar of the "silly factor." The director staged the crash landing of a bomber with elaborate, often dazzling camerawork, but the story built up to a ridiculous climax.* A young crew member (Casey Siemaszko) trapped in a plastic gunnery bubble under the plane draws cartoon wheels that magically materialize so the plane can land safely. Richard B. Matheson, who served as a story consultant on *Amazing Stories,* "had to be more honest with Spielberg than is smart to be. I told him they spent all this money on 'The Mission,' they had a great cast, and it was all based on this guy *drawing a wheel!* On *The Twilight Zone,* the stories were so interesting. There were not enough interesting or involving stories on *Amazing Stories.*"

"Steven never could make up his mind what the show was going to be, whether it was going to be scary or whether it was going to be fantasy," says writer and story consultant Bob Gale. "Every month Steven would change his mind about what direction we should go. Television is not a director's medium, and it's great that Steven got all these directors in there to do these shows, but the scripts weren't any good. He should have spent more time getting the best writers in the world to contribute, and *then* worrying about the directors."

* Menno Meyjes wrote the teleplay, based on a Spielberg story originally titled "Round Trip."

Spielberg expressed similar sentiments in his eloquent speech when accepting his Thalberg Award at the 1987 Oscar ceremony: "Most of my life has been spent in the dark watching movies. Movies have been the literature of my life. The literature of Irving Thalberg's generation was books and plays. They read the great words of great minds. And in our romance with technology and our excitement at exploring all the possibilities of film and video, I think we've partially lost something that we now have to reclaim. I think it's time to renew our romance with the word. I'm as culpable as anyone of exalting the image at the expense of the word. . . . I'm proud to have my name on this award in his honor, because it reminds me of how much growth as an artist I have ahead of me in order to be worthy of standing in the company of those who have received this before me."

I N the mid-eighties, Spielberg attempted to produce a feature film for David Lean, who had returned to directing with *A Passage to India* after a fourteen-year hiatus. Lean was considering filming J. G. Ballard's *Empire of the Sun*. The 1984 *roman à clef* dealt with the author's harrowing experiences as a boy living in Shanghai's British Protectorate and interned without his parents in a Japanese prison camp during the World War II occupation. Spielberg initially agreed to produce Lean's film version of *Empire of the Sun* for Warner Bros., which controlled the rights.*

But the elderly director became daunted by the prospect of working in China and by the problems of adapting the novel. "I worked on it for about a year," he told biographer Kevin Brownlow, "and in the end I gave it up because I thought, This is like a diary. It's bloody well written and very interesting, but I don't think it's a movie for me because it hasn't got a dramatic shape. . . . I gave it up and Steven said, 'Do you mind if I have it?' I said, 'Of course I don't.' And he did it and I must say a bit of what I felt, I felt about his film, too." (Spielberg subsequently agreed to produce Lean's planned film version of Joseph Conrad's *Nostromo* for Warner Bros., but angered Lean in February 1987 by handing him a detailed memo suggesting changes in Christopher Hampton's screenplay. "Who does he think he is?" Lean demanded, waving the memo at Hampton, who replied, "He thinks he's the producer, and he is." Spielberg withdrew from the project, Hampton said, "because he could see there would be some sort of fight between him and David and he wanted to avoid that." Lean continued preparing *Nostromo* until soon before his death in 1991.)

Spielberg's 1987 film version of *Empire of the Sun* combined Lean's epic grandeur with Spielberg's own thematic concentration on the painful process of growing up. "The kid in *E.T.* that Henry Thomas played was as much who Steven Spielberg was when he made that movie as the kid in *Empire of the*

* Harold Becker originally was to have directed the film, with former studio president Robert Shapiro producing; Shapiro eventually became the executive producer.

Sun was when he made *Empire of the Sun,"* Bob Gale observes. "By the time he made *Empire of the Sun,* Steven was cut off from normal, every-day stuff by virtue of his success and how he lived. He was the kid in the ivory tower, so to speak, the kid in the sequestered existence. He was identifying with that kid [splendidly played by thirteen-year-old Christian Bale], because that was more who he was than the kid he was when he made *E.T."*

"From the moment I read the [Ballard] novel, I secretly wanted to do it myself," Spielberg admitted. "I had never read anything with an adult setting —even *Oliver Twist*—where a child saw things through a man's eyes as opposed to a man discovering things through the child in him. This was just the reverse of what I felt—leading up to *Empire*—was my credo. And then I discovered very quickly that this movie and turning forty [in December 1986] happening at almost the same time was no coincidence—that I had decided to do a movie with grown-up themes and values, although spoken through a voice that hadn't changed through puberty as yet."

By adventuring into Lean territory and, indeed, Oedipally taking over a project from Lean himself, Spielberg was making a further declaration of artistic manhood.* When he was a schoolboy, his favorite movie was Lean's *The Bridge on the River Kwai,* which similarly takes place in a Japanese prison camp. His obsession with World War II also was stimulated by his father's stories about his experiences as a B-25 radio operator in the China-Burma-India Theater. Like J. G. [James Graham] Ballard's surrogate in the novel, Jim Graham, the young Spielberg developed an obsession with air-planes. "It's a fetish, I guess," he said in 1991. "I think it's interesting to be psychoanalyzed via my films, and I agree with this idea because I consciously like flying and have flying in all of my films. But I'm afraid to fly in real life, so there's an interesting conflict here."

To Spielberg, as to Jim, flying symbolizes both the possibility and the danger of escape. Jim's growing alienation from his prewar self and society is reflected in his hero-worship of the Japanese aviators based at the airfield adjoining the camp. "I think it's true that the Japanese were pretty brutal with the Chinese, so I didn't have any particularly sentimental view of them," Ballard recalled. "But small boys tend to find their heroes where they can. One thing there was no doubt about, and that was that the Japanese were extremely brave. One had very complicated views about patriotism [and] loyalty to one's own nation. Jim is constantly identifying himself, first with

---

* Also in 1987, Spielberg helped convince Columbia Pictures to support the Robert A. Harris–Jim Painten restoration of Lean's mutilated masterpiece *Lawrence of Arabia,* which was completed triumphantly in 1989. The project kindled Spielberg's passion for the twin causes of film preserva-tion and the moral rights of filmmakers, which he has championed along with Martin Scorsese, George Lucas, and other filmmakers. As Spielberg put it in 1988, "Moral rights are essential to protect future generations from the kind of big-business greed that doesn't care about the desecra-tion of timeless treasures."

the Japanese, then when the Americans start flying over in their Mustangs and B-29s, he's very drawn to the Americans."

The apocalyptic wartime setting and the climactic moment when Jim sees the distant white flash of the atomic bomb being dropped over Nagasaki gave Spielberg powerful visual metaphors "to draw a parallel story between the death of this boy's innocence and the death of the innocence of the entire world," he said at the time of the film's release. ". . . I don't think I've made a dark movie. But it's as dark as I've allowed myself to get, and that was perversely very compelling to me." Perhaps with this story about "the death of innocence," Spielberg was still working out his feelings about the *Twilight Zone* helicopter crash, as well as grappling with more of the unsettling "adult truths" that faced him as a husband and father. *Empire of the Sun* may have tapped into some of the same emotional anxieties in Spielberg as another story he was considering filming, one that also dealt with families being torn apart in World War II.

T H E film rights to *Schindler's List,* Thomas Keneally's Holocaust novel about the rescuing of Jews by the righteous gentile Oskar Schindler, were purchased by Universal shortly after its publication in 1982. Sid Sheinberg, who understood Spielberg's heart as well as anyone in Hollywood, sensed that the book would be challenging material for him both as a man and as an artist. Spielberg agreed, but for the next decade he agonized over whether he should direct such a "burdensome subject," as he described it in a 1989 interview: "[A] feature film about the Holocaust is going to be studied through a microscope, and it's going to be scrutinized from the Talmud to Ted Koppel. And it has to be accurate and it has to be fair and it cannot *in the least* come across as entertainment. And it's very hard, when you're making a movie, not to violate one or all of those self-imposed rules. So that's why it's been stalled for so many years."

Spielberg could not have made his Holocaust film without first having told the story of the death of Jim Graham's innocence. Seeing *Empire of the Sun* today, one is struck by the many visual correspondences between the scenes of chaos in the streets of war-torn Shanghai and in the Kraków ghetto depicted in *Schindler's List*. Both films take place largely in prison camps, although *Schindler* is far more disturbing, since it not only includes scenes taking place in the Plaszów forced-labor camp but also in the Auschwitz extermination camp. The terrifying scene of Jim being separated from his mother when he drops his toy airplane on the crowded Shanghai street in *Empire of the Sun* is multiplied a hundredfold when the Jewish mothers run screaming after the trucks bearing their unsuspecting children away to Auschwitz in *Schindler's List*.

Spielberg acknowledged that his unresolved childhood trauma resulting from the breakup of his family was reflected in his intense identification with

Jim's dilemma in being torn from his parents and forced to live in strange, hostile surroundings. The Shanghai setting also had a personal significance for Spielberg, which he did not discuss publicly. Some of his relatives on his father's side, the Chechiks, lived there after fleeing persecution in their native Russia. Like many Russian Jews, they found a temporary safe haven first in northern China and, later, in Shanghai's British Protectorate, whose thriving Jewish community managed to survive the war. Anti-Semitism enters only fleetingly into Spielberg's canvas in *Empire of the Sun,* when Jim catches a glimpse through the window of his chauffeured automobile of some men in Nazi armbands chasing children along a Shanghai street. But the images of a prewar peace being violently shattered by Axis militarism carry related emotions in both films.

Survival and loss are the predominant themes of both *Empire* and *Schindler.* The protagonists of both films outwit the enemy by adapting to wartime corruption with their formidable talents as hustlers and *machers.* The fact that the hero of *Empire* is an adolescent boy helped Spielberg ease his way into such treacherous thematic terrain using a familiar emotional compass. It was not until he came to grips with his Jewish heritage that he found a way of dealing with the agony of war from a more fully adult and more historically complete perspective.

B E S T known for his dreamlike science-fiction novels, which Spielberg admired as a boy, Ballard recreated his bizarre childhood experiences in China by conjuring up a landscape that was simultaneously a realistic portrayal of a particular time and place and an almost surrealistic evocation of a world gone mad. With his own tendency to view the world through the heightened perspective of dreams and cinematic imagery, Spielberg was especially well suited to film Ballard's hallucinatory vision.

Working with cinematographer Allen Daviau and production designer Norman Reynolds, Spielberg recreated 1941 Shanghai in images of overwhelming visual beauty, shadowed by an omnipresent sense of nightmarish danger and anxiety. Daviau's work rivals the best work of Lean and his great cinematographer, Freddie Young.* The poetic, multilayered texture of Daviau's imagery and its sensitivity to the subtle changes of light on exotic locations make *Empire* a visual feast. With the possible exception of Janusz Kaminski's black-and-white photography on *Schindler's List,* no other Spielberg film has been so magnificently photographed.

The Shanghai location shoot in the first three weeks of March 1987 required elaborate preplanning, including a year of negotiations with Chinese

---

* One day in England, Spielberg was shooting in an abandoned gasworks serving as the initial detention camp "where the boy did an Oliver Twist and went up and asked for more. It was very strange," assistant director David Tomblin recalls, "because that was the day David Lean came down. I said, 'We're doing some remakes on *Oliver Twist.*' "

officials by Kennedy and Marshall. "It was superbly prepared, one of the smoothest productions I have ever been on in my life," Daviau recalls. Made when China was actively courting the American film industry, the $30 million Warner Bros./Amblin production was the first Hollywood movie shot so extensively on Chinese locations. Much of Shanghai's landscape had remained unchanged since the 1940s; the only major changes required were the installation of signs with the old Chinese characters and the use of smokescreens to block out some modern buildings. The government took the unprecedented step of shutting down seven blocks of the city's main thoroughfare for Spielberg, and also supplied thousands of extras.

While preparing for the first day of shooting in Shanghai, assistant director David Tomblin "plotted out all the crowd movement and everything, and I planned to keep the road clear so there could be traffic movement. I drew it all out and told everyone what to do. Then five thousand people suddenly flooded the road. I went crazy. I said to Steven, 'Oh, Jesus, it's all gone wrong!' He said, 'Looks great.' So I said, 'Roll the cameras. Action!' He was happy with how it looked, and I wasn't going to argue with five thousand people. He's very good like that. He's not pedantic. Whatever is there, he makes it work."

"**I** THINK the first hour of *Empire of the Sun* is somewhere in the masterpiece class, as good as anything he ever did," says playwright Tom Stoppard, who adapted Ballard's novel.* "It's up to *Schindler's List,* the work of his I like best of all. The scenes in the streets of Shanghai were absolutely remarkable. The way the shots are put together, the balance between the work that Steven is doing against the work which I and J. G. Ballard were doing, the balance there just seemed to me to be perfect."

The major issue Stoppard and Spielberg worked out together was how to focus the second half of the story, dealing with what Ballard describes as Jim's "unsentimental education" in the Lunghua prison camp. "The book is a big canvas, with a lot of figures in the foreground," Stoppard observes. "To film all of it, you'd end up with a film which is maybe four or five hours long. And so, as normal, you make choices, and the *auteur*—the author as opposed to the screenwriter—is the person who ultimately makes these choices. When it gets to the camp, the book is about several relationships between Jim and other people, not all equally important, but you can't deal fully with all of them. Steven was most interested in Jim's relationship with Basie."

Played by John Malkovich, Basie is Jim's surrogate father figure. While showing him occasional moments of kindness, Basie also teaches the brutal

---

* Stoppard wrote the first draft of the screenplay when Harold Becker was attached as director. Spielberg hired Menno Meyjes to do an uncredited rewrite before Stoppard was brought back to write the final shooting script.

lessons of survival. As Ballard puts it, "Jim's entire upbringing could have been designed to prevent him from meeting people like Basie, but the war had changed everything." Jim's own father (Rupert Frazer) is a pampered fool of a businessman who ignores warnings to evacuate his family from Shanghai and vanishes from his son's life until the war has come to an end. By then Jim has turned into a feral, hollow-eyed little man who cannot remember what his parents look like. While admiring Basie's cynical pragmatism as a necessary tool for survival, Jim finally rejects his mentor in disgust, recognizing in Basie the Darwinian ugliness he must transcend to keep his spirit from perishing along with his childhood illusions.

Basie remains a somewhat nebulous character for the generous amount of time he is given on screen. The book's suggestions of sexual ambiguity in his character and that of his sidekick, Frank (Joe Pantoliano), and of a sexual component to their interest in Jim, remain largely unexplored on screen. Perhaps in part for that reason, the second half of the film, which takes place mostly in the prison camp,* proves a relatively pallid and conventional piece of storytelling. Some of the fault lies with the novel, which is most compelling when evoking Jim's state of mind as a solitary figure trying to come to grips with dizzying social dislocation, but less so when he interacts dramatically with other characters. The film's growing emphasis on Basie tends to take the focus away from Jim, making *Empire* more of a typical prison-camp movie, despite several visually lyrical and deeply emotional scenes dealing with Jim's experiences of the war's final stages. Among the most memorable are the scenes of Jim's twilight song and salute to the departing Japanese kamikaze pilots and his hysterical jubilation over the devastating American bomber attack on the airfield adjoining the camp.

The first half of the film is superior, Stoppard feels, because it "had a compression, a density. There was more room in it for Steven to do what *he* does. The images were very eloquent—they locked together in a way which aggregated—and not many overtly dramatic events were happening. For example, there's a moment where the boy is rude to the servant about taking something from the icebox. I didn't care for it too much on paper. But Steven always knows what he's doing. When the servant later slaps the boy's face, the two things, those two moments, are so interdependent. The boy wasn't trying to be insolent. The boy was just expressing colonialism, he was expressing the ethos of his own society."

In his *Village Voice* review, Andrew Sarris wrote, "Christian Bale as Jim gives the most electrifying child performance I have ever seen on the screen, even surpassing . . . Jean-Pierre Léaud's Antoine Doinel in *The Four Hundred Blows.*" Les Mayfield's documentary on the making of the film, *The China Odyssey,* shows Spielberg crafting the young British actor's performance in a casual but shrewdly intuitive manner, behaving more like a friend or older brother than an authority figure. Spielberg bought remote-controlled racing

---

* A set built near Trebujena, Spain.

cars so he and Bale could play with them during lunch breaks. Bale thought of the director as "just like another kid." At one point during the filming, while coaxing an open-mouthed reaction of shock from Bale, Spielberg boyishly suggested he assume "one of these real cool action-figure positions." But the director always took care to ensure that his young star understood the deeper meaning of a scene. Preparing Bale for Jim's separation from his mother, Spielberg said, "I think the reason I want you to have a plane in your hand is because you need to make a choice between your mother's hand or your airplane, which drops, and you choose your airplane. You let go of your mother to get the airplane and your mother is swept away in this force."

Before they shot the scene of Jim throwing his battered suitcase into the sea at the end of the war, it was almost as if the director was thinking aloud to Bale about his own painful maturation process: "I guess you could think your life is so simple that it's everything you once were, contained in this small box. Which is not really a fair measure of who you are, but it's interesting to think about this box as everything you *used* to be." And when the scene was completed, Spielberg told his young alter ego, "This was the only room, I think, in the story for tears, for crying, because this is the last day of his childhood, and he goes into another era after this. For the rest of his life, he will never be the same."

T H E R E was little critical consensus on *Empire of the Sun.* While Sarris was "stirred and moved on a scale I had forgotten still existed," his colleague J. Hoberman condemned Spielberg for being "shamelessly kiddiecentric . . . This is *The Sorrow and the Pity* remade as *Oliver!*" Faced with what David Ansen of *Newsweek* called "the first Spielberg adventure set in hell," many reviewers seemed at a loss for words. "You come out saying, 'What was that about?,' " wrote *The New Yorker*'s Pauline Kael, describing the film as both "majestically" directed and "mindlessly manipulative."

Even some who praised it seemed uncomfortable as they tried to deal with Spielberg's cinematic maturation process while being stuck with a warehouse of outmoded critical clichés. "There are almost too many brilliant, climactic moments; Spielberg hypes the emotions he wants to create rather than just letting them emerge from the marvelous story he's been given," thought David Denby of *New York* magazine. ". . . But what a prodigious visual imagination! *Empire of the Sun* is a great, overwrought movie that leaves one wordless and worn out." Expecting something quite different from the maker of *E.T.,* Sheila Benson complained in the *Los Angeles Times* that "we don't have a single character to warm up to. They are either illegal, immoral or fatally malnourished. . . . Surely the least sentimental young 'hero' ever to occupy the center of a massive movie, Jim isn't shaped by the horrors of his surroundings into a more loving, more admirable or more humane person. He becomes a slicker and more accomplished little con man."

Such complaints must have seemed strange to a filmmaker who previously had been pilloried by many critics for his supposed sentimentality about childhood. His latest attempt to move beyond his familiar suburban milieu was received with more of the supercilious sneering that greeted *The Color Purple:* "I hope Steven Spielberg's *Empire of the Sun* wins him that damn Oscar so he goes back to making movies that give real and lasting pleasure to people," Peter Rainer wrote in the *Los Angeles Herald-Examiner.*

Spielberg also was attacked for downplaying Ballard's details of disease and starvation in the prison camp, and for minimizing the brutality of the Japanese guards. The film "treats the hell of the prison camp as if it were the background for a coming-of-age story," Kael contended. ". . . Spielberg seems to be making everything nice, and, as with *The Color Purple,* there's something in the source material that's definitely not nice." Such comments betrayed a fundamental misunderstanding of the complexity of Spielberg's, and Ballard's, perspectives on childhood. "I have—I won't say *happy*—not unpleasant memories of the camp," Ballard explained. "I was young, and if you put 400 or 500 children together they have a good time whatever the circumstances. . . . I know my parents always had very much harsher memories of the camp than I did, because of course they knew the reality of the circumstances. Parents often starved themselves to feed their children. But I think it's true that the Japanese do like children and are very kindly toward them. The guards didn't abuse the children at all. . . . I was totally involved but at the same time saved by the magic of childhood."

Empire of the Sun was a major commercial disappointment, bringing in only $66.7 million at the worldwide box office, considerably less than even *1941.* Spielberg said he knew going in that "my large-canvas personal film . . . wasn't going to have a broad audience appeal." But he consoled himself by feeling, "I've earned the right to fail commercially."

Receiving six Academy Award nominations, all in the craft categories, *Empire* failed to win a single award. It was nominated neither for Best Picture nor for Best Director. Allen Daviau publicly complained, "I can't second-guess the Academy, but I feel very sorry that I get nominations and Steven doesn't. . . . . It's his vision that makes it all come together, and if Steven wasn't making these films, none of us would be here." Spielberg's feelings about the critics were made clear to George Lucas, with whom he was planning another Indiana Jones movie. Lucas wanted to start the movie with a sequence showing Indy as a boy, but Spielberg initially demurred because, as Lucas put it, "Steven had been really trashed by the critics for *Empire of the Sun,* and he said, 'I just don't want to do any more films with kids in them.' "

S PIELBERG admitted he was "consciously regressing" in making *Indiana Jones and the Last Crusade* (1989). If many critics and large segments of the public didn't want him to grow up or scoffed at his attempts to do so, then he would stop fighting them. His run for cover would last for the next few years, an uneven creative period that saw him indulging in various forms of cinematic and personal regression in hopes of reconnecting with his audience.

In making *Last Crusade, Always* (1989), and *Hook* (1991), Spielberg seemed to be giving up, for the time being, on courting the critics or the members of the Academy. Part of him could not help being concerned about his future as a popular artist. He knew how fickle the moviegoing public could be, and his anxiety about maintaining a high commercial profile drove him back to escapist subject matter—a pulp adventure, a ghost story, a pirate movie—as he recycled tried-and-true material from movies past.

But there was another dimension to those movies. The battering he had taken in attempting to expand his horizons forced him to turn inward, both for self-protection and as personal compensation for playing the commercial game. Those three films examined the wellsprings of his artistic personality in a more covert fashion, treating some of his most cherished psychological obsessions within the framework of genre conventions. Rather than taking daring risks with subject matter as he had with *The Color Purple* and *Empire of the Sun,* he bent traditional genres to express his own style and feelings, like the studio directors he admired from Hollywood's Golden Age. By disguising his increasingly personal filmmaking as popular entertainment, Spielberg was conducting creative experiments that would help advance him along the path toward *Schindler's List*.

In light of the major changes taking place in Spielberg's personal life during the second half of the 1980s—fatherhood, marriage, and, eventually, divorce—it's not surprising that the most interesting and unusual thematic elements in *Last Crusade, Always,* and *Hook* revolve around troubled relationships between fathers and sons or father-son surrogates. Spielberg's belated personal maturation forced him to examine the meaning of manhood as it applied to his own life, both as the son of a broken marriage and as the father in what would become a disintegrating marriage. The fact that he seemed to be imitating his own parents' failure must have caused him to rethink some of his condemnatory attitudes toward his father, as well as giving him a greater understanding of the cost of his own workaholic tendencies.

The career vs. family conflict so central to baby boomer psyches figures largely in these three films, along with Spielberg's increasingly critical examination of male characters who, like him, suffer from the "Peter Pan Syndrome." What J. Hoberman (writing of *Empire of the Sun*) sarcastically called Spielberg's "Peter Panic" became the director's explicit subject matter in the aesthetically unsatisfactory but nakedly autobiographical *Hook*. Peter Pan himself finally occupied the center stage of a Spielberg movie, but the character was no longer the rebellious little boy who won't grow up. He was a boy in the guise of a fully grown man, a perfectly miserable failure in his roles as a husband and father.

The depth of Spielberg's involvement in his characters' neuroses in these transitional films makes them resemble cinematic Rorschach inkblots. Spielberg went through psychotherapy around 1987, the first time he had done so since adolescence. "All my friends went to therapy and I thought that maybe I would learn something about myself, so I went for a year," he said. "But I can't say that I found the discoveries conclusive. Everything I learned about myself I knew already or I'd guessed for myself." Shortly after the release of *Hook,* it was reported that Spielberg had met privately with psychologist John Bradshaw. Bradshaw's emphasis on dysfunctional families and getting back in touch with one's "inner child" made him a guru for Hollywood celebrities undergoing midlife crises. Spielberg solicited Bradshaw's advice on the script of *Hook;* he also had the psychologist on the set for part of the shooting, and cast Bradshaw's daughter in the film.

Moviemaking, not formal psychotherapy, has always been Spielberg's preferred method of working out his personal problems. He may have shared his psychological discoveries somewhat sketchily in *Last Crusade,* confusedly in *Always,* and clumsily in *Hook,* but for viewers alert to reading nuances between the lines, those films are fascinating because they reveal so much about their maker.

FULFILLING his obligation to George Lucas for a final movie in the Indiana Jones trilogy meant that Spielberg had to abandon *Rain Man.* He had been working for several months in 1987 with Dustin Hoffman, Tom Cruise, and screenwriter Ronald Bass, developing the project about an autistic savant and his mutually enriching relationship with his outwardly normal but (in Spielberg's words) "emotionally autistic" younger brother.

Spielberg was not yet satisfied with the script of *Rain Man* by the time he left to begin preproduction on *Last Crusade,* which had to begin shooting in May 1988 to ensure its scheduled Memorial Day weekend release in 1989. Barry Levinson eventually took over the direction of *Rain Man,* which won Academy Awards for Best Picture, Director, Actor (Hoffman), and Screenplay (Bass and original writer Barry Morrow). "It's a shame that people who are involved with a film in its interim can't have their name[s] connected with it," Bass said. "Spielberg really did a tremendous amount." Though he could not have helped feeling somewhat jealous over the Oscars *Rain Man* received, Spielberg was not alone in finding the film "emotionally very distancing. I think I certainly would have pulled tears out of a rather dry movie. . . . I was very upset not to have been able to do *Rain Man,* mainly because I've wanted to work with Dustin Hoffman ever since I saw *The Graduate.*"

Lucas initially suggested making *Indy III* "a haunted-house movie." He had such a script written by *Romancing the Stone* screenwriter Diane Thomas before her death in a 1985 car accident, but, Lucas said, "Steven had done *Poltergeist,* and he didn't want to do another movie like that." Fearing further accusations of racism, Spielberg and Lucas both rejected the script they commissioned from Chris Columbus about an African Monkey King (half man, half monkey). Taking the safest route, they finally decided to reuse the cartoonish Nazi villains from *Raiders of the Lost Ark*. But Menno Meyjes's draft about Indy's quest for the Holy Grail, a plot device suggested by Lucas, left Spielberg dubious.

Spielberg recalled telling the producer that he would make a movie about the Holy Grail, "but I want it to be about a father and son. I want to get Indy's father involved in the thing. I want a quest for the father." In the film, Indy's father, Dr. Henry Jones, a professor of medieval literature, is cut from a sterner, more Victorian code of right and wrong. Unlike his son, whose interest in precious objects stems from a mixture of greed and intellectual curiosity, the elder Dr. Jones has a truly religious obsession with finding the Holy Grail. "I wanted to do Indy in pursuit of his father, sharing his father's dream," said Spielberg, "and in the course of searching for their dreams, they rediscover each other."

Screenwriter Jeffrey Boam gives a different account of how the storyline evolved. Boam, who wrote the final draft,* worked mostly with Lucas, since Spielberg was busy on *Empire of the Sun*. The father-son story "came from George," the writer insists. "I think maybe George has his own father fixation. I don't think Steven had a personal point of view to impose on the material at all. Steven knows these are George's movies. Steven has no problem with that. He approaches them as what John Ford used to call 'a job of work.' " In the earlier draft of *Last Crusade* by Meyjes, "the father was sort of a MacGuffin [a Hitchcockian device that provides an excuse for the plot]," recalls Boam. "They didn't find the father until the very end. I said to George, 'It doesn't make sense to find the father at the end. Why don't they find him in the middle?' Given the fact that it's the third film in the series, you couldn't just end with them obtaining the object. That's how the first two ended. So I thought, Let them *lose* the object—the Grail—and let the relationship be the main point. It's an archeological search for Indy's own identity. Indy coming to accept his father is more what it's about [than the quest for the Grail]."

The Indiana Jones movies all begin with a cliffhanger action sequence whose underlying function, Boam explains, is to "tell us something new about Indiana Jones." For *Last Crusade*, Lucas suggested, "What if we learn about his childhood?" The film opens in 1912 with the adolescent Indy, played by River Phoenix, on a trip to Monument Valley with his Boy Scout troop. Besides performing outlandish feats of derring-do atop a speeding circus train, young Indy acquires his trademark fedora hat and whip and his passion for archeology.

Despite Spielberg's nostalgia for his own formative days as a Boy Scout, "George felt Steven wouldn't go for it," Boam recalls. "Steven felt, 'I'm always doing movies about children. I did *Empire* and *E.T.*' Then Steven asked his wife [Amy] and his friends and his business associates—he was kind of

---

* Boam receives sole screenplay credit, with Lucas and Meyjes sharing story credit.

polling his constituency—and said he would do it. I think Steven was most captivated by the idea of the circus train. He had a lot of fun coming up with different gags. Steven is very good with little touches. He is inspired by what is there—he's able to make it a little funnier, a little more exciting, but he waits until the recipe is written and the meal is cooked, and then he puts his little spices in it. He's very specific about what he wants. He doesn't have any 'nagging qualms that he can't put his finger on,' like many people do. When he likes what you've done, he really shows his enjoyment. It's so gratifying to delight him. There's nothing in the least bit cynical or jaded about him. He responds like a kid with a popcorn box on his lap."

As so often happens with directors, though, Spielberg may have become *so* delighted by his writers' contributions that he began to think he had come up with at least some of them himself. Once he seized on the father-son relationship, he shaped it according to his own emotional need for a more combative relationship. Lucas thought of Indy's father as a rather ineffectual old gent, "a John Houseman kind of person." Spielberg wanted Sean Connery. The ruggedly sexy Scottish actor, in a sense, already *was* the father of Indiana Jones, since the series had sprung from the desire of Lucas and Spielberg to rival (and outdo) Connery's James Bond movies. Connery proves more than a match for his cinematic son, ordering him around and condescendingly calling him "Junior." The elder Jones, Connery observed, is "eccentric, self-centered, and quite selfish. He does not have the *Saturday Evening Post* mentality of fatherhood. He's quite indifferent to his boy's needs." At one point, Indy complains that in his childhood, "We never talked." His father retorts, "You left just when you were becoming interesting."

In the film's most memorable comic exchange, which was improvised by the actors, Indy is shocked to realize his father also had an affair with Elsa (Alison Doody), the sinuous blonde who turns out to be a Nazi spy. "I'm as human as the next man," the elder Dr. Jones insists. "I *was* the next man," his son replies. Spielberg had to overcome his own qualms about having Indy and his father sleep with the same woman, an obvious Freudian stand-in for Mom (in an even darker twist, the film also suggests that the treacherous Elsa has slept with Adolf Hitler). When Connery learned that the director, expressing concern about how women would react, had excised his sexual relationship with Elsa, Connery insisted on putting it back into the script. "I didn't want the father to be so much of a wimp," he said. In a cocky bit of screen-hero one-upmanship, Connery added, "Aside from the fact that Indiana Jones is not as well-dressed as James Bond, the main difference between them is sexual. Indiana deals with women shyly. In the first film, he's flustered when the student writes 'I love you' on her eyelids. James Bond would have had all those young coeds for breakfast."

Indiana Jones and the Last Crusade is a graceful piece of popular filmmaking, bursting with the sheer pleasure of cinematic craftsmanship and gratifyingly free of the racist overtones that blighted the two previous films in the series. Released by Paramount on May 24, 1989, to then-record opening figures, *Last Crusade* was Spielberg's biggest hit since *E.T.,* with $494.7 million in worldwide gross on a production cost of $44 million. It was respectfully received by most reviewers, including the author of this book in *Daily Variety.*

Some reviewers, however, found the film distasteful when it mixes cartoonish jokes about Nazis ("Nazis! I *hate* these guys," Indy snarls) with such real-life elements as a book-burning at a Party rally attended by Hitler (who gives Indy his autograph). "The idea about book-burning was Steven's," Boam reports. "He said, 'I really want to do a scene of them burning books.' At the time I thought, This must be a warming-up for *Schindler's List.* But I had no idea what *Schindler's List* was going to be like."

With all its masterly technique, and the added sparks emanating from the father-son relationship, *Last Crusade* is mostly a lark, a holiday outing for a director emotionally wrung out from his two previous films. It is also a farewell to a certain kind of soulless action filmmaking, pushed about as far as it can be along the scale of cinematic ambition (even if Spielberg still talks nostalgically from time to time about doing a fourth Indiana Jones movie). "I've learned more about movie craft from making the Indiana Jones films than I did from *E.T.* or *Jaws,"* he said at the time *Last Crusade* was released. "And now I feel as if I've graduated from the college of Cliffhanger U."

O N April 24, 1989, Spielberg and Amy Irving announced they would divorce after three and a half years of marriage. "Our mutual decision, however difficult, has been made in a spirit of caring," they said. ". . . And our friendship remains both personal and professional."

They agreed to share custody of their son, Max, maintaining homes near each other in Los Angeles and New York to facilitate their joint parenting responsibilities. Amy also received a large settlement. Although the amount was never officially announced, it was reported that she may have received a sum approximating half of her husband's net worth. At the time Spielberg made his first appearance on the *Forbes* 400 list of the nation's wealthiest people in 1987, his net worth was estimated at "well over $225 million." Press estimates of Amy's golden parachute ranged from $93 million to $112.5 million.

The competing stresses of their professional careers were among the primary factors in the failure of their marriage, which had been the subject of rumors in the press for months before the announcement. "I started my career as the daughter of Jules Irving," she said in 1989. "I don't want to finish it as the wife of Spielberg or the mother of Max." Writer-director Matthew Robbins has recalled, "It was no fun to go [to their house], because there was an electric tension in the air. It was competitive as to whose dining table this is, whose career we're gonna talk about, or whether he even approved of what she was interested in—her friends and her actor life. He really was uncomfortable. The child in Spielberg believed so thoroughly in the possibility of perfect marriage, the institution of marriage, the Norman Rockwell turkey on the table, everyone's head bowed in prayer—all this stuff. And Amy was sort of a glittering prize, smart as hell, gifted, and beautiful, but definitely edgy and provocative and competitive. She would not provide him any ease."

For much of their final months as a married couple, Steven was in London and Spain making *Last Crusade,* and Amy was on the New York stage in Athol Fugard's *The Road to Mecca.* They previously had agreed to alternate their work assignments, with neither accepting a job that would keep them apart while the other was working. Amy gave up film offers to spend an "isolated and miserable" time in Spain with Max and Steven for *Empire of the Sun,* and Steven accompanied her when she appeared in director Joan Micklin Silver's 1988 film *Crossing Delancey.* When Amy accepted her role in the Fugard play, however, Steven did not want to pass up the opportunity to make *Last Crusade.* They flew back and forth across the ocean to visit each other whenever they could, but found the situation "impossible," Amy said. "Everything suffered. . . . I used to think I could do it all before Max was born. Now everything's changed."

She admitted five years after the divorce that she had never managed to shake the "loss of identity" she felt as the wife of Hollywood's most powerful filmmaker: "During my marriage to Steven, I felt like a politician's wife. There were certain things expected of me that definitely weren't me. One of my problems is that I'm very honest and direct. You pay a price for that. But then I behaved myself and I paid a price too." Part of what made her uncomfortable, evidently, was their complicated, hectic, and extravagant lifestyle. A woman whose idea of heaven has long been her relatively modest adobe home in Santa Fe, Amy never became accustomed to running four additional households: their estates in Pacific Palisades and East Hampton, beach house in Malibu (which was damaged by fire in July 1988 but subsequently rebuilt), and Trump Tower apartment in Manhattan. "This is not really my style," she complained. "We're surrounded by live-in help and tennis courts and vegetable gardens. . . . the last thing I want is to be 'the lady of the house.' "

Her biggest complaint was not that she had to pass up jobs to be with her husband and son. "It's been frustrating," she acknowledged, "but it's more important that Max is with us and we're a happy group. . . . [W]ork has to be really special for us to do it now." What bothered her even more was her belief that being married to Spielberg made her something of an untouchable in Hollywood. "I know I've never gotten work because of Steven," she said in 1988. "I know I have *not* gotten work because of Steven. Certain directors' egos are such that they don't want somebody from Steven's camp on their territory. I've known of instances when I was supposed to get a part, but they started to worry about Steven Spielberg getting more of a focus on them."

At least one instance when Amy became upset over not being cast in a part involved an Amblin Entertainment production. When Joe Dante was preparing the 1987 *Innerspace,* he was having trouble casting the role of astronaut Dennis Quaid's girlfriend. "It was a very awkward situation," Dante recalls, "because Amy Irving wanted to play the part. Steven would not make me hire Amy Irving, which may have been the cause of a certain dissension in the household. I didn't think she was right for it. [The character] was supposed to be a tough reporter type. I didn't want to go through the rigmarole of meeting her and reading her. Every other actress that would come up, Steven would veto. Finally it got close to shooting the role, and [Warner Bros. executive] Lucy Fisher suggested Meg Ryan. We thought she was perfect. Amy was very upset. She sent me a letter: 'I'm not Mrs. Steven Spielberg. I'm an actress.' " Asked if part of his concern about casting Amy was what might happen if he did not get along with her, Dante conceded that was a situation he "didn't want to have on the set."

As it turned out, the only roles Amy played for Amblin during her marriage to Spielberg were the singing voice of cartoon character Jessica Rabbit in *Who Framed Roger Rabbit* and a virtually invisible cameo (along with her mother, Priscilla Pointer) as a train passenger in Spielberg's *Amazing Stories* program "Ghost Train." Following the divorce, she also played the voice of a cartoon character in *An American Tail: Fievel Goes West* (1991).

Although she has continued to do notable stage work, such as her role as a Brooklyn Jewish woman haunted by Nazism in Arthur Miller's play *Broken Glass,* Irving has played only occasional film roles since her divorce from Spielberg. "I think it hurt being Steven Spielberg's wife, and then it hurt being the ex-Mrs. Steven Spielberg," she said in 1994. "It was awkward for a while. I don't know why. I only know that I felt nonexistent. . . . I'd do a movie with Steven, but I think it would be awkward for him. Our friendship is very valuable to us, and that would probably put a strain on it." However, she has appeared in films directed by her companion Bruno Barreto, a Brazilian filmmaker she met when he cast her in *Show of Force* in March 1989, shortly before her divorce announcement.*

The press often linked Kate Capshaw with Spielberg in the months preceding that announcement, but Spielberg's spokesmen denied there was any romantic attachment between them. However, the marital problems between Steven and Amy were also denied up until the time the marriage collapsed. Kate and Steven kept a low profile together until he invited her to London at the end of June 1989 for the premiere of *Last Crusade.* They made no attempt to keep their relationship clandestine, and Steven thought Amy would have no way of finding out. But Amy read about their tryst in the *National Enquirer.*

While waiting for Steven's divorce, Kate cared for a newborn African American foster child, Theo, whom she and then also Spielberg later

---

* Amy and Bruno have a son, Gabriel, who was born in 1990.

adopted. On May 14, 1990, she gave birth to her first child with Spielberg, a daughter named Sasha. After converting to Judaism, Kate married Steven in a traditional Jewish ceremony on October 12, 1991, at their country estate in East Hampton, under a tent filled with Hollywood friends, including Steve Ross, Barbra Streisand, Richard Dreyfuss, Harrison Ford, Dustin Hoffman, and Robin Williams.

The two worst times of his life, Spielberg recalled in 1994, were the divorce of his parents and his own divorce from Amy. But he has always remained guarded about the subject of his divorce. "I've never talked [to the press] about my personal life with Amy," he said in 1989. "She talks about it." The way he has expressed his feelings is to make movies about them.

A L W A Y S can best be understood as a movie about Spielberg's acceptance of loss. His on-screen surrogate in this loose remake of the 1943 movie *A Guy Named Joe,* a reckless pilot played by Richard Dreyfuss, loses his life flying and is sent back to Earth to help his former lover and fellow pilot (Holly Hunter) find happiness with another man. In Spielberg's own life at the time he made *Always,* he was trying to come to terms with several kinds of loss—the loss of his wife, the aging of his parents, and the loss of his childhood—as well as with the inevitable feelings of failure a divorced man faces in his roles as husband and father.

Spielberg's interest in the story traces back to the time his own parents' marriage was starting to fall apart. He first watched *A Guy Named Joe* on TV in Phoenix, and later said it was "a story that touched my soul . . . the second movie, after *Bambi,* that made me cry." Written by Dalton Trumbo and directed by Victor Fleming, the MGM movie stars Spencer Tracy as a World War II pilot who dies in combat but returns to reassure his grieving widow (Irene Dunne) that it's not wrong to fall in love with another man (Van Johnson). The young Spielberg—whose fascination with airplanes always seemed to involve his feelings about his father—needed to hear the message that life would go on despite separation and loss. "I didn't understand why I cried," he said. "But I did. [The Tracy character] is powerless, unable to influence events, like a piece of furniture. As a child I was very frustrated, and maybe I saw my own parents in it. I was also short of girlfriends. And it stuck with me."

In remaking one of his most cherished childhood favorites, Spielberg also made one of his rare commercial missteps: *Always* grossed a relatively disappointing $77.1 million worldwide. The personal imperatives of the project blinded Spielberg to its irrelevance for contemporary audiences. He seemed not to understand that what gave *A Guy Named Joe* its wide appeal in 1943 was its wartime setting and its audience's shared ethos of sacrifice. A nation of grieving families and war widows hungered for that kind of emotional boost; the audience of 1989 could not be faulted for finding the situation of *Always* little more than a curiosity. Setting the remake in World War

II would not have solved the problem, but Spielberg's decision to transpose the story to the present day, among pilots fighting forest fires in Montana, robbed it of the social context that had made its self-sacrificial fantasy acceptable and meaningful in 1943. The hybrid nature of the film is emphasized by Spielberg's use of World War II–vintage airplanes, 1940s slang ("dollface," "you big lug," "moxie," "Your number is up"), and retro romantic scenes, demonstrating the director's overly literal fixation on his mood as a twelve-year-old child. From its spectacular flying sequences to its emphasis on romantic voyeurism and its obsession with surrogate fatherhood, *Always* is a smorgasbord of Spielbergian motifs and psychological hangups.

The project had begun taking shape in his mind in 1974, when he discovered that Richard Dreyfuss shared his fondness for the original movie. Although Spielberg thought of Dreyfuss as their generation's equivalent of Spencer Tracy, he hesitated about giving the role to his "alter ego," whose persona seems a bit too cerebral for the part of a rough-and-tumble pilot. The director also considered such older, more conventionally romantic stars as Paul Newman and Robert Redford. Debra Winger (an old flame of Spielberg's) was discussed for the female lead and Harrison Ford for the thankless role of the other pilot.

After the project was first announced at MGM in 1980 as *A Guy Named Joe,* Spielberg commissioned a dozen screenplays* but kept delaying the start of shooting, making *Always* seem like one of those pet projects that somehow never get off the ground. "In a lot of the earlier drafts, Richard walked through walls," Spielberg recalled. "He put his hands through things. He glowed. It was riddled with gimmicks and tricks and all the stuff that I guess I do really well. I guess that's why I didn't want to do it. . . . Every special effect that we had was written out of the movie. . . . I had a lot of false starts, but I think it all came down to the fact that I wasn't ready to make it. . . . If I had made it in 1980, I think it would have been more of a comedy. I'd have hidden all of the deep feelings."

Hiding deep feelings is part of the problem Spielberg's alter ego faces in *Always*. Dreyfuss's Pete Sandich is unable to admit he loves his girlfriend, Dorinda (Hunter), until he finds himself in the afterlife. He is brought back to Earth for a dual purpose: to serve as guardian angel to the callow young flyer Ted Baker (Brad Johnson) and to let go of his unrequited emotional attachment to Dorinda. Pete's own guardian angel is a blithe spirit named Hap, perhaps an allusion to General Henry H. (Hap) Arnold, the World War II chief of the U.S. Army Air Forces, in which Spielberg's father served. When the father figure from *Last Crusade,* Sean Connery, was unavailable to play Hap, Spielberg made the unconventional casting choice of Audrey Hepburn, figuring she "was closer to the maternal side of nature."

The fantasy framework adds a level of poignancy to a triangular romance

---

* Jerry Belson and Diane Thomas were among the writers. Ronald Bass worked on the shooting script, but Belson did the final draft and received sole screen credit.

that the director otherwise treats with the jocular tone of 1940s romantic comedy. But the fantasy elements also underscore the curiously asexual nature of what was touted as Spielberg's first "adult love story." The most moving, and most genuinely romantic, scene depends on the audience's awareness that the two lovers are unable to touch each other. Dorinda's solitary dance to "Smoke Gets in Your Eyes" is accompanied by the ghostly Pete, whom she cannot see. As Dorinda glides around her living room, wearing the clingy white "girl clothes" Pete gave her before he died, Spielberg's graceful, gently caressing camera movements wistfully express feelings of loss and remembrance.*

But for some (perhaps most) contemporary viewers, unrequited love of the sort on view in *Always* may seem more annoying than charming. And for Spielberg's detractors, this old-fashioned, asexual plot was simply another sign of his arrested development, further proof that he wouldn't—or couldn't —grow up. When Dorinda makes her first appearance in her shimmering white dress before a roomful of comically awe-stricken fliers and grease monkeys, "It's the most purely sexless moment in Spielberg's long, long career as a boy," wrote David Denby in *New York* magazine, "and it made me realize to what extent sex in his movies is a matter of dreams and idealization."

Spielberg, it is true, has yet to explore the full dimensions of adult sexuality on screen. His occasional forays in that direction, such as the lesbian love scene in *The Color Purple,* have tended to be shy and tentative. The director's handling of romantic scenes in *Always* is often marred by an excessively juvenile tone, with characters breaking into nervous giggles like high school kids embarrassed at playing grown-up. To compare Holly Hunter's girlish hysteria in *Always* with Irene Dunne's serene womanly grace in *A Guy Named Joe* is to recognize how far Spielberg still has to go in dealing with mature female sexuality.

Spielberg is more in his element dealing with male anxieties, such as Pete's possessiveness toward Dorinda, his lack of emotional commitment, his discomfort with her career, and his masochistic jealousy over watching her being courted by Ted. The director imbalances the drama, however, by making Ted a cartoonish oaf, perhaps because making Pete's rival a man of equal stature would have felt too threatening. Pete eventually realizes that the happiness of the woman he loves depends on his own willingness to accept that she has found someone else. His process of letting go is a process of emotional maturation.

It's unlikely Spielberg could have found these feelings in himself without having first experienced the pain of separation and divorce. The paternal

---

* Spielberg's witty use of the lovely old Jerome Kern ballad as the love song of the two smoke-eaters came about after the director was denied the use of Irving Berlin's haunting "Always." In a telephone conversation with Spielberg, the ninety-four-year-old Berlin said he "planned to use it in the future."

way Pete learns to treat Ted seems to reflect Spielberg's own pleasure in his newfound role as a father. And by showing Pete acting as Ted's professional mentor, Spielberg is echoing the role he likes to play with younger directors.

Photographed by Mikael Salomon, *Always* contains some of Spielberg's most ravishing images, and the aerial firefighting sequences (partly filmed during the 1988 Yellowstone fires) are far superior to the studiobound visuals of *A Guy Named Joe.* Where *Always* falters is in the wide disparity between the sophistication of its craftsmanship and the relative shallowness of its romantic relationships.

F O R a film that was widely anticipated as an artistic culmination for Spielberg—his definitive statement on the "Peter Pan Syndrome"—*Hook* mostly serves to demonstrate the middle-aged director's overwhelming sense of boredom with Peter Pan, the Lost Boys, and all they represent about the anarchic spirit of childhood. The filmmaker's passion is stimulated only by the more somber parts of the story, in which the grown-up Pan, Peter Banning (Robin Williams), movingly comes to terms with his failure as a father to his embittered young son, Jack (Charlie Korsmo). But otherwise *Hook* is a lumbering white elephant, marred by protracted, tediously chaotic tomfoolery in the pirate village and Neverland.

Perhaps Spielberg simply had waited too long to get around to making his Peter Pan movie. In one way or another, of course, he had been making it forever. Even Spielberg's first amateur feature, made twenty-eight years earlier, owes a debt to *Peter Pan,* for Tinkerbell flies around in the form of a firelight. Henry Sheehan, one of the few critics to regard *Hook* as a major Spielberg work, wrote in *Film Comment* that the movie "pulled together the many different thematic strands, visual motifs, and character types that had been haphazardly scattered through his first fifteen [*sic*] years of work, and patterned them into a rich, coherent whole." But as revealing as *Hook* may be for students of Spielberg's life and work, most of it is far more "rich" and "coherent" in the abstract than in its execution.

During the early 1980s, Spielberg developed a live-action adaptation of *Peter Pan* for Disney and, later, Paramount. He considered Michael Jackson for the title role (as a singing and dancing Pan) and Dustin Hoffman for Captain James Hook. "I decided not to make *Peter Pan* really when Max was born," the director explained in 1990, "and I guess it was just bad timing. *Peter Pan* came at a time when I had my first child and I didn't want to go to London and have seven kids on wires in front of blue screens swinging around. I wanted to be home as a dad, not a surrogate dad."

Spielberg had moved on to new problems and more adult concerns. As he showed in *Empire of the Sun,* he no longer felt comfortable with mere celebrations of childhood innocence, but now was concerned about the death of innocence and the coming of manhood. Around that same time, he briefly considered directing *Big,* his sister Anne's screenplay (in collaboration with Gary Ross) about a twelve-year-old boy who suddenly finds himself a grown man and becomes a phenomenally successful designer of toys. The boy-man played by Tom Hanks in director Penny Marshall's 1988 movie bears more than a casual resemblance to Steven Spielberg himself; indeed, *Big* can be seen as his sister's affectionately satirical commentary on his life and career. But what would have been the point of making it? He already had lived the tale, and now he was trying to outgrow it.*

Fittingly, *Hook* was the brainchild of a small boy. In 1982, screenwriter Jim V. Hart's three-year-old son, Jake, showed his family a drawing. "We asked Jake what it was," Hart recalled, "and he said it was a crocodile eating Captain Hook, but that the crocodile *really* didn't eat him, he got away. As it happens, I had been trying to crack *Peter Pan* for years, but I didn't just want to do a remake. So I went, 'Wow. Hook is not dead. The crocodile is. We've all been fooled.' Four years later, our family was having dinner and Jake said, 'Daddy, did Peter Pan ever grow up?' My immediate response was, 'No, of course not.' And Jake said, 'But what if he did?' And that unlocked all the doors that had been closed to me. I realized that Peter *did* grow up, just like all of us baby boomers who are now in our forties. I patterned him after several of my friends on Wall Street, where the pirates wear three-piece suits and ride in limos."

Hook was being developed by Hart and director Nick Castle at TriStar when the Japanese electronics giant Sony bought Columbia-TriStar in 1989. The following year, Sony hired Mike Medavoy to run TriStar. Medavoy, who had been Spielberg's first agent, sent Hart's script to Spielberg, who quickly committed to direct it. Castle, who had worked for Spielberg on *Amazing Stories,* was taken off *Hook* and given a $500,000 settlement, as well as a story credit with Hart. Spielberg received unfavorable publicity for what some took to be an arrogant power play against a less prominent director, but Medavoy says, "He didn't want anything to do with taking another director off a picture. I said, 'I've already done it.' Because Dustin and Robin weren't going to work with [Castle]."

Spielberg had no trouble seeing reflections of himself in Hart's workaholic protagonist, yuppie arbitrageur Peter Banning: "He's very representative of a lot of people today who race headlong into the future, nodding hello and good-bye to their families. I'm part of a generation that is extremely motivated by career, and I've caught myself in the unenviable position of *being* Peter Banning from time to time. I've seen myself overworked, and not spending enough time at home, and I got a couple of good lessons from making the movie."

Hart, however, found himself replaced by other writers, including Malia Scotch Marmo and actress/novelist Carrie Fisher. "I loved Jim Hart's script,"

---

* His stated reason for bowing out of the project was that he felt Anne had been "standing in my shadow long enough. . . . I began to consider the fact that if I directed it, people wouldn't give Annie any credit." She and Ross received Oscar nominations for the screenplay.

claimed Spielberg, "but I didn't feel he had written Captain Hook, and neither did Dustin. Malia rescued that." Marmo received screenplay credit along with Hart, but Fisher was uncredited for rewriting comedic dialogue for Tinkerbell (Julia Roberts). "Steven tends to use writers like paintbrushes," Hart noted. "He wants this writer for this, this writer for that. The joke was that everyone in town who had his fax number was writing for it."

Much of the press coverage generated by *Hook* came for reasons that had little to do with the story of Peter Pan growing up. The gargantuan scale of the production made it a prominent symbol of 1990s runaway excess in Hollywood, with lavish sets filling nine stages on the Sony lot in Culver City. Although, as usual, Spielberg kept the sets closed to most of the press, a constant flow of Hollywood celebrities made *Hook* the town's "in" attraction after filming began on February 19, 1991, continuing into the summer.

Spielberg, Hoffman, and Williams did not take salaries for the film. Their deal, negotiated by the Creative Artists Agency (CAA), instead called for the trio to split 40 percent of the distributor's gross revenues from all markets. They were to receive a total of $20 million from the first $50 million in gross theatrical film rentals, with TriStar keeping the next $70 million in rentals before the three resumed receiving their percentage. As Medavoy pointed out at the time, if Spielberg and the two stars "went out and got their regular salaries, they would have gotten a lot more than the aggregate of 40 percent of $50 million. A huge amount more. I think it was a fair deal for everybody." Medavoy's explanations did not stop the absurdly exaggerated gossip around Hollywood that the film would have to gross as much as $300 million to $500 million to see any profits.

When *Hook* opened with less than expected box-office numbers in December 1991, many people wrote it off as a bomb. With a production cost variously estimated at between $60 million and $80 million, far in excess of its original budget of $48 million, it is often regarded as one of the most conspicuous money-wasting debacles in Sony's profligate Hollywood spending spree. In fact, says Medavoy, "Sony made a lot of money on that picture. It did better overseas, but it did just an enormous amount here [the total worldwide theatrical gross was $288 million]. The video sold well. The studio will do somewhere between $40 million and $50 million profit." As for Spielberg, Hoffman, and Williams, "They made a lot of money," Medavoy says. "But so did everybody else."

Medavoy points out that *Hook* also was designed as a way for Sony to say to Hollywood, "Take notice. The studio is open for business, and it's going to do big movies." Unfortunately, that attitude seemed to infect everyone on the set, including Spielberg. Although he had been practicing frugality ever since his "rehab" on *Raiders of the Lost Ark,* he became intoxicated with the sheer scale of the production* and reverted to the kind of indulgence that

---

* An Amblin Entertainment film, it was produced by Kathleen Kennedy, Frank Marshall, and Gerald R. Molen (Amblin's production manager, who also served in that capacity on *Hook*).

characterized his work on *1941*. *Hook* ran forty days over its seventy-six-day shooting schedule. Among the other contributors to the laborious shooting pace were the notoriously perfectionistic Dustin Hoffman, the physically and emotionally overwrought Julia Roberts, some amateurish child actors, elaborate special effects, and crowd scenes with hundreds of extras and stuntmen. But Spielberg said, "It was all my fault. . . . Nobody else made it go over budget. I began to work at a slower pace than I usually do. . . . For some reason this movie was such a dinosaur coming out of the gate. It dragged me along behind it. . . . Every day I came on to the set, I thought, Is this flying out of control?"

H o o k "gets the prize for the most lavish, extravagant, opulent ode to simple joys and basic values ever made," quipped *Village Voice* reviewer Georgia Brown. The more intimate scenes, particularly those revolving around Peter's relationship with his son, are so far superior to the spectacle scenes that it almost seems as if another director made the rest of the movie. The lifeless and garishly photographed scenes in the pirate village, the overly ornate and pointlessly cluttered production design,* the slapdash construction of the Neverland sequences, and the forced humor involving the punk-ish Lost Boys betray what *New Yorker* reviewer Terrence Rafferty called "a profound weariness in Steven Spielberg's attitude toward his art and his audience. In this version of *Peter Pan,* the imagination seems like a burden —a terrible, crushing obligation."

Spielberg intends the audience to come away feeling that Peter is freed of his anal-retentive, Type-A behavior by immersing himself in the carefree behavior of childhood. The director's confused notion was that Peter "rescued his past. He rescued that memory of himself as a child and carried that best friend with him the rest of his life. It will never leave him again." But the movie actually seems to be saying the opposite—that Peter needs to get his infantile tendencies out of his system for once and for all, through this one last monumental effort of regression, before he can go back to his family and behave like a *mensch*. Saving his children from Captain Hook requires that he give up his wish "to be a little boy and have fun." "I can't stay and play," Peter sadly tells the Lost Boys, although he carries away from Neverland a renewed sense of the importance of play in everyday life and an awareness of the futility of a life devoted exclusively to greed and ambition.

The troubled relationship between Peter and his son, so full of echoes of Spielberg's relationship with his own father, is the emotional heart of the film. An orphan himself, raised by his Granny Wendy (Maggie Smith), Peter

* Dean Cundey was cinematographer and Norman Garwood production designer; theatrical designer John Napier was hired as the film's "visual consultant" after Spielberg saw his work on the musical *Cats*. Spielberg's animation studio, Amblimation, has been working for years on a film version of *Cats*.

says, "I knew why I grew up. I wanted to be a father." But he is a terrible failure as a husband and father, so "obsessed with success" at the expense of his family (as Captain Hook puts it) that he takes a business call during his daughter's school performance of *Peter Pan* and sends an assistant to videotape his son's Little League baseball game. When he promises to attend games in the future, adding, "My word is my bond," his son bitterly replies, "Yeah—junk bond." Scarcely repressing his hostility toward his father, Jack nevertheless retains a tender core of wounded love that he finally is able to express when his father stands against the devious, child-hating Captain Hook.

After kidnapping Jack and his sister Maggie (Amber Scott)—the latest in a long string of child abductions in Spielberg movies—Hook woos them from their family allegiance with a lecture entitled "Why Parents Hate Their Children." Hook's arguments are so persuasive because they are so accurate. "Jack and Maggie are gone because Peter has wished them gone," Henry Sheehan noted in *Film Comment*. "Hook is merely the agent of Peter's most secret, repressed desires, and as such is his mirror image. When Peter first confronts Hook and is taunted by the mustachioed pirate into attempting a rescue, his failure to do so is deeply ambiguous, the result partly of physical shortcoming [ironically, a fear of heights] but also partly of nerve and, hence, desire." In one of the most quietly affecting scenes in the movie, Peter's wife Moira (Caroline Goodall) chides him by saying, "Your children love you. They want to play with you. How long do you think that lasts? Soon Jack may not even want you to come to his games. We have a few special years with our children, when they're the ones who want *us* around. After that you're going to be running off to them for a bit of attention. So *fast,* Peter— it's a few years, then it's over. You are not being careful. And you are missing it."

That is the lesson Peter Banning learns in *Hook,* and it is one Spielberg took to heart in his own life, even while he was being pulled in the other direction by his own obsession with success. In learning to take the responsibility of fatherhood, Spielberg also learned to take greater responsibility as an artist.

"So," Granny Wendy tells Peter, "your adventures are over."

"Oh, no," he replies. "To live—to live will be an awfully big adventure!"

Sixteen

Mensch

I'VE SAID TO HIM, "WHO ARE YOU? I HARDLY KNOW YOU." BUT STEVEN JUST KEEPS GROW-
ING IN ALL DIRECTIONS.

— LEAH ADLER, 1994

W H E N he went to Poland
in 1993 to make *Schindler's List,* Spielberg was "hit in the face with my
personal life. My upbringing. My Jewishness. The stories my grandparents
told me about the Shoah. And Jewish life came pouring back into my heart.
I cried all the time." The anguish he felt while making *Schindler's List* was
translated directly to the screen. While immersed in his re-creation of the
Holocaust, the viewer can readily understand why the filmmaker felt "constantly sickened" and "frightened every day" on location in Poland. To the
almost overwhelming burden of paying witness to the history of his people
was added the personal burden of finally coming to terms with himself.
Schindler's List became the transforming experience of Spielberg's lifetime.
Making the film after more than a decade of hesitation and avoidance was
the catharsis that finally liberated him to be himself, both as a man and as an
artist, fully integrating those two, sometimes distinct-seeming halves of his
personality.

What made the day-to-day experience in Poland bearable was what made
it possible for him to undertake the project: the presence of his family. Before
undertaking his "journey from shame to honor," Spielberg "had to have a
family first. I had to figure out what my place was in the world." His second

wife, Kate, accompanied him to Poland with their five children.* His parents and his rabbi also paid visits to the location of what *Jewish Frontier* reviewer Mordecai Newman called "Spielberg's bar mitzvah movie, his cinematic initi-ation into emotional manhood."

When he finally accepted his long-overdue Academy Award for directing *Schindler's List,* Spielberg thanked Kate "for rescuing me ninety-two days in a row in Kraków, Poland, last winter when things got just too unbearable." He told the press he "would've gone crazy" without his family there. ". . . My kids saw me cry for the first time. I would come home and weep, not because I was feeling sorry for anybody—I would weep because it was *so bloody painful."* Every couple of weeks, he said, "Robin Williams would call me with comic CARE packages over the telephone to try to get me to laugh."

Even in those depths, Spielberg was never far from his more familiar niche as a crowd-pleasing commercial filmmaker. Three nights a week, he came home to the small hotel he had rented for his family in Poland, switched on a satellite dish situated in the front yard, and worked on *Jurassic Park,* which had finished principal photography barely three months before *Schindler's List* began filming on March 1, 1993.

Because *Schindler's List* had to be filmed while it was still winter in Po-land, Spielberg left many of the final postproduction chores of his dinosaur movie in the hands of George Lucas. But he reserved for himself the final decisions about the creation of computer-generated dinosaurs and the mov-ie's soundtrack. High-tech communication methods and computer technol-ogy enabled him to see evolving images at Industrial Light & Magic in northern California, along with such friendly faces as those of special-effects wizard Dennis Muren and producer Kathleen Kennedy (who shared produc-ing chores with Gerald R. Molen). Each night when they were finished, composer John Williams would transmit his score, which Spielberg played on large speakers. All this interaction was transmitted from California to Poland and back again, scrambled to avoid piracy.

Spielberg's schizoid, "culturally dislocating" existence working on both films simultaneously was "an unusual set of circumstances, and all my own doing. I don't regret it, but I spend two hours on *Jurassic Park,* and it takes a while to get back into *Schindler's List."* That bifurcated focus perfectly expressed the duality of his artistic personality at a crucial turning point in his career. His career-long balancing act between the somewhat arbitrarily defined poles of artist and entertainer, while never quite so stark as it was during those months in 1993, had made Spielberg a great popular artist. Even if the purely crowd-pleasing side of his nature often seemed dominant, his

* Including his son by Amy Irving, Max; his two children by Capshaw, Sasha and Sawyer (a son born in 1992); and their adopted son, Theo. Kate's teenaged daughter, Jessica, also worked on the film as a production assistant. In 1996, Steven and Kate added to their family a daughter, Destry Allyn, and an adopted daughter, Mikaela.

strengths as a filmmaker, like Dickens's strengths as a novelist, have always been drawn from that duality. Taking respites from the horror of *Schindler's List* to play with fantasy dinosaurs also may have helped keep him from becoming immobilized by despair while going about the task of re-creating the Holocaust in places where it actually occurred. "The test of a first-rate intelligence," wrote F. Scott Fitzgerald, "is the ability to hold two opposed ideas in the mind at the same time, and still retain the ability to function."

A three-hour, black-and-white film about the Holocaust was a highly risky commercial proposition for Universal. Although a few Hollywood films had been made on Holocaust issues,* no major-studio film had ever dealt with the subject with such a level of uncompromising, brutal realism. "I guaranteed the studio they'd lose all their money," Spielberg recalled. "I told them that the $22 million it was costing to make the film, they might as well just give it away to me to make this film, because they were never going to see anything from it. That's how pessimistic I was that there was a climate ready to accept [what is] essentially a movie about racial hatred. I was happily wrong."

Not wanting what he called "blood money," Spielberg offered to forego any salary and defer his lower-than-usual percentage of the gross film rentals until Universal recouped its production cost. All the money he earned from the film (which ultimately became a considerable box-office success) has been donated, through his Righteous Persons Foundation, to Jewish organizations and to such historical projects as the United States Holocaust Memorial Museum in Washington, D.C., and Spielberg's own nonprofit Survivors of the Shoah Visual History Foundation.

"Nobody else could have gotten any studio to say yes to this project," Spielberg said. ". . . I don't boast ever about my own accomplishments, but that was the time I said, well, thank God that I was able to become some kind of a nine-hundred-pound gorilla so I could have the ability to get this project off the ground. . . . One studio executive who shall remain nameless said, 'Why don't we just make a donation to the Holocaust Museum—would that make you happy?' I blew up when I heard that." That was a "message," Spielberg felt, which "capped my resolve to make the movie immediately."

MCA president Sid Sheinberg gave the director the go-ahead to make the picture with only one condition: he had to make *Jurassic Park* first. As Spielberg acknowledged, "He knew that once I had directed *Schindler* I wouldn't be able to do *Jurassic Park*."

• • •

* Most notably *The Diary of Anne Frank, Judgment at Nuremberg, The Pawnbroker, Sophie's Choice,* and the 1978 NBC-TV miniseries *Holocaust.*

I N the late 1980s, Spielberg bought a screenplay Michael Crichton based on his youthful experiences as a Harvard Medical School intern in the emergency ward of Massachusetts General Hospital. *ER* eventually would be transformed into Spielberg's first prime-time hit TV series. "We were talking about changes in my office one day [in October 1989]," Spielberg recalled, "and I happened to ask him what he was working on, aside from this screenplay. He said he had just finished a book about dinosaurs, called *Jurassic Park,* and that it was being proofed by his publisher. I said, 'You know, I've had a fascination with dinosaurs all my life and I'd really love to read it.' So he slipped me a copy of the galleys; and I read them and I called him the next day, and said, 'There's going to be a real hot bidding war for this, I'm sure.'

"But Michael said he wasn't really interested in getting into a bidding war. He wanted to give it to someone who would make the movie. So I said, 'I'd like to make it.' And he said, 'You mean you want to produce it or direct it?' I said, 'Both.' And he said, 'I'll give it to you if you guarantee me that you'll direct the picture.' But then the agency [Creative Artists Agency, which represented both Crichton and Spielberg] got ahold of it; and they, of course, encouraged a bidding war, even though Michael had kind of promised me the book privately. Before long, it had been sent out to every studio in town, and the bidding was fast and furious."

The novel is a hodgepodge of pulp fiction and diverting scientific speculation. Taking as his springboard the notion of cloning dinosaurs from prehistoric DNA preserved in amber, Crichton spun a yarn about a mad theme-park impresario named John Hammond who recklessly creates dinosaurs on a remote island off the coast of Costa Rica, only to see them run amok and destroy both him and the park. Although *Jurassic Park* borrows elements from Crichton's own 1973 movie *Westworld*—a sci-fi thriller about a theme park with a murderous robot gunslinger—it is even more indebted to Arthur Conan Doyle's 1912 novel *The Lost World,* whose very title Crichton cribbed for his sequel, filmed by Spielberg in 1996–97 as *The Lost World: Jurassic Park.*

Doyle's protagonist, a British explorer named Professor Challenger, discovers a South American plateau populated by dinosaurs and ape-men, a prehistoric world removed from "the ordinary laws of Nature." Like Crichton's island, most of whose denizens (notably the *Tyrannosaurus rex*) stem from the Cretaceous rather than the Jurassic Period, Doyle's lost world freely mixes creatures from several geological epochs. Adapted as a silent film in 1925, the novel also was the source of Irwin Allen's 1960 film *The Lost World,* at which the youthful Spielberg stampeded a Phoenix audience with his contagious vomiting prank. Acknowledging his debt to Doyle's work, Crichton commented, "We're both failed doctors who found storytelling more congenial than healing. Sometimes I think I've devoted my entire life to rewriting Conan Doyle in different ways."

Crichton's human characters in *Jurassic Park* are pure cardboard, however, and his dinosaur action set-pieces are far less exciting than those in Spielberg's film. But the author's blend of pseudoscientific fantasizing with old-fashioned monster-movie hokum was tailor-made for Spielberg's talents as a showman. As the director put it, "I have no embarrassment in saying that with *Jurassic* I was really just trying to make a good sequel to *Jaws*. On land."*

The film rights were put up for sale at a non-negotiable asking price of $1.5 million plus a substantial percentage of the gross. Over a three-day period in May 1990, Crichton weighed matching offers from Warner Bros. (for director Tim Burton), Columbia/TriStar (for Richard Donner), Twentieth Century–Fox (for Joe Dante), and Universal for Spielberg. After a day of telephone conversations with all four directors, Crichton settled on Spielberg, with Universal throwing in another $500,000 for a screenplay by the author. "I knew it was going to be a very difficult picture to make," Crichton said. "Steven is arguably the most experienced and most successful director of these kinds of movies. And he's really terrific at running the technology rather than letting the technology run him."

In a largely unsuccessful attempt to flesh out Crichton's characters, Spielberg commissioned rewrites by Malia Scotch Marmo, who had worked on *Hook,* and David Koepp, the writer of Robert Zemeckis's black comedy *Death Becomes Her.* Only Crichton and Koepp received screen credit for the script of *Jurassic Park;* Marmo said her principal contribution was to make Dr. Ellie Sattler (Laura Dern) and the children, Lex (Ariana Richards) and Tim (Joseph Mazzello), more assertive. The crucial change introduced in Koepp's shooting script was giving Crichton's protagonist, Dr. Alan Grant (Sam Neill), a deep-seated hostility toward children, providing a source of dramatic tension that does not exist in the novel (Crichton's Grant "liked kids—it was impossible not to like any group so openly enthusiastic about dinosaurs").

Even before the first script was written, Spielberg, in a departure from his usual order of procedure, was busy storyboarding his favorite sequences from the novel with production designer Rick Carter and several other illustrators. "We basically set up what the scenes were going to be about," Carter explained. "Once [Spielberg] knows what the space is—that's very important, to know where things are—he'll just start playing a projector in his head. He's open to contributions and he'll talk it through, but he'll actually draw these funny little frames which are incredibly detailed if you know how to look at them." When hired to do his rewrite in the spring of 1992, Koepp found the storyboards "enormously helpful. It was like having a large portion

---

* Spielberg already had produced a successful dinosaur movie, Don Bluth's animated *The Land Before Time* (1988). Less than six months after *Jurassic Park,* Amblin came out with *We're Back!: A Dinosaur's Story,* a lighthearted animated film aimed at the small children Spielberg suggested should not be allowed to see *Jurassic Park.*

of the movie just handed to you, to be able to walk around and soak up the feel of what the movie was supposed to look like."

Spielberg's careful planning kept the complex production running smoothly. "From the beginning, I was afraid that a movie like *Jurassic Park* could get away from me," he said. "There had been other pictures—*1941, Jaws,* and *Hook* —where the production simply got away from me and I was dragged behind schedule. I was determined not to let it happen this time. So I walked away from a lot of takes where, on my last picture, I might have stayed for four or five more. . . . I probably drove everyone to the brink of insanity in order to complete this movie on budget and on schedule."

Officially, the final production cost was reported at about $60 million, but *Forbes* magazine later estimated that the film's actual negative cost (including $20 million for interest and overhead) totaled $95 million. Principal photography began on the Hawaiian island of Kauai on August 24, 1992, and was completed in Hollywood on November 30, twelve days *ahead* of the original eighty-two-day shooting schedule. Even Hurricane Iniki, which struck Kauai on September 11, the last scheduled day of the three-week location shoot, barely caused a bump in the production. Spielberg and company, who rode out the storm in the ballroom of the Westin Kauai Hotel, resumed filming on the Universal lot four days later. The day of the hurricane was the thirteenth birthday of actress Ariana Richards. She recalled that "the storm knocked part of the roof in, but nobody was hurt. Steven Spielberg kept all of us kids entertained by telling ghost stories, so it actually turned out to be a pretty good birthday."

T H E sense of wonder that is part of Spielberg's *raison d'être* elevates his *Jurassic Park* to an imaginative level far beyond Crichton's cold-blooded speculations on paleo-DNA cloning. Paleontologist Stephen Jay Gould criticized the movie for trying to pass off a dinosaur revivification premise that amounts to "heaping impossibility upon impossibility." But the achievement of Spielberg and his special-effects wizards in conjuring up believable images of long-extinct creatures is genuinely "spectacular," Gould wrote. "Intellectuals too often either pay no attention to such technical wizardry or, even worse, actually disdain special effects with such dismissive epithets as 'merely mechanical.' I find such small-minded parochialism outrageous. Nothing can be more complex than a living organism, with all the fractal geometry of its form and behavior. . . . The use of technology to render accurate and believable animals therefore becomes one of the greatest all-time challenges to human ingenuity."

With its extensive employment of computer-generated imagery (CGI), *Jurassic Park* rendered obsolescent the traditional stop-motion miniature techniques developed by such special-effects masters as Ray Harryhausen and the original *King Kong*'s Willis O'Brien, as well as eclipsing the advanced go-motion techniques perfected by George Lucas's Industrial Light & Magic. An early example of CGI could be glimpsed in one of Spielberg's own productions, *Young Sherlock Holmes* (1985), for which ILM and Pixar (then the computer graphics division of Lucasfilm) conjured up a computer-animated knight springing into action from a stained-glass window. But when preproduction on *Jurassic Park* began in June 1990, Spielberg did not realize how far he could push CGI techniques to make his dinosaur movie "the most realistic of them all. . . . I thought it was possible that *someday* they might be able to create three-dimensional, live-action characters through computer graphics. But I didn't think it would happen this soon."

Hoping the art of building mechanical monsters had progressed substantially since *Jaws,* Spielberg first thought of hiring Bob Gurr, designer of the King Kong attraction for the Universal theme parks, to build full-sized, ambulatory robotic dinosaurs. But it soon became apparent that the capabilities of Gurr's creatures were far too limited. Spielberg turned to creature designer Stan Winston, who began building large animatronic dinosaurs operated with mechanized support structures, not unlike Bob Mattey's sharks for *Jaws,* but far more technically advanced. Spielberg planned to augment Winston's creatures with go-motion miniatures designed by Phil Tippett and a limited amount of computer animation by ILM. When effects supervisor Dennis Muren told Spielberg his animators could create full-sized dinosaurs with computer graphics, Spielberg replied, "Prove it."

"And," marveled Spielberg, "he went out and proved it. . . . I'll never forget the time that Dennis brought the first test down. I'd never seen movements this smooth outside of looking at *National Geographic* documentaries. But I didn't dare call [Tippett] at that time and say, 'Hey, Phil, we'd like to replace what you were going to do on this film—creating a hundred shots with the best go-motion ever done in history—with CGI.' I didn't have the heart to do it then, because I wasn't fully convinced until I saw a [CGI test of a] fleshed dinosaur, outside in the worst sunlight.

"When I saw that, and Phil saw that with me for the first time, there we were watching our future unfolding on the TV screen, so authentic I couldn't believe my eyes. It blew my mind again. I turned to Phil, and Phil looked at me, and *Phil* said, 'I think I'm extinct.' I actually used Phil's line in the movie, gave it to Malcolm [Jeff Goldblum] to say to Grant." (When they arrive at Jurassic Park and Grant says, "We're out of a job," Malcolm replies, "Don't you mean extinct?") Tippett remained on the film as what Spielberg called "the director of the CGI dinosaurs."* They filled only six and a half minutes of screen time, but, as Spielberg put it, the *Tyrannosaurus rex* became "our star," dwarfing the human performers in more ways than one. The sequence of the *Tyrannosaurus rex* attack on the children, a mixture of CGI and

---

* Tippett, Muren, Winston, and special dinosaur effects creator Michael Lantieri won Academy Awards for their Visual Effects; the film also won Oscars for Sound and Sound Effects Editing.

animatronics, so impressed Spielberg that he changed the ending (originally planned as a smaller-scale battle between two velociraptors) to bring back his star in an all-CGI climax.

To handle his new tools, Spielberg had to take a crash course in computer technology, his father's profession. He had resisted entering his father's field, and that ambivalence was reflected in the movie itself. "I hate computers" is Dr. Grant's first line, and the villain is the park's corrupt director of computer technology, Dennis Nedry (Wayne Knight), whose brief shutdown of the overloaded system has catastrophic consequences. As Richard Corliss observed in *Time,* "no film could be more personal to [Spielberg] than this one. . . . a movie whose subject is its process, a movie about all the complexities of fabricating entertainment in the microchip age. It's a movie in love with technology (as Spielberg is), yet afraid of being carried away by it (as he is)."

W H E N Crichton and Spielberg first met to discuss the adaptation, Crichton assumed they would start by talking about the technical challenges involved in creating dinosaurs. But Spielberg said, "Let's talk about the characters."

"And then," recalled Crichton, "as I scribbled hastily, he went through every character in the story, outlining their physical appearances, their motivations, their hopes and fears, their quirks and foibles. Ideas about dialogue, gestures, and costuming tumbled out. Speaking very rapidly, he went on like this for an hour.

"At last he turned to the dinosaurs, but again, he spoke of them as characters. The strength and limitations of the tyrannosaur. The quick menace of the velociraptors. The sick triceratops. Already, he had a list of telling visual touches: snorting breath fogging a glass window; a foot squishing in mud; muscles moving under skin; a pupil constricting in bright light. He was thinking about how to convey weight, speed, menace, intention. He talked about a *Tyrannosaurus* sprinting sixty miles an hour, chasing a car.

"Finally I could stand it no longer. 'Steven,' I said, 'how are you going to *do* this?'

"He shrugged, and made a little dismissing gesture with his hand. Not important. Not what we need to talk about. (Of course, it was also true he didn't then have an answer.)

"I said, 'But these effects—'

" 'Effects,' he said, 'are only as good as the audience's feeling for the characters.' "

O N E of the most revealing differences between the novel and the film is Spielberg's transformation of Hammond into a far more sympathetic figure. The director admitted that he could not help identifying with Hammond's blinkered obsession with showmanship.* Spielberg underscored his affinities with the character by casting another movie director (Richard Attenborough) as the Scottish impresario.

Spielberg also admitted that he shares the character's "dark side," an all-encompassing passion for his work, sometimes at the expense of family responsibilities. Another in the long line of irresponsible father (or grandfather) figures in Spielberg's films, Hammond is so thrilled to be able to breed dinosaurs that he doesn't stop to weigh the consequences. He even exposes his own grandchildren to mortal danger by using them as guinea pigs for his tourist park. But Hammond's essentially kindly nature in the film—as seen in his almost maternal coaxing of a baby dinosaur from its shell—makes his conduct seem more misguided than villainous. He has no conscious wish to put the children in danger, or any thought of what might happen to them until it is too late to do anything but rely on Grant to save them.

"The power of the film's coupling of children and death arises almost solely from Spielberg's obsessive invocation of it," Henry Sheehan observed in *Sight and Sound*. ". . . The two most terrifying scenes in the film revolve specifically around the children's near death at the hands first of a *Tyrannosaurus rex* and then of the velociraptors. But these encounters also serve to play out the child-murder fantasies of Dr. Grant." Grant's first scene in the film shows him sadistically teasing a young boy with a murderous fantasy about velociraptors ripping him apart. When Tim and Lex greet the celebrated paleontologist with hero-worship, Grant's response is to glower at them and wish they would disappear. He almost gets his wish. "When the *Tyrannosaurus rex* attacks the kids in their stalled car, [Grant] sits still in his own vehicle for what seems endless moments, watching in horror as his (barely) suppressed murder fantasy is played out in front of him," noted Sheehan. "When he finally does leap to the rescue of the kids, he has only partially compensated for his evil wish. The film can't end until he undergoes the exact same scenario, the velociraptor attack, that he outlined at the film's beginning. . . . Given the startling effrontery of building a film around such an unspeakable wish, the complaints over *Jurassic Park*'s lack of 'story' and 'character' sound a little off the point."

Spielberg's decision to change Hammond's motivation from heartless greed to a childlike love of spectacle helps account for why the character, as critic Peter Wollen observed, "escapes unscathed, presumably because he is too close, in some respects, to Spielberg himself." The children's ordeal as they flee from rampaging dinosaurs, and Grant's gradual acceptance of his adult responsibilities as their fatherly protector, resolve what Sheehan called Spielberg's "continuing obsession with fathers treading the line between life-giver and life-destroyer." In the final scene, with his arms around the sleeping children in a helicopter escaping the park, Grant exchanges a silent

---

* In a self-reflexive irony, *Jurassic Park: The Ride* opened in 1996 at Universal Studios Hollywood, with Spielberg serving as a consultant.

acknowledgment with Dr. Ellie Sattler that he finally has become comfortable with his fatherly feelings.

Spielberg's depiction of the dinosaurs, like his depiction of the Great White Shark in *Jaws,* contains equal parts of fascination and fear. The director's ambivalence sharpens the suspense by encouraging the audience to admire and even identify with the dinosaurs (as Grant does), while also experiencing the terror of their human prey. The resulting complexity of tone produces the kind of unsettling "attraction/repulsion" ambivalence familiar from Hitchcock films. Spielberg's lifelong fascination with dinosaurs may stem from the same underlying anxieties as his obsession with irresponsible parents. Crichton theorizes that "children liked dinosaurs because these giant creatures personified the uncontrollable force of looming authority. They were symbolic parents. Fascinating and frightening, like parents. And kids loved them, as they loved their parents."

It's fair to criticize Spielberg for failing to make the people in *Jurassic Park* as three-dimensional as the dinosaurs. While Australian actor Sam Neill fills the role of the brooding Grant in competent but uninspired fashion, Laura Dern is an annoyance as Dr. Sattler, her open-mouthed gaping and general ditziness undercutting her credibility as a paleobotanist. Spielberg's anxiety about finishing ahead of schedule may have undermined his customary care with performances, allowing the cast (including Jeff Goldblum's hipster mathematician, Ian Malcolm) to get away with too many affectless, mumbling line readings. Spielberg preferred to spend his budget on special effects rather than on his cast.* But the director's more intense creative rapport with Attenborough and the two children also suggests that the characters played by Neill and Dern simply failed to engage his full emotional involvement.

"Jurassic Park packs the thrills of a great entertainment, but it doesn't resonate like a great movie," wrote Julie Salamon of *The Wall Street Journal,* who complained that "while the dinosaurs feel real, the humans seem fake." With few exceptions, such as Henry Sheehan, reviewers tended to be indifferent or actively hostile to the director's preoccupation with the fatherhood theme. David Ansen of *Newsweek* dismissed it by writing that Grant's "aversion to children [is] predictably reversed when he must save Hammond's two movie-brattish grandchildren from becoming the dinosaurs' hors d'oeuvre." Georgia Brown of *The Village Voice* wrote that *Jurassic Park* is "too terrifying for tender psyches. Amazingly, it really roughs up its two picture book–perfect child protagonists. After *Hook*'s nauseating tribe of Lost Boys, many will appreciate this new coldness."

"W H A T is a cynic?" asked Oscar Wilde. "A man who knows the price of everything, and the value of nothing." That observation could be applied

---

* Before hiring Neill, he considered such stars as William Hurt (who turned down the role) and Kurt Russell and Richard Dreyfuss (too expensive).

to the box-office phenomenon of *Jurassic Park.* The financial numbers were so staggering, they threatened to relegate the actual movie to a footnote.

Following its opening on June 10, 1993, *Jurassic Park* took less than four months to break the previous record of $701 million set by *E.T.,* and it finished its theatrical run with a worldwide box-office gross of $913 million *(E.T.* remains champion in the domestic market, with $399.8 million to *Jurassic's* $357.1 million). *Jurassic Park* so monopolized foreign theater screens that it sparked bitter protests among French filmmakers demanding government protection for their own films over such rampaging Hollywood blockbusters. Spielberg's own share of *Jurassic* revenues also made news, with *Forbes* reporting that he "got his 'gross points,' in this case a weighted average of perhaps 20% of film revenues, until the film broke even. Once the film was in the black, Spielberg split profits 50–50. . . . Spielberg will make over $250 million from *Jurassic Park.* . . . by far the most an individual has ever made from a movie, or any other unit of entertainment."

Sarcastically skewering such journalistic hosannas to the film's financial success, Stuart Klawans wrote in *The Nation,* "Do I care? Is any of that money headed toward *my* bank account? But perhaps I've missed the point. From the tone of the news report, I can tell that *Jurassic Park's* success must surely be my success, too. As if in a potlatch, I can participate in the communal good fortune by offering my $7.50 to the next week's gross. To quote the ad campaign: 'Be a Part of Motion Picture History!' What joy all of America must feel, as the numbers rise higher and higher!"

With people reviewing his bank account rather than his movie, Spielberg once again found himself stigmatized by his own success. That bore out the truth of his reflection: "Part of me is afraid I will be remembered for the money my films have made, rather than the films themselves. Do people remember the gold medal, or do they remember what the gold medal was won for?"

Then came *Schindler's List.*

"**I** T ' L L make a helluva story," Spielberg said. "Is it true?"

Sid Sheinberg had sent him a *New York Times* review of Thomas Keneally's "nonfiction novel" about Oskar Schindler, the Nazi industrialist who spent his fortune to save his Jewish workers from the Shoah. "I was drawn to it because of the paradoxical nature of the character," Spielberg recalled. "It wasn't about a Jew saving Jews, or a neutral person from Sweden or Switzerland saving Jews. It was about a Nazi saving Jews. . . . What would drive a man like this to suddenly take everything he had earned and put it all in the service of saving these lives?"

Spielberg did not commit in 1982 to directing *Schindler's List,* but he showed enough interest that Universal bought the film rights for him that fall. The following spring, he had his first meeting with a Holocaust survivor named Leopold (Paul) Page. A Pole, born Leopold Pfefferberg, he was one of the eleven hundred Jews saved by Schindler, known to themselves as the *Schindlerjuden*. "Poldek" Pfefferberg played the black market for Schindler in Kraków before becoming a barracks leader in the Plaszów forced-labor camp, whose commandant was SS *Untersturmführer* Amon Goeth. Schindler bribed Goeth to let Pfefferberg, his wife, Mila, and the other *Schindlerjuden* work in the safety of his *Deutsche Emailwaren Fabrik* (German Enamelware Factory) on the outskirts of Kraków. When the factory was ordered disbanded in 1944, Schindler bought the workers from Goeth and established another haven, a bogus munitions plant in his hometown of Brünnlitz, Czechoslovakia.

Since coming to America in the war's aftermath, Pfefferberg had made it his life's mission to bear witness to Schindler's unlikely heroism. Pfefferberg was the first person Spielberg thanked while accepting his Oscar for directing the film: "This never could have happened—this never could have gotten started—without a survivor named Poldek Pfefferberg. . . . He has carried the story of Oskar Schindler to all of us, a man of complete obscurity who makes us wish and hope for Oskar Schindlers in all of our lives." Armed with a rich collection of documents and photographs, Pfefferberg searched indefatigably for someone to tell the story. While doing so, he also arranged with his fellow *Schindlerjuden* to support their rescuer, whose business ventures after the war all came to ruin. A deal Pfefferberg helped arrange with MGM in 1963 for a film about Schindler also fell through, but not before earning $37,500 for Schindler himself.

One day in October 1980, on his way home to Australia from a film festival in Italy, Thomas Keneally stopped briefly in Beverly Hills to sign copies of his latest novel, *Confederates*. Visiting a luggage store to buy a briefcase, he began chatting with the owner—Poldek Pfefferberg. "In the course of the conversation he found out I was a novelist," Keneally recalled. ". . . He told me that he had the best story of the century."

"I was saved by a big, good-looking Nazi named Oskar Schindler," Pfefferberg explained. "Not only was I saved from Gröss-Rosen [a concentration camp in Poland], but my wife, Mila, was saved from Auschwitz itself. So as far as I'm concerned, Oskar is Jesus Christ. But though he was Jesus Christ, he wasn't a saint. He was all-drinking, all-black-marketeering, all-screwing."

Keneally was fascinated by "Herr Schindler's strange virtue" and by Pfefferberg's documents on the bureaucratic and industrial aspects of the Holocaust. But, recalled Pfefferberg, "Keneally said he was the wrong person to write it—he was only three when World War II broke out, as a Catholic he knew little about the Holocaust, and he didn't know much about Jewish suffering. I got angry and said those were three reasons he should write the book." A shrewd insight, for Keneally's eclectic body of work has what the author calls a "preoccupation with race and the interface between different races and cultures." He traces that preoccupation to the fact that he comes from "disreputable Irish convict stock" and to his early awareness of the injustices suffered by Australian Aborigines. And, like Schindler, Keneally is a former Catholic. "I was always fascinated by the way former Catholics tended to be morally engaged," the author noted. "The first thing you do when you become a lapsed Catholic is to pork as many men or women as you can. Then you take up causes. Schindler seemed to me a typical lapsed Catholic."

With Pfefferberg acting as liaison and persuader, Keneally traveled to several countries to interview almost fifty *Schindlerjuden,* taking care to make *Schindler's List* factually accurate. "It may be a novel," he said, "but it's not fiction." The reason he cast the book in fictional form was that he thought of Schindler as "very much partaking of the paradoxes that are favored by the novel. Paradox is what turns novelists on. Linear valor is not as important to them as light and shade." As for the film, "The big fear the author of the original work would have with a film is whether or not it retains the ambiguities, and it's there in spades. I'd say it's triumphantly ambiguous."

"**P** L E A S E , when are you starting?" Poldek Pfefferberg asked Spielberg at their first meeting in 1983.

"Ten years from now," Spielberg replied.

He kept that promise precisely. Spielberg displayed a remarkable degree of self-knowledge in anticipating how hard it would be to summon up the courage to make *Schindler's List.* Throughout his decade of indecision, the project "was on my guilty conscience," he said, because Pfefferberg kept "heaping on the fact that he was going to die."* Spielberg kept stalling a commitment, ostensibly because he had trouble getting a usable screenplay (first from Keneally and then from Kurt Luedtke), but mostly because he was not yet emotionally ready to "face the responsibility I have as a filmmaker. . . . In my burning desire to entertain, I kept pushing it back." Responding to the external and internal pressures he felt to "grow up" artistically, Spielberg angrily told *The Wall Street Journal* in 1987, "I think some people would like me to make a movie that explores the dark side and provides no easy answer to make the audience feel better when they return to their cars. If those critics want more pain in my films, they can give me $2 million—that's all it would take to make a film about pain—and I'll make that movie. I won't ask Warner or Universal to subsidize my pain."

He tried to pass off *Schindler's List* to other directors. One was Roman Polanski. As a child, Polanski had been confined to the Kraków ghetto, escaping through the barbed wire on March 13, 1943, the day of the ghetto's final liquidation by the Nazis. He spent the rest of the war in hiding; his father also survived, but his mother was gassed at Auschwitz. Polanski was approached repeatedly by Spielberg to direct *Schindler's List* but decided he did not want to relive the experience. In 1988, Spielberg offered to produce

---

* Pfefferberg survived to be a consultant on the film. He is played on screen by Jonathan Sagalle.

the film for Martin Scorsese, who commissioned a new screenplay from Steven Zaillian. After surrendering artistic control, Spielberg had a change of heart. He was planning to direct a remake of the 1962 thriller *Cape Fear,* but swapped that more obviously commercial property to Scorsese for the return of *Schindler's List;* Scorsese directed *Cape Fear* for Amblin in 1992.

Another filmmaker who wanted to film Keneally's book was the legendary Billy Wilder. An Austrian-born Jew who fled Berlin when Hitler came to power in 1933, Wilder wanted to close his career with *Schindler's List* "as a memorial to most of my family, who went to Auschwitz." "He made me look very deeply inside myself when he was so passionate to do this," Spielberg acknowledged. "In a way, he tested my resolve." After he saw the film, Wilder magnanimously wrote Spielberg a long letter of appreciation. "They couldn't have gotten a better man," Wilder said. "The movie is absolutely perfection."

World events also played a role in galvanizing Spielberg to action: "There was CNN reporting every day on the equivalent to the Nazi death camps in Bosnia, the atrocities against the Muslims—and then this horrible word 'ethnic cleansing,' cousin to the 'final solution.' I thought: My God, this is happening again. . . . And on top of all that comes the media giving serious air time and print space to the Holocaust deniers, the people who claim that the Holocaust never happened, that six million weren't killed, that it's all some kind of hoax." While working on *Hook,* Spielberg "picked up Steve Zaillian's script—I hadn't read it for a year—and was leafing through it. And I suddenly turned to Kate, who was half asleep, and I said, 'I'm doing *Schindler's List* as my next film.' "

I N the process of persuading himself to tell the story of Oskar Schindler, Spielberg developed a powerful identification with the altruistic tycoon, who was addressed by his workers as "Herr Direktor." Like Schindler, Spielberg struggled for years with the conflicting urges of commercial success and social responsibility, self-interest and the service of humanity. The man who had once told Sid Sheinberg that he was in "the Steven Spielberg business" described his protagonist as a man who was in "the Oskar Schindler business." And like Schindler, Spielberg was a man driven to conform, to seek success in the approbation of others, until the price of popularity became too high.

Spielberg received some criticism for making a film about the Holocaust with a gentile protagonist, one who was a Nazi to boot. To quote Keneally, Schindler represented "a figure of the imagination somehow as popular as the golden-hearted whore: the good German." Schindler's first scene in the film shows him affixing a swastika to his lapel before going out to ingratiate himself with Nazi officers at a Kraków nightclub. The evidence suggests that Schindler joined the Party more through cynical opportunism than ideology, although it might have added another layer of complexity if the film had acknowledged that he served as an agent of German intelligence (*Abwehr*) and, later in the war, as a double agent helping the Jewish underground.

To some observers, honoring the memory of a "good German"—even one who so spectacularly redeemed himself—is inappropriate in the context of the Holocaust. Rabbi Eli Hecht found it "incredible, almost blasphemous" that Schindler was given the status of a "Righteous Gentile" by the Yad Vashem Heroes and Martyrs Memorial Authority in Jerusalem. "For the life of me," the rabbi wrote, "I can't understand what possessed Steven Spielberg to make *Schindler's List,* to glorify a latter-day Robin Hood who profited at the expense of Polish Jewry." Even one of the *Schindlerjuden* who lays stones on Schindler's grave in the epilogue, Dr. Danka Dresner Schindel, expressed discomfort at seeing him portrayed as a hero: "We owe our lives to him. But I wouldn't glorify a German because of what he did to us. There is no proportion." Cartoonist Art Spiegelman, author of the powerful Holocaust tale *Maus,* went so far as to claim that because *Schindler's List* takes a gentile businessman as its hero, "the film is not about Jews or, arguably, even the Holocaust. Jews make people uncomfortable. It's about Clinton. It's about the benign aspects of capitalism—Capitalism with a Human Face."*

Rather than making a movie centering around a victim of Nazism such as Anne Frank or a heroic opponent of Nazism such as Raoul Wallenberg, Spielberg chose to explore the mind of the enemy. A lifetime of dealing with the issues of assimilation and prejudice had made him a keen observer of *goyim,* and as survivors and victims of prejudice are often prone to do, he developed a preoccupation with the dark side of the "other." "We're perversely fascinated and frightened by [Nazism]," Spielberg commented after making *Schindler's List,* "and that fear, I think, attracts us to knowing more about it." While focusing on one atypical Nazi's gradual evolution from victimizer to rescuer, Spielberg gave almost equal dramatic attention to the unrestrained evil of Amon Goeth (Ralph Fiennes), described by Keneally as "Oskar's dark brother . . . the berserk and fanatic executioner Oskar might, by some unhappy reversal of his appetites, have become."

Perhaps the most surprising aspect of *Schindler's List* is how acutely Spielberg penetrates the twisted psyche of Goeth, even to the point of unearthing some deeply buried humanity. Rather than being content to portray Goeth as a one-dimensional monster, Spielberg even more disturbingly brings out the Nazi's perverse mixture of attraction and sadism toward his Jewish maid, Helen Hirsch (Embeth Davidtz). Goeth cannot help feeling drawn to this beautiful woman, telling her he "would like so much to reach out and touch you in your loneliness. What would that be like, I wonder? I mean, what would be wrong with that? I realize that you're not a person in the strictest

---

* Spiegelman admitted to his own "Spielberg problem," feeling that Spielberg's 1986 animated film *An American Tail,* which also portrayed mice as Jews and cats as their antagonists, was "a horrible appropriation from *Maus.*"

sense of the word." His inability to cope with forbidden feelings of tenderness is what leads him to beat her as a "Jewish bitch." Little in Spielberg's previous work anticipated such an insight into the nature of fascism, although his intimate lifelong acquaintance with the nature of terror no doubt helped him understand the personality of a psychopathic sadist such as Goeth.

In Schindler's risky double-dealing with Nazis on behalf of Jews, Spielberg could see a provocative parallel with his own need to assimilate into WASP society. He too learned to disguise his true feelings in order to manipulate and outwit those who otherwise would be hostile to him and his people. Spielberg played that game with a keen sense of showmanship, or, as Schindler calls it, "The Presentation." A case in point was Spielberg's relationship with the anti-Semitic bully he cast in one of his boyhood movies. As Spielberg told the *Jerusalem Post,* the bully "never became my real friend. I was able to stop some of the hatred by, in a way, doing what Schindler did. Which was to charm him and make him a conspirator. . . . Schindler consorted with the enemy and he got what he wanted. And I found that there was a real relationship."

Spielberg's decision to put his reputation as a filmmaker on the line to bear witness to the Holocaust took courage. He knew he was risking ridicule and, worse, personal attack for venturing so far from his public image, and he worried that his image might prejudice people's reactions to the movie. His own courage must have seemed to him a distant echo of the courage Schindler displayed in putting his life and fortune at risk for the sake of Jewish victims of the Holocaust. Still, there was enough similarity in those moral decisions to give Spielberg a shared sense of mission with his protagonist. Even though he felt "more akin to the Ben Kingsley character"—Schindler's Jewish accountant and conscience, Itzhak Stern—Spielberg said, "I aspire to be Oskar Schindler."

S CHINDLER'S List contains two dedications. The first reads: "In memory of the more than six million Jews murdered." The second, less noticed because it comes at the conclusion of the end-title sequence, reads: "For Steve Ross."

While some found it incongruous for a film on the Holocaust to be dedicated to the late Time Warner chairman (who died shortly before it began filming), Spielberg saw Ross as an inspiration for the film's characterization of Schindler. To help Irish actor Liam Neeson capture Schindler's panache, Spielberg showed Neeson his home movies of the handsome, gregarious Ross, whose personality was a similarly intricate texture of roguish business practices interwoven with lavish generosity. "I always told Steve that if he was fifteen years younger, I'd cast him as Schindler," Spielberg said. ". . . After I met Steve, I went from being a miser to a philanthropist, because I knew him, because that's what he showed me to do." Inspired by the "pleasure that [Ross] drew from his own private philanthropy," Spielberg emulated his mentor: "I have my name on a couple of buildings, because in a way that's a fund-raiser. But eighty percent of what I do is anonymous. And I get so much pleasure from that—it's one of the things that Steve Ross opened my heart to."

It was a sign of Spielberg's highly sentimental view of Ross that he thought of him as akin to George Bailey, the altruistic building-and-loan officer played by James Stewart in Ross's favorite film, Frank Capra's *It's a Wonderful Life*. When Ross was dying of cancer, Spielberg made a short film based on the Capra classic, showing him the world as it would have been if he had never lived. "I dreamt this up when we were in Hawaii, filming *Jurassic Park,*" Spielberg said. "We had [Warner Bros. executives] Bob Daly and Terry Semel as hobos, looking for food in trashcans. Clint Eastwood, instead of being the legend, was a stuntman, an extra. ([Producer] Joel Silver shoots him—and actually kills him.) Quincy [Jones] was Clarence, the angel. Chevy Chase was God. I was in a mental institution, totally enclosed in a straitjacket, just my fingers free. I was putting together in shaving foam the face of E.T. and not quite knowing what I was trying to express. I said, 'He came to me . . . he came to me . . . he was a six-foot-three E.T.!' "

The unsentimentalized truth about Ross, according to biographer Connie Bruck, was that "his extraordinary generosity was funded to a great degree by the company; his loyalty, in many cases, endured as long as people were useful to him; and—driven by a compulsion to win—he tended to put his own interest ahead of others, in situations large and small. Not only did Ross not sacrifice himself for the good of others, as did his putative soulmate, George Bailey, but the precise converse was true."

Spielberg's hero-worship blinded him to the mogul's less attractive qualities and even called his own judgment into question. What did it say about Spielberg that he chose such a dubious character as a role model? The most charitable way to look at it is that he emulated what he found good about Steve Ross and forgave the rest. In much the same way, Spielberg was able to see Oskar Schindler's extraordinary generosity as redemptive of his many failings and vices. Indeed, it can be argued that only such a man could have succeeded in manipulating his fellow Nazis for such benign purposes. "We had to accept Schindler as he was," explained one of the *Schindlerjuden,* Israeli Supreme Court Justice Moshe Bejski. "Because if he wouldn't be like he was, nobody else of the normal kind of thinking was ready to do what he has done."

D U R I N G the hectic three months of production on *Schindler's List* in the winter and spring of 1993, Spielberg, in the words of cinematographer Janusz Kaminski, "worked from his heart." Keeping his preplanning to the minimum, often not knowing how he would film a scene until he arrived on that day's location in Poland, Spielberg plunged into the experience with a controlled emotional frenzy that helped give the film its startling sense of immediacy. All his gifts as an entertainer and technician were put in the service of giving the audience the feeling of being *inside the event.*

Schindler's List gains immeasurably from being shot largely on actual locations, including the streets of Kraków, Schindler's factory and apartment building, the city's SS headquarters and prison, and the gate and railroad tracks of Auschwitz (the World Jewish Congress, fearing "a Hollywood Holocaust," refused to let Spielberg film inside the gate). Because of postwar changes at the site, the Plaszów camp had to be reconstructed by production designer Allan Starski in an open pit adjacent to the original location. The awareness that the events were being filmed at the places where they actually occurred intensified the solemn atmosphere of memorialization. When he first traveled to Poland to scout locations, Spielberg found that "to touch history, to put my hand on 600-year-old masonry, and to step back from it and look down at my feet and know that I was standing where, as a Jew, I couldn't have stood fifty years ago, was a profound moment for me in my life."

Spielberg's guiding principle was to keep himself open to the raw, unmediated emotion that each scene, each setting, each group of characters provoked in him. It was not the first time he worked without the safety net of storyboards, but this time there was a greater emotional imperative. He wanted this story, in a sense, to tell itself. Approaching it with a profound humility, he functioned more like a "reporter" than like a director: "I can't tell you the shots I did on *Schindler's List* or why I put the camera in a certain place. I re-created these events, and then I experienced them as any witness or victim would have. It wasn't like a movie." Spielberg's decision to forego the conscious process of aesthetic stylization allowed him to tap freely into the mixture of individual and collective emotions that characterizes the subconscious. Accepting the Los Angeles Film Critics Association's Best Picture Award in January 1994, Spielberg said, "After getting back from the location —from which none of us has recovered—I looked through production stills taken by David James. When I came across any still that showed the crew behind the camera, I had no recollection of those images. I knew we were making a movie and that there was a camera, but I had little recognition of the moviemaking experience."

"We want people to see this film in fifteen years and not have a sense of when it was made," Kaminski said. Spielberg hired the young Polish émigré cinematographer both because of his fluency in that country's language and because of his experience in working at breakneck speed on low-budget features and TV movies, including *Class of '61,* Amblin's 1993 TV movie pilot for an unsold series about the American Civil War. Kaminski approached *Schindler* "as if I had to photograph it fifty years ago, with no lights, no dolly, no tripod. How would I do it? Naturally, a lot of it would be handheld, and a lot of it would be set on the ground where the camera was not level. . . . It was simply more real to have certain imperfections in the camera movement, or soft images. All those elements will add to the emotional side of the movie."

Handheld cameras, used for about 40 percent of the film, give the crowd scenes a raw, documentary feeling, with quick, spontaneous panning shots and abrupt, jarring crowd movements viscerally imparting an omnipresent sensation of terror and disorientation. What Spielberg called the "passionate urgency" of the filming was dictated in part by the relatively modest budget, which allowed only seventy-two shooting days. "Most scenes we're shooting in two or three takes, and we're working real fast," Spielberg told a visiting reporter. "I think that gives the movie a spontaneity, an edge, and it also serves the subject." His decision to make the film in black-and-white (aside from a few moments of stylized poetic emphasis and the present-day epilogue) was a crucial factor in giving it a documentary feeling. Resisting Universal chairman Tom Pollock's entreaties to shoot the film on color negative stock so a color version could be released for the home-video market, Spielberg felt black-and-white was essential because most documentary footage of the Holocaust is monochromatic and "because I don't want, accidentally or subconsciously, to beautify events"; he may have been influenced in that decision by the criticism of his lushly romantic visual style in *The Color Purple*.

Kaminski accurately described the complex visual texture of *Schindler's List* as "a mixture of German Expressionism and Italian Neorealism," yet Spielberg spoke of his visual strategy in terms of denial. Stylistically, he "got rid of the crane, got rid of the Steadicam, got rid of the zoom lenses, got rid of everything that for me might be considered a safety net."

The eloquent simplicity and directness of Spielberg's visual storytelling in *Schindler's List* shows a consummate mastery of the filmmaking craft. Because the emotional effect is so overwhelming, one hardly notices the subtle use of moving camera and the terrifying lighting effects that help communicate the feelings of a group of Jewish women fearing they are about to be gassed in a shower room at Auschwitz. When a crowd of mothers runs hysterically after the trucks bearing their unsuspecting children to Auschwitz, the viewer does not consciously register that the camera is shooting from the point of view of the children racing away from their mothers' outstretched arms. The liquidation of the ghetto, an astonishing sixteen-minute sequence of boldly contrasting lighting effects, shock cuts, and maze-like choreography of Nazis hunting down their victims, is perhaps the greatest directorial *tour de force* of Spielberg's career to date. But it unfolds with the dizzying immediacy of a living nightmare, all played against a small but crucially important focus: the anguished close-ups of Schindler, on horseback, watching helplessly from a nearby hillside. Schindler's expressions provide the dramatic turning point of the story, demarcating his change from exploiter of "his" Jews to their protector.

Ben Kingsley has provided a vivid account of the filming of the ghetto liquidation: "Once they started to run in with the handheld cameras and have the tracking cameras as well, the takes were very long and the shock built up in us. Horror after horror after horror—it went on so long before you heard the Klaxon for 'Cut.' Bodies, blood, the smell of explosives in the air, and people still running and being told to stop by an AD [assistant director]—but it was like an echo of the SS. Steven wanted to get the truth into the camera, and every time he did I saw he got a tremendous kick. It was as if he was saying, 'Let them see *that*. Let them look at *that*.' "

What Spielberg found himself feeling during the making of *Schindler's List* often left him surprised and shaken. One of his most difficult experiences was filming the sequence of the Health *Aktion,* in which aging Jews are forced to run naked in circles before Nazi doctors making a selection for Auschwitz. "It was hard on me to be there," said the director. "I couldn't look at it, I had to turn my eyes away, I couldn't watch. . . . None of us looked. I said to the guy pulling the focus on a very difficult shot, 'Do you think you got that?' And he said, 'I don't know, I wasn't looking.' "

Spielberg recalled that when he paid his first visit to Auschwitz during preproduction, he "went expecting to cry buckets, and I didn't cry at all. I wasn't sad one bit. I was outraged. I was furious. It was a reaction I didn't anticipate." That feeling of smoldering rage suffuses much of the film, help-ing keep it from succumbing to the temptations of sentimentality. While unfamiliar emotional territory for a Spielberg film, this was not an altogether new feeling for Spielberg himself. His Saratoga High School friend Gene Ward Smith had been surprised by the way the teenage Spielberg "radiated [a] genuine but seemingly inexplicable rage and disgust"; Smith only later realized it was the result of Spielberg's experiences with anti-Semitic bul-lies. As Spielberg acknowledged, those still-painful memories of his ado-lescent "Hell on Earth" came rushing back to the surface when he directed *Schindler's List.* But he never lost sight of how much his own experiences, and his imagination, paled before the reality of the Holocaust.

GIVEN the nature of the subject matter, no representation of the Holo-caust, whether concrete or abstract, can be expected to do justice to the memory of the victims. No film, no book, no memorial has ever failed to arouse passionate concern about whether it is appropriate to the subject. There is even a school of thought which holds that the Holocaust is an event so unique in its evil, so incomprehensible in its ultimate meaning, that it is wrong to attempt to depict it. "After Auschwitz," argued Theodor Adorno, "to write a poem is barbaric."

Schindler's List was rapturously praised by most reviewers. "[L]ike all great works, it feels both impossible and inevitable," wrote Terrence Rafferty in *The New Yorker.* ". . . It is by far the finest, fullest dramatic (i.e., nondocu-mentary) film ever made about the Holocaust. And few American movies since the silent era have had anything approaching this picture's narrative boldness, visual audacity, and emotional directness."

"This movie will shatter you, but it earns its tears honestly," *Newsweek*'s David Ansen wrote in a cover story on the film and its director. ". . . Confronted with the horrors of Auschwitz-Birkenau, the ghastly sight of children hiding from capture in outhouse cesspools, Spielberg never loses his nerve. . . . Spielberg's very nature as a filmmaker has been transformed; he's reached within himself for a new language, and without losing any of his innate fluency or his natural-born storytelling gift, he's found a style and a depth of feeling that will astonish both his fans and those detractors who believed he was doomed to permanent adolescence."

"Mr. Spielberg has made sure that neither he nor the Holocaust will ever be thought of in the same way again," Janet Maslin declared in *The New York Times*. "[I]t's as if he understood for the first time why God gave him such extraordinary skills," wrote *New York* magazine's David Denby, who admitted, "I didn't think I could be affected this way anymore."

But the film aroused equally ardent opposition from a minority of critics who found it, for various reasons, an inadequate representation of the Holocaust. Some objections bordered on the frivolous, such as that of Simon Louvish, whose essay in the British film magazine *Sight and Sound* derided it as a "Holocaust theme park," a phrase sometimes used by European critics of the U.S. Holocaust Museum. Others raised more fundamental issues. French filmmaker Claude Lanzmann, whose austere nine-hour documentary *Shoah* explores memories of the Holocaust without showing a single frame of historical footage, criticized *Schindler's List* for allegedly putting undue emphasis on Jews who were rescued, rather than on the six million who died. "The project of telling Schindler's story confuses history," Lanzmann claimed. "All of this is to say that everything is equal, to say there were good among the Nazis, bad among the others, and so on. It's a way to make it not a crime against humanity, but a crime of humanity."

In one of his rare responses to criticism of the film, Spielberg accused Lanzmann of wanting to be "the only voice in the definitive document of the Holocaust. It amazed me that there could be any hurt feelings in an effort to reflect the truth." Spielberg watched *Shoah* several times before making *Schindler's List,* and it influenced his deceptively dispassionate-seeming, documentary-like depiction of the bureaucratic apparatus of the Holocaust. But he wanted to go further and explore the human dimensions behind what was, in fact, "a crime of humanity" as well as "a crime against humanity." For a popular filmmaker seeking to influence a far wider audience than Lanzmann's relatively elite viewership, it was essential to stimulate the audience's emotions by re-creating events and dramatizing the thought processes of those involved. Neither film should cancel out or overshadow the other; it is precisely because the Holocaust is such a central event in modern history that any attempt at prescribing or limiting its aesthetic treatment is misguided. For artists to shrink from the task of dealing with the Holocaust for any reason is to encourage historical amnesia. The real question in evaluating any dramatic treatment of the Holocaust is that posed by Elie Wiesel: "How is one to tell a tale that cannot be—but must be—told?"

Too often the terms of the debate were framed in shopworn critical clichés about Spielberg's artistic personality, *ad hominem* attacks derisively questioning his intelligence and judgment and finding him inadequate to the momentous task at hand. But the film's detractors also raised some challenging arguments. Whether or not one agrees with their assessments, the public debate helped focus attention on what Spielberg was attempting in *Schindler's List* and how he went about crafting it. In his Holocaust memoir *Night,* Wiesel recalled his father's observation that "every question possessed a power that did not lie in the answer." The often unanswerable questions raised by Spielberg's film, as well as those raised by its detractors, are a testimony to the film's extraordinary emotional influence on audiences throughout the world.

Defying all box-office predictions by grossing $321.2 million around the world ($225.1 million of it outside the U.S. and Canada),* *Schindler's List* became such a major event in the public consciousness of the Holocaust that it unexpectedly elevated Spielberg to a stature few other filmmakers have ever achieved. The leaders of the U.S., Israel, Germany, Austria, Poland, France, and other countries attended special screenings and held public and private meetings with the filmmaker, treating him as if he were a visiting diplomat on a mission to combat ethnic hatred. Spielberg rose to the occasion, accepting that role with eloquence and humility. The film even received a televised endorsement from President Bill Clinton (of whom Spielberg has been a prominent supporter). After attending the Washington preview of *Schindler's List,* Clinton told his fellow countrymen, "I implore every one of you to go see it. . . . you will see portrait after portrait of the painful difference between people who have no hope and have no rage left and people who still have hope and still have rage."

Appearing just eight months after the opening of the United States Holocaust Memorial Museum in Washington, D.C., which gives visitors a three-dimensional immersion into the actual sights and sounds and artifacts of the Holocaust, *Schindler's List* provided a remarkably similar emotional experience. Taken together, as complementary educational and memorial representations of this century's most shattering historical event, the museum and the film have helped stimulate a much broader public awareness of the urgency of Holocaust study and its relevance to contemporary life.

Spielberg's return to his roots in making *Schindler's List* was also, paradoxically, an act of liberation from his culturally imposed and self-imposed limitations. In confronting the Holocaust, he radically redefined his public image, confounding most (though not all) of the skeptics who thought him

---

* Free educational screenings also were sponsored by Universal, under the auspices of most U.S. governors, for more than 3 million students.

merely a frivolous entertainer, a child-man incapable of dealing with serious themes. But there was a double edge to their abrupt reevaluation. Annette Insdorf, author of *Indelible Shadows: Film and the Holocaust,* commented in *The Village Voice,* "Many of us were expecting him to simply apply the techniques of *Jurassic Park* to the Holocaust, but were pleasantly surprised that he transcended his reputation for a glib, feel-good approach." As Armond White wondered in a *Film Comment* essay on Spielberg's career, "Can the man who directed the most splendid, heartfelt Hollywood entertainments of the past twenty years accept that praise, that dismissal of his life's work, as reasonable?"

Nowhere was that dismissive attitude more evident than in the schizoid voting of three critics' groups—the Los Angeles Film Critics Association (LAFCA), the New York Film Critics Circle, and the National Board of Review —all of which chose *Schindler's List* as the Best Film of 1993 yet pointedly failed to honor Spielberg for directing it.* The implication was either that the film somehow directed itself, or that, as Scott Rosenberg put it in the *San Francisco Examiner,* the subject matter had caused Spielberg "to resist the urge to imprint his own sensibility on the film," an act of self-abnegation more characteristic of a producer than a director.

After Spielberg won his second Directors Guild of America award, the Academy of Motion Picture Arts and Sciences gave him his Oscar as Best Director; the film received six other Academy Awards, including Best Picture.† Backstage at the Oscars, Spielberg could not resist a touch of sarcasm: "I could have dealt with never winning an Academy Award, because I had practiced dealing with it for the last twelve years." But then he added, "So this was a wonderful honor tonight. If I hadn't gotten it, I probably would have been shattered."

While the question posed in one form or another by many critics was, "How is this film unlike any other Steven Spielberg film?," it is more enlightening to ask, "How is this film profoundly *characteristic* of Steven Spielberg?"

K E N E A L L Y observed that by taking collective responsibility for the postwar financial support of Oskar Schindler, "Oskar's children"—the *Schindlerjuden*—"had become his parents." The image of Schindler as a deeply flawed father figure who ultimately assumes responsibility for his "family" of eleven hundred Jews is at the heart of Spielberg's film. In the improbable but inspiring figure of this rescuer whose underlying humanity was brought out by the social cataclysm that threatened to engulf his "children," Spielberg

---

* The author abstained in the LAFCA voting. The National Society of Film Critics distinguished itself by naming Spielberg Best Director.

† Sharing the Best-Picture Oscar with Spielberg were fellow producers Gerald R. Molen and Branko Lustig. A Croatian who has worked in various capacities on many European productions, Lustig was an Auschwitz inmate during his childhood.

could see writ large the themes of parental responsibility that have obsessed him throughout his career. *Schindler's List* extends his preoccupation with the breakdown of the nuclear family to encompass the breakdown of European society and the destruction of Jewish family life during the second World War.

Deprived of their freedom and placed in a helpless and dependent position by the Nazis, the Schindler Jews are in a situation resembling that of abused children. At any moment, they are subject to arbitrary punishment and death at the hands of Amon Goeth and his fellow SS men. Among the most chilling scenes is that of Goeth casually shooting Plaszów inmates at random from his balcony, as if for sport, before his morning urination ("Oh, God, Amon!" whines his mistress, covering her head with a pillow during the shooting. "Amon, you're such a damn fucking child!"). When Schindler takes physical charge of "his" Jews, guarding them against the depredations of the Nazis, they still remain in an infantilized position, even though he tries to restore as much of their prewar social structure as he can under the circumstances, reuniting families and enabling a rabbi among them to conduct *Shabbat* services inside the factory. "There will be generations because of what you did," Stern tells Schindler. This truth is demonstrated in the epilogue, with its reunion of Schindler's real-life "family," a long line of his workers and their families filing past his grave in the Latin Cemetery of Jerusalem. They lay memorial stones on the grave while the following words are superimposed: "There are fewer than four thousand Jews left alive in Poland today. There are more than six thousand descendants of the Schindler Jews."

Some critics found fault with Spielberg for not spending more time rounding out the characters of individual Schindler Jews. One of the film's most vociferous opponents, Philip Gourevitch, complained in *Commentary* that it "depicts the Nazi slaughter of Polish Jewry almost entirely through German eyes. Except for Itzhak Stern . . . few Jewish figures are individuated from the mob of victims. When Jews *are* seen on their own, the camera eyes them with the detachment of a *National Geographic* ethnographic documentary." Incredibly, Gourevitch went on to accuse Spielberg of employing "Jewish caricatures" lifted "from the pages of *Der Stuermer,*" the notoriously anti-Semitic Nazi organ. Calling that charge "truly enraging," reader Ruth King of New York City responded, "The movie shows Jews—ugly, plain, beautiful. This is how we look."

In fact, not only are Stern and Helen Hirsch (Goeth's maid) among the film's central characters, Spielberg also follows the fates of many other Schindler Jews carefully throughout the story. But they are seen mostly in brief vignettes or as faces in the crowd, for the director deliberately chose not to deal expansively with the personal stories of most of the Jewish characters. While the TV miniseries *Holocaust* concentrated the viewer's attention on one Jewish family—a device that encouraged audience identification with the characters but gave the series the emotionally indulgent tone of a soap opera—Spielberg wanted to avoid that kind of narrow, melodramatic focus. Instead he set out to demonstrate in brutally direct dramatic terms how the Nazis systematically stripped Jews of their individuality, robbing them of their property and freedom, chopping off their hair, dressing them in striped uniforms, and reducing their names to numbers. The first graphic indication of what is in store for the characters in *Schindler's List* comes when a trainload of Jews leaves the Kraków station and Spielberg's camera moves into an adjacent storehouse filled with piles of suitcases, valuables, family photographs, and bloodstained teeth with gold fillings. This, said Spielberg, "wasn't the story of eight Jews from Kraków who survived—it was a conscious decision to represent the six million who died and the several hundred thousand who did survive with just sort of a scent of characters and faces we follow all through the story."

It is when Schindler unexpectedly begins seeing his Jewish workers as individuals that he begins to change his thinking about the war. The first such incident is that of the elderly one-armed machinist, Lowenstein (Henryk Bista), who interrupts Schindler at lunch to thank him for having classified him as "essential to the war effort"—a designation that has saved his life, which the Nazis regard as useless. "God bless you, sir," Lowenstein earnestly tells him. "You are a good man." Realizing that he is *not* such a good man, Schindler reacts with shame, losing his appetite and angrily demanding of Stern, "Don't ever do that to me again!" Stern, who throughout the film acts as Schindler's conscience, has arranged the meeting as one of his many careful and subtle appeals to the better angels of Schindler's nature. As Spielberg has pointed out, Stern is the "unsung hero" of the story, a man who manipulates Schindler masterfully while keeping his own emotions under almost superhuman control. Ben Kingsley's finely shaded performance, rich with understated compassion and the gallows humor of a born survivor, captures what Keneally called the "limitless calm" of a character who can never afford to utter a wrong word, because hundreds of people's lives depend on him. The unspoken message Stern hopes to convey to Schindler is the same one Spielberg repeatedly gave to Kingsley when they discussed his character. The director said simply, "Be a *mensch.*"

The one-armed man's intrusion into Schindler's comfortable existence, soon followed by his shockingly brutal public execution, crystallizes the moral issues Schindler until then has been able to ignore. Some critics complained that Spielberg fails to make clear why Schindler undergoes his change of heart. Although the evidence on screen of Schindler's growing empathy and compassion is abundantly clear to anyone who has eyes to see, this profound transformation is all the more powerful for not being spelled out in words. The climactic moment of Schindler witnessing the liquidation of the ghetto with silent horror achieves its emotional impact partly because he (and the audience) have been prepared for it by his earlier protection of Lowenstein and other victims of escalating Nazi cruelty, including the symbolically unkillable Rabbi Levartov (Ezra Dagan), who miraculously survives Goeth's repeated attempts to shoot him.

While Schindler's goodness is hardly "incomprehensible," there *is* a mystery in it that resists facile explanation. Spielberg credited screenwriter Steven Zaillian with making this the film's thematic focus: "Steve had a very strong point of view. He approached it as the Rosebud theory—the mystery as to why Schindler did what he did. . . . Even having made the movie about his life, I still don't know him very well. I ended my experience, I guess, a bit like [the newsreel reporter] in *Citizen Kane*, where I was not able to go back to my editor with the story that he wanted. Every day it was frustrating."

Honoring the memory of a rescuer stresses the importance of individual responsibility while giving the lie to the myth that Germans were powerless to resist the Nazi tyranny. "I hated the brutality, the sadism, and the insanity of Nazism," was the straightforward explanation Schindler gave after the war for his heroic actions. "I just couldn't stand by and see people destroyed. I did what I could, what I had to do, what my conscience told me I must do. That's all there is to it. Really, nothing more." But ultimately the question of why one person chooses good over evil must always remain, to some extent, a spiritual riddle. When Poldek Pfefferberg was asked in 1993 why he thought Schindler saved him, he replied, *"Who cares!* I don't give a hoot for the reasons he did it. He saved eleven hundred people." Spielberg wisely resists allowing Liam Neeson's Schindler to make any explicit declaration about his motives.

"The studio, of course, wanted me to spell everything out," Spielberg said. "I got into a lot of arguments with people saying we need that big Hollywood catharsis where Schindler falls to his knees and says, 'Yes, I know what I'm doing—now I must do it!' and goes full steam ahead. That was the last thing I wanted. . . . I'm not sure he really felt that during the war. It was a lot easier for him to define his own actions after he had taken them. I also felt that it would have been too melodramatic of me to have invented a reason for him. It would have been too easy for the sort of couch-potato tastes of American audiences, who demand easy answers to complicated questions. I felt it would have been a disservice to Schindler's deeds to have manufactured something just because I couldn't find it in real life."

Even some who admire the film object to the scene of Schindler's breakdown as he bids farewell to his workers, considering it an unfortunate lapse into the kind of sentimentality the film otherwise avoids. But Spielberg's instincts as a popular artist made him recognize that both the characters and the audience need an emotional catharsis, releasing the mingled feelings of communal solidarity and loss that have been forcibly pent up throughout the three-hour film. Presented with a gold ring in which his workers have inscribed the Talmud's words, "Whoever saves one life saves the world entire," Schindler is stricken with guilt. He confesses to Stern, "I could have got more out. I could have got more." Looking over his remaining valuables, Schindler haltingly admits his car would have been worth ten people and his gold swastika pin "would have given me two more—at least one. It would have given me one. One more. One more person. A person is dead—for this. I could have got one more person and I didn't."

Schindler's mournful litany reminds the audience that, however many persons he and others managed to save, there were millions more who perished. Any celebration of survival in the context of the Holocaust, Spielberg acknowledges, must be seen in the shadow of overwhelming loss. At key points throughout the film, he stresses this complexity in visual terms, such as showing a long line of people entering the gas chamber as Schindler's women leave the shower room alive. David Thomson claimed in *Film Comment* that "when those saved hurry to trains, the camera (or their eyes) does not pan away to note those less fortunate." But that is exactly what Spielberg does with his camera, showing another group of victims arriving in Auschwitz as the Schindler Jews hurry to their trains. While Schindler and Stern are drawing up their list of people to save from extermination, the viewer is painfully aware that in bringing the selection to an end, Schindler inevitably is condemning others to die. When Schindler ransoms his women from Auschwitz, the camp commandant tries to interest him instead in "three hundred units" of Hungarian Jews from another train; in rejecting those Jews in favor of *his* Jews, Schindler is playing God and condemning the others to death. Such are the terrible moral paradoxes of this story, insoluble dilemmas Spielberg does not shrink from acknowledging. This is the opposite of sentimentality. When Schindler humbly confesses, "I didn't do enough," he is speaking not only as a wealthy man whose virtues are inextricably mixed with human weaknesses, he is also speaking for the entire world that abandoned the Jews.

For all its emphasis on rescue and survival, the film does not provide audiences the simple and consolatory "happy ending" some of its detractors accused it of offering. "This is a movie about World War II in which all the Jews live," J. Hoberman claimed in *The Village Voice*. "The selection is 'life,' the Nazi turns out to be a good guy, and human nature is revealed to be sunny and bright. It's a total reversal." Such a grotesque caricature of *Schindler's List* illustrates not only the difficulty of communicating the complexities of the Holocaust in a popular entertainment medium, but also the stubbornly enduring resistance to Spielberg's artistry among some segments of the self-styled American intellectual elite.

One of the readers of *Commentary* who took exception to Philip Gourevitch's intemperate assault on the film was Rabbi Uri D. Herscher of Los Angeles's Hebrew Union College–Jewish Institute of Religion, who wrote: "I lost so many relatives in the Holocaust; maybe that is why I found the film so appealing and, finally, so uplifting. Is it a perfect film? What would a perfect film be about the Holocaust? For me it is enough that it is an extraordinarily—even though painfully—absorbing film which *demonstrates* the splendor of human sympathies and humanitarian passion." A Holocaust survivor, Norbert Friedman of West Hempstead, New York, wrote in his letter to *Commentary,* "No matter what the critics say, no matter what the public's reactions, for us, the survivors, there is only one response, a response usually reserved for another survivor when he concludes giving public testimony. That is appreciatively and warmly to embrace Steven Spielberg in the silent act of bonding."

Rabbi Albert Lewis, Spielberg's Hebrew school teacher during his childhood in New Jersey, sees *Schindler's List* as "Steven's gift to his mother, to his people, and in a sense to himself. Now he is a full human being, and for a long while he was alienated from his people. He wrestled with himself, in a sense; it was a little like the story in the Bible of Jacob wrestling with the angel. He suddenly realized what it's all about."

A s he approached the milestone of his fiftieth birthday—which he passed on December 18, 1996—Spielberg showed no signs of being crushed under the enormous weight of his success. Many a lesser career has collapsed from the burden of escalating expectations, and Spielberg, who still bites his fingernails and throws up before coming to the set in the morning, cannot help feeling the "horrendous" pressure of having to top himself, of simply having to be Steven Spielberg. But throughout his twenty-eight years as a professional filmmaker, he has maintained a sense of inner balance that so far has enabled him to avoid losing his nerve. He seems comfortable (even if others are not) with his own complexities and contradictions.

To some observers, it may have appeared that the choice facing Spielberg about where to take his directing career was plain and clearcut: He either could make more "message" movies like *Schindler's List* or regress to making more Indiana Jones movies and movies about dinosaurs. But though Spielberg evolved as a result of *Schindler's List,* he did not suddenly change into someone else. On the last day of principal photography on *Jurassic Park,* he said, "I feel I have a responsibility. And I want to go back and forth from entertainment to socially conscious movies." When he returned to directing after a long break to recover from the emotional and physical exhaustion of filming those two movies, he proved he meant what he said. The feature film project he chose to follow *Schindler's List* was *The Lost World,* the sequel to *Jurassic Park.**

Going back to sheer entertainment was a way of keeping his creative equilibrium. The traditional American dichotomy between art and entertainment is a stubbornly enduring part of the nation's puritan heritage, but for Spielberg, pleasing himself and pleasing his audience have almost always

---

* In between, Spielberg directed some scenes for a 1996 CD-ROM, *Steven Spielberg's Director's Chair.* Spielberg's footage of a Death Row inmate (played by filmmaker Quentin Tarantino) and his girlfriend (Jennifer Aniston) is part of an interactive program in which Spielberg walks viewers through the various steps and choices involved in making a movie. Executive producer Roger Holzberg directed the scenes in which Spielberg himself appears.

gone hand-in-hand. When high school friend Chuck Case visited him at the Long Beach Airport during the filming of *1941,* Spielberg surveyed his army of uniformed actors and World War II airplanes and said with a childlike smile, "You know, they *pay* me to do this." *Schindler's List* demonstrated that, at least in the case of a great popular artist such as Steven Spielberg, artistry and popularity need not be mutually exclusive.

"You've tackled one of the darkest chapters in history," an interviewer said to him. "Can you go back to making sunny, optimistic movies?"

"Sure I can," he replied with a laugh, "because I have a sunny, optimistic nature. But I don't think the two are mutually exclusive."

S PIELBERG'S planned year-long hiatus from directing—an event so earthshaking in Hollywood it was announced on the front page of *Daily Variety*—eventually stretched to three years. Those were among the busiest years of his life, although much of his activity took place behind the scenes on two ambitious projects that illustrate how richly divergent his interests have become. In 1994, he launched both his new studio, DreamWorks SKG, and his Survivors of the Shoah Visual History Foundation, a worldwide program to videotape the testimonies of Holocaust survivors and rescuers. He called the Shoah project "the most important job I've ever done. . . . People say, 'What are you doing after *Schindler's List?'* Well, this is my next project. . . . I've dedicated the rest of my life to being involved in taking testimony as long as there are survivors who want to volunteer it."

Seeded with $6 million of his earnings from *Schindler's List,* the nonprofit project was budgeted at $60 million for its first three years, receiving additional funding from such donors as the Lew Wasserman Foundation, MCA/Universal, Time Warner, and NBC. Spielberg's contribution was part of the estimated $40 million his Righteous Persons Foundation announced it would donate to various organizations in its first seven to ten years. Other donations it has made have included a long-term grant yielding $3 million to the U.S. Holocaust Museum; $1 million to New York City's Museum of Jewish Heritage; $500,000 to the Fortunoff Video Archive for Holocaust Testimonies at Yale University; and $300,000 to Synagogue 2000, a group developing an innovative model for synagogues in the twenty-first century. Spielberg also provided funding to Bill Moyers for a public television series on the Book of Genesis, Jon Blair for his Oscar-winning documentary *Anne Frank Remembered,* and Elizabeth Swados for a film on racism and anti-Semitism, *The Hating Pot.*

The Shoah project came about, Spielberg related, "because survivors who came to me both during the production of *Schindler's List* and after the film was released said to me, 'I have a story to tell. Will you hear my story?' At first I thought, Are you saying [that] you want me to make a movie out of your story? But what they were really saying was, 'Will you take my testimony? Can I, before I die, tell somebody—tell you, with a camera—what happened to me, so my children will know, so my friends will finally know, and so I can leave something of myself behind so the world will know.' Enough people came to me that finally my slow brain suddenly went 'Click' and I thought that this really was the reason I made *Schindler's List,* . . . to do this project."

The goal of this massive oral and visual history project has been to record as many as 50,000 survivor testimonies in the first three years. Volunteer interviewers (many of them survivors themselves) and camera crews in more than a dozen countries have gone about eliciting testimony from among the estimated 300,000 Holocaust survivors alive at the beginning of the project. Because most survivors are in their seventies and eighties, the Shoah Foundation represents what Spielberg calls "a race against the clock . . . a rescue mission. We're rescuing history." After being indexed and combined with family photographs and historical film footage, the videotaped testimonies are digitally preserved. Copies are to be deposited with five major repositories—Yad Vashem in Israel, the Fortunoff Video Archive, the U.S. Holocaust Memorial Museum, the Living Memorial to the Holocaust–Museum of Jewish Heritage, and the Simon Wiesenthal Center in Los Angeles—and ultimately are to be made more widely available through online computer services, CD-ROM educational programs, books, and documentaries.*

Even such a benevolent Spielberg enterprise is not immune from controversy. In January 1996, *The Village Voice,* which had devoted eight pages to a highly critical roundtable on *Schindler's List,* ran an article by Adam Shatz and Alissa Quart accusing Spielberg of propagating "pop monumentalism" with his Shoah project: "In a strangely compensatory sequel to *Schindler's List,* a film so enamored of a benevolent German entrepreneur that it barely portrayed the Jews he saved as characters in their own right, Steven Spielberg is promising each of the survivors of the Holocaust a permanent place in cyberspace."

Spotlighting the competitive anxiety other archives have felt over Spielberg's better-funded and -publicized project, Shatz and Quart also raised aesthetic and moral issues reminiscent of those prompted by *Schindler's List.* Questioning the propriety of a "virtual walk-through concentration camp" Spielberg has envisioned as a CD-ROM teaching tool, they wrote, "Critics wonder whether the price of making history lessons more like arcade visits could result in a student encountering the Holocaust as a morbidly thrilling game." Spielberg's practice of encouraging Holocaust survivors to bring their families before the camera at the end of their testimonies—his way of celebrating the fact that "because of their survival, whole generations have been replanted on this planet"—was criticized by Holocaust scholar Lawrence Langer as "a kind of manipulated scenario." Pointing out that many Holocaust survivors have had great difficulties returning to a normal postwar existence, Langer contended, "Having the family in the video creates the

---

* The first such documentary, the Emmy Award–winning *Survivors of the Holocaust,* played in film festivals before debuting on cable television in 1996.

impression that the Holocaust is an event people recover from and get over. It's a Hollywood spin."

While these concerns are valid, it is impossible for Spielberg or any other chronicler of the Holocaust to avoid putting his own emotional imprint onto the story. Spielberg's continuing identification with Oskar Schindler has led him to see himself as the "rescuer" of the last uncollected history of the Holocaust. If that goal is "[l]audable and self-aggrandizing in equal measure," as the authors of the *Voice* article contended, Spielberg nevertheless has the resources, and the moral imperative, to attempt it. Karen Kushell, one of the project's executive producers, reported that Spielberg "almost went through the same epiphany I think Schindler does at the end of the movie, where he said, 'No, no, I want them all. I don't want to just do the Schindler survivors, I want to get everybody's stories.' "

W H E N he and his partners in DreamWorks held a press conference to announce the creation of their film, TV, music, interactive video, and consumer products company, Spielberg, in a Freudian slip, called it "our new country." Turning his *hubris* into a joke, he added, "Maybe it will be a country. Is Belize still for sale?"

The first new Hollywood studio to be planned on such a scale since Twentieth Century–Fox was founded in 1935, DreamWorks, if all goes as Spielberg envisioned, could well become "a company that will outlive us all." With their grandiose plans for reimagining the very concept of a movie studio, Spielberg and his partners could take the lumbering, financially overextended, and creatively bankrupt movie industry on a quantum jump into the next century. DreamWorks combines Spielberg's creative vision and passion for breaking the bounds of technology with Jeffrey Katzenberg's executive savvy and David Geffen's entrepreneurial flair. In their case, the old Hollywood warning about not letting the lunatics run the asylum may be meaningless, for Katzenberg brought Disney animation to record box-office heights, Geffen's record company made him a billionaire, and Spielberg has amassed a comparable fortune.

When the partnership was announced on October 12, 1994, the location of the studio facility had not yet been decided. The company did not even have a name, although the press, prompted by Katzenberg, fawningly labeled it "The Dream Team." There were, in fact, no concrete plans to discuss at the press conference, a fact that caused some skeptical head-shaking in Hollywood.

The rough sketch for the partnership had come together with remarkable alacrity. After being forced from his post as chairman of Walt Disney Studios on August 24, Katzenberg, already a partner with Spielberg in the Dive! restaurant chain, asked Spielberg, "What do you think about starting a studio from scratch?" Spielberg was immediately receptive, although he worried about leaving his longtime home at MCA. The decisive discussions among the three partners occurred during the early morning hours of September 29 in Washington, D.C., following their attendance at a White House state dinner for Russian President Boris Yeltsin. "We're in tuxedos talking about a brand-new studio," Spielberg recalled, "and just across from us there's Yeltsin and Bill Clinton talking about disarming the world of nuclear weapons." The preliminary legal paperwork for the partnership was drawn up hurriedly during the weekend before the announcement.

"We could have built this up over a fifteen-year period," Spielberg mused. "Instead, we're trying to do it in a couple of years. After our first planning sessions, I thought about how much easier it would be to start with a single film, make it, see how it does, and if it does well, do a second picture. That's the conservative, play-it-safe side that haunts me before I fall asleep at night."

Seeming bemused at his own audacity, Spielberg told the press that he had broken two long-standing personal rules with the creation of Dream-Works. "Over the years I've had almost a religious fervor in not investing my own money in show business," he said. ". . . Now I can't think of a better place than this to invest in our own future." And recalling his fruitful business and personal relationships with Sid Sheinberg and Steve Ross, he noted, "Ten years ago this would have been inconceivable because I love having bosses in my life. . . . I needed them. But I grew up and began to foster children and have a large family. I have five children. I felt I was ready to be the father of my own business. Or at least the co-father."

There was speculation that what the three were really after was a takeover of MCA in support of Lew Wasserman and Sheinberg, who were then embattled with the firm's Japanese owners, Matsushita. That notion was fueled by reports that the DreamWorks partners sought and received the "blessing" of Wasserman and Sheinberg before announcing their new studio. Any takeover plans the trio might have had were rendered moot by the acquisition of MCA in April 1995 by Seagram, which subsequently concluded a ten-year deal with DreamWorks to distribute its films outside North America. The eighty-two-year-old Wasserman was kicked upstairs to become chairman emeritus of MCA, and Sheinberg left to form his own production company, The Bubble Factory.

Planning its own domestic distribution operation rather than relying on the traditional Hollywood system, DreamWorks, as George Lucas observed, "has the opportunity to create a whole new distribution system that may be a vast improvement over the old one." MCA's foreign distribution of DreamWorks films excludes only South Korea, where rights are reserved for that country's One World Media Corp., which invested $300 million in the new studio. That largesse was surpassed only by the $500 million investment by Microsoft co-founder Paul Allen. Spielberg, Katzenberg, and Geffen each put up $33.3 million for a combined 67 percent stake in their privately held company, with the outside investors divvying up the remaining 33 percent. DreamWorks also lined up $1 billion in loan commitments from Chemical Bank. By using their personal leverage to retain control of the company despite being minority investors, Spielberg, Katzenberg, and Geffen are attempting (in Spielberg's words) to "be the owners of our own dreams."

But there is nothing harder to create in Hollywood than a new studio that lasts, and the checkered history of creative partnerships in the film industry gives ample cause for skepticism. DreamWorks initially seemed to have little trouble commanding the enormous financial resources needed to capitalize all the start-up costs involved in such a grandiose enterprise, including the construction of physical facilities, deals with creative talent, and the underwriting of a sustained production schedule. But after spending more than two years in the planning stages, DreamWorks was still without a permanent home.

The partners wanted to build their studio in the Playa Vista section of western Los Angeles, on the 1,087-acre former site of Howard Hughes's aircraft plant where Hughes built his gigantic wooden airplane, the legendary Spruce Goose. It was a fitting choice in light of Spielberg's continuing interest in directing Warren Beatty in a *Citizen Kane*–like biographical picture about Hughes, a fellow aviation fanatic and movie producer.* With Walt Disneyish futuristic visions dancing in their heads, Spielberg and his partners planned a hundred-acre, high-tech yet pastoral environment complete with a man-made lake. The facility was to be part of a massive real-estate development that was also to include a residential community, a hotel, and retail and office space. But by the fall of 1996, the Playa Vista project had stalled due to the developer's financial problems and opposition from some environmentalists who were concerned about the project's impact on the Ballona Wetlands (some of which was to be preserved under the development plan). At presstime, it was not certain whether the project would go ahead on the site or whether DreamWorks would find another location for its studio facilities.† DreamWorks had already begun to make films and TV programs elsewhere —its first feature, *The Peacemaker,* was scheduled for 1997 release—but as a studio it was still something of an unfulfilled dream.

W HETHER the three partners will have the desire to stick with the studio over the long haul, weathering the inevitable setbacks and heavy demands on their time and energy, is another key question. Spielberg has been viewed in the press as an especially doubtful prospect for such a long-term business venture. His parallel involvement in his directing career, as well as with such creative and philanthropic activities as the Shoah project,

---

* Spielberg helped develop the as-yet-unfilmed screenplay by Bo Goldman, saying of Hughes in 1990, "Here was a man who spent his entire life living in the so-called rarefied existence of Hollywood, but living a life, or several lives, or three or four lifetimes, in a very short span of time. . . . What drove him to the seclusion? What drove him into the rooms with the curtains drawn? It's a very interesting subject."

† DreamWorks also announced plans to build a twelve-acre, Mediterranean-style animation complex in Glendale.

cannot help but make people wonder whether at some point Spielberg will begin to find the role of mogul too distracting. The fact that he has kept the right to direct movies for other companies (such as the *Jurassic Park* sequel for Universal) has raised concerns about his ultimate commitment to DreamWorks. "I go where the material is," he insisted. For admirers of his work as a director, however, the most troubling question of all is: Why would the greatest director in contemporary Hollywood want to take time away from directing movies to run a studio?

Perhaps, having made *Schindler's List,* Spielberg recognized he had reached the time of life when he needed a radically different kind of creative challenge. Making plans for his own movie studio could be seen as a welcome diversion, enabling him to take his time deciding what kind of filmmaker he wants to become in the second half of his career. When CNN interviewer Larry King suggested in 1995 that he may never top the achievement of *Schindler's List,* Spielberg replied with equanimity, "I'll be very happy if I never top this." Perhaps with that once-in-a-lifetime personal and artistic triumph behind him, it is now true of Spielberg what Lesley Blanch once wrote about the director George Cukor, that "he has not, or has passed, *ambition,* in the destructive sense. This makes him utterly free. And being perfectly sure of who he is, what he is, he does not envy—is not eaten up by competition."

One of the few constraints Spielberg accepted in starting DreamWorks was imposed by his wife. Kate showed signs of becoming a bit restless in the early 1990s, advancing her own acting aspirations in such varied projects as the flop TV sitcom *Smoldering Lust,* Tony Bill's cable TV movie *Next Door,* and Amblin's feature *How to Make an American Quilt.* Spielberg was not altogether happy with her renewed interest in her career. "We were watching *Indiana Jones and the Temple of Doom* the other night on television," Kate related in early 1994. "And I turned to Steven and I said, 'What happened to my career after that movie?' He said, 'You weren't supposed to have a career. You were supposed to be with me.' "

When it came to starting DreamWorks, however, he knew he needed her blessing as much as Lew Wasserman's. Concerned about Jeffrey Katzenberg's legendary work habits, Kate laid down the law to her husband: "I love Jeffrey. But I never want you to become Jeffrey. I don't want you to become involved in that lather of workaholism." Perhaps chastened by the failure of his previous marriage, Spielberg promised he wouldn't make that mistake again. When asked how he can manage starting a new studio while simultaneously running the Shoah project and directing movies, he said with characteristic optimism, "All important things get done in my life. . . . Somehow this is all fitting nicely into my life and I'm still home by six and I'm still home on weekends. That's the miracle."

As he goes about creating his own private moviemaking domain, Spielberg is realizing another of his lifelong dreams. His actress friend Joan Darling remembers, "What Steven wanted more than anything else when he was young was somehow to set up his life so he could just go on a soundstage and make movies." The alienated, anxiety-ridden boy who turned to filmmaking to find "a place where I felt safer: in front of my camera" has turned his refuge into a kingdom. If the promise of *Schindler's List* is fulfilled, he should rule it with wisdom and responsibility. Rabbi Albert Lewis observes that moviemaking gave Steven "the strength or the courage to be what he was . . . the opportunity to stay sort of in the shadows, i.e., behind the camera, and to be part of the outside world." And when Steven learned to use a movie camera, it "made a *mensch* out of him."

I FIRST BECAME AWARE of Steven Spielberg's prodigious filmmaking gifts in 1972, when I saw his TV movie *Something Evil*. In the twenty years that followed, I watched with bemusement as his enormous popularity left him largely without honor from his Hollywood colleagues and the critical community. As early as 1982, when *E.T.* appeared, I began thinking, Here is a good story for a biographer. The disdain of the self-styled intellectual elite for this great popular artist reminded me of the condescension with which such Golden Age directors as Hitchcock, Hawks, and Capra were treated in the prime of their careers. I reluctantly put aside the notion of a Spielberg biography at the time, realizing that it was a bit premature (he was, after all, only thirty-five), but I waited in vain during the intervening years to read a serious, in-depth biography, or even a critical study with any insight or originality. It seemed that first-rate writers on film and academic scholars were shunning Spielberg as if he were unworthy of sustained attention.

Ironically, another factor in this undervaluation of Spielberg has been his desire to control the telling of his own life story. Even writers who have approached him with the proposal of an authorized biography or an authorized book about his films have been discouraged; he was said to be planning to write his autobiography at some time in the future. Evidently the idea of writing an unauthorized biography of Hollywood's most powerful figure was out of the question for many writers. I am constantly surprised by how many people, including some in the literary world, react with automatic suspicion when they hear the phrase "unauthorized biography," as if there were something inherently dubious about a book not having the subject's seal of approval. On the contrary, what should arouse the reader's suspicions are the inevitable constraints placed on an author's integrity by the decision to allow his subject to authorize and thereby to control the writing of the book. By talking endlessly about his life in press and television interviews to promote his movies, Spielberg already has given us an autobiography of sorts, albeit a scattered, fragmentary, and sometimes misleading one; what largely has been missing from the picture is an independent examination of his character, seen not simply through his eyes alone but also through the perspectives of the people who have known and worked with him throughout his lifetime.

What finally convinced me in 1993 to write this book was the news that Spielberg finally had decided to make *Schindler's List*. Once he mustered the courage to confront the Holocaust and his own Jewish heritage, the conflicting impulses of his life and work began to resolve themselves in a way that provided dramatic shape and resolution for a biography, even if the subject still was only a middle-aged man with (one hopes) another twenty or thirty years of productivity ahead of him. There are major advantages in writing a biography when the subject is in the prime of his life. The subject and his surroundings have a vital immediacy, and if the benefit of distant perspective is somewhat lacking, it is not entirely absent. Spielberg has been making films, as boy and man, for forty years now, and if he were to stop tomorrow, his career would stand as one of the most important in the history of film. But the foremost advantage for a biographer of the fifty-year-old Steven Spielberg is being able to interview the people who knew him during his formative years—his family, friends, and neighbors, his playmates, classmates, and teachers, the people who shaped him into the man he would become—and the opportunity to hear their accounts when their memories still are relatively fresh.

Even more than for most human beings, it is true of Spielberg what Wordsworth wrote, that "The Child is father of the Man." Following the trail of Spielberg's unconventional childhood from Cincinnati to Haddon Township to Phoenix to Saratoga was a fascinating and revelatory experience; very few of the scores of people I interviewed from those years had ever before talked about him to a writer. In all, I interviewed 327 people for this book, including many of Spielberg's Hollywood coworkers, friends, and colleagues (see the list in the following section).

Spielberg himself declined to be interviewed. During my years as a reporter on *Daily Variety,* I had met him twice, first at a small, informal press conference for *Jaws* in the Universal commissary in 1975, and then for a brief conversation with him and his wife, Kate Capshaw, before he received an award from the American Cinema Editors in 1990. When I wrote Spielberg on March 1, 1994, four months after starting work on this book, I explained that while I was writing an "unauthorized, strictly independent biography," I would welcome the opportunity to interview him, as well as any other cooperation he might care to give, such as letting me see his early amateur films. His always gentlemanly spokesman, Marvin Levy, replied in a telephone call on March 18 that while Spielberg knew my work and realized that I was writing a serious book, he had a policy of not talking with anyone writing a book about him because of his plans to write his autobiography. "He'd be happy if there are *no* books" about him, Levy pointed out, but added, "He's not going to stop *you* from writing a book." Levy suggested that if I submitted factual questions in writing, Spielberg might answer them; it also might be possible, he said, to let me watch his amateur films, even though "some of [them] he's always wanted to keep locked away." When I followed up on March 24 by asking Levy for a list of titles and dates of Spielberg's amateur films and reminding him of my request to see those films, my letter went unanswered.

From some of the people I approached for interviews in the months that followed, I learned that Spielberg's office generally was not discouraging his friends and coworkers from talking with me, and that Levy himself had declared I was "kosher." That helped open some doors, although I eventually learned that Spielberg did ask a few people not to talk to me (not everyone complied with his wishes); others declined to be interviewed because the book was not authorized. One person who later gave me an interview initially was told by Spielberg's assistant, "Steven is in the throes of planning an authorized biography. Please save your recollections for that one." The confidentiality agreements Amblin Entertainment reportedly has extracted from at least some of its employees may have been a hindrance as well; such are the hurdles an independent biographer faces in dealing with a living subject who is virtually omnipotent in Hollywood terms and unabashedly describes himself as a "control freak." Among those who turned down my interview requests were Lew R. Wasserman, Kathleen Kennedy, Frank Marshall, John Williams, Ben Kingsley, John Milius, Sean Connery, Sam Neill, Liam Neeson, and Steven Bochco; others in the film industry, most notably Sidney J. Sheinberg and Richard Dreyfuss, did not respond to my letters. But I was pleasantly surprised by the degree of cooperation and candor I did receive from dozens of others who had known and worked with Spielberg throughout his career in Hollywood and were eager to help me set the record straight.

Spielberg's charming and effervescent mother, Leah Adler, chatted with me over the phone on three occasions from her Milky Way kosher restaurant but in the end declined to give me a formal interview. Although she has often talked about her son in print and on television, Mrs. Adler told me in January 1996, "The studio would rather I not do anything." "You mean Steven?" I asked. "The gods!" she replied, laughing. "The gods said nix. . . . I don't ask questions. I'm in obedience training school. Good luck with it." On the other hand, Spielberg's father, Arnold, enthusiastically granted me a candid and wide-ranging interview in January 1996. He subsequently changed his mind about loaning me family photographs for use in the book, explaining apologetically, "I have to go by my son's wishes." I remain extremely grateful to Mr. Spielberg for his many illuminating comments on Steven and the rest of his family, especially on those who were born in Russia. One especially poignant moment during our interview came when Arnold said of his son, with whom he has not always been close, "You probably know more about him than I do." After Steven dissuaded his mother from talking, I made no attempt to interview his wife, Kate; his three sisters (one of whom, Anne, I dated for several months in 1981–82); or his first wife, Amy Irving (although I have never met Irving, while she was living with Spielberg in the late 1970s she allowed me to use her name to help market a screenplay I wrote but that was not produced).

I received valuable assistance on Spielberg family history from Steven's first cousins in Cincinnati, Samuel Guttman, Daniel Guttman, and Deborah Guttman Ridenour, who passed along genealogical research compiled by their late mother, the former Natalie Spielberg (I also had the pleasure of meeting Samuel's son, Scott, who asked me to be sure to mention him in this book on the famous relative he has never met). In addition, I interviewed a distant Spielberg relative, Ruth Schuhmann Solinger, who left Germany in the wake of *Kristallnacht* and also settled in Cincinnati. Other genealogical information was generously provided by Cincinnati researcher Adele Blanton and by Dr. Ida Cohen Selavan, reference librarian of the Hebrew Union College–Jewish Institute of Religion, who translated Hebrew memorial books for me and helped guide my research into life in old-country *shtetlach*.

O N E of the rewards of writing books is that I am able to make new and enduring friendships in the course of my research. Thanks to our shared Spielberg connection, I am lucky to know such warm and delightful people as Marjorie Robbins; Don Shull and his mother, Marge; Gene Ward Smith; and Rabbi Albert Lewis. Among his many other *mitzvoth,* Rabbi Lewis researched the history of his Temple Beth Shalom congregation of Cherry Hill, New Jersey, showed me the former temple site in Haddonfield, and arranged for me to visit the United States Holocaust Memorial Museum in Washington, D.C., with my brother, Washington attorney Michael F. McBride.

The Revs. Fred Hill and James Milton, and caretaker Willie Perdue, kindly welcomed me at the Southern Baptist Church in Cincinnati's Avondale neighborhood and gave me a tour of their beautiful building, the former Adath Israel synagogue. Others who provided hospitality and showed me places where Spielberg had lived in Cincinnati and New Jersey included Leonard Bailey; Bill Dabney; Miriam Fuhrman (who also helped me research Arnold Spielberg's time at RCA), Jane Fuhrman Satanoff, Glenn Fuhrman, Dr. Mitchell Fuhrman, and Dr. Dennis Satanoff; August and Loretta Knoblach (who also provided photographs of their home); Bonita Moore; and Mildred (Millie) Friedman Tieger.

I was honored to make the acquaintance of the late historian Dr. Jacob Rader Marcus, director of the American Jewish Archives on the campus of Cincinnati's Hebrew Union College–Jewish Institute of Religion, who generously took time from his own writing in 1994 to share his knowledge about the history of Avondale and other subjects.

Throughout my three years of research, Linda Harris Mehr and her staff at the Margaret Herrick Library of the Academy of Motion Picture Arts & Sciences in Beverly Hills, including Sandra Archer, Barbara Hall, and Howard Prouty, always gave me diligent and knowledgeable assistance. Other helpful archivists and librarians included Christy

French of the California State University at Long Beach (CSULB) Library/Archives; Patricia M. Van Skaik and Anna Horton of the Public Library of Cincinnati & Hamilton County; Monica Weiner of the Museum of Television & Radio, New York; Steve Hoza of the Arizona Historical Society; Kevin Proffitt of the American Jewish Archives; and Geraldine Duclow of the Free Library of Philadelphia. Edith Cummins and Melissa Pearse of the Hamilton County (Ohio) Court went beyond the call of duty to help me research Spielberg's family history.

Information on Spielberg's attendance at Thomas A. Edison School in Haddonfield, New Jersey, was provided by the Haddonfield Board of Education and by Sharon Gurtcheff, secretary of the Haddon Township High School guidance office; Edison principal Doug Hamilton was also helpful. At Arcadia High School in Phoenix, the principal, Dr. J. Calvin Bruins, generously supplied information and gave me a tour of the school; my research was aided by Nancy Lindquist and Anita Underdown. For assistance in locating members of Spielberg's classes at Arcadia and at Ingleside Elementary School and for other information about those schools, I thank, among others, Patricia Scott Rodney, Susan Smith LeSueur, Steve Blasnek, Steve Suggs, and Bill Hoffman. At Saratoga High School in California, the principal, Dr. Kevin Skelly, graciously assisted my research, as did Kerry Mohnike, adviser for the school newspaper, *The Falcon*. Judith Hamilton Kirchick, Peter Fallico, Philip H. Pennypacker, and Carol Magnoli helped me locate members of Spielberg's Saratoga class and invited me to their thirtieth reunion in San Jose in 1995. I also received information from Los Gatos (Ca.) High School registrar Jan Helzer; the records office of CSULB; the registrar's office of the University of California, Los Angeles; and the office of academic records and registrar at the University of Southern California.

My understanding of the Holocaust was enriched by conversations with several survivors, including Eva Klein David, Peter Mora, Jakob (Alex) Schneider (a former inmate of the Plaszów camp depicted in *Schindler's List)*, Richard Zomer, and the members of Cafe Europa in Los Angeles. I thank Heidi Rechteger and Dr. Florabel Kinsler for introducing me to many of these inspiring people and for sharing their own knowledge of the Holocaust and other subjects pertaining to Jewish history and culture. Dr. Kinsler also loaned me copies of her articles and her doctoral dissertation, "An Eriksonian and Evaluative Investigation of the Effects of Video Testimonials Upon Jewish Survivors of the Holocaust" (International College, Los Angeles, 1986). Eva David, an Auschwitz survivor, not only supplied copies of articles about Spielberg and his mother that I might not otherwise have seen, but also invited me to speak with her in 1994 at Congregation Mogen David in Los Angeles and at Santa Monica College, under the auspices of Heidi Crane. I had the benefit of stimulating discussions about *Schindler's List* and the Holocaust with my editor at Da Capo Press, Yuval Taylor, whose spirited disagreements with me over Spielberg's film helped sharpen my discussion in chapter 16. Thomas Keneally, the author of the remarkable book upon which Spielberg based *Schindler's List,* also lent encouragement to this project.

Other people who kindly supplied research material and information included Susan Roper Arndt; Sheila M. Arthur of the Saratoga Chamber of Commerce; James Auer of the *Milwaukee Journal Sentinel;* Sue Barnet, coordinator of the Arizona Newspaper Project, Phoenix; Jean Weber Brill; Ralph Burris; Roxanne Camron and Karle Dickerson of *'Teen* magazine; Charles Carter; Judge Charles G. Case II; Steven DeCinzo; Tim Dietz; Nancy Engebretson and Nancy Van Leeuwen of Phoenix Newspapers, Inc.; Stephen Farber; Nancy Frishberg; Bob Gale; Davida Gale; Mark Haggard; Arlene Hellerman of the Writers Guild of America, East; Denis C. Hoffman; Richard Y. Hoffman Jr.; David Kronke; J. Wesley Leas; the Lippin Group; Howard Mandelbaum of Photofest; Richard B. Matheson; Lee Mercer; Del Merrill; Marie Nordberg of *Emergency Medical Services* magazine; Peter Z. Orton; Jennifer Pendleton; Haven Peters; Terry Peugh; Bert Pfister; San Antonio film critic Bob Polunsky; Nancy Randle; David Robb; Hubert E. (Hugh) and Connie Roberts; Jerry Roberts; Peter and Helen Rutan; Barry Sollenberger; Floyd W. Tenney; and Beth Weber Zelenski. I also thank Book Castle, Burbank, Ca.; Collectors Bookstore, Hollywood; Larry Edmunds Bookshop, Hollywood; Producers & Quantity Photo, Inc., Hollywood; and Video Still, Hollywood.

For help in contacting Spielberg collaborators, I am grateful to the Directors Guild of America, the Screen Actors Guild, and the Writers Guild of America, West. Additional research sources included the American Film Institute, Los Angeles; the Berkeley (Ca.) Public Library; the Beverly Hills Public Library; Book City, Hollywood; the Cincinnati Board of Health, Office of Vital Statistics; the Cincinnati Historical Society Research Library; the Glendale (Ca.) Public Library; the Haddonfield Public Library; the Haddon Township Library; the Los Angeles County Law Library; the Los Angeles Public Library; the Pasadena (Ca.) Public Library; the Phoenix Central Library; the San Antonio Central Library; the *San Antonio Express and News;* the Santa Clara County (Ca.) Superior Court; the Saratoga Community Library; the Scottsdale (Az.) *Progress Tribune;* the Scottsdale Public Library; the Simon Wiesenthal Center, Los Angeles; Tribune Newspapers, Mesa, Az.; the Trinity University Library, San Antonio; the San Jose Public Library; the University of Cincinnati Library; the University of Southern California libraries; the University of Oregon Press; and the Walt Disney Company Archives.

Screenings of Spielberg films and television programs were made possible by Donovan Brandt of Eddie Brandt's Saturday Matinee, North Hollywood; Joe Dante; Denis Hoffman; Frank Morriss; the Museum of Television & Radio in New York and Beverly Hills; James Pepper; Donna Ross and Lou Ellen Kramer of the UCLA Film and Television Archive; Thomas Sherak and Angela Pierce of Twentieth Century–Fox; and Vidiots, Santa Monica. Videotapes for research also were provided by Tony Bill, Harrison Engle, and the Boys and Girls Club of the East Valley, Tempe, Az.

A S the honor roll of names listed above amply indicates, it takes a village to raise a book. In my Spielberg village, there were four special people who made this book possible.

My partnership with Dr. Ruth O'Hara not only has endured but has deepened over the years. Ruth is not only a great Stanford University scholar and mother to our son, John, but also the best editor any writer could hope to have. She not only urged me to write a Spielberg biography and gave me many keen insights into Spielberg and his work, but also pitched in at a critical juncture with unflagging devotion, energy, and intellectual brilliance to help bring this book to fruition.

Jean Oppenheimer, my friend and fellow film critic, brightened my life with her companionship and sustained me with her good heart, her stimulating and challenging wit, her many research contributions, and her belief in this book, which could not have been completed without her help. Her nurturing of this project went beyond emotional and intellectual sustenance to include an unending supply of bagels and other "comfort food" from Junior's Delicatessen in West Los Angeles.

Maurice L. Muehle's formidable legal skills again played a vital role in enabling me to write the book I wanted to write. Maury's vast experience and knowledge of the law, his shrewdness and tact, and his love of writing have helped sustain me throughout the last eight years of my literary life. He is always generous with his time and advice, and he is ably assisted by, among others, Sira Windwer and Lanla Gist.

My son, John McBride, has been my greatest comfort and joy throughout the writing of this book. While constantly reminding me that there is life away from the word processor, John has been at my side as my enthusiastic research assistant and companion in watching Spielberg films and TV shows, enabling me to see them anew through the eyes of a precocious child. John has shown special delight and acumen in calling my attention to Spielberg references in other movies, and he has done his best to keep me young by serving as my personal fitness trainer.

I am proud that my daughter Jessica McBride is carrying on my late parents' tradition as a superb reporter with the *Milwaukee Journal Sentinel* and that she now has become my professional colleague. Among my siblings and their spouses, I received extraordinary support during the writing of this book from Mike and Kerin McBride; Dennis McBride and Karen Barry; and Timothy McBride and Shirley Porterfield; as well as from Dr. Patrick and Kim McBride; Genevieve McBride; and Mark McBride and Kim Stanton-McBride. Sean McBride made me think more clearly about the principles of film criticism when he interviewed me for a class project; I also take delight in my other McBride nieces and nephews: John Caspari, Catherine Caspari, and Barbara, Gabrielle, Gillian, Lauren, Lindsay, Meredith, Philip, Pierce, Raymond Erin, and Ryan McBride. My aunts Bobby Dunne, Sister M. Jean Raymond, and Mickey Lorch and my cousin Cece Lorch are always there for me with love and encouragement.

I am grateful to remain part of the remarkable O'Hara clan that has emigrated from the east coast of Ireland to grace the San Francisco Bay Area: Noel and Hetty O'Hara; Stuart and Susan Bennett; Karl, Gwenn, my nephew Karl Jr., and my niece Natasha Van Dessel; and Fiona O'Kirwan; as well as the more far-flung Una, Siúan, and David McGahan; and extended family members Lynn Garrison and Gary Holloway.

Through Jean Oppenheimer, I am delighted also to belong in spirit to the clan of those great Texas liberals, the Oppenheimers of San Antonio and Dallas: Sue and Jesse; David, Harriet, Rebecca, Daniel, and Jacob; and Barbara and John Cohn; and to share their kinship with that spirited Texas literary maven Louise Michelson.

Among my other professional colleagues and friends, I am grateful for the continuing support of Charles Champlin, F. X. Feeney, Kirk Honeycutt, Leonard Maltin, Myron Meisel, Henry Sheehan (who has written the most perceptive criticism of Spielberg's work), and the other members of the Los Angeles Film Critics Association; Kim Williamson and Ray Greene of *Boxoffice* magazine; Walter Donohue, my editor at Faber and Faber, London; Harrison Engle of Signal Hill Entertainment; my former *Daily Variety* colleagues Thomas M. Pryor, Michael Silverman, Pete Pryor, David Robb, Art Murphy, Jennifer Pendleton, and Judy Brennan; Bob Thomas, the dean of Hollywood biographers; and Richard Parks.

Friends whose loyalty and encouragement helped sustain me during the writing of this book also included Barry Allen; Glen Barrow; Edward Bernds; Dorian Carli-Jones; Felipe, Felipito, and Martha Caseres; Danny Cassidy; Marilyn Engle; Ronnie Gilbert; Gary and Jillian Graver; Kendall Hailey; Charles Horton; Penn and Elaine Jones; Jonathan Lethem; William Link; Blake Lucas and Linda Gross; Larry Mantle; Connie Martinson; Christie Milliken; Morris Polan; Lou Race; Diana Rico; Victoria Riskin, David Rintels, and Fay Wray; Jonathan Rosenbaum; Margaret Ross; John Sanford; Michael Schlesinger; Kathryn Sharp; Michael Shovers; Abraham Smith; Julia Sweeney; Gore Vidal; Edward Watz; Bob Werden; Michael Wilmington; and Fiona, Charlotte, and Sam Zomer.

Among those at Simon & Schuster who worked on this book, I thank my editor, Bob Bender; his assistant, Johanna Li; Felice Javit of the legal department; and copy editor Virginia Clark, who once again enhanced my writing with her film scholarship.

Joseph McBride
Los Angeles, California
1993–1997

Interviews by the Author

Spielberg Family Members:
Daniel Guttman, Samuel Guttman, Deborah Guttman Ridenour, Ruth Schuhmann Solinger, Arnold Spielberg

Cincinnati:
Leonard M. Bailey, Rev. Arnetta Brantley, Edith Cummins, Bill Dabney, Anastasia Del Favero, Hugo Del Favero Jr., William Del Favero, Jean Gaynor, Dr. Bernard Goldman, Rev. Fred Hill, Dolores Del Favero Huff, Terry Johnson, Dr. Jacob Rader Marcus, Roslyn Mitman, Bonita Moore, Willie Perdue, Benjamin Pritz, Louise Pritz, Dr. Ida Cohen Selavan, Meyer Singerman, Peggie Hibbert Singerman, Richard Singerman, Olga Sorrell, Mildred Friedman (Millie) Tieger

Haddon Township, Haddonfield, and Camden, New Jersey:
Veronica Adams, Mildred Bonaventura, Jane Bonaventura Caputo, Bill Davison, Jon Davison, Charles F. Devlin, Charles J. Devlin Jr., Mrs. Charles J. Devlin Jr., John DiPietropolo, Pat Berry DiPietropolo, Vincent DiPietropolo, Bill Esher, Judith Myer Flenard, Glenn Fuhrman, Miriam Fuhrman, Dr. Mitchell Fuhrman, Barbara (Bobby) Harris, August (Gus) Knoblach, Loretta Knoblach, J. Wesley Leas, Rabbi Albert Lewis, Scott MacDonald, Stanley (Sandy) MacDonald, Gerald McMullen, Robert J. Moran Jr., Robert J. Moran Sr., Jane MacDonald Morley, Edward G. Myer, Louise Bonaventura Patterson, Dr. Darryl Robbins, Grace Robbins, Marjorie Robbins, Helen Rutan, Peter Rutan, Dr. Dennis Satanoff, Jane Fuhrman Satanoff, Barbara Schwartz, George F. Schwartz Jr., George F. Schwartz Sr., Carol Adams Spinelli, Lisa Toll, Michael Toll

Phoenix and Scottsdale, Arizona:
Howard Amerson, Susan Roper Arndt, Sam Baar, Rick Barr, Rick Blakeley, Steve Blasnek, Jean Weber Brill, Phyllis Brooks, Dr. J. Calvin Bruins, Margaret Burrell, Barbara Callahan, Charles Carter, Dr. Forrest Carter, Lynda Carter, Judge Charles G. Case II, Richard E. Charland, Coette Childers, Clynn Christensen, Rick Cook, George Cowie, Phil Deppe, Mary DiCerbo, Mike DiCerbo, Tim Dietz, Jackson Drake, Betty Castleberry Edwards (Mrs. Roger Sheer), Jim Emery, Nancy Engebretson, Cynthia (Cindy) Gaines Fleetham, Richard T. Ford, Shirley Frye, Bill Gaines, Bob Gaines, Sylvia Gaines, Katherine Galwey, Rodney Gehre, Dan Harkins, Kay Harmon, Guy Hayden Jr., Guy Hayden III, Karen Hayden, Robert V. Hendricks, Bill Hoffman, Lynn Hoffman, Richard Y. (Dick) Hoffman Jr., Angela Jacobi, George Jacobi, Betty Johnson, Mike Keefe, Karen Hakes Knight, Susan Smith LeSueur, Clifford Lindblom, Nancy Hay Lindquist, Clark (Lucky) Lohr, Steve Lombard, Mike Loper, Peggy McMullin Loper, Michael W. McNamara, Vance Marshall, Warner Marshall, Terry Mechling, Del Merrill, Betty Michaud, Ferneta Miller (formerly Ferneta Sulek), Harold Millsop, Michael Neer, Lawrence Olden, Donald W. Penfield, Haven Peters, Terry Peugh, Art Piccinati, Chris Pischke, Fred Pratt, Frances

Preimsberg, Bob Proehl, Martha Rook Reedy, Pete Repp, Nina Nauman Rivera, Patricia Scott Rodney, Paul G. Rowe, James L. Seeman, Carole Sheer, Mrs. Leonard Sheer, Carol Stromme Shelton, Louis K. Sher, Brenda Simmons, Tom Simmons, William J. Simmons Jr., William J. Simmons Sr., Barry Sollenberger, Jim Sollenberger, Junia Sollenberger, Mark Sollenberger, A. D. Stromme, Steve Suggs, Sharyn Galwey Sunda, Walter Tamasauckas, Craig Tenney, Floyd Tenney, Bill Thompson, Doug Tice, Marie Tice, Walter Tice, Audrey Dalessandro Watkins, Betty Weber, Alan Wesolowski, Sherry Missner Williams, Eleanor Wolf, Beth Weber Zelenski, Frank Ziska Jr., Daniel Zusman, Dorothy Zusman, Janice Zusman, Lloyd Zusman

SARATOGA AND LOS GATOS, CALIFORNIA:
Sheila M. Arthur, Mike Augustine, Don Baroni, Bonnie Parker Bartman, Dutch Boysen, Kathy Shull Cappello, Jill Tucker Carroll, John J. Cody, Jane Craft, Diana Hart Deem, Peter Fallico, Sally Farrington, James Fletcher, Nancy Frishberg, Al Gibson, Dr. Peter Griffith, Tim Haggerty Sr., Kendra Rosen Hanson, Susan Didinger Hennings, Marilyn Holmes, Tom Holwerda, Judith Kreisberg Kirchick, Grant Koch, Leo McKenna, Carol Magnoli, Skippy Margolis, Larry Mercer, Lee Mercer Jr., Kerry Mohnike, Susan Bomen Moman, Laurie Oberhaus, Carl Pennypacker, Philip H. Pennypacker, Eloise Peters, Jim Peters Sr., Bert Pfister, Rhoda Porter, Connie Roberts, Hubert E. (Hugh) Roberts, Henry Rogalsky, Jim Roszell, Dallas Sceales Jr., George Scott, Don Shull, Marge Shull, Dr. Kevin Skelly, Connie Skipitares, Gene Ward Smith, Douglas H. Stuart, William Teplow, Leslie Watkins, Joseph Wharton, Dan Wilson, Ron Wolyn

CALIFORNIA STATE COLLEGE AT LONG BEACH:
Dan Baker, Ralph Burris, Robert Finney, Stephen Hubbert, Howard Martin, Hubert (Hugh) Morehead

FILM INDUSTRY COLLABORATORS AND COLLEAGUES:
Edward M. Abroms, Joseph Alves Jr., Margaret Avery, Stephen Bach, David Bale, Richard Belding, Peter Benchley, Tony Bill, Robert S. Birchard, Jeffrey Boam, Orin Borsten, Joseph E. Boston, Meredith Brody, Ralph Burris, Jeff Corey, Roger Corman, Joe Dante, Joan Darling, Allen Daviau, Jon Davison, George Eckstein, Sharon Farrell, Michael Finnell, Bob Gale, David Giler, William S. Gilmore Jr., Carl Gottlieb, Gary Graver, Devorah Mann Hardberger, Dean Hargrove, Donald E. Heitzer, Arthur Hill, Denis C. Hoffman, Martin Hornstein, Willard Huyck, Lawrence Kasdan, Gloria Katz, Howard Kazanjian, John Landis, Rocky Lang, William Link, Carey Loftin, Jerry McNeely, Hal Mann, James Mann, Tony Martinelli, Richard B. Matheson, Richard Christian Matheson, Mike Medavoy, Frank Morriss, George J. Nicholson, Peter Z. Orton, Jerry Pam, Michael Phillips, Carl Pingitore, John Ptak, Louis B. Race, Julie Raymond, William Sackheim, Peter Saphier, Charles A. (Chuck) Silvers, Robert Stack, Lionel Stander, Bill Stanley, Tom Stoppard, Barry Sullivan, Jeannot Szwarc, David Tomblin, Douglas Trumbull, John Veitch, Anson Williams, Richard D. Zanuck, Fred Zinnemann, Vilmos Zsigmond

OTHERS:
James Auer, Charles Champlin, Eva Klein David, Stephen Farber, Dr. Florabel Kinsler, Peter Mora, A. D. Murphy, Jennifer Pendleton, Bob Polunsky, Jerry Roberts, Jakob (Alex) Schneider, Bob Thomas, David Weddle, Michael Wilmington

STEVEN SPIELBERG INTERVIEWS AND ARTICLES BY SPIELBERG
Abbreviations used in this section and in the chapter notes include: *DV, Daily Variety,* Los Angeles; *HR, The Hollywood Reporter; LADN,* the *Los Angeles Daily News; LAHE,* the *Los Angeles Herald-Examiner; LAT,* the *Los Angeles Times;* and *NYT, The New York*

Times. References to books and articles are listed fully the first time; subsequent references include only the author's last name (and, in the case of more than one book or article by a single author, the title).

Adler, Dick. "Hitchhiking on the Road to Success," *TV Guide*, August 26, 1972.

Alward, Jennifer. "An Interview with Steven Spielberg," *The Filmex Flash*, September 1976.

Andrews, Suzanna. "The Man Who Would Be Walt," *NYT*, January 26, 1992.

Ansen, David. "Spielberg's Obsession," *Newsweek*, December 20, 1993.

Anthony, George. "King of Inner Space," *Marquee*, July–August 1982.

Austin, Chuck. "Director Steve Spielberg," *Filmmakers Newsletter*, December 1977.

Bagala, Jo Marie. "Director Wheels Way Through Bicycle Epic," *The Forty-Niner* (California State College at Long Beach), October 4, 1967.

Blair, Jon. "Spielberg Comes of Age," *Esquire* (U.K.), March 1994.

Bobrow, Andrew C. "Filming *The Sugarland Express*: An Interview with Steven Spielberg," *Filmmakers Newsletter*, Summer 1974.

Breskin, David. "The *Rolling Stone* Interview: Steven Spielberg," October 24, 1985.

Callo, Jim. "Director Steven Spielberg Takes the Wraps Off E.T., Revealing His Secrets at Last," *People*, August 23, 1982.

———. "Steven Spielberg's Musings on *Poltergeist*," November 1, 1982.

Cameron, Sue. "How to Succeed—Sneak Past the Studio Guard," *HR*, April 13, 1971.

Champlin, Charles. "Spielberg's Escape from Escapism," *LAT*, February 2, 1986.

Clark, Esther. "Teenage Cecil B.," *The Arizona Republic*, December 8, 1963.

Collins, Glenn. "Spielberg Films *The Color Purple*," *NYT*, December 15, 1985.

Combs, Richard. "Primal Scream: An Interview with Steven Spielberg," *Sight and Sound*, Spring 1977.

Cook, Bruce. "Close Encounters with Steven Spielberg," *American Film*, November 1977.

Corliss, Richard. "Steve's Summer Magic," *Time*, May 31, 1982.

———. " 'I Dream for a Living,' " *Time*, July 15, 1985.

Crist, Judith. *Take 22: Moviemakers on Moviemaking*. Viking, 1984 (includes a 1982 seminar with Spielberg).

Davidson, Bill. "Will *1941* Make Spielberg a Billion-Dollar Baby?," *NYT*, December 9, 1979.

Elkin, Michael. "On Spielberg's A-'List,' " *Jewish Exponent*, March 18, 1994.

Elkins, Merry, ed. "Steven Spielberg on *Indiana Jones and the Temple of Doom*," *American Cinematographer*, July 1984.

Forsberg, Myra. "Spielberg at 40: The Man and the Child," *NYT*, January 10, 1988.

Gallagher, John. "A First Encounter with Steven Spielberg," *Grand Illusions*, Winter 1977.

Griffin, Nancy. "Spielberg's Last Crusade," *Time Out*, May 24–31, 1989.

Gritten, David. "Grim. Black and White . . . Spielberg?" *LAT*, May 9, 1993.

Gross, Linden. "Steven Spielberg's Close Encounter with the Past," *Reader's Digest*, April 1996.

Grunwald, Lisa. "Steven Spielberg Gets Real," *Life*, December 1993.

Guthmann, Edward. "Spielberg's *List*," *San Francisco Chronicle*, December 12, 1993.

Haber, Joyce. "The Man Who Bit the Bullet on *Jaws*," *LAT*, July 13, 1975.

Harper, Suzanne. "Spielberg," *Nutshell*, Spring 1984.

Heathwood, Gail. "Steven Spielberg," *Cinema Papers*, April–June 1978.

Helpern, David. "At Sea with Steven Spielberg," *Take One*, March–April 1974.

Hirschberg, Lynn. "Will Hollywood's Mr. Perfect Ever Grow Up?" *Rolling Stone*, July 19–August 2, 1984.

Hluchy, Patricia, and Gillian MacKay. "Spielberg's Magic Screen," *Maclean's,* June 4, 1984.

Hodenfield, Chris. "The Sky Is Full of Questions!!: Science Fiction in Steven Spielberg's Suburbia," *Rolling Stone,* January 26, 1978.

———. *"1941:* Bombs Away!" *Rolling Stone,* January 24, 1980.

Hull, Bob. "22-Year-Old Tyro Directs Joan Crawford: 'A Pleasure,' " *HR,* February 17, 1969.

Hutchison, David. "Steven Spielberg: The Making of *Raiders of the Lost Ark,"* Starlog, September 1981.

Jacobs, Diane. "Interview with Steven Spielberg," *Millimeter,* November 1977.

Jagger, Bianca, and Andy Warhol. "Steven Spielberg," *Interview,* June 1982.

Janos, Leo. "Steven Spielberg: L'Enfant Directeur," *Cosmopolitan,* June 1980.

Kakutani, Michiko. "The Two Faces of Spielberg—Horror vs. Hope," *NYT,* May 30, 1982.

Klemesrud, Judy. "Can He Make the *Jaws* of Outer Space?," *NYT,* May 15, 1977.

Kramer, Rabbi William M. "My Shtetele California: Young Steve Spielberg," HERITAGE: Southwest Jewish Press, November 27, 1970, reprinted July 18, 1986.

Kroll, Jack. "Close Encounter with Spielberg," *Newsweek,* November 21, 1977.

Lane, Randall. " 'I Want Gross,' " *Forbes,* September 26, 1994.

Lightman, Herb A. "The New Panaflex Camera Makes Its Production Debut," *American Cinematographer,* May 1973.

———. "Spielberg Speaks About *Close Encounters,"* American Cinematographer, January 1978.

McCarthy, Todd. "Sand Castles," *Film Comment,* May–June 1982.

Margolis, Herbert, and Craig Modderno, *"Penthouse* Interview: Steven Spielberg," *Penthouse,* January 1978.

Maslin, Janet. "Spielberg's Journey from Sharks to the Stars," *NYT,* November 13, 1977.

Olmsted, Dan. " 'Ex–Boy Scout Makes Movies,' " *USA Weekend,* July 30, 1989.

Pancol, Katherine. "Steven Spielberg," *Hello!,* 1990.

Perlez, Jane. "Spielberg Grapples with the Horror of the Holocaust," *NYT,* June 13, 1993.

Perry, George. "Purple Raider," *London Sunday Times,* June 15, 1986.

Pile, Susan, and Tere Tereba. "Steven Spielberg: From *Jaws* to Paws," *Interview,* May 1977.

Pollock, Dale. "Spielberg Philosophical Over *E.T.* Oscar Defeat," *LAT,* April 13, 1983.

———. "Spielberg Gets Place to Settle Down," *LAT,* May 21, 1984.

Poster, Steve. "The Mind Behind *Close Encounters of the Third Kind,"* American Cinematographer, February 1978.

Rader, Dotson. " 'We Can't Just Sit Back and Hope,' " *Parade,* March 27, 1994.

Rehlin, Gunnar. "Even Steven," *Scanorama,* May 1990.

Reilly, Sue. "By Raiding Hollywood Lore and His Childhood Fantasies, Steven Spielberg Rediscovers an Ark That's Pure Gold," *People,* July 20, 1981.

Richardson, John H. "Steven's Choice, " *Premiere,* January 1994.

Rosenfield, Paul. "The Inside Man," *LAT,* December 3, 1989.

Royal, Susan. "Steven Spielberg in His Adventures on Earth," *American Premiere,* July 1982.

———. *"Always:* An Interview with Steven Spielberg," *American Premiere,* December 1989.

———. "An Interview with Steven Spielberg," *American Premiere,* Winter 1993–94.

Salamon, Julie. "Maker of Hit After Hit, Steven Spielberg Is Also a Conglomerate," *Wall Street Journal,* February 9, 1987.

———. "The Long Voyage Home," *Harper's Bazaar,* February 1994.

Savoy, Maggie. "Pennies for Perry: Young Movie Producer Aids School for Retarded," *The Arizona Republic,* July 19, 1962.

Schiff, Stephen. "Seriously Spielberg," *The New Yorker,* March 21, 1994.

Seligson, Marcia. "Steven Spielberg: The Man Behind Columbia Pictures' $19-Million Gamble," *New West,* November 7, 1977.

Shah, Diane K. "Steven Spielberg, Seriously," *LAT,* December 19, 1993.

Shay, Don. "Steven Spielberg on *Close Encounters,"* *Cinefantastique,* Vol. 7, Nos. 3–4, Fall 1978.

Siskel, Gene. "With *Purple,* Spielberg Finally Grows Up and Gets Serious," *Chicago Tribune,* December 15, 1985.

Spielberg, Steven. "The Unsung Heroes or Credit Where Credit Is Due" (on *Close Encounters of the Third Kind), American Cinematographer,* January 1978.

———. "Dialogue on Film: Steven Spielberg," *American Film,* September 1978.

———. "Directing *1941,"* *American Cinematographer,* December 1979.

———. "Of Narrow Misses and Close Calls" (on *Raiders of the Lost Ark), American Cinematographer,* November 1981.

———. "He Was the Movies" (on François Truffaut), *Film Comment,* February 1985.

———, as told to Denise Worrell, "The Autobiography of Peter Pan," *Time,* July 15, 1985.

———. "Dialogue on Film," *American Film,* June 1988.

———. "Sometimes We Take the Abuse in Silence" (letter), *San Jose Mercury News,* January 11, 1994.

Spillman, Susan. *"Schindler's List* a work for history," *USA Today,* December 10, 1993.

Sragow, Michael. *"Raiders of the Lost Ark:* The Ultimate Saturday Matinee," *Rolling Stone,* June 25, 1981.

———. "A Conversation with Steven Spielberg," *Rolling Stone,* July 22, 1982.

Stettin, Monte. "From Television to Features . . . Steven Spielberg," *Millimeter,* March 1975.

Thronson, Ron. "Student to Direct 12th Film," *The Forty-Niner,* April 12, 1967.

Tuchman, Mitch. "Close Encounter with Steven Spielberg," *Film Comment,* January–February 1978.

Tugend, Tom. "Spielberg's Remembrance of Things Past," *The Jerusalem Post,* December 10–16, 1993.

Turner, George E. "Steven Spielberg and *E.T. The Extra-Terrestrial,"* *American Cinematographer,* January 1983.

———. "Spielberg Makes 'All Too Human' Story," *American Cinematographer,* February 1986.

Ventura, Michael. "Spielberg on Spielberg," *L.A. Weekly,* June 11–17, 1982.

Warga, Wayne. "The Short Subjects—Much in Little," *LAT,* December 22, 1968.

———. "Spielberg Keeps His Touch in Transition," *LAT,* April 3, 1974.

Weinraub, Bernard. "Steven Spielberg Faces the Holocaust," *NYT,* December 12, 1993.

Wuntch, Philip. "Spielberg Frames a New Image," *Dallas Morning News,* December 12, 1993.

Zimmerman, Paul D. "Hard Riders," *Newsweek,* April 8, 1974.

BOOKS ON STEVEN SPIELBERG

Baxter, John. *The Unauthorised Biography: Steven Spielberg.* London: HarperCollins, 1996.

Brode, Douglas. *The Films of Steven Spielberg.* Citadel Press, 1995.

Collins, Tom. *Steven Spielberg, Creator of E.T.* Dillon Press, 1983 (children's biography).

Conklin, Thomas. *Meet Steven Spielberg.* Random House, 1994 (children's biography).

Crawley, Tony. *The Steven Spielberg Story: The Man Behind the Movies*. London: Zomba Books, and New York: Quill Press, 1983.

Ebert, Roger, and Gene Siskel. *The Future of the Movies: Interviews with Martin Scorsese, Steven Spielberg, and George Lucas*. Andrews and McMeel, 1991.

Fernández, Marcial Cantero. *Steven Spielberg*. Madrid: Ediciones Cátedra, 1993.

Godard, Jean-Pierre. *Spielberg*. Paris: 1987.

Goldau, Antje, and Hans Helmut Prizler. *Spielberg: Film als Spielzeug*. Berlin: 1985.

Hargrove, Jim. *Steven Spielberg: Amazing Filmmaker*. Children's Press, 1988 (children's biography).

Johnson, Barbara Pearce, Sam L. Grogg Jr., and Annette Bagley. *Steven Spielberg Study Guide*. American Film Institute, 1979.

Kolker, Robert Philip. *A Cinema of Loneliness: Penn, Kubrick, Scorsese, Spielberg, Altman*. Oxford University Press, 1980 (revised edition, 1988).

Lara, Antonio. *Spielberg: maestro del cine de hoy*. Madrid: Espasa-Calpe, 1990.

Leather, Michael C. *The Picture Life of Steven Spielberg*. Franklin Watts, 1988 (children's biography).

Mabery, D. L. *Steven Spielberg*. Lerner Publications Co., 1986.

McAllister, Marcia L. *Steven Spielberg: He Makes Great Movies*. Rourke Enterprises, 1989 (children's biography).

Mott, Donald R. and Cheryl McAllister Saunders. *Steven Spielberg*. Twayne Publishers, 1986.

Pye, Michael, and Lynda Myles. *The Movie Brats: How the Film Generation Took Over Hollywood*. London: Faber and Faber, and New York: Holt, Rinehart & Winston, 1979.

Sanello, Frank. *Spielberg: The Man, The Movies, The Mythology*. Taylor, 1996.

Schneider, Wolf, ed. *Steven Spielberg* (American Film Institute Life Achievement Award program booklet). AFI, 1995.

Sinyard, Neil. *The Films of Steven Spielberg*. London: Bison Books, 1987.

Somazzi, Claudio. *Steven Spielberg: Dreaming the Movies*. E/K/S Group, 1994.

Taylor, Philip M. *Steven Spielberg: The Man, His Movies, and Their Meaning*. London: Batsford, and New York: Continuum, 1992 (revised Continuum edition, 1994).

Van Gunden, Kenneth. *Postmodern Auteurs: Coppola, Lucas, De Palma, Spielberg and Scorsese*. McFarland, 1991.

Weiss, Ulli. *Das Neue Hollywood: Francis Ford Coppola, Steven Spielberg, Martin Scorsese*. Munich: 1986.

BOOKS AND PAMPHLETS ON SPIELBERG FILMS AND TV SHOWS

Balaban, Bob. *"Close Encounters of the Third Kind" Diary*. Introduction by Steven Spielberg. Paradise Press, 1977.

Blake, Edith. *On Location on Martha's Vineyard (The Making of the Movie "Jaws")*. Ballantine, 1975.

Duncan, Jody. *"The Flintstones": The Official Movie Book*. Modern Publishing, 1994.

Durwood, Thomas, ed. *"Close Encounters of the Third Kind": A Document of the Film*. Introduction by Ray Bradbury. Ariel/Ballantine, 1978.

Erickson, Glenn, and Mary Ellen Trainor. *The Making of "1941."* Ballantine, 1980.

Farber, Stephen, and Marc Green. *Outrageous Conduct: Art, Ego, and the "Twilight Zone" Case*. Arbor House/Morrow, 1988.

Fensch, Thomas, ed. *Oskar Schindler and His List: The Man, the Book, the Film, the Holocaust and Its Survivors*. Introduction by Herbert Steinhouse. Paul S. Eriksson, 1995.

Gottlieb, Carl. *The "Jaws" Log*. Dell, 1975.

Klastorin, Michael, and Sally Hibbin. *"Back to the Future": The Official Book of the Complete Movie Trilogy*. Mallard Press, 1990.

LaBrecque, Ron. *Special Effects: Disaster at "Twilight Zone": The Tragedy and the Trial.* Charles Scribner's Sons, 1988.

Millar, Al. *E.T.—You're More Than a Movie Star.* Privately published, 1982 (pamphlet).

Pourroy, Janine. *Behind the Scenes at "ER."* Ballantine, 1995.

Reed, Rochelle, ed. *"The Sugarland Express"—Spielberg, Barwood and Robbins, Zsigmond.* American Film Institute, 1974.

Shay, Don, and Jody Duncan. *The Making of "Jurassic Park."* Ballantine, 1993.

Spielberg, Steven (introduction). *Letters to E.T.* G. P. Putnam's Sons, 1983.

Taylor, Derek. *The Making of "Raiders of the Lost Ark."* Ballantine, 1981.

Walker, Alice. *The Same River Twice: Honoring the Difficult* (on Spielberg's filming of her novel *The Color Purple*). Charles Scribner's Sons, 1996.

CHAPTER NOTES

EPIGRAPH

Michael Crichton's comment is from his article "Across Time and Culture" in Schneider.

PROLOGUE: "CECIL B. DESPIELBERG" (PP. 11–15)

"Firelights Capture Earthlings in Film Premiering Tuesday" was the headline of a March 1964 article in *The Arizona Republic*. Spielberg's boyhood friend Jim Sollenberger told the author that Steven's mother called him "Cecil B. DeSpielberg"; the "Spielbug" nickname was recalled by Rick Cook, his classmate at Arcadia High School in Phoenix. Spielberg's ambition to be "the Cecil B. DeMille of science fiction" was reported by *Firelight* crew member Jean Weber Brill.

Sources on *Firelight* include the author's interviews with Brill and twelve other people who worked on it: Susan Roper Arndt, Judge Charles G. Case II, Bill Hoffman, Clark (Lucky) Lohr, Warner Marshall, Haven Peters, Chris Pischke, Paul G. Rowe, Carol Stromme Shelton, Arnold Spielberg, Betty Weber, and Beth Weber Zelenski (who also described the filming in a March 4, 1994, letter to the author, and to Bill Jones in "Star of Spielberg's 1st Feature Remembers 'Hands-Off' Director," *Arizona Republic,* May 12, 1996). The author also interviewed Charles A. (Chuck) Silvers, then with the editorial department of Universal Pictures and later executive vice-president of Dunhill Media Services of Valencia, Ca.; Silvers consulted with Spielberg during the making of *Firelight* and saw it after its premiere. The premiere was recalled by various people who worked on *Firelight,* as well as by others in attendance, including George Cowie, Richard Y. Hoffman Jr., Lynn Hoffman, Vance Marshall, and Doug Tice; copies of the premiere program and Spielberg's undated shooting script were supplied by Zelenski. Allen Daviau also described the film to the author.

Brief clips from *Firelight* were included in *Citizen Steve,* a parody biographical film made by Spielberg's Amblin Entertainment as a birthday present for him in 1987; *The Barbara Walters Special* (ABC-TV, March 21, 1994); and *The American Film Institute Salute to Steven Spielberg* (NBC-TV/A&E, 1995). *Firelight* was reviewed by Larry Jarrett in *The Arizona Journal,* "Young Movie Maker Premieres Own Film," March 26, 1964. The making of the film was covered by *The Arizona Republic* in Clark; Paul Dean, "Encounter with Success Began at Arcadia High," March 8, 1978; Michael Clancy and Dolores Tropiano, "Early Spielberg Effects Weren't All That Special," July 14, 1993; and Jones, "Spielberg's Spark," May 12, 1996. Spielberg's denigration of the film (1974) is from Zimmerman. Spielberg's mother, Leah Adler, recalled his filmmaking in Paula Parisi, "Wunderkind in the Making," *HR* Spielberg tribute issue, March 10, 1994. Leah's description of her son as "a terrible student" is from Margy Rochlin, "So Says Leah Adler," *LAT,* December 22, 1985.

Steven's 1963–64 comments on his filmmaking ambitions are from Clark; Jarrett; and "Firelights Capture Earthlings in Film Premiering Tuesday."

1. "HOW WONDROUS ARE THY WORKS" (PP. 16–34)

Leah Posner Spielberg (Mrs. Bernard Adler) recalled her parents and her Uncle Boris in Fred A. Bernstein, *The Jewish Mothers' Hall of Fame,* Doubleday, 1986. Sources on Spielberg and Posner family history also include the author's interviews with Arnold Spielberg, Samuel Guttman, Daniel Guttman, and Deborah Guttman Ridenour, and genealogical material compiled by the late Natalie Spielberg Guttman. Natalie was interviewed by Carol Sanger in "E.T.'s Cincinnati Roots," *The Cincinnati Enquirer,* August 22, 1982. Additional genealogical material was provided by Cincinnati researcher Adele Blanton. Also useful were birth, death, and marriage records of family members in Cincinnati; the Cincinnati city directories, 1905ff; and obituaries and marriage listings from various Cincinnati newspapers. Information about Spielberg's family history also came from the author's interviews with family friends who knew Steven's grandparents, including Millie Tieger and Edith Cummins; and from Barry M. Horstman, "Spielberg's Roots: Avondale Years Shaped *Schindler,*" *Cincinnati Post,* January 13, 1994. Arnold Spielberg talked about his family history and his own moviemaking in Julie Salamon's memoir of her family, *The Net of Dreams: A Family's Search for a Rightful Place,* Random House, 1996.

Documents on Samuel Spielberg's estate are from the Probate Court, Hamilton County, Ohio, including his Last Will and Testament, January 2, 1946; Inventory of Estate, May 7, 1946; and Account of Estate, November 29, 1946. Steven Spielberg's fortune was estimated in "The *Forbes* Four Hundred," *Forbes,* October 14, 1996. The marriage license of Arnold Spielberg and Lea [*sic*] Posner was filed in the Probate Court on February 23, 1945.

Among the books on Jewish, Russian, and Jewish-American history consulted were Mark Zborowski and Elizabeth Herzog, *Life Is with People: The Culture of the Shtetl,* International Universities Press, 1952; Werner Keller, translated by Richard and Clara Winston, *Diaspora: The Post-Biblical History of the Jews,* Harcourt, Brace & World, 1969; Irving Howe, *World of Our Fathers,* Harcourt Brace Jovanovich, 1976; Chaim Potok, *Wanderings: Chaim Potok's History of the Jews,* Knopf, 1978; Neal Gabler, *An Empire of Their Own: How the Jews Invented Hollywood,* Crown, 1988; Benjamin Pinkus, *The Jews of the Soviet Union: The History of a National Minority,* Cambridge University Press, 1988; Ronald Sanders, *Shores of Refuge: A Hundred Years of Jewish Emigration,* Henry Holt, 1988; Jonathan D. Sarna and Nancy H. Klein, *The Jews of Cincinnati,* Hebrew Union College–Jewish Institute of Religion, 1989; Martin Gilbert, *The Atlas of Jewish History,* Morrow, 1992 (revised edition), and *Atlas of Russian History,* Oxford University Press, 1993 (second edition); Howard M. Sachar, *A History of the Jews in America,* Knopf, 1992; and Edward S. Shapiro, *A Time for Healing: American Jewry Since World War II (The Jewish People in America,* Vol. 5), Johns Hopkins University Press, 1992. Abraham Cahan's observation about immigrant Jews' vision of America is quoted in Sachar.

Information about Kamenets-Podolsk is from various histories and reference works on Russia and from a post–World War II Jewish memorial book translated from the Hebrew for the author by Dr. Ida Cohen Selavan: Abraham Rozen, H. Sarig, and Y. Bernshtain, *Kamenets-Podolsk and Environs,* Tel Aviv, 1965. Information about Spielberg relatives killed in the Holocaust is from Arnold Spielberg; Weinraub; and Salamon, "The Long Voyage Home" and *The Net of Dreams.*

Sources on Cincinnati history included the author's interviews with the late Dr. Jacob Rader Marcus and others who lived there at the same time as Spielberg and his parents. Among books of local history consulted were John Clubbe, *Cincinnati Observed: Architecture and History,* Ohio State University Press, 1992; Federal Writers Project, Works Progress Administration, *The WPA Guide to Cincinnati,* 1943, reprinted in 1987 by the Cincinnati Historical Society; B. J. Foreman, *CCM 125: College–Conservatory of Music*

1867–1992, University of Cincinnati, 1992; Reginald C. McGrane, *The University of Cincinnati: A Success Story in Urban Higher Education*, Harper & Row, 1963; Sarna and Klein, *The Jews of Cincinnati;* and Iola Hessler Silberstein, *Cincinnati Then and Now*, League of Women Voters of the Cincinnati Area, 1982. Also helpful were various interviews in the National Council of Jewish Women–American Jewish Archives Oral History Project, 1980–81 (Cincinnati Historical Society).

Additional sources on the Avondale neighborhood included articles in Cincinnati papers: "Avondale: A Suburb That Appreciates Its Natural Endowments," *Commercial Gazette*, May 24, 1892; Robert Heidler, "Avondale . . . One of City's Most Populous Areas," *Times Star*, November 18, 1950; L. Robert Liebert, "Avondale," *Enquirer*, October 28, 1951; George Amick, "A Changing Avondale," *Enquirer* series, February 22–26, 1959; and Steven Rosen, "Avondale's Memories Preserved," *Enquirer*, July 29, 1984.

Spielberg described his earliest memory in Corliss's *Time* cover story " 'I Dream for a Living.' " Cincinnati's Adath Israel Synagogue was described in *The WPA Guide;* Sarna and Klein, *The Jews of Cincinnati;* and "Synagogue Presents Neo-Classic Style; History of Avondale Society Is Recalled," *Cincinnati Enquirer*, August 12, 1929.

David Lyman reported on Spielberg's film project *I'll Be Home* in the *Cincinnati Post:* "Spielberg Planning Movie in Cincinnati," December 11, 1989; "Spielberg Movie in Cincinnati Doubtful This Year," August 13, 1990; and "Spielberg Pledges: He'll Film Here," December 5, 1991. Spielberg commented on the project in Ebert and Siskel, *The Future of the Movies*. See also Mason Wiley's November 1990 *Cosmopolitan* article "The Women Who Write the Scripts," which includes a section on Anne Spielberg.

Pauline Kael's comments on *Close Encounters* and Spielberg's influence on other filmmakers are from her review "The Greening of the Solar System,"*The New Yorker*, November 28, 1977, and from David Blum, "Steven Spielberg and the Dread Hollywood Backlash," *New York*, March 24, 1986. *Schindler's List* was heralded as Spielberg's maturation by Schiff and by Mordecai Newman, "Spielberg's Bar Mitzvah," *Jewish Frontier*, January–February 1994; Spielberg's response was made to Elkin. He discussed his Jewish heritage in various published interviews around the time of *Schindler's List* and in the "Spielberg's Oskar" segment of *Eye to Eye with Connie Chung* (CBS-TV), December 9, 1993. The religious practices of the Spielbergs and the Posners were described to the author by Arnold Spielberg. Vincent Canby's description of Spielberg as "the poet of suburbia" is quoted in Ebert and Siskel.

Steven's mother discussed her music and its influence on her son to Bernstein and Reilly. Steven's comment about "genetic overload" and the story about his father's oscilloscope are from Horstman. John Williams remarked on Spielberg's musical instincts in Shay and Duncan, *The Making of "Jurassic Park."*

2. *"MAZIK"* (PP. 35–49)

Natalie Guttman's description of her nephew as a *"mazik"* and her other comments on his childhood are from Sanger.

Spielberg's correct birthdate, December 18, 1946, is established by his Certificate of Live Birth, Ohio Department of Health, No. 15473: Steven Allan Spielberg (Cincinnati Board of Health). His birth was reported in *The American Israelite*, December 26, 1946, and his bar mitzvah was announced in *The Phoenix Jewish News*, December 25, 1959. His age also was reported correctly in such early articles as Clark; Jarrett; "Universal Pacts Pamela McMyler, Steve Spielberg," *HR*, and "Univ. Pacts Pair," *DV*, December 12, 1968; Ray Loynd, "Shorts Makers Get Short Cut to Success Via Short," *HR*, December 13, 1968; Hull; and Kramer. Incorrect ages were given in such articles as "Spielberg Pacted to Produce for U," *DV*, December 28, 1970; Cameron; Adler; and Fred Schruers, "Peter Pandemonium," *Premiere*, December 1991.

Incorrect dates for Spielberg's arrival at Universal were reported in the Adler article and in Tuchman; Hirschberg; Corliss, " 'I Dream for a Living' "; and Gross. Spielberg's actual arrival at Universal in late 1963 or early 1964 was established by the author's interview with Charles A. Silvers and by Jarrett's 1964 article. Spielberg's 1968 comment to Sid Sheinberg was reported in Shah.

Patricia Goldstone uncovered Spielberg's deception about his birthdate in "Movie Directors Can Stay Forever Young," *LAT,* March 8, 1981. Spielberg's representatives confirmed his correct age in James Bates, "Spielberg's Legal Dispute Adds a Year to His Life," *LAT,* October 27, 1995.

The author of this book first interviewed Denis C. Hoffman about Spielberg on September 12, 1994. *Denis C. Hoffman vs. Steven Spielberg* was filed October 25, 1995, in Los Angeles County Superior Court; *Heights Investment Co. Inc. and Steven Spielberg vs. Denis Hoffman* was filed in the same court on October 24, 1995. A copy of Spielberg's September 28, 1968, agreement with Hoffman is contained in Hoffman's suit, as are copies of Hoffman's Short Form Assignment of *Amblin'* rights to Spielberg, December 30, 1976, and Assignment of Rights, January 3, 1977; Hoffman's March 16, 1970, distribution agreement with United Productions of America; his June 15, 1970, distribution agreement with Excelsior Distributing Co.; and his U.K. distribution agreement with Four Star, November 14, 1972. Other articles on Hoffman's claim against Spielberg include (1995): Ted Johnson, "Spielberg Sues *Amblin* [sic] Investor," *DV,* and Donna Parker, "Spielberg Sues Donut Guy over *Amblin* [sic] Dough," *HR,* October 25; "Spielberg Charges Aired," *DV,* October 27; Jonathan Davies, "Doughnut Guy Returns Fire," *HR,* October 27–29; "Director vs. Donut Man," *Time,* November 6; and (1996): *"1941* Will Now Be Known as *1942,"* *Premiere,* February. Hoffman's attorneys Robert C. Rosen and Pierce O'Donnell issued an October 26, 1995, press release, "Steven Spielberg Sued for Fraud by Producer Who Launched His Career."

Leah Adler's quip about having "my uterus bronzed" is from David Ferrell, "Mother's Day," *LAT,* March 23, 1994. She also discussed Steven's childhood in Bernstein; John Skow, "Staying Five Moves Ahead," *Time,* May 31, 1982; Jeff Silverman, "They Are What They E.T.—Or, a Close Encounter of the Spielberg Kind," *LAHE,* June 24, 1982; Corliss, " 'I Dream for a Living' "; and Rochlin. She jokingly described herself as "certifiable" in Karen S. Schneider and Kristina Johnson, "That's My Boy," *People,* April 25, 1994. Steven's description of himself as "a victim of the Peter Pan Syndrome" is from Jerry Buck, "Spielberg: Raider of the Lost Art of Anthologies," *LADN,* June 28, 1995. Dr. Dan Kiley's 1983 book *The Peter Pan Syndrome: Men Who Have Never Grown Up* was published by Dodd, Mead, 1983. Dustin Hoffman's remark about Spielberg's insecurity is from Schruers. Henry Sheehan analyzed Spielberg's films in his two-part *Film Comment* essay "The Panning of Steven Spielberg," May–June 1992, and "Spielberg II," July–August 1992.

Spielberg recalled hearing about Nazis and the Holocaust as a child in various interviews around the time of *Schindler's List* and in "Production Information," *Schindler's List* press kit, Universal Pictures, 1993. Steven's mother told Weinraub and Horstman about hearing stories from Holocaust survivors. Her comments about raising her children largely among gentiles are from Bernstein and Horstman. She described Judaism as having been "a very nothing part of our lives" in Schneider and Johnson. David Halberstam's comments on postwar America are from *The Fifties,* Villard Books, 1993.

Information on the Spielbergs' move from Cincinnati to Camden and Haddon Township, New Jersey, is from the author's interviews with Arnold Spielberg; their New Jersey neighbors Miriam Fuhrman, Jane Fuhrman Satanoff, and Glenn Fuhrman; and Helen and Peter Rutan, who sold the Spielbergs their home in Haddon Township in August 1952. Information on the births of Spielberg's sisters is from Arnold Spielberg. Sources on Haddonfield and Haddon Township include the author's interviews with other Spielberg neighbors; Haddonfield City Directories, 1952, 1954–55, and 1956; and Robert

Strauss, "Take a Walk on the Mild Side by Hoofing It in Haddonfield," *The Philadelphia Inquirer,* July 15, 1994. Spielberg's time in Haddon Township was discussed in Strauss and in Tillie Clement, "Master of Big-Screen Fantasy Adventures Has a Local Link," *The Haddon Gazette,* August 8, 1985.

3. *"MESHUGGENEH"* (PP. 50-65)

The late Arnold Fuhrman's description of the young Steven Spielberg as *"meshug-geneh"* and his other comments about Steven were reported by Fuhrman's sister Miriam, his daughter Jane Satanoff, and his son Glenn. Anne Spielberg's observation about *Jaws* is from Reilly.

Information on the Spielbergs' home on Crystal Terrace in Haddon Township is from the author's interviews with Helen and Peter Rutan, and with August and Loretta Knoblach, who bought the house from the Spielbergs in February 1957. Information on Temple Beth Shalom was provided by Rabbi Albert Lewis, who researched the temple's history in its bulletins, *Temple Talk,* 1953–57. Steven's memory of Hebrew school and his other comments on Jewish education are from Guthmann and from Karen W. Arenson, "From *Schindler's List,* a Jewish Mission," *NYT,* September 24, 1995.

Steven's recollections of Christmastime on Crystal Terrace to Salamon in "The Long Voyage Home" are similar to stories he told his California high school classmate Gene Ward Smith, who recalled them in interviews with the author and in February 25 and March 28, 1994, letters to the author.

Arnold Spielberg told the author about his work for RCA, as did Rabbi Lewis and Arnold's RCA colleagues J. Wesley Leas, Bill Davison, and Miriam Fuhrman. Although in "The Autobiography of Peter Pan," Steven says he was around eleven years old when he swallowed his father's transistor, which would place the incident in Arizona, Leas says that Arnold received his first transistor while working at RCA in about 1955, which would indicate that Steven was eight or nine when the incident supposedly occurred. Arnold described his influence on Steven's storytelling abilities to the author and in Corliss, " 'I Dream for a Living.' "

Information on the *Hadrosaurus foulkii* is from John R. Horner and James Gorman, *Digging Dinosaurs,* Workman, 1988; "Fossil Site Designated Landmark," *NYT,* November 27, 1994; and the author's interview with Jon Davison. Sources on Spielberg's early interest in dinosaurs include the author's interview with Scott MacDonald and Spielberg's comments on the 1993 Bravo cable-TV program *Opening Shot:* "Dinosaurs." Spielberg remembered his first visit to Disneyland in "60 Candles," *People,* November 7, 1988.

4. *"A WIMP IN A WORLD OF JOCKS"* (PP. 66-93)

The chapter title is Spielberg's self-description in Sragow, "A Conversation with Steven Spielberg." The Spielbergs' North Forty-ninth street address in Phoenix is listed in the Phoenix and Scottsdale city directories, 1958–63.

Leah Adler recalled moving to Arizona in Baxter; she talked about Steven's room, neighborhood children's anti-Semitism, and her marriage to Bernard Adler in Bernstein, *The Jewish Mothers' Hall of Fame.* She also spoke of her second husband in Schneider and Johnson, "That's My Boy"; his obituaries appeared in *LAT,* October 3, 1995, and *NYT,* October 8 and 15, 1995. Leah discussed Steven's relationship with his sisters (Anne, Sue, and Nancy) in Reilly and in Rochlin. Sue and Nancy talked about their family in Corliss, " 'I Dream for a Living' "; Anne talked about Steven to Schiff and to Reilly. Steven confessed his *Lost World* prank and his "six-month fling as a juvenile delinquent" to Margolis and Modderno.

Sources on Spielberg's Boy Scouting include the author's interviews with Arnold Spielberg, Scout leader Richard Y. Hoffman Jr., and various members of Ingleside's

Troop 294. Hoffman also was interviewed in Bill Jones, " 'Mr. Wizard' Inspired Filmmaker's Creative Fire," *The Arizona Republic,* May 12, 1996, which includes Steven's 1985 description of him as "Mr. Wizard." Spielberg's most detailed comments about his Scouting experiences are in Olmsted's article " 'Ex–Boy Scout Makes Movies.' "

Spielberg's most extensive interview about his early filmmaking is Poster, "The Mind Behind *Close Encounters of the Third Kind"*; contemporaneous printed sources include Savoy's 1962 article "Pennies for Perry" and Clark's 1963 profile "Teenage Cecil B." Arnold Spielberg's memories of Steven's filmmaking are from an interview with the author. Leah Adler talked about her son's filmmaking in "Leah Adler," Steven Spielberg tribute issue, *HR,* March 10, 1994. Barry Sollenberger reminisced about their filmmaking activities to the author and in *Citizen Steve.*

A Day in the Life of Thunder was described to the author by Doug Tice and his mother, Marie Tice; former Ingleside Elementary School principal Richard T. Ford was among those who remembered *Steve Spielberg's Home Movies;* the filming of *Scary Hollow* was reported to the author by Betty Castleberry Edwards (Roger Sheer's widow). The making of *Fighter Squad* was recalled by Edwards (who preserved the single surviving print), Arnold Spielberg, and cast members Jim Sollenberger, Barry Sollenberger, Steve Suggs, Doug Tice, and Mike McNamara. Clips from *Fighter Squad* were shown in *The Barbara Walters Special* (1994) and *The American Film Institute Salute to Steven Spielberg* (A&E expanded version, 1995).

Sources on Steven's early film screenings include the Savoy and Clark articles and the author's interviews with Arnold Spielberg and neighborhood children who attended the screenings. Paul Campanella's story about Steven painting his ladies' room is from *Citizen Steve.*

Spielberg's comments on David Lean's influence are quoted in Taylor and in L. Robert Morris and Lawrence Raskin, *"Lawrence of Arabia": The 30th Anniversary Pictorial History,* Anchor Books, 1992; Haven Peters recalled Spielberg's classroom discussion of *The Bridge on the River Kwai* in a letter to the author on February 12, 1994. Spielberg reminisced about the *Wallace & Ladmo* show in *Ladmo Remembered: A Wallace & Ladmo Special* (KPHO, Phoenix, 1994); other sources include the author's interview with Bill Thompson ("Wallace"); Mark J. Scarp, "Spielberg Remains True to Local Roots," and Jeffrey Crane, "Ladmo Memorials Still Coming into Club," *Scottsdale Progress Tribune,* March 19, 1994. Ray Bradbury's comments on Spielberg are from his introduction to Durwood, ed., *"Close Encounters of the Third Kind": A Document of the Film.*

Ingleside's 1961 eighth-grade graduation ceremonies are documented in the program for that event and in teacher Patricia Scott Rodney's "Class Prophesy [*sic*] 1961."

5. "BIG SPIEL" (PP. 94–111)

Sources on Phoenix's Arcadia High School, which Spielberg attended from September 1961 through March 1964, include the author's interviews with the current Arcadia principal, Dr. J. Calvin Bruins; former principal Jackson Drake; and other past and present staff, faculty members, and students. Also helpful were the school newspaper, *The Arcadian,* 1961–64, and yearbook, *The Olympian,* 1962–64; and booklets commemorating the twentieth and thirtieth reunions of the Class of 1965. Arcadia was profiled by Mary Jo Clements in "School's a Blast in Arizona!" *'Teen,* April 1962.

Spielberg reminisced about the incident with the frogs in Corliss, "Steve's Summer Magic," and in the 1996 MCA Home Video laserdisc documentary *The Making of "E.T. The Extra-Terrestrial,"* directed by Laurent Bouzereau. Spielberg's theatrical activities at Arcadia were recalled by faculty members including Drama Club adviser Phil Deppe, vocal director Harold Millsop, and art teacher Margaret Burrell; and by Phyllis Brooks, who worked on costumes for the school plays and is the wife of former school band director Reginald Brooks. The author also interviewed the following students who were involved with Spielberg in school plays and/or in the Drama Club and theater-arts class: Jean Weber Brill, Karen Hayden, Bill Hoffman, Clifford Lindblom, Clark (Lucky) Lohr, Peggy McMullin Loper, Haven Peters, Paul G. Rowe, Carol Stromme Shelton, Sherry Missner Williams, and Beth Weber Zelenski. Peters also recalled Spielberg's work with stage director Dana Lynch in his 1994 letter to the author. Other sources on Spielberg's theatrical activities include *The Olympian,* 1963, 1964; Jarrett; Spielberg, "Dialogue on Film: Steven Spielberg"; and articles in *The Arcadian,* including Melinda Milar, "Crews Arrange Sets for Play" *(Guys and Dolls),* February 15, 1963; "Crews Named for First Play" *(See How They Run),* September 27, 1963; "*I Remember Mama* Tryouts Completed," November 8, 1963; Lynn Davis, "*I Remember Mama* Opens Next Week," December 6, 1963; and "Drama Students Become Arcadia's Thespians," March 6, 1964. *The Olympian* also lists Spielberg's membership in the Junior Varsity Band (1963) and the Titan Marching Band (1964).

Sources on the filming of *Escape to Nowhere* include the author's interviews with Arnold Spielberg, Jim Sollenberger, Barry Sollenberger, and Chris Pischke; and also Crawley; Taylor; the Clark, Jarrett, Janos, and Rader articles; and Poster's interview with Spielberg. Barry Sollenberger also recalled the filming in *Citizen Steve.* Clips from *Escape to Nowhere* were shown in *The Barbara Walters Special* (1994) and *The American Film Institute Salute to Steven Spielberg* (A&E version). For sources on *Firelight,* see notes for the Prologue.

Spielberg's involvement with Ernest G. Sauer's film *Journey to the Unknown* was recalled by its lead actor, Haven Peters, who also provided a copy of the premiere program. Spielberg recalled his visit to the set of *PT 109* in Army Archerd's column, *DV,* December 1, 1992.

The principal sources on Spielberg's first visit to Universal Studios are the author's interviews with Charles A. (Chuck) Silvers and Arnold Spielberg. Steven's various accounts of his first visit are from the articles by Hull (1969), Kramer (1970), Cameron (1971), Adler (1972), Corliss (1985), and Gross (1996). He recalled obtaining a gate pass in Loynd, "Shorts Makers Get Short Cut to Success Via Short." *HR.*

6. "HELL ON EARTH" (PP. 112–34)

The chapter title and some of Spielberg's other comments about his senior year at Saratoga (Ca.) High School are from his January 11, 1994, letter to the *San Jose Mercury News,* "Sometimes We Take the Abuse in Silence."

Spielberg's attendance dates, September 1964–June 1965, were provided by the school's current principal, Dr. Kevin Skelly. Other information on the school came from the author's interviews with Spielberg's fellow students and Saratoga faculty members, and from *The Falcon* (school newspaper), 1964–65; *The Talisman* (yearbook), 1965; and the *Saratoga News,* 1964–65. Information about Spielberg's academic record is from faculty members and from Don Shull. The dates of Spielberg's prior attendance at Los Gatos High School, March–June 1964, were provided by that school's registrar, Jan Helzer. The Spielbergs' Sarahills Drive address in Saratoga was documented in a December 16, 1964, *Saratoga News* column on newly arrived residents.

Background on Saratoga is drawn largely from the author's interviews with Spielberg's friends, neighbors, classmates, and Saratoga High faculty members, especially former social studies teacher Hubert E. (Hugh) Roberts. Other sources on Saratoga include Florence R. Cunningham, *Saratoga's First Hundred Years,* Panorama West Books, 1967; League of Women Voters of Los Gatos–Saratoga–Monte Sereno, *Saratoga,*

1991; Elizabeth Ansnes, *Saratoga's Heritage: A Survey of Historic Resources,* City of Saratoga Heritage Preservation Commission, 1993; and Leigh Weimers, *Guide to Silicon Valley: An Insider's Tip for Techies and Tourists,* Western Tanager Press, 1993.

Spielberg's memories of Saratoga are from his letter to the *Mercury News; The Barbara Walters Special* (1994); and the articles by Ansen, "Spielberg's Obsession"; Spillman; Weinraub; and Wuntch. The reactions of some of his former classmates were reported by Connie Skipitares in "Spielberg Anti-Semitism Charges Disturb Saratogans," *Mercury News,* December 18, 1993, which also quoted Spielberg spokesman Marvin Levy. *Falcon* writer Austiaj Parineh commented on the controversy in "Spielberg's Claims Illogically Rattle Saratogans," January 21, 1994. Don Shull's letter to the *Mercury News,* "If Spielberg Had Been Hurt, I Would Have Known," was printed on January 1, 1994; Gene Ward Smith's letter to the paper, "Teen-age Spielberg Aspired to Reach a Mass Audience," appeared on January 15, 1994. Smith's other comments on Spielberg and Saratoga are from his interviews with the author and from his February 25 and March 28, 1994, letters to the author; Spielberg also recalled his senior year in a January 14, 1994, letter to Smith.

Spielberg's revelation about his sexual initiation was reported in "Spielberg Defers to Prophet Lucas," *Variety,* June 2, 1982. His work on *The Falcon* in 1964–65 was remembered by his journalism teacher, Bert Pfister; the paper's editor, Bonnie Parker Bartman; and by other fellow staff members: Mike Augustine, Diana Hart Deem, James Fletcher, Nancy Frishberg, and Philip H. Pennypacker. Spielberg's *Falcon* articles include "Shull Travels" (on Don Shull and his family), October 2, 1964; "Athlete's Feat," October 23, 1964; and "Fluke Plagues Varsity," March 12, 1965. His journalistic bent was mentioned in the class prophecy, "Twenty Years Hence," *The Falcon,* June 16, 1965.

Information on the school play *Twelve Angry Jurors* (1965) is from the author's interview with Mike Augustine; *The Talisman;* "Senior Play," *The Falcon,* February 5; and Karen Mitchell's column, *Saratoga News,* February 17. Information on Spielberg's *Senior Sneak Day* film is from interviews with various classmates and the Skipitares article; the dates and place of the senior party are from Mitchell's column of June 23, 1965.

Sources on Universal Studios include *DV*'s Universal Pictures 75th anniversary issue, February 6, 1990, which includes Joseph McBride, "Business 101" (on the studio's theatrical films from 1970 through 1990). Other background on Universal includes Clive Hirschhorn, *The Universal Story,* Crown, 1983; and Dan E. Moldea, *Dark Victory: Ronald Reagan, MCA, and the Mob,* Viking, 1986.

Spielberg's 1977 comment to Ray Bradbury was reported by Bradbury in "The Turkey That Attacked New York," his introduction to Jim Wynorski, ed., *They Came from Outer Space,* Doubleday, 1980. Quotes on Jewish humor are from Albert Memmi, *The Liberation of the Jew,* Orion Press, 1966; and Leo Rosten, *The Joys of Yiddish,* McGraw-Hill, 1968. Friedrich Nietzsche's observation on a joke being "an epitaph on an emotion" is from his *Miscellaneous Maxims and Opinions* (1879). Lenny Bruce's remark "Negroes are all Jews" is quoted in Alan M. Dershowitz, *Chutzpah,* Little, Brown, 1991. Spielberg recalled his first viewing of *Dr. Strangelove* in Eric Lefcowitz, *"Dr. Strangelove* Turns 30. Can It Still Be Trusted?" *NYT,* January 30, 1994; the film's first showings in San Jose were listed in the *Mercury News* for the weekend of March 20–22, 1964. Spielberg's comment on growing up in the 1960s is quoted in Taylor. He told Hodenfield about seeing a psychiatrist and not being part of the drug culture in "The Sky Is Full of Questions!!" His comment about staying in college to avoid the draft is quoted in Crawley. Saratoga classmate Douglas H. Stuart recalled Spielberg's failure to take the ACT exam.

Information on the divorce of Spielberg's parents is from documents in the Santa Clara County (Ca.) Superior Court: *Leah Spielberg vs. Arnold Spielberg* Complaint for Divorce, No. 178192, April 11, 1966, including a Property Settlement Agreement, April

1, 1966; Interlocutory Judgment of Divorce, April 20, 1966; and Final Judgment of Divorce, April 17, 1967. Other sources include the author's interviews with Arnold Spielberg and Don Shull; and Steven's comment in Margolis and Modderno.

7. "A HELL OF A BIG BREAK" (PP. 135-66)

"The Film School Generation" has been covered in the segment of that title in the 1995 TV series *American Cinema* (PBS) and in such books as Michael Pye and Lynda Myles, *The Movie Brats: How the Film Generation Took Over Hollywood;* Dale Pollock, *Skywalking: The Life and Films of George Lucas,* Harmony Books, 1983; David Thompson and Ian Christie, eds., *Scorsese on Scorsese,* Faber and Faber (London), 1989; Peter Cowie, *Coppola,* Scribner's, 1990; Kevin Jackson, ed., *Schrader on Schrader,* Faber and Faber, 1990; Mary Pat Kelly, with forewords by Spielberg and Michael Powell, *Martin Scorsese: A Journey,* Thunder's Mouth Press, 1991; Van Gunden, *Postmodern Auteurs: Coppola, Lucas, De Palma, Spielberg and Scorsese;* and Charles Champlin, with forewords by Spielberg and Francis Coppola, *George Lucas: The Creative Impulse: Lucasfilm's First Twenty Years,* Harry N. Abrams, 1992. *Time* spotted the trend in "The Student Movie Makers," February 2, 1968.

Spielberg recalled his first encounter with Lucas in his foreword to Champlin's book and in "The Film School Generation"; their donations to USC were reported in Dale Pollock, "Lucas & Spielberg—Investing in Film-School Futures," *LAT,* September 6, 1981. Information on Spielberg's honorary doctorate from USC and his election to the school's board of trustees is from "Spielberg New USC Trustee," *DV,* September 17, 1996. Lucas recalled the "credo of film school" to Audie Bock, "George Lucas: An Interview," *Take One,* May 1979. The author interviewed such 1960s USC film school graduates as Gloria Katz, Willard Huyck, and Howard Kazanjian, and also Mike Medavoy, who became the agent for Spielberg and other prominent filmmakers of that generation.

Spielberg's attendance dates at California State College (now California State University) at Long Beach, September 1965–January 1969, were provided by the school's records office. Other information about Spielberg's college years came from the school paper, *The Forty-Niner,* 1965–69, and yearbook, *The Prospector,* 1966–69 (his picture appears among the members of Theta Chi in the 1966 yearbook). Articles about Spielberg in *The Forty-Niner* include Bruce Fortune, *"Great Race* to Be Filmed by Students," February 18, 1966; Thronson; and Bagala. Spielberg's boast that he "didn't learn a bloody thing" at the school was made to Howard Priest in *"Jaws, Duel* Directing Product of Former LB Student," *The Forty-Niner,* November 13, 1974.

Sources on Spielberg's 1965–67 filmmaking and his visits to Universal during his college years include the author's interviews with Chuck Silvers, Arnold Spielberg, Tony Martinelli, Carl Pingitore, Richard Belding, Ralph Burris, Don Shull, Jeff Corey, Allen Daviau (also quoted from Crawley and from David Chell, *Moviemakers at Work,* Microsoft Press, 1987), and Tony Bill (who also spoke about Spielberg in 1967 to Bagala). Spielberg reported on his experiences at Universal in an undated letter to Shull; internal evidence, including references to the shooting of *The Chase* and construction work at Universal, establishes that Spielberg wrote the letter in June 1965. Charlton Heston's recollection of Spielberg's visit to the set of *The War Lord* is from *In the Arena: An Autobiography,* Simon & Schuster, 1995. Sources on Spielberg's attendance at Jeff Corey's acting studio include the author's interviews with Corey and Bill, as well as Patrick McGilligan, *Jack's Life: A Biography of Jack Nicholson,* Norton, 1994.

Information on Universal TV programs of that period is from Larry James Gianakos, *Television Drama Series Programming: A Comprehensive Chronicle 1959–1975,* Scarecrow Press, 1978; James Robert Parish and Vincent Terrace, *The Complete Actors' Television Credits 1948–1988* (second edition), Scarecrow Press, 1989; and Christopher

Wicking and Tise Vahimagi, *The American Vein: Directors and Directions in Television,* Dutton, 1979. Shooting dates on *Torn Curtain* are from Donald Spoto, *The Dark Side of Genius: The Life of Alfred Hitchcock,* Little, Brown, 1983. Spielberg reminisced to Ventura about his experiences with John Cassavetes; other information on *Faces* is from C. Robert Jennings, "Hollywood's Accidental Artist of *Faces,*" *LAT,* February 16, 1969, and Ray Carney, *The Films of John Cassavetes: Pragmatism, Modernism and the Movies,* Cambridge University Press, 1994. American Cinema Editors president George Grenville's comment about Spielberg's respect for editors is from Paula Parisi, "Spielberg ACE's Filmmaker of '80s," *HR,* February 2, 1990.

Sources on *Amblin'* include the author's interviews with Silvers, Denis C. Hoffman, Julie Raymond, Burris, Daviau, Donald E. Heitzer, Hal Mann, James Mann, Devorah Mann Hardberger, Belding, Pingitore, Martinelli, and Jerry Pam. Other sources include (1968): "Universal Pacts Pamela McMyler, Steve Spielberg"; "Univ. Pacts Pair"; Loynd, "Shorts Makers Get Short Cut to Success Via Short"; "Pact-Winning Short Will Open Next Week," *DV,* December 17; advertisement for opening engagement at Crest Theater in Westwood, *LAT,* December 18; "Short Subject *Amblin'* on Crest Screen," *LAT,* December 19; and Warga, "The Short Subjects—Much in Little"; also, Atlanta International Film Festival program book, 1969; Morton Moss, "She's a Sad, Glad Girl" (on McMyler), *LAHE,* December 28, 1971; and Peter Rainer, "Student Films of Welles, Scorsese and Spielberg Offer Lessons in Ambition," *LAHE,* February 24, 1984. Business documents on *Amblin'* are contained in Hoffman's 1995 lawsuit against Spielberg (see notes for chapter 2). Spielberg's claim about Hoffman wanting the possessory credit is from Crawley.

Sources on Sidney J. Sheinberg as a TV executive include Cecil Smith, "There's No Biz Like TV Film Biz," *LAT,* January 9, 1969, and "He Makes Universal's TV Moves," *LAT,* April 1, 1971; and "Sidney J. Sheinberg," *DV* Universal issue, February 6, 1990. Sheinberg's initial meeting with Spielberg was recalled by Silvers and Medavoy in their interviews with the author and by Sheinberg to Hirschberg and Shah; Spielberg's recollection is quoted in Crawley. Spielberg's gift to the Cedars–Sinai Medical Center was reported in "Cedars–Sinai Gets Spielberg Donation," *DV,* March 29, 1989.

8. "THIS TREMENDOUS MEATGRINDER" (PP. 167–98)

See notes for previous chapter on the release of *Amblin'* and Spielberg's signing by Universal. Information on film festival screenings of *Amblin'* (1969) is from the author's interview with Denis C. Hoffman; the Atlanta Film Festival program book; "Universal Enters Short, *Amblin',* Atlanta Fest," *HR,* June 2; "*Amblin* [sic] to Venice," *DV,* June 17; "Hoffman's *Amblin* [sic] Wins," *HR,* June 30; and Hoffman, letter to the editor, *HR,* July 24, 1969. Information on the Oscar campaign is from the author's interviews with Hoffman and the film's publicist, Jerry Pam; the trade advertisement featuring marijuana ran in *DV,* December 23, 1968. The terms of Spielberg's initial contract with Universal are from the author's interview with his agent, Mike Medavoy, and from Cameron. Spielberg's description of that contract as "the biggest mistake of my life" and information on his amended 1970 agreement with Universal are from Reed; the new contract was reported in "Spielberg Pacted to Produce for U," *DV,* December 28, 1970.

Information about Spielberg's departure from Long Beach State is from the CSULB records office. The date he began rehearsing his *Night Gallery* segment "Eyes" is from the author's interview with Barry Sullivan and from Army Archerd's column, *DV,* February 6, 1969, which also includes Crawford's comment about Spielberg's age and information about her illness. Universal's firing of Bette Davis was reported by Julie Raymond. The story of Spielberg's first meeting with Crawford is from the author's interview with Chuck Silvers and from Bob Thomas, *Joan Crawford: A Biography,* Simon & Schuster, 1978 (which also contains an account of the filming, based on Thomas's interview with Spielberg). Other sources on *Night Gallery* include the author's interviews with William

Sackheim and Edward M. Abroms; Joel Engel, *Rod Serling: The Dreams and Nightmares of Life in the Twilight Zone*, Contemporary Books, 1989; Gordon F. Sander, *Serling: The Rise and Twilight of Television's Last Angry Man*, Dutton, 1992; Marc Scott Zicree, *The Twilight Zone Companion* (second edition), Silman-James Press, 1992; "U's *Night Gallery* First Joan Crawford 2-Hr Vidpic," *DV,* January 23, 1969; Hull's *HR* interview with Spielberg on the final day of shooting; and "Lady in the Dark," *TV Guide,* August 16, 1969.

Spielberg's tour of Universal for Michael Crichton was reported by Rick Du Brow, "Beyond Blood and Yucks," *LAT,* November 6, 1994. The director's comment on Serling was quoted by Marc Wielage in "Spielberg's Unknown Video Movies," *Video Review,* December 1982. Spielberg's memorial tribute to Crawford is from Kevin Thomas, "Academy Pays Radiant Tribute to Joan Crawford," *LAT,* June 27, 1977. He commented on the editing of "Eyes" in Tay Garnett, ed. by Anthony Slide, *Directing: Learn from the Masters,* Scarecrow Press, 1996. Sources on the *Snow White* project (based on the Donald Barthelme novella published in *The New Yorker,* February 18, 1967) include the author's interviews with Medavoy and David Giler; Hull; and A. H. Weiler, *"Snow White* Swings," *NYT,* February 23, 1969.

The genesis of *The Sugarland Express* was related by co-screenwriter Hal Barwood in Reed's booklet on the film. The article that first attracted Spielberg's attention, "New Bonnie 'n [*sic*] Clyde," *Hollywood Citizen-News,* May 2, 1969, was identified by Spielberg in his interview with Helpern. Other articles on the actual Texas incident include: "Hostage Patrolman Rescued," *San Antonio Evening News,* May 2, 1969; "Policeman's Captor Slain by Officers," *San Antonio Express and News,* May 3, 1969; "Policeman Abductor Dies of Gun Wounds," *LAT,* May 3, 1969; "Dent First Shot by Sheriff," *San Antonio Express and News,* May 4, 1969; and "Texas Lawmen Dispute *Sugarland,"* *LAT,* November 14, 1975.

Spielberg's comment about being in a "despondent" state at Universal in 1969 and his subsequent praise of Sid Sheinberg and other executives are from Cameron. Sheinberg recalled Spielberg's "avant-garde" reputation to Hirschberg. The executive commented on his role in Spielberg's TV career in Aaron Latham, "MCA's Bad Cop Shoots from the Hip," *Manhattan, Inc.,* July 1988, and praised "Par for the Course" to Kramer.

Spielberg's representation by Mike Medavoy and Creative Management Associates was discussed with the author by Medavoy; other sources include Spielberg's comments in Reed, and Claudia Eller, "A Former Agent's Field(s) of Dreams" (on CMA partner Freddie Fields), *LAT,* June 16, 1995. Carl Gottlieb recalled his and Spielberg's film projects in an interview with the author and in his book *The "Jaws" Log;* Spielberg's interest in directing *The Christian Licorice Store* was reported by Allen Daviau. Sources on *Ace Eli and Rodger of the Skies* include the author's interviews with Medavoy, Richard D. Zanuck, and Daviau; "Trio Form Co. for Filming of *Ace Eli* Pic," *HR,* and *"Ace* Filming Planned," *DV,* January 6, 1970; "Pseudonyms Take Credit (or Blame) for *Ace Eli & Rodger of the Skies?" DV,* February 26, 1973; and reviews by *Murf.* (A. D. Murphy), *Variety,* May 2, 1973, and Vincent Canby, *NYT,* March 2, 1974. Spielberg's opinion of *Ace Eli* is from Reed.

The order in which Spielberg directed his episodic TV shows is from Tuchman, in which Spielberg identifies "Par for the Course" and "Murder by the Book" as his two best TV episodes. The airdates are from sources including Gianakos, *Television Drama Series Programming,* and reviews in *DV* and *HR.* Wielage reported the partial reshooting of "Make Me Laugh" by Jeannot Szwarc. Information on *Whispering Death* is from the author's interview with Jeff Corey and from Donna Witzleben, ed., *Television Programming Source Books, Vol. 2: Films M–Z, 1994–95,* North American Publishing Co., 1994. *DV* reviews of Spielberg's TV shows include: *Daku.* (Dave Kaufman), *Night Gallery* ("Eyes"), November 10, 1969; *Helm.* (Jack Hellman), *The Name of the Game* ("LA 2017"),

January 18, 1971; and *Tone.* (Tony Scott), *Columbo* ("Murder by the Book") and *The Psychiatrist* ("Par for the Course"), September 16, 1971. John Mahoney reviewed *Night Gallery* in *HR* on November 11, 1969. NBC promoted "LA 2017" with a full-page advertisement in *DV,* January 15, 1971. The trade ad for "Par for the Course" was printed in *DV* and *HR* on March 10, 1971; Cecil Smith wrote about that program in "A Career Switch for Joan Darling," *LAT,* January 3, 1973. Joseph E. Boston recalled working with Spielberg on *Marcus Welby* in an interview with the author and in a September 15, 1994, letter to the author.

Sources on Richard Levinson, William Link, and *Columbo* include the author's interview with Link; Levinson and Link, *Stay Tuned: An Inside Look at the Making of Prime-Time Television,* St. Martin's Press, 1981; Levinson and Link, *Off Camera: Conversations with the Makers of Prime-Time Television,* New American Library, 1986; Mark Dawidziak, *The Columbo Phile: A Casebook,* The Mysterious Press, 1989; and David Marc and Robert J. Thompson, *Prime Time, Prime Movers,* Little, Brown, 1992. Peter Falk's comment on Spielberg is from Michael Leahy, "Raincoat Man," *TV Guide,* December 14, 1991.

Spielberg recalled "some bad experiences with TV stars" in Paul Rosenfield, *The Club Rules,* Warner Books, 1992. His 1995 summation of his period as a TV contract director is from "The Film School Generation" segment of *American Cinema* (PBS). The February 9, 1971, southern California earthquake was reported in various *LAT* articles, February 10–11. Information on Spielberg's house in Laurel Canyon is from Klemesrud and the author's interviews with Ralph Burris and Joan Darling.

9. "THE STEVEN SPIELBERG BUSINESS" (PP. 199–225)

The comments on Spielberg by Billy Wilder and Barry Diller are from Haber.

Sources on *Duel* include the author's interviews with Richard Matheson, George Eckstein, Frank Morriss, Carey Loftin, and Joan Darling; "Richard Burton Matheson," *Contemporary Authors,* Gale Research Co., 1981; Cecil Smith, "The Making of a 4-Wheel Monster," *LAT,* November 8, 1971; "French Prize to *Duel,*" *DV,* February 22, 1973; "New Award to *Duel,*" *DV,* July 27, 1973; "Spielberg Ducks Politics," *Variety,* September 12, 1973; "Universal Sets *Duel* Release, 1st Spielberg Pic," *DV,* February 14, 1983; Jack Searles, "Can 12-Year-Old TV Film Make It in Theaters?" *LAHE,* February 15, 1983; Deborah Caulfield, "Spielberg's TV *Duel* Revived for Theaters," *LAT,* February 16, 1983; and "No Sale," *LAHE,* July 21, 1983. Matheson's short story was published in *Playboy,* April 1971; his teleplay is dated September 1, 1971. Shooting dates and information about the filming of the climactic scene are from notes in Morriss's cutting script. Critical commentary includes Stephen King, *Danse Macabre,* Everest House, 1981, and reviews by *Tone.* (Tony Scott), *DV,* November 15, 1971, and Dilys Powell, *Sunday Times of London,* October 1972, reprinted in Christopher Cook, ed., *The Dilys Powell Film Reader,* Oxford University Press, 1992. Full-page advertisements promoting *Duel* appeared in *DV* and *HR* on November 12, 1971. David Lean's comment is from Corliss, " 'I Dream for a Living.' "

Directorial assignments on *McKlusky* (released as *White Lightning*) were reported in "Steve Spielberg Directs UA Film," *HR,* March 1, 1972, and "Sargent to Direct Reynolds' *McKlusky,*" *DV,* April 28, 1972. Sources on *Something Evil* include the author's interviews with Jeff Corey, Margaret Avery, and Darling, and an interview with Bill Butler in Dennis Schaefer and Larry Salvato, *Masters of Light: Conversations with Contemporary Cinematographers,* University of California Press, 1984; the review by *Daku.* (Dave Kaufman) appeared in *DV,* January 25, 1972. Sources on *Savage* include the author's interviews with William Link and Barry Sullivan; Martin Landau's comments in Lee Goldberg, *Unsold Television Pilots: 1955 through 1988,* McFarland, 1990; and the *DV* review by *Tone.* (Tony Scott), April 2, 1973.

Spielberg's relationship with Jennings Lang was recalled by the executive's son Jennings Rockwell (Rocky) Lang as well as by his assistant, Peter Saphier, and Orin Borsten. Other sources include Rosenfield, *The Club Rules;* "Meet the Executives: Jennings Lang," *Universal City Studios News,* December 1965; Wayne Warga, "He Keeps His Assets Moving," *LAT,* December 22, 1974; Mel Gussow, "Jennings Lang, 81, Executive on High-Gross Disaster Films," *NYT,* and Myrna Oliver, "Jennings Lang: Produced *Earthquake, Airport* Movies," *LAT,* May 31, 1996 (obituaries). *Clearwater* was announced by Universal as a Spielberg project in an *LAT* item, November 5, 1973.

See notes for the previous chapter on the genesis of *The Sugarland Express* (working title: *Carte Blanche*). The second-draft screenplay of *The Sugarland Express* by Hal Barwood and Matthew Robbins, from a story by Spielberg, Barwood, and Robbins, is dated October 18, 1972. A novelization by Henry Clement was published by Popular Library in 1974. Information on the film's development by Universal is from the author's interviews with Saphier, Rocky Lang, Richard D. Zanuck, and William S. Gilmore Jr.; Reed's booklet on the film; and Wayne Warga, "Spielberg Keeps His Touch in Transition," *LAT,* April 3, 1974.

Sources on Zanuck and David Brown, in addition to the author's interview with Zanuck, include John Gregory Dunne, *The Studio,* Farrar, Straus & Giroux, 1969; Zanuck and Brown, American Film Institute seminar (April 17, 1975), in Joseph McBride, ed., *Filmmakers on Filmmaking,* Vol. 1, J. P. Tarcher, 1983; Stephen Farber and Marc Green, *Hollywood Dynasties,* Delilah, 1984; Marlys J. Harris, *The Zanucks of Hollywood: The Dark Legacy of an American Dynasty,* Crown, 1989; Brown, *Let Me Entertain You,* Morrow, 1990; Anthony Haden-Guest, "The Rise, Fall and Rise of Zanuck-Brown," *New York,* December 1, 1975; and "Son of Darryl F., He Made His Own Name with Hollywood's Most Toothsome Grosser Ever," *People,* December 29, 1975. Spielberg's comment on Zanuck and Brown is from Alan R. Howard, *"Sugarland* Tough Sell," *HR,* April 29, 1974. The film was announced on October 17, 1972, in *"Carte Blanche* at U for Zanuck, Brown," *DV,* and "Zanuck, Brown Set *Carte Blanche* for Filming in January," *HR;* the title *The Sugarland Express* was announced in *"Carte Blanche* Retitled," *Boxoffice,* November 13, 1972.

The author interviewed the following people who worked on the film: Zanuck, Gilmore, Joseph Alves Jr., Vilmos Zsigmond, Carey Loftin, and Edward S. Abroms; and also Bob Polunsky. Other sources on the filming include (1973): Lightman, "The New Panaflex Camera Makes Its Production Debut"; Bobrow; "Filming of *Sugarland Express* Begins in S.A. Monday," *San Antonio Express and News,* January 27; Ron White, "Filming Site of Movie Resembles Lawmen's Meeting," *Express and News,* January 31; White, "Crash, Wham, Crunch—Carey Loftin at Work," *Express and News,* February 15; Jerry Deal, "Goldie Grabs Hot One," *Express and News,* February 26; Jeff Millar, *"Sugarland* Role a Departure for Sweet Goldie Hawn," *LAT,* March 4; " 'Thanks, S.A.,' says producer of movie," *Express and News,* April 4; and Paul Vangelisti, "Almost 5,000 Extras Carried Aboard *Sugarland Express,"* *HR,* April 18. Spielberg's comment on Goldie Hawn is from Mary Murphy, "All That Giggles Is Not Goldie Hawn," *LAT,* September 26, 1974; Hawn on Spielberg is from Millar; other information is from Tom Burke, "All That Glitter Is Goldie's," *NYT,* January 28, 1973, and Universal's pressbook for the film (1974). Rocky Lang remembered the mementos Spielberg brought back from location. Colonel Wilson Speir's criticism of the film was reported in "Texas Lawmen Dispute *Sugarland."*

Reviews (1974) include Pauline Kael, "Sugarland and Badlands," *The New Yorker,* March 18; Vincent Canby, "Fascinated with Young Couples on the Lam," *NYT,* April 7; Zimmerman, "Hard Riders"; Stephen Farber, "Something Sour," *NYT,* April 28; and Dilys Powell, "Westerns on Wheels," *The Times* (London), June 16. Henry Sheehan's essay "A Father Runs from It" was published in *DV,* December 7, 1993. Box-office figures for *Sugarland* (and subsequent Spielberg films through *Hook*) are from "Filmography: Films

Directed by Steven Spielberg," *DV,* December 7, 1993, and Paula Parisi, "Spielberg's
List," *HR,* March 10, 1994. *Sugarland* postmortems included Spielberg's 1974 comments
to Murphy and to Howard, who also reported on the industry preview screenings.

10. "A PRIMAL SCREAM MOVIE" (PP. 226–60)

Spielberg's comment on his agent's dealmaking is from Reed. His rejection on *The
Taking of Pelham One Two Three* was reported to the author by Steven Bach, former
head of creative affairs for Palomar Pictures, which made the film with Palladium Productions. Richard D. Zanuck discussed Spielberg's rejection of *MacArthur* with the
author; David Brown's report about Spielberg passing on another project is from his
memoir, *Let Me Entertain You.* Information on Spielberg's 1973 development deal with
Columbia for *Watch the Skies* is from the author's interview with Michael Phillips; David
McClintick, *Indecent Exposure: A True Story of Hollywood and Wall Street,* Morrow,
1982; and a February 22, 1974, IFA document outlining the terms of Michael and Julia
Phillips' deal to produce what was then titled *The Close Encounter of the Third Kind.*
Paul Schrader discussed his work on Spielberg's UFO project in Jackson, *Schrader on
Schrader & Other Writings;* other sources include Phillips; and a December 12, 1973,
IFA document giving the terms of Schrader's writing deal with Columbia for his version
of the script, *Kingdom Come.* Information on David Begelman is from McClintick's book
and his article "Final Exposure," *Vanity Fair,* November 1995; and from Corie Brown,
"Final Exposure," *Premiere,* November 1995. Additional sources on Spielberg's relation-
ships with Phillips, his wife Julia, and their coterie include the author's interviews with
Gloria Katz and Willard Huyck; Julia Phillips, *You'll Never Eat Lunch in This Town
Again,* Random House, 1991; Jackson; and Cook (which includes Michael Phillips's
1977 comment on Spielberg). Wallace Reyburn's *Flushed with Pride: The Story of
Thomas Crapper* was published in 1969 by Macdonald and Company (London).

The author interviewed the following participants in the making of *Jaws:* Peter
Benchley, Richard D. Zanuck, William S. Gilmore Jr., Carl Gottlieb, and Joseph Alves Jr.,
as well as observers including Katz, Huyck, Michael Phillips, Peter Saphier, William Link,
Rocky Lang, Joan Darling, Allen Daviau, Vilmos Zsigmond, Orin Borsten, and Bob Gale
(the author also attended the April 24, 1975, preview of *Jaws* at Hollywood's Cinerama
Dome). Benchley's novel *Jaws* was published by Doubleday, 1974; his final screenplay
draft is undated. The making of *Jaws* has been the subject of two books, Gottlieb's *The
"Jaws" Log* and Edith Blake's *On Location on Martha's Vineyard (The Making of the
Movie "Jaws").* Oral histories were compiled in the MCA Home Video laserdisc *The
Making of Steven Spielberg's "Jaws,"* produced by Laurent Bouzereau, 1995 (which also
includes Spielberg's home movies of the filming); and Nancy Griffin, "In the Grip of
Jaws," Premiere, October 1995.

Spielberg's most extensive location interview about the film was with Helpern.
Brown wrote about *Jaws* in *Let Me Entertain You;* he and Zanuck discussed the film in
McBride, *Filmmakers on Filmmaking,* Vol. 1; Zanuck also recalled the production in
Susan Royal, "Interview with *Cocoon* Producers Richard and Lili Fini Zanuck of Zanuck/
Brown Productions," *American Premiere,* June 1985. Other accounts by participants in
Jaws include "Dialogue on Film: Verna Fields," *American Film,* June 1978; Fields's
American Film Institute seminar (December 3, 1975) in *Filmmakers on Filmmaking,* Vol.
1; Valerie Taylor, "The Filming for *Jaws,"* in Ron and Valerie Taylor, with Peter Goadby,
Great Shark Stories, Harper & Row, 1978; and cinematographer Bill Butler's interview
in Schaefer and Salvato, *Masters of Light.* Richard Dreyfuss recalled his reluctance about
appearing in *Jaws* to Michael Rogers, "Jawing with Richard Dreyfuss," *Rolling Stone,*
July 31, 1975; Dreyfuss's comment on Spielberg's direction of actors is from Cook.
Gottlieb's comments on Dreyfuss are from his essay "Richard Dreyfuss: Forceful Intel-
lect," in Danny Peary, ed., *Close-Ups: The Movie Star Book,* Workman, 1978. Gottlieb

also recalled the filming in Ray Loynd, "In the Teeth of the Storm," *LAHE,* August 3, 1975.

Articles published about *Jaws* during production include (1974): "Hunting the Shark," *Newsweek,* June 24; Robert Riger, "On Location with *Jaws*—'Tell the Shark We'll Do It One More Time!' " *Action,* July–August; Gregg Kilday, "Books, Lines and Clinkers on Martha's Vineyard," *LAT,* July 7; and "Introducing Bruce," *Time,* September 2; also, Mik Cribben, "On Location with *Jaws,* " *American Cinematographer,* March 1975.

The genesis of Benchley's novel was discussed in Richard Ellis and John E. McCosker, *Great White Shark,* Stanford University Press, 1991. Information on Universal's purchase of the film rights (1973) includes: Peter Saphier's memo to Lew R. Wasserman recommending the purchase of the novel, April 16; a synopsis of the novel by Universal story department reader Dennis McCarthy, April 17; the MCA deal memo regarding the film rights, Paul Miller to Joe DiMuro, May 1; and a May 8 IFA document outlining the terms of Benchley's deal with Universal and Zanuck–Brown. Spielberg's hiring was announced in "Spielberg Signed for Zanuck–Brown *Jaws* Production," *HR,* June 21, 1973. Robert Shaw's comment on Benchley's novel is from the *Time* cover story on the film, "Summer of the Shark," June 23, 1975, which also includes comments by Dreyfuss and Brian De Palma. Additional information on Shaw is from Karen Carmean and Georg Gaston, *Robert Shaw: More Than a Life,* Madison Books, 1994.

Spielberg commented on Benchley's novel in "Hunting the Shark" and in Stettin; Benchley's criticisms of Spielberg appeared in Kilday. Benchley's letter to Spielberg is quoted in *The "Jaws" Log.* Spielberg's worry that *Jaws* could be a "turkey" was related to Desmond Ryan, *"Jaws* Director Raises His Sights—to UFOs," *Philadelphia Inquirer,* April 10, 1977. His phrase "a primal scream movie" is from Combs; his comments on fear are from Ryan and "Spielberg Spanks Sequels as 'Cheap, Carnival Trick,' " *Variety,* October 29, 1975, in which he also remarked that *Jaws* could have been a "laugh riot."

Sources on Spielberg's interest in directing *Lucky Lady* include Reed and the author's interviews with Zanuck, Rocky Lang, and *Lucky Lady* screenwriters Huyck and Katz; Sid Sheinberg told Latham of his insistence that Spielberg make *Jaws* and his description of the film as *"Duel* with a shark." Sheinberg's denial that Universal was thinking of canceling the film or firing Spielberg is from Griffin, "In the Grip of *Jaws."* The charges of nepotism over the hiring of Lorraine Gary in *Jaws* and two sequels were reported in Sue Ellen Jares, "Lorraine Gary Got a Big Bite of *Jaws 2*—But Not, She Insists, Because She's the Boss's Wife," *People,* August 7, 1978; Zanuck's suggestion of casting Linda Harrison was reported in "All in the Family," *New York,* October 6, 1975, and in Harris, *The Zanucks of Hollywood.*

Verna Fields's role in the making of *Jaws* was discussed in Mary Murphy, "Fields: Up from the Cutting Room Floor," *LAT,* July 24, 1975; "Making It in Film" (advertisement), *Millimeter,* June 1976; Paul Rosenfield, "Women in Hollywood," *LAT,* July 13, 1982; Todd McCarthy, "Oscar-Winning Film Editor Verna Fields Dies of Cancer," *DV,* December 2, 1982; Margy Rochlin, "In the Editing Room, Many Propose, Few Dispose," *NYT,* July 23, 1995; and Gottlieb, *"Jaws* Did Not Need Saving" (letter replying to Rochlin), *NYT,* August 6, 1995. Fields's promotions by Universal were reported in studio press releases, "Verna Fields—Biography," June 5, 1975, and "Verna Fields Named a Vice President of Universal Pictures," February 18, 1976. Spielberg's decision not to work with Fields on *Close Encounters of the Third Kind* was reported in Phillips, *You'll Never Eat Lunch in This Town Again;* Schrader's remarks about Spielberg resenting his helpers are from Crawley.

Jaws reviews (1975) include *Murf.* (A. D. Murphy), *DV,* June 12; Frank Rich, "Easy Living," *New Times,* June 27; Molly Haskell, "The Claptrap of Pearly Whites in the Briny Deep," *The Village Voice,* June 23; and William S. Pechter, "Man Bites Shark (& Other Curiosities)," *Commentary,* November. Universal's quote ad appeared in *Variety* on

September 24, 1975. Pauline Kael's comments are from "Notes on Evolving Heroes, Morals, Audiences," *The New Yorker,* November 8, 1976. Jane E. Caputi's essay *"Jaws* as Patriarchal Myth" is from *Journal of Popular Film,* Vol. VI, No. 4, 1978.

Articles on *"Jaws*mania" (1975) include: "Summer of the Shark"; John Charnay and Doug Mirell, "Ripping Response to *Jaws," HR,* June 26; Peter Goldman, *"Jaws*mania: The Great Escape," *Newsweek,* July 28; Robert E. Dallos, "Sharks: Jaws of Fear Open on All Shores," *LAT,* July 12; and John Getze, *"Jaws* Swims to Top in Ocean of Publicity," *LAT,* September 28. Fidel Castro's interpretation of the film and Spielberg's response were reported by Tuchman. Ellis and McCosker commented on the film's impact in *Great White Shark;* Cleveland Amory reported on the protest against Universal souvenirs in "Sharks Have Feelings Too," *TV Guide,* November 27, 1976. Spielberg's proposal for chocolate sharks was recalled by Joan Darling.

The date on which *Jaws* turned a profit was reported to the author by Gilmore. Its box-office record was reported in "U Claims Rental Record as *Jaws* Passes *Godfather," DV,* September 10, 1975; see also *"Star Wars* Zaps *Jaws* in Grosses," *LAT,* December 2, 1977, and Spielberg's advertisement congratulating George Lucas in *HR,* December 2, 1977. Alfred Hitchcock's reaction to the success of *Jaws* was reported by the author in "Hitchcock: a Defense and an Update," *Film Comment,* May–June 1979. Spielberg discussed the film's release strategy in "Ripping Response to *Jaws."* Peter Biskind discussed the "blockbuster syndrome" in his essay "Blockbuster: The Last Crusade," in Mark Crispin Miller, ed., *Seeing Through Movies,* Pantheon, 1990.

Information on Spielberg's profit percentages on *Jaws* is from the author's interviews with Zanuck and Michael Phillips; Getze's article; and Klemesrud's interview with Spielberg. His contract renegotiation was reported in "Spielberg, Universal in Four-Film Deal," *HR,* July 11, 1975; "Spielberg, Universal Sign Four-Picture Agreement," *LAT,* July 14, 1975; and Deborah Caulfield, *"E.T.* Gossip: The One That Got Away?" *LAT,* July 18, 1982. Sheinberg's prediction that Spielberg would win an Oscar is from Haber; Spielberg's reaction to the nominations is recorded in *TVTV Looks at the Oscars* (TVTV/KCET, Los Angeles, 1976).

Sources on *Jaws 2* include the author's interviews with the film's director, Jeannot Szwarc, and Alves, its production designer and associate producer; Ray Loynd, *The "Jaws 2" Log,* Dell, 1978; "Spielberg Spanks Sequels as 'Cheap, Carnival Trick' "; and Joseph McBride, "Director Avers *Jaws 2* Not a 'Rip-Off Sequel,' " *DV,* May 13, 1977 (interview with John Hancock, who later was fired from the film).

11. WATCH THE SKIES (PP. 261–92)

See notes for previous chapter for material on the genesis of *Close Encounters of the Third Kind.* The author interviewed the following people who worked on the film: Michael Phillips, John Veitch, Vilmos Zsigmond, Joseph Alves Jr., Douglas Trumbull, Allen Daviau, and David Giler (as well as discussing the film with François Truffaut during production); and others including Robert S. Birchard (who worked on the 1980 *Special Edition*), Robert Stack, and Bob Gale. The production of *Close Encounters* was chronicled in Balaban, with an introduction by Spielberg, *"Close Encounters of the Third Kind" Diary;* Forrest J. Ackerman, *"Close Encounters of the Third Kind": Official Authorized Edition* (magazine), Warren Publishing Co., 1977; Durwood, ed., *"Close Encounters of the Third Kind": A Document of the Film;* Julia Phillips, *You'll Never Eat Lunch in This Town Again;* and *Making "Close Encounters,"* a 1990 documentary produced by Isaac Mizrahi and Morgan Holly, included in the Criterion Collection laserdisc edition (which contains both the original 1977 release version of *Close Encounters* and scenes added for the 1980 *Special Edition*).

Dell published a novelization, credited to Spielberg, in 1977, and a "Fotonovel" adaptation of the film in 1978. Screenplay extracts are included in *Making "Close En-*

counters"; the shooting script, credited to Spielberg, is dated May 12, 1976. Sources on the other writers who contributed to the screenplay include the author's interviews with Michael Phillips and Giler; Schrader's comments in Crawley and in Jackson, *Schrader on Schrader & Other Writings; You'll Never Eat Lunch in This Town Again;* Will Tusher, "Phillips' *Close Encounters* Cost on \$11 Mil Space Trip," *HR,* April 22, 1976; Shay, "Steven Spielberg on *Close Encounters";* Lane Maloney, "Michael Phillips on Lucky Streak with Tyro Directors," *DV,* October 2, 1981; and the Jagger–Warhol interview with Spielberg. Julia Phillips' 1991 comment on Spielberg's relationship with writers is from Sally Ogle Davis, "Attack of the Killer Tomato," *Los Angeles,* March.

Included in the January 1978 special issue of *American Cinematographer,* "The Making of *Close Encounters of the Third Kind,"* are: Spielberg, "The Unsung Heroes or Credit Where Credit Is Due"; Herb A. Lightman, "My Close Encounter with *CE3K";* Lightman, "Spielberg Speaks About *Close Encounters";* Alves, "Designing a World for UFO's, Extraterrestrials and Mere Mortals"; Trumbull, "Creating the Photographic Special Effects for *Close Encounters of the Third Kind";* Frank Warner, "The Sounds of Silence and Things That Go 'Flash' in the Night"; Zsigmond, "Lights! Camera! Action! for *CE3K";* and "From the Producers' Point of View." *Cinefantastique,* Fall 1978, contains Don Shay's "Steven Spielberg on *Close Encounters," "Close Encounters* Extraterrestrials," and *"Close Encounters* at Future General." *Filmmakers Newsletter,* December 1977, includes Chuck Austin, "Director Steve Spielberg"; Judith McNally, "Making *Close Encounters";* and Steve Mitchell, "Special Effects: Douglas Trumbull."

Writings by Dr. J. Allen Hynek include *The UFO Experience: A Scientific Inquiry,* Regnery, 1972; foreword to Jacques and Janine Vallee, *The UFO Enigma: Challenge to Science,* Regnery, 1966; "Are Flying Saucers Real?" *The Saturday Evening Post,* December 17, 1966, reprinted in Jay David, ed., *The Flying Saucer Reader,* Signet, 1967; and "Twenty-one Years of UFO Reports," in Carl Sagan and Thornton Page, eds., *UFO's—A Scientific Debate,* Norton, 1974. Hynek was quoted on *Close Encounters* in Cook and profiled by Peter Gwynne in "The Galileo of UFOlogy," *Newsweek,* November 21, 1977.

Other books on ufology include C. G. Jung, trans. by R.F.C. Hull, *Flying Saucers: A Modern Myth of Things Seen in the Skies,* Princeton University Press, 1978 (originally published in 1959); Curtis Peebles, *Watch the Skies!: A Chronicle of the Flying Saucer Myth,* Smithsonian Institution Press, 1994; C. D. B. Bryan, *Close Encounters of the Fourth Kind: Alien Abduction, UFOs, and the Conference at M.I.T.,* Knopf, 1995; Phil Cousineau, *UFOs: A Manual for the Millennium,* HarperCollins West, 1995 (which quotes Ronald Reagan's alleged comment to Spielberg). The allegation that *Close Encounters* and *E.T.* were part of a military plot to indoctrinate the public is made in Brad Steiger and Sherry Hansen Steiger, *The Rainbow Conspiracy,* Pinnacle Books, 1994. Sources on Spielberg's involvement with META include "Taking a Long Look for a Real E.T.," *LAHE,* September 30, 1985; his appearance with his son Max on the TV special *Nova:* "Is Anybody Out There?" (WGBH, Boston, 1986); and Thomas R. McDonough, *The Search for Extraterrestrial Intelligence: Listening for Life in the Cosmos,* John Wiley & Sons, 1987; see also Walter Sullivan, *We Are Not Alone: The Continuing Search for Extraterrestrial Intelligence* (revised edition), Plume, 1994. Ray Bradbury wrote about *Close Encounters* in his introduction to Durwood's book (first published in *LAT,* November 20, 1977, as "Opening the Beautiful Door of True Immortality") and in "The Turkey That Attacked New York"; *The Martian Chronicles* was published by Doubleday, 1950.

Additional articles on *Close Encounters* (1977) include Frank Rich, "The Aliens Are Coming!" *Time,* November 7; Jack Kroll, "The UFO's Are Coming!" *Newsweek,* November 21; Gregg Kilday, "Special Encounter on Effects," *LAT,* December 5. Melinda Dillon's comments on the filming are from "A Wedding for Dillon," *Horizon,* January 1978. Richard Dreyfuss's comments are from Durwood, *"Close Encounters of the Third Kind":* *A Document of the Film,* and from Steve Grant, "Blithe Spirit," *Time Out,* January 10–

17, 1990. The influence of *The Searchers* on *Close Encounters* was discussed in Stuart Byron, *"The Searchers:* Cult Movie of the New Hollywood," *New York,* March 5, 1979.

Information on the budget and production cost of *Close Encounters* is from the author's interviews with Michael Phillips, Veitch, and Trumbull; and other sources including *You'll Never Eat Lunch in This Town Again;* Will Tusher, *"Encounter* Budget to Top $7 Million," *HR,* November 14, 1975; Tusher, "Phillips' *Close Encounters* Cost on $11 Mil Space Trip"; "How Close the Encounter to a Profit," *Variety,* November 9, 1977; and "From the Producers' Point of View." Spielberg's earnings on *Close Encounters* were estimated by Lane. Sources on Columbia's finances include the author's interview with A. D. Murphy; McClintick, *Indecent Exposure;* and Bernard F. Dick, "From the Brothers Cohn to Sony Corp.," in Dick, ed., *Columbia Pictures: Portrait of a Studio,* University Press of Kentucky, 1992. Spielberg's comment on David Begelman is from Brown, "Final Exposure." Information on the 1975 start date is from Phillips; "Shelter Deadlines Possible Reasons for Odd Pic Starts," *DV,* December 31, 1975; and Shay, *"Close Encounters* at Future General." The title *Close Encounter of the Third Kind* is mentioned in an August 15, 1975, Columbia press release and trade press articles including "Col. Lineup Nears Peak," *HR,* March 29, 1974, and "Spielberg's New *Close Encounter* First Since *Jaws,"* *HR,* August 12, 1975.

The *Star Wars* screening was described to the author by Gloria Katz and Willard Huyck; see also Pollock, *Skywalking: The Life and Films of George Lucas.* Information on Spielberg's Hawaiian vacation with Lucas and their decision to make *Raiders of the Lost Ark* is from Pollock; Taylor, *The Making of "Raiders of the Lost Ark";* and Champlin, *George Lucas: The Creative Impulse.*

Information on *Close Encounters* previews is from Michael Phillips, Veitch, and Trumbull; Crawley; *Making "Close Encounters";* and 1977 articles: Gregg Kilday, October 10, November 5 (*"Close Encounters:* Go or No-Go?"), and November 9, *LAT;* "Col Delays Press Preview of *Close Encounters,"* *DV,* October 11; "Columbia Disputes Magazine's Views on *Third Kind,"* *HR,* November 2; William Flanagan, "An Encounter with *Close Encounters,"* *New York,* November 7, and letter to the editor, *New York,* November 21; Rich; Geri Fabrikant, "Wall Street Vigil; Col Stock Peaks with *Encounters,"* *HR,* November 8; and "Col Holds Bally Rally in N.Y. for *Encounters* Launching," *Variety,* November 9. See also Shay, "Steven Spielberg on *Close Encounters."*

Julia Phillips's claim that her cocaine problem began on *Close Encounters* is from Joyce Wadler, "A Hollywood Outcast Treats the Stars to an Acid-Dip Memoir," *People,* March 18, 1991. Spielberg's no-comment reaction to her book is from Larry Rohter, "Hollywood Memoir Tells All, and Many Don't Want to Hear," *NYT,* March 14, 1991.

Close Encounters reviews (1977) include Rich; Charles Champlin, "Saucer Sorcery," *LAT,* November 18; Kroll; Stephen Farber, *"Close Encounters:* Smooth Takeoff, Bumpy Landing," *New West,* December 5; and Molly Haskell, "The Dumbest Story Ever Told," *New York,* December 5; also, Arthur Schlesinger Jr., "Close Encounters of a Benign Kind," *Saturday Review,* January 7, 1978. Spielberg's 1994 comment on the film is from *The Barbara Walters Special.*

Spielberg wrote about Truffaut in "He Was the Movies." Writings by Truffaut on *Close Encounters* include "En tournant pour Spielberg," preface to Tony Crawley, *L'Aventure Spielberg* (1984 French edition of *The Steven Spielberg Story*), reprinted in Truffaut's *Le Plaisir des yeux,* Flammarion, Paris, 1987; Dominique Rabourdin, trans. by Robert Erich Wolf, *Truffaut by Truffaut,* Harry N. Abrams, 1987; and Truffaut, ed. by Gilles Jacob and Claude de Givray, trans. by Gilbert Adair, *Correspondence 1945–1984,* The Noonday Press, 1990. Other sources include "François Truffaut Moves to Other Side of Camera for *Close Encounters of the Third Kind,"* Columbia Pictures pressbook, 1977; Bridget Byrne, "Truffaut Savors Hollywood Treatment," *LAHE,* December 13, 1977; Heathwood; Larry Van Dyne, "His Mind Is a Camera, His Life Is Film," *The Chronicle Review,* March

19, 1979; William Kowinski, "François Truffaut, the Man Who Loved Movies," *Rolling Stone,* June 14, 1979; and David Lees, "Checking In," *Playboy,* October 1981. Truffaut criticized Julia Phillips in James F. Clarity, "François Truffaut—A Man for All Festivals," *NYT,* September 26, 1976; Spielberg responded in a letter to the editor, October 24, and Phillips in *You'll Never Eat Lunch in This Town Again;* Truffaut made additional remarks in "Truffaut, Part V," *The New Yorker,* October 18, 1976. Jean Renoir's comment on the film is from his March 7, 1978, letter to Truffaut, in Renoir's *Letters,* ed. by Lorraine LoBianco and David Thompson, Faber and Faber, London, 1994.

Spielberg's two versions of *Close Encounters* are compared in Laurent Bouzereau, *The Cutting Room Floor,* Citadel Press, 1994. Articles on the *Special Edition* include Aljean Harmetz, *"Close Encounters* to Get Even Closer," *NYT,* December 6, 1978; "Col *Encounters* Plans News to Steven Spielberg," *DV,* October 24, 1979; and (1980): *Cart.* (Todd McCarthy), "New *Encounters* a Refinement of Original Version," *DV,* August 1; Miles Beller, "The High Cost of Going Inside the Alien Spaceship," *LAHE,* August 1; Arthur Knight, *HR* review, August 1; Charles Champlin, *"Encounters* Even Closer in Revision," *LAT,* August 3; Vincent Canby, *"Close Encounters* Has Now Become a Classic," *NYT,* August 31; and Pauline Kael, "Who and Who," *The New Yorker,* September 1. Gail Rentzer's lawsuit was reported in "Columbia Sued over Film's Ads," *NYT,* August 9, 1980.

12. "REHAB" (PP. 293–322)

Sources on Amy Irving include Laurent Bouzereau, *The De Palma Cut,* Dembner Books, 1988; Phillips, *You'll Never Eat Lunch in This Town Again;* Kerry Segrave, *The Post-Feminist Hollywood Actress: Biographies and Filmographies of Stars Born After 1939,* McFarland, 1990; Cherie Burns, "Amy Irving's Enjoying a Close Encounter of Two Kinds: Love with Steven Spielberg and Stardom in *The Fury,"* People, March 27, 1978; Roderick Mann, "An Encounter for Amy, Steve," *LAT,* March 13, 1979; "Amy Irving's Voices," *Look,* April 2, 1979; Janos; Andrea Chambers, "She's Streisand's Sweetie in *Yentl,* But Amy Irving Says Her Heart Belongs to Broadway," *People,* January 16, 1984; Stephen Farber, "Once in Love with Amy . . . ," *Cosmopolitan,* March 1985; Meme Black, "Amy Irving's 'Charmed Life,' " *McCall's,* June 1985; and Cliff Jahr, "Amy Irving: Mom Is Her Real Starring Role," *Ladies' Home Journal,* March 1989. Information on Spielberg's Coldwater Canyon house is from the author's interview with Bob Gale and various articles including Klemesrud; Seligson, "Steven Spielberg: The Man Behind Columbia Pictures' $19-Million Gamble"; and Royal, "Steven Spielberg in His Adventures on Earth."

Information on Spielberg's pirate movie project is from A. H. Weiler, "Spielberg Weighs Two Projects," *NYT,* June 9, 1974; his involvement in *The Bingo Long Traveling All-Stars and Motor Kings* is from the author's interview with Joseph Alves Jr. and from Bruce Cook, "The Saga of Bingo Long and the Traveling All-Stars," *American Film,* July–August 1976. Spielberg discussed *Magic* in his introduction to Andy Dougan, *The Actors' Director: Richard Attenborough Behind the Camera,* Mainstream Publishing Co., Edinburgh, 1994; his plans to direct a TV production of *Twelve Angry Men* were mentioned in "Dialogue on Film: Steven Spielberg."

Sources on Gale and Robert Zemeckis and their projects with Spielberg include the author's interview with Gale; the June 23, 1978, Zemeckis–Gale screenplay *After School;* Balaban, *"Close Encounters of the Third Kind" Diary;* "Steven Spielberg's 'Broker' Position as Newcomers Film at Universal," *Variety,* November 30, 1977; Ray Loynd, "Surprising Turns for Two Hit Filmmakers," *LAHE,* December 9, 1977; "Studios Cheat Us All, Sez Spielberg," *Variety,* February 22, 1978; "Spielberg Modest Cost for Universal; Actors' Maximum Age Is 14," *Variety,* March 1, 1978; *"Used Cars* Tells Sleazy Side; 2d 'Sale' for Young Scripters," *Variety,* November 21, 1979; Gregg Kilday, "The *1941* Campaign

Revisited," *LAHE,* December 14, 1979; and Paul Attanasio, "The Zooming Zemeckis," *Washington Post,* July 3, 1985. Truffaut's urging Spielberg to make a movie about "keeds" is from Spielberg, "He Was the Movies." Information on the Oak Tree Gun Club is from the author's interviews with Gale, Robert Stack, and Arnold Spielberg; the author's 1975 visit to the club with John Milius; Hodenfield, *"1941:* Bombs Away!"; and Attanasio. Charlton Heston's comment on Hollywood gun enthusiasts is from *In the Arena: An Autobiography.*

The author interviewed the following people involved in the making of *1941:* Milius (in 1975), Gale, Stack, John Veitch, and Lionel Stander. The production was chronicled in Glenn Erickson and Mary Ellen Trainor, *The Making of "1941,"* Ballantine Books, 1980, and the 1996 MCA Home Video laserdisc documentary *The Making of "1941,"* produced by Laurent Bouzereau (the laserdisc also contains the 146-minute restoration of the film, outtakes, and Spielberg's home movies of the filming). The ninth-draft screenplay by Zemeckis and Gale, from their story with Milius, is dated August 28, 1978. Gale's novelization of the film, Ballantine Books, 1979, includes his preface, "About This Book." Spielberg wrote about the film in his September 1979 introduction to *"1941": The Illustrated Story* by Stephen Bissette and Rick Veitch, adapted by Allan Asherman, *Heavy Metal*/Pocket Books; and in "Directing *1941,"* *American Cinematographer,* December 1979. That issue also contains A. D. Flowers, "Mechanical Special Effects for *1941"*; Gregory Jein, "The Mini-World of *1941"*; and "Photographing *1941."* See also David S. Reiss, *"1941:* A Conversation with DP William A. Fraker, ASC," *Filmmakers Monthly,* December 1979.

The first mention of *1941* in print, under the project's original title *The Night the Japs Attacked,* was in McBride, "Milius Says *Apocalypse Now* Is a 'Descent Into Hell,' " *DV,* September 2, 1975; Milius told the author about Spielberg sending him a copy of the article. Objections to the original title were mentioned in "Col Signs Spielberg for *1941,"* *DV,* May 3, 1977; see also Gallagher and *"Rising Sun* New Title for Spielberg," *HR,* January 13, 1978.

Information on "The Great Los Angeles Air Raid" and Japanese attacks on the U.S. mainland is from Bert Webber, *Retaliation: Japanese Attacks and Allied Countermeasures on the Pacific Coast in World War II,* Oregon State University Press, 1975, and *Silent Siege: Japanese Attacks Against North America in World War II,* Ye Galleon Press, 1984; *LAT* coverage, February 22–27, 1942, including "Submarine Shells Southland Oil Field" (February 24), "L.A. Area Raided!" (February 25 extra edition), and "Army Says Alert Real" (February 26); and Sally Ogle Davis, "How Many Japanese Attackers Does It Take to Throw L.A. into a Panic?" *Los Angeles,* November 1979.

General Joseph W. Stilwell's activities in late 1941, including his viewing of *Dumbo,* are documented in *The Stilwell Papers,* ed. by Theodore H. White, William Sloane Associates, 1948. Samuel Fuller's objection to playing Stilwell was reported by Fuller to the author in 1978 and to Lee Server, *Sam Fuller: Film Is a Battleground,* McFarland, 1994. John Wayne's reaction to the script was recalled by Spielberg in *The Making of "1941"* and in Joe Morgenstern, "Bob Z Can Read Your Mind," *Playboy,* August 1995.

Additional reports on the filming of *1941* include "H'wood & Vine *1941* Location Lensing Nixed," *DV,* July 24, 1978; Army Archerd columns, *DV,* December 20, 1978, and May 17, 1979; Chris Hodenfield, "Masters of Illusion," *Rolling Stone,* February 8, 1979, and *"1941:* Bombs Away!"; Wayne Warga, "Remembering Pearl Harbor with Steven Spielberg," *LAT,* March 11, 1979; and "Animal House Goes to War," *Time,* April 16, 1979. Spielberg's description of *1941* as "a celebration of paranoia" is from the pressbook for the film, Columbia/Universal, 1979. The budget and final cost, and the film's ramifications for Spielberg's career, were discussed with the author by Veitch and Gale, and by Michael Finnell, Howard Kazanjian, A. D. Murphy, and David Tomblin. Spielberg's self-criticisms are from "Of Narrow Misses and Close Calls"; Anthony; and Royal, "Steven

Spielberg in His Adventures on Earth." Press coverage of the cost also includes Charles Schreger, "Milius' A-Team Prods. Prepping Six Projects, One for Orion," *DV,* March 6, 1978; Stuart Byron, "Rules of the Game," *The Village Voice,* June 27, 1979; Andrew Epstein, *"1941* Gets a Bad Press, But Payoff Is Promising," *LAT,* April 20, 1980; and "Tanen Says U Will Recoup on *1941* Release," *DV,* May 12, 1980. The European reception was discussed by Veitch; Epstein; and in *"1941* Doing Well in Europe Theatres," *HR,* April 2, 1980, and an item in *New York,* April 7, 1980. Drug use by John Belushi and others who worked on *1941,* Spielberg's notion of casting Belushi as the Japanese submarine commander, and Spielberg's buyout price for *Continental Divide* are discussed in Bob Woodward, *Wired: The Short Life and Fast Times of John Belushi,* Simon & Schuster, 1984.

Sources on previews of *1941* include Gale and Veitch; Bouzereau, *The Cutting Room Floor;* and 1979 articles: Dale Pollock, *"1941* Openings Cancelled as Pic Undergoes Surgery," *DV,* October 24; "Col & U: Opinions Differ on Spielberg's *1941," DV,* October 25; "Re-Edit of *1941* Proceeding; Spielberg Sanguine Re Tightening," *Variety,* October 31; "Minimum Run on *1941* Shortened," *Variety,* December 12; and Pollock, "Spielberg Cuts *1941* 17 Mins.," *Variety,* December 19.

Reviews (1979) include Ron Pennington, *HR,* December 13; Charles Champlin, "Spielberg's Pearl Harbor," *LAT,* December 14; Michael Sragow, *"1941:* World War II, *Animal House* style," *LAHE,* December 14; and in 1980, Stephen Farber, "Nuts!" *New West,* January 14. Spielberg's comment about Adolf Eichmann is from Rehlin.

Information on the premiere of *1941* and Spielberg's trip to Japan with Amy Irving is from Woodward, *Wired;* Archerd column, *DV,* December 17, 1979; Janos; Black; and Jahr. Rumors about Irving and Willie Nelson were mentioned in Chambers, Farber, and Jahr. Spielberg commented on Kathleen Carey in Skow, "Staying Five Moves Ahead"; their relationship also was discussed in "As *E.T.* Grows, Spielberg Cools Out and Mulls the Sequel," *People,* August 23, 1982. A photo of Valerie Bertinelli on a date with Spielberg appeared in *US,* June 10, 1980; they also were seen together on *The American Film Institute Salute to James Stewart* (CBS-TV, March 1980).

The author interviewed the following people who worked on *Raiders of the Lost Ark:* Gary Graver, Lawrence Kasdan, Kazanjian, and Tomblin. Information on the cost and schedule is from Kazanjian. Kasdan's screenplay, based on a story by George Lucas and Philip Kaufman, was published in 1995 by O.S.P. Publishing as part of the *Premiere* magazine series The Movie Script Library. The revised third draft of the screenplay is dated August 1979. A children's storybook adaptation by Les Martin was published by Random House, 1981.

The production was chronicled in Taylor, *The Making of "Raiders of the Lost Ark";* Ann Heller, ed., *"Raiders of the Lost Ark": Collector's Album,* George Fenmore Associates, 1981; and the 1981 Lucasfilm documentaries *Great Movie Stunts: "Raiders of the Lost Ark"* (directed by Robert Guenette) and *The Making of "Raiders of the Lost Ark"* (directed by Phillip Schuman). Other information appears in Pollock, *Skywalking: The Life and Films of George Lucas;* Alan McKenzie, *The Harrison Ford Story,* Arbor House, 1984; Thomas G. Smith, *Industrial Light and Magic: The Art of Special Effects,* Del Rey, 1986; Champlin, *George Lucas: The Creative Impulse;* and Mark Cotta Vaz and Shinji Hata, *From "Star Wars" to Indiana Jones: The Best of the Lucasfilm Archives,* Chronicle Books, 1994.

Spielberg wrote about the filming of *Raiders* in "Of Narrow Misses and Close Calls," *American Cinematographer,* November 1981, which also includes "Making Sure the Action Never Stopped" (interview with stunt coordinator Glenn Randall). Other articles on *Raiders* include Pollock, "Paramount Floating Lucasfilm's *Ark," DV,* November 30, 1977; "Paramount in Deal with Lucas for *Lost Ark* and Four Sequels," *Variety,* December 5, 1979; item in *HR,* May 9, 1980 (on Tom Selleck); "Harrison Ford *Lost Ark* Star," *DV,*

June 10, 1980; and in 1981, Janet Maslin, "How Old Movie Serials Inspired Lucas and Spielberg," *NYT,* June 7; David Ansen, "Cliffhanger Classic," *Newsweek,* June 15; Richard Schickel, "Slam! Bang! A Movie Movie," *Time,* June 15; Michael Sragow, *"Raiders of the Lost Ark:* The Ultimate Saturday Matinee," *Rolling Stone,* June 25; James H. Burns, "Harrison Ford: The Name of the Game Is 'Hero,' " *Starlog,* July; Mitch Tuchman and Anne Thompson, " 'I'm the Boss': George Lucas Interviewed," *Film Comment,* July–August; Ben Stein, "A Deal to Remember," *New West,* August; and Peter Sullivan, "Raiders of the Movie Serials," *Starlog,* August.

Additional information on Kasdan's script is from Robert F. Moss, "New Epic, Big Stakes," *Saturday Review,* June 1981; James H. Burns, "Lawrence Kasdan: Part I," *Starlog,* September 1981; and "Kasdan on Kasdan," ed. by Graham Fuller, in John Boorman and Walter Donohue, eds., *Projections 3: Film-makers on Film-making,* Faber and Faber, London, 1994. Information on eliminated sequences is from the author's interviews with Kasdan, Gloria Katz, and Willard Huyck; and Kasdan's third-draft screenplay of *Raiders,* August 1979.

Sources on Frank Marshall include his publicity biography, Paramount Pictures (1995), and Robert Greenberger, "Meet Frank Marshall," *Starlog,* January 1983. Kathleen Kennedy's comment on Spielberg's problem with intimacy is from Schiff. Other sources on Kennedy include her publicity biographies, Universal (1986) and Paramount (1995); and Alexandra Brouwer and Thomas Lee Wright, "Kathleen Kennedy" (interview), *Working in Hollywood,* Crown, 1990.

Reviews of *Raiders* (1981) include Sheila Benson, *"Lost Ark:* Back to Saturday Matinees," *LAT,* June 7; David Denby, "Movie of Champions," *New York,* June 15; Robert Asahina, "Contrived Comic Books," *The New Leader,* June 29; Victoria Geng, "Spielberg's Express," *Film Comment,* July–August; and Molly Haskell, "Lucas–Spielberg: An *Ark* de Triomphe," *Playgirl,* September.

13. "ECSTASY AND GRIEF" (PP. 323–58)

Sources on *E.T. The Extra-Terrestrial* (working titles: *E.T. and Me, A Boy's Life)* include the author's interviews with Allen Daviau and John Veitch; the 1996 documentary *The Making of "E.T. The Extra-Terrestrial,"* including footage shot by John Toll during the film's production in 1981 (the laserdisc also includes outtakes from the film); Melissa Mathison's shooting script, *A Boy's Life,* August 21, 1981; and articles in *American Cinematographer,* January 1983: George E. Turner, "Steven Spielberg and *E.T. The Extra-Terrestrial";* Lloyd Kent, "The Photography of *E.T.";* and Allen D. Lowell, "Production Design for *E.T."* Book tie-ins include William Kotzwinkle, *ET: The Extra-Terrestrial in His Adventures on Earth,* Berkley Books, 1982 (novelization); Kotzwinkle, based on the screenplay by Mathison, *E.T.—The Extra-Terrestrial Storybook,* G. P. Putnam's Sons, 1982; Spielberg (introduction), *Letters to E.T.,* G. P. Putnam's Sons, 1983; and Kotzwinkle, based on a story by Spielberg, *E.T.: The Book of the Green Planet,* Berkley Books, 1985. The Spielberg-Mathison treatment "E.T. II: Nocturnal Fears" is discussed in John M. Wilson, "E.T. Returns to Test His Midas Touch," *LAT,* June 16, 1985.

Information on the *Night Skies* project is from Veitch; Crawley; and Steven Ginsberg, "Col Plans 20 Features for Year," *DV,* April 21, 1980. Sources on Mathison include "Production Notes" for *E.T.,* Universal, 1982; Philip Wuntch, "Spielberg Isn't All There Is to *E.T.," LAHE,* July 12, 1982; Andrew Epstein, "Melissa Mathison: The Hands of *E.T.," LAT,* July 24, 1982; Deborah Caulfield, *"E.T.* Author Mathison on *E.T.," LAT,* March 23, 1983; David Robb, *"E.T.* Scripter Awarded 5% of Merchandising," *DV,* March 1, 1989; and Bruce Ramer, "Credit on Creation of *E.T."* (letter to the editor), *DV,* March 6, 1989. Spielberg's childhood wish that "strange creatures" would change his life was related to Roger Ebert, *"E.T.:* The Second Coming," *Movieline,* August 9–15, 1985; his wish for a best friend was recalled in "Personal Glimpses," *Reader's Digest,* November 1982. Donald Richie's comments on *Shane* are from his book *George Stevens: An American Romantic*, Museum of Modern Art, 1970. Allegations that *E.T.* was plagiarized were reported in 1983 by the *LAT*'s Caulfield in "Satyajit Ray Questions *E.T.* Origins," March 16; "Authorship Claim Stirs the Studios," March 18; and *"E.T.* Author Mathison on *E.T.*"; and on June 23 in "Judge Rules *E.T.* Not an Infringement" *(DV)* and "Spielberg, Universal win *E.T.* lawsuit" *(HR)*.

Information on Carlo Rambaldi is from "Creating a Creature," *Time*, May 31, 1982; Jane Hartnell, "A Wide-Eyed Wonder: The Creation of a Lovable Alien," *Marquee*, July–August 1982; Callo, "Director Steven Spielberg Takes the Wraps Off E.T., Revealing His Secrets at Last"; Ed Naha, "Inside E.T.," *Starlog*, October 1982; and Carlo Rambaldi Enterprises, *"E.T.* Clarification" (advertisement), *DV*, February 11, 1983.

Sources on Columbia's rejection of *E.T. and Me* include Veitch and Caulfield, *"E.T.* Gossip: The One That Got Away?" Information on Spielberg's *Reel to Reel* project is from the author's interview with Howard Kazanjian and Army Archerd's column, *DV*, April 18, 1983.

The cover title *A Boy's Life* was mentioned in Archerd columns, *DV*, June 12, July 14, and September 21, 1981; "Fourth encounters?" *LAHE*, July 13, 1981; and "Spielberg's Secret Film," *Rolling Stone*, November 12, 1981. The misleading description of the film was published in *Motion Picture Product Digest*, December 2, 1981. The secrecy surrounding the production also was reported in "Raiders of the Boss' Art," *People*, December 21, 1981, and Richard Turner, "Steven Spielberg: His Stories Aren't Amazing Enough . . . Yet," *TV Guide*, August 2, 1986. Information on the production cost is from Daviau and from Charles Michener and Katrine Ames, "A Summer Double Punch," *Newsweek*, May 31, 1982. Audience figures and the length of the original run are from Universal's "Production Notes" for the 1985 reissue. Sid Sheinberg commented on the Houston preview in Latham, "MCA's Bad Cop Shoots from the Hip"; Ebert's description of the Cannes premiere is from *"E.T.:* The Second Coming."

The White House, United Nations, and royal benefit premiere showings were reported (1982) in "E.T. Phone (First) Home?" *LAHE*, June 25; Jeff Silverman, "Spaced Out . . ." *LAHE*, June 30; *"E.T.* Goes to the U.N.," *NYT*, September 16; *HR* item, November 4; and in February 1983, "U.N. Finds *E.T.* O.K.," *The Twilight Zone Magazine*. Spielberg's comments on the Reagans' reactions are from Callo, "Director Steven Spielberg Takes the Wraps Off E.T. . . ." The *Rolling Stone* cover story is "A Star Is Born," July 22, 1982. Spielberg's protest, in the form of a "Letter from E.T.: Don't Portray Me Glorifying Vice," *LAT*, June 23, 1985, was in response to the June 16 cover of the *LAT* Calendar section; Charles Champlin wrote "Our Response: The Joke That Turned Out to Be on Us," June 23.

Reviews and commentary (1982) include Millar, *E.T.—You're More Than a Movie Star*; Stanley Kauffmann, "The Gospel According to St. Steven," *The New Republic*, July 5; Michael Sragow, "Extra-terrestrial Perception," *Rolling Stone*, July 8; George F. Will, "Well, *I* Don't Love You, E.T.," *Newsweek*, July 19; William Deerfield, "Is *E.T.* a Religious Parable?," letter to *NYT*, August 15; and Andrew Sarris, "Is There Life After *E.T.?*" *The Village Voice*, September 21. The *Time* profile is Corliss, "Steve's Summer Magic"; the bumping of Spielberg from the cover was reported by John A. Meyers, "A Letter from the Publisher," *Time*, July 15, 1985 (the issue that finally featured Spielberg on its cover). Universal's Christmas 1982 ad for *E.T.* appeared in *NYT*. Jimmy Swaggart's denunciation of *E.T.* was reported in Bill Quinn, "E.T., Phone Hell," *L.A. Weekly*, November 8–14, 1985. Spielberg's comment on *E.T.* 's religious overtones is from Crist, *Take 22*.

Information on *E.T.* merchandising and tie-ins (1982) is from Stephen J. Sansweet, "MCA Inc. Expects *E.T.* Merchandise to Outsell the Movie," *Wall Street Journal*, July 19; David Van Biema, "Life Is Sweet for Jack Dowd as Spielberg's Hit Film Has *E.T.* Lovers Picking Up the (Reese's) Pieces," *People*, July 26; Bernice Kanner, "The Selling of *E.T.*,"

New York, August 9; "MCA Ties 43 Merchandisers to *E.T.* Windfall; Women's Undies?" *Variety,* August 11; and "Start Your Christmas Shopping Here" (Universal Studios advertisement for E.T. Earth Center), *LAT,* December 3; see also, "Universal Quietly Shutters $1 Mil *E.T.* Facility," *DV,* January 27, 1983; Wilson, "E.T. Returns to Test His Midas Touch"; and "U Tours' E.T. Stops with Spielberg Aboard," *DV,* June 3, 1991. Michael Ventura's comments are from "Steven Spielberg: the Vision and the Nightmare," *L.A. Weekly,* June 1–7, 1984.

Spielberg's earnings from the film were reported in "Spielberg's Creativity," *NYT,* December 25, 1982; Callo gave the figure at $1 million per day in "Director Steven Spielberg Takes the Wraps Off E.T. . . ." Spielberg's 1982 real estate purchases were reported in *"Phone Home?* How Can You Phone Home When It's Not Built Yet?" *LAHE,* October 1; *LAHE* item, October 30; and *HR* items, November 3 and 17. "Quelle Barn" was described in Kurt Andersen, "Architecture: Gwathmey Siegel & Associates: Steven Spielberg and Amy Irving's East Hampton Residence," *Architectural Digest,* May 1988; see also Suzanne Stephens, "Architecture: Gwathmey Siegel: Steven Spielberg's Guesthouse in East Hampton," *Architectural Digest,* November 1994. Spielberg's 1982 purchase of a sled from *Citizen Kane* was reported in "Spielberg Acquires Original 'Rosebud' Sled," *DV,* June 11; Caulfield, "Citizen Spielberg," *LAT,* June 11; and "Citizen Spielberg's Purchase," *NYT,* June 13.

Sources on *Poltergeist* include the author's interviews with David Giler and Bob Gale; Callo, "Steven Spielberg's Musings on *Poltergeist"*; and the 1982 MGM/UA documentary *The Making of "Poltergeist,"* directed by Frank Marshall. The screenplay, n.d., by Spielberg, Michael Grais, and Mark Victor, based on Spielberg's story, was novelized by James Kahn, Warner Books, 1982. Richard B. Matheson's comments on "Little Girl Lost" are from his interview with the author and from Zicree, *The "Twilight Zone" Companion.* Spielberg commented on *The Texas Chain Saw Massacre* and the genesis of *Poltergeist* in MGM's 1982 *Poltergeist* "Production Notes" and press release, "Steven Spielberg Takes Terror to the Suburbs in MGM's *Poltergeist."*

Articles on the film and the authorship controversy between Spielberg and Tobe Hooper include (1981): Jeff Silverman, "Well, You Don't Expect *Every* Spirit to Just Sit in the Background Quietly . . . ," *LAHE,* June 2, and "Those Noisy Spirits Never Rest," *LAHE,* June 5; and in 1982, Gregg Kilday, "Hooper's Vision of the Otherworld,"*LAHE,* May 14; Dale Pollock, *"Poltergeist:* Whose Film Is It?" *LAT,* May 24; Aljean Harmetz, "Film Rating System Under New Fire," *NYT,* June 2; Army Archerd column, *DV,* June 3; "DGA Looking into *Poltergeist* But Is Not Saying Why," *DV,* June 15; Jack Searles, "Hooper Gets Some Recognition," *LAHE,* June 19; and Jim Harwood, "Hooper Awarded 15G Damages for 'Slight'; Confirm Spielberg Spat," *Variety,* June 23. MGM's advertisement featuring Spielberg over Hooper is in the pressbook for the film; the studio's ad apologizing to Hooper about the trailer is from *HR,* July 9, 1982; Spielberg's June 2, 1982, letter to Hooper was published as an ad in *Variety* on June 9. Information on the cost of the film and the shooting dates is from (1981): Army Archerd column, *DV,* May 8; "Hollywood Soundtrack," *Variety,* August 12; and Roderick Mann, "A Scene Seen Leads to *Poltergeist* Role," *LAT,* August 13; and from Pollock, *"Poltergeist:* Whose Film Is It?" Reviews (1982) include David Ehrenstein, "The Hollow Horror of Spielberg's *Poltergeist,"* *L.A. Reader,* June 4; and Pauline Kael, "The Pure and the Impure," *The New Yorker,* June 14.

Information on *Gremlins* is from the author's interviews with Joe Dante and Michael Finnell; an interview with Dante in Maitland McDonagh, *Filmmaking on the Fringe: The Good, The Bad, and the Deviant Directors,* Citadel Press, 1995; David Chute, "Dante's Inferno," *Film Comment,* June 1984; and David Ansen, "Little Toyshop of Horrors," *Newsweek,* June 18, 1984. Spielberg's comment about helping younger filmmakers is from David Blum, "Steven Spielberg and the Dread Hollywood Backlash," *New York,* March 24, 1986.

The author interviewed the following people who worked on *Twilight Zone—The Movie:* Dante, Daviau, Jon Davison, Finnell, John Landis, and Richard B. Matheson. The production, the fatal 1982 accident, the investigation, and the trial were chronicled in two 1988 books: Farber and Green, *Outrageous Conduct: Art, Ego, and the "Twilight Zone" Case,* and Ron LaBrecque, *Special Effects: Disaster at "Twilight Zone": The Tragedy and the Trial.* Farber and Green also published three articles in the August 28, 1988, *LAT:* "Trapped in the Twilight Zone," "Trials of the Prosecution," and "The Forgotten Man." The text of Spielberg's December 1, 1982, letter to the National Transportation Safety Board was printed in sources including David Robb, "Spielberg Denies Presence at Fatal *Twilight* Crash," *DV,* December 10, 1982; "Spielberg Denies He Was at *Twilight* Chopper Crash Scene," *Variety,* December 15, 1982; and the book by Farber and Green. Harland W. Braun's seven-page letter to Gilbert Garcetti, chief deputy district attorney of Los Angeles County, is dated November 20, 1985.

Additional information on the origin of *Twilight Zone—The Movie* is from Engel, *Rod Serling: The Dreams and Nightmares of Life in the Twilight Zone;* Sander, *Serling: The Rise and Twilight of Television's Last Angry Man;* Zicree, *The Twilight Zone Companion* (second edition); Jim Robbins, "Spielberg Re-Enters *Twilight Zone,"* DV, May 25, 1982; Serling, "Notes for a *Twilight Zone* Movie," *The Twilight Zone Magazine,* April 1983; and Robert Martin, "From Down Under to '20,000 Feet'" (George Miller interview), *The Twilight Zone Magazine,* June 1983. Robert Bloch's novelization of the film was published in 1983 by Warner Books. Before the accident, Paul M. Sammon observed the filming of Landis's Vic Morrow segment for his article "On the Set of *Twilight Zone,"* *The Twilight Zone Magazine,* October 1983; the same issue contains Sammon's "TZ Interview: John Landis." With Don Shay, Sammon wrote about the film's special effects in "Shadow and Substance," *Cinefex,* October 1983.

Articles on the filming and its aftermath also include (1982): Jerry Belcher and Charles P. Wallace, "Vic Morrow, 2 Children Die in Film Accident," *LAT,* July 24; Lennie La Guire and Andy Furillo, "Death on the *Twilight Zone* Set," *LAHE,* July 24; Army Archerd columns, *DV,* November 18 and December 6; Robb, "D.A. Wants Crash Re-Creation," *DV,* November 23; Robb, "Spielberg Again in *Zone* Focus," *DV,* November 30; Furillo, *"Twilight Zone* Story Revealed," *LAHE,* December 1; Dale Pollock, *"Twilight Zone* Allegations Denied," *LAT,* December 2; Furillo, "Spielberg Says He Wasn't on *Twilight* Set," *LAHE,* December 11; "Director Denies Presence at Fatal Movie Crash," *NYT,* December 12;

And (1983): Furillo, "Warners: Child *Twilight* Victim 'Assumed the Risk,'" *LAHE,* May 13; Furillo, "Are *Twilight Zone* Crew members on a Blacklist?" *LAHE,* August 7; and Robb, *"Twilight Zone* Witness Is Still 'Missing,'" *DV,* December 16; (1984): Robb, "Welder's Hood Impairs Sight of *Zone* Spec-Effects Man," *DV,* January 25; and Randall Sullivan, "Death in the Twilight Zone," *Rolling Stone,* June 21; (1985): Robert W. Stewart, "Attorney Pressed on *Twilight Zone* Allegations," *LAT,* November 1; Nancy Hill-Holtzman and Furillo, "Spielberg Dragged into *Twilight Zone* Case," *LAHE,* November 1; "Deputy DA Says Spielberg Not Tied to *Twilight Zone,"* *LAHE,* November 2; Stewart, "Movie Deaths —Spielberg 'Not Involved,'" *LAT,* November 3; Robb, "Former *Zone* Prosecutor Denies Spielberg 'Conspiracy' Involvement," *DV,* November 4; and Stewart, "Prosecutors Accused of Curbing *Twilight* Probe," *LAT,* November 21;

And (1986): Paul Feldman and Bill Farr, "Witness in Film Deaths Eludes D.A.," *LAT,* July 10; Furillo, "Technician Tells Role in Fatal Copter Scene," *LAHE,* December 2; Furillo, *"Twilight* Witness Surprises Defense," *LAHE,* December 3; Feldman, "Fired Mortars Without Watching Copter, *Twilight* Aide Says," *LAT,* December 3; and "Witness Says He Approved Explosion in Film," *NYT,* December 3; (1987): Feldman, "Landis Admits Hiring Children Illegally in Filming Fatal Scene," *LAT,* February 19; Cynthia Gorney, "Risk and Reality: Hollywood on Trial," *Washington Post,* March 18; AP, *"Twilight Zone*

Tragedy Ups H'wood Concern for Safety," *HR*, May 5; Kathleen A. Hughes, *"Twilight Zone* Case, Nearing a Close, Has Made Film Makers More Cautious," *Wall Street Journal*, May 12; Caulfield and Michael Cieply, *"Twilight* Aftermath: It's Caution on the Movie Set," *LAT*, May 20; Terry Pristin, "Ethnically Diverse *Twilight* Jury Came Together on Very First Ballot," *LAT*, May 30; Feldman, "Outraged: Landis Relieved but Calls Prosecution Dishonest," *LAT*, June 2; and Gay Jervey, "Misfire in the Twilight Zone," *The American Lawyer*, December;

And (1988): Robb, "Landis, Allingham, Cohn Cited for *Zone* Conduct," *DV*, January 19; Lea Purwin D'Agostino, "Twilight Zone," and Gary Kesselman, "Twilight Zone II" (letters to the editor), *The American Lawyer*, April; (1990): Sean Mitchell, *"Twilight Zone:* A Word from the Producer," *LAT*, July 18; and (1992): Kathleen O'Steen, "Danger 'Zone' Still Exists, Film Pros Say" and *"Zone* testimony takes its toll," *DV*, July 23.

Reviews of *Twilight Zone—The Movie* (1983) include Richard Corliss, "Bad Dreams," *Time*, June 20; Vincent Canby, *"Twilight Zone* Is Adapted to the Big Screen," *NYT*, June 24; David Ansen, "Twilight's Last Gleaming," *Newsweek*, June 27; and J. Hoberman, "Zoned Again," *The Village Voice*, July 5. Spielberg reflected on the accident and on the 1983 Academy Awards in Pollock, "Spielberg Philosophical over *E.T.* Oscar Defeat," *LAT*, April 13, 1983. The comments by Spielberg and Richard Attenborough about the DGA Awards are from Dougan, *The Actors' Director: Richard Attenborough Behind the Camera*.

The author interviewed the following people involved in the filming of *Indiana Jones and the Temple of Doom* (working title: *Indiana Jones and the Temple of Death)*: Willard Huyck, Gloria Katz, Louis B. Race, and David Tomblin. The screenplay by Huyck and Katz, from a story by George Lucas, was published in 1995 by O.S.P. Publishing as part of the *Premiere* magazine series The Movie Script Library. An uncredited draft of the screenplay is dated March 10, 1983. In 1984, a novelization by James Kahn was published by Ballantine, and a children's story adaptation by Les Martin was published by Random House.

Other sources on the filming include Champlin, *George Lucas: The Creative Impulse;* Pollock, "Spielberg Gets Place to Settle Down," *LAT*, May 21, 1984; Hluchy and MacKay, "Spielberg's Magic Screen"; Elkins, "Steven Spielberg on *Indiana Jones and the Temple of Doom"*; Thomas McKelvey Cleaver, "Frank Marshall Adventuring Alongside *Indiana Jones and the Temple of Doom,"* *Starlog*, June 1984; George E. Turner, "Visual Effects for *Indiana Jones and the Temple of Doom,"* *American Cinematographer*, July 1984; and Adam Pirani, "Robert Watts: Secrets of the *Temple of Doom,"* *Starlog*, May 1985.

Sources on the controversy over the film's violence and its PG rating (and over the PG rating for *Gremlins)* include the author's interviews with Huyck, Katz, Tomblin, and Dante; Caulfield, "Spielberg Is Upset; So Is the Rating," *LAT*, May 7, 1982; Pollock, "Spielberg Gets Place to Settle Down"; Chute; Harmetz, "Hollywood Plans New Rating to Protect Children Under 13," *NYT*, June 20, 1984; "Revising the Rating System," *Newsweek*, July 2, 1984; and Jacqueline R. Smetak, "Steven Spielberg: Gore, Guts, and PG-13," *Journal of Popular Film & Television*, Spring 1986. Other commentary on *Temple of Doom* includes Ralph Novak's review in *People*, June 4, and Henry Sheehan's essay "The Panning of Steven Spielberg." Bruno Bettelheim's comments on fairy tales are from his book *The Uses of Enchantment*, Knopf, 1976.

14. "ADULT TRUTHS" (PP. 359-78)

Sources on Kate Capshaw include: Segrave, *Up and Coming Actresses;* Vance Muse, *We Bombed in Burbank: A Joyride to Prime Time*, Addison-Wesley, 1994; Roderick Mann, "Kate Capshaw Gets Plum Role in *Indiana Jones,"* *LAT*, March 29, 1983; 1984 articles by Michael J. Bandler, "Kate Capshaw," *Moviegoer*, June; Nancy Griffin, "Jungle Chums: Indy and Willie in a Race with Doom," *Life*, June; Thomas McKelvey Cleaver,

"Meet Kate Capshaw: Companion in High Adventure," *Starlog,* June; Phoebe Sherman, "Kate Who?" *Marquee,* June–July; Mann, "Capshaw: Her Career Is Not Constricting," *LAT,* June 10; Pat H. Broeske, "Kate Capshaw: *Indiana Jones* Heroine Lights the Screen with Four New Films," *Drama-Logue,* June 14–20; Jeff Jarvis, "Who's That Woman in the Summer's Smash Movie With What's-His-Name? It's Newcomer Kate Capshaw," *People,* July 2 (which quotes Gene Siskel on her role in *Indiana Jones and the Temple of Doom);* Lois Draegin, "Beginner's Guts," *Self,* August; and Stephen Farber, "Caps Off to Capshaw," *Cosmopolitan,* October; also, Donald Chase, "Kate Capshaw's 'Comeback,' " *Movieline,* February 7–13, 1986; Salamon, "The Long Voyage Home"; Schiff; Melina Gerosa, "Kate Capshaw: Loving Steven," *Ladies' Home Journal,* October 1994; Johanna Schneller, "Kate Capshaw," *US,* February 1996; and Cindy Pearlman, "My Funny Valentine," *Premiere,* March 1996. Leo Rosten's *The Joys of Yiddish* was published in 1968 by McGraw-Hill.

Sources on Amy Irving's reunion with Spielberg, their son Max, and their marriage include Barbara Walz and Jill Barber, *Starring Mothers: 30 Portraits of Accomplished Women,* Doubleday, 1987; Hirschberg; "Amy Irving and Steven Spielberg Collaborate on a Little Gremlin," *People,* November 19, 1984; Black; "Filmmaker Steven Spielberg and Actress Amy Irving Exchange Vows at Private Ceremony in Santa Fe, N.M." (press release), Warner Bros., November 1985; "Spielberg, Irving Marry," *Haddonfield (N.J.) Courier-Post,* November 1985; Roger Ebert, "Director in Focus: Spielberg," *Movieline,* December 27, 1985–January 2, 1986; "Amy Irving and Max," *Redbook,* August 1986; Jahr; and Schiff. The birth of Max Samuel Spielberg was reported in Gregg Kilday, "It's a Boy!" *LAHE,* June 14, 1985; Spielberg called him "my best production yet" in Eric Sherman, "What's Hot: Couples," *Ladies' Home Journal,* February 1988. Their Pacific Palisades home was described by *Architectural Digest* in Harry Hurt III, *"Architectural Digest* Visits: Steven Spielberg and Amy Irving," May 1989, and Pilar Viladas, "Steven Spielberg: The Director Expands His Horizons in Pacific Palisades," April 1994. Information on Spielberg and *Yentl* is from Shaun Considine, *Barbra Streisand: The Woman, the Myth, the Music,* Delacorte, 1985; Randall Riese, *Her Name Is Barbra,* Birch Lane Press, 1993; and James Spada, *Streisand: Her Life,* Crown, 1995.

Information on the 1984 formation of Amblin Entertainment and on Spielberg's complex at Universal is from Dale Pollock, "Spielberg Gets Place to Settle Down," *LAT,* May 21, 1984; Jack Kroll and David T. Friendly, "The Wizard of Wonderland," *Newsweek,* June 4, 1984; "Terrestrial Sphere: Steven Spielberg's Hollywood Headquarters," *Architectural Digest,* May 1985; and Nancy Griffin and Ann Bayer, "Spielberg: Husband, Father and Hitmaker," *Life,* May 1986. For sources on Steve Ross, see notes for chapter 15.

The Color Purple is based on the novel by Alice Walker, Washington Square Press, 1983. Menno Meyjes's third-draft shooting script was dated May 31, 1985, and titled *Moon Song.* The author interviewed Allen Daviau and Margaret Avery. Walker commented on the film in her 1996 book *The Same River Twice: Honoring the Difficult,* Charles Scribner's Sons, 1996 (which includes her 1984 journal entry; her unused 1984 screenplay adaptation, *Watch For Me in the Sunset, or The Color Purple;* and her July 21, 1989, letter to Spielberg); and in her *Ms.* articles "Finding Celie's Voice," December 1985, and "In the Closet of the Soul," November 1986. She was interviewed in 1985 by William Goldstein, "Alice Walker on the Set of *The Color Purple," Publishers Weekly,* September 6; and Mona Gable, "Author Alice Walker Discusses *The Color Purple," Wall Street Journal,* December 19. Walker was quoted on *E.T.* in Karen Jaehne, "The Final Word," *Cineaste,* 15, No. 1, 1986.

Reports on the filming of *The Color Purple* include Susan Dworkin, "The Strange and Wonderful Story of the Making of *The Color Purple," Ms.,* December 1985; Elena Featherston, "The Making of *The Color Purple," San Francisco Focus,* December 1985; Collins, "Spielberg Films *The Color Purple";* and February 1986 *American Cinematogra-*

pher articles by George Turner, "Spielberg Makes 'All Too Human' Story," and Al Harrell, "The Look of *The Color Purple."* Also quoted is Jean Oppenheimer's 1991 interview with Daviau. Meyjes was interviewed by Marie Saxon Silverman, "Dutch Scripter Found Universality of People Key to *Purple* Project," *Variety,* March 12, 1986. Additional data on the filming are from "Production Information," Warner Bros., 1985.

Sources on Whoopi Goldberg include Philip Wuntch, "Celebrity Status Makes Whoopi a Little Uneasy," *Chicago Tribune,* December 21, 1985; "Whoopi Goldberg," *People,* December 23, 1985; Cathleen McGuigan, "Whoopee for Whoopi," *Newsweek,* December 30, 1985; Carinthia West, "Purple Reign," *US,* January 13, 1986; Steve Erickson, "Whoopi Goldberg," *Rolling Stone,* May 8, 1986, and David Rensin, *"Playboy* Interview: Whoopi Goldberg," June 1987. Sources on Oprah Winfrey include her syndicated TV show *Oprah,* May 22, 1996, on which Spielberg appeared and she read from her 1985 journal; Robert Waldron, *Oprah!,* St. Martin's Press, 1987; "Yes, Sir, Steven . . . " *Chicago Tribune,* September 5, 1985; Jane Galbraith, "Winfrey Tickled Pink by *Purple* Role," *DV,* January 31, 1986; Bruce Cook, "Oprah Winfrey Enjoying Sweet Success," *LADN,* March 17, 1986; and Gary Ballard, "Oprah Winfrey," *Drama-Logue,* March 20–26, 1986. See also (1986): Jack Mathews, "3 *Color Purple* Actresses Talk About Its Impact," *LAT,* January 31, and Nan Robertson, "Actresses' Varied Roads to *The Color Purple," NYT,* February 13.

Articles on the controversy over the film include (1985): Jeffrey Ressner, "Media Monitoring Group to Protest *Color Purple* Pic," *HR,* November 1; Emily Gibson, "Black Like She," *L.A. Weekly,* November 1; "Black Marchers Protest Film," *LAHE,* November 10; Mathews, "Some Blacks Critical of Spielberg's *Purple," LAT,* December 20; and Charles Champlin, "Spielberg's Primary 'Colors,' " *LAT,* December 28; and in 1986: "Does *Purple* Hate Men?" *Chicago Tribune,* January 5; E. R. Shipp, "Blacks in Heated Debate over *The Color Purple," NYT,* January 27; Lynn Norment, *"The Color Purple," Ebony,* February; Jacqueline Trescott, "The Passions over *Purple," Washington Post,* February 5; Legrand H. Clegg II, "Bad Black Roles in *Purple,"* letter to *LAT,* February 16; and John Stark, "Seeing Red Over *Purple," People,* March 10.

Reviews (1985) include Peter Rainer, "One Wonders Why Spielberg Wanted to Do *Color Purple," LAHE,* December 18; John Powers, "Sister, Where Art Thou?" *L.A. Weekly,* December 20; Rita Kempley, *"Purple:* Making Whoopi a Star," *Washington Post,* December 20; Siskel, *"Color Purple*—Powerful, Daring, Sweetly Uplifting," *Chicago Tribune,* December 20; Richard Corliss, "The Three Faces of Steve," *Time,* December 23; J. Hoberman, "Color Me Purple," *The Village Voice,* December 24; David Ansen, "We Shall Overcome," *Newsweek,* December 30; and Pauline Kael, "Sacred Monsters," *The New Yorker,* December 30. The description of the film as *"Close Encounters with the Third World"* is from "The Color Spielberg," *LAHE,* December 12, 1985. Armond White's comments are from his essay "Toward a Theory of Spielberg History," *Film Comment,* March–April 1994. The critical reception of *The Color Purple* was analyzed in 1985 articles by Pat H. Broeske and John M. Wilson, "Seeing Red Over *Purple," LAT,* December 22; Martin Grove, "Hollywood Report," *HR,* December 26; and Broeske, "Color *Purple* Different Shades," *LAT,* December 29; information on top-ten lists is from Pat McGilligan and Mark Rowland, "Critics Went Gunning for Stallone in '85," *LAT,* January 19, 1986.

Articles on Spielberg's omission from the 1986 Academy Award directing nominations, and his subsequent Directors Guild of America award, include Army Archerd column, *DV,* February 6; Mathews, "Spielberg Upstages Oscar Race," *LAT,* February 7; Kroll, "The Snubbing of Spielberg," *Newsweek,* February 17; letters to the editor, *DV,* by Andre de Toth, February 18, and Sy Gomberg, February 19; "Seeing Red Over *Purple";* David T. Friendly, "Spielberg's Revenge—Hollywood Style," *LAT,* March 10; Desmond Ryan, "Why Does Oscar Keep Slighting Spielberg?" *Philadelphia Inquirer,* March 26;

"Spielberg Speaks Out on Acad's *Color* Snub," *DV,* April 1; and Perry. Spielberg also commented in 1996 on *Oprah.* Additional articles on the film's treatment by the Academy include (March 26, 1986): Bruce Cook, "Oscar Snub of *Purple* Called Bias," *LADN;* "Academy Denies NAACP Charges Re *Color Purple,"* *DV;* and "NAACP Files Protest re *Purple* Shutout," *HR;* and March 27: Friendly, "Academy Hits Racism Accusation," *LAT;* David Colker, "Black Coalition Says It's Glad *Color Purple* Didn't Win Oscar," *LAHE;* and Yardena Arar, "NAACP Defends *Purple* Position," *LADN.*

15. "AN AWFULLY BIG ADVENTURE" (PP. 379–413)

Spielberg discussed fatherhood in a June 6, 1985, interview with Gene Shalit on *Today* (NBC-TV), quoted in that day's *LAHE* item by Gregg Kilday, "He Deserves a Break Today"; Andrews; and *The Barbara Walters Special* (1994). Amy Irving called him "a great father" in "Amy Irving and Max."

Spielberg was described as a "one-man entertainment conglomerate" by Salamon in "Maker of Hit After Hit, Steven Spielberg Is Also a Conglomerate." Other information is from Klastorin and Hibbin, *"Back to the Future": The Official Book of the Complete Movie Trilogy;* Skow; Chute; Lee Goldberg, "Bob Zemeckis: It's a Wonderful Time!" *Starlog,* October 1985; Blum, "Steven Spielberg and the Dread Hollywood Backlash"; Kim Masters, "The Futures Back to Back," *Premiere,* December 1989; and Andrews. A. D. Murphy's caveat about Spielberg's producing was expressed to the author in the early 1980s. Spielberg's Thalberg Award (1987) was reported in Jack Mathews, "Academy Finally Taps Spielberg," *LAT,* February 9, and Aljean Harmetz, "Steven Spielberg Wins Movies' Thalberg Award," *NYT,* March 31. Pauline Kael's review of *Young Sherlock Holmes,* "Lasso and Peashooter," appeared in *The New Yorker,* January 27, 1986.

Spielberg recalled his meeting with John Ford in Lane, " 'I Want Gross.' " Information on Spielberg's lunch with Orson Welles is from the author's interview with Gary Graver and from Jonathan Rosenbaum, "Afterword" to Welles, *The Cradle Will Rock: An Original Screenplay,* ed. by James Pepper, Santa Teresa Press, 1994; the comments by Spielberg and Welles on Spielberg's purchase of a Rosebud sled are quoted in Frank Brady, *Citizen Welles: A Biography of Orson Welles,* Charles Scribner's Sons, 1989.

Information on Spielberg's relationship with Steve Ross is from Connie Bruck, *Master of the Game: Steve Ross and the Creation of Time Warner,* Simon & Schuster, 1994, and "A Mogul's Farewell," *The New Yorker,* October 18, 1993; and from Roger Cohen, "A $78 Million Year: Steve Ross Defends His Paycheck," *NYT,* March 22, 1992. The Warner Bros. "Celebration of Tradition" party was covered by Joseph McBride in "Past, Present Converge on WB Lot," *DV,* June 4, 1990. Spielberg's involvement in *Strokes of Genius* (PBS) is described in "The Story Behind the Series," *The Dial,* May 1984.

Sources on Spielberg's TV series *Amazing Stories* include the author's interviews with Joe Dante, Bob Gale, Richard B. Matheson, Richard Christian Matheson, Peter Z. Orton, and Joan Darling; and articles including Leslie Bennetts, "Spielberg to Produce Adventure Series for NBC," *NYT,* July 31, 1984; Eric Mankin, "Spielberg to Return to TV with a Weekly Anthology," *LAHE,* July 31, 1984; "MCA, NBC Say Spielberg Will Produce TV Series," *Wall Street Journal,* July 31, 1984; Buck, "Spielberg: Raider of the Lost Art of Anthologies"; Morgan Gendel, "It Came from Beyond to NBC," *LAT,* July 21, 1985; Steve Pond, "Making Little Movies," *US,* September 23, 1985; Elvis Mitchell, "Amazing Anthologies," *Film Comment,* September–October 1985; Paul Bartel, "My Amazing Story," *American Film,* October 1985; Breskin; Michael Kaplan, "NBC's 800-Pound Turkey," *L.A. Reader,* January 10, 1986; Tom Carson, "Boy Wonder," *L.A. Weekly,* January 10, 1986; Blum; Aljean Harmetz, *"Amazing Stories* Tries New Tactics," *NYT,* June 2, 1986; and Turner, "Steven Spielberg: His Stories Aren't Amazing Enough . . . Yet." Sid Sheinberg reacted to Turner's article in Pat H. Broeske, "Amazing Story," *LAT,* August 10, 1986. Sources on David Lean's visit to the set of "Ghost Train" include Breskin and

Royal, *"Always:* An Interview with Steven Spielberg." Kael's comment on *Amazing Stories* is from Blum.

Sources on *Empire of the Sun* include the author's interviews with Tom Stoppard, Allen Daviau, David Tomblin, David Bale (father of actor Christian Bale), and Gale; additional information is from Jean Oppenheimer's 1991 interview with Daviau. The film is based on the novel by J. G. Ballard, Simon & Schuster, 1984. Ballard described the filming in his sequel, *The Kindness of Women,* HarperCollins, London, 1991. The fourth-draft shooting script by Tom Stoppard (and Menno Meyjes, who did not receive screen credit) is dated February 2, 1987. Ballard talked about his childhood in *The China Odyssey: "Empire of the Sun," a Film by Steven Spielberg,* Les Mayfield's documentary about the making of the film (Warner Bros., CBS-TV, 1987); and in "From Shanghai to Shepperton," an interview in *Foundation,* No. 24, February 1982, reprinted in V. Vale and Andrea Juno, eds., *Re/Search: J. G. Ballard,* Re/Search Publications, 1984.

Information on Spielberg's involvement in the restoration of *Lawrence of Arabia* is from Morris and Raskin, *"Lawrence of Arabia": The 30th Anniversary Pictorial History*. Spielberg's comment on filmmakers' moral rights is from David Robb, "Battle over Berne Copyright Treaty Is Heating Up," *DV,* February 19, 1988; see also Robb, "Mr. Spielberg Goes to Washington," *DV,* November 18, 1987. Sources on David Lean's involvement with *Empire of the Sun* and Spielberg's with Lean's *Nostromo* project include the author's interviews with Daviau and Tomblin; Stephen M. Silverman, *David Lean,* Harry N. Abrams, 1989; Alain Silver and James Ursini, *David Lean and His Films,* Silman-James Press, 1992 (revised edition); and Kevin Brownlow, *David Lean: A Biography,* Richard Cohen Books (London) and St. Martin's Press (New York), 1996.

Articles on the filming of *Empire of the Sun* include Army Archerd's column, *DV,* February 15, 1985; Todd McCarthy, *"Sun* Rises on Bob Shapiro's Prod'n Sked," *DV,* July 26, 1985; "Shapiro, Amblin Option *Empire," HR,* May 2, 1986; James Greenberg, "Spielberg to Direct Amblin Film in China," *DV,* January 21, 1987; Charles Champlin, "New Day Dawns for *Sun* Writer Tom Stoppard," *LAT,* December 10, 1987; Dale Kutzera, *"Empire of the Sun*—an Exotic Journey," *American Cinematographer,* January 1988; Cathleen McGuigan, "Not Just Child's Play," *Newsweek,* February 22, 1988; Jeffrey Jolson-Colburn, *"Empire* Cinematographer Defends Spielberg," *HR,* March 3, 1988; "Theatrical Cinematography Noted by ASC, Academy," *American Cinematographer,* April 1988; and Nora Lee, "Reflections 4: Daviau," *American Cinematographer,* August 1988. Spielberg's comment on his airplane "fetish" is from Bob Strauss, *"Peter Pan* Takes a Flying Leap," *LADN,* December 8, 1991. Spielberg's comment to George Lucas on "films with kids" is from Champlin, *George Lucas: The Creative Impulse*.

Reviews (1987) include Sheila Benson, *"Empire of the Sun* Charts a Boy's Survival During War," *LAT,* December 9; Peter Rainer, "Spielberg's New *Empire," LAHE,* December 9; David Denby, "Empire Builders," *New York,* December 14; David Ansen, "A Childhood Lost to War," *Newsweek,* December 14; Andrew Sarris, "A Boy's Own Story," *The Village Voice,* December 15; J. Hoberman, *The Village Voice,* December 22; and Pauline Kael, "Religious Experiences," *The New Yorker,* December 28.

Spielberg talked about his psychotherapy in Pancol, "Steven Spielberg." His involvement with John Bradshaw was reported in Sally Ogle Davis, "Oh, Pablum!" *Los Angeles,* April 1992, and Stephen Farber and Marc Green, *Hollywood on the Couch,* Morrow, 1993.

Information on Spielberg's involvement in *Rain Man* is from sources including an interview with Ronald Bass in William Froug, *The New Screenwriter Looks at the New Screenwriter,* Silman-James Press, 1991; Anne Thompson, "Risky Business," *L.A. Weekly,* July 24, 1987; Mitchell Fink, "Spielberg Begs Off," *LAHE,* October 14, 1987; *LAT* item, November 17, 1987; Donald Chase, "On the Road with Hoffman and Cruise," *NYT,* December 11, 1988; Griffin, "Spielberg's Last Crusade"; and Royal, *"Always:* An Interview with Steven Spielberg." Royal reported on the development of *Schindler's List* in the 1980s; also see notes for chapter 16.

Sources on *Indiana Jones and the Last Crusade* include the author's interviews with Jeffrey Boam, David Tomblin, Gloria Katz, and Willard Huyck. The screenplay by Boam, from a story by George Lucas and Menno Meyjes, was published in 1995 by O.S.P. Publishing as part of *Premiere* magazine's series The Movie Script Library. Boam's third revised draft of the screenplay, titled *Indy III*, is dated March 1, 1988. In 1989, a novelization by Rob MacGregor was published by Ballantine and a children's adaptation by Les Martin was published by Random House. A documentary film, *Great Adventurers & Their Quests: "Indiana Jones and the Last Crusade,"* was directed by Les Mayfield and William Rus for Paramount and CBS-TV (1989). Additional information on the story and screenplay of *Last Crusade* is from sources including Champlin, *George Lucas: The Creative Impulse,* and (1989): Richard B. Woodward, "Meanwhile, Back at the Ranch," *NYT,* May 21; Richard Corliss, "What's Old Is Gold: A Triumph for *Indy 3,"* *Time,* May 29; and David Heuring, *"Indiana Jones and the Last Crusade," American Cinematographer,* June. Other 1989 articles include Philip Wuntch, "Actor Connery Feels Bond with New Film Image," *The Hartford Courant,* June 4; Richard Gold, "Door Left Ajar for *Indiana 4,"* *Variety,* June 5; and Ben Fong-Torres, "Indiana Jones' Final Adventure," *Stars and Stripes,* June 19. Reviews (1989) include *Mac.* (Joseph McBride), *DV,* May 19, and Henry Sheehan, *L.A. Reader,* June 2.

The Spielberg–Irving divorce was disclosed in "Spielberg, Irving Agree to Divorce," *HR,* April 25, 1989, and "Legal File," *LAT,* June 30, 1989. Spielberg's net worth of "well over $225 million" was reported in "The 400 Richest People in America," *Forbes,* October 26, 1987. Estimates of Irving's settlement were made in "Bermuda Shorts," *LAHE,* May 31, 1989 ($93 million), and "Steven Spielberg Finally Suffers a Big-Budget Flop— His Marriage," *People,* May 8, 1989 ($112.5 million). Amy's comment "I started my career . . ." is from "No Family Ties," *People,* April 3, 1989. Matthew Robbins discussed the marriage in Schiff. Rumors about Spielberg–Irving marital problems were printed in Cyndi Stivers, "Unswerving Irving," *US,* October 3, 1988; Liz Smith column, LAT, November 3, 1988; Jahr; "Morning Report," *LAT,* March 24, 1989; Mitchell Fink, "The Altar of Doom," *LAHE,* April 25, 1989; and "A Year of Rumors Becomes a Fact," *USA Today,* April 25, 1989. Their agreement to alternate work assignments was reported in Maureen Orth, "Amy Irving," *Vogue,* March 1988, and Leslie Bennetts, "Amy Irving," *Cosmopolitan,* November 1988. Amy also discussed her problems balancing career and marriage in Jahr and Patrick Pacheco, "The Amy Chronicles," *LAT,* April 17, 1994. Their Malibu house fire was reported in "Spielberg's Beach House Catches Fire," *LAHE,* July 25, 1988, and *Variety* item, August 3, 1988.

Kate Capshaw was linked to Spielberg in such articles as Fink's "The Spielberg Watch," *LAHE,* August 10, 1988, and "The Altar of Doom" (which also reported on denials of marital problems and a Spielberg–Capshaw romance). Capshaw recalled their 1989 London stay in Salamon, "The Long Voyage Home." Kate's adoption of Theo was reported in an *LAHE* item, May 17, 1989; Salamon reported the child's subsequent adoption by Spielberg. Information on the birth of Sasha Spielberg (1990) is from Army Archerd's column, *DV,* May 15, and "Born," *Time,* June 4. The Spielberg–Capshaw wedding (1991) was reported in "Close Encounter," *LAT,* October 14; "Spielberg–Capshaw," *HR,* October 14; Liz Smith column, *LAT,* October 15; "And Daddy Makes Three," *Newsweek,* October 28; and *People* item, October 28. Information on Amy's relationship with Bruno Barreto and on their son, Gabriel, is from Archerd's column, *DV,* April 25, 1989; Ann Trebbe, "Spielberg and Irving to Divorce," *USA Today,* April 25, 1989; "Cash Is Better," *LAHE,* August 31, 1989; Beth Kleid, "Crossing Motherhood," *LAT,* May 7, 1990; "Born," *Time,* May 21, 1990; Leslie Marshall, "Desert Bloom," *In Style,* January 1996; and Dotson Rader, " 'I Have a New Life,' " *Parade,* March 24, 1996. Spielberg's comment on the two worst times in his life was made on *The Barbara Walters Special* (1994). His 1989 comment on Amy is from Griffin, "Spielberg's Last Crusade."

The revised shooting script of *Always* by Jerry Belson and Ron Bass (based on the 1943 film *A Guy Named Joe*) is dated May 4, 1989; Bass did not receive screen credit (Diane Thomas also worked on the script without credit). Information on the film includes MGM's announcement of the project as *A Guy Named Joe, HR,* July 10, 1980; Army Archerd's column, *DV,* October 9, 1981; Robert Osborne, "Rambling Reporter," *HR,* February 1, 1985, and October 29, 1987; Joy Horowitz, "Development Hell," *American Film,* November 1987; "Rewrite of a Rewrite," *LAHE,* April 4, 1989; "Short Takes," *DV,* June 1, 1989; Charles Fleming, *"Always* on Time," *LAHE,* August 18, 1989; "Role Reversal," *People,* August 21, 1989; Christopher Perez, "A Close Encounter with Steven Spielberg," *The Village View,* December 22–28, 1989; and Steve Dollar, " 'Boy Wonder' Director of *Jaws* Grows Up," *Long Beach Press-Telegram,* December 23, 1989. Reviews and commentary include *Mac.* (Joseph McBride), *DV,* December 18, 1989; Henry Sheehan, "Spielberg: *Sometimes* Brilliant," *L.A. Reader,* January 5, 1990; David Denby, "Flying Low," *New York,* January 8, 1990; and Harvey R. Greenberg, M.D., "Spielberg on the Couch," *Movieline,* December 1991, reprinted in Greenberg's book *Screen Memories: Hollywood Cinema on the Psychoanalytic Couch,* Columbia University Press, 1993. Diane Thomas's death was reported in Leonard Greenwood, "Writer of *Romancing the Stone* Killed," *LAT,* October 23, 1985.

The screenplay of *Hook* by Jim V. Hart and Malia Scotch Marmo (and Carrie Fisher, uncredited), from a story by Hart and Nick Castle, is based on J. M. Barrie's play *Peter Pan* (1904) and his novels *The Little White Bird* (1902), *Peter Pan in Kensington Gardens* (1906), and *Peter and Wendy* (1911). Hart's first revised draft of the screenplay (June 21, 1990) is titled *Hook!: The Return of the Captain.* Two novelizations of the film, one by Terry Brooks and the other by Geary Gravel, were published by Ballantine Books, 1991. Sources on *Hook* include the author's interview with Mike Medavoy; "Production Information" (TriStar, 1991); and articles including (1991): Schruers, "Peter Pandemonium"; Ivor Davis, " 'I Won't Grow Up!' " *Los Angeles,* December; Graham Fuller, "Hook, Line, and Spielberg," *Interview,* December; Richard W. Stevenson, "Waiting to See If *Hook* Will Fly," *NYT,* December 7; Hilary De Vries, "A *Peter Pan* for the New-Age," *NYT,* December 8; Strauss, "Spielberg Panning for Gold in *Hook,"* *LADN,* December 8; Clifford Terry, "Spielberg in Neverland," *Chicago Tribune,* December 8; Davis, "Boys on the Never Never," *The Sunday Times* (London), December 8; Tom Provenzano, *"Hook:* Making It Fly," *Drama-Logue,* December 12–18; John Evan Frook and Joseph McBride, "Sony Crows, but Jury's Out on Whether *Hook* Will Fly," *DV,* December 13; Michael Church, "Dreams Flying High on the Never-Never," *London Observer,* December 15; McBride, *"Hook* Bow Fails to Wow," *DV,* December 16; David Lyman, "With *Hook,* It Was the Look," *Long Beach Press-Telegram,* December 17; Jeannie Park, "Ahoy! Neverland!" *People,* December 23; and (1992): Robert Hofler, "The Look of *Hook,"* *US,* January; Martin A. Grove, "Hollywood Report," *HR,* January 23; and John Calhoun, *"Hook," Theatre Crafts,* February. Reviews and commentary include Georgia Brown, "Hangin' with the Lost Boys," *The Village Voice,* December 17, 1991; Terrence Rafferty, "Fear of Flying," *The New Yorker,* December 30, 1991; and Sheehan, "The Panning of Steven Spielberg" and "Spielberg II."

16. MENSCH (PP. 414–48)

The epigraph is from Horstman, "Spielberg's Roots: Avondale Years Shaped *Schindler."* The birth of Sawyer Spielberg (1992) was reported in Army Archerd's column, *DV,* March 12; "A Boy for Spielbergs," *Long Beach Press-Telegram,* March 12; and *People* item, March 23. The birth of Destry Allyn Spielberg was reported in Claudia Puig, "Quick Takes," *LAT,* December 3, 1996, and Mikaela Spielberg's adoption in Casey Davidson,

"Monitor," *Entertainment Weekly,* April 12, 1996. Kate Capshaw's comments on the eclipse of her career are from Schiff; her edict about Spielberg's work schedule was reported by Bernard Weinraub and Geraldine Fabrikant in "A Hollywood Recipe: Vision, Wealth, Ego," *NYT,* October 16, 1994.

Jurassic Park is based on the novel by Michael Crichton, Knopf, 1990. The continuity script by David Koepp, based on adaptations by Crichton and Malia Scotch Marmo, is dated December 11, 1992 (Crichton and Koepp shared script credit onscreen). The making of the film was chronicled in Shay and Duncan, *The Making of "Jurassic Park";* the documentary *The Making of "Jurassic Park"* (Universal/Amblin/MCA Home Video, 1995, directed by John Schultz); the *Behind the Scenes of "Jurassic Park"* exhibit, Universal Studios Hollywood Tour, 1994; and the *Filmscapes* exhibit, Academy of Motion Picture Arts & Sciences, Beverly Hills, 1994. Koepp, production designer Rick Carter, and cinematographer Dean Cundey discussed the making of the film in the Academy's "Filmscapes" seminar on October 6, 1994. Information on dinosaurs is from John R. Horner and James Gorman, *Digging Dinosaurs,* and from Horner and Don Lessem, *The Complete* T. rex, Simon & Schuster, 1993.

Crichton recalled his story conference with Spielberg in "Across Time and Culture." Information on Crichton's *ER* screenplay and his first conversation with Spielberg about *Jurassic Park* is from Shay and Duncan, *The Making of "Jurassic Park,"* and Janine Pourroy, *Behind the Scenes at "ER,"* Ballantine, 1995. Sources on the sale of the *Jurassic Park* film rights include the author's interview with Joe Dante; and (1990), Andrea King, "4 Studio-Director Teams Bid $1.5 Mil for Crichton's *Park,"* *HR,* May 24; King, "Spielberg to Helm Dino Sci-Fier *Park* with Crichton Scripting," *HR,* May 25; Will Tusher, "U Pays $2 Mil for *Jurassic,"* *DV,* May 25; and Alan Citron, "Hollywood Agency Adds New Twist to Bidding on Story," *LAT,* May 25. Malia Scotch Marmo's screenplay rewrites were discussed in Shay and Duncan, *The Making of "Jurassic Park";* "The *Jurassic* Job," *New York,* March 2, 1992; and "Todd Graff and Malia Scotch Marmo," *On Writing,* No. 1, 1993. Crichton's sequel to *Jurassic Park, The Lost World,* was published by Knopf in 1995.

Additional articles on *Jurassic Park* include (1992): Christian Moerk, *"Jurassic* Looks Like an F/X Classic," *Variety,* September 7; Andy Marx, "Hawaiian Hurricane Shuts Down Prod'n on *Jurassic,"* *DV,* September 14; Donna Parker, "Storm Blows *Jurassic Park* to Costa Rica," *HR,* September 14; and Army Archerd column, *DV,* September 15; (1993): Matt Rothman, "Computer Effects Leap Ahead," *DV,* January 12; Don Lessem, ed., *Jurassic Park* Special Edition, *The Dino Times,* Spring; Richard Corliss, "Behind the Magic of *Jurassic Park,"* *Time,* April 26; Bob Fisher, *"Jurassic Park:* When Dinosaurs Rule the Box Office," *American Cinematographer,* June; Malcolm W. Browne, "Visiting *Jurassic Park* for Real," *NYT,* June 6; Sharon Begley, "Here Come the DNAsaurs," and David A. Kaplan, "Believe in Magic," *Newsweek,* June 14; Jody Duncan, "The Beauty in the Beasts," *Cinefex,* August; Ron Magid, "After *Jurassic Park,* Traditional Techniques May Become Fossils," *American Cinematographer,* December; and Rex Weiner, "SSFX (Special Spielberg Effects)," *DV,* December 7; also, Rod Bennett, *"Jurassic Park* and the Death of Stop-Motion Animation," *Wonder,* Winter 1994–95. Information on Spielberg's satellite hookup in Poland (1993) is from Matt Rothman, "ILM Beams F/X to Spielberg in Poland," *DV,* March 29; Paula Parisi, "Dinosaurs Make Long-Distance Call," *HR,* March 30; and David Gritten, "Cue the Dinosaurs: Editing Via Satellite," *LAT,* May 9. George Lucas's supervision of the film's postproduction was reported in Archerd columns, *DV,* December 1, 1992, and January 13, 1993. F. Scott Fitzgerald's comment on the "test of a first-rate intelligence" is from his 1936 essay "The Crack-Up," in *The Crack-Up,* ed. by Edmund Wilson, New Directions, 1945.

Sources on the shooting schedule include Shay and Duncan, *The Making of "Jurassic Park";* the August 24, 1992, production callsheet, *Behind the Scenes of "Jurassic Park";*

Archerd column, *DV,* December 1, 1992; and Universal advertisement, *HR,* December 2, 1992. The official production cost was reported in Thomas R. King, *"Jurassic Park* Offers a High-Stakes Test of Hollywood Synergy," *Wall Street Journal,* February 20, 1993. Other estimates of the cost (1992) appeared in Doris Toumarkine, "Spielberg Sked: *Jurassic, List,"* HR, August 24 ($80 million); Joseph McBride, "Spielberg's *Jurassic* Rolls Today in Kauai," *DV,* August 24 ($90–100 million); and Moerk ($100 million); *Fortune*'s $95-million estimate is from Lane, " 'I Want Gross,' " which also estimated Spielberg's earnings from the film. Data on the *Jurassic Park* vs. *E.T.* box-office competition are from *Variety:* Leonard Klady, "Spielberg's Lizards Eat E.T.," October 18, 1993; "Top 100 All-Time Domestic Grossers," October 17, 1994; and "Foreign Leverage" chart, August 28, 1995. Oscar Wilde's definition of a cynic is from his play *Lady Windermere's Fan* (1892).

Stephen Jay Gould discussed *Jurassic Park* in "Dinomania," *The New York Review of Books,* August 12, 1993, and *"Jurassic Park,"* in Mark C. Carnes, ed., *Past Imperfect: History According to the Movies,* Henry Holt, 1995. Other reviews and commentary (1993) include Julie Salamon, "Watch Out! There's Trouble in Dinosaurland," *Wall Street Journal,* June 10; David Ansen, "Monsters to Haunt Your Dreams," *Newsweek,* June 14; Georgia Brown, "Prospero Cooks," *The Village Voice,* June 22; Henry Sheehan, "The Fears of Children," and Peter Wollen, "Theme Park and Variations," *Sight and Sound,* July; Stuart Klawans, *The Nation,* July 19; and Sheehan, "A Father Runs From It," *DV,* December 7.

Schindler's List is based on the novel by Thomas Keneally, Simon & Schuster, 1982 (published in England as *Schindler's Ark).* The third-draft screenplay by Steven Zaillian is dated March 24, 1992. Universal Pictures, in 1993, published a *Schindler's List* photo album, with an introduction by Spielberg; and "Production Information" in the film's pressbook. Oskar Schindler's life also was the subject of Jon Blair's documentary film *Schindler* (1983). The making of *Schindler's List* was documented in the "Spielberg's Oskar" segment of *Eye to Eye with Connie Chung* (1993) and in "The Film Makers," *Nightline* (ABC-TV), March 21, 1994. Spielberg discussed the film in 1994 on *The Barbara Walters Special* and in his July 18 appearance at the National Governors' Association meeting in Boston (cablecast on C-SPAN). A *Viewer's Guide to "Schindler's List"* was published in 1994 by the Martyrs Memorial and Museum of the Holocaust, Los Angeles.

Articles on the film were collected in Fensch, ed., *Oskar Schindler and His List: The Man, the Book, the Film, the Holocaust and Its Survivors.* See also Abraham Zuckerman, *A Voice in the Chorus: Memories of a Teenager Saved by Schindler,* Longmeadow Press, 1991; and Elinor J. Brecher, foreword by Keneally, *Schindler's Legacy: True Stories of the List Survivors,* Penguin, 1994. Other books on the Holocaust consulted for this study include Elie Wiesel, trans. by Stella Rodway, *Night,* Hill & Wang, 1960; Hannah Arendt, *Eichmann in Jerusalem: A Report on the Banality of Evil,* Viking, 1963; Primo Levi, trans. by Stuart Woolf, *Survival in Auschwitz: The Nazi Assault on Humanity,* Collier, 1969; Annette Insdorf, *Indelible Shadows: Film and the Holocaust,* Vintage, 1983; David S. Wyman, *The Abandonment of the Jews: America and the Holocaust 1941–1945,* Pantheon, 1984; Claude Lanzmann, *Shoah: An Oral History of the Holocaust: The Complete Text of the Film,* Pantheon, 1985; Art Spiegelman, *Maus I: A Survivor's Tale: My Father Bleeds History,* Pantheon, 1986, and *Maus II: A Survivor's Tale: And Here My Troubles Began,* Pantheon, 1991; Michael Berenbaum, *The World Must Know: The History of the Holocaust as Told in the United States Holocaust Memorial Museum,* Little, Brown, 1993; Deborah E. Lipstadt, *Denying the Holocaust: The Growing Assault on Truth and Memory,* The Free Press, 1993; James E. Young, *The Texture of Memory: Holocaust Memorials and Meaning,* Yale University Press, 1993; Eva Fogelman, *Conscience & Courage: Rescuers of Jews During the Holocaust,* Doubleday, 1994; Lawrence

L. Langer, *Admitting the Holocaust: Collected Essays,* Oxford University Press, 1995; and Edward T. Linenthal, *Preserving Memory: The Struggle to Create America's Holocaust Museum,* Viking, 1995.

Keneally commented on his book *Schindler's List* and the film version in his article "It's the Story of a Hero in Hell," *LAT,* December 12, 1993; and "Creating *Schindler's List,* " a lecture at Saddleback College, Mission Viejo, Ca., September 20, 1994. See also Deirdre Donahue, "How Thomas Keneally Drew Up *Schindler's List,* " *USA Today,* December 23, 1993; Valerie Takahama, *"Schindler's* Author Gives Film a Standing Ovation," *Orange County Register,* January 2, 1994; Pedro E. Ponce, "Making Novels of Life's Ethical Dilemmas," *The Chronicle of Higher Education,* February 2, 1994; Fritz Lanham, "Keneally's Luck," *Houston Chronicle,* April 24, 1994; and Tom Tugend, "The Neverending Story," *Jerusalem Post,* January 13, 1995.

Other articles and interviews about the film, Oskar Schindler, and the Schindler Jews include: Archerd columns, *DV,* December 1, 1992, and June 17, 1993; and (1993): David Gritten, "Grim. Black and White . . . Spielberg?" *LAT,* May 9; Zoe Heller, "The Real Thing," *The Independent on Sunday* (London), May 23; Perlez, "Spielberg Grapples with the Horror of the Holocaust"; Grunwald, "Steven Spielberg Gets Real"; Tugend, "Spielberg's Remembrance of Things Past"; Elaine Dutka, "They Made the 'List' and Lived," *LAT,* December 12; Weinraub, "Steven Spielberg Faces the Holocaust"; Guthmann, "Spielberg's List"; Shah, "Steven Spielberg, Seriously"; Ansen, "Spielberg's Obsession," Jonathan Alter, "After the Survivors," and Mark Miller, "The Real Schindler," *Newsweek,* December 20; Harry Sumrall, "Schindler's Legacy," *San Jose Mercury News,* December 23; "Interview: Ray Stella, SOC," *The Operating Cameraman Magazine,* Winter; and Royal, "An Interview with Steven Spielberg";

And (1994): Richardson, "Steven's Choice"; Karen Erbach, *"Schindler's List* Finds Heroism Amidst Holocaust," *American Cinematographer,* January; Rabbi Eli Hecht, "When Will Jews Let It Rest?" *LAT,* January 2; Michael Wilmington, "Redefining Spielberg," *The Arizona Republic,* January 9; Kirk Honeycutt, "Despite Quake, Show Must Go On at L.A. Critics Fete," *HR,* January 20; Anne Thompson, "How Steven Spielberg Brought *Schindler's List* to Life," *Entertainment Weekly,* January 21; Peter Rainer, "Why the *Schindler's List* Backlash?" *LAT,* January 30; Brian Case, "The Reich Stuff," *Time Out* (London), February 9–16; Blair, "Spielberg Comes of Age"; Andrew Nagorski, *"Schindler's List* Hits Home," *Newsweek,* March 14; Richard Wolin, *"Schindler's List* and the Politics of Remembrance," *In These Times,* March 21–April 3; Diana Jean Schemo, "Good Germans: Honoring the Heroes. And Hiding the Holocaust," *NYT,* June 12 (including Claude Lanzmann's criticism); "Florida Will Teach Holocaust," *B'nai B'rith Messenger,* August 26; "Spielberg Donates *Schindler's* Profits to Foundation," and Sue Fishkoff, "More Schools Turn to *Schindler's List* as Educational Tool," *Jewish Bulletin,* September 16; (1995): Rabbi Marvin Hier, "Heroes Aren't the Story, Villainy Is," *LAT,* January 19; Sherry Amatenstein, " 'A Rescue Mission with a Time Clock,' " *USA Weekend,* May 5–7; Catherine Jordan and Lisa de Moraes, "Humor of *Schindler* Spoof Lost on Spielberg," *HR,* September 18, 1995; and (1996): Leopold Page, "Remembering Schindler's Humanity," *LAT,* May 6.

Information on Roman Polanski's experiences in the Kraków ghetto liquidation is from his autobiography *Roman by Polanski,* Morrow, 1984, and Lawrence Weschler, "Artist in Exile," *The New Yorker,* December 5, 1994 (which also reported on Spielberg offering him *Schindler's List).* Billy Wilder's interest in making the film was reported in Shah and in Archerd's column, *DV,* December 21, 1993. Scorsese's involvement was reported by Richardson. Bruck, *Master of the Game,* reported on Spielberg's film for Steve Ross.

Schindler's List reviews and commentaries include (1993): David Denby, "Unlikely Hero," *New York,* December 13; Janet Maslin, "Imagining the Holocaust to Remember

It," *NYT,* December 15; Scott Rosenberg, "The Paradox of a Candle," *San Francisco Examiner,* December 15; Henry Sheehan, "The Family Values of Steven Spielberg," *Orange County Register,* December 19; Terrence Rafferty, "A Man of Transactions," *The New Yorker,* December 20; Newman, "Spielberg's Bar Mitzvah"; and (1994): Philip Gourevitch, "A Dissent on *Schindler's List,*" *Commentary,* February; Bob Strauss, "Surprise! Oscar Goes Conventional," *LADN,* February 10; Simon Louvish, "Witness," *Sight and Sound,* March; David Thomson, "Presenting Enamelware," and White, "Toward a Theory of Spielberg History," *Film Comment,* March–April; J. Hoberman et al., "*Schindler's List:* Myth, Movie, and Memory," *The Village Voice,* March 29 (including Art Spiegelman's comments); and Norbert Friedman, Rabbi Uri D. Herscher, and Ruth King, letters to the editor, *Commentary,* June. President Bill Clinton's comment on the film is from "Spielberg's Oskar." Articles about the voting of critics' groups (1993) include Todd McCarthy, "L.A. Crix Tap *List, Piano,*" *DV,* December 13, and "Crix Crux Is a Crock," *Variety,* December 27; Martin A. Grove, "L.A. Spielberg Snub Tops List of Party Buzz," *HR,* December 15; Kirk Honeycutt, "*Schindler* Takes N.Y., but Critics Hear *Piano,*" *HR,* December 16; Jack Mathews, "N.Y. Writers Pick *List* but Bypass Spielberg," *LAT,* December 16; and Donna Parker, "L.A. Critics: No Snub of Director Spielberg," *HR,* December 17–19. Box-office figures on *Schindler's List* are from *Variety*'s August 28, 1995, "Foreign Leverage" chart.

Sources on Spielberg's Shoah project include Allan Holzman's 1996 documentary films *Survivors of the Shoah Visual History Foundation* (Turner Home Entertainment) and *Survivors of the Holocaust* (Turner Original Productions). Spielberg TV interviews about the project include *20/20* (ABC, July 14, 1995), *Larry King Live* (CNN, August 2, 1995), and *Oprah* (syndicated, May 22, 1996). Articles include (1994): Connie Benesch, "Spielberg's List: The Survivors," *HR,* September 1; "*List* Director Seeks to Preserve Holocaust History," *LADN,* September 1; Rosanne Keynan, "Spielberg Leads Huge Holocaust On-Line Project," *LAT,* October 1; Bernard Weinraub, "Spielberg Is Recording Holocaust Survivors' Stories," *NYT,* November 10; and Laura Shapiro, " 'A Race Against Time,' " *Newsweek,* November 21; (1995): Michael Haile, "Reminting *Schindler's* Gold," *Boxoffice,* April; Trip Gabriel, "Spielberg Braves Society for a Cause," *NYT,* August 18; Karen W. Arenson, "From *Schindler's List,* a Jewish Mission," *NYT,* September 24; and Robin Abcarian, "The Worst of Times—on the Record," *LAT,* October 18; and (1996): Adam Schatz and Alissa Quart, "Spielberg's List," *The Village Voice,* January 9; and David Usborne, "Spielberg Builds Huge Holocaust Database," *The Independent on Sunday* (London), January 7; Anick Jesdanum, "Spielberg's Holocaust Project Gets Boost from U.S. Senate," *LADN,* July 24; and "War and Remembrance," *USA Today,* July 24.

Articles on the establishment of DreamWorks SKG include (1994): Anita M. Busch, "Three Men & Their Baby," *DV,* October 12; Alan Citron and Claudia Eller, " 'Dream Team' Trio Outline Plans for Studio," and James Bates and Elaine Dutka, "Bravos and Shudders Greet Moguls' Plan for New Studio," *LAT,* October 13; John Brodie and Anita M. Busch, "Troika Sets Town Atwitter," *DV,* October 13; Kirk Honeycutt, "Hollywood's 'Dream Team,' " *HR,* October 13; Bernard Weinraub, "3 Holywood Giants Team Up to Create Major Movie Studio," *NYT,* October 13; Weinraub and Fabrikant, "A Hollywood Recipe: Vision, Wealth, Ego"; Robert W. Welkos, "Big News, but Where Are the Big Plans?" *LAT,* October 21; Jim Impoco, "Hollywood's Dream Team," *U.S. News & World Report,* October 24; Richard Corliss, "A Studio Is Born," *Time,* October 24; Michael Meyer and Charles Fleming, "Hollywood Poker," *Newsweek,* October 24; Citron and Eller, " 'Dream Team's' 1st Project: Mastering Spin Control," *LAT,* October 25; (1995): Corliss, "Hey, Let's Put On a Show!" (cover story), *Time,* March 27; Kim Masters, "What's Ovitz Got to Do with It?" *Vanity Fair,* April; Henry Chu, "DreamWorks Studio Stirs Rivalry of Civic Suitors," *LAT,* April 1; Martin Peers, "DreamWorks Gets Coin in Line," *DV,* April 25; Honeycutt, "The Rights of DreamWorks," *HR,* May 1; Bates and Eller,

"DreamWorks, MCA Ally on Distribution," *LAT,* June 14; and Thomas R. King, "MCA, DreamWorks Reach Wide-Ranging Distribution Accord," *Wall Street Journal,* June 14; (1996): Wade Major, "Dream in the Works: A Complete Update on the SKG Co-Venture," *Boxoffice,* April; Lee Condon, "DreamWorks, Glendale Deal Nearing Completion," *LADN,* May 18; James Bates and Jesus Sanchez, "Playa Vista: A Project in Frustration," *LAT,* November 1; and J. William Gibson, "All Wet at Ballona Creek," *L.A. Weekly,* December 6–12; and (1997): Jeff Stockwell, "Getting Swamped," *Premiere,* January.

Information on *Steven Spielberg's Director's Chair* is from David Kronke, "ROMantics," *Premiere,* August 1996; a review by Ann Kwinn, *Boxoffice,* October 1996; and Bob Strauss, "Electric Chair," *Entertainment Weekly,* October 11, 1996. Spielberg discussed his Howard Hughes film project in Ebert and Siskel, *The Future of the Movies.* Lesley Blanch's comment on George Cukor is quoted in Gavin Lambert, *On Cukor,* G.P. Putnam's Sons, 1972.

FILMOGRAPHY
AND VIDEOGRAPHY

Code: DIST: Distributor; P: Producer; D: Director; SCR: Screenwriter; CAM: Cinematographer; WITH: Principal Cast Members; R: Release Date (for theatrical films); AIR: Original Airdate (for TV shows); L: Length (where known); S: Steven Spielberg; U: Universal; WB: Warner Bros.

AMATEUR FILMS (PARTIAL LIST)
Running times and some dates approximate; in 8mm unless otherwise indicated. See text for information on other early filmmaking by S.

1957 *The Last Train Wreck.* D-CAM: S. L: 3 min.

1958 *The Last Gunfight* (aka *The Last Gun, The Last Shootout, Gunsmog*). D-CAM: S, Arnold Spielberg. WITH: Jim Sollenberger, Barry Sollenberger. L: 9 min.

1958 *A Day in the Life of Thunder.* D-CAM: S. WITH: Thunder (S's cocker spaniel).

1959 Documentary on Soviet Union. D-CAM: Arnold Spielberg. EDITING and TITLES: S.

1959 Western. D-CAM: S, Terry Mechling. WITH: Steve Swift. L: 6 min.

1959 Films of Ingleside Elementary School (Phoenix, Az.) flag football games. D-CAM: S.

1960 (begun in 1959) *Fighter Squad.* D: S. CAM: S, Jim Sollenberger. WITH: Jim Sollenberger, Roger Sheer, Mike McNamara, Steve Suggs, S. L: 15 min.

1960 *Film noir* in wide-screen. D-CAM: S. WITH: Jim Sollenberger.

1960 *Steve Spielberg's Home Movies* (slapstick comedy for Ingleside Halloween carnival). D-CAM: S.

1961 Western made for Patricia Scott's eighth-grade class "career exploration" project at Ingleside. D-CAM: S.

1961 *Scary Hollow* (film of Ingleside school play). D-CAM: S, Roger Sheer. WITH: Sheer.

1962 (begun in 1959) *Escape to Nowhere.* D-CAM: S. WITH: Haven Peters, Jim Sollenberger, Barry Sollenberger, George Mills, Leah Spielberg. L: 40 min.

1964 (begun in 1963) *Firelight.* P: Arnold Spielberg, Leah Spielberg (for American Artist Productions). D-SCR-CAM: S. WITH: Robert Robyn, Beth Weber, Clark (Lucky) Lohr, Margaret Peyou, Nancy Spielberg. R: March 24, 1964 (Phoenix Little Theatre). L: 135 min.

1964 Films of Saratoga (Ca.) High School football games. D-CAM: S.

1964–65 Film about John F. Kennedy. D-CAM: S (with Mike Augustine). L: 3 min.

1965 *Senior Sneak Day* (documentary filmed in Santa Cruz, Ca.). D-CAM: S. WITH: Members of Saratoga High School Class of '65.

1965–66 *Encounter* (16mm). D-CAM: S (with Charles [Butch] Hays). WITH: Roger Ernest, Peter Maffia. L: 20 min.

1966 *The Great Race* (16mm). D-CAM: S (with Charles [Butch] Hays). WITH: Roger Ernest, Halina Junyszek.

1967 *Slipstream* (35mm). P: Ralph Burris (for Playmount Productions). D: S. SCR: S,

Roger Ernest. CAM: Serge Haignere, Allen Daviau. WITH: Tony Bill, Roger Ernest, Peter Maffia, Andre (Andy) Oveido, Jim Baxes. (Uncompleted; parts shown in the 1987 documentary *Citizen Steve.*)

1968 *Amblin'* (35mm). DIST: Sigma III; Four Star Excelsior Releasing Co.; UPA (nontheatrical). P: Denis C. Hoffman (with Ralph Burris, "in charge of production"). D-SCR: S. CAM: Allen Daviau. WITH: Pamela McMyler, Richard Levin. R: December 18, 1968. L: 26 min.

TELEVISION PROGRAMS AS DIRECTOR (IN ORDER OF AIRING)

1969 *Night Gallery:* "Eyes" (one segment of a three-part TV movie pilot; other segments directed by Boris Sagal, Barry Shear). P: William Sackheim (for U-TV). D: S. SCR: Rod Serling, from his own short story. CAM: Richard Batcheller. WITH: Joan Crawford, Barry Sullivan, Tom Bosley. AIR: November 8, 1969, NBC World Premiere. L: 95 min. ("Eyes": 26 min.)

1970 *Marcus Welby, M.D.:* "The Daredevil Gesture." P: David J. O'Connell (for U-TV). D: S. SCR: Jerome Ross. CAM: Walter Strenge. WITH: Robert Young, Frank Webb, James Brolin, Elena Verdugo, Marsha Hunt. AIR: March 17, 1970, ABC. L: 52 min.

1971 *Night Gallery:* "Make Me Laugh." P: Jack Laird (for U-TV). D: S (and Jeannot Szwarc, uncredited). SCR: Rod Serling. CAM: Richard C. Glouner. WITH: Godfrey Cambridge, Tom Bosley, Jackie Vernon, Al Lewis, Sidney Clute. AIR: January 6, 1971, NBC (as part of the *Four-in-One* series). L: 24 min.

1971 *The Name of the Game:* "LA 2017." P: Dean Hargrove (for U-TV). D: S. SCR: Philip Wylie. CAM: Richard A. Kelley. WITH: Gene Barry, Barry Sullivan, Edmond O'Brien, Sharon Farrell, Severn Darden. AIR: January 15, 1971, NBC. L: 74 min.

1971 *The Psychiatrist:* "The Private World of Martin Dalton." P: Jerrold Freedman (for U-TV). D: S. SCR: Bo May. CAM: Lloyd Ahern. WITH: Roy Thinnes, Jim Hutton, Kate Woodville, Stephen Hudis, Pamelyn Ferdin. AIR: February 10, 1971, NBC (as part of the *Four-in-One* series). L: 52 min. (U-TV combined this program with a *Psychiatrist* episode directed by Jeff Corey to make up an 88-min. feature, *Whispering Death,* released in European theaters by CIC in 1971 and given its American premiere on CBS in 1980.)

1971 *The Psychiatrist:* "Par for the Course." P: Jerrold Freedman (for U-TV). D: S. SCR: Thomas Y. Drake, Herb Bermann, Jerrold Freedman, Bo May, from a story by Drake. CAM: Lloyd Ahern. WITH: Roy Thinnes, Clu Gulager, Joan Darling, Michael C. Gwynne. AIR: March 10, 1971, NBC (as part of the *Four-in-One* series). L: 52 min.

1971 *Columbo:* "Murder by the Book." P: Richard Levinson, William Link (for U-TV). D: S. SCR: Steven Bochco. CAM: Russell L. Metty. WITH: Peter Falk, Jack Cassidy, Martin Milner, Rosemary Forsyth, Barbara Colby. AIR: September 15, 1971, NBC Mystery Movie. L: 76 min.

1971 *Owen Marshall, Counselor at Law:* "Eulogy for a Wide Receiver." P: Jon Epstein (for U-TV). D: S. SCR: Richard Bluel. CAM: Harkness Smith. WITH: Arthur Hill, Lee Majors, Stephen Young, Anson Williams, Joan Darling. AIR: September 30, 1971, ABC. L: 52 min.

1971 *Duel.* P: George Eckstein (for U-TV). D: S. SCR: Richard Matheson, based on his story. CAM: Jack A. Marta. WITH: Dennis Weaver, Carey Loftin, Dale Van Sickle, Jacqueline Scott, Lucille Benson. AIR: November 13, 1971, ABC Movie of the Weekend. L: 73 min. (An expanded, 91-min. version, including additional scenes directed by S in 1972, was released theatrically by CIC in Europe, 1972–73, and in U.S. by Universal, 1983, as well as being shown on TV in the U.S. from August 15, 1973, to the present. The longer version also has been released by MCA Home Video on videocassette and laserdisc.)

1972 *Something Evil.* P: Alan Jay Factor (for CBS). D: S. SCR: Robert Clouse. CAM: Bill Butler. WITH: Sandy Dennis, Darren McGavin, Ralph Bellamy, Johnny Whitaker, Jeff Corey. AIR: January 21, 1972, CBS Friday Night Movie. L: 72 min.

1973 *Savage.* P: Paul Mason (for U-TV). D: S. SCR: Richard Levinson, William Link, Mark Rodgers. CAM: Bill Butler. WITH: Martin Landau, Barbara Bain, Will Geer, Barry Sullivan, Michele Carey. AIR: March 31, 1973, NBC World Premiere. L: 76 min. (Working title: *The Savage Report.*)

1984 *Strokes of Genius.* A series of profiles of artists: Willem de Kooning, Arshile Gorky, Jackson Pollock, David Smith, and Franz Kline. P: Courtney Sale Ross, Karen Lindsay (for Cort Productions/KERA, Dallas–Fort Worth). D: Charlotte Zwerin, Amanda C. Pope, Jay Freund, Carl Colby. CAM: Francis Kenny. AIR: May 1984, PBS. (S directed the introductory segments hosted by Dustin Hoffman.)

1985 *Amazing Stories:* "Ghost Train." P: David E. Vogel (for U-TV/Amblin Television). D: S. SCR: Frank Deese, from a story by S. CAM: Allen Daviau. WITH: Roberts Blossom, Scott Paulin, Gail Edwards, Lukas Haas, Renny Roker. AIR: September 29, 1985, NBC. L: 25 min.

1987 (filmed in 1985) *Amazing Stories:* "The Mission." P: David E. Vogel (for U-TV/Amblin Television). D: S. SCR: Menno Meyjes, from a story by S. CAM: John McPherson. WITH: Kevin Costner, Casey Siemaszko, Kiefer Sutherland, Jeffrey Jay Cohen, John Philbin. AIR: May 15, 1987, NBC. L: 50 min. (Working title: "Round Trip.") ("The Mission" also became part of *Amazing Stories: The Movie,* released theatrically outside the U.S. by CIC in 1987 and subsequently to TV syndication in the U.S.; the other parts are "Go to the Head of the Class," directed by Robert Zemeckis, and "Mummy Dearest," directed by William Dear and based on a story by S.)

FEATURE FILMS AS WRITER (BUT NOT DIRECTOR)

1973 (filmed in 1971) *Ace Eli and Rodger of the Skies.* DIST: Twentieth Century–Fox. P: Boris Wilson (Robert Fryer, James Cresson). D: Bill Sampson (John Erman). SCR: Chips Rosen (Claudia Salter), from a story by S. CAM: David M. Walsh. WITH: Cliff Robertson, Pamela Franklin, Eric Shea, Rosemary Murphy, Bernadette Peters. R: April 1, 1973. L: 92 min.

1985 *The Goonies.* DIST: WB. P: Richard Donner, Harvey Bernhard. D: Donner. SCR: Chris Columbus, from a story by S. CAM: Mike McLean. WITH: Sean Astin, Josh Brolin, Jeff Cohen, Corey Feldman, Ke Huy Quan. R: June 7, 1985. L: 111 min.

1986 *Poltergeist II: The Other Side.* DIST: MGM/UA. P: Mark Victor, Michael Grais. D: Brian Gibson. SCR: Grais, Victor, based on S's story for the original 1982 film *Poltergeist* (see below). CAM: Andrew Laszlo. WITH: JoBeth Williams, Craig T. Nelson, Heather O'Rourke, Oliver Robins, Zelda Rubinstein. R: May 23, 1986. L: 91 min.

1988 *Poltergeist III.* DIST: MGM. P: Barry Bernardi. D: Gary Sherman. SCR: Gary Sherman, Brian Taggert, based on S's story for *Poltergeist.* CAM: Alex Nepomniaschy. WITH: Tom Skerritt, Nancy Allen, Heather O'Rourke, Zelda Rubinstein, Lara Flynn Boyle. R: June 10, 1988. L: 97 min.

FEATURE FILM AS CREW MEMBER

1968 (begun in 1965) *Faces.* DIST: Walter Reade Organization. P: Maurice McEndree. D-SCR: John Cassavetes. CAM: Al Ruban. WITH: John Marley, Gena Rowlands, Lynn Carlin, Seymour Cassel, Fred Draper. R: October 1968. L: 130 min. (S was an uncredited production assistant.)

THEATRICAL FEATURE FILMS AS DIRECTOR

1964 *Firelight* (see credits above).

1972 *Duel* (expanded theatrical version of 1971 TV movie; see above).

1974 *The Sugarland Express.* DIST: U. P: Richard D. Zanuck, David Brown. D: S. SCR: Hal Barwood, Matthew Robbins, from a story by Barwood and S. CAM: Vilmos Zsigmond.

WITH: Goldie Hawn, Ben Johnson, Michael Sacks, William Atherton, Louise Latham. R: April 5, 1974. L: 109 min. (Working title: *Carte Blanche.)*

1975 *Jaws.* DIST: U. P: Richard D. Zanuck, David Brown. D: S. SCR: Carl Gottlieb, Peter Benchley (and Howard Sackler, John Milius, Robert Shaw, uncredited), from the novel by Benchley. CAM: Bill Butler. WITH: Roy Scheider, Richard Dreyfuss, Robert Shaw, Lorraine Gary, Murray Hamilton. R: June 20, 1975. L: 125 min. (Additional footage included as supplement to 1995 MCA Home Video laserdisc edition.)

1977 *Close Encounters of the Third Kind.* DIST: Columbia. P: Julia Phillips, Michael Phillips. D: S. SCR: S (and Paul Schrader, John Hill, Jerry Belson, David Giler, Hal Barwood, Matthew Robbins, uncredited). CAM: Vilmos Zsigmond (additional photography by William A. Fraker, Douglas Slocombe, John A. Alonzo, Laszlo Kovacs, Frank W. Stanley). WITH: Richard Dreyfuss, François Truffaut, Teri Garr, Melinda Dillon, Cary Guffey. R: November 16, 1977. L: 135 min. (Working titles: *Watch the Skies, Close Encounter of the Third Kind.)* (On July 31, 1980, Columbia released *The Special Edition of Close Encounters of the Third Kind,* a reedited, 132-min. version with additional scenes directed by S, photographed by Michael Butler and Allen Daviau. Both versions are included in the 1990 Voyager laserdisc edition.)

1979 *1941.* DIST: U/Columbia. P: Buzz Feitshans. D: S. SCR: Robert Zemeckis, Bob Gale, from a story by Zemeckis, Gale, and John Milius. CAM: William A. Fraker. WITH: Bobby Di Cicco, Dianne Kay, Wendie Jo Sperber, Robert Stack, John Belushi. R: December 14, 1979. L: 118 min. (Working titles: *The Night the Japs Attacked, The Night the Japanese Attacked, The Rising Sun.)* (A 146-min. restored version, including additional scenes previously shown in an expanded TV version of the film, was released on laserdisc in 1996 by MCA Universal Home Video.)

1981 *Raiders of the Lost Ark.* DIST: Paramount. P: Frank Marshall (for Lucasfilm). D: S. SCR: Lawrence Kasdan, from a story by George Lucas, Philip Kaufman. CAM: Douglas Slocombe. WITH: Harrison Ford, Karen Allen, Paul Freeman, Ronald Lacey, John Rhys-Davies. R: June 12, 1981. L: 115 min.

1982 *Poltergeist.* DIST: MGM/UA. P: S, Frank Marshall. D: Tobe Hooper (and S, uncredited). SCR: S, Michael Grais, Mark Victor, from a story by S. CAM: Matthew F. Leonetti. WITH: Craig T. Nelson, JoBeth Williams, Beatrice Straight, Dominique Dunne, Heather O'Rourke. R: June 4, 1982. L: 114 min.

1982 *E.T. The Extra-Terrestrial.* DIST: U. P: S, Kathleen Kennedy. D: S. SCR: Melissa Mathison. CAM: Allen Daviau. WITH: Dee Wallace, Henry Thomas, Peter Coyote, Robert Macnaughton, Drew Barrymore. R: June 11, 1982. L: 115 min. (Working titles: *E.T. and Me, A Boy's Life.)* (Additional footage included as supplement to 1996 MCA Home Video laserdisc edition.)

1983 *Twilight Zone—The Movie.* DIST: WB. P: S, John Landis. D: S ("Kick the Can" segment), Landis, Joe Dante, George Miller. Additional credits for "Kick the Can": SCR: George Clayton Johnson, Richard Matheson, Josh Rogan (Melissa Mathison), from a story by George Clayton Johnson (originally filmed for *The Twilight Zone* CBS-TV series and aired February 9, 1962). CAM: Allen Daviau. WITH: Scatman Crothers, Bill Quinn, Martin Garner, Selma Diamond, Priscilla Pointer. R: June 24, 1983. L: 102 min. ("Kick the Can": 23 min.).

1984 *Indiana Jones and the Temple of Doom.* DIST: Paramount. P: Robert Watts (for Lucasfilm). D: S. SCR: Willard Huyck, Gloria Katz, from a story by George Lucas. CAM: Douglas Slocombe. WITH: Harrison Ford, Kate Capshaw, Ke Huy Quan, Amrish Puri, Roshan Seth. R: May 23, 1984. L: 118 min. (Working title: *Indiana Jones and the Temple of Death.)*

1985 *The Color Purple.* DIST: WB. P: S, Kathleen Kennedy, Frank Marshall, Quincy Jones. D: S. SCR: Menno Meyjes, from the novel by Alice Walker. CAM: Allen Daviau.

with: Whoopi Goldberg, Danny Glover, Margaret Avery, Oprah Winfrey, Willard Pugh. r: December 18, 1985. L: 152 min. (Working title: *Moon Song*.)

1987 *Empire of the Sun.* DIST: WB. P: S, Kathleen Kennedy, Frank Marshall. D: S. SCR: Tom Stoppard (and Menno Meyjes, uncredited), from the novel by J. G. Ballard. CAM: Allen Daviau. WITH: Christian Bale, John Malkovich, Miranda Richardson, Joe Pantoliano, Rupert Frazer. R: December 9, 1987. L: 152 min.

1989 *Indiana Jones and the Last Crusade.* DIST: Paramount. P: Robert Watts (for Lucasfilm). D: S. SCR: Jeffrey Boam, from a story by George Lucas, Menno Meyjes. CAM: Douglas Slocombe. WITH: Harrison Ford, Sean Connery, Denholm Elliott, Alison Doody, River Phoenix. R: May 24, 1989. L: 127 min.

1989 *Always.* DIST: U/United Artists. P: S, Frank Marshall, Kathleen Kennedy. D: S. SCR: Jerry Belson (and Diane Thomas, Ronald Bass, uncredited), based on the 1943 film *A Guy Named Joe,* written by Dalton Trumbo from a story by Chandler Sprague and David Boehm, adapted by Frederick Hazlitt Brennan. CAM: Mikael Salamon. WITH: Richard Dreyfuss, Holly Hunter, Brad Johnson, John Goodman, Audrey Hepburn. R: December 22, 1989. L: 123 min. (Working title: *A Guy Named Joe*.)

1991 *Hook.* DIST: TriStar. P: Kathleen Kennedy, Frank Marshall, Gerald R. Molen. D: S. SCR: Jim V. Hart, Malia Scotch Marmo (and Carrie Fisher, uncredited), from a story by Hart and Nick Castle, based on the play *Peter Pan* and the novels *The Little White Bird, Peter Pan in Kensington Gardens,* and *Peter and Wendy* by J. M. Barrie. CAM: Dean Cundey. WITH: Dustin Hoffman, Robin Williams, Julia Roberts, Bob Hoskins, Maggie Smith. R: December 10, 1991. L: 142 min.

1993 *Jurassic Park.* DIST: U. P: Kathleen Kennedy, Gerald R. Molen. D: S. SCR: Michael Crichton, David Koepp (and Malia Scotch Marmo, uncredited), from the novel by Crichton. WITH: Sam Neill, Laura Dern, Jeff Goldblum, Richard Attenborough, Joseph Mazzello. R: June 10, 1993. L: 127 min.

1993 *Schindler's List.* DIST: U. P: S, Gerald R. Molen, Branko Lustig. D: S. SCR: Steven Zaillian, from the novel by Thomas Keneally. CAM: Janusz Kaminski. WITH: Liam Neeson, Ben Kingsley, Ralph Fiennes, Caroline Goodall, Embeth Davidtz. R: December 15, 1993. L: 197 min.

1997 *The Lost World: Jurassic Park.* P: Gerald R. Molen, Colin Wilson. D: S. SCR: David Koepp, based on the novel *The Lost World* by Michael Crichton. CAM: Janusz Kaminski. WITH: Jeff Goldblum, Julianne Moore, Richard Attenborough, Arliss Howard, Pete Postlethwaite. DIST: U.

THEATRICAL FILMS AS PRODUCER OR EXECUTIVE PRODUCER (BUT NOT DIRECTOR)

1978 *I Wanna Hold Your Hand* (D: Robert Zemeckis; U).

1980 *Used Cars* (D: Robert Zemeckis; Columbia).

1980 *Home Movies* (D: Brian De Palma; United Artists Classics; S was investor only).

1981 *Continental Divide* (D: Michael Apted; U).

1984 *Gremlins* (D: Joe Dante; WB).

1985 *Fandango* (D: Kevin Reynolds; WB).

1985 *The Goonies* (D: Richard Donner; WB).

1985 *Back to the Future* (D: Robert Zemeckis; WB).

1985 *Young Sherlock Holmes* (D: Barry Levinson; Paramount).

1986 *The Money Pit* (D: Richard Benjamin; U).

1986 *An American Tail* (D: Don Bluth; U; animated).

1987 *Innerspace* (D: Joe Dante; WB).

1987 *Harry and the Hendersons* (D: William Dear; U).

1987   *batteries not included* (D: Matthew Robbins; U).

1987   *Citizen Steve* (P: Amy Irving/Amblin Entertainment).

1988   *The Land Before Time* (D: Don Bluth; U; animated).

1988   *Who Framed Roger Rabbit* (D: Robert Zemeckis; Touchstone; part animated).

1989   *Back to the Future Part II* (D: Robert Zemeckis; U).

1989   *Dad* (D: Gary David Goldberg; U).

1990   *Dreams* (D: Akira Kurosawa; WB).

1990   *Back to the Future Part III* (D: Robert Zemeckis; U).

1990   *Gremlins II: The New Batch* (D: Joe Dante; WB).

1990   *Joe Versus the Volcano* (D: John Patrick Shanley; WB).

1990   *Arachnophobia* (D: Frank Marshall; Hollywood Pictures).

1991   *An American Tail: Fievel Goes West* (D: Phil Nibbelunk, Simon Wells; U; animated).

1991   *Cape Fear* (D: Martin Scorsese; U).

1992   *Noises Off* (D: Peter Bogdanovich; Touchstone).

1993   *A Far-Off Place* (D: Mikael Salamon; Disney).

1993   *We're Back!: A Dinosaur's Story* (D: Dick Zondag, Ralph Zondag, Phil Nibbelink, Simon Wells; U; animated).

1993   *A Dangerous Woman* (D: Stephen Gyllenhaal; U).

1994   *I'm Mad!* (D: Rich Arons, Audu Paden, Dave Marshall; WB; animated short).

1994   *The Flintstones* (D: Brian Levant; U).

1994   *Little Giants* (D: Duwayne Dunham; WB).

1994   *The Little Rascals* (D: Penelope Spheeris; U).

1994   *To Wong Foo, Thanks for Everything, Julie Newmar* (D: Beeban Kidron; U).

1995   *Casper* (D: Brad Silberling; U).

1995   *The Bridges of Madison County* (D: Clint Eastwood; WB).

1995   *How to Make an American Quilt* (D: Jocelyn Moorhouse; U).

1995   *Balto* (D: Simon Wells; U; animated).

1995   *Anne Frank Remembered* (D: Jon Blair; Sony Pictures Classics; S was part-sponsor only of this documentary).

1996   *Twister* (D: Jan De Bont; WB/U).

1996   *The Trigger Effect* (D: David Koepp; Gramercy).

1996   *Dear Diary* (D: David Frankel; DreamWorks; short).

1997   *Men in Black* (D: Barry Sonnenfeld; Columbia).

1997   *The Peacemaker* (D: Mimi Leder; DreamWorks).

TV, VIDEO, LASERDISC, AND CD-ROM PROGRAMS

Unless otherwise indicated, S served as an executive producer, officially or unofficially, on most of these programs. From 1984 until the 1994 formation of DreamWorks SKG, his programs usually were made for Amblin Television or, in the case of animated programs, for Amblimation. Some of these programs also have been released or repackaged for the home-video and laserdisc markets.

1982   *The Making of "Poltergeist"* (D: Frank Marshall; MGM/UA).

1985-87   *Amazing Stories* (U-TV, NBC series; S also received story credit on some segments).

1987   *The China Odyssey: "Empire of the Sun," a Film by Steven Spielberg* (D: Les Mayfield; WB, CBS special).

1989   *Great Adventurers & Their Quests: "Indiana Jones and the Last Crusade"* (D: Les Mayfield, William Rus; Paramount, CBS special).

1990   *Making "Close Encounters"* (P: Isaac Mizrahi, Morgan Holly; Voyager laserdisc).

1990-   *Tiny Toon Adventures* (WB, syndicated 1990–92, Fox 1992–; animated series).

1991-93 *Back to the Future* (U, CBS; animated series spin-off from the 1985 feature, with live-action introductions by Christopher Lloyd).

1991 *A Wish for Wings That Work* (U, CBS; D: Skip Jones; animated special).

1992 *The Plucky Duck Show* (Fox; animated series).

1992 *The Water Engine* (Cable TV movie, D: Steven Schachter; TNT Screenworks).

1992-93 *Fievel's American Tails* (U-TV, CBS; animated series).

1993 *American Masters:* "George Lucas: Heroes, Myths and Magic" (Paley/Price Prods./Thirteen/WNET; PBS; D: Jane Paley, Larry Price; S and Kate Capshaw appeared on this documentary special).

1993 *Class of '61* (TV movie pilot for unsold series, D: Gregory Hoblit; MCA-TV).

1993 *Family Dog* (WB-TV, U-TV; CBS; animated series spin-off from a 1987 *Amazing Stories* segment of the same title).

1993- *Animaniacs* (Fox 1993–95, WB 1995–, syndicated; animated series).

1993-95 *seaQuest DSV* (U-TV; NBC series).

1994-95 *Earth 2* (U-TV; NBC series).

1994- *ER* (WB-TV; NBC series).

1994 *American Cinema* (New York Center for Visual History/KCET/BBC; PBS limited series; S was part-sponsor).

1995 *The Making of "Jurassic Park"* (D: John Schultz; NBC special; expanded laserdisc version released by MCA Home Video).

1995 *Fudge-A-Mania* (TV movie, MTE; ABC).

1995- *Fudge* (MTE; ABC series).

1995 *seaQuest 2032* (U-TV; NBC series; retitled version of *seaQuest DSV*).

1995- *Pinky & the Brain* (WB; syndicated; animated series).

1995- *Freakazoid!* (WB; syndicated; animated series).

1995 *The Making of Steven Spielberg's "Jaws"* (D: Laurent Bouzereau; MCA Home Video laserdisc).

1996 *Champs* (ABC series).

1996- *High Incident* (ABC series).

1996- *Majority Rules* (KPNX, Phoenix; game-show series).

1996 *The Dig* (Interactive CD-ROM; D: Sean Clark; story and design developed in collaboration with S; LucasArts Entertainment).

1996 *Survivors of the Holocaust* (D: Allan Holzman; Turner special).

1996 *Survivors of the Shoah Visual History Foundation* (EDITOR: Allan Holzman; Turner Home Entertainment videocassette and laserdisc).

1996 *The Making of "1941"* (D: Laurent Bouzereau; MCA Home Video laserdisc).

1996 *The Making of "E.T. The Extra-Terrestrial"* (D: Laurent Bouzereau; MCA Home Video laserdisc).

1996 *Spin City* (ABC series).

1996 *Ink* (CBS series).

1996 *The Neverhood* (Interactive CD-ROM; DreamWorks Interactive).

1996 *Steven Spielberg's Director's Chair* (Interactive CD-ROM; S hosts and directed some scenes; Knowledge Adventure/DreamWorks Interactive).

APPEARANCES IN FILMS AND TV, VIDEO, AND LASERDISC PROGRAMS (PARTIAL LIST)

1963 *Journey to the Unknown* (D: Ernest G. Sauer; S also was credited with the special effects).

1971 *Duel* (D: S).

1972 *Something Evil* (D: S).

1976 *TVTV Looks at the Oscars* (TVTV/KCET, Los Angeles).

1980 *The Blues Brothers* (D: John Landis; U).

1981   *Great Movie Stunts: "Raiders of the Lost Ark"* (D: Robert Guenette; Lucasfilm, CBS).

1981   *The Making of "Raiders of the Lost Ark"* (D: Phillip Schuman; Lucasfilm).

1982   *The Making of "Poltergeist."*

1982   *Chambre 666* (D: Wim Wenders).

1984   *Gremlins* (D: Joe Dante).

1984   *Indiana Jones and the Temple of Doom* (D: S).

1987   *The China Odyssey: "Empire of the Sun," a Film by Steven Spielberg.*

1987   *Citizen Steve.*

1989   *Great Adventurers & Their Quests: "Indiana Jones and the Last Crusade."*

1989   *The Tracey Ullman Show:* "The Gate" (D: Ted Bessell; S played himself in a comedy sketch with Ullman; Fox).

1990   *Listen Up: The Lives of Quincy Jones* (D: Ellen Weissbrod; WB).

1990   *Making "Close Encounters."*

1991   *Here's Looking at You, Warner Bros.* (D: Robert Guenette; WB).

1992   *The Magical World of Chuck Jones* (D: George Daugherty; WB).

1992   *Your Family Matters:* "Shattered Lullabies" (Lifetime Television special hosted by S and Kate Capshaw).

1993   *François Truffaut: 25 Years, 25 Films* (P: Michael Kurcfeld; Voyager laserdisc).

1994   *American Cinema:* "The Film School Generation" (D: Steve Jenkins).

1994   *Ladmo Remembered: A Wallace & Ladmo Special* (KPHO, Phoenix).

1995   *The Making of "Jurassic Park."*

1995   *The American Film Institute Salute to Steven Spielberg* (D: Louis J. Horvitz; NBC; expanded version on A&E).

1995   *The Making of Steven Spielberg's "Jaws."*

1996   *Survivors of the Holocaust.*

1996   *Survivors of the Shoah Visual History Foundation.*

1996   *The Making of "1941."*

1996   *The Making of "E.T. The Extra-Terrestrial."*

1996   *Steven Spielberg's Director's Chair* (D of scenes in which S appears: Roger Holzberg).

INDEX **521**

Planetary Society Megachannel Extraterrestrial
Assay (META), 265
Playboy, 200
Playhouse 90, 62
Playmount Productions, 22, 152
Pointer, Priscilla, 293, 405
Poland, 22, 24, 26, 88, 414–15
Polanski, Roman, 426
Pollock, Dale, 350
Pollock, Tom, 228, 310, 432
Poltergeist, 18, 63, 115, 323, 336–40, 355, 356
autobiographical elements in, 53, 72, 89,
336, 338
direction of, 336–40, 341
financing and production of, 338, 384
public and critical response to, 339–40
screenplay of, 63, 337
Polunsky, Bob, 216
Porter, Cole, 354
Posner, Anna Fildman
(great-great-grandmother), 25
Posner, Bernard "Bernie" (uncle), 25, 32
Posner, Boris (great-uncle), 25–26
Posner, Ezekiel (great-great-grandfather), 25
Posner, Jennie Fridman (grandmother), 25, 26,
28, 40, 43, 47
Posner, Miriam "Mary" Rasinsky
(great-grandmother), 25
Posner, Philip "Fievel" (grandfather), 16, 20,
21–22, 24–25, 28, 34, 47, 286
Steven's relationship with, 21, 25, 26, 196,
388
Posner, Simon (great-grandfather), 25
Poster, Steven, 273
Potemkin, 24
Powell, Dilys, 207, 223
Powers, John, 373
Premiere, 37
Preminger, Otto, 167
Pretty Maids All in a Row, 189
Price, Frank, 311, 326
Pride of the Yankees, The, 376
Pritz, Bella, 29
Proehl, Bob, 79
Psychiatrist, The, 149, 183, 185–86, 187, 193–
196, 215
"Par for the Course" episode of, 185–86,
191, 192–96, 201
"The Private World of Martin Dalton"
episode of, 193
Psycho, 81, 120
Ptak, John, 231
PT 109, 102, 148
Pugh, Willard, 369–70
Pulitzer Prize, 238, 365
Pye, Michael, 136

Quaid, Dennis, 405
Quan, Ke Huy, 353, 357
Quart, Alissa, 443
Quatermass II, 103
Quayle, J. Danforth "Dan," 67
Quiet Man, The, 109
Quirk, Lawrence J., 172

Race, Louis B., 355
racism, 123, 142, 355, 366
Radford, Bonne, 347
Radioland Murders, 353
Rafferty, Terrence, 412, 433
Raiders of the Lost Ark, 19, 61, 107, 287, 309–
322, 324, 327, 353, 354, 355, 381
Ark of the Covenant theme in, 19, 287, 309,
312, 321
casting of, 315–16
financing and production of, 310–11, 321
Indiana Jones in, 312–13, 316–18, 322
Jewish mysticism and, 19, 313
screenplay of, 310–11, 313–15, 316–17
special effects of, 107, 320, 321
Rainer, Peter, 366, 398
Rain Man, 400
Rambaldi, Carlo, 279–80, 325
Ramer, Bruce, 38, 241, 326
Rasinsky, Benjamin (great-great-grandfather),
25
Ray, Satyajit, 334
Raymond, Julie, 112–13, 114, 156, 159
RCA, 46–48, 55–56, 58, 62, 63
Reagan, Nancy, 334
Reagan, Ronald, 266, 318, 334
Rear Window, 120
Redgrave, Michael, 296
Reel to Reel, 327
Reivers, The, 222
Renoir, Jean, 290, 333
Renoir, Pierre Auguste, 280
Repertory Theatre of Lincoln Center, 293
Republic Pictures, 109
Return of the Secaucus Seven, The, 325
Reyburn, Wallace, 228
Reynolds, Burt, 208–9, 240–41
Reynolds, Kevin, 389
Reynolds, Norman, 394
Rich, Frank, 256, 288, 289
Richards, Ariana, 418, 419
Richards, Dick, 232
Richie, Donald, 330
Richie, Lionel, 371
Righteous Persons Foundation, 416, 442
Riley, Michael, 206
Ring, Kenneth, 264
Ritchie, Michael, 177, 180
Rivera, Nina Nauman, 90, 96
Rizzo, Carl, 234–35
Road to Mecca, The (Fugard), 404
Robbins, Grace, 57, 58
Robbins, Marjorie, 53–54
Robbins, Matthew, 137, 211, 213, 221, 222,
226–27, 263, 268, 286, 296, 314, 403–4
Roberts, Hubert E. "Hugh," 115, 117
Roberts, Julia, 411, 412
Robertson, Cliff, 102, 180, 181, 296
Robyn, Robert, 103
Rodgers, Mark, 209
Rodney, Patricia Scott, 18, 69, 73, 74, 84–85,
88, 91, 92–93
Rollercoaster, 212
Rolling Stone, 127, 132, 333, 334, 340